W9-BCQ-510

WRITING COACH Online

INTERACTIVE WHITEBOARD READY!

To preview Writing Coach Online, follow these easy steps:

1. Go to www.phwritingcoach.com
2. Click on "Preview Writing Coach Online."
3. Register for a free demo account and explore.

Access online demonstrations of the following student resources:

- Interactive Writing Coach™ for paragraph and essay scoring
- Online Journal for writing notes, ideas, and drafts
- Interactive Graphic Organizers for help planning your writing
- Videos on effective writing strategies
- Interactive Models of Mentor Texts and Student Models with audio
- Resources for additional support and information

- Student Edition eText
- Grammar Tutorials
- Grammar Practice

DIMENSION L™ Powered By PEARSON

Video game to help you master grammar

www.phwritingcoach.com/DimensionL

Prentice Hall

Writing COACH

Writing and Grammar for the 21st Century

PEARSON

Upper Saddle River, New Jersey
Boston, Massachusetts
Chandler, Arizona
Glenview, Illinois

WRITING COACH

Acknowledgments appear on page R58, which constitute an extension of this copyright page.

PEARSON

0-13-253143-7

978-0-13-253143-6

1 2 3 4 5 6 7 8 9 10 V063 14 13 12 11 10

WELCOME TO Writing COACH

Seven Great Reasons to Learn to Write Well

1 Writing is hard, but hard is **rewarding**.

2 Writing helps you **sort things out**.

3 Writing helps you **persuade** others.

4 Writing makes you a **better reader**.

5 Writing makes you **smarter**.

6 Writing helps you get into and through **college**.

7 Writing **prepares you** for the world of work.

AUTHORS

The contributing authors guided the direction and philosophy of *Prentice Hall Writing Coach*. Working with the development team, they helped to build the pedagogical integrity of the program and to ensure its relevance for today's teachers and students.

Program Authors

Jeff Anderson

Jeff Anderson has worked with struggling writers and readers for almost 20 years. His works integrate grammar and editing instruction into the processes of reading and writing. Anderson has written articles in NCTE's ***Voices from the Middle, English Journal***, and ***Educational Leadership.*** Anderson won the NCTE Paul and Kate Farmer Award for his ***English Journal*** article on teaching grammar in context. He has published two books, ***Mechanically Inclined: Building Grammar, Usage, and Style into Writer's Workshop*** and ***Everyday Editing: Inviting Students to Develop Skill and Craft in Writer's Workshop*** as well as a DVD, ***The Craft of Grammar.***

Grammar gives me a powerful lens through which to look at my writing. It gives me the freedom to say things exactly the way I want to say them.

Kelly Gallagher

Kelly Gallagher is a full-time English teacher at Magnolia High School in Anaheim, California. He is the former co-director of the South Basin Writing Project at California State University, Long Beach. Gallagher is the author of ***Reading Reasons: Motivational Mini-Lessons for the Middle and High School, Deeper Reading: Comprehending Challenging Texts 4–12, Teaching Adolescent Writers,*** and ***Readicide.*** He is also featured in the video series, ***Building Adolescent Readers.*** With a focus on adolescent literacy, Gallagher provides training to educators on a local, national and international level. Gallagher was awarded the Secondary Award of Classroom Excellence from the California Association of Teachers of English—the state's top English teacher honor.

The best swimmers swim the most; the best writers write the most. There's only one way to become a good writer: write!

Contributing Authors

Evelyn Arroyo

Evelyn Arroyo is the author of **A+RISE,** Research-based Instructional Strategies for ELLs (English Language Learners). Her work focuses on closing the achievement gap for minority students and English language learners. Through her publications and presentations, Arroyo provides advice, encouragement, and practical success strategies to help teachers reach their ELL students.

Your rich, colorful cultural life experiences are unique and can easily be painted through words. These experiences define who you are today, and writing is one way to begin capturing your history. Become a risk-taker and fall in love with yourself through your own words.

When you're learning a new language, writing in that language takes effort. The effort pays off big time, though. Writing helps us generate ideas, solve problems, figure out how the language works, and, above all, allows us to express ourselves.

Jim Cummins, Ph.D.

Jim Cummins is a Professor in the Modern Language Centre at the University of Toronto. A well-known educator, lecturer, and author, Cummins focuses his research on bilingual education and the academic achievement of culturally diverse students. He is the author of numerous publications, including ***Negotiating Identities: Education for Empowerment in a Diverse Society.***

Grant Wiggins, Ed.D.

Grant Wiggins is the President of Authentic Education. He earned his Ed.D. from Harvard University. Grant consults with schools, districts, and state education departments; organizes conferences and workshops; and develops resources on curricular change. He is the co-author, with Jay McTighe, of ***Understanding By Design,*** the award-winning text published by ASCD.

I hated writing as a student—and my grades showed it. I grew up to be a writer, though. What changed? I began to think I had something to say. That's ultimately why you write: to find out what you are really thinking, really feeling, really believing.

Concepts of grammar can sharpen your reading, communication, and even your reasoning, so I have championed its practice in my classes and in my businesses. Even adults are quick to recognize that a refresher in grammar makes them keener—and more marketable.

Gary Forlini

Gary Forlini is managing partner of the School Growth initiative ***Brinkman—Forlini—Williams,*** which trains school administrators and teachers in Classroom Instruction and Management. His recent works include the book ***Help Teachers Engage Students*** and the data system ***ObserverTab*** for district administrators, ***Class Acts: Every Teacher's Guide To Activate Learning***, and the initiative's workshop ***Grammar for Teachers***.

CONTENTS IN BRIEF

WRITING

WRITING GAME PLAN

Writing without grammar only goes so far. Grammar and writing work together. To write well, grammar skills give me great tools.

CORE WRITING CHAPTERS

GRAMMAR

GRAMMAR GAME PLAN

Find It FIX IT 20 Major Grammatical Errors and How to Fix Them

CORE GRAMMAR CHAPTERS

Writing COACH : How to Use This Program

This program is organized into two distinct sections: one for WRITING and one for GRAMMAR.

In the **WRITING** section, you'll learn strategies, traits, and skills that will help you become a better writer.

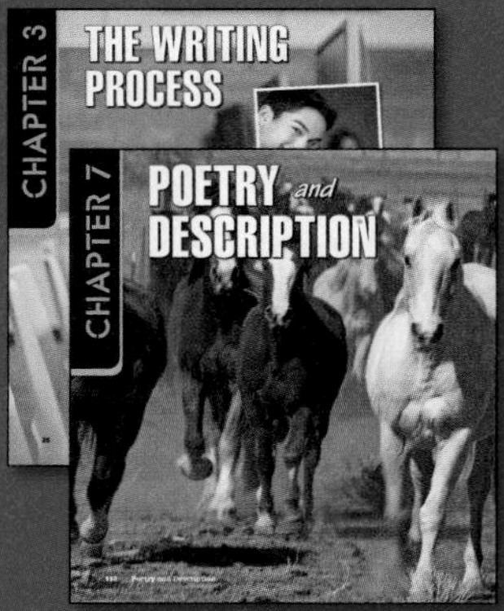

In the **GRAMMAR** section, you'll learn the rules and conventions of grammar, usage, and mechanics.

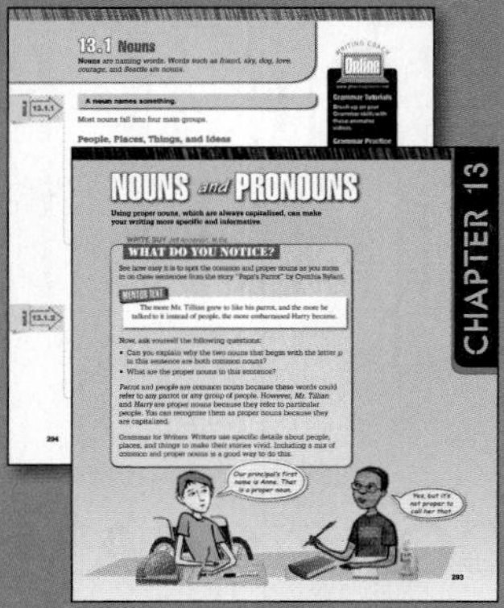

What DIGITAL writing and grammar resources are available?

The Writing Coach Online boxes will indicate opportunities to use online tools.

In **Writing,** use the **Interactive Writing Coach™** in two ways to get personalized guidance and support for your writing.

- Paragraph Feedback and
- Essay Scorer

WRITING COACH Online
www.phwritingcoach.com

Interactive Writing Coach™

- Choosing from the Topic Bank gives you access to the Interactive Writing Coach™.
- Submit your writing and receive instant personalized feedback and guidance as you draft, revise, and edit your writing.

WRITING COACH Online
www.phwritingcoach.com

Grammar Tutorials
Brush up on your grammar skills with these animated videos.

Grammar Practice
Practice your grammar skills with Writing Coach Online.

Grammar Games
Test your knowledge of grammar in this fast-paced interactive video game.

In **Grammar,** view grammar tutorials, practice your grammar skills, and play grammar video games.

What will you find in the WRITING section?

Writing Genre

Each chapter introduces a different **writing genre.**

Learn about the key characteristics of the **genre** before you start writing.

Focus on a single form of the genre with the **Feature Assignment**.

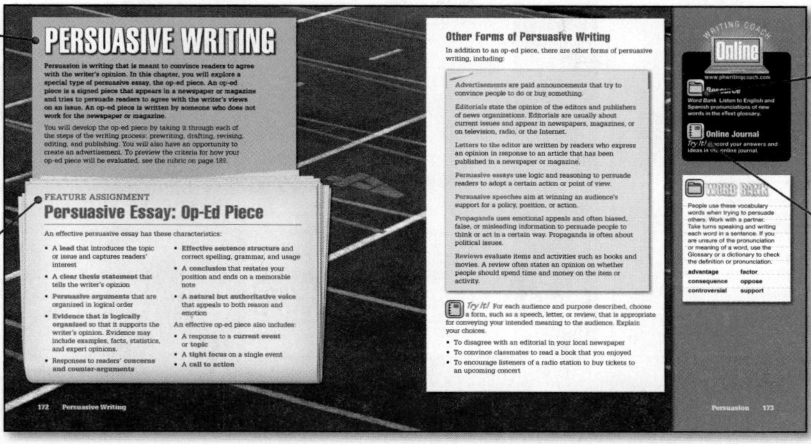

Writing Coach Online

- View the **Word Bank** words in the eText glossary, and hear them pronounced in both English and Spanish.
- Use your **Online Journal** to record your answers and ideas as you respond to ***Try It!*** activities.

Mentor Text and Student Model

The **Mentor Text** and **Student Model** provide examples of the genre featured in each chapter.

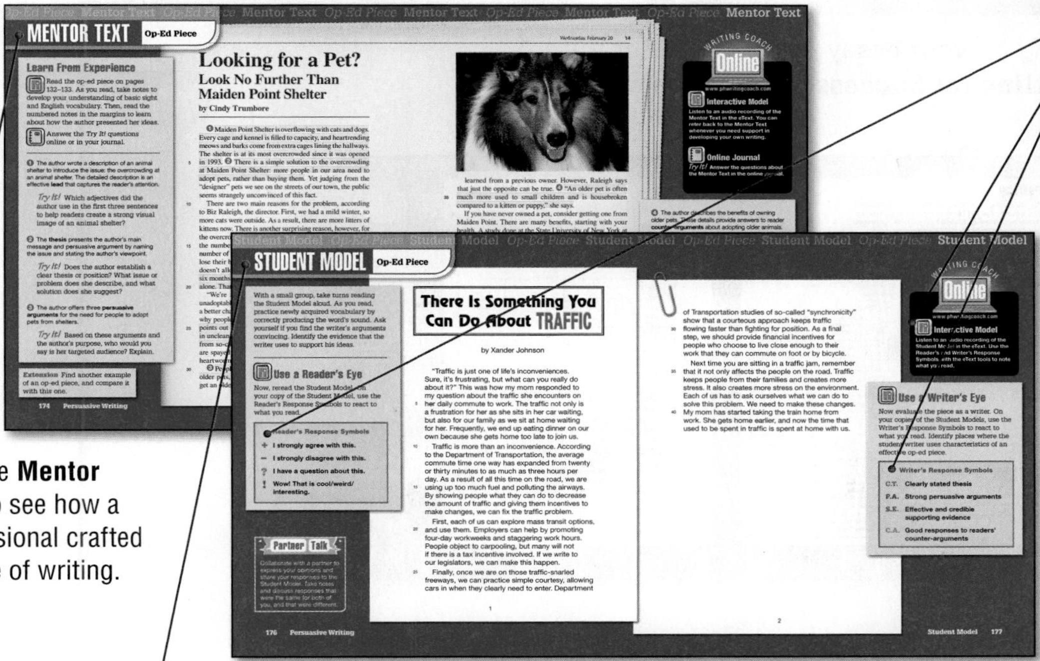

Use the **Mentor Text** to see how a professional crafted a piece of writing.

Review the **Student Model** as a guide for composing your own piece.

Writing Coach Online

- Use the **Interactive Model** to mark the text with Reader's and Writer's Response Symbols.
- Listen to an audio recording of the **Mentor Text** or **Student Model**.

Topic Bank — PREWRITING

The **Topic Bank** provides prompts for the **Feature Assignment.**

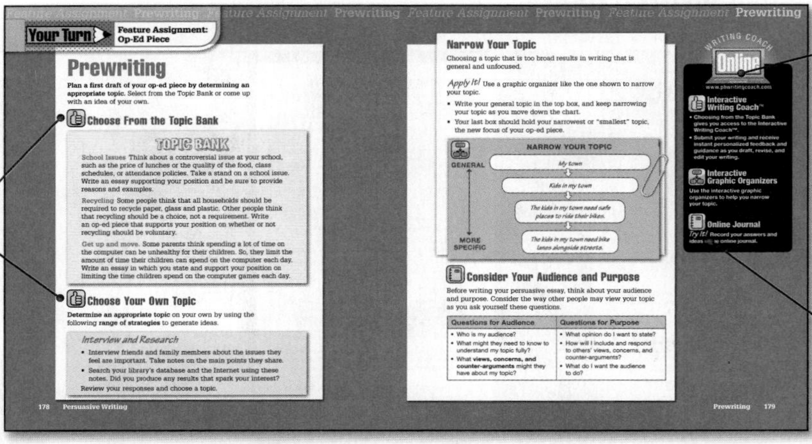

Choose from a bank of topics, or follow steps to find an idea of your own.

Writing Coach Online

- As you narrow your topic, get the right type of support! You'll find three different forms of graphic organizers—one model, one with step-by-step guidance, and one that is blank for you to complete.
- Use *Try It!* ideas to practice new skills. Use ***Apply It!*** activities as you work on your own writing.

Outline for Success — DRAFTING

Whether you are working on your essay drafts online or with a pen and paper, an **Outline for Success** can get you started.

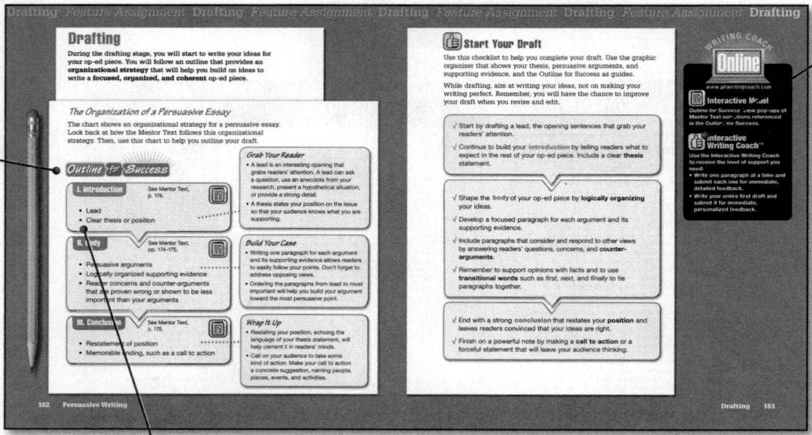

Consult this **outline** for a quick visual specific to the writing task assigned in each chapter.

Follow the bulleted suggestions for each part of your draft, and you'll be on your way to success.

Writing Coach Online

- Start with just a paragraph and build up to your essay draft, or if you are ready, go straight to submitting your essay. The choice is yours!

Revision RADaR

REVISING

You can use the **Revision RADaR** strategy as a guide for making changes to improve your draft.

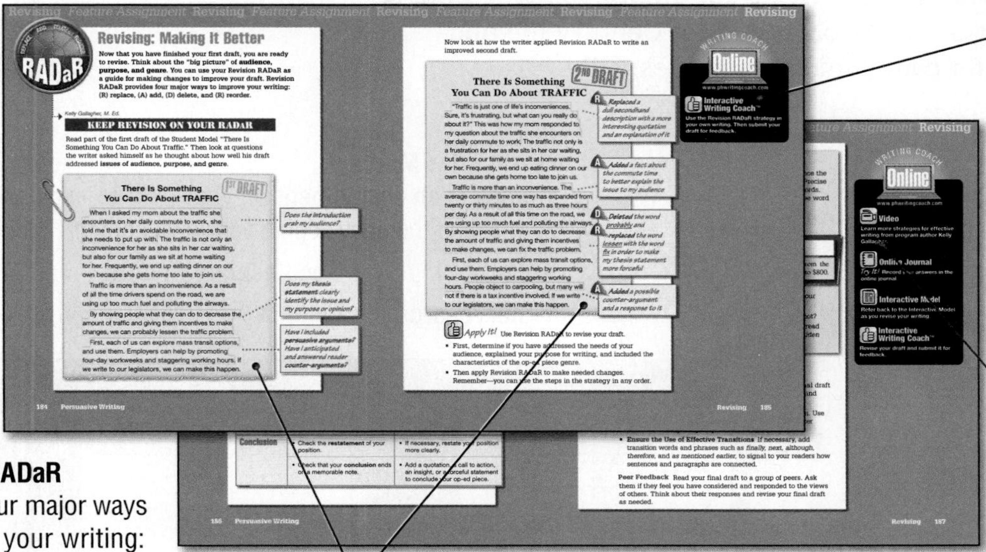

Revision RADaR provides four major ways to improve your writing:

- **R**eplace
- **A**dd
- **D**elete
- **R**eorder

Check out these example drafts to see how to apply **Revision RADaR.**

Writing Coach Online

- With **Interactive Writing Coach™**, submit your paragraphs and essays multiple times. View your progress in your online writing portfolio. Feel confident that your work is ready to be shared in peer review or teacher conferencing.
- View **videos** with strategies for writing from program author **Kelly Gallagher.**

What Do You Notice?

EDITING PUBLISHING

In the editing stage, **What Do You Notice?** and **Mentor Text** help you zoom in on powerful sentences.

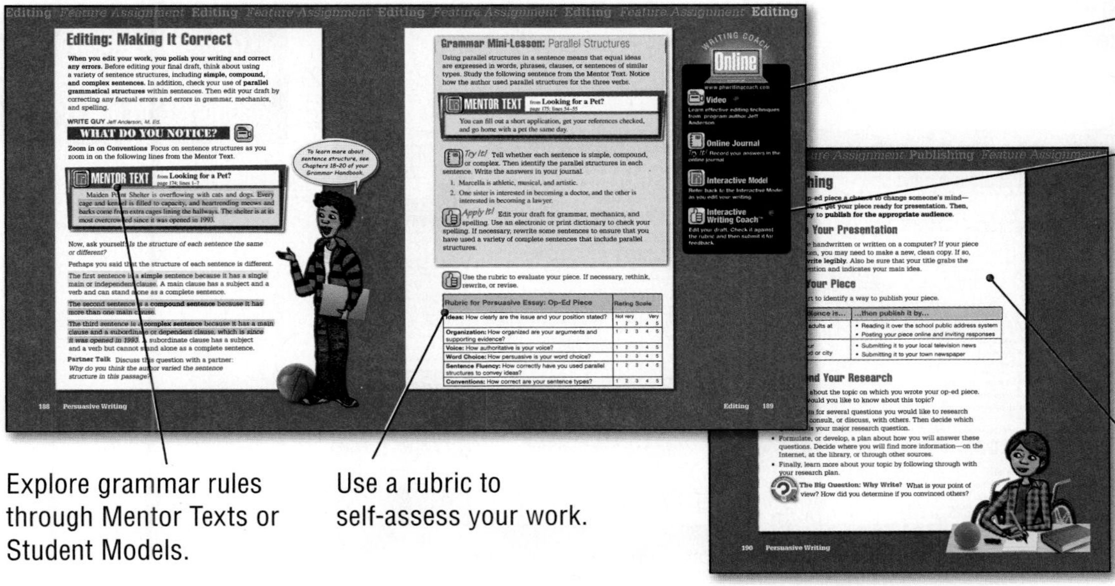

Explore grammar rules through Mentor Texts or Student Models.

Use a rubric to self-assess your work.

Find the best way to share your writing with others.

Writing Coach Online

- View **videos** with strategies for writing from program author **Jeff Anderson.**
- Submit your essay for feedback and a score.

How do end-of-chapter features help you apply what you've learned?

21st Century Learning

In **Make Your Writing Count** and **Writing for Media** you will work on innovative assignments that involve the 21st Century life and career skills you'll need for communicating successfully.

Make Your Writing Count
Work collaboratively on project-based assignments and share what you have learned with others. Projects include:

- Debates
- TV Talk Shows
- News Reports

Writing for Media
Complete an assignment on your own by exploring media forms, and then developing your own content. Projects include:

- Blogs
- Storyboards
- Documentary Scripts
- Multimedia Presentations

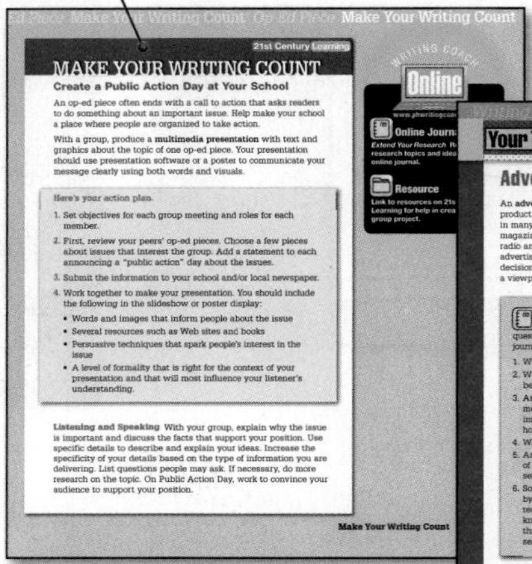

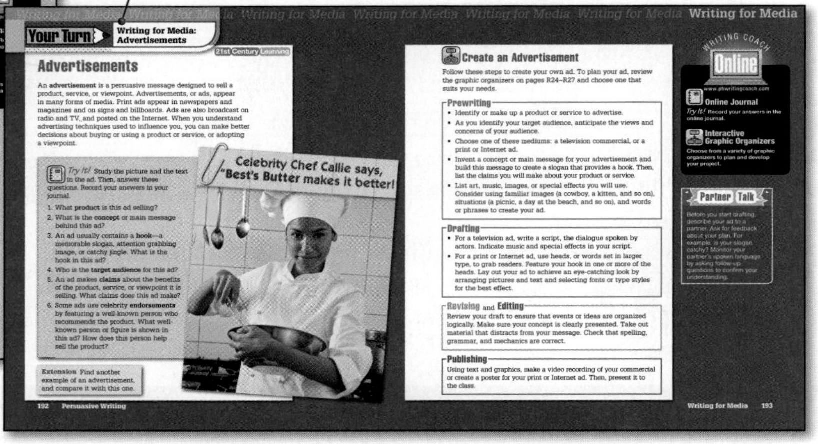

Test Prep

The **Writing for Assessment** pages help you prepare for important standardized tests.

Notice these icons that emphasize the types of writing you'll find on high-stakes tests.

Use **The ABCDs of On-Demand Writing** for a quick, memorable strategy for success.

Writing Coach Online
Submit your essay for feedback and a score.

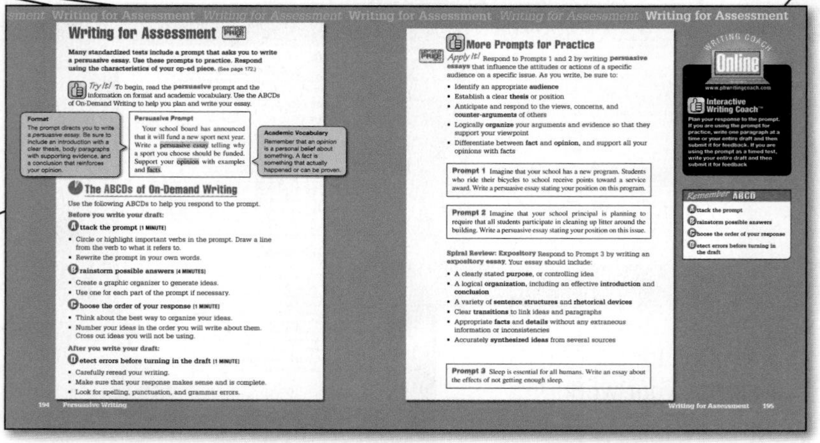

What will you find in the GRAMMAR section?

Grammar Game Plan

The **Find It/Fix It** reference guide helps you fix the **20** most common errors in student writing.

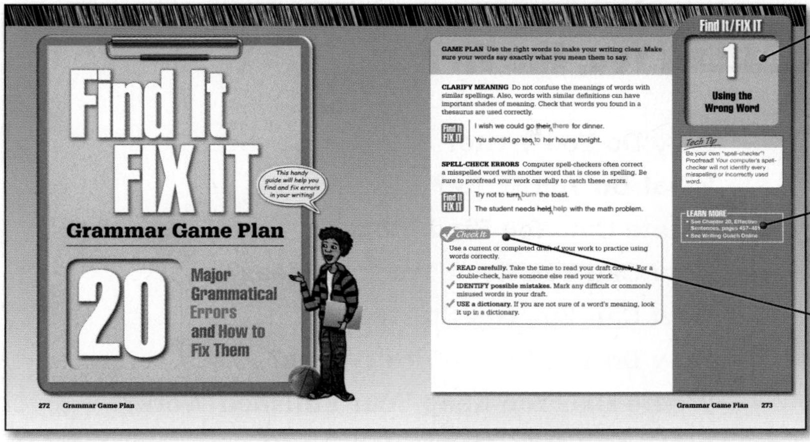

Study each of the 20 common errors and their corrections, which are clearly explained on each page.

Follow cross-references to more instruction in the grammar chapters.

Review the **Check It** features for strategies to help you avoid these errors.

Grammar Chapters

Each grammar chapter begins with a **What Do You Notice?** feature and **Mentor Text.**

Use the **Mentor Text** to help you zoom in on powerful sentences. It showcases the correct use of written language conventions.

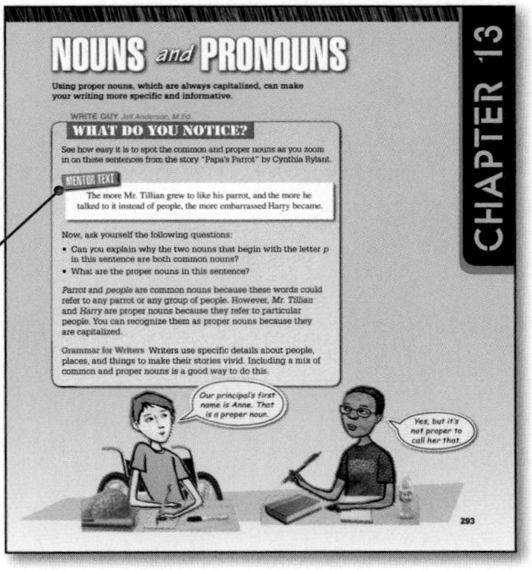

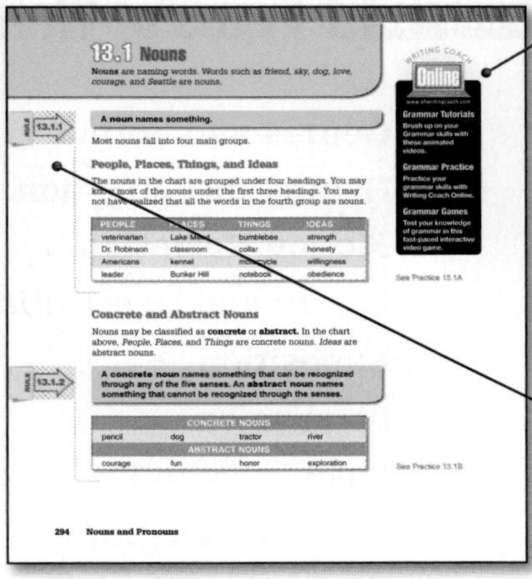

Writing Coach Online

The **Writing Coach Online** digital experience for Grammar helps you focus on just the lessons and practice you need.

Use the grammar section as a quick reference handbook. Each **grammar rule** is highlighted and numbered.

Try **Practice** pages and **Test Warm-Ups** to help you check your progress.

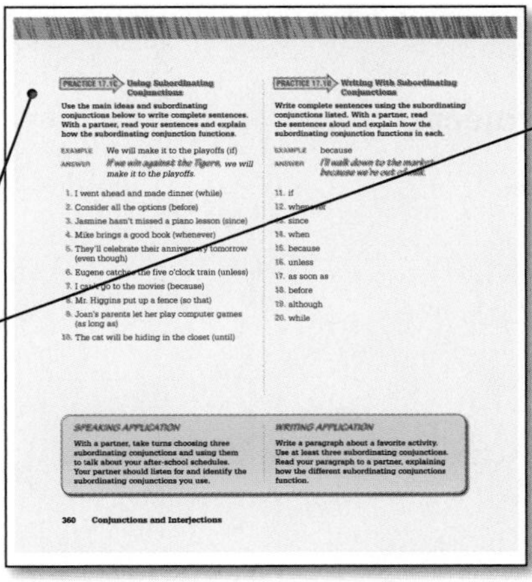

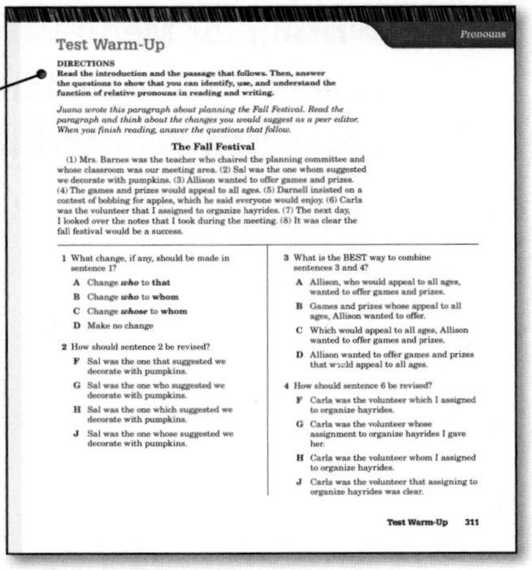

CONTENTS

WRITING

WRITING GAME PLAN

CHAPTER 1 You, the Writer 2

CHAPTER 2 Types of Writing 8

WRITING COACH Online

www.phwritingcoach.com

All content available online

- Interactive Writing Coach™
- Interactive Graphic Organizer
- Interactive Models
- Online Journal
- Resources
- Video

WRITING

Connect to the Big Questions

- **What do you think?**
  What makes a good story?
- **Why write?**
  What should we put in and leave out to be accurate and honest?

Connect to the Big Questions

- **What do you think?**
  Can we do anything we truly set out to do?
- **Why write?**
  What can fiction do better than nonfiction?

WRITING COACH Online
www.phwritingcoach.com

All content available online
- Interactive Writing Coach™
- Interactive Graphic Organizer
- Interactive Models
- Online Journal
- Resources
- Video

WRITING

Connect to the Big Questions

- **What do you think?**
  Can every important experience be communicated in words?
- **Why write?**
  How do we best convey feelings through words on a page?

Connect to the Big Questions

- **What do you think?**
  What is the best way to come up with a solution to a problem?
- **Why write?**
  What should we tell and what should we describe to make information clear?

WRITING COACH **Online**

www.phwritingcoach.com

All content available online

- Interactive Writing Coach™
- Interactive Graphic Organizer
- Interactive Models
- Online Journal
- Resources
- Video

WRITING

Connect to the Big Questions

- **What do you think?**
  What are our responsibilities to our communities?
- **Why write?**
  What is your point of view? How will you know if you've convinced others?

Connect to the Big Questions

- **What do you think?**
  What can we learn from others' reactions?
- **Why write?**
  What should you write about to make others interested in a text?

WRITING COACH Online
www.phwritingcoach.com

All content available online

- Interactive Writing Coach™
- Interactive Graphic Organizer
- Interactive Models
- Online Journal
- Resources
- Video

WRITING

Connect to the Big Questions

- **What do you think?**
  How does technology affect our lives?
- **Why write?**
  Do you understand your subject well enough to write about it?

Connect to the Big Questions

- **What do you think?**
  When is accuracy most important in writing?
- **Why write?**
  What do daily workplace communications require of format, content, and style?

Writing Coach Online

www.phwritingcoach.com

All content available online

- Interactive Writing Coach™
- Interactive Graphic Organizer
- Interactive Models
- Online Journal
- Resources
- Video

GRAMMAR GAME PLAN

Find It/Fix It The 20 Errors

GRAMMAR

CHAPTER 15 Phrases and Clauses 355

CHAPTER 16 Effective Sentences 397

WRITING COACH Online

www.phwritingcoach.com

All content available online

- Grammar Tutorials
- Grammar Practice
- Grammar Games

GRAMMAR

USAGE

CHAPTER 17 Verb Usage 423

WRITING COACH Online

www.phwritingcoach.com

All content available online

- Grammar Tutorials
- Grammar Practice
- Grammar Games

GRAMMAR

MECHANICS

WRITING COACH Online
www.phwritingcoach.com

All content available online

- Grammar Tutorials
- Grammar Practice
- Grammar Games

GRAMMAR

WRITING COACH Online

www.phwritingcoach.com

All content available online

- Grammar Tutorials
- Grammar Practice
- Grammar Games

STUDENT RESOURCES

ONFICTION NARRATION *Personal Narrative* FICTION NARRATION *Rea*
ontrast Essay PERSUASION *Persuasive Essay* RESPONSE TO LITERATURE
low-To Essay, Thank You Letter, Friendly Letter NONFICTION NARRATION
oem and Haiku EXPOSITION *Compare-and-Contrast Essay* PERSUASION *Pe*
ional Research Report WORKPLACE WRITING *How-To Essay, Thank You Lette*
ION *Realistic Short Story* POETRY *Rhyming Poem and Haiku* EXPOSITION
URE *Letter to an Author* RESEARCH *Informational Research Report* WORKPLA
ION *Personal Narrative* FICTION NARRATION *Realistic Short Story* POET
ION *Persuasive Essay* RESPONSE TO LITERATURE *Letter to an Author* RESE

Writing

CHAPTER 1

YOU, THE WRITER

Why Do You Write?

Writing well is one of the most important life skills you can develop. Being a good writer can help you achieve success in school and beyond. Most likely, you write for many reasons. You write:

To Share

You probably often write to **share** your experiences with others. Writing can be an easy way to **reach out** to people and connect with them.

To Persuade People

Writing can also be an effective way to **persuade** people to consider your opinions. For example, you may find it's easier to convince someone of your point of view when you've effectively organized your thoughts in an essay or a letter.

To Inform

Another reason to write is to **inform.** Perhaps you want to tell an audience how you built your computer network or how you finally got your e-mail to function properly.

To Enjoy

Personal fullfillment is another important motivation for writing, since writing enables you **to express** your thoughts and feelings. In addition, writing can also help you recall an event, or let you escape from everyday life.

Fortunately, writing well is a skill you can learn and one that you can continue to improve and polish. This program will help you improve your writing skills and give you useful information about the many types of writing.

What Do You Write?

Writing is already an important part of your everyday life. Each day is full of opportunities to write, allowing you to capture, express, think through, and share your thoughts and feelings, and demonstrate what you know. Here are some ways you might write.

- Recording thoughts in a journal
- Texting friends or posting on social networking sites
- E-mailing thank-you notes to relatives
- Creating lists of things to do or things you like
- Writing research reports, nonfiction accounts, fiction stories, and essays in school

How Can You Find Ideas?

The good news is that ideas are all around you. You just need to be aware of the rich resources that are available.

By Observing

Observing is a good way to start to find ideas. Did you see anything interesting on your way to school? Was there something unusual about the video game you played last night?

By Reading

Reading is another useful option—look through newspaper articles and editorials, magazines, blogs, and Web sites. Perhaps you read something that surprised you or really made you feel concerned. Those are exactly the subjects that can lead to the ideas you want to write about.

By Watching

Watching is another way to get ideas—watch online videos or television programs, for example.

WRITING COACH **Online**

www.phwritingcoach.com

Online Journal

Try It! **Record your notes, answers, and ideas in the online journal. You can also record and save your answers and ideas on pop-up sticky notes in the eText.**

“ Writer to Writer ”

I write when I want to be heard or connect. Writing lets me be a vital part of my community and reach outside it as well. All the while, I get to be me—my unique self.

—Jeff Anderson

How Can You Keep Track of Ideas?

You may sometimes think of great writing ideas in the middle of the night or on the way to math class. These strategies can help you remember those ideas.

Start an Idea Notebook or a Digital Idea File

Reserving a small **notebook** to record ideas can be very valuable. Just writing the essence of an idea, as it comes to you, can later help you develop a topic or essay. A **digital idea file** is exactly the same thing—but it's recorded on your computer, cell phone, or other electronic device.

Keep a Personal Journal

Many people find that keeping a **journal** of their thoughts is helpful. Then, when it's time to select an idea, they can flip through their journal and pick up on the best gems they wrote—sometimes from long ago.

Maintain a Learning Log

A **learning log** is just what it sounds like—a place to record information you have learned, which could be anything from methods of solving equations to computer shortcuts. Writing about something in a learning log might later inspire you to conduct further research on the same topic.

Free Write

Some individuals find that if they just let go and write whatever comes to mind, they eventually produce excellent ideas. **Free writing** requires being relaxed and unstructured. This kind of writing does not require complete sentences, correct spelling, or proper grammar. Whatever ends up on the paper or on the computer screen is fine. Later, the writer can go back and tease out the best ideas.

How Can You Get Started?

Every writer is different, so it makes sense that all writers should try out techniques that might work well for them. Regardless of your personal writing style, these suggestions should help you get started.

Get Comfortable

It's important to find and create an environment that encourages your writing process. Choose a spot where interruptions will be minimal and where you'll find it easy to concentrate. Some writers prefer a quiet library. Others prefer to work in a room with music playing softly on their computer.

Have Your Materials Ready

Before starting to write, gather all the background materials you need to get started, including your notes, free writing, reader's journal, and portfolio. Make sure you also have writing tools, such as a pen and paper or a computer.

Spend Time Wisely

Budgeting your available writing time is a wise strategy. Depending on your writing goal, you may want to sketch out your time on a calendar, estimating how long to devote to each stage of the writing process. Then, you can assign deadlines to each part. If you find a particular stage takes longer than you estimated, simply adjust your schedule to ensure that you finish on time.

October
SUNDAY
MONDAY
TUESDAY
WEDNESDAY
THURSDAY
FRIDAY
SATURDAY
1 Start Research
2 Finish Research
3 Write Outline
4
5
6
7
8 Finish First Draft
9 Finish Revising
10 Finish Proof-reading
11
12
13
14 DUE DATE
15
16
17
18
19
20
21
22
23
24
25
26
27
28
29
30
31

How Do You Work With Others?

If you think of writing as a solitary activity, think again. Working with others can be a key part of the writing process.

Brainstorming

Brainstorming works when everyone in a group feels free to suggest ideas, whether they seem commonplace or brilliant.

Cooperative Writing

Cooperative writing is a process in which each member of a group concentrates on a different part of an assignment. Then, the group members come together to discuss their ideas and write drafts.

Peer Feedback

Peer feedback comes from classmates who have read your writing and offered suggestions for improvements. When commenting on a classmate's work, it's important to provide constructive, or helpful, criticism.

21st Century Learning

Collaborate and Discuss

In **collaborative writing,** each group member takes an assigned role on a writing project. A collaborative group may decide on such possible roles as leader, facilitator, recorder, and listener. The roles may change as the group discusses and works through the writing process. The goal, however, is to work and rework the writing until all members feel they have produced the best result.

Possible Roles in a Collaborative Writing Project

LEADER
Initiates the discussion by clearly expressing group goals and moderates discussions

FACILITATOR
Works to move the discussion forward and clarify ideas

COMPROMISER
Works to find practical solutions to differences of opinion

LISTENER
Actively listens and serves to recall details that were discussed

Using Technology

Technology allows collaboration to occur in ways that were previously unthinkable.

- By working together on the Internet, students around the world have infinite opportunities to collaborate online on a wide range of projects.
- Collaboration can range from projects that foster community cooperation, such as how to improve debates during local elections, to those that increase global awareness, such as focusing on how to encourage more recycling.
- Being able to log in and to contribute to media, such as journals, blogs, and social networks, allows you to connect globally, express your views in writing, and join a world-wide conversation.

Where Can You Keep Your Finished Work?

A **portfolio,** or growing collection of your work, is valuable for many reasons. It can serve as a research bank of ideas and as a record of how your writing is improving. You can create a portfolio on a computer or in a folder or notebook. You'll learn more about managing a portfolio in chapter 3.

A **Reader's Journal,** in which you record quotes and ideas from your reading, can also be used to store original ideas. Your journal can be housed on a computer or in a notebook.

Reflect on Your Writing

Analyzing, making inferences, and drawing conclusions about how you find ideas can help you become a better, more effective writer. Find out more about how you write by asking yourself questions like these:

- Which strategies have I found most effective for finding good ideas for writing?
- What pieces of writing represent my best work and my weakest work? What do the pieces in each group have in common?

Partner Talk

With a partner, talk about your collaborative writing experiences. Be sure to share your responses to such questions as these: What project did you work on as a collaborative effort? What did you learn that you might not have discovered if you were developing a writing project by yourself?

CHAPTER 2

TYPES *of* WRITING

Genres and Forms

Genres are types, or categories, of writing.

- Each genre has a specific **purpose,** or goal. For example, the purpose of persuasive writing is to convince readers to agree with the writer's point of view.
- Each genre has specific **characteristics.** Short stories, for example, have characters, a setting, and a plot.

In this chapter, you will be introduced to several genres: nonfiction narratives, fiction narratives, poetry and descriptive writing, expository writing, persuasive writing, responses to literature, and workplace writing.

Forms are subcategories of genres that contain all the characteristics of the genre plus some unique characteristics of their own. For example, a mystery is a form of short story. In addition to plot, characters, and setting, it has a mystery to be solved.

Selecting Genres

In some writing situations, you may need to select the correct genre for conveying your intended meaning.

- To **entertain,** you may choose to write a short story or a humorous essay.
- To **describe** an emotion, writing a poem may be best.
- To **persuade** someone to your point of view, you may want to write a persuasive essay or editorial.

Each genre has unique strengths and weaknesses, and your specific goals will help you decide which is best.

Nonfiction Narration

Nonfiction narratives are any kind of literary text that tells a story about real people, events, and ideas. This genre of writing can take a number of different forms but includes well-developed conflict and resolution, interesting and believable characters, and a range of literary strategies, such as dialogue and suspense. Examples include Issac Bashevis Singer's "The Washerwoman" and Rudolfo A. Anaya's "A Celebration of Grandfathers."

Personal Narratives

Personal narratives tell true stories about events in a writer's life. These types of writing are also called **autobiographical essays.** The stories may tell about an experience or relationship that is important to the writer, who is the main character. They have a clearly defined focus and communicate the reasons for actions and consequences.

Biographical Narratives

In a **biographical narrative,** the writer shares facts about someone else's life. The writer may describe an important period, experience, or relationship in that other person's life, but presents the information from his or her own perspective.

Blogs

Blogs are online journals that may include autobiographical narratives, reflections, opinions, and other types of comments. They may also reflect genres other than nonfiction such as expository writing, and they may include other media, such as photos, music, or video.

WRITING COACH **Online**

www.phwritingcoach.com

Online Journal

Try It! **Record your notes, answers, and ideas in the online journal. You can also record and save your answers and ideas on pop-up sticky notes in the eText.**

Diary and Journal Entries

Writers record their personal thoughts, feelings, and experiences in **diaries** or **journals.** Writers sometimes keep diaries and journals for many years and then analyze how they reacted to various events over time.

Eyewitness Accounts

Eyewitness accounts are nonfiction writing that focus on historical or other important events. The writer is the narrator and shares his or her thoughts about the event. However, the writer is not the main focus of the writing.

Memoirs

Memoirs usually focus on meaningful scenes from writers' lives. These scenes often reflect on moments of a significant decision or personal discovery. For example, many modern U.S. presidents have written memoirs after they have left office. These memoirs help the public gain a better understanding of the decisions they made while in office.

Reflective Essays

Reflective essays present personal experiences, either events that happened to the writers themselves or that they learned about from others. They generally focus on sharing observations and insights they had while thinking about those experiences. Reflective essays often appear as features in magazines and newspapers.

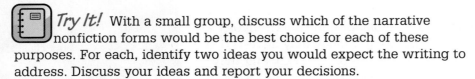

Try It! With a small group, discuss which of the narrative nonfiction forms would be the best choice for each of these purposes. For each, identify two ideas you would expect the writing to address. Discuss your ideas and report your decisions.

- To tell about seeing a championship kite-flying tournament
- To write about one of the first astronauts to walk in space
- To record personal thoughts about a favorite teacher

Fiction Narration

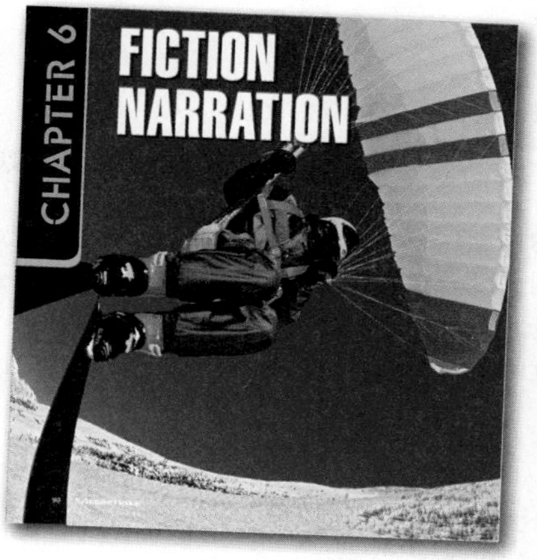

Fiction narratives are literary texts that tell a story about imagined people, events, and ideas. They contain elements such as characters, a setting, a sequence of events, and often, a theme. As with nonfiction narratives, this genre can take many different forms, but most forms include well-developed **conflict** and **resolution.** They also include **interesting and believable elements** and a range of **literary strategies,** such as dialogue and suspense. Examples include Edgar Allan Poe's "The Cask of Amontillado" or Richard Connell's "The Most Dangerous Game."

Realistic Fiction

Realistic fiction portrays invented characters and events in everyday situations that most readers would find familiar. Although characters may be imaginary, writers sometimes use real individuals in their own lives as a basis for the fictional ones. Because the focus is on everyday life, realistic fiction often presents problems that many people face and solutions they devise to solve them.

Fantasy Stories

Fantasy stories stretch the imagination and take readers to unreal worlds. Animals may talk, people may fly, or characters may have superhuman powers. Good fantasy stories have the elements of narrative fiction and manage to keep the fantastic elements believable.

Historical Fiction

Historical fiction is about imaginary people living in real places and times in history. Usually, the main characters are fictional people who know and interact with famous people and participate in important historical events.

Mystery Stories

Mystery stories present unexplained or strange events that characters try to solve. These stories are popular, probably because they are often packed full of suspense and surprises. Some characters in mystery stories, such as Sherlock Holmes, have become so famous that many people think of them as real people.

Myths and Legends

Myths and **legends** are traditional stories, told in cultures around the world. They were created to explain natural events that people could not otherwise explain or understand. They may, for example, tell about the origin of fire or thunder. Many myths and legends include gods, goddesses, and heroes who perform superhuman actions.

Science Fiction

Science fiction stories tell about real and imagined developments in science and technology and their effects on the way people think and live. Space travel, robots, and life in the future are popular topics in science fiction.

Tall Tales

You can tell a **tall tale** from other story types because it tells about larger-than-life characters in realistic settings. These characters can perform amazing acts of strength and bravery. One very famous hero of tall tales is Pecos Bill, who could ride just about anything—even a tornado!

Try It! Think about what you've read about narrative fiction and narrative nonfiction genres. Then, discuss in a group which **genre** would be best if you were planning a first draft and had these purposes in mind. **Select the correct genre** for conveying your intended meaning to your audiences. Then, identify two or three ideas that you would expect to include in a first draft. Be sure to explain your choices.

- To tell about a Texas rancher who can lasso lightning
- To share a true story about a famous person
- To tell the story of your most exciting day at school

Poetry and Description

Poetry and other kinds of descriptive literature express ideas and feelings about real or imagined people, events, and ideas. They use rhythm, rhyme, precise language, and sensory details—words that appeal to the senses—to create vivid images. In addition, they use figurative language—writing that means something beyond what the words actually say—to express ideas in new, fresh, and interesting ways.

Structural elements, such as line length and stanzas, also help the poet express ideas and set a mood. Some examples of poetry include Langston Hughes's "Dreams" and Walter Dean Myers's "Summer."

Ballad

A **ballad** is a form of lyric poetry that expresses the poet's emotions toward someone or something. Ballads rhyme, and some have refrains that repeat after each stanza, which makes them easy to translate into songs.

In many places, traditional folk ballads were passed down as oral poems or songs and then later written. Some ballads tell about cultural heroes. Other ballads tell sad stories or make fun of certain events.

Free Verse

Free verse is poetry that has no regular rhyme, rhythm, or form. Instead, a free verse poem captures the patterns of natural speech. The poet writes in whatever form seems to fit the ideas best. A free verse poem can have almost anything as its subject.

Writer to Writer

Anyone can write a first draft, but revision is where the paper comes to life.

—Kelly Gallagher

Partner Talk

Think about an example of fiction that you've especially enjoyed reading. Then, choose a partner and report your choices to each other. Be sure to explain what made the fiction piece so enjoyable, interesting, or exciting.

Prose Poem

A **prose poem** shares many of the features of other poetry, since it has rhythm, repetition, and vivid imagery. However, it is different from other poetry in one important way: it takes the form of prose or non-verse writing. Therefore, a prose poem may look like a short story on a page.

Sonnet

The **sonnet** is a form of rhyming lyric poetry with set rules. It is 14 lines long and usually follows a rhythm scheme called iambic pentameter. Each line has ten syllables and every other syllable is accented.

Haiku

Haiku is a form of non-rhyming poetry that was first developed in Japan hundreds of years ago. Many poets who write haiku in English write the poems in three lines. The first line has seven syllables, the second line has five syllables, and the third line has seven syllables. Haiku poets often write about nature and use vivid visual images.

Other Descriptive Writing

Descriptive writing includes descriptive essays, travel writing, and definition essays.

- **Descriptive essays** often use words that involve the senses to create a clear picture of a subject. For example, a descriptive essay about a freshly grilled hamburger might use adjectives such as *juicy*, *spicy*, *steamy*, *fragrant*, *hot*, and *glistening* to paint a word picture.
- A **travel essay** uses sensory words to describe a place.
- A **definition essay** can draw on a writer's emotional experience to describe something abstract, like friendship or happiness.

The qualities of description can also be used in other types of writing. For example, a short story can be more realistic or compelling when it includes strong description.

Try It! Now that you've learned more about poetry and description, discuss which specific **genre** would be best for each of these purposes. **Select the correct genre** for conveying your intended meaning to your audiences. Then, identify two or three types of information that you would want to include in a first draft. Be ready to explain your thinking.

- To tell about a trip to a beach in Mexico
- To describe a drop of rain
- To tell the story of a character who lives in the wilderness

Exposition

Exposition is writing that seeks to communicate ideas and information to specific audiences and for specific purposes. It relies on facts to inform or explain.

- Effective expository writing reflects an organization that is well planned—with effective introductory paragraphs, body paragraphs, and concluding paragraphs.
- In addition, good expository writing uses a variety of sentence structures and rhetorical devices—deliberate uses of language for specific effects.

Examples of expository writing include Sally Ride's "Single Room, Earth View" and John Raven's "Early Texas Cuisine."

Analytical Essay

An **analytical essay** explores a topic by supplying relevant information in the form of facts, examples, reasons, and valid inferences to support the writer's claims.

- An **introductory paragraph** presents a thesis statement, the main point to be developed.
- The **body of the essay** provides facts about the topic, using a variety of sentence structures and transitions to help the writing flow.
- The **concluding paragraph** sums up ideas, helping readers understand why the topic is important.

Compare-and-Contrast Essay

A **compare-and-contrast** essay explores similarities and differences between two or more things for a specific purpose. As with other expository essays, the compare-and-contrast essay offers clear, factual details about the subject.

Cause-and-Effect Essay

A **cause-and-effect essay** traces the results of an event or describes the reasons an event happened. It is clearly organized and gives precise examples that support the relationship between the cause and effect.

"Writer to Writer"

Expository forms can shape my thinking and help my writing gel. I find the expository patterns clarifying my thoughts and filling in gaps that I may have otherwise missed.

—Jeff Anderson

Partner Talk

Choose a different partner this time. Discuss a poem that you've read in class. Share your thoughts about the poem and describe what made the piece successful.

Classification Essay

In a **classification essay,** a writer organizes a subject into categories and explains the category into which an item falls.

- An effective classification essay **sorts** its subjects—things or ideas—into several categories.
- It then offers **examples** that fall into each category. For example, a classification essay about video games might discuss three types of video games—action, adventure, and arcade.
- The essay might conclude with a statement about how the items classified are different or about how they are similar.

Problem-Solution Essay

A **problem-solution essay** presents a problem and then offers solutions to that problem. This type of essay may contain opinions, like a persuasive essay, but it is meant to explain rather than persuade.

- An effective problem-solution essay presents a clear statement of the problem, including a summary of its causes and effects.
- Then, it proposes at least one realistic solution and uses facts, statistics, or expert testimony to support the solution.
- The essay should be clearly organized, so that the relationship between the problem and the solution is obvious.

Pro-Con Essay

A **pro-con essay** examines arguments for and against an idea or topic.

- It has a topic that has two sides or points of view. For example, you might choose the following as a topic: Is it right to keep animals in zoos?
- Then, you would develop an essay that tells why it's good to keep animals in zoos, as well as why it's harmful to keep animals in zoos.
- It's important to be sure to give a clear analysis of the topic.

Newspaper and Magazine Articles

Newspaper and **magazine articles** offer information about news and events. They are typically factual and do not include the writer's opinions. They often provide an analysis of events and give readers background information on a topic. Some articles may also reflect genres other than the analytical essay, such as an editorial that aims to persuade.

Internet Articles

Articles on the **Internet** can supply relevant information about a topic.

- They are often like newspaper or magazine articles but may include shorter sentences and paragraphs. In addition, they include more visuals, such as charts and bulleted lists. They may also reflect genres other than analytical essays.
- It's always wise to consider the source when reading Internet articles because only the most reputable sources should be trusted to present correct facts.

On-Demand Writing

Because essay questions often appear on school tests, knowing how to write to **test prompts**, especially under time limits, is an important skill.

Test prompts provide a clear topic with directions about what should be addressed. The effective response to an essay demonstrates not only an understanding of academic content but also good writing skills.

Try It! Think about what you've learned about expository writing and consider the other genres you've discussed. Then, discuss in a group which **genre** would be best if you were planning a first draft with these purposes in mind. **Select the correct genre** for conveying your intended meaning to your audiences. Then, identify two or three key ideas that you would want to include in a first draft. Be sure to explain your choices.

- To weigh the benefits of two kinds of pets
- To imagine what life would be like on the moon

Partner Talk

Share your experiences with writing expository essays with a partner. Talk about strategies that worked well for you, as well as those that weren't as successful. Be sure to include your analysis of why certain strategies worked better than others.

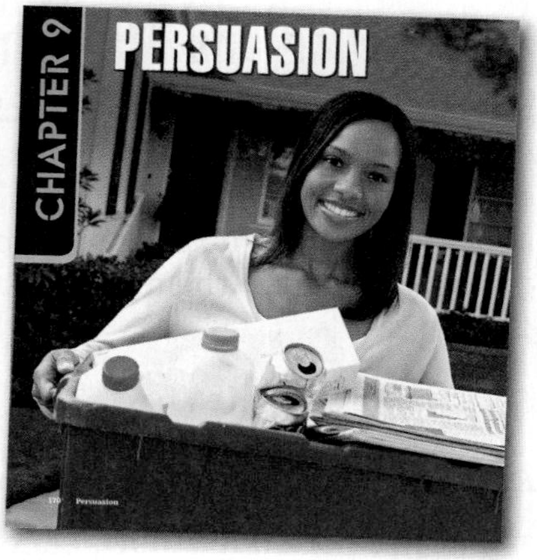

Persuasion

Persuasive writing aims to influence the attitudes or actions of a specific audience on specific issues. A strong persuasive text is logically organized and clearly describes the issue. It also provides precise and relevant evidence that supports a clear thesis statement. Persuasive writing may contain diagrams, graphs, or charts. These visuals can help to convince the reader. Examples include Pete Hammill's "Libraries Face Sad Chapter" or Franklin Delano Roosevelt's "First Inaugural Address."

Persuasive Essays or Argumentative Essays

A **persuasive essay** or **argumentative essay** uses logic and reasoning to persuade readers to adopt a certain point of view or to take action. A strong persuasive essay starts with a clear thesis statement and provides supporting arguments based on evidence. It also anticipates readers' counter-arguments and responds to them as well.

Persuasive Speeches

Persuasive speeches are presented aloud and aim to win an audience's support for a policy, position, or action. These speeches often appeal to emotion and reason to convince an audience. Speakers sometimes change their script in order to address each specific audience's concerns.

Editorials

Editorials, which appear in newspapers, in magazines, or on television, radio, or the Internet, state the opinion of the editors and publishers of news organizations. Editorials usually present an opinion about a current issue, starting with a clear thesis statement and then offering strong supporting evidence.

Op-Ed Pieces

An **op-ed, or opposite-editorial, piece** is an essay that tries to convince the readers of a publication to agree with the writer's views on an issue. The writer may not work for the publication and is often an expert on the issue or has an interesting point of view. The writer is identified so that people can judge his or her qualifications.

Letters to the Editor

Readers write **letters to editors** at print and Internet publications to express opinions in response to previously published articles. A good letter to the editor gives an accurate and honest representation of the writer's views.

Reviews

Reviews evaluate items and activities, such as books, movies, plays, and music, from the writer's point of view. A review often states opinions on the quality of an item or activity and supports those opinions with examples, facts, and other evidence.

Advertisements

Advertisements in all media—from print to online sites to highway billboards—are paid announcements that try to convince people to buy something or do something. Good advertisements use a hook to grab your attention and support their claims. They contain vivid, persuasive language and multimedia techniques, such as music, to appeal to a specific audience.

Propaganda

Propaganda uses emotional appeals and often biased, false, or misleading information to persuade people to think or act in a certain way. Propaganda may tap into people's strongest emotions by generating fear or attacking their ideas of loyalty or patriotism. Because propaganda appears to be objective, it is wise to be aware of the ways it can manipulate people's opinions and actions.

Try It! Think about what you have learned about exposition, description, and persuasion. Form a group to discuss and draw conclusions about which **genres** would be best if you were planning a first draft with each of these intentions in mind. **Select the correct genre** for conveying your intended meaning to your audiences. Then, identify two or three types of information that you would want to include in a first draft.

- To explain how an event happened
- To describe a beautiful landscape
- To encourage teens to buy teeth-whitening toothpaste

Partner Talk

Share your experiences with various types of persuasive texts with a partner. Talk about the types of persuasive text that you think are most effective, honest, and fair. Be sure to explain your thinking.

Responses to Literature

Responses to literature analyze and interpret an author's work. They use clear **thesis statements** and **evidence from the text using embedded quotations to support the writer's ideas.** They also evaluate how well authors have accomplished their goals. Effective responses to literature extend beyond literal analysis to evaluate and discuss how and why the text is effective or not effective.

Critical Reviews

Critical reviews evaluate books, plays, poetry, and other literary works. Reviews present the writer's opinions and support them with specific examples. The responses may analyze the aesthetic effects of an author's use of language in addition to responding to the content of the writing.

Compare-and-Contrast Essays

Compare-and-contrast essays explore similarities and differences between two or more works of literature. These essays provide relevant evidence to support the writer's opinions.

Letters to Authors

Readers write **letters to authors** to share their feelings and thoughts about a work of literature directly.

Blog Comments

Blog comments on an author's Web site or book retailer pages let readers share their ideas about a work. Readers express their opinions and give interpretations of what an author's work means.

Partner Talk

Interview your partner about his or her experiences writing interpretative responses. Be sure to ask questions such as these:

- How did you support your opinion of the author's work?
- How did you choose evidence, such as quotes, to support your analysis or opinion?

Try It! As a group, decide which **genre** would be most appropriate if you were planning a first draft for each of these purposes. **Select the correct genre** for conveying your intended meaning to your audiences. Then, identify two or three key questions that you would want to answer in a first draft.

- To tell an author why you think her book is excellent
- To write an opinion about a newspaper article
- To imagine how a certain landform came to be

Research Writing

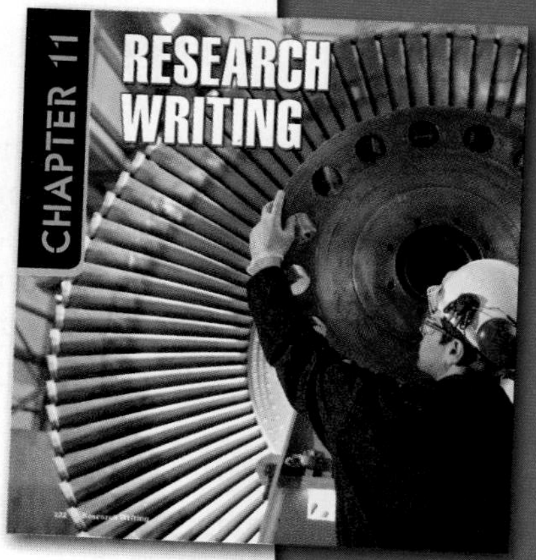

Research writing is based on factual information from outside sources. Research reports organize and present ideas and information to achieve a particular purpose and reach a specific audience. They present evidence in support of a clear thesis statement.

Research Reports and Documented Essays

Research reports and **documented essays** present information and analysis about a topic that the writer has studied. Start with a clear thesis statement. Research reports often include graphics and illustrations to clarify concepts. Documented essays are less formal research writings that show the source of every fact, quote, or borrowed idea in parentheses.

Experiment Journals and Lab Reports

Experiment journals and **lab reports** focus on the purposes, procedures, and results of a lab experiment. They often follow a strict format that includes dates and specific observation notes.

Statistical Analysis Reports

A **statistical analysis report** presents numerical data. Writers of this type of report must explain how they gathered their information, analyze their data, tell what significance the findings may have, and explain how these findings support their thesis statement.

Annotated Bibliographies

An **annotated bibliography** lists the research sources a writer used. It includes the title, author, publication date, publisher, and brief notes that describe and evaluate the source.

Try It! Discuss which kinds of reports you might write if you were planning a first draft for these purposes. **Select the correct form** for conveying your intended meaning to your audiences. Then, identify two or three key questions that you would want to answer in a first draft. Explain your choices.

- To accompany a project you plan to enter in a science fair
- To write about a poll taken to predict the results of a local election

Partner Talk

Share with a partner the kinds of research writing you've done in school. Explain which projects you've enjoyed and why.

Workplace Writing

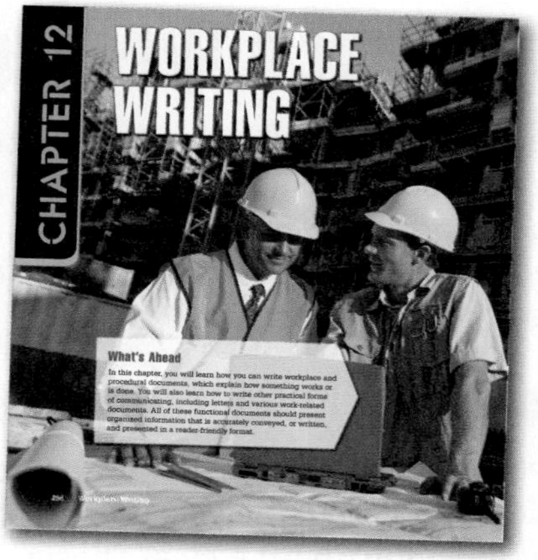

Workplace writing is writing done on the job or as part of a job, often in an office setting. It usually communicates details about a particular job or work project. This type of writing features organized and accurately conveyed information and should include reader-friendly formatting techniques, such as clearly defined sections and enough blank space for easy reading.

Business Letters and Friendly Letters

A **business letter** is a formal letter written to, from, or within a business. It can be written to make requests or to express concerns or approval. For example, you might write to a company to ask about job opportunities. Business letters follow a specific format that includes an address, date, formal greeting, and closing.

In contrast, a **friendly letter** is a form of correspondence written to communicate between family, friends, or acquaintances. For example, you might write a thank-you note for a gift.

Memos

Memos are short documents usually written from one member of an organization to another or to a group. They are an important means of communicating information within an organization.

E-mails

E-mail is an abbreviation for "electronic mail" and is a form of electronic memo. Because it can be transmitted quickly allowing for instant long-distance communication, e-mail is a very common form of communication that uses a computer and software to send messages.

Forms

Forms are types of workplace writing that ask for specific information to be completed in a particular format. Examples include applications, emergency contact information forms, and tax forms.

Instructions

Instructions are used to explain how to complete a task or procedure. They provide clear, step-by-step guidelines. For example, recipes and user manuals are forms of instructions.

Project Plans

Project plans are short documents usually written from one member of an organization to another. They outline a project's goals and objectives and may include specific details about how certain steps of a project should be achieved.

Résumés

A **résumé** is an overview of a person's experience and qualifications for a job. This document lists a person's job skills and work history. Résumés can also feature information about a person's education.

College Applications

College applications are documents that ask for personal information and details about someone's educational background. College administrators use this information to decide whether or not to accept a student.

Job Applications

Job applications are similar to résumés in that they require a person to list work experience and educational background. Most employers will require a completed job application a part of the hiring process.

Try It! As a group, discuss which form of workplace writing would be best for each of these purposes. Select the correct form for conveying your intended meaning to your audiences. Identify two or three types of information you would expect to include in a first draft.

- To inform the company that made your cell phone that it does not work properly
- To prepare information about your qualifications for a job search
- To create a plan for your group assignment in science class

Partner Talk

Share with a partner your experience with workplace and procedural writing. For example, have you ever written instructions, created a résumé, or completed a job application? What do you find are particular challenges with this type of writing?

Writing for Media

The world of communication has changed significantly in recent years. In addition to writing for print media such as magazines and books, writers also write for a variety of other **media,** in forms such as:

- Scripts for screenplays, video games, and documentaries
- Storyboards for graphic novels and advertisements
- Packaging for every kind of product
- Web sites and blogs

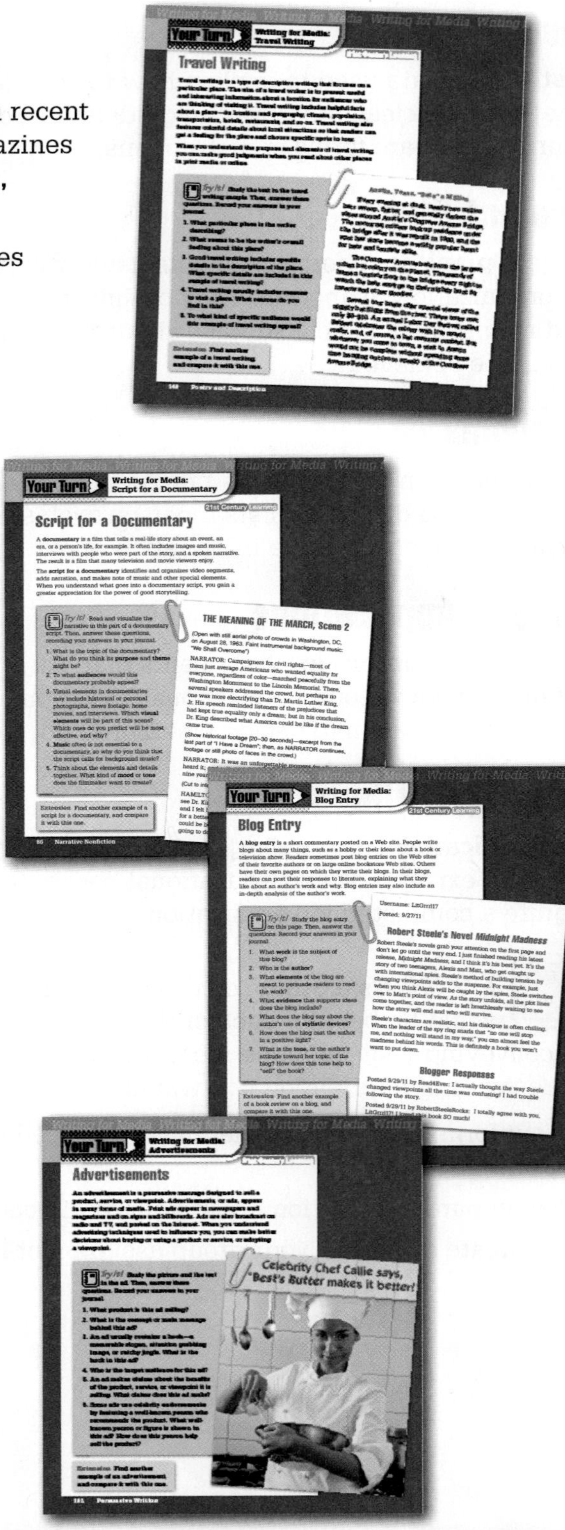

Scripts

Scripts are written for various media, such as documentaries, theater productions, speeches, and audio programs. Movies, television shows, and video games also have scripts.

- A good script focuses on a clearly expressed or implied **theme** and has a specific **purpose.**
- It also contains interesting details, which contribute to a definite **mood or tone.**
- A good script also includes a clear **setting**, **dialogue**, and well-developed **action**.

Blogs

Blogs address just about every purpose and interest. For example, there are blogs about local issues, pets, or food.

Advertisements

Advertisements are designed to persuade someone to buy a product or service. Advertisements use images, words, and music to support their message. Writers write the content of advertisements. In addition, they may help create music and design the sound and the images in the ad.

Creating Multimedia Projects

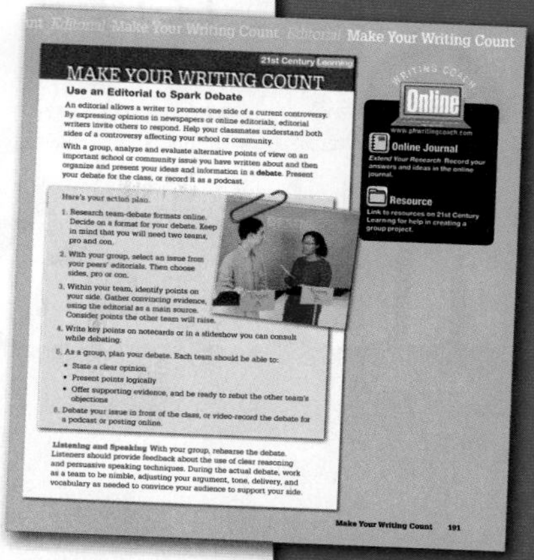
Make Your Writing Count Editorial Make Your Writing Count

21st Century Learning

MAKE YOUR WRITING COUNT

Use an Editorial to Spark Debate

An editorial allows a writer to promote one side of a current controversy. By expressing opinions in newspapers or online editorials, editorial writers invite others to respond. Help your classmates understand both sides of a controversy affecting your school or community.

With a group, analyze and evaluate alternative points of view on an important school or community issue you have written about and then organize and present your ideas and information in a **debate**. Present your debate for the class, or record it as a podcast.

Here's your action plan.

1. Research team-debate formats online. Decide on a format for your debate. Keep in mind that you will need two teams, pro and con.
2. With your group, select an issue from your peers' editorials. Then choose sides, pro or con.
3. Within your team, identify points on your side. Gather convincing evidence, using the editorial as a main source. Consider points the other team will raise.
4. Write key points on notecards or in a slideshow you can consult while debating.
5. As a group, plan your debate. Each team should be able to:
   - State a clear opinion
   - Present points logically
   - Offer supporting evidence, and be ready to rebut the other team's objections
6. Debate your issue in front of the class, or video-record the debate for a podcast or posting online.

Listening and Speaking With your group, rehearse the debate. Listeners should provide feedback about the use of clear reasoning and persuasive speaking techniques. During the actual debate, work as a team to be nimble, adjusting your argument, tone, delivery, and vocabulary as needed to convince your audience to support your side.

Writing Coach Online
www.phwritingcoach.com

Online Journal
Extend Your Research Record your answers and ideas in the online journal.

Resource
Link to resources on 21st Century Learning for help in creating a group project.

Make Your Writing Count 191

A **multimedia project** or presentation uses sound, video, and other media to convey a point or entertain an audience. No matter what type of project you choose as your own multimedia project, it is important to follow these steps:

- Decide on the project's **purpose** and your target **audience.**
- Choose **media** that will effectively convey your **message.**
- **Plan** your presentation. Will you work alone or with a partner or group? If you work with others, how you will assign the tasks?
- What **equipment** will you need? Will you produce artwork, record audio, and take photographs? Should you produce a storyboard to show the sequence of details in your presentation? Be sure to allow enough time to produce the text and all the other elements in your project.
- Keep the **writing process** in mind. There should be working and reworking along the way.
- **Assess** the progress of the project as you work. Ask questions, such as: Does my project incorporate appropriate writing genres? Will the presentation interest my audience? Have I kept my purpose in mind?
- **Rehearse!** Before presenting your project, be sure to do several "practice runs" to weed out and correct any errors.
- Keep an electronic record of your presentation for future reference.
- After your presentation, have others assess the project. Their critique will help you to do an even better job next time!

Partner Talk

Share with a partner your experience with writing for media or multimedia projects. Have you created a Web site or contributed to one? Have you had to complete multimedia projects for a class assignment or for a personal project on which you worked? Talk about how writing for media presents different challenges from more traditional writing and how you have dealt with those challenges.

Reflect on Your Writing

Learning more about the different types of writing can help you focus on the characteristics of each type so you can keep improving your own writing. Think about what you've learned in Chapter 2 as you answer these questions:

- What type of writing most interests you?
- What type of writing do you think is most useful? Why?

CHAPTER 3

THE WRITING PROCESS

Writing Traits

Good writing has specific qualities, or traits. In this chapter you will learn about these traits and how to use rubrics to evaluate your writing in terms of them. You will also learn how to address them during the writing process.

Ideas

The best writing is built from strong ideas. It shows original thinking and provides readers with interesting, significant information. It also sends a strong message or presents a clear "angle" or point of view on a subject. In good writing, ideas are well developed, or explained and supported with examples and other details.

Organization

A well-organized paper has an obvious plan. Ideas move from sentence to sentence and paragraph to paragraph in a logical way. For example, events in a story often appear in chronological order, the order in which they occurred. Some expository writing presents ideas in order of importance. Descriptive writing may use a spatial organization, describing something from top to bottom or left to right.

Voice

Voice is the combination of word choice and personal writing style that makes your writing unique. It shows your personality or "take" on a story. Voice connects a reader to the writer. While the content of your writing is critical, effective writing features a strong voice.

Word Choice

To best achieve your purpose in writing, choose words carefully. When you choose precise words, you choose words that express your exact meaning. When you choose vivid words, you choose words that create pictures for readers, words that describe how a subject looks, sounds, smells, and so on. You may also use figures of speech (direct or indirect comparisons of unlike things) to create memorable images of your subject.

Sentence Fluency

Sentence fluency refers to the rhythm and flow of writing. Keep the rhythm of your writing fresh by varying sentence patterns, and create flow by choosing sentence structures that match your meaning. For example, you might show the connection between two ideas by joining them in one longer sentence, or you might create emphasis by breaking off a series of long sentences with one short sentence.

Conventions

By following the rules of spelling, capitalization, punctuation, grammar, and usage, you help readers understand your ideas.

Overview of Writing Traits	
Ideas	• Significant ideas and informative details • Thorough development of ideas • Unique perspective or strong message
Organization	• Obvious plan • Clear sequence • Strong transitions
Voice	• Effective word choice expressing personality or perspective • Attention to style
Word Choice	• Precise, not vague, words • Vivid, not dull, words • Word choices suited to audience and purpose
Sentency Fluency	• Varied sentence beginnings, lengths, and structures • Smooth sentence rhythms used to support meaning
Conventions	• Proper spelling and capitalization • Correct punctuation, grammar, usage, and sentence structure

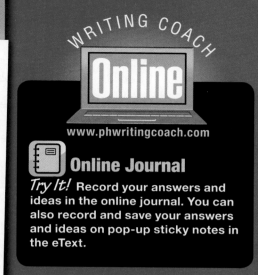

WRITING COACH **Online**

www.phwritingcoach.com

Online Journal

Try It! **Record your answers and ideas in the online journal. You can also record and save your answers and ideas on pop-up sticky notes in the eText.**

"Writer to Writer"

Good writing is a symphony of traits—all coming together to make the paper sing.

—Kelly Gallagher

Rubrics and How to Use Them

You can use rubrics to evaluate your writing. A rubric allows you to score your writing on a scale for each trait. You will use a six-point rubric like this to help evaluate your writing in chapters 5–12.

Writing Traits	Rating Scale
Ideas: How interesting, significant, or original are the ideas you present? How well do you develop, or explain, support, and extend, ideas?	Not very Very 1 2 3 4 5 6
Organization: How logically is your piece organized? How much sense do your transitions, or movements from idea to idea, make?	1 2 3 4 5 6
Voice: How authentic and original is your voice?	1 2 3 4 5 6
Word Choice: How precise and vivid are the words you use? How well does your word choice help achieve your purpose?	1 2 3 4 5 6
Sentence Fluency: How well do your sentences flow? How strong and varied is the rhythm they create?	1 2 3 4 5 6
Conventions: How correct is your punctuation? Your capitalization? Your spelling?	1 2 3 4 5 6

Each trait to be assessed appears in the first column. The rating scale appears in the second column. The higher your score for a trait, the better your writing exhibits that trait.

Using a Rubric on Your Own

A rubric can be a big help in assessing your writing while it is still in process. Imagine you are about to start writing a piece of narrative fiction. You consult a rubric, which reminds you that narrative fiction should have characters, a setting, and a conflict and resolution. As you write, you try to incorporate and develop each element. After drafting, you might check the rubric again to make sure you are on track. For example, after reviewing the rubric again, you might decide that you have not developed the conflict or its resolution well. You would then go back and revise to improve your writing and get a better score.

Narrative Fiction Elements	Rating Scale
	Not very Very
Interesting characters	1 2 3 4 5 6
Believable setting	1 2 3 4 5 6
Literary strategies	1 2 3 4 5 6
Well-developed conflict	1 2 3 4 5 6
Well-developed resolution	1 2 3 4 5 6

Try It! If you checked your story against the rubric and rated yourself mostly 1s and 2s, what actions might you want to take?

Using a Rubric With a Partner

In some cases, building your own rubric can help you ensure that your writing will meet your expectations. For example, if your class has an assignment to write a poem, you and a partner might decide to construct a rubric to check one another's work. A rubric like the one shown here can help point out whether you should make any changes. Extra lines allow room for you to add other criteria.

Poetry Elements	Rating Scale
	Not very Very
Good sensory details	1 2 3 4 5 6
Colorful adjectives	1 2 3 4 5 6
	1 2 3 4 5 6
	1 2 3 4 5 6
	1 2 3 4 5 6

Try It! What other elements might you add to the rubric?

Using a Rubric in a Group

It is also helpful to use a rubric in a group. That way you can get input on your writing from many people at the same time. If the group members' ratings of your piece are similar, you will probably have an easy time deciding whether to make changes. If the responses vary significantly, you might want to discuss the results with the group. Then, analyze what led to the differing opinions and make careful judgments about what changes you will make.

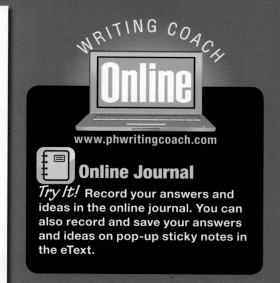

WRITING COACH Online

www.phwritingcoach.com

Online Journal

Try It! Record your answers and ideas in the online journal. You can also record and save your answers and ideas on pop-up sticky notes in the eText.

What Is the Writing Process?

The five steps in the writing process are prewriting, drafting, revising, editing, and publishing. Writing is a process because your idea goes through a series of changes or stages before the product is finished.

Study the diagram to see how moving through the writing process can work. Remember, you can go back to a stage in the process. It does not always have to occur in order.

Prewriting
In prewriting, you will:
• Explore ideas
• Choose a purpose and an audience
• Gather details
• Sequence ideas
Drafting
In drafting, you will:
• Put ideas down
• Develop a thesis or controlling idea
• Structure ideas in a sustained way
Revising
In revising, you will:
• Re-read draft to see what works and what does not
• Use a rubric to evaluate
• Analyze what you want to change or improve
• Make changes
Editing
In the editing phase, you will:
• Check the accuracy of facts
• Correct errors in spelling, grammar, usage, and mechanics
Publishing
In publishing, you will:
• Produce a final polished copy of your writing
• Share your writing

Why Use the Writing Process?

Writing involves careful thinking, which means you will make changes as you write. Even professional writers don't just write their thoughts and call it a finished work of art. They use a process. For example, some writers keep going back to the revising stage many times, while others feel they can do the revision in just one step. It is up to each writer to develop the style that works best to produce the best results.

You might find that the writing process works best for you when you keep these tips in mind:

- Remember that the five steps in the writing process are equally important.
- Think about your audience as you plan your paper and develop your writing.
- Make sure you remember your topic and stick to your specific purpose as you write.
- Give your writing some time to "rest." Sometimes it can be good to work on a piece, walk away, and look at it later, with a fresh eye and mind.

The following pages will describe in more detail how to use each stage of the writing process to improve your writing.

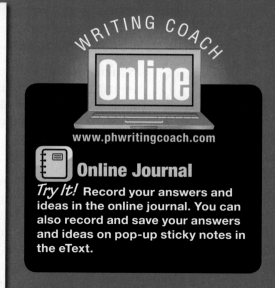

WRITING COACH Online

www.phwritingcoach.com

Online Journal

Try It! Record your answers and ideas in the online journal. You can also record and save your answers and ideas on pop-up sticky notes in the eText.

"Writer to Writer"

Writing process gives us the freedom to write like mad, tinker like an engineer, evaluate like a judge—playing different roles at different stages. Most importantly it gives us the freedom to get our words out of our heads and into the world.

—Jeff Anderson

Prewriting

No matter what kind of writing you do, planning during the prewriting stage is crucial. During prewriting, you determine the topic of your writing, its purpose, and its specific audience. Then, you narrow the topic and gather details.

Determining the Purpose and Audience

What Is Your Purpose?

To be sure your writing communicates your ideas clearly, it is important to clarify why you are writing. Consider what you want your audience to take away from your writing. You may want to entertain them, or you may want to warn them about something. Even when you write an entry in a private journal, you're writing for an audience—you!

Who Is Your Audience?

Think about the people who will read your work and consider what they may already know about your topic. Being able to identify this group and their needs will let you be sure you are providing the right level of information.

Choosing a Topic

Here are just a few of the many techniques you can use to determine an appropriate topic.

- **Brainstorm**
  You can brainstorm by yourself, with a partner, or with a group. Just jot down ideas as they arise, and don't rule out anything. When brainstorming in a group, one person's idea often "piggy-backs" on another.

- **Make a Mind Map**
  A mind map is a quick drawing you sketch as ideas come to you. The mind map can take any form. The important thing is to write quick notes as they come to you and then to draw lines to connect relationships among the ideas.

- **Interview**
  A fun way to find a writing topic is to conduct an interview. You might start by writing interview questions for yourself or someone else. Questions that start with *what*, *when*, *why*, *how*, and *who* are most effective. For example, you might ask, "When was the last time you laughed really hard?" "What made you laugh?" Then, conduct the interview and discover the answers.

- **Review Resources and Discuss Ideas**
  You can review resources, such as books, magazines, newspapers, and digital articles, to get ideas. Discussing your initial ideas with a partner can spark even more ideas.

Narrowing Your Topic

Once you have settled on a topic idea you really like, it may seem too broad to tackle. How can you narrow your topic?

- **Use Graphic Organizers**
  A graphic organizer can help narrow a topic that's too broad. For example, you might choose "Animals" as a topic. You might make your topics smaller and smaller until you narrow the topic to "The Habitat of Emperor Penguins."

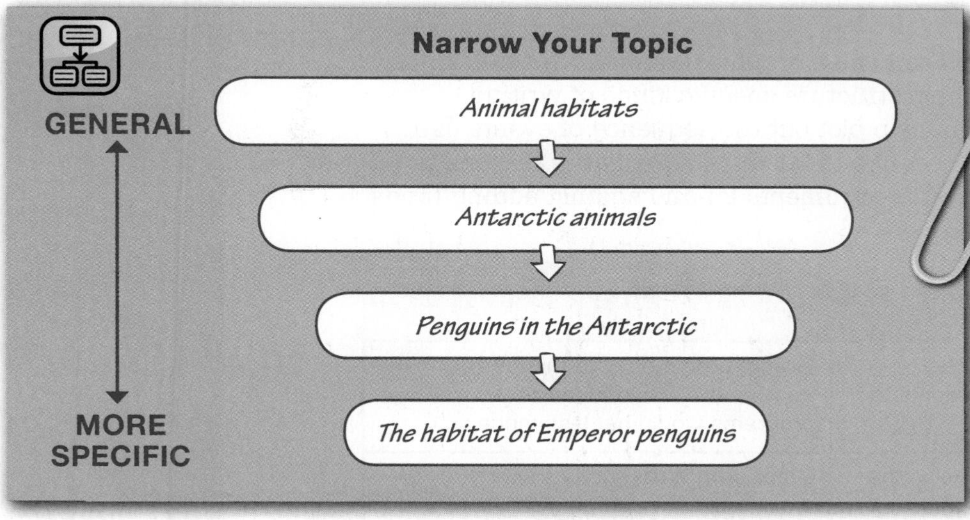

WRITING COACH Online
www.phwritingcoach.com

Online Journal

Try It! Record your answers and ideas in the online journal. You can also record and save your answers and ideas on pop-up sticky notes in the eText.

Writer to Writer

Put something down. Anything. Then, magic will happen.

—Jeff Anderson

Prewriting (continued)

- **Use Resource Materials**
  The resource materials you use to find information can also help you narrow a broad topic. Look up your subject online in an encyclopedia or newspaper archive. Scan the resources as you look for specific subtopics to pursue.

Gather Details

After you decide on a topic, you will want to explore and develop your ideas. You might start by looking through online resources again, talking with people who are knowledgeable about your topic, and writing everything you already know about the topic. It will be helpful to gather a variety of details. Look at these types:

- Facts
- Statistics
- Personal observations
- Expert opinions
- Examples
- Descriptions
- Quotations
- Opposing viewpoints

After you have narrowed your topic and gathered details, you will begin to plan your piece. During this part of prewriting, you will develop your essay's thesis or controlling idea—its main point or purpose. If you are writing a fiction or nonfiction story, you will outline the events of the story.

As you plan your piece, you can use a graphic organizer. Specific kinds of graphic organizers can help structure specific kinds of writing. For example, a plot map can help plot out the sequence of events in a mystery story. A pro-con chart like this one can clarify the reasons for and against an idea. It presents arguments for and against adding funds to a school music program.

Pro	Con
Adding funds to the school music budget would allow more students to learn to play instruments.	Giving more money to the music department would mean other programs would get less money.
Research shows that music helps the brain become more flexible.	Other programs, such as sports, are important in keeping students physically healthy.
Band members could stop selling gift-wrap materials at holiday time.	The school board has already approved the current budget allocations.

Drafting

In the drafting stage, you get your ideas down. You may consult an outline or your prewriting notes as you build your first draft.

Prewriting
Drafting
Revising
Editing
Publishing

WRITING COACH Online
www.phwritingcoach.com

Online Journal

Try It! **Record your answers and ideas in the online journal. You can also record and save your answers and ideas on pop-up sticky notes in the eText.**

The Introduction

Most genres should have a strong introduction that immediately grabs the reader's attention and includes the thesis. Even stories and poems need a "hook" to grab interest.

Try It! Which of these first sentences are strong openers? Read these examples of first sentences. Decide which ones are most interesting to you. Explain why they grab your attention. Then, explain why the others are weak.

- Have you ever wondered what it would be like to wake up one morning to find you're someone else?
- There are many ways to paint a room.
- Yogi Berra, the famous baseball star, said, "You got to be careful if you don't know where you're going, because you might not get there."
- Autumn is a beautiful season.
- On Sunday, we went to the store.
- When I woke up that morning, I had no idea that it would be the best day of my life.

The Body

The body of a paper develops the main idea and details that elaborate on and support the thesis. As you tell your story or build an argument these details may include interesting facts, examples, statistics, anecdotes or stories, quotations, personal feelings, and sensory descriptions.

The Conclusion

The conclusion typically restates the thesis and summarizes the most important concepts of a paper.

Revising: Making It Better

No one gets every single thing right in a first draft. In fact, most people require more than two drafts to achieve their best writing and thinking. When you have finished your first draft, you're ready to revise.

Revising means "re-seeing." In revising, you look again to see if you can find ways to improve style, word choice, figurative language, sentence variety, and subtlety of meaning. As always, check how well you've addressed the issues of purpose, audience, and genre. Carefully analyze what you'd want to change and then go ahead and do it. Here are some helpful hints on starting the revision stage of the writing process.

Take a Break

Do not begin to revise immediately after you finish a draft. Take some time away from your paper. Get a glass of water, take a walk, or listen to some music. You may even want to wait a day to look at what you've written. When you come back, you will be better able to assess the strengths and weaknesses of your work.

Put Yourself in the Place of the Reader

Take off your writer's hat and put on your reader's hat. Do your best to pretend that you're reading someone else's work and see how it looks to that other person. Look for ideas that might be confusing and consider the questions that a reader might have. By reading the piece with an objective eye, you may find items you'd want to fix and improve.

Read Aloud to Yourself

It may feel strange to read aloud to yourself, but it can be an effective technique. It allows you to hear the flow of words, find errors, and hear where you might improve the work by smoothing out transitions between paragraphs or sections. Of course, if you're more comfortable reading your work aloud to someone else, that works, too.

Share Your Work to Get Feedback

Your friends or family members can help you by reading and reacting to your writing. Ask them whether you've clearly expressed your ideas. Encourage them to tell you which parts were most and least interesting and why. Try to find out if they have any questions about your topic that were not answered. Then, evaluate their input and decide what will make your writing better.

Use a Rubric

A rubric might be just what you need to pinpoint weaknesses in your work. You may want to think about the core parts of the work and rate them on a scale. If you come up short, you'll have a better idea about the kinds of things to improve. You might also use a rubric to invite peer review and input.

21st Century Learning

Collaborate and Discuss

When presenting and sharing drafts in the revision stage with a small group, it may be wise to set some ground rules. That way, the group is more likely to help each other analyze their work and make thoughtful changes that result in true improvements.

Here are some suggestions for reviewing drafts as a group:

- Cover the names on papers the group will review to keep the work anonymous.
- Print out copies for everyone in the group.
- Show respect for all group members and their writing.
- Be sure all critiques include positive comments.
- While it is fine to suggest ways to improve the work, present comments in a positive, helpful way. No insults are allowed!
- Plan for a second reading with additional input after the writer has followed selected suggestions.

WRITING COACH Online

www.phwritingcoach.com

Online Journal

Try It! **Record your answers and ideas in the online journal. You can also record and save your answers and ideas on pop-up sticky notes in the eText.**

Partner Talk

After a group revision session, talk with a partner to analyze each other's feeling on how the session went. Discuss such issues as these: Did the group adhere to the ground rules? What suggestions could you and your partner make to improve the next session?

Revision RADaR

The Revision RADaR strategy, which you will use throughout this book, is an effective tool in helping you conduct a focused revision of your work.

You can use your Revision RADaR to revise your writing. The letters **R**, **A**, **D**, and **R** will help you remember to **r**eplace, **a**dd, **d**elete, and **r**eorder.

To understand more about the Revision RADaR strategy, study the following chart.

R	A	D and	R
Replace . . . • Words that are not specific • Words that are overused • Sentences that are unclear	**Add . . .** • New information • Descriptive adjectives and adverbs • Rhetorical or literary devices	**Delete . . .** • Unrelated ideas • Sentences that sound good, but do not make sense • Repeated words or phrases • Unnecessary details	**Reorder . . .** • So most important points are last • To make better sense or to flow better • So details support main ideas

R Replace

You can strengthen a text by replacing words that are not specific, words that are overused, and sentences that are unclear. Take a look at this before and after model.

BEFORE As I ran to the finish line, my heart was beating.
AFTER As I sprinted to the finish line, my heart was pounding in my chest.

Apply It! **How did the writer replace the overused verb *ran*? What other replacements do you see? How did they improve the text?**

A Add

You can add new information, descriptive adjectives and adverbs, and rhetorical or literary devices to make your piece more powerful. Study this before and after model.

BEFORE Shadows made the night seem scary.
AFTER Ominous shadows made the dark night seem even more sinister.

Apply It! **How did the second sentence make you feel, compared with the first? Explain.**

D Delete

Sometimes taking words out of a text can improve clarity. Analyze this before and after model.

BEFORE The candidates talked about the issues, and many of the issues were issues that had been on voters' minds.
AFTER The candidates talked about the issues, many of which had been on voters' minds.

Apply It! **Describe the revision you see. How did taking out unnecessary repetition of the word *issues* help the sentence flow more naturally?**

R Reorder

When you reorder, you can make sentences flow more logically. Look at this example.

BEFORE Put the sunflower seeds over the strawberries, which are on top of the pineapple in a bowl. You'll have a delicious fruit salad!
AFTER To make a delicious fruit salad, cut pineapple into a bowl. Add strawberries and then sprinkle a few sunflower seeds over the top.

Apply It! **Which of the models flows more logically? Why?**

WRITING COACH Online

www.phwritingcoach.com

Online Journal

Try It! **Record your answers and ideas in the online journal. You can also record and save your answers and ideas on pop-up sticky notes in the eText.**

Writer to Writer

Anyone can write a first draft, but revision is where the paper comes to life.

—Kelly Gallagher

USING TECHNOLOGY

Most word processing programs have a built-in thesaurus tool. You can use the thesaurus to find descriptive words that can often substitute for weaker, overused words.

Revision RADaR (continued)

Prewriting
Drafting
Revising
Editing
Publishing

Read the first draft of the Student Model—a review of the book *Technology Drives Me Wild!* Think about how you might use your Revision RADaR to improve the text in a second draft.

Kelly Gallagher, M. Ed.

KEEP REVISION ON YOUR RADAR

Technology Book Drives Reviewer Wild

1ST DRAFT

As a technology fan, I always look for new books about the latest in technology, as soon as they come out. So, when I bought *Technology Drives Me Wild!* by James Frank, after reading other books by Mr. Frank, I had high hopes this would be another winner that would improve my life. Those high hopes were not met by reading this disappointing book.

Does my introduction grab reader interest?

This book, which dashed my high hopes of learning some new stuff, has many mistakes. One error is that computers were not invented in the early 1800s. Did Thomas Jefferson use a computer when he was president? I don't think so.

The one good thing about *Technology Drives Me Wild!* is the fact that it is a very short book. That way, you won't waste too much time, if you decide not to take my advice and read this boring book after all.

It would have helped to show more pictures when explaining how computer chips work. Besides that, the text is boring and there are no diagrams or photos to keep the text from being boring. In addition, the boring text is very wordy and many of the explanations are unclear and impossible to understand. Also, the photograph of Mr. Frank on the book jacket is out of focus.

Are my word choices varied?

Here's a summary of my recommendation about this book: don't read it! Use your time to find better information about technology in other sources.

After writing the first draft, the student used Revision RADaR and asked questions like these:

- What could I **replace**?
- What could I **add**?
- What words might I **delete**?
- Should I **reorder** anything?

The student writer created this second draft after using Revision RADaR.

2ND DRAFT

Technology Book Drives Reviewer Wild

There's no doubt about it. I find the expansion of technology fascinating. I'm always anxious to read the latest developments and to consider how they might enhance my own life. Having read James Frank's previous excellent books on technology, I rushed out to buy his latest—*Technology Drives Me Wild!* Unfortunately, this book turned out to be a be grave disappointment.

R *Replaced opening with more engaging sentences*

I'd hoped to glean new information and a fresh understanding of improvements in global positioning systems, netbooks, and cell phones from the book. What I discovered instead was a substandard account, fraught with errors. For example, I am quite certain that while some people may have dreamed of computers in the 1800s, I doubt any actually existed. Mr. Frank should have checked his facts.

Perhaps additional diagrams, photographs, and other visuals would have helped clarify the weak explanations of how, for example, computer chips work. The addition of lively text would have also helped.

D *Deleted repetitive words*

A *Added details about what would improve the text*

It's fortunate that *Technology Drives Me Wild!* is a short book. That way, even if you pick it up in error, you will not have wasted much of your valuable time.

Try It! What other words did the writer replace? Add? Delete? Reorder?

WRITING COACH Online

www.phwritingcoach.com

Online Journal

Try It! Record your answers and ideas in the online journal. You can also record and save your answers and ideas on pop-up sticky notes in the eText.

Partner Talk

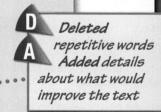

Work with a partner to write as many substitutions for the verb *walk* as possible. Remember to consider the different ways people walk. For example, how does a young child walk? How does a successful team captain walk? How might a very elderly person walk? Discuss the value of using more specific words in your writing.

Editing: Making It Correct

Prewriting
Drafting
Revising
Editing
Publishing

Editing is the process of checking the accuracy of facts and correcting errors in spelling, grammar, usage, and mechanics. Using a checklist like the one shown here can help ensure you've done a thorough job of editing.

Editing Checklist

Task	Ask Yourself
Check your facts and spelling	❑ Have I checked that my facts are correct? ❑ Have I used spell check or a dictionary to check any words I'm not sure are spelled correctly?
Check your grammar	❑ Have I written any run-on sentences? ❑ Have I used the correct verbs and verb tenses? ❑ Do my pronouns match their antecedents, or nouns they replace?
Check your usage	❑ Have I used the correct form of irregular verbs? ❑ Have I used object pronouns, such as *me*, *him*, *her*, *us*, and *them* only after verbs or prepositions? ❑ Have I used subject pronouns, such as *I*, *he*, *she*, *we*, and *they* correctly—usually as subjects?
Check for proper use of mechanics	❑ Have I used correct punctuation? ❑ Does each sentence have the correct end mark? ❑ Have I used apostrophes in nouns but not in pronouns to show possession? ❑ Have I used quotation marks around words from another source? ❑ Have I used correct capitalization? ❑ Does each sentence begin with a capital letter? ❑ Do the names of specific people and places begin with a capital letter?

Using Proofreading Marks

Professional editors use a set of proofreading marks to indicate changes in a text. Here is a chart of some of the more common proofreading marks.

Proofreader's Marks

b.f.	boldface
⌐	break text start new line
caps	capital letter
⁀‿	clos e up
e	deletes
a/	insert word
,/	insert comma
=/	insert hyphen
t/	insert leter
⊙/	insert period
ital	italic type
stet	let stand as is
l.f.	lightface
l.c.	Lower case letter
[	move left
]	move right
¶	new paragraph
rom	roman type
	run text up
sp	spell out whole word
	transpoes

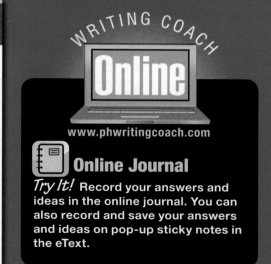

WRITING COACH Online
www.phwritingcoach.com

Online Journal

Try It! Record your answers and ideas in the online journal. You can also record and save your answers and ideas on pop-up sticky notes in the eText.

USING TECHNOLOGY

Many word processing programs have automatic spelling and grammar checks. While these tools can be helpful, be sure to pay attention to any suggestions they offer. That's because sometimes inappropriate substitutes are inserted automatically!

Editing: Making It Correct (continued)

Prewriting
Drafting
Revising
Editing
Publishing

WRITE GUY *Jeff Anderson, M. Ed.*

WHAT DO YOU NOTICE?

Using an editing checklist is a great way to check for correct grammar. However, using a checklist is not enough to make your writing grammatically correct. A checklist tells you what to look for, but not how to correct mistakes you find. To do that, you need to develop and apply your knowledge of grammar.

Looking closely at good writing is one way to expand your grammar know-how. The *What Do You Notice*? feature that appears throughout this book will help you zoom in on passages that use grammar correctly and effectively.

As you read this passage, from "One Dog's Feelings," zoom in on the sentences in the passage.

> Bo clearly shows when he is angry. He gnashes his teeth, growls, and sometimes even spits! On the other hand, Bo, who can simultaneously chew on two pairs of shoes, is usually content. When he's happy, he simply smiles.

Now, ask yourself: *What do you notice about the sentences in this passage?*

Maybe you noticed that the writer uses sentences of varying lengths and with different structures. Or perhaps you noticed that the writer varies the way sentences begin.

After asking a question that draws your attention to the grammar in the passage, the *What Do You Notice*? feature provides information on a particular grammar topic. For example, following the passage and question, you might read about simple and complex sentences, which are both used in the passage.

The *What Do You Notice*? feature will show you how grammar works in actual writing. It will help you learn how to make your writing correct.

One Dog's Feelings

Some people wonder if animals feel and show emotions. However, I am absolutely positive that dogs experience a full range of emotions. I owe this knowledge to my dog, Bo.

Bo clearly shows when he is angry. He gnashes his teeth, growls, and sometimes even spits! On the other hand, Bo, who can simultaneously chew on two pairs of shoes, is usually content. When he's happy, he simply smiles. The colors on his tan and white face seem to glow.

He and my cat often rest together on the mat near the door. When they are together, they both purr with happiness. Neither Bo nor the cat minds that cool air seeps under the door. They're just happy to be with one another.

If my brothers or I want to play fetch, Bo is always up for a game. We often throw a ball into the woods, where it sometimes gets buried under leaves and sticks. Bo always rushes for the ball. And running back to us with the stick in his mouth is obviously his great joy. As for the sticks, few are ever left unfound.

When I leave for school in the morning, Bo whimpers—an obvious sign of sadness. That makes me feel miserable. However, the big payoff comes when I return home. Then Bo jumps up on the door, his tail wagging enthusiastically with excitement. Everybody wants to be loved like that!

Try It! Read "One Dog's Feelings." Then, zoom in on two more passages. Write a response to each question in your journal.

1 What do you notice about the pronouns (*he, they, one, another*) in the third paragraph?

2. How does the writer use transitions, such as the word *however,* to connect ideas in the last paragraph?

WRITING COACH Online

www.phwritingcoach.com

Online Journal

Try It! **Record your answers and ideas in the online journal. You can also record and save your answers and ideas on pop-up sticky notes in the eText.**

Writer to Writer

If I wonder how to write any kind of writing, I look at models—well-written examples of the kind of writing I want to do. Models are the greatest how-to lesson I have ever discovered.

—Jeff Anderson

Publishing

Prewriting
Drafting
Revising
Editing
Publishing

When you publish, you produce a final copy of your work and present it to an audience. When publishing you'll need to decide which form will best reach your audience, exhibit your ideas, show your creativity, and accomplish your main purpose.

To start assessing the optimal way to publish your work, you might ask yourself these questions:

- What do I hope to accomplish by sharing my work with others?
- Should I publish in print form? Give an oral presentation? Publish in print form and give an oral presentation?
- Should I publish online, in traditional print, or both?
- What specific forms are available to choose from?

The answers to most of these questions will most likely link to your purpose for writing and your audience. Some choices seem obvious. For example, if you've written a piece to contribute to a blog, you'll definitely want to send it electronically.

Each publishing form will present different challenges and opportunities and each will demand different forms of preparation. For example, you may need to prepare presentation slides of your plan to give a speech, or you may want to select music and images if you will be posting a video podcast online.

Ways to Publish

There are many ways to publish your writing. This chart shows some of several opportunities you can pursue to publish your work.

Genre	Publishing Opportunities	
Narration: Nonfiction	• Blogs • Book manuscript • Audio recording	• Private diary or journal entries • Electronic slide show
Narration: Fiction	• Book manuscript • Film	• Audio recording • Oral reading to a group
Poetry and Description	• Bound collection • Visual display	• Audio recording • Oral reading to a group
Exposition and Persuasion	• Print or online article • Web site • Slide show • Visual display	• Film • Audio recording • Oral reading or speech
Response to Literature	• Print or online letters • Visual displays	• Blogs • Slide show
Research Writing	• Traditional paper • Print and online experiment journals	• Multimedia presentation

Reflect on Your Writing

Think about what you learned in Chapter 3 as you answer these questions:

- What did you learn about the writing process?
- What steps in the writing process do you already use in your writing?
- Which stage do you think is the most fun? Which one may be most challenging for you? Explain.

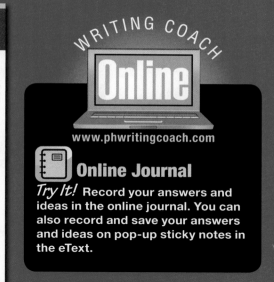

WRITING COACH Online

www.phwritingcoach.com

Online Journal

Try It! **Record your answers and ideas in the online journal. You can also record and save your answers and ideas on pop-up sticky notes in the eText.**

Partner Talk

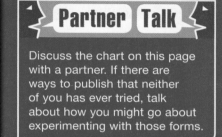

Discuss the chart on this page with a partner. If there are ways to publish that neither of you has ever tried, talk about how you might go about experimenting with those forms.

SENTENCES, PARAGRAPHS, and COMPOSITIONS

Good writers know that strong sentences and paragraphs help to construct effective compositions. Chapter 4 will help you use these building blocks to structure and style excellent writing. It will also present ways to use rhetorical and literary devices and online tools to strengthen your writing.

The Building Blocks: Sentences and Paragraphs

A **sentence** is a group of words with two main parts: a subject and a predicate. Together, these parts express a complete thought.

A **paragraph** is built from a group of sentences that share a common idea and work together to express that idea clearly. The start of a new paragraph has visual clues—either an indent of several spaces in the first line or an extra line of space above it.

In a good piece of writing, each paragraph supports, develops, or explains the main idea of the whole work. Of course, the traits of effective writing—ideas, organization, voice, word choice, sentence fluency, conventions—appear in each paragraph as well.

Writing Strong Sentences

To write strong paragraphs, you need strong sentences. While it may be your habit to write using a single style of sentences, adding variety will help make your writing more interesting. Combining sentences, using compound elements, forming compound sentences, and using subordination all may help you make your sentences stronger, clearer, or more varied.

Combine Sentences

Putting information from one sentence into another can make a more powerful sentence.

BEFORE
Video games can be effective educational tools. They can help teach many subjects.

AFTER
Video games, which can help teach many subjects, can be effective educational tools.

Use Compound Elements

You can form compound subjects, verbs, or objects to help the flow.

BEFORE
Students can play video games on their laptops. Students can also play video games on their cell phones.

AFTER
Students can play video games on their laptops and cell phones.

Form Compound Sentences

You can combine two sentences into a compound sentence.

BEFORE
Video games can motivate students to learn. They must have educational value.

AFTER
Video games can motivate students to learn, but they must have educational value.

Use Subordination

Combine two related sentences by rewriting the less important one as a subordinate clause.

BEFORE
Video games can take time away from exercise. That can be unhealthy.

AFTER
Video games can take time away from exercise, which can be unhealthy.

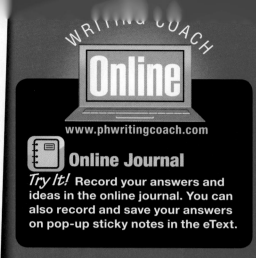

WRITING COACH **Online**

www.phwritingcoach.com

Online Journal

Try It! **Record your answers and ideas in the online journal. You can also record and save your answers on pop-up sticky notes in the eText.**

LEARN MORE

For more on sentence combining see Chapter 16.

Writing Strong Paragraphs

If all the sentences in a paragraph reflect the main idea and work together to express that idea clearly, the result will be a strong paragraph.

Express Your Main Idea With a Clear Topic Sentence

A **topic sentence** summarizes the main idea of a paragraph. It may appear at the beginning, middle, or end of a paragraph. It may even be unstated. When the topic sentence comes at the beginning of a paragraph, it introduces the main idea and leads the reader naturally to the sentences that follow it. When it appears at the end of a paragraph, it can draw a conclusion or summarize what came before it. If the topic sentence is unstated, the rest of the paragraph must be very clearly developed, so the reader can understand the main idea from the other sentences.

Think about the topic sentence as you read this paragraph.

> Without a doubt, hiking must be the best sport in the world. Hiking is good exercise and makes me feel totally free. When I'm out on the trail, I can think more clearly than anywhere else. Even solving problems that seemed totally unsolvable at home becomes possible. I also use all of my senses when I hike. I hear birds singing, I notice strange plants, and I feel the soft underbrush beneath my boots. Sometimes I even think I can smell and taste the fresh air.

Try It! Look back at the sample paragraph to answer these questions.

1. What is the topic sentence?
2. Does the topic sentence introduce the main idea or draw a final conclusion? Explain.
3. What makes this topic sentence strong?

Write Effective Supporting Sentences

A clear topic sentence is a good start, but it needs to be accompanied by good details that support the paragraph's main idea. Your supporting sentences might tell interesting facts, describe events, or give examples. In addition, the supporting sentences should also provide a smooth transition, so that the paragraph reads clearly and logically.

Think about the topic sentences and supporting details as you read this paragraph.

> What was life like before cell phones? It's barely imaginable! People were tied to land lines and could make and take calls only in homes, offices, or on pay phones. If there were an emergency, there could be unavoidable delays as people searched for an available phone. If they wanted to chat with friends, they usually had to wait until they got home. How ever did they live without being able to text? Some people send text messages to their friends about 50 times a day. What a different world it was way back then.

Try It! Look at the paragraph and answer these questions.

1. What is the topic sentence of the paragraph?
2. Do you think it's an effective topic sentence? Why or why not?
3. What supporting details does the writer provide?
4. If you were the writer, what other supporting details might you add to strengthen the paragraph?
5. Which sentence in the paragraph breaks up the flow of ideas and does not provide a smooth transition to the next sentence?

WRITING COACH Online

www.phwritingcoach.com

Online Journal

Try It! **Record your answers and ideas in the online journal. You can also record and save your answers on pop-up sticky notes in the eText.**

Include a Variety of Sentence Lengths, Structures, and Beginnings

To be interesting, a paragraph should include sentences of different lengths, types, and beginnings. Similarly, if every sentence has the same structure—for example, article, adjective, noun, verb—the paragraph may sound boring or dry.

21st Century Learning

Collaborate and Discuss

With a group, study this writing sample.

The scene was tense as Carlos stepped to the plate. Looking confident, he took a few practice swings. Then he stopped and stared straight at the pitcher. The first pitch zoomed over home plate at about 90 miles an hour—right past Carlos. Strike one! The second pitch was high and outside. Ball one! Next Carlos took a deep breath; it was obvious he meant business now. He stared down the pitcher and raised his bat. Crack! Carlos hit that ball right over the fence behind second base and the game was over. It was a 4-2 victory for the home team, thanks to Carlos!

Discuss these questions about the paragraph.

1. What is the topic sentence? How does it draw in the reader?
2. What details support the topic sentence in each paragraph?
3. Point out some examples of varying sentence lengths and beginnings.
4. What examples can you find of sentences with a variety of sentence structures?
5. Which words help the transitions and flow of the paragraphs?

Partner Talk

Work with a partner to take another look at the writing sample on this page. Talk about what you think the writer did well. Then, discuss what might make the paragraph even stronger.

USING TECHNOLOGY

It's often better to use the tab key, rather than the space bar, to indent a paragraph. Using the tab key helps to ensure that the indents in all paragraphs will be uniform.

Composing Your Piece

You've learned that the building blocks of writing are strong sentences and paragraphs. Now it's time to use those building blocks to construct an effective composition. While the types of writing vary from short poems to long essays and research papers, most types have a definite structure with clearly defined parts.

The Parts of a Composition

Writers put together and arrange sentences and paragraphs to develop ideas in the clearest way possible in a composition. Some types of writing, such as poetry and advertisements, follow unique rules and may not have sentences and paragraphs that follow a standard structure. However, as you learned in Chapter 3, most compositions have three main sections: an introduction, a body, and a conclusion.

I. Introduction

The introduction of a composition introduces the focus of the composition, usually in a thesis statement. The introduction should engage the reader's interest, with such elements as a question, an unusual fact, or a surprising scene.

II. Body

Just as supporting statements develop the ideas of a topic sentence, the body of a composition develops the thesis statement and main idea. It provides details that help expand on the thesis statement. The paragraphs in the body are arranged in a logical order.

III. Conclusion

As the word implies, the conclusion of a composition concludes or ends a piece of writing. A good way to ensure the reader will remember your thesis statement is to restate it or summarize it in the conclusion. When restating the thesis, it's usually most effective to recast it in other words. Quotations and recommendations are other ways to conclude a composition with memorable impact. The conclusion should provide a parting insight or reinforce the importance of the main idea.

"Writer to Writer"

Strong, varied sentences and unified paragraphs are the building blocks of effective writing.

—Kelly Gallagher

Rhetorical and Literary Devices

Like any builders, good writers have a set of tools, or devices, at their fingertips to make their writing interesting, engaging, and effective. Writers can use the rhetorical devices of language and their effects to strengthen the power of their style. This section presents some tools you can store in your own writing toolbox to develop effective compositions.

Sound Devices

Sound devices, which create a musical or emotional effect, are most often used in poetry. The most common sound devices include these:

- **Alliteration** is the repetition of consonant sounds at the beginning of words that are close to one another.

  Example: Bees buzzed by both bouquets.

- **Assonance** is the repetition of vowel sounds in words that are close to one another.

  Example: My kite flew high into the sky.

- **Consonance** is the repetition of consonants within or at the end of words.

  Example: Each coach teaches touch football after lunch.

Structural Devices

Structural devices determine the way a piece of writing is organized. Rhyme and meter are most often used to structure poetry, as are stanzas and many other structural devices.

- **Rhyme** is the repetition of sounds at the ends of words. Certain poetry forms have specific rhyme schemes.
- **Meter** is the rhythmical pattern of a poem, determined by the stressed syllables in a line.
- **Visual elements**, such as stanzas, line breaks, line length, fonts, readability, and white space, help determine how a piece of writing is read and interpreted. These elements can also affect the emotional response to a piece.

Other Major Devices

You can use these devices in many forms of writing. They help writers express ideas clearly and engage their readers.

Device	Example
Figurative language is writing that means something beyond what the words actually say. Common forms of figurative language include these:	
• A **simile** compares two things using the words *like* or *as*.	*The fallen autumn leaves were like colorful jewels.*
• A **metaphor** compares two things by mentioning one thing as if it is something else. It does not use *like* or *as*.	*Her smile was a beacon of good cheer.*
• **Personification** gives human characteristics to a non-human object.	*Shadows crawled over the sand just before dusk.*
Hyperbole is exaggeration used for effect.	*The elephant was as big as a house.*
Irony is a contradiction between what happens and what is expected.	In a famous story, a wife cuts her hair to buy her husband a watch fob, and he sells his watch to buy her a brush.
Paradox is a statement that contains elements that seem contradictory but could be true.	George Orwell said, "Ignorance is strength."
An **oxymoron** is word or phrase that seems to contradict itself.	I had jumbo shrimp for dinner.
Symbolism is an object that stands for something else.	An owl is often used as a symbol for wisdom.
An **allegory** is a narrative that has a meaning other than what literally appears.	Some say that his sci-fi story is actually an allegory for the effects of war.
Repetition (or tautology) occurs when content is repeated, sometimes needlessly—for effect.	The forest was dense, dense and dark as coal.

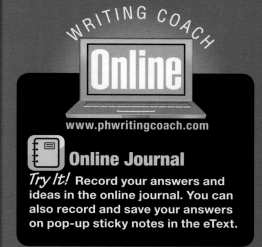

WRITING COACH Online

www.phwritingcoach.com

Online Journal

Try It! **Record your answers and ideas in the online journal. You can also record and save your answers on pop-up sticky notes in the eText.**

USING TECHNOLOGY

Most word processing programs have a built-in thesaurus tool. You can use the thesaurus to find descriptive words that can often substitute for weaker, overused words.

Partner Talk

There are many online tools that can help you strengthen your writing. For example, you can search for examples of figurative language and sound devices. Then you can model your own writing after the samples. Just be sure that you don't plagiarize or copy the written work of others.

Using Writing Traits to Develop an Effective Composition

You read about rubrics and traits in Chapter 3. Now it's time to look at how they function in good writing.

Ideas

In an excellent piece of writing, the information presented is significant, the message or perspective is strong, and the ideas are original. As you read the sample, think about the ideas it presents and how it develops them.

Leaves of Three

Leaves of three. Let them be! It's an old rhyme that warns against the dangers of poison ivy—a plant with three waxy-looking leaves. If you've ever had a poison ivy rash, you know that the itching and pain it can cause are nothing to sneeze at. You may not know that the rash is caused by a colorless oil called urushiol or that not all people are allergic to this substance. However, those who are allergic never forget its effects.

Contracting the rash is, unfortunately, all too easy. Perhaps you've been outside, pulling up weeds on a sunny weekend. Because of the way poison ivy leaves bend down, you might not have even noticed them. Then it might have taken 12 to 48 hours before you felt a sharp itch and saw the telltale red blisters caused by even a brief brush with the plant.

What can you do for the discomfort of poison ivy? Applying ice helps some people. Others need anti-itch medication, especially if the reaction is intense or covers a large area. However, the best idea is to keep that old rhyme in mind and to be careful not to let those leaves of three ever come close to thee!

Try It! Think about ideas in the sample as you respond to these prompts.

1. List two details that help readers relate to the topic.
2. List two significant pieces of information the writer includes.
3. List two details that clearly convey the writer's perspective.

Organization

A well-organized composition flows easily from sentence to sentence and paragraph to paragraph. It smoothly progresses from one idea to the next, indicating the connections between ideas with transitions. The paper also avoids needless repetition.

Think about organization as you reread "Leaves of Three" on page 56.

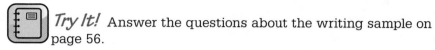

Try It! Answer the questions about the writing sample on page 56.

1. Identify the transition the writer uses to move from the ideas in the first paragraph to the ideas in the second.
2. List three details in the third paragraph. Explain how each detail supports the first sentence in the paragraph.
3. Identify the topic of each paragraph, and explain whether the topics are presented in logical order.

Voice

Voice is the individual "sound" of a writer's writing, reflecting the writer's personality and perspective. A well-written piece has a distinctive voice that expresses the writer's individuality.

Read the writing sample. Think about voice as you read.

What is it like to know a person who looks exactly like you? As identical twins, my brother, Ben, and I can tell you that it's totally great. There are many reasons why.

First, it's great to have a special non-verbal communication with another person. Sometimes it's even scary. Take this morning. Ben and I never dress alike, since we like to show that we're individuals. So, each of us got dressed in our own room and then skipped down the stairs for breakfast. You guessed it! We'd chosen exactly the same clothes—right down to our striped socks.

Second, we can have fun fooling people by pretending to be each other. It's great fun to see Dad's expression when he finds he's treated the wrong twin to a reward.

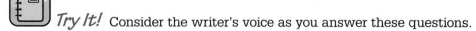

Try It! Consider the writer's voice as you answer these questions.

1. Describe the writer's tone—his attitude toward his subject.
2. Which words and phrases create a voice in this sample? Explain.

WRITING COACH Online

www.phwritingcoach.com

Online Journal

***Try It!* Record your answers and ideas in the online journal. You can also record and save your answers on pop-up sticky notes in the eText.**

Partner Talk

Analyze the composition about poison ivy on page 56 with a partner. Discuss how well it might score for the traits of ideas and organization—from ineffective (1), to somewhat effective (2), to fairly effective (3), to effective (4), to highly effective in parts (5), to highly effective throughout (6).

Word Choice

By choosing words with precision, and by using vivid words to create images, good writers give their writing energy and help readers understand their exact meaning.

Think about the writer's word choice as you read these two drafts:

> **1ST DRAFT**
>
> Sally and Alice ran until they reached a place to make a turn. They headed off to the left, where the flowers were pretty and smelled nice.

> **2ND DRAFT**
>
> Sally and Alice jogged at a steady pace on the dirt path along the lake until they reached a fork in the trail. Without breaking stride, the two turned in unison and headed left, bound by their silent understanding that left was best—left, where the cream-and-gold honeysuckle blossoms, drooping with fragrance, filled the air with a drowsy sweetness.

Try It! Answer the question about the two drafts.

1. List two vague or imprecise words in the first draft.
2. Explain which words in the second draft replace the words you listed. What do the words in the second draft help you understand?

Sentence Fluency

When you read the best writing aloud, you will find that the sentences flow smoothly; they do not sound choppy or awkward. The meaning and the rhythm of the sentences work together. To create and control rhythm in writing, good writers use a variety of sentence structures and patterns. Think about the rhythm of the sentences as you read this draft:

> Since I first joined the student council in the ninth grade, I have been a tireless advocate for many important student causes. My experience makes me a good candidate for president of the council; my advocacy makes me a great one. No one else matches my record.

Try It! Answer the question about the sample.

Describe the rhythm created by the sentences. How does the writer emphasize the final sentence?

Conventions

If a piece of writing reflects a good command of spelling, capitalization, punctuation, grammar, usage, and sentence structure, it is much more likely to communicate clearly to readers.

Pay attention to spelling, capitalization, punctuation, grammar, usage, and sentence structure in the following first draft.

Super-Hero III Doesn't Fly (1ST DRAFT)

If you're among the thousands who have been waiting for the latest installment of the popular Super-Hero movie series, you'are in for a big disappointment. This sequel misses the boat—literally.

Me and my companion couldn't believe it! At the very beginning of the movie, as usual, our "hero" runs for the ship on his quest to capture the evil warlord. However, this time he misreads, the schedule and it took off for asia without his assistant and he.

Now, read this section of the reviewer's second draft.

Super-Hero III Doesn't Fly (2ND DRAFT)

If you're among the thousands who have been waiting for the latest installment of the popular Super-Hero movie series, you're in for a big disappointment. This sequel misses the boat—literally.

My companion and I couldn't believe it! At the very beginning of the movie, as usual, our "hero" runs for the ship on his quest to capture the evil warlord. However, this time he misreads the schedule, and the ship takes off for Asia without his assistant and him.

Try It! Answer these questions about both drafts.

1. What errors in convention did the writer correct in the second draft?
2. Why is the last sentence easier to read in the second draft?

WRITING COACH Online

www.phwritingcoach.com

Online Journal

Try It! Record your answers and ideas in the online journal. You can also record and save your answers on pop-up sticky notes in the eText.

Partner Talk

Work with a partner to make sure you both found every error the move reviewer corrected in the second draft.

Using Interactive Writing Coach

As you learned in Chapter 3, you can use rubrics and your Revision RADaR to check how well your paragraphs and essays read. With Writing Coach, you also have another tool available to evaluate your work: the Interactive Writing Coach.

The Interactive Writing Coach is a program that you can use anywhere that you have Internet access. Interactive Writing Coach functions like your own personal writing tutor. It gives you personalized feedback on your work.

The Interactive Writing Coach has two parts: **Paragraph Feedback** and **Essay Scorer**.

- Paragraph Feedback gives you feedback on individual paragraphs as you write. It looks at the structure of sentences and paragraphs and gives you information about specific details, such as sentence variety and length.
- Essay Scorer looks at your whole essay and gives you a score and feedback on your entire piece of writing. It will tell you how well your essay reflects the traits of good writing.

This chart shows just a few questions that Paragraph Feedback and Essay Scorer will answer about your writing. The following pages explain Paragraph Feedback and Essay Scorer in more detail.

Sentences	• Are sentences varied in length? • Do sentences have varied beginnings? • Which sentences have too many ideas? • Are adjectives clear and precise? • Is the sentence grammatically correct? • Is all spelling correct in the sentence?
Paragraphs	• Does the paragraph support its topic? • Does the paragraph use transitions? • Does the paragraph contain the right amount of ideas and information?
Compositions	• Does the essay reflect characteristics of the genre? • Does it demonstrate the traits of good writing? • Is the main idea clear? • Is the main idea well supported? • Is the essay cohesive—does it hold together?

Interactive Writing Coach and the Writing Process

You can begin to use Essay Scorer during the drafting section of the writing process. It is best to complete a full draft of your essay before submitting to Essay Scorer. (While you are drafting individual paragraphs, you may want to use Paragraph Feedback.) Keep in mind, however, that your draft does not need to be perfect or polished before you submit to Essay Scorer. You will be able to use feedback from Essay Scorer to revise your draft many times. This chart shows how you might use the Interactive Writing Coach and incorporate Essay Scorer into your writing process.

Prewriting
In prewriting, you will:
Generate ideas using Interactive Graphic Organizers
Drafting
In drafting, you will:
• Use Paragraph Feedback while you draft
• Use Essay Scorer when your first draft is complete
Revising
In revising, you will:
• Use Essay Scorer feedback to revise your draft
• Submit your work to Essay Scorer again
• Revise and submit your draft again as needed
Editing
In the editing phase, you will:
Use feedback from Essay Scorer to correct any grammar and spelling errors
Publishing
In publishing, you will:
Submit to Essay Scorer again to ensure your draft is final and polished

Paragraph Feedback With Interactive Writing Coach

The Paragraph Feedback assesses the ideas and topic support for each paragraph you write. You can enter your work into Paragraph Feedback one paragraph at a time. This makes it easy to work on individual paragraphs and get new feedback as you revise each one. Here are some things that Paragraph Feedback will be able to tell you.

Overall Paragraph Support	• Does the paragraph support the main idea? • Which sentences do not support the main idea?
Transitions	• Which sentences contain transition words? • Which words are transition words?
Ideas	• How well are ideas presented? • Which sentences have too many ideas?
Sentence Length and Variety	• Which sentences are short, medium, and long? • Which sentences could be longer or shorter for better sense or variety? • Are sentences varied?
Sentence Beginnings	• How do sentences begin? • Are sentence beginnings varied?
Sentence Structure	• Are sentence structures varied? • Are there too many sentences with similar structures?
Vague Adjectives	• Are any adjectives vague or unclear? • Where are adjectives in sentences and paragraphs?
Language Variety	• Are words repeated? • Where are repeated words located? • How can word choice be improved?

Essay Scoring With Interactive Writing Coach

Essay Scorer assesses your essay. It looks at the essay as a whole, and it also evaluates individual paragraphs, sentences, and words. Essay Scorer will help you evaluate the following traits.

Ideas	• Are the ideas original? Is a clear message or unique perspective presented? • Is the main idea clearly stated? • Is the main idea supported by informative details?
Organization	• Is the organization logical? • Is the introduction clear? Is the conclusion clear? • What transitions are used, and are they effective?
Voice	• Does the writer create a unique voice, expressing his or her personality or perspective? • Does the tone match the topic, audience, and purpose?
Word Choice	• Are precise words used? • Are vivid words used? • Do the word choices suit the purpose and audience?
Sentence Fluency	• Are sentence beginnings, lengths, and structures varied? • Do the sentences flow smoothly?
Conventions	• Is spelling correct? • Is capitalization used properly? • Is all punctuation (ending, internal, apostrophes) accurate? • Do subjects and verbs agree? • Are pronouns used correctly? • Are adjectives and adverbs used correctly? • Are plurals formed correctly? • Are commonly confused words used correctly?

Whenever you see the Interactive Writing Coach icon you can go to Writing Coach Online and submit your writing, either paragraph by paragraph or as a complete draft, for personalized feedback and scoring.

WRITING COACH Online

www.phwritingcoach.com

Interactive Writing Coach™

Interactive Writing Coach provides support and guidance to help you improve your writing skills.

- **Select a topic to write about from the Topic Bank.**
- **Use the interactive graphic organizers to narrow your topic.**
- **Go to Writing Coach Online and submit your work, paragraph by paragraph or as a complete draft.**
- **Receive immediate, personalized feedback as you write, revise, and edit your work.**

CHAPTER 5

NONFICTION NARRATION

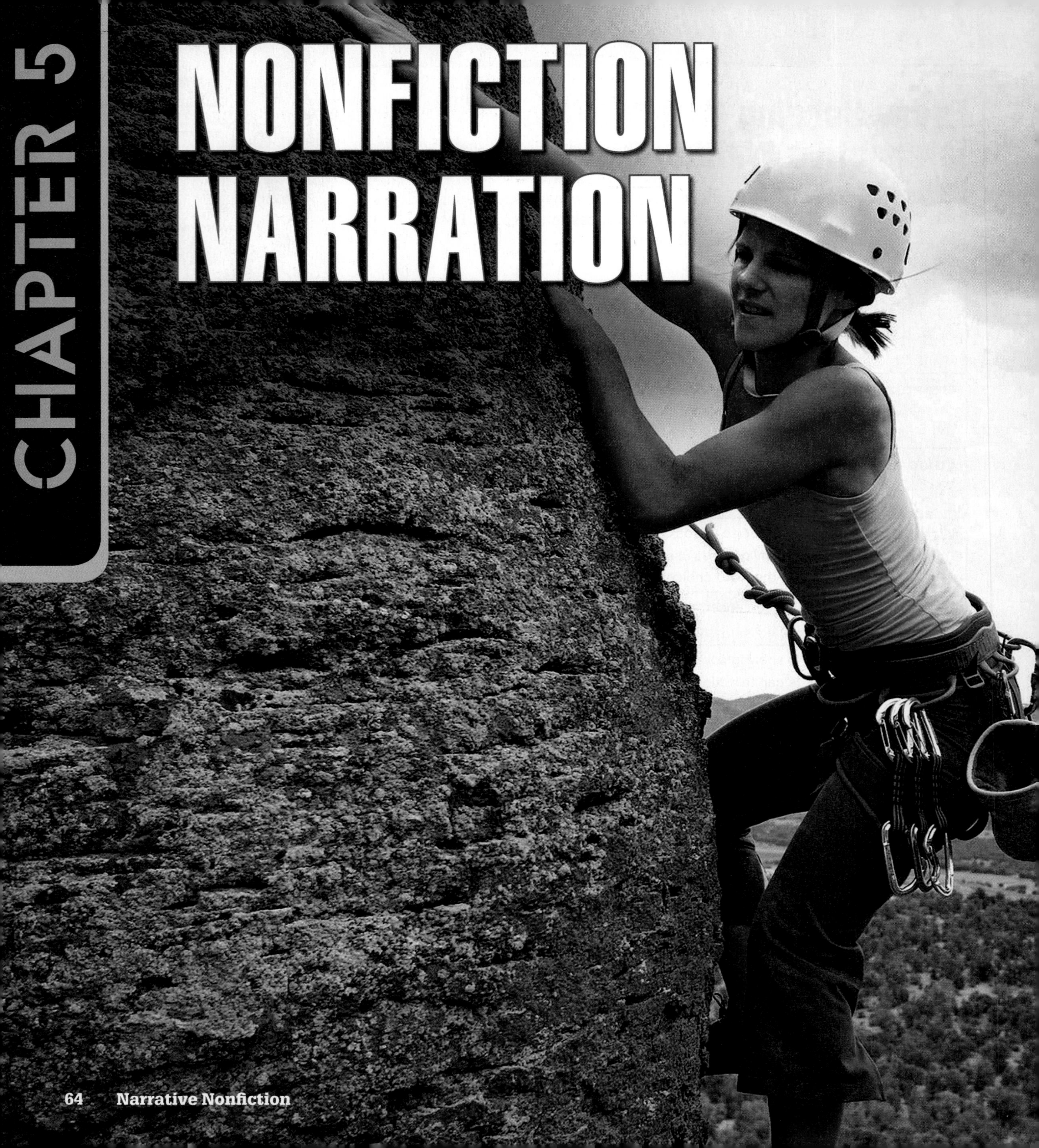

What Do You Remember?

Why are memories important? What would make other people want to hear about your memories? An interesting retelling of events often includes a conflict, or problem, that leads to a resolution, or solution.

In order to tell another person about an event from your life, you will need to remember vivid details and tell them in a way that builds interest. You will also want to describe conflict. One way you can do this is by telling about your struggles to accomplish a goal.

Try It! Think about an event that happened in your life. What details would help to build interest in the story? List those details.

Consider these questions as you participate in an extended discussion with a partner. Take turns expressing your ideas and feelings.

- What happened?
- What was your challenge or problem?
- How did you overcome or solve the problem?

Review the list you made, and then think about how you could use these details to build your story. Tell your story to a partner. As you tell what happened, tell it in a way that the outcome is uncertain until the end.

What's Ahead

In this chapter, you will review two strong examples of an autobiographical narrative: a Mentor Text and a Student Model. Then, using the examples as guidance, you will write an autobiographical narrative of your own.

Online

www.phwritingcoach.com

Online Journal

Try It! Record your answers and ideas in the online journal.

You can also record and save your answers and ideas on pop-up sticky notes in the eText.

Connect to the Big Questions

Discuss these questions with your partner:

1 **What do you think?** What makes a good story?

2 **Why write?** What should we put in and leave out to be accurate and honest?

NARRATIVE NONFICTION

In this chapter, you will explore a special type of narrative nonfiction: the autobiographical narrative. An autobiographical narrative gives you the chance to present writing in which YOU are the leading character. By sharing a true personal experience, you can let readers know something about who you are—and perhaps you can encourage them to look inside themselves as well!

You will develop the autobiographical narrative by taking it through each of the steps of the writing process: prewriting, drafting, revising, editing, and publishing. You will also have an opportunity to write a script for a documentary. To preview the criteria for how your autobiographical narrative will be evaluated, see the rubric on page 83.

FEATURE ASSIGNMENT

Narrative Nonfiction: Autobiographical Narrative

An effective narrative nonfiction essay has these characteristics:

- An **engaging story** that holds readers' attention
- A **well-developed conflict**, or problem, that shows why a situation created a problem for you
- A **well-developed resolution**, the outcome of the conflict, that shows the result and consequences of your or others' actions
- **A range of literary strategies and devices to enhance the plot**, such as dialogue and suspense, that can make the quality of your narrative stand out
- **Sensory details** that help readers feel connected to the story
- **Effective sentence structure** and correct spelling, grammar, and usage

An autobiographical narrative also includes:

- Specific **details** about your personal experiences
- Strong **characterization** of real people, that shows who they are and why they are important to the narrative
- A **theme** that shares a lesson learned

Other Forms of Narrative Nonfiction

In addition to an autobiographical narrative, there are other forms of narrative nonfiction, including:

Biographical narratives are stories that share facts about someone else's life. They often focus on famous people, but they can also be about someone the writer knows personally.

Blogs, or comments that writers share in online forums, may include autobiographical narratives, reflections, opinions, and other types of comments. Blogs often invite responses, and they usually are not considered a "permanent" form of writing.

Diary entries, which are highly personal, include experiences, thoughts, and feelings—but the audience is private, unless writers choose to share the entries.

Narrative essays use one or more biographical or autobiographical narratives to illustrate or prove a point—the main idea.

Memoirs contain a writer's reflections on an important person or event from his or her own life. Book-length memoirs by famous people often are quite popular.

Reflective essays present personal experiences that are either events that happened to the writers themselves or events that they learned about from others. However, they focus more on sharing the observations and insights that writers had while thinking about those experiences. Reflective essays often appear as features in magazines and newspapers.

Try It! For each audience and purpose described, choose a form, such as a reflective essay, memoir, or blog, that is appropriate for conveying your intended meaning to multiple audiences. Explain your choices.

- To let classmates know your feelings about a new pet
- To tell the Spanish Club about how visiting Mexico changed you
- To share with online friends a funny story about what happened to you on the way home from school

WRITING COACH **Online**

www.phwritingcoach.com

Resource

Word Bank **Listen to English and Spanish pronunciations of new words in the eText glossary.**

Online Journal

Try It! **Record your answers and ideas in the online journal.**

WORD BANK

People often use these vocabulary words when they talk about writing narrative nonfiction. Work with a partner. Take turns saying or writing each word in a sentence. If you are unsure of the meaning of a word, use a reference guide, such as the Glossary or a dictionary to check the definition.

autobiographical	**engaging**
biographical	**resolution**
consequences	**strategies**

MENTOR TEXT

Autobiographical Narrative

Learn From Experience

After reading the autobiographical narrative on pages 68–69, read the numbered notes in the margins to learn about how the author presented her ideas.

Answer the *Try It!* questions online or in your notebook.

❶ In the introduction, the author hints at the **conflict,** or main struggle, that will be presented in the story.

Try It! What is the story's conflict? What challenges related to the conflict do you think the author might face?

❷ The author presents interesting, believable **characters** in the story.

Try It! What does this passage tell you about the characters? How does this make them believable?

❸ The author uses literary strategies, such as **suspense,** to enhance the plot.

Try It! How does this sentence create suspense for the reader? How did it make you feel when you read it?

Extension Find another autobiographical narrative, and compare it with this one. How do the structures and themes compare?

A Wild Ride

by Callie McCafferty

❶ Have you ever had one of "those" days? I mean, a day when anything that can go wrong, does, in fact, go wrong? I had one on a sunny, summer day back when I was in high school. A canoe trip with my family ended up being far more dramatic than we'd ever thought possible!

That morning, the sun kissed our shoulders as we unloaded the canoes. My brother, Aidan, and my cousin Nicolas hopped into a canoe with Uncle Frank. My cousin Nora and I were to ride with Aunt Rae. The guys agreed to keep the cooler with the sandwiches and sodas in their canoe, to give us a little more room in ours. Since there were only two seats in the canoe, I settled into the bottom of the canoe. Nora and I would switch places farther down the river.

The trip started off great enough. The trees lining the river were wearing their summer greenery, and their branches waved at us as we traveled the swiftly moving river. ❷ Small islands with trees dotted the center of the river, and we often steered our canoes to opposite sides of the islands, just for the joy of saying, "Whoa! Fancy meeting you here!" when we rejoined on the other side.

Yet then, we traveled around one island … and the guys' canoe was nowhere to be seen. We paddled on. Still nothing. We didn't see them again until the trip was over. It was around noon at this point, and Aunt Rae, Nora, and I were starving. The sandwiches were in the guys' canoe, and we still had a three-hour trip to the rendezvous point. With hunger clawing at our insides, we paddled on.

After a while, we decided to pull over to an island so Nora and I could switch places. As we pulled up, the powerful river current slammed us up against the brush-filled island, lodging us in deep water against thick bushes and a fallen log. No amount of paddling could get us out of there; the current was too strong. We also couldn't get out of the canoe, because the island brush was too thick.

❸ At this point, my worst nightmare took form. Spiders began falling from an overhanging branch into our canoe. A lot of spiders. Cue the screaming. And screaming. And more screaming. None of us were fans of our fellow eight-legged creatures.

Nora and I began to whack the spiders in the canoe with the oars. In our zeal, we managed to smack each other in the head a couple times. I remember thinking, "Wow. I might keel over from fear or a whack on the head. Fantastic."

4 Aunt Rae finally gathered her wits about her and leapt into brown, murky river water up to her neck. With nearly super-human strength, she pulled our canoe out of its jam and back into the river at large. As she hoisted herself back into the canoe, we capsized. So again, cue screaming. And more screaming. It took us a while to realize that we were all wearing life jackets, so we weren't exactly in danger. At last, we managed to get back in the canoe. We were soaking wet but intensely grateful the capsizing had drowned any remaining spiders lurking in our canoe.

So, wet, hungry, and traumatized, we continued on our way. Then, things got even worse. Huge, black storm clouds rolled in. Menacing thunder growled. Lightning flashed in the heavens. So there we were, in a *metal* canoe, in the middle of a *river,* during a *lightning* storm. Knowing that metal and water are great conductors of electricity, I was absolutely, positively sure we were not going to make it.

5 Somehow, miraculously, we survived. We reached the rendezvous point, where the guys were waiting and eating *our* sandwiches. Oftentimes, after days like these, people are reminded of the famous quote: "That which does not kill us makes us stronger." I'm not so sure about that; I still don't like spiders, and now I'm not so fond of canoes either.

WRITING COACH **Online**

www.phwritingcoach.com

Interactive Model

Listen to an audio recording of the Mentor Text in the eText. You can refer back to the Mentor Text whenever you need support in developing your own writing.

Online Journal

Try It! Answer the questions about the Mentor Text in the online journal.

4 The author gives **specific details** to make her story come alive.

Try It! Which details help you picture the scene?

5 In the **resolution,** or final outcome, the author reflects on what happened.

Try It! What does the author realize about herself? What insights into your own fears or strengths did the narrative give you?

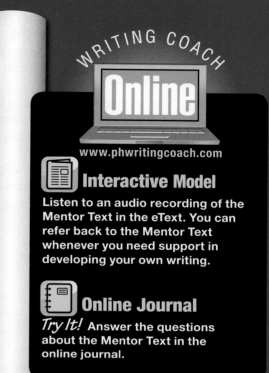

STUDENT MODEL Autobiographical Narrative

With a small group, take turns reading the Student Model aloud. As you read, practice newly acquired vocabulary by correctly producing the word's sound. Also, notice how the writing interweaves personal examples and ideas with factual information and how the described event holds your interest.

Use a Reader's Eye

Now, reread the Student Model. On your copy of the Student Model, use the Reader's Response Symbols to react to what you read.

Reader's Response Symbols

- **+ I like where this is going.**
- **– This isn't clear to me.**
- **? What will happen next?**
- **! Wow! That is really cool/weird/interesting!**

Partner Talk

Discuss your opinions, ideas, and feelings about the autobiographical narrative. Are there changes you would make? What are they and why?

A Lemonade NIGHT

by Tamara Fiero

Have you ever heard someone say, "When life gives you lemons, make lemonade"? Well, sometimes life gives you the lemonade, too!

This past June, as a birthday present, my parents gave me four tickets to see Future Focus, my favorite local band. One ticket was for Dad, our chauffeur; the other three were for me and for Kim and Isabel, my best friends.

"Wouldn't it be spectacular if we could MEET them?" I asked with enthusiasm.

"Get real, Tamara," Kim scoffed. "We don't stand a chance."

"However," Isabel commented, "I've read that occasionally they'll sign autographs. Maybe if we wait at the stage door?"

When the night of the concert arrived, Future Focus belted out their hits and introduced new songs that had us jumping in the aisles. The crowd roared so much that the band came out for two encores—but by then, Dad had led us to the stage door. There we waited, ready for a meeting!

We waited as the music stopped and then as people streamed into the parking lot. "They HAVE to come out," I said, trying to keep my voice from quivering.

Suddenly a guard opened the door. "Sorry, kids," he announced, "but the band has left. Maybe next time, right?"

1

"Too bad." Dad tried to make us feel better as we shuffled to the car. "How about some pizza to cheer ourselves up?"

Soon we were sitting in a booth at Romano's, eating a spicy, sizzling pizza. We were the only diners there.

"It's not fair," Kim complained as she helped herself to a slice. "We waited and waited, and all for nothing."

Just then, there was a commotion at the front door. We looked up—and there stood Future Focus! "Man, I'm starved!" Dylan Reynolds, the lead singer, exclaimed as the band headed toward some tables in the back.

We could hardly keep from squealing, but Dad made us stay put as he went over and politely asked if we could get a few autographs. When he waved to us, it was a dream come true! We ran to their table, got autographs and pictures, and then let them enjoy their meal.

On the drive home, while we still were numb with excitement, Dad grinned and exclaimed, "Awesome!"

WRITING COACH

Online

www.phwritingcoach.com

Interactive Model

Listen to an audio recording of the Student Model in the eText. Use the Reader's and Writer's Response Symbols with the eText tools to note what you read.

Use a Writer's Eye

Now, evaluate the piece as a writer. On your copy of the Student Model, use the Writer's Response Symbols to react to what you read. Identify places where the student writer uses characteristics of an effective autobiographical narrative.

Writer's Response Symbols

E.S.	**Engaging story**
C.R.	**Clear, well-developed conflict and resolution**
B.C.	**Believable characters**
S.D.	**Specific and vivid details**

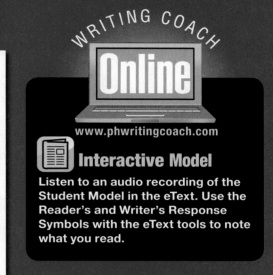

Your Turn **Feature Assignment: Autobiographical Narrative**

Prewriting

Plan a first draft of your autobiographical narrative **by determining an appropriate topic.** You may select from the Topic Bank or come up with an idea of your own.

Choose From the Topic Bank

TOPIC BANK

What's So Funny? Write an autobiographical narrative that tells the story of a humorous mix-up or misunderstanding that you have experienced. In addition to details showing what happened, include your thoughts and feelings about the event.

Game On! Think of an exciting competition. It could be one that you were part of or one that you witnessed. Write an autobiographical narrative in which you describe the competitive event and explain why it was so exciting.

Not-So-Everyday Unusual events can transform an average day into something special. Write an autobiographical narrative that tells about something unusual that happened to you on an otherwise ordinary day.

Choose Your Own Topic

Determine an appropriate topic on your own by using the following **range of strategies** to generate ideas.

Interview and Reflect

- Interview some friends, asking them to recall a story about you; then, consider telling that story from your perspective.
- List some personal interests and then circle one that sparks a memory of an event that you could share.
- If you post to social networking sites, review what you have posted lately. Could you develop a post into a story starring you?

Review your responses and choose a topic.

Narrow Your Topic

Choosing a topic that is too broad can make your writing confusing, and it can keep readers from identifying with your personal story.

Apply It! Use a graphic organizer like the one shown to narrow your topic.

- Record your general topic—your broadest story idea—in the top box. Then, narrow your topic as you move down the chart.
- Your final box should hold your narrowest story idea, the focus of your autobiographical narrative.

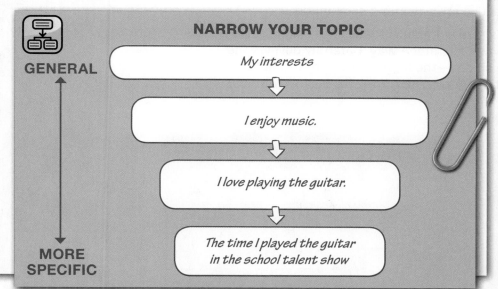

NARROW YOUR TOPIC

GENERAL

My interests

↓

I enjoy music.

↓

I love playing the guitar.

↓

The time I played the guitar in the school talent show

MORE SPECIFIC

Consider Multiple Audiences and Purposes

Before writing, think about your audiences and purposes. Consider how your writing will convey your intended meaning to multiple audiences. Consider the views of others as you ask yourself these questions.

Questions for Audience	Questions for Purpose
• Who are the people in my audiences? • Will the topic of my narrative engage each audience's interest? • What might each audience want to know about me—and why?	• What is my purpose? Do I want to be humorous, thought-provoking, or something else? • As I develop my purpose, how much about myself do I want to share with each audience?

Record your answers in your writing journal.

WRITING COACH Online

www.phwritingcoach.com

Interactive Writing Coach™

- Choosing from the Topic Bank gives you access to the Interactive Writing Coach™.
- Submit your writing and receive instant personalized feedback and guidance as you draft, revise, and edit your writing.

Interactive Graphic Organizers

Use the interactive graphic organizers to help you narrow your topic.

Online Journal

Try It! Record your answers and ideas in the online journal.

Plan Your Piece

You will use the graphic organizer to develop your plot, including the conflict, climax, and resolution. When it is completed, you will be ready to write your first draft.

Develop Your Theme To develop a theme, or controlling idea, for your writing, think about what you learned from the experience or what you want your audience to learn. In narrative nonfiction, your theme is the lesson that came from experiencing an event. For instance, the person who created the graphic organizer identified his or her theme as the lesson that passion and practice are a winning combination.

Map Out Your Plot Events Use a graphic organizer to help develop a draft that **structures ideas in a sustained way**. Carefully develop the events that will lead to the climax—the highest point in the **conflict**—and then reveal the **resolution**, or outcome. You may make additional notes here, too.

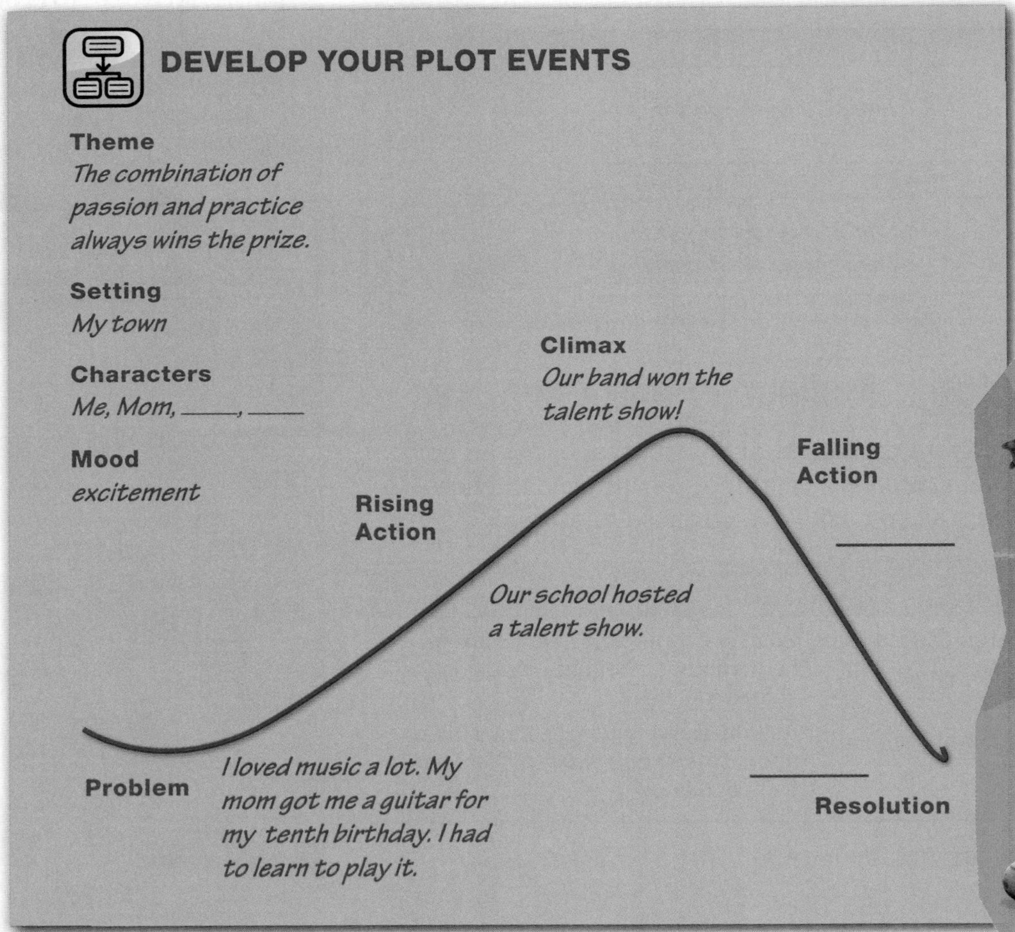
DEVELOP YOUR PLOT EVENTS
Theme
The combination of passion and practice always wins the prize.
Setting
My town
Characters
Me, Mom, ____, ____
Mood
excitement
Rising Action
Our school hosted a talent show.
Climax
Our band won the talent show!
Falling Action
Problem
I loved music a lot. My mom got me a guitar for my tenth birthday. I had to learn to play it.
Resolution

Gather Details

Autobiographical writers usually build on the **story elements** of character, setting, and plot by using **literary devices,** such as dialogue, mood, and suspense. These devices can provide more detail about the characters' personalities, the mood of the setting, and the plot. They can also illustrate a theme. Look at these examples:

- **Dialogue:** *"Since you love music so much, I wanted you to learn to play an instrument," Mom explained.*
  "Excellent, Mom!" I shrieked. "You got me a guitar for my birthday?"
- **Mood:** *The darkened auditorium was filled with students waiting restlessly for the talent show to begin. I stood nervously with my guitar on the stage, shielding my eyes from the glare of the lights.*
- **Suspense:** *This was it—the moment we'd been waiting for. Principal Michaels read the list of the top three acts in the talent show. We weren't third. We weren't second. My head drooped. But then she said, "And in first place is the band Rock the House!" My head snapped up. That was us! We'd won!*

Try It! Read the Student Model excerpt and identify how the author's opening engages the readers' interest and suggests a theme.

STUDENT MODEL from **A Lemonade Night**
page 70; lines 1–6

Have you ever heard someone say, "When life gives you lemons, make lemonade"? Well, sometimes life gives you the lemonade, too!

This past June, as a birthday present, my parents gave me four tickets to see Future Focus, my favorite local band.

Apply It! As you review the literary elements that narrative writers often use, think about how your story details can include these elements.

- Decide which details are most likely to help you write an engaging story with **interesting** and **believable** characters, setting, and action.
- Add these details to your graphic organizer, matching each detail to the right part of the story.
- Determine which **literary strategies and devices,** such as suspense and dialogue, you will use to **enhance the plot**.

WRITING COACH **Online**

www.phwritingcoach.com

Interactive Graphic Organizers

Use the interactive graphic organizers to help you create a plan for your writing.

Interactive Model

Refer back to the Interactive Model in the eText as you plan your writing.

Drafting

During the drafting stage, you will start to write your ideas for your autobiographical narrative. You will follow an outline that provides **an organizational strategy** that will help you write **an engaging autobiographical narrative with a well-developed conflict.**

The Organization of a Nonfiction Narrative

The chart shows an organizational strategy for a nonfiction narrative. Look back at how the Mentor Text follows this organizational strategy. Then, use this chart to help you outline your draft.

Outline for Success

I. Beginning

See Mentor Text, p. 68.

- Engaging opening
- Theme

II. Middle

See Mentor Text, pp. 68–69.

- Well-developed conflict
- Literary devices and strategies that enhance the plot (such as suspense, dialogue)
- Specific details

III. End

See Mentor Text, p. 69.

- Well-developed resolution
- Ending that reflects the theme

Grab Your Reader

- An engaging opening catches your readers' attention; for example, a question or quotation often adds interest here.
- An autobiographical narrative has a theme or point. The opening may give a hint about this idea.

Develop Your Plot

- Plot events are generally presented in chronological, or time, order.
- Dialogue and other strategies, such as suspense, help develop the plot and connect readers to your story.
- Vivid details—about the characters, setting, and action—help the reader visualize, or see, the story.

Wrap It Up

- The resolution shows how the problem was solved or how events ended it.
- The ending often explains how the story reflects the theme or main point.

Start Your Draft

Use this checklist to help you complete your draft. Use the Plot Structure Map that shows your conflict, rising action, and resolution, and the Outline for Success as guides.

While drafting, aim at writing your ideas, not on making your writing perfect. Remember, because writing is an open-ended process, you will have the chance to improve your draft when you revise and edit.

√ Start by drafting an attention-getting opening sentence. Use **rhetorical devices**, such as vivid images and lively language, to convey meaning and immediately draw readers into your story.

√ Continue your **beginning** by giving details that hint at the theme of your narrative. Introduce readers to the major **conflict** that you will be struggling to resolve throughout the narrative.

√ Develop the **middle** of your autobiographical narrative. Present a series of plot events that build the conflict. These events should develop the conflict by demonstrating how you struggled with the growing problem.

√ Illustrate the climax, the moment you took an action or made a major decision that led to a resolution.

√ Enhance the narrative using **literary strategies and devices.** Provide interesting and believable details about the characters and their actions, as well as detailed descriptions of any settings. Use dialogue to capture people's words and the way they sounded. Build suspense by revealing information slowly so that the reader wonders what will happen.

√ At the **end** of your narrative, show the **resolution**—how the conflict worked out.

√ Finish in a way that is satisfying and that recalls the beginning of your true story. Share with your reader how the events of your narrative affected you or your life.

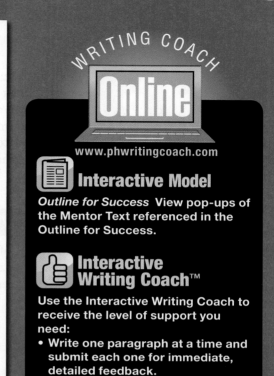

WRITING COACH **Online**

www.phwritingcoach.com

Interactive Model

Outline for Success **View pop-ups of the Mentor Text referenced in the Outline for Success.**

Interactive Writing Coach™

Use the Interactive Writing Coach to receive the level of support you need:

- **Write one paragraph at a time and submit each one for immediate, detailed feedback.**
- **Write your entire first draft and submit it for immediate, personalized feedback.**

REPLACE ADD DELETE and REORDER
RADaR

Revising: Making It Better

Now that you have finished your first draft, you are ready to revise. Think about the "big picture" of **audience, purpose, and genre.** You can use Revision RADaR as a guide for making changes to improve your draft. Revision RADaR provides four major ways to improve your writing: (R) replace, (A) add, (D) delete, and (R) reorder.

Kelly Gallagher, M. Ed.

KEEP REVISION ON YOUR RADaR

Read part of the first draft of the Student Model "A Lemonade Night." Then, look at questions the writer asked herself as she thought about how well her draft **addressed issues of audience, purpose, and genre.**

1ST DRAFT

A Lemonade Night

When the night of the concert arrived, Future Focus sang their hits and introduced new songs that were great. The crowd was so happy that the band came out for two encores—but by then, Dad had taken us to the stage door. There we waited, ready for a meeting!

*Do my details help my **audience** clearly visualize or picture the settings and the action?*

We waited as the music stopped and then as people streamed into the parking lot. "They HAVE to come out," I said, trying to keep my voice from quivering.

Suddenly a guard opened the door. "Sorry, kids," he announced, "but the band has left. Maybe next time, right?"

*My **purpose** here is to show our disappointment, but is that clear?*

Soon we were sitting in a booth at Romano's, eating a sizzling pizza. We were the only diners there.

I don't understand why things like that happen. Bands should pay more attention to the fans who make them rich!

*My **genre** is narrative nonfiction, but this paragraph sounds like I'm making an argument. Does it really belong?*

Now look at how the writer applied Revision RADaR to write an improved second draft.

2ND DRAFT

A Lemonade NIGHT

...When the night of the concert arrived, Future Focus belted out their hits and introduced new songs that had us jumping in the aisles. The crowd roared so much that the band came out for two encores—but by then, Dad had led us to the stage door. There we waited, ready for a meeting!

We waited as the music stopped and then as people streamed into the parking lot. "They HAVE to come out," I said, trying to keep my voice from quivering.

Suddenly a guard opened the door. "Sorry, kids," he announced, "but the band has left. Maybe next time, right?"

"Too bad," Dad said consolingly as we shuffled to the car. "How about some pizza to cheer ourselves up?"

Soon we were sitting in a booth at Romano's, eating a sizzling pizza. We were the only diners there.

"It's not fair," Kim complained as she helped herself to a slice. "We waited and waited, and all for nothing."

R ***Replaced*** *some details to make the concert scene and Dad's action more vivid*

A ***Added*** *information that shows our disappointment by saying we shuffled to the car and by using words like consolingly.*

D ***Deleted*** *my opinion about the band*
A ***Added*** *dialogue to focus more on the plot of the narrative*

WRITING COACH Online

www.phwritingcoach.com

Interactive Writing Coach™

Use the Revision RADaR strategy in your own writing. Then submit your paragraph or draft for feedback.

Apply It! Use your Revision RADaR to revise your draft.

- First, determine if you have addressed the interests of your **audience,** used plot events and details to achieve your **purpose,** and included the characteristics of the narrative nonfiction **genre.**
- Then, apply the Revision RADaR srategy to make needed changes. Remember—you can use the steps in the strategy in any order.

RADaR
REPLACE ADD DELETE and REORDER

Look at the Big Picture

Use the chart to evaluate how well each section of your autobiographical narrative addresses **purpose, audience, and genre.** When necessary, use the suggestions in the chart to revise your piece.

Section	Evaluate	Revise
Beginning	• Decide whether your **opening** sentence is engaging, making your audience want to read on.	• Add a question, a quotation, or some other detail that stirs readers' curiosity.
	• Consider your **theme**. Readers should know why you're writing, even if it is subtle.	• Sum up the theme, or main point of your narrative, in one sentence; then decide whether you want to include that sentence or just hint at its idea.
Middle	• Review the plot of your narrative. Do you have a well-developed **conflict?** Do the events clearly present a problem that involves you?	• Rearrange events to ensure chronological order. Add, change, or even delete details to keep readers in suspense about the conflict's outcome.
	• Underline details that show your real-life **characters** in action in one or more settings. Do specific details make the characters and settings interesting and believable?	• To help readers identify with the people in your narrative and the settings, add vivid descriptive details about both.
	• Look at the middle as a whole and evaluate your use of a range of **literary strategies and devices** to enhance the plot and hold readers' interest.	• Review the dialogue and the level of suspense. If necessary, add suspense and dialogue. Make sure that your additions help develop the theme or main focus of your narrative.
End	• Check for a well-developed **resolution**—one that clearly reveals the conflict's outcome.	• Add or revise details to show how the problem was solved or how events ended it.
	• Evaluate your **closing** to see if it reflects the beginning and brings the narrative full circle.	• Add details or ideas that connect the theme with the outcome of the conflict. Leave readers with a sense of closure and a life lesson.

Focus on Craft: Sentence Variety

Think about **sentence variety** when you write. Sentences can have varying lengths. A paragraph or any essay composed of all short sentences will be choppy. Using too many long sentences will make your essay boring and difficult to follow. Try to vary sentences to create a rhythm and emphasize your most important points.

Think about variety in sentence length as you read these sentences from the Student Model.

STUDENT MODEL from **A Lemonade Night**
page 70; lines 9-12

"Wouldn't it be spectacular if we could MEET them?" I asked with enthusiasm.

"Get real, Tamara," Kim scoffed. "We don't stand a chance."

Try It! Now, ask yourself these questions. Record your answers in your journal.

- Does the variety in sentence length provide a rhythm to the conversation? Why or why not?
- Would the conversation be more or less real if the first sentence read: "'Let's meet them' I said"? Explain.

Fine-Tune Your Draft

Apply It! Use the revision suggestions to prepare your final draft **after thinking how well questions of purpose, audience, and genre have been addressed.**

- **Ensure Sentence Variety** Raise the interest level by including both long and short sentences, as well as various sentence types and sentence structures.
- **Improve Subtlety of Meaning** Refine your meaning and make your writing more precise by using words that are specific. For instance, notice how the writer of the Student Model uses the word *scoffed*, rather than *said*, to communicate the speaker's emotion. Use **transition words**, such as *next* and *finally*, to connect ideas and clarify meaning.

Peer Feedback Read your final draft to a group of peers. Ask classmates which events and ideas were most memorable. Think about their responses and revise your final draft as needed.

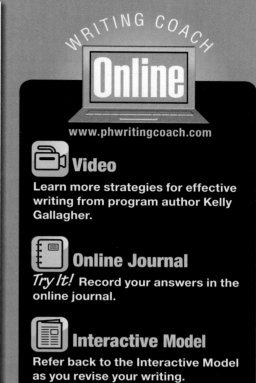

WRITING COACH **Online**

www.phwritingcoach.com

Video

Learn more strategies for effective writing from program author Kelly Gallagher.

Online Journal

Try It! Record your answers in the online journal.

Interactive Model

Refer back to the Interactive Model as you revise your writing.

Interactive Writing Coach™

Revise your draft and submit it for feedback.

Editing: Making It Correct

Editing your draft means polishing your work and correcting errors. You may want to read through your work several times, looking for different errors and issues each time.

Before editing your draft, think about using **a variety of correctly structured sentences,** including **compound, complex,** and **compound-complex** sentences. You should also be aware of the **correct punctuation** for each sentence, including **comma placement in clauses.** Then, edit your final draft by correcting any factual errors and errors in **grammar, mechanics, and spelling. Use a dictionary to check your spelling.**

WRITE GUY *Jeff Anderson, M. Ed.*

WHAT DO YOU NOTICE?

Zoom in on Conventions Focus on sentence structures as you zoom in on these sentences from the Mentor Text.

MENTOR TEXT from **A Wild Ride**
page 68–69; lines 22–24, 52–54

The sandwiches were in the guys' canoe, and we still had a three-hour trip to the rendezvous point. . . .Knowing that metal and water are great conductors of electricity, I was absolutely, positively sure we were not going to make it.

To learn more about sentence structures, see Chapter 14 of your Grammar Handbook.

Now, ask yourself: *How is each sentence like or unlike the other*?

Perhaps you said that each sentence has a different structure.

The first sentence is a **compound** sentence because it has two independent clauses. An independent clause has a subject and a verb and can stand alone as a complete sentence.

The second sentence is a **complex** sentence because it has one independent clause and one subordinate clause. A subordinate clause contains a subject and a verb but cannot stand alone as a sentence. The subordinate clause is *Knowing that metal and water are great conductors of electricity.*

A **compound-complex** sentence contains two or more independent clauses and at least one subordinate clause.

Partner Talk With a partner, break up the Mentor Text excerpt into all simple sentences. Then, discuss this question with your partner: Which form of the excerpt is more effective? Why?

Grammar Mini-Lesson: Commas With Clauses

To learn more, see Chapter 23.

Commas may be used to separate elements in a sentence or to set off part of a sentence, such as a **clause.**

- In compound and compound-complex sentences, place a comma before the conjunction linking the independent clauses.
- In complex and compound-complex sentences, place a comma after a subordinate clause that begins a sentence.

Notice the comma placement in this compound-complex sentence from the Mentor Text.

MENTOR TEXT from **A Wild Ride**
page 68; lines 13-15

The trees lining the river were wearing their summer greenery, and their branches waved at us as we traveled the swiftly moving river.

Try It! Copy each sentence into your journal, placing commas where needed.

1. Charles wants to meet with Kathy but she has other plans. (Compound sentence)
2. While you used the computer I visited the library. (Complex sentence)
3. Since you are home I want to make dinner but I know you want to rest. (Compound-Complex sentence)

Apply It! **Edit your draft for grammar, mechanics, capitalization and spelling**. If necessary, rewrite or combine sentences to ensure that you have used a **variety of sentences**. Fix **comma placement in clauses**, as needed.

Use the rubric to evaluate your piece. If necessary, rethink, rewrite, or revise.

Rubric for Narrative Nonfiction: Autobiographical Narrative	Rating Scale
Ideas: How well do the dialogue and setting support the plot?	Not very Very 1 2 3 4 5 6
Organization: How clearly organized is the sequence of events?	1 2 3 4 5 6
Voice: How effectively have you created a unique voice in your narrative?	1 2 3 4 5 6
Word Choice: How effective is your word choice in creating tone and style?	1 2 3 4 5 6
Sentence Fluency: How well have you used sentence variety to build rhythm?	1 2 3 4 5 6
Conventions: How correct are your sentence structures?	1 2 3 4 5 6

WRITING COACH **Online**

www.phwritingcoach.com

Video

Learn effective editing techniques from program author Jeff Anderson.

Online Journal

Try It! Record your answers in the online journal.

Interactive Model

Refer back to the Interactive Model as you edit your writing.

Interactive Writing Coach™

Edit your draft. Check it against the rubric and then submit it for feedback.

Publishing

Introduce yourself to an audience and let readers get to know you by publishing your autobiographical narrative. First, get your piece ready for presentation; then, choose ways to **publish for appropriate audiences.**

Wrap Up Your Presentation

Is your narrative handwritten or written on a computer? If your narrative is handwritten, you may need to make a new, clean copy. If so, be sure to **write legibly.** Also, be sure to add a title to your narrative that grabs the reader's attention and conveys your topic.

Publish Your Piece

Use the chart to identify ways to publish your autobiographical narrative.

If your audience is...	...then publish it by...
Classmates and teachers at school	• Reading it aloud as a dramatic monologue • Submitting it to the school literary magazine
People in your town or around the world that you may never meet	• Posting it to a blog for people who share one of your interests • Submitting it to a print or online magazine that publishes first-person, true-life accounts. Add photographs or illustrations to support the narrative.

Reflect on Your Writing

Now that you are done with your autobiographical narrative, read it over and use your writing journal to answer these questions.

- Do you think your autobiographical narrative was a success? Why?
- Are any parts weak—dull, for example, or unrealistic? If so, what can you focus on in your next writing assignment?

Manage Your Portfolio You may wish to include your published autobiographical narrative in your writing portfolio. If so, consider what this piece reveals about your writing and your growth as a writer.

The Big Question: Why Write? What did you decide to put in or leave out to be accurate and honest?

21st Century Learning

MAKE YOUR WRITING COUNT

Get Your Autobiographies on Library Shelves

Publishers sometimes package autobiographical narratives into an anthology, a bound collection of similar types of writing. Build up your local library by creating an appealing **anthology** of your own autobiographical narratives.

Package your anthology for publication by creating a book cover and other parts of the anthology including a table of contents, a foreword, and information about the author.

Here's your action plan.

1. Each group member should have a role in this project and a deadline for completing a part of the book.
2. In a group, decide which narratives to include in your anthology.
3. Together, brainstorm for a title and image reflecting a common theme in the narratives.
4. When each element of the anthology is ready, arrange them in an appealing design.
   - Consult book publishers' Web sites to see the latest trends in cover design.
   - Include the title and the names of the contributors, as well as the cover image, on the front.
   - Prepare a table of contents in book order. Include a summary of the contents and a biography of each writer.
5. Present your anthology to a local library.

Listening and Speaking With your group, hold a "debriefing" about the process you used to create the anthology. Ask yourselves: What worked in the process? What didn't work? Then, plan to present your book to the library. Arrange with the library staff for your group to give readings from your book in a presentation ceremony.

WRITING COACH Online

www.phwritingcoach.com

Online Journal

Reflect on Your Writing **Record your answers and ideas in the online journal.**

Resource

Link to resources on 21st Century Learning for help in creating a group project.

Your Turn **Writing for Media: Script for a Documentary**

21st Century Learning

Script for a Documentary

A **documentary** is a film that tells a real-life story about an event, an era, or a person's life, for example. It often includes images and music, interviews with people who were part of the story, and a spoken narrative. The result is a film that many television and movie viewers enjoy.

The **script for a documentary** identifies and organizes video segments, adds narration, and makes note of music and other special elements. When you understand what goes into a documentary script, you gain a greater appreciation for the power of good storytelling.

Try It! Read and visualize the narrative in this part of a documentary script. Then, answer these questions, recording your answers in your journal.

1. What is the topic of the documentary? What do you think its **purpose** and **theme** might be?
2. To what **audiences** would this documentary probably appeal?
3. Visual elements in documentaries may include historical or personal photographs, news footage, home movies, and interviews. Which **visual elements** will be part of this scene? Which ones do you predict will be most effective, and why?
4. **Music** often is not essential to a documentary, so why do you think that the script calls for background music?
5. Think about the elements and details together. What kind of **mood** or **tone** does the filmmaker want to create?

Extension Find another example of a script for a documentary, and compare it with this one.

THE MEANING OF THE MARCH, Scene 2

(Open with still aerial photo of crowds in Washington, DC, on August 28, 1963. Faint instrumental background music: "We Shall Overcome")

NARRATOR: Campaigners for civil rights—most of them just average Americans who wanted equality for everyone, regardless of color—marched peacefully from the Washington Monument to the Lincoln Memorial. There, several speakers addressed the crowd, but perhaps no one was more electrifying than Dr. Martin Luther King, Jr. His speech reminded listeners of the prejudices that had kept true equality only a dream; but in his conclusion, Dr. King described what America could be like if the dream came true.

(Show historical footage [20–30 seconds]—excerpt from the last part of "I Have a Dream"; then, as NARRATOR continues, footage or still photo of faces in the crowd.)

NARRATOR: It was an unforgettable moment for all who heard it; and college professor Louisa Hamilton, who was nine years old that day, remembers it well.

(Cut to interview footage of LOUISA HAMILTON.)

HAMILTON: Papa set me on his shoulders so that I could see Dr. King. As we listened, I saw tears on peoples' faces, and I felt like crying, too—not with sorrow but with hope for a better tomorrow. For the first time, I really felt that life could be better for all Americans, and I decided that I was going to do what I could to help make it happen.

Create a Script for a Documentary

Follow these steps to create a 5-minute scene for your own documentary script. Keep in mind the **theme, or main idea** of the documentary, as well as the **mood or tone** you hope to convey. Decide if you will **explicitly** state your theme in the narration or if you will **implicitly** tell, or hint at it. Review the graphic organizers on pages R24–R27 and choose one that suits your needs.

Prewriting

- Choose a genre for your documentary, such as a how-to, or a day-in-the-life documentary. To choose a topic, think about what interests you. In addition, select a topic that would appeal to your audience.
- Research your topic, gathering information for the narration as well as for the visual elements, music, and so on. As you research, document your sources for later reference.
- Decide on your purpose. Think about the theme you want to develop. You may want to state your theme directly or explictly, or you may decide to present it implicitly, letting readers get your main idea through the details you include.
- List the kinds of elements that you might include—narration, still or moving images, music, location, and camera angle direction. All the details you include should contribute to a definitive mood and tone.

Drafting

- Write a script that identifies the placement of each element and uses narration to connect the story line.
- Organize the elements in a way that is varied but still makes sense.
- Keep your purpose, audience, and theme in mind as you draft.

Revising and Editing

- Review your draft to ensure that your documentary is accurate and appealing; add or remove details as needed.
- Create a clean copy of your script and share it with some classmates by acting it out. Ask them to describe the documentary they "see." You may want to adjust your script after hearing their feedback.
- Check that spelling, grammar, and mechanics are correct. Also make sure that the narrator's words are specific and interesting.

Publishing

Before recording, you might want to spend some time planning and talking with the subjects of your documentary. Afterward, present it to the class. Use your script to video-record your documentary.

WRITING COACH Online

www.phwritingcoach.com

Online Journal

Try It! **Record your answers in the online journal.**

Interactive Graphic Organizers

Choose from a variety of graphic organizers to plan and develop your project.

Partner Talk

Before you start drafting, explain your documentary to a partner and ask for feedback. What ideas about the film's elements does your partner have? Use specific details to describe and explain your ideas. Increase the specificity of your details based on the type of information you are delivering.

Writing for Assessment

Some prompts ask you to write an autobiographical narrative. Use these prompts to practice. Respond using the characteristics of an autobiographical narrative. (See page 66).

Try It! Read the **narrative nonfiction** prompt and the information on format and academic vocabulary; then, write a narrative by following the instructions in the ABCDs of On-Demand Writing.

Format

The prompt directs you to write a *nonfiction narrative*. Include a beginning that introduces your main idea, a middle whose narrative develops a conflict, and an end that presents a resolution and reflects your main idea.

Narrative Nonfiction Prompt

Teachers do more than present facts and formulas—they challenge your thinking and can even change your life! Choose one such teacher and write a nonfiction narrative that describes a teacher's impact on you. Support your choice by telling a personal story whose conflict and resolution show this teacher's influence.

Academic Vocabulary

A *conflict* is a problem to be solved or a clash to be settled; a *resolution* is the outcome of that conflict. Your nonfiction narrative should include a well-developed conflict and resolution.

The ABCDs of On-Demand Writing

Use the following ABCDs to help you respond to the prompt.

Before you write your draft:

Attack the prompt [1 MINUTE]

- Circle or highlight important verbs in the prompt. Draw a line from the verb to what it refers to.
- Rewrite the prompt in your own words.

Brainstorm possible answers [4 MINUTES]

- Create a graphic organizer to generate ideas.
- Use one for each part of the prompt if necessary.

Choose the order of your response [1 MINUTE]

- Think about the best way to organize your ideas.
- Number your ideas in the order you will write about them. Cross out ideas you will not be using.

After you write your draft:

Detect errors before turning in the draft [1 MINUTE]

- Carefully reread your writing.
- Make sure that your response makes sense and is complete.
- Look for spelling, punctuation, and grammar errors.

More Prompts for Practice

Apply It! Respond to Prompts 1 and 2 in a timed or open-ended situation by writing **nonfiction narratives** that present an engaging story. As you write, be sure to:

- Identify an appropriate audience for your intended purpose
- Use a plot structure map to organize your ideas
- Give your narrative a well-developed **conflict** and **resolution**
- Establish **characters** that are **interesting** and **believable**
- Include a range of **literary devices,** such as dialogue and suspense, to enhance the plot of the narrative
- Use **sentence variety** and appropriate **rhetorical devices,** such as figurative language, to keep the essay interesting
- Include **transitions** to connect ideas

Prompt 1 What was your first day of high school like—exciting, frightening, or perhaps hilarious? Create a statement that sums up your feelings about that day; then write a nonfiction narrative in which you recount one or more personal experiences that support that statement.

Prompt 2 Most schools offer extracurricular activities. Think about a school club to which you belong, a school sports team, or other activity in which you had some responsibility. In a nonfiction narrative, discuss the importance of your role in that extracurricular event or activity.

Spiral Review: More Strategies for Writing for Assessment

- Consider several possible topics and quickly list details that you might use in your response. Then, choose the topic for which you have the strongest ideas.
- If you do not understand any words in the prompt, use context clues to help you determine the meaning of unfamiliar words.
- Be sure to follow the ABCDs of writing to a prompt. Planning is an important part of writing. Don't just start writing right away.
- Make sure to reread your piece after you have completed it. This will give you time to find and correct errors. If you are in a timed situation, be sure to leave enough time for this step.

WRITING COACH **Online**

www.phwritingcoach.com

Interactive Writing Coach™

Plan your response to the prompt. If you are using the prompt for practice, write one paragraph at a time or your entire draft and then submit it for feedback. If you are using the prompt as a timed test, write your entire draft and then submit it for feedback.

Remember **ABCD**

Attack the prompt

Brainstorm possible answers

Choose the order of your response

Detect errors before turning in the draft

CHAPTER 6

FICTION NARRATION

What's the Story?

What is happening in the photo? What do you think will happen next? What story can you tell about it?

Many stories have realistic settings. Believable details about setting, such as a description of snow, help get the reader interested and add to the story. Conflict is also important. Conflict is a challenge or problem the main character faces.

Try It! Think about the events of this person's day. What events led up to this moment?

Consider these questions as you participate in an extended discussion with a partner. Take turns expressing your ideas and feelings.

- Who is the person in the photo?
- Why is this person parachuting onto a snowy mountain?
- How do you think this person feels?
- Is this a normal day for this person or an extraordinary one? Why do you think that?

Review your notes. Use your notes to tell a story about the skier. Be sure to use many details to make your story believable.

What's Ahead

In this chapter, you will review two strong examples of a fiction story: a Mentor Text and a Student Model. Then, using the examples as guidance, you will write a short story of your own.

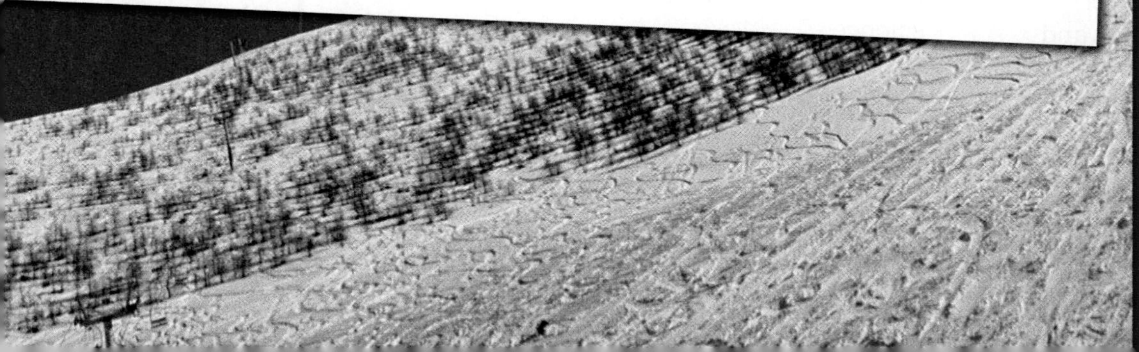

WRITING COACH Online

www.phwritingcoach.com

Online Journal

Try It! Record your answers and ideas in the online journal.

You can also record and save your answers and ideas on pop-up sticky notes in the eText.

Connect to the Big Questions

Discuss these questions with your partner:

1. **What do you think?** Can we do anything we truly set out to do?
2. **Why write?** What can fiction do better than nonfiction?

SHORT STORY

A short story is a brief work of fiction that presents characters in a conflict that is first developed and then resolved. In this chapter, you will explore a special type of short story, the science fiction story. Science fiction stories focus on real or imagined developments in science and technology and their effects on the way people think and live. Space travel, robots, and life in the future are popular topics for science fiction.

You will develop the science fiction story by taking it through each of the steps of the writing process: prewriting, drafting, revising, editing, and publishing. You will also have an opportunity to create a script for a graphic story with text and art. To preview the criteria for how your science fiction story will be evaluated, see the rubric on page 111.

FEATURE ASSIGNMENT

Short Story: Science Fiction

An effective and imaginative short story has these characteristics:

- A specific, believable **setting** created through the use of details
- A clear, engaging **plot**, or storyline
- **A well-developed conflict**, or problem, **and resolution**, or outcome
- One or more **interesting and believable characters**
- A **range of literary strategies and devices**, such as dialogue and suspense, to **enhance the plot** or develop the story
- A consistent **point of view**, or perspective from which the story is told
- **Effective sentence structure** and correct spelling, grammar, and usage

An effective science fiction story also includes:

- A **setting** that features more advanced technical abilities and scientific knowledge than existed when the story was written
- An action-packed **plot** that centers on a **conflict** between people's needs and technology. Some sci-fi stories feature a conflict between people from Earth and fictional aliens
- A **theme** about an aspect of the relationship between humans and science

Other Forms of Short Stories

In addition to science fiction, there are other forms of short stories, including:

Fantasy stories stretch the imagination and take readers to unreal worlds. Animals may talk, people may fly, or characters may have superhuman powers.

Historical fiction tells about imaginary people living in real places and times in history. Usually, the main characters are fictional people who know and interact with famous people in history and participate in important historical events.

Mystery stories focus on unexplained or strange events that one of the characters tries to solve. These stories are often full of suspense and surprises.

Myths and legends are traditional stories that different cultures have told to explain natural events, human nature, or the origins of things. They often include gods and goddesses from ancient times and heroes who do superhuman things.

Realistic fiction portrays invented characters and events in everyday life that most readers would find familiar.

Tall tales tell about larger-than-life characters in realistic settings. The characters perform amazing acts of strength, bravery, or silliness. The main character often solves a problem or reaches a goal by doing something wild or fantastic.

Try It! For each audience and purpose described, choose a story form, such as tall tale, realistic fiction, or mystery, that is appropriate for conveying your intended meaning to the audience. Explain your choices.

- To describe the experience of attending high school in a large city
- To follow detectives on the trail of a criminal
- To explain how a friendly giant wrestles a tornado to save a community

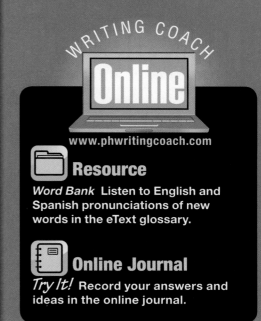

WRITING COACH **Online**

www.phwritingcoach.com

Resource

Word Bank **Listen to English and Spanish pronunciations of new words in the eText glossary.**

Online Journal

Try It! **Record your answers and ideas in the online journal.**

WORD BANK

People often use these vocabulary words when they talk about short story writing. Work with a partner. Take turns saying each word aloud. Then write one sentence using each word. If you are unsure of the meaning of a word, use the Glossary or a dictionary to check the definition.

characterization	**plot**
dialogue	**setting**
engaging	**theme**

MENTOR TEXT

Science Fiction Story

Learn From Experience

Read the science fiction story on pages 94–97. As you read, take notes to develop your understanding of basic sight and English vocabulary. Then, read the numbered notes in the margins to learn about how the author presented her ideas.

Answer the *Try It!* questions online or in your notebook.

1 The **point of view** of the narrator, or "voice" telling the story, is revealed in the first paragraph.

Try It! From what point of view is the story told: first person or third person? How do you know?

2 Through the use of **detail,** the author hints at the **setting** of the story.

Try It! Where do you think the story is set? Why do you think so?

3 The narrator is the only **character** in the story.

Try It! What is unusual about the narrator's description of herself? How does the description compare to descriptions of characters in other stories you have read?

4 The narrator does not reveal to whom she is speaking. This device helps **sustain reader interest** in the story.

Try It! In your opinion, would it improve the story if you knew from the start who the narrator was and to whom she was speaking? Explain.

Homelanding

by Margaret Atwood

1 Where should I begin? After all, you have never been there; or if you have, you may not have understood the significance of what you saw, or thought you saw. A window is a window, but there is looking out and looking in. 2 The native you glimpsed, disappearing behind the curtain, or into the bushes, or down the manhole in the main street—my people are shy—may have been only your reflection in the glass. My country specializes in such illusions.

Let me propose myself as typical. 3 I walk upright on two legs, and have in addition two arms, with ten appendages, that is to say, five at the end of each. On the top of my head, but not on the front, there is an odd growth, like a species of seaweed. Some think this is a kind of fur, others consider it modified feathers, evolved perhaps from scales like those of lizards. It serves no functional purpose and is probably decorative.

4 My eyes are situated in my head, which also possesses two small holes for the entrance and exit of air, the invisible fluid we swim in, and one larger hole, equipped with bony protuberances called teeth, by means of which I destroy and assimilate certain parts of my surroundings and change them into my self. This is called eating. The things I eat include roots, berries, nuts, fruits, leaves, and the muscle tissues of various animals and fish. Sometimes I eat their brains and glands as well. I do not as a rule eat insects, grubs, eyeballs or the snouts of pigs, though these are eaten with relish in other countries.

***

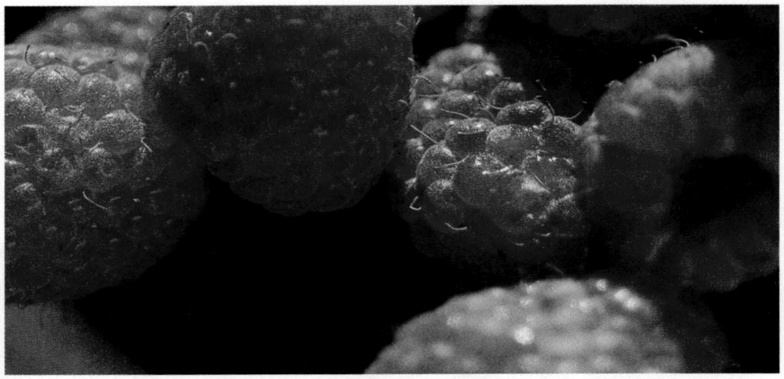

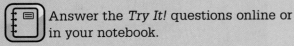

5 As for the country itself, let me begin with the sunsets, which are long and red, resonant, splendid and melancholy, symphonic you might almost say; as opposed to the short boring sunsets of other countries, no more interesting than a lightswitch. We pride ourselves on our sunsets. "Come and see the sunset," we say to one another. This causes everyone to rush outdoors or over to the window.

Our country is large in extent, small in population, which accounts for our fear of large empty spaces, and also our need for them. 6 Much of it is covered in water, which accounts for our interest in reflections, sudden vanishings, the dissolution of one thing into another. Much of it however is rock, which accounts for our belief in Fate.

WRITING COACH Online

www.phwritingcoach.com

Interactive Model

Listen to an audio recording of the Mentor Text in the eText. You can refer back to the Mentor Text whenever you need support in developing your own writing.

Online Journal

Try It! Answer the questions about the Mentor Text in the online journal.

5 **Sensory details** help create a **believable setting** and set a particular **tone.**

Try It! From the details in the paragraph, where does the story seem to take place? What **tone** do you think the details create?

6 The imaginative description suggests more than it directly states.

Try It! What do you think the narrator means when she says that she and her people believe in Fate because their country is covered in rock? What does rock have to do with Fate? What does the description suggest about the culture in which the narrator lives?

Extension Find another example of a science fiction story, and compare it with this one.

7 This description makes everyday events seem mysterious.

Try It! To what two seasons of the year does the passage refer? How can you tell?

8 The narrator finds a similarity between her and "her people" and the beings to whom she is speaking.

Try It! What is the similarity? Why might that particular similarity make the narrator keep communicating with the beings, even though it is very difficult?

7 In summer we lie about in the blazing sun, almost naked, covering our skins with fat and attempting to turn red. But when the sun is low in the sky and faint, even at noon, the water we are so fond of changes to something hard and white and cold and covers up the ground. Then we cocoon ourselves, become lethargic, and spend much of our time hiding in crevices. Our mouths shrink and we say little.

Before this happens, the leaves on many of our trees turn blood red or lurid yellow, much brighter and more exotic than the interminable green of jungles. We find this change beautiful. "Come and see the leaves," we say, and jump into our moving vehicles and drive up and down past the forests of sanguinary trees, pressing our eyes to the glass.

We are a nation of metamorphs.

Anything red compels us.

Sometimes we lie still and do not move. If air is still going in and out of our breathing holes, this is called sleep. If not, it is called death. When a person has achieved death a kind of picnic is held, with music, flowers and food. The person so honoured, if in one piece, and not, for instance, in shreds or falling apart, as they do if exploded or a long time drowned, is dressed in becoming clothes and lowered into a hole in the ground, or else burnt up.

These customs are among the most difficult to explain to strangers. Some of our visitors, especially the young ones, have never heard of death and are bewildered. They think that death is simply one more of our illusions, our mirror tricks; they cannot understand why, with so much food and music, the people are sad.

But you will understand. 8 You too must have death among you. I can see it in your eyes.

I can see it in your eyes. If it weren't for this I would have stopped trying long ago, to communicate with you in this halfway language which is so difficult for both of us, which exhausts the throat and fills the mouth with sand; if it weren't for this I would have gone away, gone back. It's this knowledge of death, which we share, where we overlap. Death is our common ground. Together, on it, we can walk forward.

Partner Talk

Discuss this story with a partner. How does the author's use of language compare with the style and voice of other literary works you have read?

9 By now you must have guessed: I come from another planet. But I will never say to you, *Take me to your leaders.* Even I—unused to your ways though I am—would never make that mistake. We ourselves have such beings among us, made of cogs, pieces of paper, small disks of shiny metal, scraps of colored cloth. I do not need to encounter more of them.

Instead I will say, take me to your trees. Take me to your breakfasts, your sunsets, your bad dreams, your shoes, your nouns. Take me to your fingers; take me to your deaths.

These are worth it. These are what I have come for.

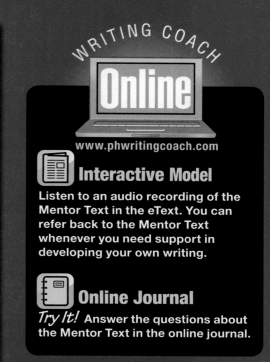

WRITING COACH Online

www.phwritingcoach.com

Interactive Model

Listen to an audio recording of the Mentor Text in the eText. You can refer back to the Mentor Text whenever you need support in developing your own writing.

Online Journal

Try It! Answer the questions about the Mentor Text in the online journal.

9 In this passage, the narrator finally reveals that she is from another planet—that is, one different from that of the imagined reader.

Try It! How would you describe the narrator and the planet she inhabits? How does withholding information until the end of the story help build suspense? What does this story suggest about the historical period in which it was written?

STUDENT MODEL Science Fiction

With a small group, take turns reading this Student Model aloud. Note how the characters interact with technology. Think about how the culture the characters live in influences that interaction.

Use a Reader's Eye

Now, reread the Student Model. On your copy of the Student Model, use the Reader's Response Symbols to react to what you read.

Reader's Response Symbols

- **+ This is a good description.**
- **– This isn't clear to me.**
- **! This is really cool/weird/interesting!**
- **? What will happen next?**

Partner Talk

Participate in an extended discussion with a partner. Express your opinions and share your responses to the Student Model. Discuss how the author's word choices set the mood of the story and create imagery, or pictures in your mind.

Dance on Air

by Devin Curtis

Ever since Rexx got his new Aircar, he's never late to pick me up anymore. He loves driving that thing! And it works for me, too, because I don't like waiting. So I was psyched to see him hovering outside the spaceport on our home pod. I waved goodbye to the parental units and jetted. We were out of there!

How did we ever live without the Aircar? I read somewhere that once it took people hours or days to drive to other sectors, which were called states. Days!? That's ridiculous. The Anti-Gravity Dance Jam was in another sector, but it would only take us a few micro-minutes to get there.

We sailed along the pathways and were micro-seconds away from arriving at the dance when a major jam got in the way—a power jam. Rexx freaked, but the cause was clear. It was a flock of bug-rats. They had flown straight into the wind units on both wings. It's a drag, but everyone with an Aircar knows that this is one of the dangers of travel.

I thought everyone also knew how to fix this kind of problem. But no—Rexx sat there, mystified. The control panel left him completely confused. He just stared at the red lights flashing along both wing icons. I snapped my fingers in front of his face, but he wouldn't snap out of it. That's when I knew I had to take over.

Have you ever cleared the wind units of an Aircar after a bug-rat collision? It's not pretty. Thankfully, Rexx's new Aircar had come equipped with the wind wand that's needed to blow out the units. Wow, do those bug-rats stink!

1

When I got back in the Aircar, I remembered that I had a can of fresh oxygen in my bag, so I was all set. I opened the can, and it drew the remaining stink off my togs. I mean, come on! The Anti-Gravity Dance Jam is only held once a month, and we weren't going to let a little bug-rat collision get in our way.

"Okay, man! Let's jet!" I said to Rexx.

"You got it!" he replied.

He powered up the wind units, and we were off to dance on air!

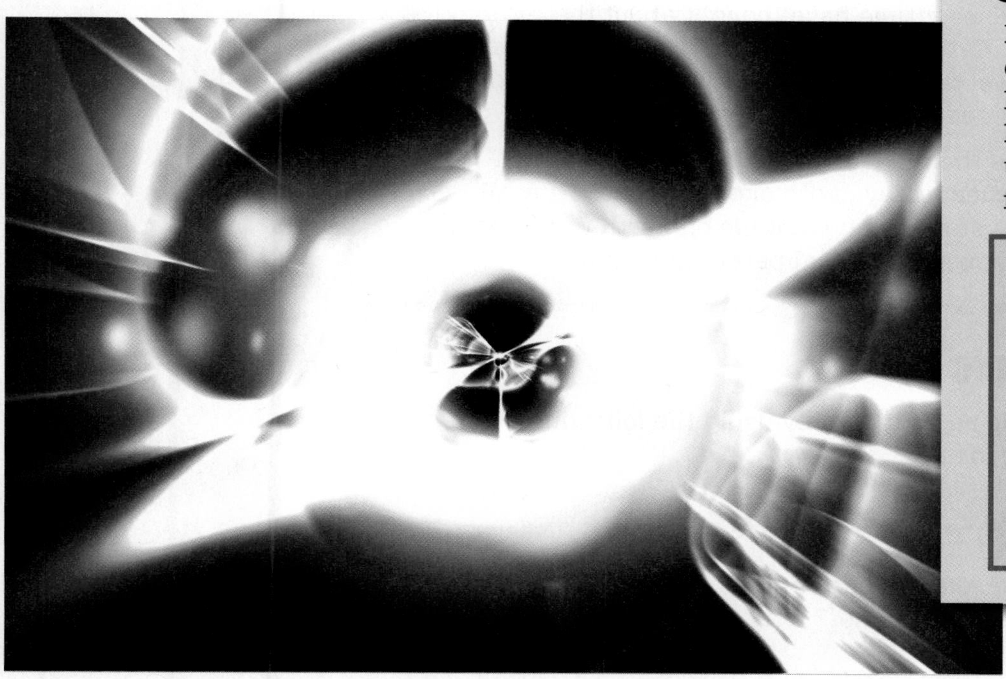

WRITING COACH Online

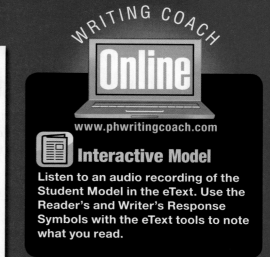

www.phwritingcoach.com

Interactive Model

Listen to an audio recording of the Student Model in the eText. Use the Reader's and Writer's Response Symbols with the eText tools to note what you read.

Use a Writer's Eye

Now, evaluate the piece as a writer. On your copy of the Student Model, use the Writer's Response Symbols to react to what you read. Identify places where the student writer uses characteristics of an effective science fiction story.

Writer's Response Symbols	
R.D.	Realistic and believable dialogue
S.D.	Vivid sensory details
W.C.	Well-developed, interesting characters
E.S.	Engaging story

Your Turn **Feature Assignment: Science Fiction**

Prewriting

Plan a first draft of your science fiction story **by determining an appropriate topic.** You can select from the Topic Bank or come up with an idea of your own.

Choose From the Topic Bank

TOPIC BANK

Future Trip What is your community like today? Now imagine what it will be like in 100 years. Write a story about your own community, set 100 years in the future.

Time Traveler Many people over time have thought about the possibilities of time travel. Write a story in which a main character discovers the ability to travel through time. What vehicle crosses the time barrier? To what era does your main character travel?

Superpower People Picture this: Earth, just like we know it today. People, just like we know them today...with one exception. They all have super powers. Write a story about what life on Earth would be like if people with super powers were a normal part of human life.

Choose Your Own Topic

Determine an appropriate topic on your own by using the following **range of strategies** to generate ideas.

Tap Into Personal Interests and Discuss

- Think about topics that make you curious. About which events, structures, or customs do you wonder? Note some topics that especially intrigue you.
- Think about something you know well. Do you love working on bicycles, cooking, or taking care of animals? Can you recount yesterday's football game play by play?
- With a group of friends, discuss some ways to take your interests into the future of science or technology. Brainstorm for story ideas that incorporate your interests.

Review your responses and choose a topic.

Narrow Your Topic

If the topic for your science fiction story is too broad, you may end up with a wandering story line that is hard for your readers to follow.

Apply It! Use a graphic organizer like the one shown to narrow your topic.

- Write the main topic of your science fiction story in the top box. Move down the chart, narrowing your topic to help focus your plot.
- Your last box should hold the details that will be your story's focus.

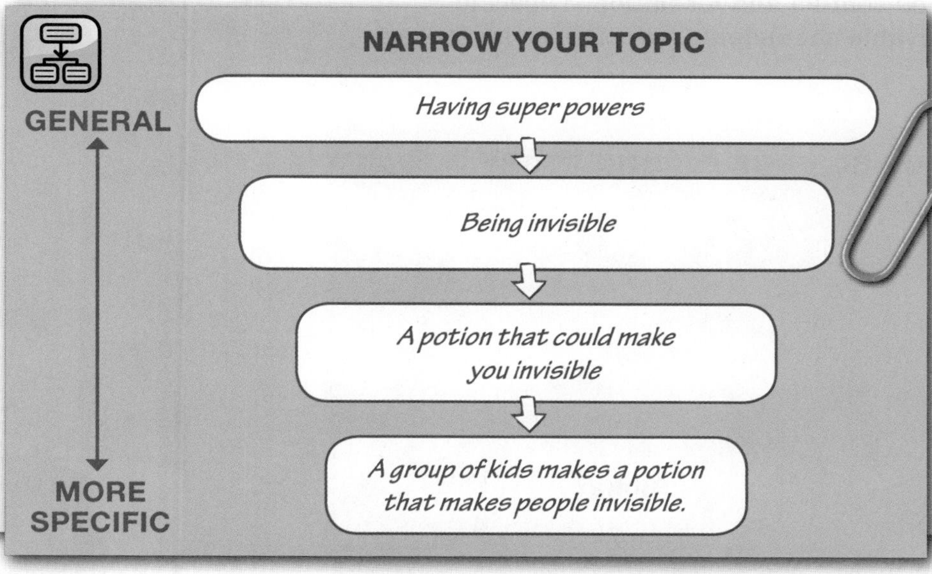

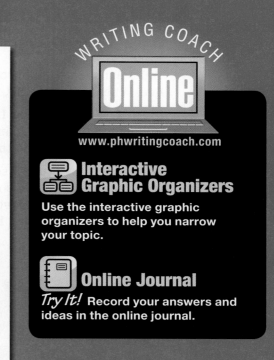

Consider Your Audience and Purpose

Before writing, think about your audience and purpose. Consider how your writing will convey the intended meaning to multiple audiences. Consider the views of others as you ask yourself these questions. Ask yourself what your audiences need and want to know about your story.

Questions for Audience	Questions for Purpose
• Who are my audiences? What are their interests? • What kinds of story lines will my audiences find engaging? • What background information will my audiences need to understand my story?	• Why am I writing the story? To surprise my audiences? To make them laugh? Think? Something else? • What conflict and resolution will best develop the plot? • What literary strategies and devices can I use to enhance the story?

Record your answers in your writing journal.

WRITING COACH Online

www.phwritingcoach.com

Interactive Graphic Organizers

Use the interactive graphic organizers to help you narrow your topic.

Online Journal

Try It! Record your answers and ideas in the online journal.

Plan Your Piece

You will use the graphic organizer to organize your details and your story line. When it is complete, you will be ready to write your first draft.

Identify Your Premise In a few words, identify the controlling idea or unique feature of the science fiction world of your story. As you draft, you will include details that help build and reinforce this premise.

Organize Your Story Use a graphic organizer to structure your ideas in a **sustained** way. This means your ideas will build on each other logically. Plan **a well-developed conflict and resolution**, a specific setting, and **interesting, believable characters**. Use complete sentences to fill in the spaces.

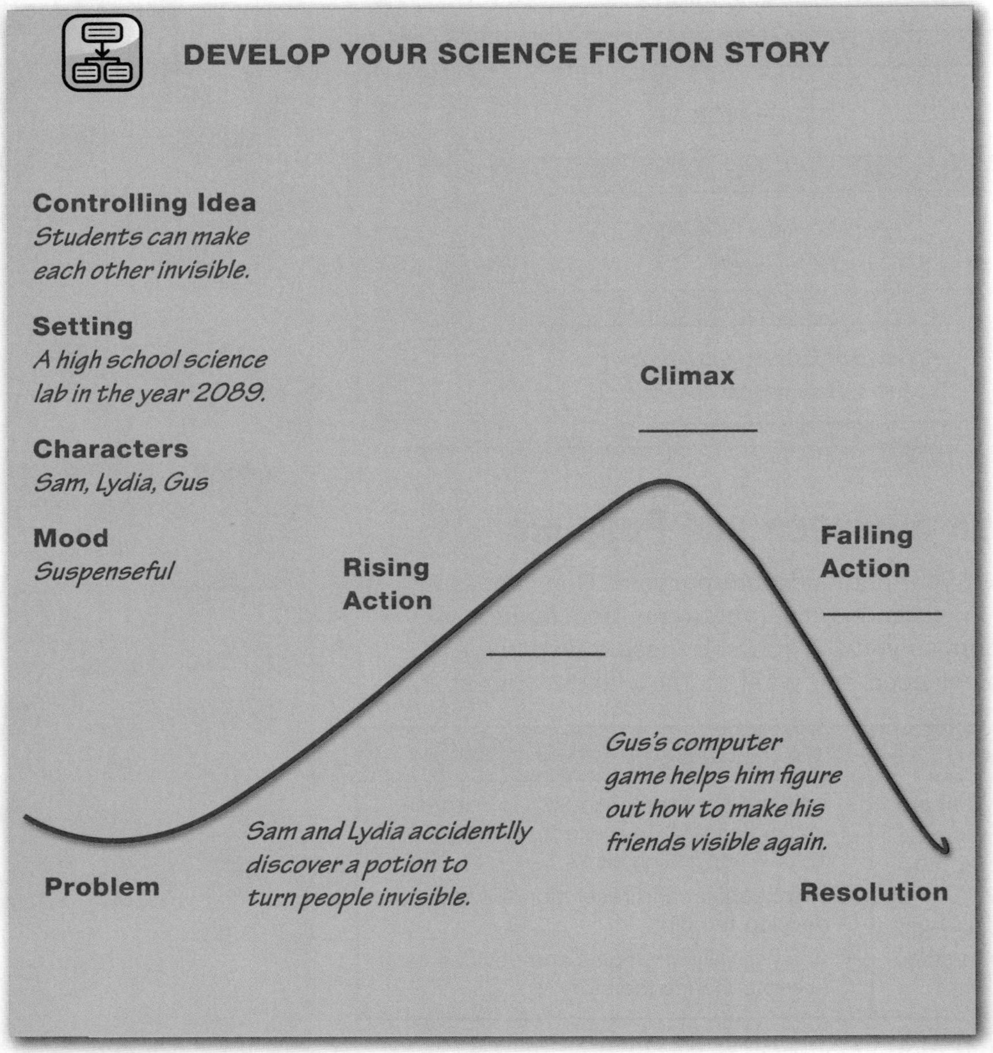
DEVELOP YOUR SCIENCE FICTION STORY
Controlling Idea
Students can make each other invisible.
Setting
A high school science lab in the year 2089.
Characters
Sam, Lydia, Gus
Mood
Suspenseful
Climax
Rising Action
Falling Action
Gus's computer game helps him figure out how to make his friends visible again.
Sam and Lydia accidentlly discover a potion to turn people invisible.
Problem
Resolution

Gather Details

To make the audience want to keep reading, develop interesting characters and a believable setting through the use of sensory details. Look at these examples of how writers use sensory details that appeal to the senses:

- **Sight:** *the shiny glass countertops in the chemistry lab*
- **Sound:** *Lydia's calm, soft voice*
- **Taste:** *Gus chews sweet-and-salty granola*
- **Smell:** *the aroma of the chemicals in the experiment*
- **Touch:** *the tight pinch of the lab goggles*

Writers also use a variety of **literary strategies and devices** to enhance the plot. Look at these examples.

- **Dialogue:** *"Sam, where are you?" Gus asked. "Right here in front of you!" Sam replied.*
- **Suspense:** *It had been two hours since Gus started puzzling out the solution. Were his friends doomed to a life as the Invisible Duo?*
- **Interesting Comparisons:** *Sam was feeling desperate, as though he were underwater and running out of oxygen.*

Try It! Read the Student Model excerpt and identify which kinds of details and literary strategies or devices the author uses to move the plot forward.

STUDENT MODEL from Dance on Air

page 99; lines 33–38

I opened the can, and it drew the remaining stink off my togs. I mean, come on! The Anti-Gravity Dance Jam is only held once a month, and we weren't going to let a little bug-rat collision get in our way.

"Okay, man! Let's jet!" I said to Rexx.

"You got it!" he replied.

Apply It! Review the types of details a short story writer can use. Then, write at least one detail you can apply to each section of your story.

- Add vivid sensory details to bring your story to life.
- Include **literary strategies and devices** that will **enhance your plot,** such as dialogue, suspense, and interesting comparisons.
- Then, add this information to your graphic organizer.

WRITING COACH Online

www.phwritingcoach.com

Interactive Graphic Organizers

Use the interactive graphic organizers to help you create a plan for your writing.

Interactive Model

Refer back to the Interactive Model in the eText as you plan your writing.

Drafting

During the drafting stage, you will start to write your ideas for your short story. You will follow an outline that provides an organizational strategy that will help you write a focused, organized, and coherent science fiction story.

The Organization of a Short Story

The chart shows an organizational strategy for a short story. Look back at how the Mentor Text follows this organizational strategy. Then, use this chart to help you outline your draft.

Outline for Success

I. Beginning

See Mentor Text, p. 94.

- Setting and characters
- Conflict

Set the Scene

- Sensory details help to create a specific setting and to develop interesting and believable characters. Telling a story in the first person is one way to show a character's personality.
- The beginning of the story should set up an engaging plot by hinting at the main problem.

II. Middle

See Mentor Text, pp. 95–97.

- Plot with well-paced action
- Climax when the suspense is at its highest point
- Use of language that includes rhetorical and literary devices

Build Suspense

- The action should stay focused to hold reader interest. The story's pace is kept interesting with one or two sentences for each event up to and including the climax.
- Literary strategies and devices, such as dialogue and suspense, help to make your writing interesting and move the plot forward.

III. End

See Mentor Text, p. 98.

- Resolution
- The results of the character's action

Wrap It Up

- The resolution shows what happens after the conflict or problem is solved. All of the story's loose ends should be tied up in the resolution.
- The resolution may also describe something permanent that remains as evidence of the events.

Start Your Draft

Use the checklist to help complete your draft. Use the graphic organizer that shows the beginning, middle, and end of your story, and the Outline for Success as guides.

While drafting, aim at writing your ideas, not on making your writing perfect. Remember, because writing is an open-ended process, you will have the chance to improve your draft when you revise and edit.

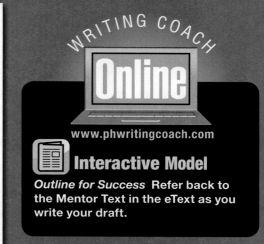

- √ Start drafting your **beginning** with the opening of your science fiction story. Describe the setting and create interesting, believable **characters.** Include sensory details that will engage your readers and draw them into the story.
- √ Continue by hinting at the **conflict,** or problem, to come.

- √ Create an **engaging** story line by building a well-developed conflict that builds suspense.
- √ Use vivid sensory details and a range of **literary strategies** and devices, such as dialogue, to help readers experience what the characters experience and to enhance the plot.
- √ Use **rhetorical devices**, such as analogies and rhetorical questions, to convey meaning to your audience. Well-placed rhetorical devices will also make your writing livelier and more interesting.
- √ Keep the **action** in the **middle** of your story moving at a good pace and focused on the conflict. Describe events in time order, building to the climax.

- √ **End** your story by writing a well-developed **resolution.** Describe what happens after the main character solves the problem. Tell readers a lasting result of the character's actions.

WRITING COACH Online

www.phwritingcoach.com

Interactive Model

Outline for Success **Refer back to the Mentor Text in the eText as you write your draft.**

REPLACE ADD DELETE and REORDER RADaR

Revising: Making It Better

Now that you have finished your first draft, you are ready to revise. Think about the "big picture" of audience, purpose, and genre. You can use your Revision RADaR as a guide for making changes to improve your draft. Revision RADaR provides four major ways to improve your writing: (R) replace, (A) add, (D) delete, and (R) reorder.

Kelly Gallagher, M. Ed.

KEEP REVISION ON YOUR RADaR

Read part of the first draft of the Student Model "Dance on Air." Then look at questions the writer asked herself as she thought about how well her draft **addressed issues of audience, purpose, and genre.**

1ST DRAFT

Dance on Air

We drove along in Rexx's Aircar for micro-seconds until we had a problem. A flock of Bug-rats flew into the wind units on both wings. This is a danger of air travel; everyone knows it.

*Does this description hold my audience's attention and create **suspense**?*

And I thought everyone knew how to fix the problem, but obviously Rexx didn't, so I had to.

*Is my writing lively and **interesting**?*

I cleared the wind units, I got back in the Aircar, and we were on our way! We really wanted to go to the Anti-Gravity Dance Jam because it only takes place once a month.

*Is the **action** well paced and does it build toward a resolution? Have I included **sensory details** to make my audience feel as if they are a part of the story?*

Bug-rats stink, and you have to use a special tool to clear the wind units. Luckily they include this tool with every new Aircar. It's called a wind wand.

*Are my ideas organized in a **clear and logical** way?*

Now look at how the writer applied Revision RADaR to write an improved second draft.

2ND DRAFT

Dance on Air

We sailed along the pathways and were micro-seconds away from arriving at the dance when a major jam got in the way—a power-jam. Rexx freaked, but the cause was clear. It was a flock of bug-rats. They had flown straight into the wind units on both wings. It's a drag, but everyone with an Aircar knows that this is one of the dangers of travel.

A *Added descriptive language to set the scene and create suspense*

I thought everyone also knew how to fix this kind of problem. But no—Rexx sat there, mystified. The control panel left him completely confused. He just stared at the red lights flashing along both wing icons. I snapped my fingers in front of his face, but he wouldn't snap out of it. That's when I knew I had to take over.

D *__Deleted__ dull language and __replaced__ it with stronger words for a better description*

Have you ever cleared the wind units of an Aircar after a bug-rat collision? It's not pretty. Thankfully, Rexx's new Aircar had come equipped with the taser wand that's needed to blow out the units. Wow, do those bug-rats stink!

R *__Replaced__ more general language with sensory details and more detailed descriptions*

When I got back in the Aircar, I remembered that I had a can of fresh oxygen in my bag, so it was no worries. I opened the can, and it drew the remaining stink off my togs. I mean, come on! The Anti-Gravity Dance Jam is only held once a month, and we weren't going to let a little bug-rat collision get in our way.

R *__Reordered__ ideas to lead to a clear resolution*

WRITING COACH **Online**

www.phwritingcoach.com

Video

Learn more strategies for effective writing from program author Kelly Gallagher.

Apply It! Use your Revision RADaR to revise your draft.

- First, determine if you have engaged your audience and included all the genre characteristics of a short story. Think back to prewriting and your writing purpose and check that you have met it.
- Then, apply the Revision RADaR strategy to make needed changes. Remember—you can use the steps in the strategy in any order.

Look at the Big Picture

Use the chart and your analytical skills to evaluate how well each section of your short story addresses **purpose, audience, and genre.** When necessary, use the suggestions in the chart to revise your piece.

Section	Evaluate	Revise
Beginning	• Check the **opening.** Will it grab readers' attention and make them want to read more?	• Introduce science or technology details to reinforce your controlling idea. Use precise word choice and vivid images.
	• Introduce the characters and the **conflict.**	• Include dialogue and characters' thoughts to help set up the problem.
	• Introduce the **setting.**	• Use sensory details to describe where the action takes place.
Middle	• Check that the action is well-paced and the **plot** clear.	• Show events in time order leading up to the climax.
	• Underline details that build **suspense.** Draw a line from each one to the climax.	• Reorder details as necessary to better build suspense. Delete or replace details that don't contribute to building the story.
	• Confirm that you have included enough **details** that build the science fiction side of your narrative.	• Consider creating new words to describe unusual objects or behaviors. Add details that remind readers of your unique setting or characters.
End	• Check that **loose ends** of the story are tied up.	• Answer questions such as *What happened then? What did the characters do after the problem was solved?*
	• Make sure you described the **results** of the main character's actions.	• Explain the result of what the character learned from the experience or how it affected him or her.

Focus on Craft: Style

Style is the particular way an author uses language. Diction, or an author's choice of words, is an important element of style. Authors may also use varying sentence lengths to achieve a particular style. An author's tone —whether serious or comical—can be an effective tool to relay style. Finally, the author's use of figurative language and rhetorical devices, such as rhetorical questions, can affect how information is interpreted by the reader.

Think about an effective writing style for science fiction as you read the following sentences from the Student Model.

STUDENT MODEL from **Dance on Air**
page 98; lines 26-30

Have you ever cleared the wind units of an Aircar after a bug-rat collision? It's not pretty. Thankfully, Rexx's new Aircar had come equipped with the wind wand that's needed to blow out the units. Wow, do those bug-rats stink!

Try It! Now, ask yourself these questions. Record your answers in your journal.

- How do the varying sentence lengths add to the comical style?
- Would the second sentence be more or less comical if it read "It is messy and difficult"? Explain.

Fine-Tune Your Draft

Apply It! Use the revision suggestions to prepare your final draft **after rethinking how well questions of purpose, audience, and genre have been addressed**.

- **Convey Clear Style** Combine varying sentence structure, word choice, and tone to create a clear writing style.
- **Improve Figurative Language** Look for places where you could make your writing stronger by using a simile or metaphor.
- **Improve Subtlety of Meaning** Tone, word choice, and writing style combine to create exactly the meaning and feeling a writer wants. Confirm that you have chosen exactly the words you mean. Then, use transitions such as *then* and *next* to organize your writing in a logical sequence.

Peer Feedback Read your final draft to a group of peers. Ask if you have **interesting and believable characters**. Think about their responses and revise your final draft as needed.

WRITING COACH Online

www.phwritingcoach.com

Online Journal

Try It! **Record your answers in the online journal.**

Interactive Model

Refer back to the Interactive Model as you revise your writing.

Editing: Making It Correct

Read your draft carefully when editing to check for correct spelling and grammar. It can be helpful to read your story out loud to listen for places that need correction.

Before editing your final draft, think about the way you are using **restrictive and nonrestrictive relative clauses.** Relative clauses, which cannot stand on their own as complete sentences, modify nouns in a sentence. Once you have checked for relative clauses in your story, you can identify which clauses are **restrictive and nonrestrictive**. You can also **place commas correctly in these clauses.** Then, edit your final draft for any errors in **grammar, mechanics, and spelling.**

WRITE GUY *Jeff Anderson, M. Ed.*

WHAT DO YOU NOTICE?

Zoom in on Conventions Focus on relative clauses as you zoom in on lines from the Mentor Text.

To learn more about clauses, see Chapter 15 of your Grammar Handbook.

MENTOR TEXT from **Homelanding**
page 95; lines 26–27

> As for the country itself, let me begin with the sunsets, which are long and red....

Now, ask yourself: *Which part of the sentence gives more information about the sunsets?*

Perhaps you said the relative clause *which are long and red.* A relative clause begins with a relative pronoun, such as *that, which, who, whom,* and *whose.* It modifies, or describes, a subject, such as *sunsets*, in this case.

There are two kinds of relative clauses. A restrictive relative clause gives necessary information that identifies the person or thing it modifies. If you remove a restrictive relative clause, the sentence will be unclear or misleading.

A nonrestrictive relative clause gives information that is not essential to identifying the person or thing it modifies. You can read a sentence without the nonrestrictive clause and it should still make sense.

Grammar Mini-Lesson: Commas in Relative Clauses

To learn more, see Chapter 23.

Commas are often used to set off part of a sentence, such as a clause. **Restrictive relative clauses** do not require a comma, but **nonrestrictive relative clauses** do. The text set off by the commas can be removed and the sentence will still make sense. Notice how a comma sets off the nonrestrictive relative clause in the Mentor Text.

MENTOR TEXT from **Homelanding**
page 95; lines 33–34

Our country is large in extent, small in population, which accounts for our fear of large empty spaces....

Try It! Identify the restrictive and nonrestrictive relative clauses in the sentences. Then add commas to the sentence with the nonrestrictive clause. Write the answers in your journal.

1. Bring down the tents that are in the attic and load them in the car.
2. Our guide who was once a chef moved here from the city.

Apply It! Edit your draft for grammar, mechanics, and spelling. If necessary, rewrite some sentences to ensure that you have used restrictive and nonrestrictive relative clauses correctly. Check that you use commas with nonrestrictive clauses.

Use the rubric to evaluate your piece. If necessary, rethink, rewrite, or revise.

Rubric for Short Story: Science Fiction	Rating Scale
Ideas: How well do the dialogue and setting support the plot?	Not very Very 1 2 3 4 5 6
Organization: How clearly organized is the sequence of events?	1 2 3 4 5 6
Voice: How effectively have you created a unique voice in your narrative?	1 2 3 4 5 6
Word Choice: How effective is your word choice in creating tone and style?	1 2 3 4 5 6
Sentence Fluency: How well have you used sentence variety to build rhythm?	1 2 3 4 5 6
Conventions: How correct are your clauses?	1 2 3 4 5 6

WRITING COACH Online
www.phwritingcoach.com

Video
Learn effective editing techniques from program author Jeff Anderson.

Online Journal
Try It! Record your answers in the online journal.

Interactive Model
Refer back to the Interactive Model as you edit your writing.

Publishing

Share your science fiction story with others by publishing it. First, get the story ready for presentation. Then choose a way to publish it for the appropriate audiences.

Wrap Up Your Presentation

Create a final draft. If you have typed your story on a computer, be sure to choose a font that is easy to read. When your story is printed, your readers can enjoy it more easily. Also be sure to check that your title grabs the reader's attention and hints at your story's main idea.

Publish Your Piece

Use this chart to identify a way to publish your written work.

If your audience is...	...then publish it by...
Students or adults at your school	• Expressing your ideas by presenting it with friends as Reader's Theater • Creating a class book of science fiction for the library • Posting it to your school Web site with illustrations and background sound effects
Younger children at the local library	• Making it into a puppet show or short animated film • Drawing large, colorful illustrations to use as you read it aloud

Reflect on Your Writing

Now that you are done with your science fiction story, read it over and use your writing journal to answer these questions. Use specific details to describe and explain your reflections. Increase the specificity of your details based on the type of information requested.

- What is your favorite part of the story? Your least favorite? What can you focus on improving the next time you write a story?
- Do you think knowing how to write fiction is an important skill to possess? Explain.

The Big Question: Why Write? What can fiction do better than non-fiction?

Manage Your Portfolio You may wish to include your published science fiction story in your writing portfolio. If so, consider what this story reveals about your writing and your growth as a writer.

21st Century Learning

MAKE YOUR WRITING COUNT

Create a Graphic Sci-Fi Novel

Science fiction writers create startling images of fantastic creatures, machines, and entire worlds. Retell a group member's sci-fi tale through words and images by creating a **graphic novel**.

A graphic novel tells a dramatic story in a traditional comic-book fashion. Present your graphic novel in a dramatic performance, or share it electronically using presentation software.

Here's your action plan.

1. Choose roles, such as artist, writer, and editor.
2. Choose a peer's story to adapt.
3. Review a selection of graphic novels to get a sense of the variety of styles. Takes notes on the unique presentation and flow of information.
4. Determine the point of view from which you will express the story—first person narrator, for example. Choose an illustration style for the specific audience you want to entertain. For example, manga and U.S. comics are two popular styles.
5. To draft your graphic novel:
   - Choose a medium. Pen and ink are traditional, but a computer graphics program makes the novel easier to publish electronically.
   - Draft the dialogue and narration and sketch the images that will appear in each panel.
6. As a group, discuss revisions before moving into the final drafting stage.
7. Present your final product to the class.

Listening and Speaking Share the distinctive point of view of your sci-fi graphic novel through an inventive **multimedia presentation,** integrating sound, images, and words that convey your specific point of view and appeal to your specific audience. Scan each panel into a slideshow application, add sound effects, and project it onto a large screen. Alternatively, dramatically read each panel for the class as they view the paper comic.

WRITING COACH Online

www.phwritingcoach.com

Online Journal

Reflect on Your Writing **Record your answers and ideas in the online journal.**

Resource

Link to resources on 21st Century Learning for help in creating a group project.

Your Turn Writing for Media: Graphic Story Script

21st Century Learning

Graphic Story Script

A **graphic story** is much like a comic book. It tells a story with both images and words. Writers create scripts for graphic stories that explain the story with both words and images. These scripts are called storyboards. The images show what each frame of the story will look like, including the characters' expressions and other actions. Like other stories, graphic story scripts have a setting, characters, plot, and well-paced action. They also include a theme, or big idea that runs throughout the story. The theme can be **explicit** and directly stated or **implicit** and just suggested or implied, leaving readers to draw conclusions.

Try It! Study the sample script. Then, answer these questions. Record your answers in your journal.

1. To what **audience** is this scene most likely aimed?
2. Is the **story line of** "New Neighbors" **engaging?** Explain why or why not.
3. What is the **purpose** of "New Neighbors"?
4. How would you describe the **pace of events?**
5. Which **character** is most interesting to you? Why?
6. How could the **images** be described more clearly?
7. What is the **mood,** the overall feeling created by the text, of the script? What is the **tone,** or attitude, of the script? Which **details** define the mood and tone?
8. What is the **theme** of the script? Is it **implicit** or **explicit**?

Extension Find another example of a graphic story, and compare it with this one.

New Neighbors

1

<Shot 1 Image: Space capsule in upper left of a field. Aliens (non threatening) are exiting. Tent with open flaps in lower right of field. Two teen males inside tent in sleeping bags. One is sitting up awake; the other is rubbing eyes, appears sleepy, etc.>

<Dialogue> John: What was THAT?
Bill: Hey, I was sleeping!

2

<Shot 2 Image: Aliens stand outside tent which has begun to levitate. Rays are beaming from the aliens' foreheads. John looks worried and Bill looks relaxed. Show squiggly lines to note movement of levitating. >

<Dialogue> John: Did you feel that?
Bill: Dude, relax and go back to sleep!

3

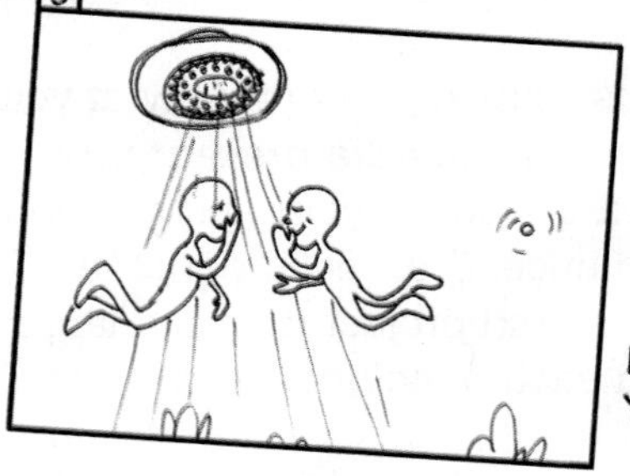

<Shot 3 Image: Aliens rise up to the space capsule, looking relieved and gesturing to each other.>

<Dialogue> John: Thank goodness they're leaving! I guess they think we look scary!

Bill: Wake up, John! You've been screaming in your sleep. You must be having a nightmare.

Create a Script

Follow these steps to create your own script. To plan your script or storyboard, review the graphic organizers on pages R24–R27 and choose one that suits your needs.

Prewriting

- Identify and narrow a topic, and identify your target audience.
- Determine your purpose and theme. Decide if the theme will be implicit or explicit.
- Create a realistic, yet out-of-this-world, setting with characters for your script. Match your characters to the setting.
- Outline the story line—the beginning, middle, and end of your script.

Drafting

- Use the proper format to draft your script. For instance, draw a sketch of what you intend each image to be in its final form. Then, write what appears in each image. Provide dialogue that will appear in speech bubbles in the graphic story.
- Draft an opening that grabs your audience. Be sure to use details that contribute to a definitive mood or tone.
- Include details that help to define the mood or tone of your script. For instance, in "New Neighbors," the descriptions of the aliens standing silently beside the tent create a spooky mood.
- Develop an engaging story line with well-developed conflict and resolution. Keep in mind that in a graphic story, the plot is developed through images and through what the characters say. For instance, in "New Neighbors," readers think the characters might be in trouble when the tent begins to levitate.
- Write clear and specific descriptions of the images that will enhance the story. For instance, in "New Neighbors," the words, "the other... appears sleepy" give readers a clear visual image.

Revising and Editing

- Review your draft to make sure events are organized logically. Make sure the conflict, or problem, is clear and that the images are clearly described.
- Check that spelling, grammar, and mechanics are correct.

Publishing

- Create the images you described in the script, either drawing them by hand or creating them with a computer graphics program. Add the dialogue to the speech bubbles and tie the pages together to create a book.
- You may also want to make a video recording of you and classmates acting out the script.

WRITING COACH **Online**

www.phwritingcoach.com

Online Journal

Try It! **Record your answers in the online journal.**

Interactive Graphic Organizers

Choose from a variety of graphic organizers to plan and develop your project.

Partner Talk

Before you start drafting, describe your story idea to a partner in specific detail. Ask for feedback about your plan. For example, ask your partner's opinion about whether your story will sustain reader interest. Monitor your partner's spoken language by asking follow-up questions to confirm your understanding.

Writing for Assessment

You can use the prompts on these pages to practice writing short stories. Your responses should include the same characteristics as your science fiction story. (See page 92.)

Try It! To begin, read the **short story** prompt and the information on format and academic vocabulary. Use the ABCDs of On-Demand Writing to help you plan and write your story.

Format

The prompt directs you to write a *short story.* Start with a beginning that introduces the characters and conflict. Then, develop an engaging story line. End by tying up loose ends of the story.

Short Story Prompt

Write a short story about a character who gets drawn into a video game. Describe what the video game was like and how the character was drawn into it. Remember to use literary devices, such as dialogue and foreshadowing, in your story.

Academic Vocabulary

A *literary device* is a technique or literary element that authors use to create meaning. *Dialogue* is the conversation between two or more characters in a work of literature. *Foreshadowing* is an author's use of hints or clues about something that will happen later in the story.

The ABCDs of On-Demand Writing

Use the following ABCDs to help you respond to the prompt.

Before you write your draft:

Attack the prompt [1 MINUTE]

- Circle or highlight important verbs in the prompt. Draw a line from the verb to what it refers to.
- Rewrite the prompt in your own words.

Brainstorm possible answers [4 MINUTES]

- Create a graphic organizer to generate ideas.
- Use one for each part of the prompt if necessary.

Choose the order of your response [1 MINUTE]

- Think about the best way to organize your ideas.
- Number your ideas in the order you will write about them. Cross out ideas you will not be using.

After you write your draft:

Detect errors before turning in the draft [1 MINUTE]

- Carefully reread your writing.
- Make sure that your response makes sense and is complete.
- Look for spelling, punctuation, and grammar errors.

More Prompts for Practice

Apply It! Respond to Prompts 1 and 2 by writing **short stories** with engaging story lines that hold the reader's interest.

- Establish an engaging story line with a well-developed **conflict** and **resolution**
- Develop logical and **well-paced action**
- Create a specific **setting**
- Develop **interesting and believable characters**
- Use a range of **literary strategies and devices** to enhance your plot and make your writing interesting

Prompt 1 Write a short story about a character who can see 500 years into the future. Develop an engaging story with a cohesive plot through beginning, middle, and end. Make sure to include a believable setting and interesting characters.

Prompt 2 Write a short story about a new kind of technology that makes life easier. Create a new technological invention that is specific and believable, and develop a story line about the effect of the new technology on your characters—whether for good or ill. Does the new technology present some kind of problem or solve a problem, or both?

Spiral Review: Narrative Respond to Prompt 3 by writing a **narrative nonfiction** essay that includes a well-developed **conflict** and **resolution**. Use a range of **literary devices,** such as dialogue and suspense, to enhance the plot. Make sure that your story includes all the characteristics on page 66. Like short stories, narrative nonfiction essays usually include an interesting and believable **character** who faces a problem—but in this narrative nonfiction essay, the character will be you.

Prompt 3 Think about a time when you accepted responsibility for a mistake. Write an engaging narrative essay that describes what the mistake was and why and how you took responsibility for it.

WRITING COACH Online

www.phwritingcoach.com

Interactive Writing Coach™

Plan your response to the prompt. If you are using the prompt for practice, write one paragraph at a time or your entire draft and then submit it for feedback. If you are using the prompt as a timed test, write your entire draft and then submit it for feedback.

Remember ABCD

- **A**ttack the prompt
- **B**rainstorm possible answers
- **C**hoose the order of your response
- **D**etect errors before turning in the draft

CHAPTER 7

POETRY AND DESCRIPTION

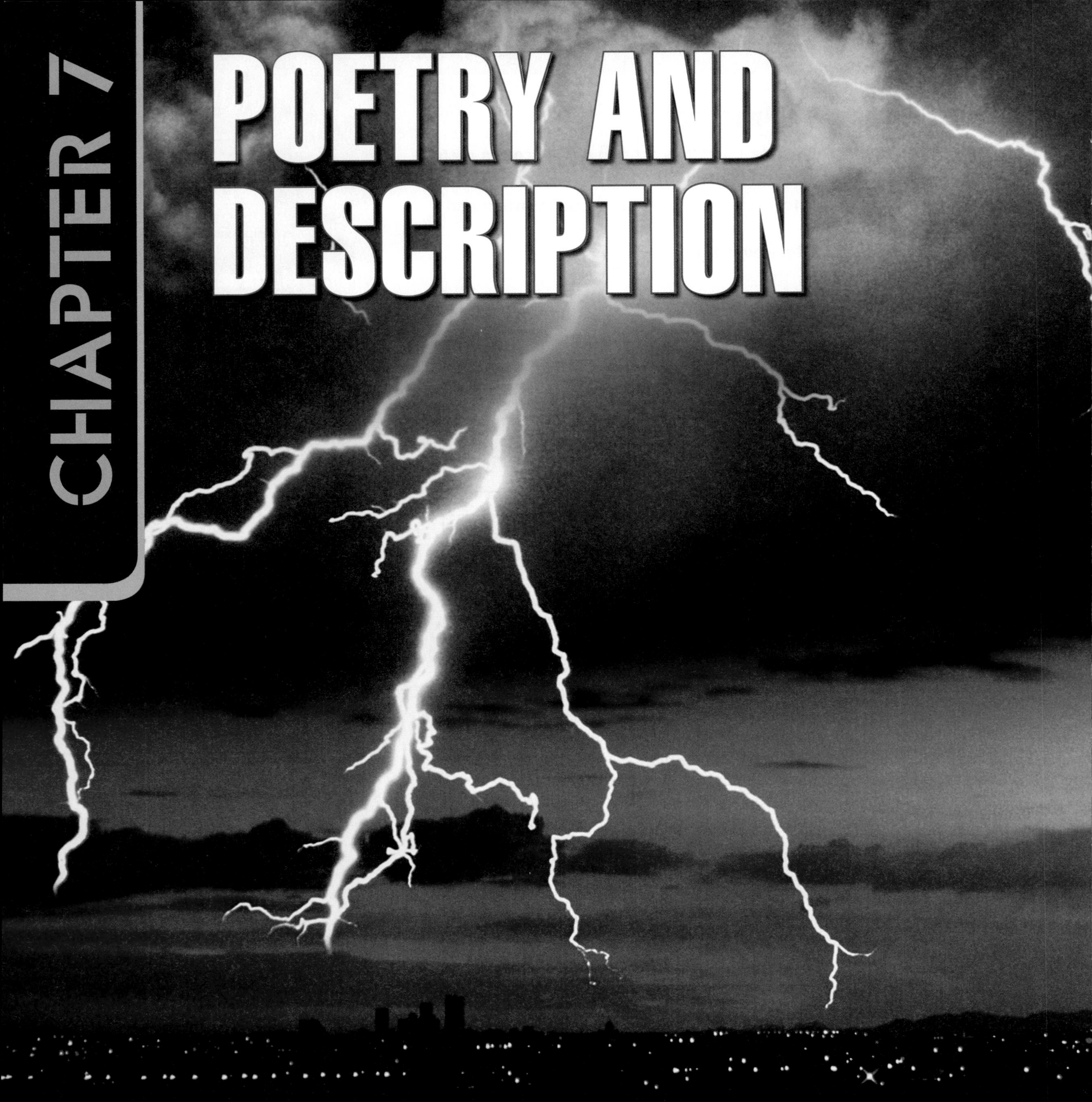

What Do You See?

People see different things when they look at something. Some people may look at this photograph and see lightning. Others might see the power of nature or danger.

People use different words to describe what they see. Words can be a powerful way to capture the beauty or danger of nature.

Try It! Take a few minutes to list what you see in the photograph of the lightning. Consider these questions as you participate in an extended discussion with a partner. Take turns expressing your ideas and feelings.

- What do you actually see?
- What emotions does this photograph make you feel?
- How would you feel if you were in this storm?

Review the list you made. Use your list to describe to a partner what you see in this photograph. Think about how you would use these words to make a poem.

What's Ahead

In this chapter, you will review some strong examples of poems: Mentor Texts and Student Models. Then, using the examples as guidance, you will write a poem of your own.

WRITING COACH Online

www.phwritingcoach.com

Online Journal

Try It! **Record your answers and ideas in the online journal.**

You can also record and save your answers and ideas on pop-up sticky notes in the eText.

Connect to the Big Questions

Discuss these questions with your partner:

1. **What do you think?** Can every important experience be communicated in words?
2. **Why Write?** How do we best convey feeling through words on a page?

POETRY AND DESCRIPTION

In this chapter, you will focus on writing a poem. Poetry is a concise form of writing that uses imaginative language, rhythm, and often rhyme to communicate ideas and feelings. To make every word count, a poet carefully chooses language that is vivid, precise, and often musical, or pleasing to hear. An especially important part of poetry—and most other kinds of writing—is description. Descriptive details create imagery that helps readers picture what something looks like or imagine its aroma, sound, texture, or taste.

You will develop a poem by taking it through each stage of the writing process: prewriting, drafting, revising, editing, and publishing. To preview the criteria for how your poem will be evaluated, see the rubric on page 137. You will also have an opportunity to apply the elements of descriptive writing to another form—an eyewitness account, or description of an event told by someone who saw an event occur.

FEATURE ASSIGNMENT

Poem

An effective poem has these characteristics: (See page 129 for additional information).

- A clear **topic, theme,** or **controlling idea**
- A variety of **poetic techniques,** such as structural elements, figurative language, and sound devices
- **Structural elements**, such as rhyme and meter
- **Figurative language**, such as similes, metaphors, and personification
- **Sensory details** that allow the reader to see, smell, hear, taste, and feel what the poet describes
- **Sound devices** that create a musical or emotional effect

A ballad also has these characteristics:

- A simple **rhyme pattern** and regular rhythm
- A narrative that tells **a story,** often an adventure or romance
- A song-like **structure,** often with a refrain, or a regularly repeated line or group of lines

Free verse also has these characteristics:

- Text written to mimic the patterns of **natural speech**
- No specific rhyme pattern
- No specific meter
- No specific length

Forms of Poetry and Description

There are many forms of poetry and description, including these:

Ballads are poems that tell a story and are usually meant to be sung. Ballads often contain repetition and have a simple, regular rhyme pattern and meter, or "beat."

Descriptive essays use imagery and vivid details to help readers imagine a person, place, thing, or event. Like all essays, they are made up of an introduction, body, and conclusion. They include forms such as eyewitness accounts or travel writing.

Free verse is poetry that imitates the rhythms of everyday speech. Freed of set rhythm and rhyme patterns, free verse uses figurative language and sound devices to convey ideas and feelings.

Haiku are three-line poems that originated in Japan. In a haiku, the first and last lines consist of five syllables, and the middle line consists of seven syllables. Classic haiku are usually about nature.

Lyric poems are poems that express a speaker's feelings about a particular person, place, thing, or event. Unlike ballads, lyric poems usually do not tell a story. Sonnets and free verse poems are types of lyric poems.

Prose poems look like prose, or regular text you might find in a story or essay, but use poetic techniques to create a memorable description of a person, place, thing, or event.

Sonnets are 14-line poems written in a regular meter and pattern of rhyme. One kind of sonnet—the English sonnet—consists of three four-line stanzas and a final couplet, or two rhyming lines. In each stanza, alternating lines rhyme.

Try It! For each audience and purpose described, choose a form, such as ballad, haiku, or lyric poem, that is appropriate for conveying your intended meaning to the audience. Explain your choices.

- To help classmates picture the beauty of a sunset, using only a few words
- To entertain young children with a story about a hero
- To express your feelings about someone, you might consider thanking that person for being your friend

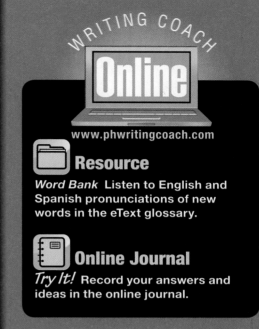

WRITING COACH Online

www.phwritingcoach.com

Resource

Word Bank Listen to English and Spanish pronunciations of new words in the eText glossary.

Online Journal

Try It! Record your answers and ideas in the online journal.

WORD BANK

People often use these basic and content-based vocabulary words when they talk about poetry. Work with a partner. Take turns saying each word aloud. Then, write one sentence using each word. If you are unsure of the meaning of a word, use the Glossary or a dictionary to check the definition.

describe	rhyme
emotion	rhythm
feeling	sensory

Learn From Experience

After reading the poems on pages 122–123, read the numbered notes in the margins to learn about how the poets presented their ideas.

Answer the *Try It!* questions online or in your notebook.

---

1 Like most **ballads,** this one tells a **story.** Here, the setting and the situation are introduced, and **sensory imagery** makes the scene more vivid.

Try It! What is the sensory image in the first stanza? To which of the five senses does it appeal?

2 **Rhyming words** create a musical effect. So does the **regular rhythm,** or "beat."

Try It! Read aloud the first two stanzas. Do the same lines rhyme in the first stanza as in the second stanza? Is this rhyme scheme, or pattern, used throughout the ballad? Explain.

3 Here, **conflict** is introduced into the story the ballad tells.

Try It! What is the conflict? What does conflict add to the story?

Extension Find another example of a poem, and compare it to these.

Sir Patrick Spens

traditional ballad

1 The king sits in Dumferline town,
Drinking the blood-red wine;
"O where shall I get a good sailor
To sail this ship of mine?"

2 Up and spoke an older knight,
Sat at the king's right knee:
"Sir Patrick Spens is the best sailor
That sailed upon the sea."

The king has written a broad letter,
And signed it with his hand;
And sent it to Sir Patrick Spens,
Was walking on the sand.

The first line that Sir Patrick read,
A loud laugh laughed he;
The next line that Sir Patrick read,
A tear blinded his eye.

"O who is this has done this deed,
This ill deed done to me;
To send me out this time of the year,
To sail upon the sea?"

3 "Make haste, make haste, my merry men all,
Our good ship sails the morn";
"O say not so, my dear master,
For I fear a deadly storm."

O the Scot's lords were right loathe
To wet their cork-heeled shoes;
But long ere a' the play were played,
Their hats they swam aboone.

O long, long may the ladies stand,
With their gold combs in their hair,
Waiting for their own dear lords,
For they'll see them no more.

O long, long, may the ladies stand
With their fans in their hands,
Before they see Sir Patrick Spens
Come sailing to the land.

Half over, half over, to Aberdour,
It's fifty fathoms deep,
And there lies good Sir Patrick Spens
With the Scot's lords at his feet.

Special Glasses

by Billy Collins

I had to send away for them
because they are not available in any store.

They look the same as any sunglasses
with a light tint and silvery frames,
(4) but instead of filtering out the harmful
rays of the sun,

they filter out the harmful sight of you—
you on the approach,
you waiting at my bus stop,
you, face in the evening window.

Every morning I put them on
and step out the side door
whistling a melody of thanks to my nose
and my ears for holding them in place, just so,

singing a song of gratitude
to the lens grinder at his heavy bench
and to the very lenses themselves
because they allow it all to come in, all but you.

(5) How they know the difference
between the green hedges, the stone walls,
and you is beyond me,

(5) yet the schoolbuses flashing in the rain
do come in, as well as the postman waving
and the mother and daughter dogs next door,

(5) and then there is the tea kettle
about to play its chord—
everything sailing right in but you, girl.

(5) Yes, just as the night air passes through the screen,
but not the mosquito,
and as water swirls down the drain,
but not the eggshell,
so the flowering trellis and the moon
pass through my special glasses, but not you.

Let us keep it this way; I say to myself,
as I lay my special glasses on the night table,
pull the chain on the lamp,
and say a prayer—unlike the song—
that I will not see you in my dreams.

WRITING COACH Online

www.phwritingcoach.com

Interactive Model

Listen to an audio recording of the Mentor Text in the eText. You can refer back to the Mentor Text whenever you need support in developing your own writing.

Online Journal

Try It! Answer the questions about the Mentor Text in the online journal.

(4) The poet **repeats** the word *you* to make a point.

Try It! What point does the repetition help make?

(5) The poet uses **sensory details** and **figurative language** to express his ideas.

Try It! How does the author's use of literal and figurative language shape the perceptions of readers?

STUDENT MODEL

Ballad and Free Verse Poem

With a small group, take turns reading the Student Models aloud. As you read, practice newly acquired vocabulary by correctly producing the word's sound. Also note the poems' structures and elements of poetry. You may want to take a look at the Poet's Toolbox on page 129. Ask yourself how the poetic language informs and shapes your understanding of the poems.

Use a Reader's Eye

Now, reread the Student Models. On your copies of the Student Models, use the Reader's Response Symbols to react to what you read.

Reader's Response Symbols

- **+ I can picture this.**
- **- This image could be stronger.**
- **? I wonder what this means.**
- **! This is cool!**

Partner Talk

Express your opinions and feelings about the Student Models with a partner. On what do you agree? How do your feelings and opinions about the poems differ?

Fire to Fight

A Ballad by Carmen Ramos

Flames orange and red licked into the sky,
Reaching amazing height.
Rosa's excitement was there, she couldn't deny,
As she leapt from her truck, a fire to fight.

The cries of a family came through thundering roars—
Wood crashing, flames crackling, all coming to light.
Rosa fought her way in, breaking down heavy doors,
As she tromped through the flames, a fire to fight.

She scooped up a child, calmed him through tears,
As his grateful mother held Rosa's hand tight.
Rosa's calmness and strength quieted fears,
And she led them out, still more fire to fight.

The team worked together, the fire was out;
Rosa had helped save a family that night.
They'd always remember her, there is no doubt,
And she knew she'd help others, more fires to fight.

1

Cat Dog

A Free Verse Poem by Jake Gomez

My dog is a little strange.
She sleeps on her back,
with her legs straight as broomsticks
and her feet in the air.
She looks like a dog statue
that has been turned upside down.

My dog is a little strange
because when she is scared
the hairs on her back
stand straight up
just like a cat's.

Strangest of all,
when I rub my nose
against my dog's velvety neck,
she softly hums
deep down in her throat,
and it sounds like purring.

Maybe my dog
was secretly raised
by cats.

2

WRITING COACH Online

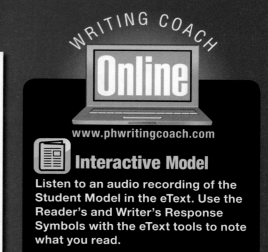

www.phwritingcoach.com

Interactive Model

Listen to an audio recording of the Student Model in the eText. Use the Reader's and Writer's Response Symbols with the eText tools to note what you read.

Use a Writer's Eye

Now, evaluate each piece as a writer. On your copies of the Student Models, use the Writer's Response Symbols to react to what you read. Identify places where the student writers use characteristics of an effective ballad or an effective free verse poem.

Writer's Response Symbols

R.R.	**Rhythm or rhyme fits the poem's form**
S.D.	**Effective use of sound devices**
F.L.	**Figurative language conveys a mood**
I.D.	**Images and details appeal to the senses**

Your Turn Feature Assignment: Ballad or Free Verse Poem

Prewriting

Plan a first draft of your poem by deciding which form of poem you want to write—a ballad, a free verse poem, or another form of your choice. Then, **determine an appropriate topic.** Select a topic from the Topic Bank or come up with an idea of your own.

Choose From the Topic Bank

TOPIC BANK

Nature or Important Person Write a poem to describe a person or something in nature. The person could be a family member, friend, or a celebrity. If you write a nature poem instead, describe a lake, the sky, or something else in nature that you think is beautiful.

Event or Performance Write a poem about a sporting event, music concert, or community event. Describe the event or performance, the crowd that was there, and your reactions.

Art or Hobby Describe a favorite piece of music, work of art, or hobby. Tell why it is important to you, what it reminds you of, or what you like about it. Make sure your description is specific and detailed.

Choose Your Own Topic

Determine an appropriate topic of your own by using the following **range of strategies** to generate ideas.

Brainstorm, Discuss, and Read

- With a partner, brainstorm for a list of people, things in nature, events, or "favorites" that might make good topics.
- Discuss your list. Cross out topics that do not interest you, and circle topics that do.
- Look through a literature book or poetry collection to see what topics published poets choose. Choose a topic that inspires you.

Review your responses and choose a topic.

Narrow Your Topic

Vivid poems contain specific details. Narrow your topic to make it easier to focus on precise details.

Apply It! Use a graphic organizer like the one shown to narrow your topic.

- Write your general topic in the top box, and keep narrowing your topic as you move down the chart.
- Your last box should hold your narrowest or "smallest" topic, the new focus of your poem.

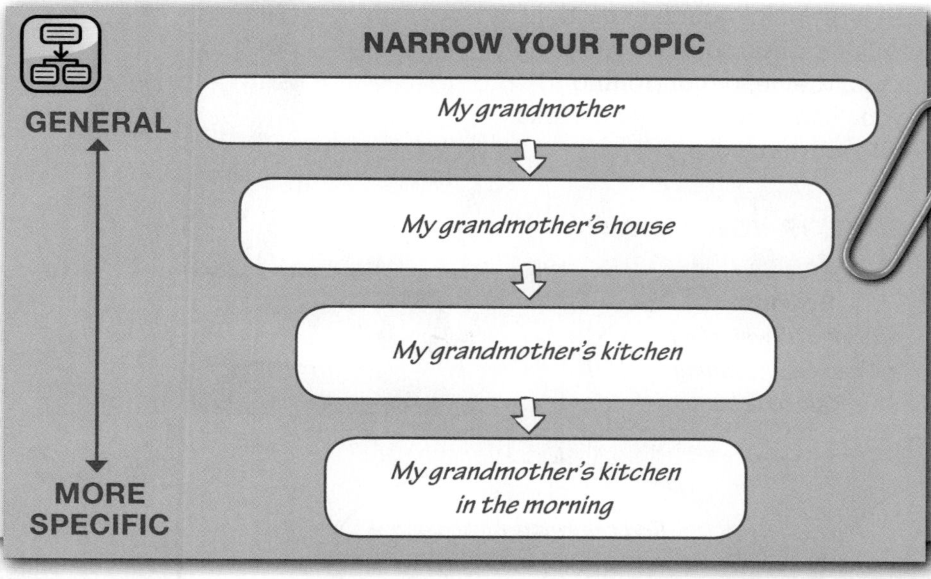

Consider Multiple Audiences and Purposes

Before writing, think about your audiences and purposes. Consider how the form you selected can convey the intended meaning to multiple audiences. Consider the views of others as you ask yourself these questions.

Questions for Audience	Questions for Purpose
• Who will read my poem? My teacher? My classmates? A family member? Someone else? • What will my readers need to know to understand my poem? • What poetic form would best convey my meaning to them?	• Why am I writing? Do I want to entertain my readers by making them laugh? Move my readers by making them see and feel what I saw and felt? Something else? • What kinds of poetic techniques will help me fulfill my purpose? • How can the poetic form help me fulfill my purpose?

Record your answers in your writing journal.

WRITING COACH Online

www.phwritingcoach.com

Interactive Graphic Organizers

Use the interactive graphic organizers to help you narrow your topic.

Online Journal

Try It! Record your answers and ideas in the online journal.

Plan Your Piece

You will use a graphic organizer like the one shown to organize your poem and to help you **structure ideas in a consistent, or sustained, way.** When it is complete, you will be ready to write your first draft.

Develop a Topic, Theme, or Controlling Idea To focus your poem, review your notes and write a clear statement of your topic, theme, or controlling idea. Name the most important idea or feeling you want to communicate. Add your statement to the center of a graphic organizer like the one shown.

Develop Ideas and Details Use a graphic organizer to identify ideas, feelings, and sensory details—sights, sounds, tastes, smells, touch—related to your topic, theme, or controlling idea. Write whatever comes to you. Then, evaluate your ideas. Underline the ones that best fulfill your purpose.

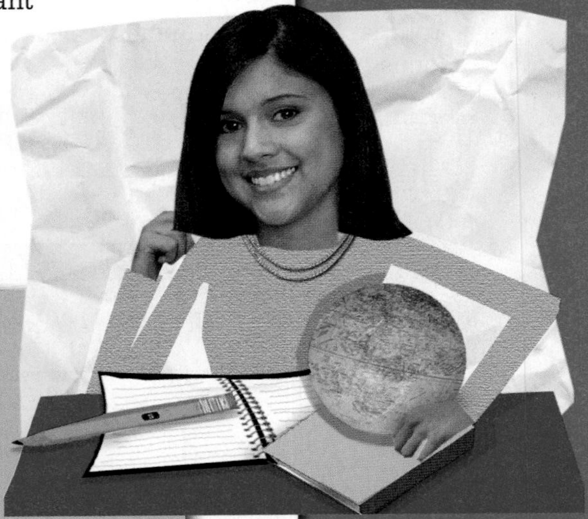

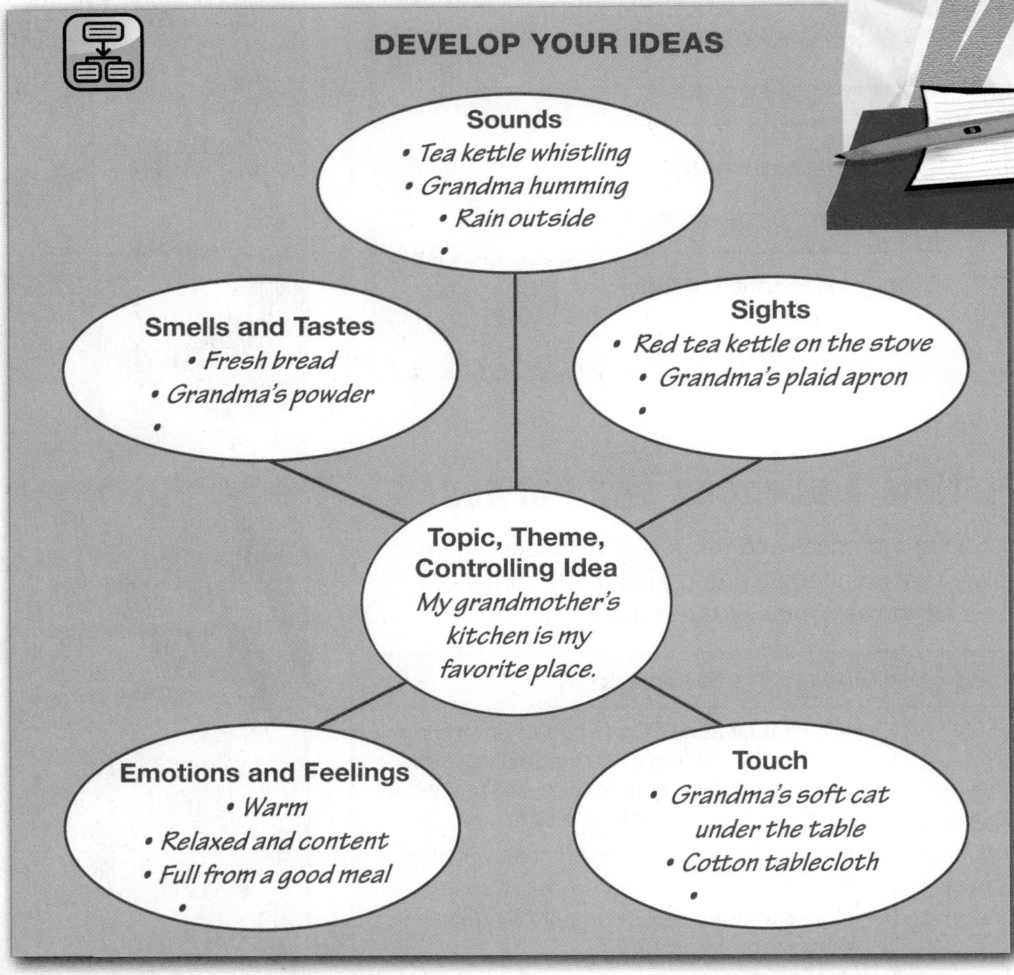

DEVELOP YOUR IDEAS
Sounds
• Tea kettle whistling
• Grandma humming
• Rain outside
•
Smells and Tastes
• Fresh bread
• Grandma's powder
•
Sights
• Red tea kettle on the stove
• Grandma's plaid apron
•
Topic, Theme, Controlling Idea
My grandmother's kitchen is my favorite place.
Emotions and Feelings
• Warm
• Relaxed and content
• Full from a good meal
•
Touch
• Grandma's soft cat under the table
• Cotton tablecloth
•

Poet's Toolbox

Poets use a variety of techniques to make their ideas vivid and clear. These techniques highlight the topic and **controlling idea** and help describe emotions, feelings, and ideas. Here are some techniques you might use.

Figurative Language is writing that means something beyond what the words actually say.	
Simile: comparison using *like* or *as*	*The tea kettle is like an angry red dragon.*
Metaphor: comparison made by saying that one thing is something else	*The whistling tea kettle is my alarm clock at Grandma's house.*
Personification: human characteristics applied to non-human objects	*The tea kettle whistled its familiar tune.*
Symbols add depth and insight to poetry.	
An object that stands for something else	The tea kettle could symbolize the joy of spending time with Grandma.
Sound Devices create a musical or emotional effect	
Alliteration: repetition of consonant sounds at the beginning of nearby words	*Grandma **p**oured **p**erfect **p**ots of tea.*
Assonance: repetition of vowel sounds in nearby words	*The squ**ea**k of the t**ea** kettle woke m**e** up.*
Consonance: repetition of consonants in the middle or at the end of words	*Gran**d**ma woul**d** knea**d** brea**d** dough each week.*
Structural Elements help build the framework for poetic language.	
Rhyme: repetition of sounds at the ends of lines of poetry	*A big breakfast of eggs and **ham*** *Is part of a special morning with **Gram.***
Meter: rhythmical pattern of a poem. It is determined by stressed syllables in a line. Some forms of poetry have specific patterns of stressed syllables.	*I **love** to **spend** a **day** with **Gram.*** *We **bake** our **pies** and **make** our **jam.***
Graphic Elements position the words on a page.	
Arrangement of words on a page	capital letters, line spacing, and line breaks

Apply It! Review the ideas, feelings, and sensory details in the graphic organizer you created.

- Decide what **techniques** from the Poet's Toolbox you would like to use in your poem.
- Keep in mind that some poetic techniques are used in specific **forms**.

As you draft your poem, you will use the characteristics of your form and finalize the techniques you will use.

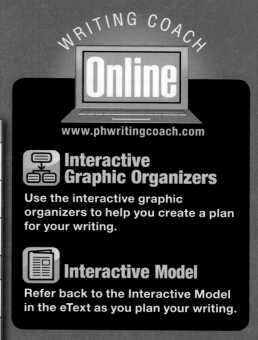

WRITING COACH Online

www.phwritingcoach.com

Interactive Graphic Organizers

Use the interactive graphic organizers to help you create a plan for your writing.

Interactive Model

Refer back to the Interactive Model in the eText as you plan your writing.

Drafting

During the drafting stage, you will start to write your ideas for your ballad, free verse poem, or other poetic form you chose. You will use the ideas you developed in prewriting to create a well-crafted poem.

Drafting a Free Verse Poem or Ballad

Each poetic form has specific characteristics. You will write your poem using these characteristics, the techniques from the Poet's Toolbox, and the ideas, feelings, and sensory details you developed in your graphic organizer.

These charts show the characteristics of each form. Review the characteristics. Then, answer the questions in the right column as you draft your poem.

Free Verse Characteristics	Questions to Answer While Drafting
• Varied number of lines • Varied number of stanzas • No meter used; follows natural patterns of speech • Rhyme not often used • Poetic techniques may be used • Feeling or emotion conveyed • Vivid descriptions	• How long do I want my poem to be? **Tip:** You don't have to decide on an exact number of stanzas and lines. • What sound devices will I use? • What poetic techniques will I use? • What feelings or emotions will I express? • How will I make my descriptions vivid?

Ballad Characteristics	Questions to Answer While Drafting
• Varied length, but usually 4 stanzas or more • Tells a story • Rhyme often used • Regular rhythm • Refrain often repeated • Poetic and narrative techniques, such as plot, used • Feeling or emotion conveyed • Vivid descriptions	• What story will I tell? • What do I want to describe or express in each stanza? • What words will I rhyme in each stanza? **Tip:** Consult a rhyming dictionary and thesaurus. • Do my lines follow a regular rhythm? **Tip:** Read aloud as you write to confirm the beat. • What poetic and narrative techniques will I use? • What feelings or emotions will I express? • How will I make my descriptions vivid?

Start Your Draft

Writing poetry is different than creating most other genres. The process is more open. Use the graphic organizer that shows your topic, ideas, and sensory details, and the Poet's Toolbox as guides, but be open to experimenting with your draft.

While developing your poem, aim at writing your ideas, not on making your writing perfect. Remember, because you are writing in an open-ended situation, you will have the chance to improve your poem when you revise and edit.

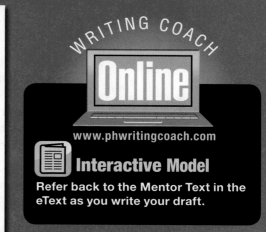

Before You Write

√ Choose the **poetic form** you want to use—free verse, a ballad, or another poetic form.

√ Review the **characteristics** of your poetic form that are listed in Drafting a Free Verse Poem or Ballad. Make sure you use these characteristics when you write your draft.

√ Think of a a striking image, **figurative language**, or other poetic technique to start your poem that will attract your readers' attention.

While You Write

√ State or imply the **theme,** topic, or controlling idea. It does not have to be apparent in each line, but it should show in the poem as a whole.

√ Include your ideas from prewriting. If a feeling, emotion, **sensory detail,** or other idea does not seem to work, you may decide not to keep it in your poem.

√ Review the poetic techniques in the Poet's Toolbox. Use a variety of these **poetic techniques** to support your ideas. If you experiment with a technique that does not seem to work, try another.

√ Include **figurative language,** such as similes, metaphors, and personification, to convey meaning to your audience and to keep your writing interesting.

√ As you draft, pay attention to the **sound** and **rhythm** of the language you use.

WRITING COACH Online

www.phwritingcoach.com

Interactive Model

Refer back to the Mentor Text in the eText as you write your draft.

Revising: Making It Better

Now that you have finished your first draft, you are ready to revise. Think about the "big picture" of audience, purpose, and genre. You can use Revision RADaR as a guide for making changes to improve your draft. Revision RADaR provides four major ways to improve your writing: (R) replace, (A) add, (D) delete, and (R) reorder.

Kelly Gallagher, M. Ed.

KEEP REVISION ON YOUR RADaR

Read part of the first draft of the Student Model "Cat Dog." Then look at questions the writer asked himself as he thought about how well his draft **addressed issues of audience, purpose, and genre.**

1ST DRAFT

Cat Dog

My dog sleeps on her back,
with her legs straight as broomsticks
and her feet in the air.
She looks really weird.

My dog is a little strange
because when she is scared
the hairs on her back
stand straight up.
It's weird!

Did I state or hint at my theme or controlling idea?

Does the fourth line help my audience picture what I am describing? Can I build a stronger image?

Do these lines clearly develop my theme or controlling idea?

Now, look at how the writer applied Revision RADaR to write an improved second draft.

2ND DRAFT

Cat Dog

My dog is a little strange.
She sleeps on her back,
with her legs straight as broomsticks
and her feet in the air.
She looks like a dog statue
that has been turned upside down.

My dog is a little strange
because when she is scared
the hairs on her back
stand straight up
just like a cat's.

A *Added a clear statement of theme*

R *Replaced a general description with a figure of speech*

D **A** *Deleted unnecessary information and added a line to make it clearer why he thinks his dog is like a cat*

Apply It! Use Revision RADaR to revise your draft.

- First, determine whether you have addressed questions of purpose, audience, and genre, and included the characteristics of a ballad or a free verse poem.
- Then, apply your Revision RADaR to make needed changes. Remember—you can use the Revision RADaR steps in any order.

WRITING COACH Online
www.phwritingcoach.com

Video
Learn more strategies for effective writing from program author Kelly Gallagher.

RADaR: REPLACE, ADD, DELETE and REORDER

Look at the Big Picture

Use the chart and your analytical skills to evaluate how well each section of your poem **addresses purpose, audience, and genre.** When necessary, use the suggestions in the chart to revise your piece.

	Evaluate	Revise
Topic and Sensory Details	• Make sure your controlling idea or **theme** is clear in the poem.	• Think about the most important idea or feeling you want to convey. If needed, add a statement of theme.
	• Check that your **sensory details** all support the controlling idea or theme.	• Replace sensory details that do not support the controlling idea with new details that help paint a clearer picture.
Structural Elements	• Ensure that the **elements** of your chosen poetic form have been included in your poem.	• Review the poetic traditions for your chosen poetic form. Revise your poem to include any missing characteristics.
	• Check the **rhythm** and **rhyme** if you are writing a ballad.	• Use a rhyming dictionary to help you find replacement rhymes.
	• Consider whether to include a refrain if you are writing a ballad.	• Add a refrain, if appropriate.
	• If you are writing a free verse poem, check to see if the language reflects **normal speech patterns.**	• Read your poem aloud. Replace, add, delete, or reorder words to make the language sound like natural speech patterns, if necessary.
Poetic Techniques	• Make sure your figurative language and **word choices** help convey your meaning and purpose to your audience.	• Replace dull or vague words with figurative language, vivid words, and sensory details.
	• Read aloud to check that your **sound devices** are effective and sound correct.	• Use a dictionary or thesaurus to find words to create better assonance or alliteration.

Focus on Craft: Figurative Language

Figurative language, such as similes and metaphors (see page 129), helps readers see everyday things in fresh, new ways. Carefully chosen figurative language can also help set the mood of a description. Consider the differences between these examples:

Simile: Rain as soft as a feather

Metaphor: Rain fell in sharp daggers

Look at the figurative language in these lines from the Student Model.

STUDENT MODEL from **Cat Dog**
page 125; lines 2–6

She sleeps on her back,
with her legs straight as broomsticks
and her feet in the air.
She looks like a dog statue
that has been turned upside down.

Try It! Now, ask yourself these questions. Record your answers in your journal.

- What two things are being compared in the first three lines?
- How would the poem's mood change if the last two lines were revised to say that the dog "looks frozen and lifeless"?

Fine-Tune Your Draft

Apply It! Use the revision suggestions to prepare your final draft after rethinking how well questions of purpose, audience, and genre have been addressed.

- **Improve Figurative Language** Get creative! Find words and phrases that don't enhance the poem's mood or help to convey your meaning. Replace these items with figurative language, such as similes, metaphors, and personification, that can strengthen your writing.
- **Improve Word Choice** Use a dictionary or thesaurus to choose the best words or best-sounding words to convey your meaning.

Teacher Feedback Read your poem aloud to your teacher. Ask for advice and feedback about the theme you convey. Think about your teacher's feedback and revise your final draft as needed.

WRITING COACH **Online**
www.phwritingcoach.com

Online Journal
Try It! Record your answers in the online journal.

Interactive Model
Refer back to the Interactive Model as you revise your writing.

Editing: Making It Correct

Editing your draft means polishing your work and correcting errors. You may want to read through your work several times, looking for different errors and issues each time.

Before editing, think about your use of **verbals,** such as **gerunds, infinitives,** and **participles.** A verbal is a verb form that functions as another part of speech, such as a noun, adjective, or adverb. Keep in mind the spelling rules for verbals, which may involve adding suffixes, especially *-ing* and *-ed*. Then edit your draft by correcting any errors in **grammar, mechanics, and spelling**. Use a dictionary or other resource to check your spelling.

WRITE GUY *Jeff Anderson, M. Ed.*

WHAT DO YOU NOTICE?

Zoom in on Conventions Focus on verbals—gerunds, infinitives, and participles—as you zoom in on these lines from the Student Model.

STUDENT MODEL from **Fire to Fight**
page 124, lines 5, 8

The cries of a family came through thundering roars–

As she tromped through the flames, a fire to fight.

To learn more about verbals, see Chapter 15 of your Grammar Handbook.

Now, ask yourself: *What do the highlighted items have in common?*

Perhaps you said that they are verbs that act as another part of speech.

The two highlighted items are **verbals**, forms of a verb that function as another part of speech. The second item, *to fight,* is an **infinitive**, formed from the verb *fight* and the word *to.* In the sentence, this verbal acts as an adjective. An infinitive can also act as a noun or an adverb.

The first item, *thundering,* is a **participle.** A participle is a verbal that functions as an adjective. Participles can end in *-ing, -ed,* or irregular endings such as *-t* and *-en.*

A gerund is the *-ing* form of a verb used as a noun. For example, the Student Model "Cat Dog" describes a sound the dog makes as being like "purring." In this case, "purring" is used as a noun. It is a gerund.

Partner Talk Discuss this question with a partner: *How do verbals help to make writing more effective and powerful?*

Grammar Mini-Lesson: Spelling Verbals

To learn more, see Chapter 15.

A suffix is a word part added to the end of a base.

- When a suffix (e.g., *-ing, -ed*) is added to a word that ends in one consonant with one vowel before it, double the last letter (*jogged*).
- If the word ends in one consonant with two vowels before it, or two or more consonants, do not double the last letter (*screaming, jumping*).
- When a word ends in a silent *e*, the *e* may be dropped (*racing*).
- When adding *-ed* to a word ending in *y*, change the *y* to an *i* (*varied*).
- When adding *-ing* to a word ending in *y*, keep the *y* (*studying*).
- If you are not sure of the spelling, check a dictionary. Notice the spelling of the **verbals** in the Mentor Text.

MENTOR TEXT from **Special Glasses** page 123; lines 22–23

yet the schoolbuses flashing in the rain
do come in, as well as the postman waving

Try It! Use the correct verbal form for each verb in the sentences. Write the sentences in your journal.

1. (Flip) pancakes requires skill, but (eat) them doesn't.
2. The (leak) raft began to sink, as the (giggle) kids swam to the side of the pool.

Apply It! **Edit your draft for grammar, mechanics, and spelling**. Be sure that you use **correctly spelled verbals**, including **gerunds, infinitives**, and **participles**.

Use the rubric to evaluate your piece. If necessary, rethink, rewrite, or revise.

Poetry: Ballad or Free Verse Poem	Rating Scale
Ideas: How well do your ideas develop the specific focus of the poem?	Not very Very 1 2 3 4 5 6
Organization: How organized are your ideas?	1 2 3 4 5 6
Voice: How effectively have you created a unique voice in your poem?	1 2 3 4 5 6
Word Choice: How effectively do you use figurative language and poetic techniques?	1 2 3 4 5 6
Sentence Fluency: How naturally does your writing flow?	1 2 3 4 5 6
Conventions: How correct is your use of verbals?	1 2 3 4 5 6

WRITING COACH **Online**

www.phwritingcoach.com

Video

Learn effective editing techniques from program author Jeff Anderson.

Online Journal

Try It! Record your answers in the online journal.

Interactive Model

Refer back to the Interactive Model as you edit your writing.

Publishing

Publish your poem so it can move someone else, make people think, or make them chuckle. First, get your poem ready for presentation. Then, choose a way to **publish your work for appropriate audiences**.

Wrap Up Your Presentation

Is your poem handwritten or written on a computer? If your poem is handwritten, you may need to make a new, clean copy. If so, be sure to **write legibly**. Also be sure to add a title to your poem that grabs the reader's attention and indicates your poem's topic.

Publish Your Piece

Use this chart to identify a way to publish your poem.

If your audience is...	...then publish it by...
A small group of close friends	• Reciting it from memory, using movements and facial expressions to add dramatic interest • Recording it with background music as a podcast and sending it to your friends
Teachers and students at your school	• Submitting it to a class poetry anthology • Writing it on a poster for a hallway poetry display • Posting it on a class or school blog

Reflect on Your Writing

Now that you are done with your poem, read it over and use your writing journal to answer these questions. Use specific details to describe and explain your reflections. Increase the specificity of your details based on the type of information requested.

- Which parts of the poem do you feel are the strongest? Which are the weakest? What can you focus on in your next writing assignment?
- How does writing a poem help you appreciate the work of other poets?

The Big Question: Why Write? How do we best convey feeling through words on a page?

Manage Your Portfolio You may wish to include your published poem in your writing portfolio. If so, consider what this piece reveals about your writing and your growth as a writer.

21st Century Learning

MAKE YOUR WRITING COUNT

Use Poetic Language to Promote a Product

Poets convey a point of view through striking images, deliberate word choice, and rhythmic patterns. Advertisers use the same tools when creating **advertisements,** although their purpose is different—they aim to sell products.

As a group, create your own **multimedia presentation** to advertise a real or imaginary product inspired by one of your peers' poems. Produce your ad using text, graphics, and sound to reveal a distinctive point of view and appeal to a specific audience. Present your ad in person, or create an online ad using Web authoring tools.

Here's your action plan.

1. Assign responsibilities, including writer, artist, and director.
2. Identify a product you want to sell and your target audience.
3. Look at online advertisements aimed at your target audience to see how Web ads use text, sound, and images to appeal to this group.
4. Choose your group's most effective poem. Analyze the poem's language and structure.
5. Using that poem as a model, write a new poem about your product. To create your ad:
   - Select images or sound effects or music to accompany your ad
   - Assemble your text, graphics, and sound elements for presentation
6. Present your ad, either in person, using handmade visuals and live sound, or by projecting your online ad onto a large screen.

Listening and Speaking Plan to present your **multimedia** ad to your class. Rehearse to make sure the sounds, images, text, and graphics work well together and reinforce your ad's point of view. Discuss the presentation with your group, and listen for important feedback. In your presentation, keep your peers' feedback in mind as they will be your audience. As a class, discuss which elements in the ads would persuade their target audiences.

WRITING COACH Online

www.phwritingcoach.com

Online Journal

Reflect on Your Writing **Record your answers and ideas in the online journal.**

Resource

Link to resources on 21st Century Learning for help in creating a group project.

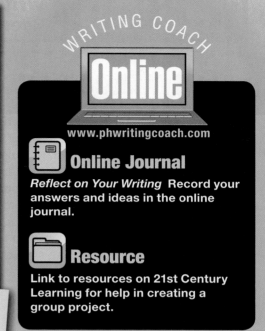

Your Turn — Writing for Media: Eyewitness Account

21st Century Learning

Eyewitness Accounts

While poetry is not often featured as writing for media, the poet's attention to detail is critical in other forms of writing. An **eyewitness account** is a description of an event told by someone who saw the event take place. Investigators such as news reporters and police detectives interview witnesses and use their descriptions to help learn the truth about something that happened. Television news programs often feature such interviews. However, eyewitness accounts can also be as simple as a friend telling you about something funny he saw on the way to school. When you understand the factors that influence an eyewitness account, you can make better judgments about what to believe and what to question.

Try It! Study the text in the sample eyewitness interview. Then, answer these questions. Record your answers in your journal.

1. What **event** are the eyewitnesses describing?
2. Good eyewitness accounts include specific **details** in the description of the event. What specific details are included in these accounts?
3. Eyewitness accounts of the same event often differ because they are told from each individual's distinctive **point of view**. How does point of view explain for the differences in these accounts?
4. If you were to describe this event in a **poem**, what would you emphasize?
5. What kind of specific **audience** would this eyewitness account best help? How would the audience for a poem differ?

Television Eyewitness Interview

Reporter: We're here at the scene with Joe Jones, who was standing across the street when a sign fell off the roof, injuring one person. Mr. Jones, what did you see?

Joe Jones: I was just standing here, minding my own business, when all of a sudden this huge sign crashed onto the sidewalk. It just missed landing on about six people, and grazed the foot of the guy over there.

Reporter: Mr. Jones, could you tell why the sign fell?

Joe Jones: No, it just crashed down. As I said, I was just minding my own business.

Reporter: Thank you for your time, sir. How about you, Miss? Where were you when the sign fell?

Young Woman: I was in my office on the fourth floor of this building behind us.

Reporter: Could you tell why the sign fell?

Young Woman: I did notice it rocking back and forth in this terrible wind. It was creaking pretty loudly. That's why I looked down on it from my window. And in just seconds it ripped off its supports and came crashing down to the sidewalk. Those people are lucky they weren't killed!

Extension Find another example of an eyewitness account, and compare it with this one.

Create an Eyewitness Account

Follow these steps to create your own eyewitness account. To plan your eyewitness account, review the graphic organizers on R24–R27 and choose one that suits your needs.

Prewriting

- Identify or make up an event to be described. Think like a poet and visualize the event. List the sensory details you will include in your description.
- Identify a specific audience. Plan questions about the event that will appeal to that specific audience.
- Invent a reporter and an eyewitness, planning a distinctive point of view for the eyewitness. What kind of person is he/she? Where was the witness? What kinds of things would the witness have been able and unable to observe?

Drafting

- Format the interview as a script, using the Television Eyewitness Interview as a model.
- First, write the reporter's questions. Then, from the point of view of the witness, answer the questions. Consider what the witness could and could not have observed. Make sure your eyewitness's explanation of the event is specific and detailed.
- Write a thorough, detailed description of the event in logical order.

Revising and Editing

- Review your draft to ensure that the description is logically organized and the details and images make sense.
- Make sure the witness's specific point of view is consistent. Take out details that do not line up with the witness's account.
- Check that spelling, grammar, and mechanics are correct.

Publishing

Use your script to help you develop a multimedia presentation of your interview. Include graphics, images, and sound to present your eyewitness's point of view to a specific audience—your classmates and teacher. For example, you could make a video recording of you and a classmate acting out the interview.

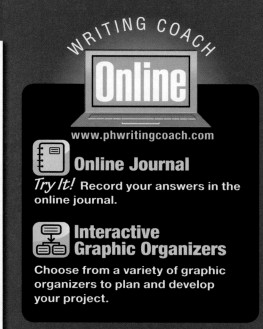

WRITING COACH **Online**

www.phwritingcoach.com

Online Journal

Try It! **Record your answers in the online journal.**

Interactive Graphic Organizers

Choose from a variety of graphic organizers to plan and develop your project.

Partner Talk

Before you start drafting, describe the event to a partner as your invented witness would. Use specific details to describe and explain your ideas. Increase the specificity of your details based on the type of information you are delivering. Ask for feedback about the description. For example, does it make sense?

Writing for Assessment

Writing a good poem can take a lot of practice. You can use these prompts to do just that—practice writing poems. Your responses should include the same characteristics as your free verse poem or ballads. (See page 120.)

Try It! To begin, read the prompt and the information on format and academic vocabulary. Then, use the ABCDs of On-Demand Writing to help you plan and write your **poem**.

Format

The prompt directs you to write a *poem.* Develop your topic, theme, or controlling idea by deciding on ideas and sensory details you would like to use in your poem.

Poetry Prompt

Think about a specific family member or a family activity or custom that is important to you. Write a poem describing that aspect of your family and how you feel about it. Choose a poetic form and use a variety of poetic techniques.

Academic Vocabulary

Use a specific *poetic form*, such as a sonnet, lyric poem, ballad, or free verse. Remember that *poetic techniques*, such as figurative language, sensory details, and sound devices, are the tools poets use to convey their ideas.

The ABCDs of On-Demand Writing

Use the following ABCDs to help you respond to the prompt.

Before you write your draft:

Attack the prompt [1 MINUTE]

- Circle or highlight important verbs in the prompt. Draw a line from the verb to what it refers to.
- Rewrite the prompt in your own words.

Brainstorm possible answers [4 MINUTES]

- Create a graphic organizer to generate ideas.
- Use one for each part of the prompt if necessary.

Choose the order of your response [1 MINUTE]

- Think about the best way to organize your ideas.
- Number your ideas in the order you will write about them. Cross out ideas you will not be using.

After you write your draft:

Detect errors before turning in the draft [1 MINUTE]

- Carefully reread your writing.
- Make sure that your response makes sense and is complete.
- Look for spelling, punctuation, and grammar errors.

More Prompts for Practice

Apply It! Respond to Prompt 1 by writing a **poem**. As you write, be sure to:

- Identify your audience
- Choose a specific **poetic form** and include all of the characteristics of that form
- Establish a clear topic, theme, or controlling idea
- Use **a variety of poetic techniques** to develop ideas; be sure to include **rhetorical devices,** which are forms of figurative language such as metaphors, similes, and personification
- Use **transitions to convey meaning** and connect ideas, especially if you are writing a ballad or other poem that tells a story.

Prompt 1 Poets write about all kinds of love, including love for homeland, love for family and friends, and love of sports. Write a poem about some kind of love. Choose a poetic form that will best convey your meaning to your audience. Support your ideas with poetic techniques.

Spiral Review: Narrative Respond to Prompt 2 by writing an **autobiographical narrative**.

Your narrative should:

- Develop an engaging **story,** including a well-developed **conflict** that is resolved
- Present **interesting and believable characters**
- Use a range of **literary strategies** and **devices** to enhance the plot
- Include sensory details that define the mood and tone

Prompt 2 We've all had times in our lives when something has startled or frightened us. Write an autobiographical narrative about a time when you had that experience. Be sure to include literary devices, such as dialogue, to enhance your story. In your conclusion, be sure to show how you overcame your fear.

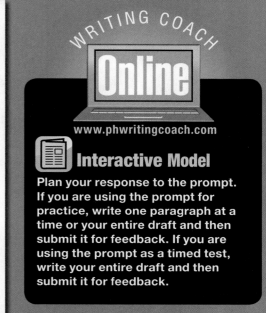

WRITING COACH Online

www.phwritingcoach.com

Interactive Model

Plan your response to the prompt. If you are using the prompt for practice, write one paragraph at a time or your entire draft and then submit it for feedback. If you are using the prompt as a timed test, write your entire draft and then submit it for feedback.

Remember **ABCD**

- **A**ttack the prompt
- **B**rainstorm possible answers
- **C**hoose the order of your response
- **D**etect errors before turning in the draft

CHAPTER 8

EXPOSITION

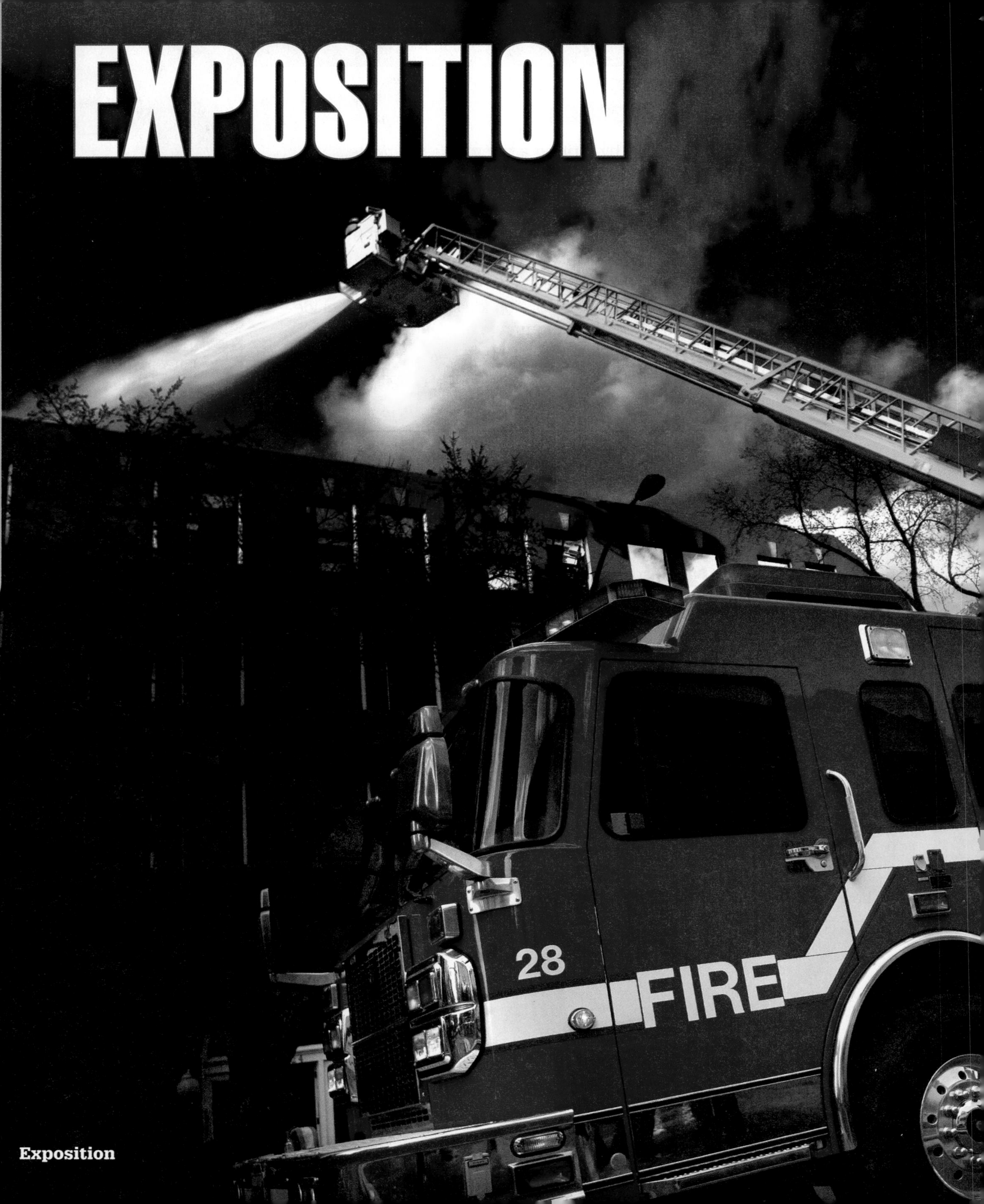

How Can You Explain This?

What do you know about fires and firefighting? What information and ideas could you share with others?

Information can be presented many ways. For example, you can compare two things, you can discuss causes and effects, or you can present a problem and a solution.

Try It! Imagine that your fire department has a problem. It needs more volunteer firefighters. What solutions, or answers to the problem, can you come up with?

Consider these questions as you participate in an extended discussion with a partner. Take turns expressing your ideas and feelings.

- Why does the fire department need more volunteers?
- What are benefits of being a volunteer firefighter?
- What solutions can you propose to solve the problem?
- What reasons and examples can you provide to support your solutions?

Review the ideas you wrote. Tell your partner your explanation of what happened. See if your partner can identify the problem and solution included in your explanation.

What's Ahead

In this chapter, you will review two strong examples of an analytical essay: a Mentor Text and a Student Model. Then, using the examples as guides, you will write an analytical essay in the problem-solution form.

Online

www.phwritingcoach.com

Online Journal

Try It! Record your answers and ideas in the online journal.

You can also record and save your answers and ideas on pop-up sticky notes in the eText.

THE BIG QUESTION

Connect to the Big Questions

Discuss these questions with your partner:

1 **What do you think?** What is the best way to come up with a solution to a problem?

2 **Why write?** What should we tell and what should we describe to make information clear?

ANALYTICAL ESSAY

An analytical essay is a type of expository essay that explores a topic by supplying relevant, or important and related, information on a given topic. In this chapter, you will learn to write a type of analytical essay known as a problem-solution essay. A problem-solution essay explores a particular problem and presents one or more possible solutions to it. It may address concerns related to personal issues; businesses or consumers; or the local, national, or global community. It may contain opinions, like a persuasive essay, but its purpose is to explain rather than persuade.

You will develop your problem-solution essay by taking it through each of the steps of the writing process: prewriting, drafting, revising, editing, and publishing. You will also have an opportunity to write a question-and-answer column. To preview the criteria for how your problem-solution essay will be evaluated, see the rubric on page 163.

FEATURE ASSIGNMENT

Analytical Essay: Problem-Solution Essay

An effective analytical essay has these characteristics:

- **Effective introductory** and **concluding paragraphs**
- A **controlling idea** or **thesis**
- An **organizing structure** that is logical and appropriate to the **purpose, audience,** and **context**
- **Relevant information**—such as facts, examples, and reasons— that is related to your controlling idea or supports the thesis
- A **variety of sentence structures** and **rhetorical devices,** such as analogies or comparisons, that help express ideas clearly and effectively
- **Smooth transitions** between paragraphs and ideas
- Correct **spelling, grammar,** and **usage**

A problem-solution essay also includes:

- A statement of the problem in the **thesis**
- A clear **analysis** of the problem
- One or more possible **solutions**

Other Forms of Analytical Essays

In addition to a problem-solution essay, there are other forms of analytical essays, including:

Cause-and-effect essays trace the results of an event or the reasons an event happened.

Classification essays organize a subject into categories or explain the category into which an item falls.

Compare-and-contrast essays explore similarities and differences between two or more people, places, things, or ideas.

Newspaper and magazine articles that are printed or published on the Internet supply relevant information about a particular topic by analyzing the topic's elements. They may also reflect genres other than analytical essays, such as persuasive writing or narrative nonfiction writing.

Pro-con essays examine the arguments for and against a particular action or decision.

Try It! For each audience and purpose described, choose a form, such as a compare-and-contrast essay or a pro-con essay, that is appropriate for conveying your intended meaning to each audience. Share your responses with a partner. Explain your choices.

- To describe the impact of a flood to students in your social studies class
- To explain to a younger sibling the categories into which different animals are grouped
- To explain to voters the benefits and risks of a political proposal

WRITING COACH **Online**

www.phwritingcoach.com

Resource

Word Bank Listen to English and Spanish pronunciations of new words in the eText glossary.

Online Journal

Try It! Record your answers and ideas in the online journal.

WORD BANK

People often use these words when they talk about expository writing. Work with a partner. Take turns using each word in a sentence. If you are unsure of the meaning of a word, use the Glossary or a dictionary to check the definition.

analyze	**improve**
challenge	**problem**
goal	**solution**

MENTOR TEXT Analytical Essay

Learn From Experience

After reading the analytical essay on pages 148–149, read the numbered notes in the margins to learn how the author presented her ideas. Later you will read a Student Model, which shares these characteristics and also has the characteristics of a problem-solution essay.

Answer the *Try It!* questions online or in your notebook.

❶ The **introductory paragraphs** present an anecdote, or story that makes a point, to grab readers' attention.

Try It! How effective is the anecdote in grabbing readers' attention? What other attention-getting devices have you seen in the introductions to essays? How do they compare to the anecdote?

❷ The author **identifies the topic to be analyzed** and clearly states her **thesis**.

Try It! In your own words, write the thesis of this essay. What do you think will be discussed in the rest of the essay?

❸ The **organizing structure** is clear. Here, the topic shifts from teens' new role in buying decisions to a different aspect of the topic.

Try It! From the topic sentence, what will this section be about?

Extension Find another example of an analytical essay, and compare it with this one.

From Big Decisions in Little Hands

by Marilyn Gardner

❶ Stacy DeBroff considers herself a savvy shopper. But on some subjects, her 13-year-old daughter is even savvier, as Ms. DeBroff discovered when the two went shopping for a cellphone.

Teenager Kyle Remy told her with cool authority, "Mom, these are the features you have to look for." Then, DeBroff recalls, "She started quizzing the sales rep about text messaging, the amount of photos you can send your friends for free, the quality of the pictures, the ring tones, the cover case choices, and the battery life. I was speechless. She was asking questions that I wouldn't have even known to ask."

DeBroff's 11-year-old son, Brooks Remy, is equally knowledgeable about the features he wants on an iPod.

Shopping—that all-American pastime—is undergoing a subtle but profound role reversal within families. Instead of the old dictatorial approach, which assumed that parents know best, there's a new mood of collaboration. ❷ Children are upstaging parents with a sophisticated knowledge of products, wielding impressive influence that goes beyond their own purchases to include family items.

"Historically, moms have made the majority of family purchasing decisions, but now it's the mom and kids," says Greg Livingston, coauthor of the forthcoming book, "Marketing to the New Super Consumer: Mom & Kid." Women account for 80 percent of retail spending, he adds.

It all adds up to big bucks. Children and teens influence $600 billion a year of their parents' money and spend $20 billion a year of their own, says Georganne Bender, a retailing analyst in Algonquin, Ill.

❸ Consumer experts trace the generational shift in consumer decision making to a variety of social changes. The Internet, they note, gives young people a wealth of information on products. Greater affluence also encourages families to spend. Even family bonds play a role.

"These kids like their parents," Ms. Bender says. "They like to hang out with their parents. They're partners picking something out together."

Mr. Livingston also sees a "much more involved parenting style." Noting that today's parents were the first of the latchkey children, he says, "Now that they are having kids, they're trying to make their family time as enjoyable as possible for everyone."

Because time is short in many two-career families and single-parent households, parents "try to make certain aspects of their life easier and smoother by getting consensus before moving forward," Livingston says. "That could be anything from dinner tonight to where to go on vacation."

Pressure from children has transformed the consumer behavior of parents—sometimes adding an element of tension, DeBroff says. While previous generations of offspring balked at shopping for household items, today's young consumers insist on going along, and not just for the ride.

❹ "It used to be parents would just go out and get something without ever soliciting opinions," DeBroff says. "Now if you don't solicit opinions, there will be bitter recriminations and criticisms for the life of that object. They'll say, 'What were you thinking when you picked this car? Everybody else has a DVD player. Do you know how important this is?'"

As the author of "The Mom Club: 4,278 Tips From Moms to Moms," she has interviewed several hundred mothers. Many report similar experiences.

❺ "If you go shopping for a couch, kids want to come along," DeBroff says. "They want to decide if it's…comfy enough to sack out and watch TV on Friday nights. They might say, 'I just think the pillows aren't as comfortable as they could be.'"

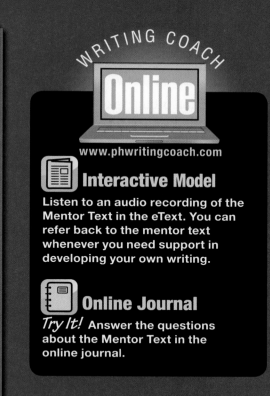

WRITING COACH **Online**

www.phwritingcoach.com

Interactive Model

Listen to an audio recording of the Mentor Text in the eText. You can refer back to the mentor text whenever you need support in developing your own writing.

Online Journal

Try It! Answer the questions about the Mentor Text in the online journal.

❹ **Relevant examples** support the author's belief that teens now have a greater say in buying decisions.

Try It! What example does the author use here? What makes this example relevant?

❺ The **concluding paragraph** provides a funny and memorable image to support the thesis of the essay.

Try It! What makes this paragraph funny? How does it support the author's thesis?

STUDENT MODEL Problem-Solution Essay

With a small group, take turns reading this Student Model aloud. Ask yourself if the explanation of the problem makes sense and if the solution offered could actually solve the problem.

Use a Reader's Eye

Now, reread the Student Model. On your copy of the Student Model, use the Reader's Response Symbols to react to what you read.

Reader's Response Symbols

- **+** **Aha! That makes sense to me.**
- **—** **This isn't clear to me.**
- **?** **I have a question about this.**
- **!** **Wow! That is cool/weird/interesting.**

Partner Talk

Participate in an extended discussion with a partner. Express your opinions and share your responses to the Student Model. Discuss the main purpose and likely audience of the essay. Decide whether or not the essay seems appropriate for that purpose and audience.

Preventing Computer "Hogging" at the LIBRARY

by Elena Marco

Last week when I visited the local library, I had to wait more than an hour before I could use a computer. During that time, two people at the computers never left their seats. Meanwhile, I just waited . . . and waited . . . and waited.

Clearly, our local library has a serious problem with people who take over the five computers. Sometimes these "computer hogs" stay at the terminals for hours. The library has tried to solve the problem by posting signs. The signs say that people are limited to only 30 minutes when others are waiting. Nevertheless, some people ignore the signs; others don't even see them.

How can the library solve this problem? One option would be to have an employee assigned to monitor computer use. This person would tell people when their time is up. However, the library has a tight budget and is short staffed already. It probably cannot afford to use staff for this chore.

So here's a better idea: Use the computers themselves to monitor computer use. The library can purchase and install, at a reasonable cost, special software that limits individuals' computer access. This software works very simply: When a person sits down and begins typing, a box opens that asks the user to type in his or her library card number and password. The library staff will program the computer so it can only be used for a specific period of time (say, 30 minutes). When the time is up, the computer shuts down. The software won't allow the person with

1

that library card number and password to use the library's computers again for the next few hours.

Our school library already uses this software, and it works wonderfully. "I'm very happy with the software," said Mrs. Vargas, the head librarian at the school library. "Not only does it allow more people to use the computers, but it also helps prevent arguments among students trying to access the computers."

The goal of public libraries is to serve all the citizens, not just a handful of people who abuse the system. Courtesy demands that every person give up his or her computer after 30 minutes. However, courtesy has failed. I request that the library install software that limits computer usage. With this software, the library should be able to solve the problem of "computer hogs" and give more people a share of free computer time.

WRITING COACH Online

www.phwritingcoach.com

Interactive Model

Listen to an audio recording of the Student Model in the eText. Use the Reader's and Writer's Response Symbols with the eText tools to note what you read.

Use a Writer's Eye

Now evaluate the piece as a writer. On your copy of the Student Model, use the Writer's Response Symbols to react to what you read. Identify places where the student writer uses characteristics of an effective problem-solution essay.

Writer's Response Symbols

C.T.	**Clearly stated thesis**
I.C.	**Effective introduction and conclusion**
R.D.	**Good use of rhetorical devices**
S.E.	**Effective supporting evidence**

Your Turn **Feature Assignment: Problem-Solution Essay**

Prewriting

Choose from the Topic Bank or come up with an idea of your own.

Choose From the Topic Bank

TOPIC BANK

Recycling Most communities encourage residents to recycle paper and metals. Some communities have laws requiring people to recycle because they might not do so voluntarily. Write an essay in which you suggest a solution for the problem of lack of interest in voluntary recycling in your community.

School Dress The problem of inappropriate student dress in school is a frequently discussed issue. Some schools have addressed the problem by requiring student uniforms, while others have adopted dress codes. Write an essay in which you suggest a solution to the problem of inappropriate student dress.

Pollution Around the Globe Research the problem of pollution in a country or geographical location of your choosing. Identify some possible solutions that are specific to that area. Write a problem-solution essay in which you describe how the problem of pollution is affecting the area you've chosen and explain a possible solution to the problem.

Choose Your Own Topic

Determine an appropriate topic on your own by using the following **range of strategies** to generate ideas.

Investigate and Observe

- Listen to TV or radio newscasts, listing problems they mention. Then, discuss the problems in class. Choose one problem, and research possible solutions. Be sure to keep careful records of all the outside sources you use.
- Be on the lookout for recurring problems with parts of your daily routine, such as taking a bus or using your school locker. What problems do you notice? How can they be solved?

Review your responses and choose a topic.

Narrow Your Topic

When the topic of a problem-solution essay is too broad, the problem may be too big to be solved in a brief essay. Narrow your topic to focus on a problem with one or two effective solutions.

Apply It! Use a graphic organizer like the one shown to narrow your topic to an appropriate size.

- Write your general topic, or larger problem, in the top box, and keep narrowing the problem as you move down the chart.
- Your last box should hold one problem. This is your essay topic.

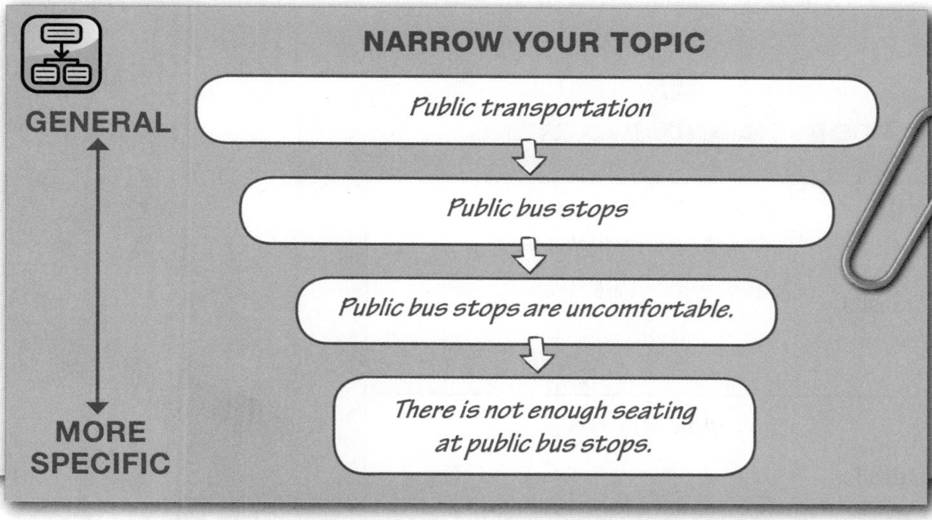

NARROW YOUR TOPIC
GENERAL
Public transportation
Public bus stops
Public bus stops are uncomfortable.
There is not enough seating at public bus stops.
MORE SPECIFIC

Consider Multiple Audiences and Purposes

Before writing, think about your audiences and purposes. Consider how your writing conveys the intended meaning to multiple audiences. Consider the views of others as you ask these questions.

Questions for Audience	Questions for Purpose
• Who are my possible audiences? • How familiar are these audiences with this problem? • What questions might these audiences have about my solution?	• How can I make the problem clear to my audiences? • How will I explain this solution to my audiences?

Record your answers in your writing journal.

WRITING COACH Online

www.phwritingcoach.com

Interactive Writing Coach™

- Choosing from the Topic Bank gives you access to the Interactive Writing Coach™.
- Submit your writing and receive instant personalized feedback and guidance as you draft, revise, and edit your writing.

Interactive Graphic Organizers

Use the interactive graphic organizers to help you narrow your topic.

Online Journal

Try It! Record your answers and ideas in the online journal.

Plan Your Piece

You will use a graphic organizer to **develop your thesis** and **structure your ideas** in a sustained, or consistent, way. When the graphic organizer is complete, you will be ready to write your first draft.

Develop a Clear Thesis The controlling idea or thesis in a problem-solution essay should clearly state the problem you intend to solve. Add your thesis statement to a graphic organizer like the one shown.

Develop Your Solution(s) Evaluate the possible solutions to your problem, and decide which are the most practical or effective. List your solutions on the graphic organizer. This chart will help ensure that your draft will have an **organizing structure** appropriate to its purpose, audience, and context.

DEVELOP YOUR PROBLEM AND SOLUTIONS

Clear Thesis That States the Problem	*Our city's public bus stops do not have enough seats.*
Supporting Evidence/Details	
First Solution	*Install more seats.*
Supporting Evidence/Details	
Second Solution	*Repair or replace broken seats.*
Supporting Evidence/Details	

Gather Details

To provide support for your problem-solution essay, there are several kinds of details you might use. Look at these examples:

- **Fact:** *According to the city transit department, over 10 percent of bus stop seats are damaged.*
- **Example:** *Yesterday, when I was at the bus stop at Ninth Street and Walnut Avenue, there were not enough seats for all the elderly riders waiting there.*
- **Valid Inference:** *Many people say they do not like standing to wait for the bus, so they drive to work. If more seats were fixed or installed, people would be more likely to take the bus.*
- **Logical Reasoning:** *The bus stops may not have room for expansion, but repairing and replacing broken seats would increase available seating, too.*

Try It! Read the Student Model excerpt. Identify and take notes about which kinds of details the author used to support her ideas.

STUDENT MODEL from **Preventing Computer "Hogging" at the Library** page 150; lines 13–18

How can the library solve this problem? One option would be to have an employee assigned to monitor computer use. This person would tell people when their time is up. However, the library has a tight budget and is short staffed already. It probably cannot afford to use staff for this chore.

Apply It! Review the types of support you can use to develop an analytical essay. Then identify **relevant information** to support the problem identified in your thesis statement and each of your proposed solutions.

- Use an organizing structure that first clearly states the problem and then clearly states the solution or solutions. Be sure your organizational plan is appropriate to your **audience** and **purpose**.
- For your problem, list details that provide evidence of its significance.
- As you describe each situation, help your readers see why you think your ideas work. Include facts, examples, and reasons that support the solution, but also explain the **valid inferences,** or conclusions you draw from the facts.

WRITING COACH **Online**

www.phwritingcoach.com

Interactive Graphic Organizers

Use the interactive graphic organizers to help you create a plan for your writing.

Interactive Model

Refer back to the Interactive Model in the eText as you plan your writing.

Drafting

During the drafting stage, you will start to write ideas for your problem-solution essay. Drafting is an open-ended process, and every writer will produce a unique essay. You will follow an outline that provides an organizational strategy that will help you write a focused, organized, and coherent problem-solution essay.

The Organization of an Analytical Essay

The chart shows an organizing structure for an analytical essay. As you adapt it for your particular problem-solution essay, be sure to keep in mind your audience and purpose.

Outline for Success

I. Introduction

See Student Model, p. 150.

- Identification of a problem
- Clear controlling idea or thesis
- Details supporting the thesis

II. Body

See Student Model, pp. 150–151.

- Statement of possible solution(s)
- Logically organized details about the solution(s)
- Possible reader questions or concerns, and responses to address the questions or concerns

III. Conclusion

See Student Model, p. 151.

- Restatement of thesis
- Summary of solutions
- Added information to stress importance of solution

Capture Attention

- The thesis makes the subject clear to the reader. It tells the main point of the essay. For a problem-solution essay, the problem is introduced here.
- Relevant details about the problem make its importance or urgency clear.

Develop Your Ideas

- If you have more than one solution, each solution and its support should be addressed in its own paragraph. If you have one solution and several different supporting details, those details can be explained in separate paragraphs.
- Reader questions and concerns are those details or issues a reader might not understand or might not agree with. Responses should answer the questions or explain why the concerns are not valid.

Sum It Up

- An effective conclusion restates the thesis and summarizes the solutions.
- A conclusion should also provide a new insight or an additional value to the solutions.

Start Your Draft

Use the checklist to help complete your draft. Use your graphic organizer and the Outline for Success as guides.

Before drafting, express your opinions and ideas aloud with a partner. Then, while drafting, aim at writing your ideas, not on making your writing perfect. You will have the chance to improve your draft when you revise and edit.

√ Start with **opening** sentences that explain the problem and get your reader's attention.

√ Continue building an effective **introduction** by making clear what the reader can expect. Include a **thesis** that states the problem you intend to solve.

√ Develop the **body** of your problem-solution essay by describing your **solutions**.

√ Evaluate your ideas and decide on **relevant information** and valid inferences to include—details that will clarify and support each solution and address your audience's likely questions and concerns.

√ Be sure to include **transitions** between paragraphs to connect ideas and use short and long sentences for a variety of sentence structures to keep your writing interesting and lively.

√ Use an **organizing structure** that is appropriate to your purpose, audience, and context. If a solution has several steps, put them in chronological order. If you give more than one solution, put them in order of importance, saving the best for last.

√ Use **rhetorical devices**, such as analogies and rhetorical questions, to help convey your meaning and make your ideas memorable.

√ End with an effective **conclusion** that **restates** your problem and reminds the audience of the value of the solution you offer.

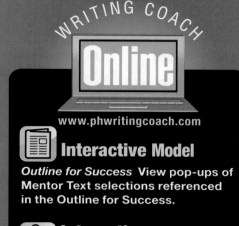

WRITING COACH **Online**

www.phwritingcoach.com

Interactive Model

Outline for Success **View pop-ups of Mentor Text selections referenced in the Outline for Success.**

Interactive Writing Coach™

Use the Interactive Writing Coach to receive the level of support you need:

- **Write one paragraph at a time and submit each one for immediate, detailed feedback.**
- **Write your entire first draft and submit it for immediate, personalized feedback.**

Revising: Making It Better

Now that you have finished your first draft, you are ready to revise. Think about the "big picture" of audience, purpose, and genre. You can use your revision RADaR as a guide for making changes to improve your draft. RADaR revision provides four major ways to improve your writing: (R) replace, (A) add, (D) delete, and (R) reorder.

Kelly Gallagher, M. Ed.

KEEP REVISION ON YOUR RADaR

Read part of the first draft of the Student Model "Preventing Computer 'Hogging' at the Library." Then look at questions the writer asked herself as she thought about how well her draft addressed issues of audience, purpose, and genre.

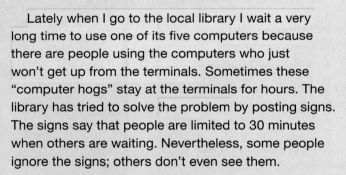

1ST DRAFT

Preventing Computer "Hogging" at the Library

Lately when I go to the local library I wait a very long time to use one of its five computers because there are people using the computers who just won't get up from the terminals. Sometimes these "computer hogs" stay at the terminals for hours. The library has tried to solve the problem by posting signs. The signs say that people are limited to 30 minutes when others are waiting. Nevertheless, some people ignore the signs; others don't even see them.

Does the introduction grab my audience and explain the problem?

Have I developed a thesis that clearly states the problem?

How can the library solve this problem? One option would be to have an employee assigned to monitor computer use. That person would tell people when their time is up. However, the library would probably have a hard time finding a worker who would be available to do this.

Can I make this drawback to the first solution clearer?

So here's a better idea: Use the computers themselves to monitor computer use. The library can purchase and install special software that limits individuals' computer access.

Have I included relevant information in the second solution?

Now look at how the writer applied Revision RADaR to write an improved second draft.

Preventing Computer "Hogging" at the LIBRARY

2ND DRAFT

Last week when I visited the local library, I had to wait over an hour before I could use a computer. During that time, two people at the computers never left their seats. Meanwhile, I just waited . . . and waited . . . and waited.

R *Replaced introduction with an interesting anecdote*

Clearly, our local library has a serious problem with people who take over the five computers. Sometimes these "computer hogs" stay at the terminals for hours. The library has tried to solve the problem by posting signs. The signs say that people are limited to only 30 minutes when others are waiting. Nevertheless, some people ignore the signs; others don't even see them.

A *Added a thesis that clearly states the problem and* *R* *reordered to put thesis in second paragraph*

How can the library solve this problem? One option would be to have an employee assigned to monitor computer use. That person would tell people when their time is up. However, the library has a tight budget and is short staffed already. It probably cannot afford to use staff for this chore.

A *Added more specific details to make clearer why this first solution is not as practical as the second*

So here's a better idea: Use the computers themselves to monitor computer use. The library can purchase and install, at a reasonable cost, special software that limits individuals' computer access.

A *Added a detail that anticipates a possible audience concern about the second solution*

WRITING COACH Online

www.phwritingcoach.com

Interactive Writing Coach™

Use the Revision RADaR strategy in your own writing. Then submit your paragraph or draft for feedback.

Apply It! Use your Revision RADaR to revise your draft.

- Include all the appropriate characteristics of the analytical essay genre, such as an effective introduction and a clear thesis statement, using details that address the purpose of your essay and are appropriate for your audience.
- Exchange drafts with a partner. Listen as your partner provides direction for how to improve your work.
- Then apply your Revision RADaR to make needed changes. Remember—you can use the Revision RADaR steps in any order.

REPLACE ADD DELETE and REORDER
RADaR

Look at the Big Picture

Use the chart and your analytical skills to evaluate how well each section of your problem-solution essay addresses **purpose**, **audience**, and **genre**. When necessary, use the suggestions in the chart to revise your piece.

Section	Evaluate	Revise
Introduction	• Make sure your **thesis** clearly identifies the problem you are examining.	• For an effective introduction, write a thesis that clearly answers the question "What problem am I addressing?"
	• Be sure to include **details** that explain the problem thoroughly.	• Add relevant information (facts, examples, reasons) and valid inferences as needed to explain the problem.
Body	• Check that you clearly identify one or more **solutions** to the problem.	• Add words such as *solve, improve,* and *better* to make sure each suggested solution is clear.
	• Check that you have **organized the structure** of your solution or solutions in a logical way that makes sense for your purpose, audience, and context.	• Rearrange steps in chronological order, if applicable. Consider rearranging multiple solutions from least to most important to reinforce your strongest idea.
	• Check that you have used **transitions** between paragraphs and ideas.	• Add transitional words and phrases, such as *however* and *for example.*
	• Underline **inferences** that are valid and that support your solution or solutions.	• Remove inferences that are not accurate or that do not support your ideas. Add relevant inferences that make each solution stronger and clearer.
	• Check that you have addressed possible questions and concerns of your **audience**.	• Include any drawbacks to your solution that the reader needs to know.
	• Check that you have used a variety of **sentence structures.**	• Rewrite sentences to combine ideas and add a variety of sentence types.
Conclusion	• Check that you have restated the problem and summed up your solution or solutions.	• Rewrite to sum up your main points for an effective conclusion. Your essay should be of sufficient length to explain your solution effectively.
	• Make sure that your essay ends on a memorable note.	• Add rhetorical devices, such as analogies. Analogies compare two things, often by using the words *like* and *as*.

Focus on Craft: Subtlety of Meaning

Your writing will be more effective if you are alert to the **subtlety of meaning.** The details in your writing show exactly, in sometimes small ways, what you want your audience to understand. Your tone, word choice, and writing style combine to create exactly the meaning and feeling that is appropriate to your essay's audience, purpose, and genre. In these examples, notice how the sentence acquires more strength and precision as it is revised:

Draft 1: The bicycle was broken.

Draft 2: The old bicycle had two flat tires and hadn't been ridden in a long time.

Draft 3: The old bicycle's red paint chips flaked off onto the garage floor; the bicycle, which had two flat tires, hadn't been ridden in years.

Think about subtlety of meaning as you read the following sentences from the Student Model.

STUDENT MODEL

from **Preventing Computer "Hogging" at the Library** page 150; lines 6–8

Clearly, our local library has a serious problem with people who take over the five computers. Sometimes these "computer hogs" stay at the terminals for hours.

Try It! Now, ask yourself these questions. Record your answers in your journal.

- What kind of tone is set in the first sentence? Which word or words help to set the tone?
- Would the second sentence be more or less effective if it were written as follows? *Sometimes these people stay at the terminals for hours.*

Fine-Tune Your Draft

Apply It! Use these revision suggestions to prepare your final draft **after rethinking how well questions of purpose, audience, and genre have been addressed**.

- **Improve Subtlety of Meaning** Use tone, precise word choice, and your writing style to clarify meaning and make your writing sharper.
- **Choose Effective Transitions** Use transitions such as *however, but,* or *next* to connect ideas within and between paragraphs.

Teacher Feedback After submitting your final draft for teacher review, revise it in response to feedback.

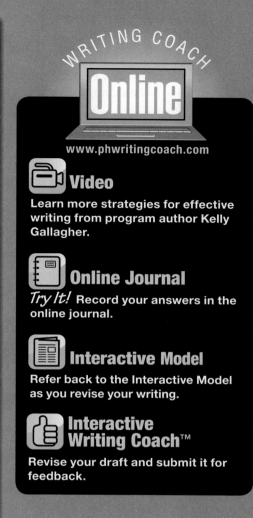

WRITING COACH Online

www.phwritingcoach.com

Video

Learn more strategies for effective writing from program author Kelly Gallagher.

Online Journal

Try It! Record your answers in the online journal.

Interactive Model

Refer back to the Interactive Model as you revise your writing.

Interactive Writing Coach™

Revise your draft and submit it for feedback.

Editing: Making It Correct

Use the editing process to polish your work and correct errors. It is often helpful to work with a partner when editing your drafts.

Before editing your draft, think about verb moods, or ways in which a verb can express an action or condition. For example, the **subjunctive mood** can be used to express **doubts, wishes, and possibilities**. Then, correct any factual errors and errors in capitalization, **grammar, mechanics, and spelling**.

WRITE GUY *Jeff Anderson, M. Ed.*

WHAT DO YOU NOTICE?

Zoom in on Conventions Focus on the verbs as you zoom in on this line from the Student Model.

STUDENT MODEL from **Preventing Computer "Hogging" at the Library** page 150; lines 42–43

I request that the library install software that limits computer usage.

To learn more about
the subjunctive mood,
see Chapter 17 of your
Grammar Handbook.

Now, ask yourself: *Which verb expresses the action that the author wishes the library would perform?*

Perhaps you said that the verb *install* expresses the author's wish.

You also may have noticed that *install* does not end in -s, even though the subject *library* is a singular subject. This is because the verb *install* is in the subjunctive mood. Writers use the **subjunctive mood** to express doubts, wishes, and possibilities. For example, in the Student Model, the verb *request* lets you know that the author is stating a wish.

You can also use the subjunctive mood in clauses beginning with *if* or *that* when the situation they describe is unlikely to occur. For example:

I would ride my bike if it were less windy.

The subjunctive mood can also be used in clauses beginning with *that* to express a demand or proposal. For example:

Alice demanded that Carl arrive promptly at noon.

The committee proposes that the issue move forward for a vote.

Partner Talk Discuss this question with a partner: *Why might the subjunctive mood be helpful when writing a persuasive essay?*

To learn more, see Chapter 17.

Grammar Mini-Lesson: Subjunctive Mood

In the **subjunctive mood,** present tense singular verbs do not take the *-s* or *-es* ending. Also, the subjunctive form of *to be* is *be* in the present tense and *were* in the past tense, regardless of the subject. Notice how the writer forms the subjunctive mood in the Student Model.

STUDENT MODEL from **Preventing Computer "Hogging" at the Library** page 150; lines 26–28

The library staff will program the computer so that it can only be used for a specific period of time (say, 30 minutes).

Try It! Rewrite each sentence, changing the correct verb to the **subjunctive mood**. Write the answers in your journal.

1. My father wishes that he was a teacher.
2. I prefer that Tony arrives at noon.

Apply It! **Edit your draft for grammar, mechanics, capitalization and spelling**. If necessary, change verbs to the **subjunctive mood to express doubts, wishes, and possibilities**.

Use the rubric to evaluate your piece. If necessary, rethink, rewrite, or revise.

Rubric for Expository Writing: Problem-Solution Essay	Rating Scale
Ideas: How clearly are the problem and its possible solutions defined and explained?	Not very — Very 1 2 3 4 5 6
Organization: How well are your ideas organized?	1 2 3 4 5 6
Voice: How well have you engaged your reader?	1 2 3 4 5 6
Word Choice: How effective is your word choice in conveying your specific meaning?	1 2 3 4 5 6
Sentence Fluency: How well do you use transitions to create sentence fluency?	1 2 3 4 5 6
Conventions: How well have you used the subjunctive mood?	1 2 3 4 5 6

WRITING COACH Online

www.phwritingcoach.com

Video
Learn effective editing techniques from program author Jeff Anderson.

Online Journal
Try It! Record your answers in the online journal.

Interactive Model
Refer back to the Interactive Model as you edit your writing.

Interactive Writing Coach™
Edit your draft. Check it against the rubric and then submit it for feedback.

Publishing

Give your problem-solution essay a chance to actually solve the problem. Get it ready for presentation. Then, choose a way to publish it for the appropriate audiences.

Wrap Up Your Presentation

Adding images to your problem-solution essay can provide readers with visual support to illustrate the evidence you presented. Think of some images you can include to bring your essay to life.

Publish Your Piece

Use the chart to identify a way to publish your problem-solution essay.

If your audience is...	...then publish it by...
Classmates and others at your school	• Submitting it to the school newspaper or a school-related blog • Reading and discussing it at a school meeting
Your local community	• Submitting it to a local newspaper • Reading and discussing it on local public-access TV
The larger community	• Posting it online and inviting responses • Developing a multimedia presentation using pictures, music, and images to convey your ideas

Extend Your Research

Think more about the topic on which you wrote your problem-solution essay. What else would you like to know about this topic?

- Brainstorm for several questions you would like to research and then consult, or discuss, with others. Then decide which question is your major research question.
- Formulate, or develop, a plan about how you will answer these questions. Decide where you will find more information—on the Internet, at the library, or through other sources.
- Finally, learn more about your topic by following through with your research plan.

The Big Question: Why Write? What should we tell and what should we describe to make information clear?

21st Century Learning

MAKE YOUR WRITING COUNT

Stage a Problem-Solution Newscast

A problem-solution essay identifies a problem that affects an individual or a community and presents several possible solutions. Help your schoolmates learn more about a local problem and its possible solutions by presenting a **problem-solution newscast.**

With a group, identify a problem from your essays that affects your school or community. Then, work together to produce a newscast to communicate your message about the problem and its solutions. This will be the theme of your newscast. Consider if you will state it directly and explicitly or if you will state it implicitly and only suggest the theme to your audience.

Here's your action plan.

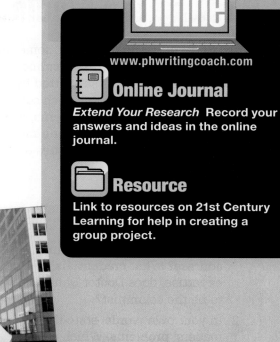

1. Set objectives for group meetings and choose roles, such as reporters, editors, photographers, or artists.
2. View available newscasts online to see how information is presented visually.
3. Review your peers' problem-solution papers. Identify one that interests the group. Use information from that paper as the basis for your newscast.
4. Take notes about what you think works best. Find still images that will illustrate the problem and possible solutions and help set a definite mood or tone.
5. Each script should do the following:
   - Introduce and provide information about a problem and its solutions
   - Include notes about when and how to incorporate visuals
   - Provide camera directions, such as "Cut to image" or "Read into camera," if you are recording your newscast
6. Rehearse your presentations. Record the video if needed. Practice pacing and matching words to visuals.

Listening and Speaking Before you begin rehearsing, talk about how and why scripted news sounds different from regular conversation. Then read your script aloud. Try to sound like a professional newscaster. Accept feedback from listeners and adjust your delivery accordingly.

WRITING COACH Online

www.phwritingcoach.com

Online Journal

Extend Your Research **Record your answers and ideas in the online journal.**

Resource

Link to resources on 21st Century Learning for help in creating a group project.

Your Turn **Writing for Media: Question-and-Answer Column**

21st Century Learning

Writing for Media

A **question-and-answer column**, sometimes called an **advice column**, is a regularly published print or online article in which a knowledgeable writer answers questions submitted by readers. Newspapers and magazines often have several such columns. Their topics range from health to chess to personal concerns, such as relationships or parenting. Readers usually send in letters or e-mails to ask questions about problems they have, and the columnist writes and publishes solutions to them.

Try It! Study this sample question-and-answer column. Then answer the questions about it. Record your answers in your journal.

1. What topic does this column address? What **credentials,** or expertise, does Doctor Dana have to be the columnist?
2. In your own words, state the two readers' **problems**. Which reader is more certain that he or she has a problem?
3. What **solutions** does Doctor Dana suggest to *Anxious in Austin?* What facts, examples, or reasons does she give to support her response? How would you describe her tone?
4. What **solution** does Doctor Dana suggest to *Dog Lover in Dallas?* What concern does she address in her last sentence?
5. Who is the **audience** for this column? What **advice** might it need?

Wednesday, February 20 14

Ask Doctor Dana

Dear Dr. Dana, My friend Angie, who is going away with her family this summer, wants to leave the family hamster with me. I have a cat. Will that be a problem?
—Anxious in Austin

Dear Anxious: Yes. Even the best-behaved cats rarely overcome their instinct to attack small furry creatures like hamsters. The cat could get its paws through the cage or knock it over. Take the hamster only if you can keep the cage in a room that the cat cannot enter. Otherwise, visit your friend's home or apartment with an adult every day and care for the hamster there, or tell your friend to ask someone else for help.

Dear Dr. Dana, My dog suddenly started scratching herself all the time. I don't see any fleas or flea bites. What do you think the problem is?
—Dog Lover in Dallas

Dear Dog Lover: Your dog could be suffering from any number of ailments. Your best bet is to get her quickly to a veterinarian. If you cannot afford a private vet, phone the local animal shelter and ask if they can help.

Dana Van Zandt has practiced veterinary medicine for over 20 years.

Extension Find another example of a question-and-answer column, and compare it with this one.

Create a Question-and-Answer Column

Follow these steps to create a question-and-answer column that communicates ideas and information to your specific audience. To plan your column, review the graphic organizers on R24–R27 and choose one that suits your needs.

Prewriting

- Identify a topic for the column. It might be a sport or a game you play, a hobby you enjoy, or something else you know about or do regularly. Your knowledge makes you an "expert." Devise a catchy name for the column that indicates its topic.
- Then, identify one or more solutions to each problem. Think of two problems related to your topic. Invent names for two writers asking about these problems.
- List facts, examples, and reasons to support your solutions.

Drafting

- Begin the column by adding the title at the top of the page. Organize your column using a question-and-answer format.
- Write two short letters. In each letter, identify the problem and ask for the columnist's advice. Use informal language, and sign each letter with the name you chose.

Revising and Editing

- Make sure that problems and solutions are clearly stated, with smooth transitions that show the relationships between ideas.
- Be sure that the advice uses an appropriate tone and uses correct terminology that shows knowledge of the topic.

Publishing

- Submit your column to an online student newspaper.
- Pool your column with classmates' columns, printing them in a class "advice magazine."

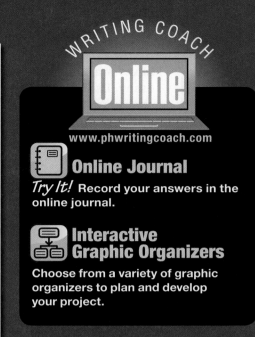

WRITING COACH **Online**

www.phwritingcoach.com

Online Journal

Try It! **Record your answers in the online journal.**

Interactive Graphic Organizers

Choose from a variety of graphic organizers to plan and develop your project.

Partner Talk

Discuss your topic with a partner. Ask what problems or questions he or she might have on the topic of your column. Monitor your partner's spoken language by asking follow-up questions to confirm your understanding.

Writing for Assessment

Many standardized tests ask you to write an expository or analytical essay. Use the prompts on these pages to practice. Your responses should include most of the same characteristics as a problem-solution essay. Look back at page 146 to review these characteristics.

Try It! To begin, read the **analytical essay** prompt and the information on format and academic vocabulary. Use the ABCDs of On-Demand Writing to help you plan and write your essay.

Format

The prompt directs you to write a *problem-solution analytical essay.* Be sure to include an introduction that clearly states your thesis, body paragraphs supported by relevant information, and a conclusion that restates your key ideas.

Analytical Prompt

Many children today are reading fewer books outside of school. Write a problem-solution analytical essay that addresses this problem and offers a possible solution.

Academic Vocabulary

Remember that an *analytical* prompt asks you to *analyze*, or closely study a topic. When you *analyze* you break something into smaller parts.

The ABCDs of On-Demand Writing

Use the following ABCDs to help you respond to the prompt.

Before you write your draft:

Attack the prompt [1 MINUTE]

- Circle or highlight important verbs in the prompt. Draw a line from the verb to what it refers to.
- Rewrite the prompt in your own words.

Brainstorm possible answers [4 MINUTES]

- Create a graphic organizer to generate ideas.
- Use one for each part of the prompt if necessary.

Choose the order of your response [1 MINUTE]

- Think about the best way to organize your ideas.
- Number your ideas in the order you will write about them. Cross out ideas you will not be using.

After you write your draft:

Detect errors before turning in the draft [1 MINUTE]

- Carefully reread your writing.
- Make sure that your response makes sense and is complete.
- Look for spelling, punctuation, and grammar errors

More Prompts for Practice

Apply It! Respond to Prompts 1 and 2 in open-ended or timed situations by writing **expository** or **analytical essays** according to these guidelines.

- Keep your **audience and purpose** in mind as you write.
- Grab readers' attention with **effective introductory paragraphs**, including a **thesis** or controlling idea.
- Use a variety of **sentence structures** and **rhetorical devices** to help make your writing interesting and to clearly convey your ideas.
- For your body, choose an **organizing structure** that logically orders your ideas and is appropriate to your audience, purpose, and context.
- Include **relevant information** for the topic and provide **valid inferences** based on the evidence you mention.
- Use **transitions** between paragraphs to convey meaning and make relationships clear.
- Create a memorable end with **effective concluding paragraphs**.

Prompt 1 In many neighborhoods, newspapers and plastic bags blow in the breeze and litter clogs the gutters. Write a problem-solution analytical essay that identifies a clear problem with litter in your town and provides an effective solution.

Prompt 2 Teens across the country drop out of high school every day. Because of this, their futures are severely limited. Write a problem-solution analytical essay that addresses this problem and offers possible solutions.

Spiral Review: Poetry Respond to Prompt 3 by writing a **poem**. Review the characteristics described on page 120. Then write a poem in the **form** of your choice using a variety of **poetic techniques** such as figurative language and sound devices.

Prompt 3 Write a poem about the way a particular animal moves. Use vivid imagery and powerful diction, or word choice, to make your poem interesting and visual.

WRITING COACH **Online**

www.phwritingcoach.com

Interactive Writing Coach™

Plan your response to the prompt. If you are using the prompt for practice, write one paragraph at a time or your entire draft and then submit it for feedback. If you are using the prompt as a timed test, write your entire draft and then submit it for feedback.

Remember **ABCD**

- **A**ttack the prompt
- **B**rainstorm possible answers
- **C**hoose the order of your response
- **D**etect errors before turning in the draft

CHAPTER 9

PERSUASION

What Do You Think?

Recycling is a topic on which most people have an opinion. Some people recycle everything. Others think recycling is a hassle.

You probably have an opinion on this topic. You may want to convince someone to share your opinion. In order to persuade someone to share your opinion, you must use facts and details to support your point of view.

Try It! List reasons why people should or should not be required to recycle. Consider these questions as you participate in an extended discussion with a partner. Take turns expressing your ideas and feelings.

- What are the benefits of recycling?
- What are some of the difficulties of recycling?
- What are some facts or details that support your point of view?

Review the list you made. Choose a position on the issue by deciding which side to take. Write a sentence that states which position, or side, you will take. Then, take turns talking about your ideas and positions with a partner.

What's Ahead

In this chapter, you will review two strong examples of an argumentative essay: a Mentor Text and a Student Model. Then, using the examples as guidance, you will write an argumentative essay of your own.

WRITING COACH Online

www.phwritingcoach.com

Online Journal

Try It! Record your answers and ideas in the online journal.

You can also record and save your answers and ideas on pop-up sticky notes in the eText.

THE BIG QUESTION

Connect to the Big Questions

Discuss these questions with your partner:

1 **What do you think?** What are our responsibilities to our communities?

2 **Why write?** What is your point of view? How will you know if you've convinced others?

ARGUMENTATIVE ESSAY

In this chapter, you will explore a special type of argumentative essay, the editorial. An editorial is a piece of writing that is published in a newspaper or magazine and is intended to present a view of a particular issue. The viewpoint expressed in an editorial is usually that of the editorial board of the publication. The editorial attempts to persuade readers to agree with that viewpoint.

You will develop the editorial by taking it through each of the steps of the writing process: prewriting, drafting, revising, editing, and publishing. You will also have an opportunity to create persuasive product packaging. To preview the criteria for how your editorial will be evaluated, see the rubric on page 189.

FEATURE ASSIGNMENT

Argumentative Essay: Editorial

An effective argumentative essay has these characteristics:

- **A clear description** of the issue
- **A clear thesis statement, based on logical reasons**, that expresses an opinion about the issue
- **Logical, precise, and relevant evidence** that supports the thesis. Evidence may include examples, facts, statistics, and expert opinions.
- **Consideration of the whole range of information and views** on the topic and an **accurate and honest representation of these views**
- **Counter-arguments**, based on evidence, that anticipate and address objections
- **An organizing structure** that is appropriate to purpose (to persuade), audience, and context
- An analysis of the **relative value of specific data**, **facts, and ideas,** which involves identifying which information is more important than others
- **Vivid**, **persuasive language** to appeal to your audience
- **Effective sentence structure** and correct spelling, grammar, and usage

An editorial may also include:

- A **lead** that introduces the topic or issue and captures readers' interest
- **A natural but strong voice** that helps persuade readers

Other Forms of Argumentative Writing

In addition to an editorial, there are other forms of argumentative writing, including:

Advertisements are paid announcements that try to convince people to do or buy something.

Letters to the editor are written by readers expressing an opinion about material previously published in a periodical. A letter to the editor may offer an opposing view to an editorial or op-ed piece.

Op-ed pieces appear in periodicals and express the views of professional columnists and public figures, among others. Unlike editorials, op-ed pieces do not necessarily represent the views of the publication's editorial board.

Persuasive essays use logic and reasoning to persuade readers to adopt a certain action or point of view.

Persuasive speeches attempt to convince a listening or viewing audience to support a particular policy, position, or action.

Propaganda uses emotional appeals and often biased, false, or misleading information to persuade people to act or think in a certain way. Propaganda is often about political issues.

Reviews evaluate items and activities, such as books and movies. A review often states an opinion on whether people should spend time and money on the item or activity.

Try It! For each audience and purpose described, choose a form, such as a speech, review, or op-ed piece, that is appropriate for conveying your intended meaning to the audience. Explain your choices.

- To persuade classmates to attend a movie you enjoyed
- To give reasons why people should live close to their workplaces
- To convince your city council to hold a music festival in your town or city

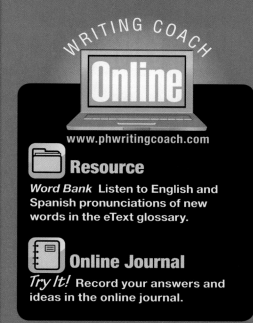

WRITING COACH **Online**

www.phwritingcoach.com

Resource

Word Bank Listen to English and Spanish pronunciations of new words in the eText glossary.

Online Journal

Try It! Record your answers and ideas in the online journal.

WORD BANK

People often use these basic and content-based vocabulary words when they talk about persuasive writing. Work with a partner. Take turns saying and writing each word in a sentence. If you are unsure of the meaning of a word, use the Glossary or a dictionary to check the definition.

agree	**opinion**
concern	**reasonable**
logical	**valid**

STUDENT MODEL Editorial

With a small group, take turns reading the Student Model aloud. As you read, practice newly acquired vocabulary by correctly producing the word's sound. Also ask yourself if you find the writer's arguments convincing.

Use a Reader's Eye

Now, reread the Student Model. On your copy of the Student Model, use the Reader's Response Symbols to react to what you read.

Reader's Response Symbols

- **+ I strongly agree with this.**
- **– I strongly disagree with this.**
- **? I have a question about this.**
- **! Wow! That is cool/weird/interesting.**

Partner Talk

With a partner, discuss your responses to the Student Model and your opinion on the topic. How were your responses to the writer's position similar and different?

Year-Round School

by Anabel Rodriguez

Oh, how we love those lazy, hazy, crazy, and long, long days of summer! However, the traditional school calendar, with its lengthy summer break, is no longer useful. Summer break was originally started long ago so that young people would be free in the summer to help their parents tend crops. Today, most families do not live on farms, especially in our area. I believe that our school district should shift from the traditional calendar to one that runs all year round.

Many school districts across the country have already started to use a year-round school calendar. In most cases, this schedule doesn't increase the number of school days. Instead, districts rearrange the times when students are in school. Year-round schedules can be different, but a typical calendar has students attending school for 9-week terms, with 2- or 3-week breaks in between.

This type of schedule can be great for parents, students, teachers, and schools. Families in which all adults work outside the home—now over 70% of our population—would not need to find child care during the long summer vacation. Most schools also benefit from the year-long calendar by planning their classes in shifts. That is, some students attend school while others are on break. This way, the schools can have more students without building more classrooms, which saves money for the schools.

Most importantly, the year-round calendar would help students to remember what they learn. Many teachers have noticed that over the summer students forget a lot of what they learned during the school year. According to a study by Dr. Harris Cooper, a well-known education expert, students on year-round schedules are better able to remember math and reading skills than students on traditional schedules. Dr. Cooper's report also showed

1

students', parents', and teachers' positive attitudes toward the year-round schedule. Most people seemed to enjoy the shorter terms and more frequent vacations.

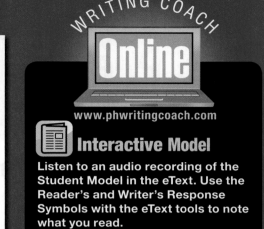

Yes, there are some disadvantages to the year-round schedule. Students couldn't have full-time summer jobs. However, they could still work part-time after school and full-time during their multiple breaks. Families taking long summer vacations would have to change their plans. While a long summer break gives young people needed "down time," that time is all bunched together. The year-round schedule gives students the same amount of free time, but it's spread out over the year. These shorter but more frequent breaks offer students (and teachers) enough time to relax, but not enough to vegetate.

I urge our local Board of Education to use a year-round calendar. This schedule is a better fit for today's society than the older, farming society. And for students, on any given school day, those lazy, crazy, hazy days of vacation would be just a few short weeks away, no matter the season!

2

WRITING COACH **Online**

www.phwritingcoach.com

Interactive Model

Listen to an audio recording of the Student Model in the eText. Use the Reader's and Writer's Response Symbols with the eText tools to note what you read.

Use a Writer's Eye

Now evaluate the piece as a writer. On your copy of the Student Model, use the Writer's Response Symbols to react to what you read. Identify places where the student writer uses characteristics of an effective editorial.

Writer's Response Symbols	
C.T.	**Clearly stated thesis**
P.A.	**Strong persuasive arguments**
S.E.	**Effective and credible supporting evidence**
C.A.	**Good responses to readers' counter-arguments**

Record your answers in your writing journal.

Your Turn **Feature Assignment: Editorial**

Feature Assignment Prewriting Feature Assignment Prewriting

Plan Your Piece

You will use the graphic organizer to state your thesis, organize your arguments, and identify details. When it is complete, you will be ready to write your first draft.

Develop a Clear Thesis To keep your readers focused on your position, review your notes and develop a clear **thesis**, or controlling idea. Write one sentence stating your viewpoint or summing up your argument. Add your thesis statement to a graphic organizer like the one shown.

Logically Organize Your Arguments Use a graphic organizer to **structure your arguments in a persuasive way:** in order of importance. In addition, **anticipate and address reader objections and concerns with counter-arguments.**

DEVELOP YOUR PERSUASIVE ARGUMENTS

Clear Thesis	*Our neighborhood should set up an online network to build relationships and community spirit.*
First Persuasive Argument	*Neighborhood safety would be improved if neighbors reported crimes and suspicious activity to each other.*
Supporting Evidence/Details	
Second Persuasive Argument	*People would find it easier to make neighborhood improvements and handle emergencies if they communicated regularly.*
Supporting Evidence/Details	
Readers' Objections	*Online communication cannot take the place of face-to-face interaction.*
Counter-argument to Objections	

Gather Details

Good persuasive writers support their arguments with logical, precise, and relevant evidence. Look at these examples:

- **Logical Reasons:** *Crime has recently increased in our neighborhood. An online network would allow neighbors to share information about suspicious activity and contact police more quickly, reducing crime.*
- **Statistics:** *A recent survey conducted in our city showed that 73% of the households in our neighborhood have Internet access.*
- **Expert Opinions:** *City Council member Alessio, who lives in our neighborhood, has said that other neighborhoods have used their online networks to organize clean-ups and other local improvements.*
- **Personal Observations:** *When my family moved here, it was hard for me to feel connected to the community at first.*

Try It! Read the Student Model excerpt and identify which details the author used to support her argument.

STUDENT MODEL from **Year-Round School**
pages 176–177; lines 28–38

Most importantly, the year-round calendar would help students to remember what they learn. Many teachers have noticed that over the summer students forget a lot of what they learned during the school year. According to a study by Dr. Harris Cooper, a well-known education expert, students on year-round schedules are better able to remember math and reading skills than students on traditional schedules are. Dr. Cooper's report also showed the students', parents', and teachers' positive attitudes toward the year-round schedule. Most people seemed to enjoy the shorter terms and more frequent vacations.

Apply It! Review the types of evidence that support persuasive writing. Then identify at least one piece of evidence for each of your arguments. Remember, your goal is to influence the attitudes and actions of your specific audience on your specific issue.

- Review the evidence you have decided to use. Make sure that each piece of evidence is **logical,** or makes sense, **precise,** or is specific instead of general, and **relevant,** or truly applies to the issue.
- Add these pieces of evidence to your graphic organizer. Match each piece to a persuasive argument so that you present a consideration of the whole range of **views** and **information** on the topic and an **accurate** and **honest representation** of those views.

WRITING COACH **Online**

www.phwritingcoach.com

Interactive Graphic Organizers

Use the interactive graphic organizers to help you create a plan for your writing.

Interactive Model

Refer back to the Interactive Model in the eText as you plan your writing.

Drafting

During the drafting stage, you will start to write your ideas for your editorial. You will **structure ideas in a persuasive way** by following an outline that provides an **organizational strategy**. This strategy will help you write a focused editorial appropriate for your **purpose, audience, and context.**

The Organization of an Argumentative Essay

This chart shows an effective organizing strategy for an argumentative essay. Look back to see how the Mentor Text follows this strategy. Then, use this chart to help you create an outline for your draft.

Outline for Success

I. Introduction

See Mentor Text, p. 174.

- Lead
- Clear thesis or position

Grab Your Reader

- A strong lead grabs the reader's attention with a lively opening. For example, you can start off with a memorable quotation, vivid detail, surprising statistic, or a personal anecdote.
- A clear statement of your thesis or position ensures that your audience understands your point of view.

II. Body

See Mentor Text, pp. 174–175.

- Persuasive arguments
- Logically organized arguments
- Counter-arguments to address other points of view

Build Your Case

- In an argumentative essay, each paragraph discusses one persuasive argument. The most important argument is usually last.
- Not everyone will agree with your point of view. Addressing counter-arguments shows how readers' objections or concerns are less important or wrong and why readers should agree with you.

III. Conclusion

See Mentor Text, p. 175.

- Restatement of position
- Memorable ending

Close the Deal

- A conclusion restates your position or thesis statement.
- Memorable conclusions end with interesting facts or quotations and tell the audience what action they should take.

Start Your Draft

Use the checklist to help you complete your draft. Use the graphic organizer that shows your thesis, persuasive arguments, and supporting evidence, and the Outline for Success as guides.

While drafting, aim at writing your ideas, not on making your writing perfect. Remember, you will have the chance to improve your draft when you revise and edit.

√ Begin by drafting a strong opening for your editorial—a sentence or two that will grab your readers' attention.

√ Develop your **introduction** by presenting information about your topic and telling readers what to expect in the rest of your editorial. Include your **thesis statement** that clearly states your position.

√ Shape the **body** of your editorial. Use an **organizing structure** that is appropriate to your purpose, audience, and context.

√ Write one paragraph for each persuasive argument. Make sure each argument supports the thesis and is based on logical reasoning and precise, relevant **evidence.**

√ Analyze the **relative value** of specific data, facts, and ideas. To do this, use phrases such as "most importantly" to show that certain pieces of evidence are more important than others.

√ Consider the whole range of information and views on the topic. When you anticipate and address readers' possible objections, support your **counter-arguments** with evidence to explain why others' views aren't valid.

√ Make sure you represent other points of view **accurately** and **honestly.**

√ End with a powerful **conclusion** that restates your position or thesis statement.

WRITING COACH **Online**

www.phwritingcoach.com

Interactive Model

Outline for Success **View pop-ups of Mentor Text selections referenced in the Outline for Success.**

Interactive Writing Coach™

Use the Interactive Writing Coach to receive the level of support you need:

- **Write one paragraph at a time and submit each one for immediate, detailed feedback.**
- **Write your entire first draft and submit it for immediate, personalized feedback.**

REPLACE ADD DELETE and REORDER
RADaR

Revising: Making It Better

Now that you have finished your first draft, you are ready to revise. Think about the "big picture" of audience, purpose, and genre. You can use Revision RADaR as a guide for making changes to improve your draft. Revision RADaR provides four major ways to improve your writing: (R) replace, (A) add, (D) delete, and (R) reorder.

Kelly Gallagher, M. Ed.

KEEP REVISION ON YOUR RADaR

Read these separate, excerpted paragraphs of the first draft of the Student Model "Year-Round School." Then look at questions the writer asked herself as she thought about how well her draft **addressed issues of audience, purpose, and genre.**

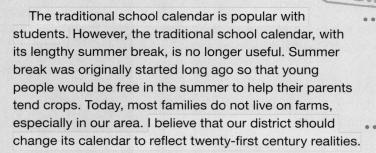

1ST DRAFT

Year-Round School

The traditional school calendar is popular with students. However, the traditional school calendar, with its lengthy summer break, is no longer useful. Summer break was originally started long ago so that young people would be free in the summer to help their parents tend crops. Today, most families do not live on farms, especially in our area. I believe that our district should change its calendar to reflect twenty-first century realities.

*Does the **introduction** grab my audience?*

*Does the **thesis statement** clearly identify the issue and my views of it?*

Most importantly, the year-round calendar would help students to remember what they learn. Many teachers have noticed that over the summer students forget a lot of what they learned during the school year. Students going to school year-round are more likely to remember their learning.

*Have I included persuasive **arguments** and logical, precise, and relevant evidence?*

Now look at how the writer applied Revision RADaR to write an improved second draft, refining her ideas and using language more effectively and precisely.

Year-Round School

2ND DRAFT

Oh, how we love those lazy, hazy, crazy, and long, long days of summer! However, the traditional school calendar, with its lengthy summer break, is no longer useful. Summer break was originally started long ago so that young people would be free in the summer to help their parents tend crops. Today, most families do not live on farms, especially in our area. I believe that our school district should shift from the traditional calendar to one that runs all year round.

R *Replaced a boring, straightforward statement with a catchy phrase to make the beginning livelier*

R *Replaced the thesis statement in the first draft with a clearer one*

Most importantly, the year-round calendar would help students to remember what they learn. Many teachers have noticed that over the summer students forget a lot of what they learned during the school year. According to a study by Dr. Harris Cooper, a well-known education expert, students on year-round schedules are better able to remember math and reading skills than students on traditional schedules are. Dr. Cooper's report also showed students', parents', and teachers' positive attitudes toward the year-round schedule. Most people seemed to enjoy the shorter terms and more frequent vacations.

A *Added more specific supporting information to the argument about students remembering what they've learned*

Apply It! Use your Revision RADaR to revise your draft.

- First, determine how well you have addressed the needs of your audience, explained your **purpose** for writing, and included the characteristics essential to the persuasive writing **genre.**
- Then apply your Revision RADaR to make needed changes. Remember—you can use the steps in Revision RADaR in any order.

WRITING COACH **Online**

www.phwritingcoach.com

Interactive Writing Coach™

Use the Revision RADaR strategy in your own writing. Then submit your paragraph or draft for feedback.

RADaR
REPLACE ADD DELETE and REORDER

Look at the Big Picture

Use the chart and your analytical skills to evaluate how well each section of your editorial addresses your **purpose, audience, and genre.** When necessary, use the suggestions in the chart to revise your piece.

Section	Evaluate	Revise
Introduction	• Check the opening of your editorial. Will it grab readers' attention and draw them in?	• Make the opening more compelling by adding a question, anecdote, quotation, statistic, or other interesting detail.
	• Make sure that the **thesis statement** clearly describes the issue and states your opinion about it.	• To state the issue and your opinion more forcefully, replace the thesis with a question and answer it by expressing your opinion in new words.
Body	• Check that you have **organized** your editorial logically, persuasively, and in a way that will be clear to your audience.	• Reorder arguments so that your second strongest argument comes first, the weaker arguments follow, and your strongest argument is last.
	• Underline each item of information that offers supporting **evidence.** Draw a line from each piece of evidence to the argument it supports.	• Reorder any piece of evidence that is not near the argument it supports. Delete any point that is unnecessary.
	• Check that the supporting evidence is **logical, precise,** and **relevant** to the issue.	• Add new specific evidence to strengthen your arguments. Indicate as strong or weak the relative value of specific facts, details, and ideas.
	• Review reader **concerns**. Determine whether you have anticipated and addressed each objection adequately.	• Restate reader concerns and objections as questions. Answer them again, and try to improve your counter-arguments.
Conclusion	• Check the restatement of your position.	• Compare the restatement to your original thesis to make sure it is consistent but fresh.
	• Check that your conclusion ends on a memorable note.	• Add a question, call to action, quotation, or forceful statement to increase the power of your conclusion.

Focus on Craft: Style

Style is the particular way an author uses language. A clear, lively, fluid writing style is a powerful tool for influencing your audience. Diction, or an author's choice of words, is an important element of style. Using engaging and interesting language can improve your **subtletly of meaning,** or language that hints at or reveals something about your meaning and purpose, and can make your arguments more convincing to readers.

Think about a clear and lively writing style as you read the following sentence from the Student Model.

STUDENT MODEL from **Year-Round School**
page 177; lines 47–49

These shorter but more frequent breaks offer students (and teachers) enough time to relax, but not enough to vegetate.

Try It! Now, ask yourself these questions. Record your answers in your journal.

- Does the style help you to connect with the author's point of view?
- Would the sentence be more or less interesting if it read "Shorter but more frequent vacations offer students (and teachers) enough free time to relax, but not enough to be bored"? Explain.

Fine-Tune Your Draft

Apply It! Use the revision suggestions to prepare your final draft after **rethinking how well questions of purpose, audience, and genre have been addressed.**

- **Improve Your Style** Substitute more precise and livelier words for vague or generic ones. For example, change *bad* to *disastrous* or *dangerous*.
- **Include Transitions to Convey Meaning** If necessary, add transition words and phrases such as *first*, *then*, *at last*, and *therefore*, to signal connections between your sentences and paragraphs.
- **Improve Figurative Language** Look for places where you could make your writing stronger by using a simile or metaphor.
- **Improve Subtlety of Meaning** Use exact language to clarify meaning and make your writing sharper and more precise.

Peer Feedback Read your final draft to a group of peers. Ask if you have considered a range of **information and views** on your topic and represented them **accurately**. Consider their responses and revise your final draft as needed.

WRITING COACH **Online**
www.phwritingcoach.com

Video
Learn more strategies for effective writing from program author Kelly Gallagher.

Online Journal
Try It! Record your answers in the online journal.

Interactive Model
Refer back to the Interactive Model as you revise your writing.

Interactive Writing Coach™
Revise your draft and submit it for feedback.

Editing: Making It Correct

To edit your work, read your draft carefully to correct errors in spelling and grammar. It can also be helpful to read your draft aloud.

Before editing your final draft, consider using **more complex active and passive tenses** to add clarity and variety to your writing. **Active voice** verbs express the action taken by the subject of the sentence. **Passive voice** verbs express an action that is performed upon the subject of the sentence. Then, edit your final draft for errors in **grammar, mechanics, and spelling**.

WRITE GUY *Jeff Anderson, M. Ed.*

WHAT DO YOU NOTICE?

Zoom in on Conventions Focus on the verb's voice as you zoom in on this sentence from the Student Model.

To learn more about active and passive voice, see Chapter 17 of your Grammar Handbook.

STUDENT MODEL from **Year-Round School**
page 176; lines 29–31

Many teachers have noticed that over the summer students forget a lot of what they learned during the school year.

Now, ask yourself: *Does this sentence focus on the people doing the action or the action itself?*

Perhaps you said the focus is on the teachers, or the subject doing the action.

The verb "have noticed" expresses the action taken by teachers—they *have noticed*—so it is in the **active voice.** Using the active voice puts emphasis on the subject, the person or thing taking the action. In general, active voice makes writing stronger. It expresses ideas directly and persuasively.

Passive voice is less direct than active voice. The **passive voice** is constructed by adding a form of *be* to the past participle of a verb. When the sentence above is written in passive voice, it becomes: *That over the summer students forget a lot of what they learned during the school year <u>was noticed</u> by many teachers.*

The use of passive voice moves the emphasis from the subject to the action performed upon the subject or the result of the action. The passive voice may be used when the person or thing performing the action is unknown or to shift emphasis when the person performing the action is unimportant. This rhetorical effect may be used for persuasive purposes.

To learn more, see Chapter 17.

Grammar Mini-Lesson: Voice in Complex Tenses

Active and **passive voice** can be used with all verb tenses, even the more **complex tenses**. The active voice of the present perfect (*has/have* + past participle), past perfect (*had* + past participle), and future perfect (*will have* + past participle) can be changed to passive voice by adding a form of *be* after the helping verb(s).

The following sentence is written in the active voice present perfect tense: *He has seen his mother*. The sentence could be rewritten in the passive voice present perfect tense: *His mother has been seen by him*. Notice how the author uses the active voice of the present perfect tense in the Mentor Text.

MENTOR TEXT from **Riding the Waves with Whales**
page 174; lines 5–7

The popularity of whale-watching cruises has spread across the globe.

Try It! Change each sentence from the passive voice to the active voice. Be sure to maintain the same complex tense. Write the answers in your journal.

1. By the end of next year, a third book will have been published by Marlena.
2. The door had been opened and closed by the children several times.

Apply It! **Edit your draft for grammar, mechanics, and spelling.** If necessary, rewrite some sentences to ensure that you have used more complex active and passive tenses.

Use the rubric to evaluate your piece. If necessary, rethink, rewrite, or revise.

Rubric for Argumentative Essay: Editorial	Rating Scale
Ideas: How clearly are the issue and your position stated and developed?	Not very — Very 1 2 3 4 5 6
Organization: How organized are your arguments and supporting evidence?	1 2 3 4 5 6
Voice: How authoritative and persuasive is your voice?	1 2 3 4 5 6
Word Choice: How persuasive is the language you have used?	1 2 3 4 5 6
Sentence Fluency: How well have you used transitions to convey meaning?	1 2 3 4 5 6
Conventions: How correct are your complex tenses?	1 2 3 4 5 6

WRITING COACH Online
www.phwritingcoach.com

Video
Learn effective editing techniques from program author Jeff Anderson.

Online Journal
Try It! Record your answers in the online journal.

Interactive Model
Refer back to the Interactive Model as you edit your writing.

Interactive Writing Coach™
Edit your draft. Check it against the rubric and then submit it for feedback.

Publishing

Make the world just a little bit better by spreading a good idea—publish your editorial! First prepare it for presentation to others. Then choose a way to **publish it for appropriate audiences.**

Wrap Up Your Presentation

Is your editorial handwritten or written on a computer? If your editorial is handwritten, you may need to make a new, clean copy. If so, be sure to **write legibly**. Also be sure to add a title that grabs the reader's attention and indicates the topic of your editorial.

Publish Your Piece

Use the chart to identify a way to publish your editorial.

If your audience is...	...then publish it by...
Students or adults at school	• Placing a copy on the bulletin board in your school's library • Making a multimedia presentation, such as a podcast, that includes graphics, images, and sound, and uploading it to your school's Web site
People in your neighborhood or city	• Applying to read it on a local radio station • Submitting it to a local television station

Extend Your Research

Think more about the topic on which you wrote your editorial. What else would you like to know about this topic?

- Brainstorm for several questions you would like to research and then consult, or discuss, with others. Then decide which question is your major research question.
- Formulate, or develop, a plan about how you will answer these questions. Decide where you will find more information—on the Internet, at the library, or through other sources.
- Finally, learn more about your topic by following through with your research plan.

THE BIG QUESTION

The Big Question: Why Write? What is your point of view? How will you know if you've convinced others?

21st Century Learning

MAKE YOUR WRITING COUNT

Use an Editorial to Spark Debate

An editorial allows a writer to promote one side of a current controversy. By expressing opinions in newspapers or online editorials, editorial writers invite others to respond. Help your classmates understand both sides of a controversy affecting your school or community.

With a group, analyze and evaluate alternative points of view on an important school or community issue you have written about and then organize and present your ideas and information in a **debate**. Present your debate for the class, or record it as a podcast.

Here's your action plan.

1. Research team-debate formats online. Decide on a format for your debate. Keep in mind that you will need two teams, pro and con.
2. With your group, select an issue from your peers' editorials. Then choose sides, pro or con.
3. Within your team, identify points on your side. Gather convincing evidence, using the editorial as a main source. Consider points the other team will raise.
4. Write key points on notecards or in a slideshow you can consult while debating.
5. As a group, plan your debate. Each team should be able to:
   - State a clear opinion
   - Present points logically
   - Offer supporting evidence, and be ready to rebut the other team's objections
6. Debate your issue in front of the class, or video-record the debate for a podcast or posting online.

Listening and Speaking With your group, rehearse the debate. Listeners should provide feedback about the use of clear reasoning and persuasive speaking techniques. During the actual debate, work as a team to be nimble, adjusting your argument, tone, delivery, and vocabulary as needed to convince your audience to support your side.

WRITING COACH

Online

www.phwritingcoach.com

Online Journal

Extend Your Research **Record your answers and ideas in the online journal.**

Resource

Link to resources on 21st Century Learning for help in creating a group project.

Your Turn **Writing for Media: Product Packaging**

21st Century Learning

Product Packaging

Product packaging refers to the container for items sold to the public. The packaging must protect the product and be convenient for the consumer to use. In addition, the package should help persuade the targeted audience to buy the product, by using words and graphic elements, such as colors, lines, and pictures, to appeal to consumers.

Product packaging is a subtle form of persuasion intended to influence the actions of a specific audience, or the targeted consumer. When you understand how packaging helps sell products, you can make more informed decisions as a consumer.

Try It! Take a good look at the packaged product shown here. Pay attention to the way the packaging uses words and graphic elements. Then, answer the questions. Record your answers in your journal.

1. What **product** is shown here?
2. What impression does the packaging create of its product? Point out the **words** and **visual elements,** such as colors, shapes, pictures, photos, that create this impression.
3. Who seems to be the target **audience** for this product? How can you tell?
4. What seems to be the main **selling point** emphasized by the packaging? Identify details that communicate this selling point.

Extension Find another example of product packaging, and compare it with this one.

SUNNY START
ORANGE JUICE
Begin your day the right way!

Create Product Packaging

Follow these steps to write a plan describing the packaging for an existing or made-up product. Be sure to structure your ideas in a persuasive way.

Prewriting

- Identify an existing product or make up one of your own. Describe that product.
- Identify the target audience. Anticipate, or predict, the audience's needs, values, and tastes by considering what you know about them.
- State the main selling point that the packaging will emphasize.
- List various colors, shapes, and images likely to appeal to the target audience.

Drafting

- Describe the type of packaging to be used, for example, a small or large cardboard box, aluminum can, plastic bag, and so on.
- Explain the physical design of the packaging—the colors, shapes, and image(s) you will use and their placement on the packaging.
- Decide how the product's name will appear, including color, size, type style, and location.
- Write additional words to appear on the package, such as a short slogan or other positive phrases that will help influence consumers to buy the product.

Revising and Editing

Review your written plan for product packaging. Make sure that the words and graphic elements are persuasive, clear, and attractive. Eliminate anything that makes the packaging cluttered, creates a false or confusing impression, or detracts from the selling point.

Publishing

Based on your written description, create your product package. You may draw or paint it on an actual surface or use computer graphics to create a virtual image. You may also construct a three-dimensional model. Then present it to the class.

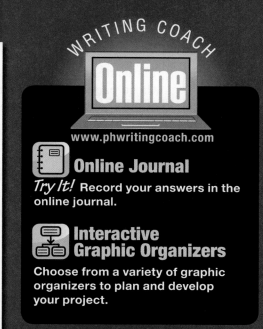

WRITING COACH Online

www.phwritingcoach.com

Online Journal

Try It! Record your answers in the online journal.

Interactive Graphic Organizers

Choose from a variety of graphic organizers to plan and develop your project.

Partner Talk

Before you start drafting your plan, describe your product packaging to a partner. Use specific details to describe and explain your ideas. Increase the specificity of your details based on the type of information you are delivering. Ask for feedback about your plan.

Writing for Assessment

SAT®/PSAT PREP ACT

Many standardized tests include writing prompts. Use the prompts on these pages to practice responding to persuasive prompts. Your response should include the same characteristics as your editorial. (See page 172.)

Try It! Read the prompt and the information on format and academic vocabulary. Then write an **argumentative essay** using the ABCDs of On-Demand Writing.

Format

The prompt asks you to write an *argumentative essay.* Be sure to include an introduction, body paragraphs with evidence supporting your position, and a strong conclusion.

Persuasive Prompt

Some people today believe that watching violent television shows can harm children. What do you think? Write an argumentative essay to persuade others that watching such shows does or does not affect children. Support your opinion with evidence.

Academic Vocabulary

Remember that an *opinion* is a personal belief about something. An opinion cannot be proven, but it can be supported with valid *evidence.* Evidence is valid when it is gathered from trustworthy sources.

The ABCDs of On-Demand Writing

Use the following ABCDs to help you respond to the prompt.

Before you write your draft:

Attack the prompt [1 MINUTE]

- Circle or highlight important verbs in the prompt. Draw a line from the verb to what it refers to.
- Rewrite the prompt in your own words.

Brainstorm possible answers [4 MINUTES]

- Create a graphic organizer to generate ideas.
- Use one for each part of the prompt if necessary.

Choose the order of your response [1 MINUTE]

- Think about the best way to organize your ideas.
- Number your ideas in the order you will write about them. Cross out ideas you will not be using.

After you write your draft:

Detect errors before turning in the draft [1 MINUTE]

- Carefully reread your writing.
- Make sure that your response makes sense and is complete.
- Look for spelling, punctuation, and grammar errors.

More Prompts for Practice

SAT®/PSAT PREP ACT

Apply It! Respond to Prompt 1 by writing an **argumentative essay** meant to **influence the attitudes and actions of specific audiences on a specific issue.** As you write, be sure to:

- Identify your purpose and an appropriate audience
- Establish **a clear thesis** or position based on logical reasons
- Support your persuasive arguments with **precise and relevant evidence,** and analyze the **relative value** of your data, facts, and ideas
- **Anticipate and address the objections** of others with **counter-arguments**
- Create a **persuasive organizing structure** appropriate to your purpose, audience, and context
- **Consider the whole range of information and views on the topic,** including views different from your own, and **give an accurate and honest representation of them**

Prompt 1 You may know people who are looking forward to getting their driver's licenses. Consider your opinion about the current legal driving age in your state. Then write an argumentative essay to persuade others to either raise or lower the age at which people can get their first driver's license.

Spiral Review: Expository Respond to Prompt 2 by writing a problem-solution **analytical essay**. Make sure your essay reflects all the characteristics described on page 146, including:

- Effective **introductory** and **concluding paragraphs**
- A variety of **sentence structures, rhetorical devices,** and **transitions** between paragraphs
- A controlling idea or **thesis** in an essay of sufficient length to develop it effectively
- **An organizing structure** appropriate to purpose, audience, and context
- **Relevant information** and **valid inferences**

Prompt 2 Think about your school, and any problems there that might need to be fixed. For example, perhaps the cafeteria doesn't offer enough healthy food options, or perhaps the amount of time in between classes isn't enough to make it to your next class. Write a problem-solution essay about a problem in your school, offering possible solutions to fix it.

WRITING COACH Online

www.phwritingcoach.com

Interactive Writing Coach™

Plan your response to the prompt. If you are using the prompt for practice, write one paragraph at a time or your entire draft and then submit it for feedback. If you are using the prompt as a timed test, write your entire draft and then submit it for feedback.

Remember ABCD

- **Attack the prompt**
- **Brainstorm possible answers**
- **Choose the order of your response**
- **Detect errors before turning in the draft**

RESPONSE *to* LITERATURE

What Do You Think?

Authors have purposes for writing. Some authors write to inform. Some write to entertain. Others write to persuade.

Part of being an active reader is analyzing the author's purpose. You think about the author's purpose and use details to show how the author achieves that purpose.

Try It! Think about your favorite book. What do you think the author was trying to achieve by writing this book? Take notes as you consider these questions. Then participate in an extended discussion with a partner. Take turns expressing your ideas and feelings.

- How did you feel when reading this book?
- How did the author achieve his or her purpose?
- Do you think the author did a good job achieving his or her purpose? Why or why not?

What's Ahead

In this chapter, you will review two strong examples of an interpretative response essay: a Mentor Text and a Student Model. Then, using the examples as guides, you will write an interpretative response essay of your own.

WRITING COACH Online

www.phwritingcoach.com

Online Journal

Try It! Record your answers and ideas in the online journal.

You can also record and save your answers and ideas on pop-up sticky notes in the eText.

Connect to the Big Questions

Discuss these questions with your partner:

1 **What do you think?** What can we learn from others' reactions?

2 **Why write?** What should you write about to make others interested in a text?

INTERPRETATIVE RESPONSE

An interpretative response is a kind of writing in which you take a close look at an author's work and explain and support your reactions to it. You share your thoughts and feelings about what you have read and discuss what the work communicated to you. In this chapter, you will explore one kind of interpretative response, a letter to an author.

You will develop your letter to the author by taking it through each of the steps of the writing process: prewriting, drafting, revising, editing, and publishing. You will also have an opportunity to write an interpretative blog entry. To preview the criteria for how your letter to an author will be evaluated, see the rubric on page 215.

FEATURE ASSIGNMENT

Interpretative Response: Letter to an Author

An effective interpretative response has these characteristics:

- A **clear thesis statement** that expresses the main idea of the writer's response to the author's work
- A careful study of what the work means, so that the response **goes beyond a summary and literal analysis** of what happens to explain why it happens
- **Valid inferences,** or interpretations about what the work means, and **examples** from the text to explain the inferences
- **Relevant evidence** from the author's work, including quotations and examples that support the writer's opinions
- Analysis of the **aesthetic effects,** or beautiful or pleasing result of the author's use of **stylistic or rhetorical devices** to discuss how the writer's style affected the work
- **Effective sentence structure** and correct spelling, grammar, and usage

A letter to an author also includes:

- A greeting and closing
- Direct discussion with the author
- An introduction of the letter writer

Other Forms of Interpretative Response

In addition to a letter to an author, there are other forms of interpretative response, including:

Blog comments on an author's Web site share readers' ideas about an author's work. Readers express their opinions and give their interpretations of what an author's work means.

Comparison essays explore similarities and differences between two or more works of literature. For example, a comparison essay may compare how main characters in two different stories handle a similar problem.

Critical reviews evaluate books, plays, poetry, and other literary works. They appear in newspapers and magazines, on television and radio, and on the Internet. These kinds of interpretative works present the writer's opinions and support them with specific examples.

Response to literature essays analyze and interpret an author's work. These kinds of essays examine what an author states directly and indirectly and what those statements mean. Response to literature essays also evaluate how well an author has accomplished what he or she has set out to do.

Try It! For each audience and purpose described, choose a form, such as a critical review or a comparison essay, that is appropriate for conveying your intended meaning to the audience. Discuss your ideas with a partner. Explain your choices.

- To convince readers that a book is worth reading
- To demonstrate to a teacher how two plays are alike
- To explain to your classmates that a seemingly simple story has a deeper meaning

WRITING COACH Online

www.phwritingcoach.com

Resource

Word Bank **Listen to English and Spanish pronunciations of new words in the eText glossary.**

Online Journal

Try It! **Record your answers and ideas in the online journal.**

WORD BANK

A root word is the most basic part of a word, for example *press*. An affix is a word part that is added to the beginning of a word, as a prefix, for example *impress*, or at the end of a word, as a suffix, for example *pressure*. Prefixes and suffixes change the meaning of the root word in some way.

People often use these vocabulary words when they talk about response to literature writing. Work with a partner. Take turns using each word in a sentence. If you are unsure of the meaning of a word, use the Glossary or a dictionary to check the definition.

analysis	**interpret**
demonstrate	**quotation**
infer	**style**

MENTOR TEXT

Response to Literature Essay

Learn From Experience

Read the response to literature essay on pages 200–201. As you read, take notes to develop your understanding of basic sight and English vocabulary. Then, read the numbered notes in the margins to learn about how the author presented her ideas. Later, you will read a Student Model, which shares these characteristics and also has the characteristics of a letter to an author.

Answer the *Try It!* questions online or in your notebook.

---

1 The **introduction** includes **quotations** from an interview with Toni Cade Bambara.

Try It! How do the quotations help create interest in reading more?

2 The **thesis statement captures the main idea** of the interpretative response.

Try It! What does the reviewer think are Bambara's greatest accomplishments? Put them in your own words.

3 The interpretative response goes **beyond summarizing or literal analysis** to make a more complex **analysis** of the grandmother's character.

Try It! What does Granny's paperweight suggest about her?

Extension Find another example of a critical review, and compare it with this one.

From Overview of "Blues Ain't No Mockin Bird"

by Theresa M. Girard

1 The short story, as a literary form, is unique in that it "does what it does in a hurry," as Toni Cade Bambara said in an interview with Beverly Guy-Sheftall, in 1979. Bambara also commented that "it's quick, it makes a modest appeal for attention, it can creep up on you on your blind side." Those are a few of the reasons that Bambara prefers to write short stories as well as read them. The short story "Blues Ain't No Mockin Bird" was written in 1971 and, as Bambara says, manages to take you by surprise and blindside you. Toni Cade Bambara accomplishes many things in focusing on short stories in her writing. 2 She is able to, among other things, tell stories of experience which hold interest; teach the young and/or ill-informed about the pride of a people; and, carry on the story-telling oral tradition of blacks, while transposing it into the written form. Above all, she spins a story in "Blues Ain't No Mockin Bird" which seems to be lifted right out of someone's life.

* * *

3 The action centers around the grandmother of the narrator and how she interacts with a variety of people, some of whom are characters in the story and some whom are only referred to as past experiences. Initial introductions to Granny, by the narrator, reveal a complex woman. She owns and likes nice things. As the children crack the ice in the puddle, the narrator (whose name is never known), lets us know that it resembles the crystal paperweight Granny has in her parlor. That the paperweight is crystal is significant, as is merely having something as frivolous as a paperweight.

The other important bit of information revealed about Granny is that she has moved a great deal: from the Judson's woods, to the Cooper place, at the dairy, to where they are now residing. . . . Reasons for Granny's moves need to be explained to the children and this also accomplishes the informing of the reader. Granny was a proud woman who did not like to have her privacy intruded upon by well-intentioned, ill-mannered, pompous people. Bambara expresses her familial background on this issue, in an interview with Beverly Guy-Sheftall. She states, simply, "people of my household were big on privacy." So, when the two men begin to film Granny's yard without her permission, Granny becomes quite upset.

. . . ❹ After a few exchanges which finally force the men to realize that they had made several errors in manners and decorum, Granny lets them know, in no uncertain terms, that she does mind if they shoot their film at her home. She also gathers her pride and dignity when they condescendingly call her "aunty." She responds quietly but firmly with, "Your mama and I are not related." With that, the men begin to understand that they cannot take advantage of this woman.

* * *

The film men make one further major error. They encounter Granny's husband and think that they will be able to circumvent Granny's objections by appealing to her tall, silent, kingly husband. Once again they assume incorrectly. Granny merely states in a low, moaning voice, "Get them persons out of my flower bed, Mister Cain" and Granddaddy Cain puts out his hand to the camera man and says, "Good day, gentlemen." The man hands Granddaddy his camera, and after destroying the film, Grandaddy hands it back to the man after the man politely asks for his camera back while adding, "Please, sir." The men learn a valuable lesson.

❺ Bambara does not waste an opportunity to instruct her characters or her readers. She tells stories to that end and embedded in her written stories are the oral stories. She gives clues to indicate features, but encourages the readers to figure it out on their own. By duplicating the story telling within the story, she raises the value of oral tradition and its place in the culture of the black community is secure.

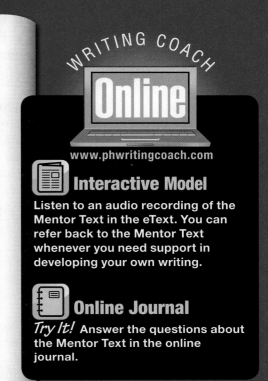

WRITING COACH

Online

www.phwritingcoach.com

Interactive Model

Listen to an audio recording of the Mentor Text in the eText. You can refer back to the Mentor Text whenever you need support in developing your own writing.

Online Journal

Try It! Answer the questions about the Mentor Text in the online journal.

❹ The response includes **relevant evidence** from the story, including a **quotation.**

Try It! How does the evidence in this paragraph support the thesis of the interpretative response?

❺ The **conclusion** brings readers full circle, back to the thesis.

Try It! How does the conclusion support the thesis?

STUDENT MODEL Letter to an Author

With a small group, take turns reading this Student Model aloud. As you read, practice newly acquired vocabulary by correctly producing the word's sound. Ask yourself what key points the writer presents and whether she has expressed them clearly. Look for evidence in the text that supports your conclusions.

Use a Reader's Eye

Now, reread the Student Model. On your copy of the Student Model, use the Reader's Response Symbols to react to what you read.

Reader's Response Symbols

- **+ I agree with this point.**
- **– This isn't clear to me.**
- **? I have a question about this.**
- **! Well said!**

Partner Talk

Participate in an extended discussion with a partner. Express your opinions and share your responses to the Student Model. Focus on parts of it that you felt were very well written. Why do you feel those parts were well written? Use details to explain your ideas.

O. Henry's "The Gift of the Magi"

Dear Mr. O. Henry:

Your story "The Gift of the Magi" held my attention from the first word to the last. Your tale of two people so in love that they give up their most prized possessions to buy each other presents shows that love is life's greatest gift.

I was caught up in your story from the very start. I felt sorry for poor Della, who wants so much to buy her husband a Christmas gift but just doesn't have enough money. When you say that "life is made up of sobs, sniffles, and smiles, with sniffles predominating," you perfectly express how Della feels.

When I realized that Della was about to sell her long, shining hair to get money for a present, I admired her. At the same time, I wondered if I could have done what she did. Clearly, her love for Jim was strong enough to make it possible for her to do something totally unselfish. As Della later tells Jim, "Maybe the hairs of my head were numbered . . . but nobody could ever count my love for you."

By buying Jim a fob chain for his pocket watch, Della puts Jim's happiness before her own. She does not want to cut and sell her hair, but buying Jim the special gift is much more important to her than her hair. Buying the gift expresses her love for Jim.

The beauty—and irony—of your story lies in what happens next. Jim comes home with the present he knew Della so badly wanted: combs for her hair. To purchase the gift, Jim, too, had to make a sacrifice: he sold the gold watch that had been handed down to him by his father and grandfather.

1

In the end, the fact that Della and Jim cannot immediately use their gifts doesn't matter. As you write at the end of the story, "let it be said that of all who give gifts these two were the wisest." I agree. It's clear that their love for each other is the most important gift of all. It is a gift much more precious than material possessions, and Della and Jim realize it.

I really appreciate the story you wrote. It is one of my favorite stories ever.

Sincerely,

Luisa Gomez

2

WRITING COACH Online

www.phwritingcoach.com

Interactive Model

Listen to an audio recording of the Student Model in the eText. Use the Reader's and Writer's Response Symbols with the eText tools to note what you read.

Use a Writer's Eye

Now evaluate the piece as a writer. On your copy of the Student Model, use the Writer's Response Symbols to react to what you read. Identify places where the student writer uses characteristics of an effective letter to an author.

Writer's Response Symbols	
C.T.	Clearly stated thesis
I.A	In-depth analysis
S.E.	Effective supporting evidence
E.Q.	Effective quotations

Your Turn

Feature Assignment: Letter to an Author

Prewriting

Plan a first draft of your letter to an author **by determining an appropriate topic.** You can select from the Topic Bank or come up with an idea of your own.

Choose From the Topic Bank

TOPIC BANK

Reaction to an Author's Work Write a letter to an author explaining your reaction to his or her book, play, or story. In your letter, use specific evidence from the work of literature to support your opinion. Include questions that your own analysis has left you unable to answer.

Response to a Plot Choose a piece of writing that had a memorable plot. Write a letter to the author in which you describe your reaction to the plot and explain why you thought the plot was especially effective or memorable.

Response to a Mentor Text Read "Homelanding" by Margaret Atwood on page 94. Write a letter to the author in which you describe your reaction to the narrator and the point of view from which the story was written.

Choose Your Own Topic

Determine an appropriate topic on your own by using the following **range of strategies** to generate ideas.

Discussion and Personal Interests

- Discuss an author's work with classmates. Take notes about classmates' ideas and reactions.
- Think about your favorite work by an author. Identify reasons why this work has special meaning for you.

Review your responses and choose a topic.

Narrow Your Topic

Choosing a topic that is too broad results in writing that is too general and unfocused.

Apply It! Use a graphic organizer like the one shown to narrow your topic.

- Write your general topic in the top box, and keep narrowing your topic as you move down the chart.
- Your last box should hold your narrowest or "smallest" topic, the new focus of your letter to the author.

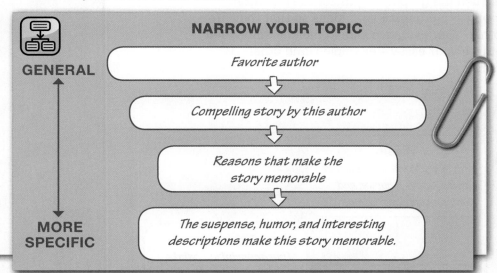

NARROW YOUR TOPIC

GENERAL

Favorite author

↓

Compelling story by this author

↓

Reasons that make the story memorable

↓

The suspense, humor, and interesting descriptions make this story memorable.

MORE SPECIFIC

Consider Multiple Audiences and Purposes

Before writing, think about your audiences and purposes. Consider how your letter can convey the intended meaning to multiple audiences—the author, but also classmates, your teacher, and other possible readers. Ask yourself what your audiences need and want to know about your topic.

Questions for Audience	Questions for Purpose
• Who will read my letter: My teacher? Classmates? The author? All of them? • What will readers need to know to understand my reaction to the work?	• What do I want my readers to understand about the work? • What thoughts and feelings do I want to convey in my letter? • What response do I hope to get from readers?

Record your answers in your writing journal.

WRITING COACH Online

www.phwritingcoach.com

Interactive Writing Coach™

- Choosing from the Topic Bank gives you access to the Interactive Writing Coach™.
- Submit your writing and receive instant personalized feedback and guidance as you draft, revise, and edit your writing.

Interactive Graphic Organizers

Use the interactive graphic organizers to help you narrow your topic.

Online Journal

Try It! Record your answers and ideas in the online journal.

Plan Your Piece

You will use the graphic organizer to state your thesis and organize your evidence. When it is complete, you will be ready to write your first draft.

Develop a Clear Thesis Think about your reaction to the author's work. Then state your thoughts in a **clear thesis or controlling idea.** Add your thesis statement to a graphic organizer like the one shown.

Logically Organize Your Supporting Evidence Fill in the graphic organizer to help you organize evidence from the author's work to support your response. Also use the graphic organizer to **structure your ideas in a sustained way**—to organize your ideas so that they are clear and build on one another. Your evidence should include embedded quotations—quotations set into your essay—examples, and other specific details from the work.

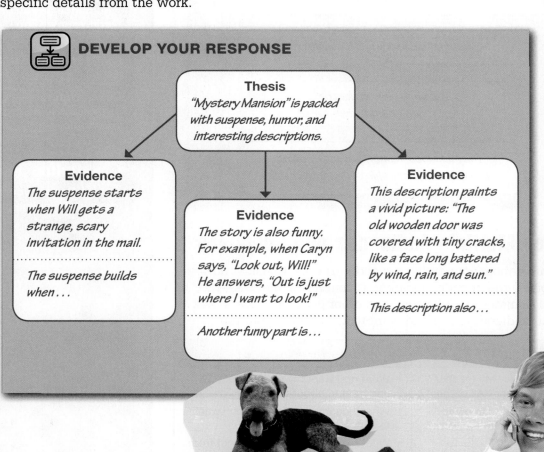

DEVELOP YOUR RESPONSE

Thesis
"Mystery Mansion" is packed with suspense, humor, and interesting descriptions.

Evidence
The suspense starts when Will gets a strange, scary invitation in the mail.

The suspense builds when . . .

Evidence
The story is also funny. For example, when Caryn says, "Look out, Will!" He answers, "Out is just where I want to look!"

Another funny part is . . .

Evidence
This description paints a vivid picture: "The old wooden door was covered with tiny cracks, like a face long battered by wind, rain, and sun."

This description also . . .

Gather Details

To support their opinions and organize their ideas, writers use various kinds of evidence. Look at these examples:

- **Embedded Quotations:** *"I'm too frightened to knock on the door!" Will whispered. "This place gives me the creeps!"*
- **Examples:** *A scary situation occurs when Will leans on a wall to catch his breath, and the wall swings open to reveal a hidden staircase.*
- **Descriptive Details:** *Covered in spider webs and a carpet of dust, "the old staircase smelled musty, like something that had never seen the sunlight."*
- **Personal Observations:** *What makes the story so original is that it is funny and scary at the same time.*
- **Relevant Information and Valid Inferences:** *First, Will gets a strange invitation to the mansion. Then, when he arrives at the mansion, strange things slowly begin to happen. Readers begin to expect that bad things will happen soon.*

Try It! Read the Student Model excerpt and identify the evidence that the author uses to support her first sentence.

STUDENT MODEL

from **O. Henry's "The Gift of the Magi"** page 202; lines 13–20

When I realized that Della was about to sell her long, shining hair to get money for a present, I admired her. At the same time, I wondered if I could have done what she did. Clearly, her love for Jim was strong enough to make it possible for her to do something totally unselfish. As Della later tells Jim, "Maybe the hairs of my head were numbered . . . but nobody could ever count my love for you."

Apply It! Review the types of supporting evidence that can be used in an analytical essay or a letter to an author. Then identify and write one piece of relevant evidence of each type.

- Review your evidence to make certain it supports your response. Remember to include one or more pieces of evidence of each kind.
- Add your supporting evidence to your graphic organizer in order to logically organize your ideas. Choose **quotations** from the text to embed, and consider how your evidence can be used to **address the writing skills of an analytical essay.** (See page 146.)
- Be sure to explain how your evidence supports your ideas to show that the **inferences** and conclusions you have drawn are **valid,** or accurate.

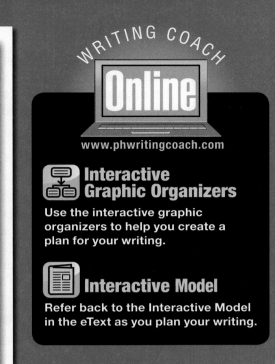

WRITING COACH **Online**

www.phwritingcoach.com

Interactive Graphic Organizers

Use the interactive graphic organizers to help you create a plan for your writing.

Interactive Model

Refer back to the Interactive Model in the eText as you plan your writing.

Drafting

During the drafting stage, you will start to write your ideas for your letter to an author. You will follow an outline that provides an organizational strategy that will help you write a focused, organized, and coherent letter to an author.

The Organization of an Interpretative Response

The chart shows an organizational strategy for an interpretative response. Look back at how the Mentor Text follows this organizational strategy. Then, use this chart to help you outline your draft. Notice that this outline includes the same type of guidelines as one for an analytical essay might—that's because an interpretative response requires much of the same type of writing.

Outline for Success

I. Introduction

See Mentor Text, p. 200.

- Interesting opening statements
- Name of work and author
- Clear thesis

II. Body

See Mentor Text, pp. 200–201.

- In-depth analysis and interpretation
- Relevant, logically organized evidence
- Consideration of the author's writing style

III. Conclusion

See Mentor Text, p. 201.

- Restatement of thesis, or main points
- Explanation of the significance of those points

Grab Your Reader

- Interesting openings often have a strong statement, ask a question, or refer to a character or event in the work.
- The name of the work being discussed and its author should always be included in the introduction.
- A clear thesis statement expresses the main idea of your response.

Develop Your Ideas

- The ideas that support your thesis should appear in the body.
- Each idea should be supported by relevant, or related evidence from the text.
- Sentences and paragraphs should be ordered so that they flow logically.
- A careful study of the artistic effects of the author's style tells how the author's writing choices affected the way you viewed and understood the story.

Wrap It Up

- The thesis should be briefly restated in slightly different language.
- An explanation of the significance of the main points leaves readers with a clear understanding of your feelings and ideas. This explanation can include what you learned by reading the author's work.

Start Your Draft

Use this checklist to help you complete your draft. Refer to the graphic organizer that shows your thesis, analysis and interpretation of the work, supporting evidence, and analysis of aesthetics, or author's style. You can also use the Outline for Success as a guide.

While drafting, aim at writing your ideas, not on making your writing perfect. Remember, you will have the chance to improve your draft when you revise and edit.

- √ Begin with a **salutation,** or greeting to the author.
- √ Identify the work you're discussing in your **introduction**.
- √ Present your thesis statement.

- √ Use the **body** of your letter to develop your ideas. Organize your paragraphs and structure your ideas in a clear and logical way.
- √ Go **beyond a summary and literal analysis** of the author's work by adding your analysis and interpretation of the selection.
- √ Support your ideas with evidence from the text, including **embedded quotations** that prove your points.
- √ Note the author's use of **stylistic and rhetorical devices,** such as rhetorical questions and analogies, and analyze their aesthetic, or artistic, effects. By noting the author's use of language, you will clearly describe how the writer's choices affected the text.
- √ Use the **writing skills** you would use in an analytical essay and formal language to support your points. (See page 146.)
- √ Include **rhetorical devices** in your letter to convey meaning to your audience. For example, you might set up an analogy that compares an element in the work with something that happened in your own life, or you might ask a rhetorical question.

- √ In your **conclusion**, restate or paraphrase your thesis. End with a memorable final statement that clearly expresses your ideas.
- √ End your letter with a **closing,** such as "Sincerely," and sign your name.

WRITING COACH **Online**

www.phwritingcoach.com

Interactive Model

Outline for Success **View pop-ups of Mentor Text selections referenced in the Outline for Success.**

Interactive Writing Coach™

Use the Interactive Writing Coach to receive the level of support you need:

- **Write one paragraph at a time and submit each one for immediate, detailed feedback.**
- **Write your entire first draft and submit it for immediate, personalized feedback.**

Revising: Making It Better

Now that you have finished your first draft, you are ready to revise. Think about the "big picture" of audience, purpose, and genre. You can use your Revision RADaR as a guide for making changes to improve your draft. Revision RADaR provides four major ways to improve your writing: (R) replace, (A) add, (D) delete, and (R) reorder.

Kelly Gallagher, M. Ed.

KEEP REVISION ON YOUR RADaR

Read part of the first draft of the Student Model "O. Henry's 'The Gift of the Magi.'" Then look at questions the writer asked herself as she thought about how well her draft **addressed issues of audience, purpose, and genre.**

1ST DRAFT

O. Henry's "The Gift of the Magi"

Your story "The Gift of the Magi" is really interesting. The relationship between Della and Jim made me think about life and other things.

*Does the introduction grab my reader's attention? Does my **thesis statement** clearly express the main idea of my response?*

I was caught up in your story from the very start. I felt sorry for poor Della, who wants so much to buy her husband a Christmas gift but just doesn't have enough money. Della and her husband are kind of poor, so they can't afford presents, which makes them feel bad. When you say that "life is made up of sobs, sniffles, and smiles, with sniffles predominating," you perfectly express how Della feels.

Have I included an analysis of the work that is more than just a summary or restatement?

When I realized that Della was about to sell her long, shining hair, I admired her. At the same time, I wondered if I could have done what she did. Clearly, her love for Jim was strong enough to make it possible for her to do something totally unselfish. In fact, later in the story, Della tells Jim that even though you could count the hairs on her head, you could never count her love for him.

Have I included relevant evidence to support my opinions?

Now look at how the writer applied Revision RADaR to write an improved second draft.

2ND DRAFT

O. Henry's "The Gift of the Magi"

Your story "The Gift of the Magi" held my attention from the first word to the last. Your tale of two people so in love that they give up their most prized possessions to buy each other presents shows that love is life's greatest gift.

A *Added specific information so that the opening is more interesting and the thesis statement more clearly expresses my main idea*

I was caught up in your story from the very start. I felt sorry for poor Della, who wants so much to buy her husband a Christmas gift but just doesn't have enough money. Not being able to buy a present makes her sad. When you say that "life is made up of sobs, sniffles, and smiles, with sniffles predominating," you perfectly express how Della feels.

D ***Deleted** unnecessary repetition to make room for a specific statement that goes beyond summarizing*

When I realized that Della was about to sell her long, shining hair, I admired her. At the same time, I wondered if I could have done what she did. Clearly, her love for Jim was strong enough to make it possible for her to do something totally unselfish. As Della later tells Jim, "Maybe the hairs of my head were numbered . . . but nobody could ever count my love for you."

R *Replaced general language with a quotation from the text to provide stronger supporting evidence*

WRITING COACH **Online**

www.phwritingcoach.com

Interactive Writing Coach™

Use the Revision RADaR strategy in your own writing. Then submit your paragraph or draft for feedback.

Apply It! Use your Revision RADaR to revise your draft.

- First, determine how well you have addressed the needs of your audience, made clear your purpose for writing, and included the characteristics of the interpretative response genre.
- Then, apply your Revision RADaR to make needed changes. Remember—you can use the steps in Revision RADaR in any order.

Look at the Big Picture

Use the chart and your analytical skills to evaluate how well each section of your letter to an author addresses **purpose, audience, and genre.** When necessary, use the suggestions in the chart to revise your letter.

Section	Evaluate	Revise
Introduction	• Check the **opening**. It should grab readers' attention and make them want to read on.	• Make your opening more interesting by writing a strong first sentence or asking a question.
	• Make sure the **thesis** clearly expresses the main idea of your response.	• Reread your letter, keeping your thesis in mind. Did you make points that are not covered in the thesis? If so, rewrite your thesis so that it covers all of your main points.
Body	• Check that you have presented ideas to support your **thesis.**	• Add ideas as needed to support the main idea of your response.
	• Make sure that you have supported each idea with relevant **evidence** from the text, including embedded **quotations.**	• Skim the story to find additional related examples and quotations, and insert them as necessary to help your reader understand your ideas.
	• Make sure your analysis goes beyond summarizing and literal **analysis**.	• Don't just tell what happens; also tell why it happens or what it means, suggests, or reveals.
	• Check that you have **logically ordered** sentences and paragraphs and structured your ideas in a sustained way.	• Reorder text as needed to improve flow. Move or combine sentences and paragraphs so that your ideas build on one another, are connected, and flow logically.
	• Make sure you have analyzed the **aesthetic effects** of the author's use of stylistic or rhetorical devices.	• Identify some use of language that you think the author did especially well. Then tell how that technique makes the work enjoyable.
	• Check that you have written in a formal style, addressing **writing skills** for an analytical essay.	• Identify places when you inferred what something means. Did you include relevant information from the work to prove that your inferences are valid? If not, add an example or quotation to accurately support your ideas.
Conclusion	• Check the **restatement** of your thesis.	• If necessary, discuss your restatement with a classmate and ask for suggestions.
	• Check that your **conclusion** leaves readers with a clear understanding of your ideas.	• Add a final statement that sums up how you feel about the work or why it is meaningful to you.

Focus on Craft: Word Choice

When responding to literature, making precise **word choices** is an important step. Precise words ensure you are accurately reflecting your purpose, your audience, and your attitude toward the literary work. Compare, for example, the vague and precise words in these word pairs: *happy/ecstatic, fast/abruptly, slowly/cautiously.*

Think about word choice as you read the following example from the Student Model.

STUDENT MODEL from **O. Henry's "The Gift of the Magi"** page 202; lines 27–31

Jim comes home with the present he knew Della so badly wanted: combs for her hair. To purchase the gift, Jim, too, had to make a sacrifice: he sold the gold watch that had been handed down to him by his father and grandfather.

Try It! Now, ask yourself these questions:

- How does this version of the second sentence differ from the example? *To buy the gift, Jim had to give up something: he sold his gold watch that had been in his family.*
- Which version is more interesting to read? Explain why.

Fine-Tune Your Draft

Apply It! Use the revision suggestions to prepare your final draft **after rethinking how well questions of purpose, audience, and genre have been addressed.**

- **Improve Word Choice** Use precise language in place of vague words. For example, replace *good* with *surprising, interesting,* or *dramatic.*
- **Vary Sentence Structure and Length** Avoid writing a letter of all short sentences. Add sentence variety by using simple, complex, and compound sentences within each paragraph.
- **Improve Style** Make changes to word choice, language use, and sentence patterns to better reflect your unique way of writing.
- **Use Transitions** If necessary, add transition words and phrases such as *although* and *finally* to convey meaning to readers.

Teacher Feedback Share your final draft in a conference with your teacher. Listen carefully, think about your teacher's feedback, and revise your final draft as needed.

WRITING COACH **Online**

www.phwritingcoach.com

Video

Learn more strategies for effective writing from program author Kelly Gallagher.

Online Journal

Try It! Record your answers in the online journal.

Interactive Model

Refer back to the Interactive Model as you revise your writing.

Interactive Writing Coach™

Revise your draft and submit it for feedback.

Editing: Making It Correct

Use the editing process to polish your draft. When you edit, check spelling and fix mistakes in grammar and punctuation.

As you edit your work, think about the conventions of **capitalization** and your use of punctuation marks. Keep in mind that **quotation marks** may sometimes be used to indicate **sarcasm or irony.** Then edit your draft by correcting any factual errors and errors in **grammar, mechanics, and spelling.** Use a dictionary to check your spelling.

WRITE GUY *Jeff Anderson, M. Ed.*

WHAT DO YOU NOTICE?

Zoom in on Conventions Focus on conventions of capitalization as you zoom in on this passage from the Student Model.

STUDENT MODEL

from **O. Henry's "The Gift of the Magi"**
page 202; lines 1–10

Your story "The Gift of the Magi" held my attention from the first word to the last. Your tale of two people so in love that they give up their most prized possessions to buy each other presents shows that love is life's greatest gift.

I was caught up in your story from the very start. I felt sorry for poor Della, who wants so much to buy her husband a Christmas gift but just doesn't have enough money.

To learn more about conventions of capitalization, see Chapter 22 of your Grammar Handbook.

Now, ask yourself: *Which words in the text did the writer capitalize?*

Perhaps you said that the writer capitalized the beginnings of sentences and the names of particular things.

The first word of a sentence is always capitalized. Also, the pronoun I is always capitalized, whether or not it is the first word of a sentence.

The first word and key words in the titles of books, poems, stories, and other works of art are always capitalized. Prepositions and articles (*a, an, the*) are not capitalized unless they are the first or last word in a title or contain four or more letters.

Also, proper nouns—nouns that name a particular person, place, or thing—are capitalized. Proper nouns also include street names, mountain ranges, lakes, and monuments.

Partner Talk Discuss this question with a partner: *What purpose do capital letters serve in writing?*

Grammar Mini-Lesson: Quotation Marks

To learn more, see Chapter 23.

Quotation marks set off direct quotations, dialogue, and certain types of titles, such as short stories. Sometimes quotation marks are used to express **sarcasm or irony**. Irony is using words to express something other than their literal meaning. Sarcasm is a cutting or bitter remark that often uses ironic language. Notice how the writer uses quotation marks to set off dialogue in the Student Model.

STUDENT MODEL from O. Henry's "The Gift of the Magi"

page 202; lines 18–20

As Della later tells Jim, "Maybe the hairs of my head were numbered . . . but nobody could ever count my love for you."

Try It! Write these sentences in your journal. Then use quotation marks to set off quotations, titles, and a word or words meant to express sarcasm or irony. Capitalize words when necessary.

1. His so-called triumph was a poorly written short story called my first car.
2. The student walked in ten minutes after the bell. Mrs. williams thanked him for arriving early.

Apply It! **Edit your draft for grammar, mechanics, and spelling**. Be sure to follow the **conventions of capitalization**. Where appropriate, use quotation marks to indicate sarcasm or irony.

Use the rubric to evaluate your piece. If necessary, rethink, rewrite, or revise.

Rubric for Interpretative Response: Letter to an Author	Rating Scale
Ideas: How well does your response present a focused statement and analysis of the work?	Not very Very 1 2 3 4 5 6
Organization: How clearly organized is your analysis?	1 2 3 4 5 6
Voice: How well have you engaged the reader and sustained his or her interest?	1 2 3 4 5 6
Word Choice: How precisely do your word choices reflect your purpose?	1 2 3 4 5 6
Sentence Fluency: How well have you varied sentence structure and length?	1 2 3 4 5 6
Conventions: How correct is your use of punctuation, quotation marks, and capitalization?	1 2 3 4 5 6

WRITING COACH Online

www.phwritingcoach.com

Video

Learn effective editing techniques from program author Jeff Anderson.

Online Journal

Try It! Record your answers in the online journal.

Interactive Model

Refer back to the Interactive Model as you edit your writing.

Interactive Writing Coach™

Edit your draft. Check it against the rubric and then submit it for feedback.

Publishing

Share the feelings and thoughts expressed in your letter to an author—publish it! First, get your letter ready for presentation. Then, choose a way to publish it for appropriate audiences.

Wrap Up Your Presentation

Now that you have finished your draft, add the final details. Be sure to include page numbers on each page of your letter.

Publish Your Piece

Use the chart to identify a way to publish your letter to an author.

If your audience is...	...then publish it by...
A living author	• Mailing or e-mailing it to the author through his or her publishing company • Submitting it to the author's Web site
Students at school	• Reading it aloud in English class • Posting your piece online and inviting responses • Working with classmates to create a binder of letters, including images to make the anthology more attractive

Extend Your Research

Think more about the topic on which you wrote your letter to an author. What else would you like to know about this topic? Use specific details to describe and explain your ideas. Increase the specificity of your details based on the type of information.

- Brainstorm for several questions you would like to research and then consult, or discuss, with others. Then decide which question is your major research question.
- Formulate, or develop, a plan about how you will answer these questions. Decide where you will find more information—on the Internet, at the library, or through other sources.
- Finally, learn more about your topic by following through with your research plan.

The Big Question: Why Write? What should you write about to make others interested in a text?

21st Century Learning

MAKE YOUR WRITING COUNT

Review a Book for Television

Sending a letter to a book's author is one way that readers can respond to literature that is meaningful to them. Work with others to share your responses to literature in a **television report** for a wider audience.

With a group, plan a book-review program in the form of a **multimedia presentation** using text, graphics, images, and sound to convey a distinctive point of view. Use your author letters as a starting point, but keep your program's opinion-driven structure and purpose in mind as you develop a plan. When choosing elements to include in your presentation, consider your audience and what it will find appealing. Give your presentation live, or video-record it.

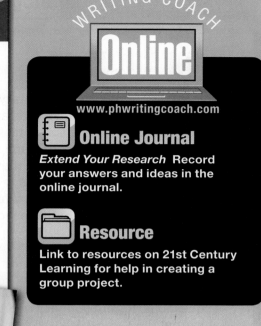

Here's your action plan.

1. Choose roles, such as director, artist, and up to four critics.
2. First, review your peers' letters to authors. Then, choose a piece of literature you think an audience of your classmates would enjoy.
3. Look online at movie or book review shows for inspiration.
4. Create a storyboard—a series of sketches representing the visual elements of each scene. Although your show will be unscripted, your storyboard should include the critic's discussion points. Also include sketches of or notes on the timing and placement of:
   - Graphics, such as the show's title
   - Images of the author and/or book cover
   - A final summing up, including the critic's overall recommendation
5. Using the storyboard as a guide, prepare your visuals, rehearse, and then present your live or recorded show to the class.

Listening and Speaking As a group, rehearse your presentation. While you practice, talk about how a speaker's persuasive purpose affects both the speaker's style and audience's response. After viewers provide feedback, critics should adjust their delivery. During the presentation, try to convince a specific audience to read the literature you review.

WRITING COACH Online

www.phwritingcoach.com

Online Journal

Extend Your Research **Record your answers and ideas in the online journal.**

Resource

Link to resources on 21st Century Learning for help in creating a group project.

Your Turn Writing for Media: Blog Entry

21st Century Learning

Blog Entry

A **blog entry** is a short commentary posted on a Web site. People write blogs about many things, such as a hobby or their ideas about a book or television show. Readers sometimes post blog entries on the Web sites of their favorite authors or on large online bookstore Web sites. Others have their own pages on which they write their blogs. In their blogs, readers can post their responses to literature, explaining what they like about an author's work and why. Blog entries may also include an in-depth analysis of the author's work.

Try It! Study the blog entry on this page. Then, answer the questions. Record your answers in your journal.

1. What **work** is the subject of this blog?
2. Who is the **author**?
3. What **elements** of the blog are meant to persuade readers to read the work?
4. What **evidence** that supports ideas does the blog include?
5. What does the blog say about the author's use of **stylistic devices**?
6. How does the blog cast the author in a positive light?
7. What is the **tone,** or the author's attitude toward her topic, of the blog? How does this tone help to "sell" the book?

Extension Find another example of a book review on a blog, and compare it with this one.

Username: LitGrrrl17

Posted: 9/27/11

Robert Steele's Novel *Midnight Madness*

Robert Steele's novels grab your attention on the first page and don't let go until the very end. I just finished reading his latest release, *Midnight Madness*, and I think it's his best yet. It's the story of two teenagers, Alexis and Matt, who get caught up with international spies. Steele's method of building tension by changing viewpoints adds to the suspense. For example, just when you think Alexis will be caught by the spies, Steele switches over to Matt's point of view. As the story unfolds, all the plot lines come together, and the reader is left breathlessly waiting to see how the story will end and who will survive.

Steele's characters are realistic, and his dialogue is often chilling. When the leader of the spy ring snarls that "no one will stop me, and nothing will stand in my way," you can almost feel the madness behind his words. This is definitely a book you won't want to put down.

Blogger Responses

Posted 9/29/11 by Read4Ever: I actually thought the way Steele changed viewpoints all the time was confusing! I had trouble following the story.

Posted 9/29/11 by RobertSteeleRocks: I totally agree with you, LitGrrrl17! I loved this book SO much!

Write a Blog Entry for an Author's Web Site

Follow these steps to create your own entry for an author's blog. To plan your entry, review the graphic organizers on R24–R27 and choose one that suits your needs.

Prewriting

- Choose a book that you have recently read and enjoyed. Determine whether the book is fiction or nonfiction. Then think about the kind of book it is, such as an adventure tale or a sports biography.
- Identify the audience for the book. Consider not only which readers are sure to like the book but also which readers *might* enjoy it. Then, think about how best to grab readers' attention. For example, you might begin with a question or start with an exciting excerpt.
- Plan ways to persuade readers to read the book. Consider what evidence, including embedded quotations, you might include.
- Write ideas to help you cast the author in a positive light. For example, has he or she won any awards? Think about what you might say about the author's style.

Drafting

- Begin with a strong opening statement to grab your readers' attention.
- Write a brief entry that makes the book sound appealing to your target audience. Include quotations and other relevant evidence to prove your points. Be sure to extend your comments to provide an in-depth analysis of the work by answering the questions *How*? and *Why*?
- Discuss the aesthetic, or artistic, effects of the author's unique style.

Revising and Editing

Review your draft to ensure that your ideas flow logically and that you have presented them in a persuasive way.

- Be sure that you have used a positive tone and done all you can to "sell" the book and the author.
- Check that spelling, grammar, and mechanics are correct.

Publishing

Find an appropriate site where you can post your entry, such as a school Web site, a bookstore site, or the author's site. Invite your classmates to read the entry. Check the site regularly to see when others have posted responses to your ideas.

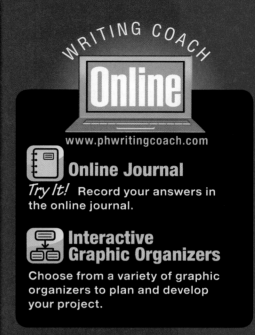

WRITING COACH Online

www.phwritingcoach.com

Online Journal

Try It! Record your answers in the online journal.

Interactive Graphic Organizers

Choose from a variety of graphic organizers to plan and develop your project.

Partner Talk

Before you start drafting, describe your planned blog entry to a partner, and ask for feedback. For example, you might ask whether your opening will grab readers' attention. Monitor your partner's spoken language by asking follow-up questions to confirm your understanding.

Writing for Assessment

You may see a prompt that asks you to write an essay in which you respond to, analyze, or interpret literature. You can use the prompts on these pages to practice. Your responses should include the same characteristics as your letter to an author. (See page 198.)

Try It! To begin, read the **interpretative** prompt and the information on format and academic vocabulary. Then use the ABCDs of On-Demand Writing to help you plan and write your essay.

Format
The prompt directs you to write a *critical review*. Include a clear thesis, or main idea, and supporting evidence.

Interpretative Prompt
Write an essay that is a critical review of a short story, book, or poem you have read. Analyze and evaluate the work. Support your analysis and evaluation with specific details, such as examples and quotations from the work. [30 minutes]

Academic Vocabulary
When you *evaluate* a story, book, or poem, you give and support your opinion about its strengths and weaknesses. Your *evaluation* of a work is your opinion or analysis.

The ABCDs of On-Demand Writing

Use the following ABCDs to help you respond to the prompt.

Before you write your draft:

A ttack the prompt [1 MINUTE]

- Circle or highlight important verbs in the prompt. Draw a line from the verb to what it refers to.
- Rewrite the prompt in your own words.

B rainstorm possible answers [4 MINUTES]

- Create a graphic organizer to generate ideas.
- Use one for each part of the prompt if necessary.

C hoose the order of your response [1 MINUTE]

- Think about the best way to organize your ideas.
- Number your ideas in the order you will write about them. Cross out ideas you will not be using.

After you write your draft:

D etect errors before turning in the draft [1 MINUTE]

- Carefully reread your writing.
- Make sure that your response makes sense and is complete.
- Look for spelling, punctuation, and grammar errors.

More Prompts for Practice

Apply It! Respond to Prompt 1 in open-ended or timed situations by writing an **interpretative response** that **interprets a literary or expository text.** As you write, be sure to:

- Express the main idea of your response in a clear **thesis** statement.
- Include ideas that provide analysis and insight and **extend beyond summary and literal analysis.**
- Include **supporting evidence** from the text, embedding quotations if possible.
- Look at the language in the selection to help you analyze the **aesthetic effects** of the author's use of stylistic or rhetorical devices.
- Address the **writing skills** for an analytical essay. (See page 146.)
- Clearly convey meaning by using **rhetorical devices,** such as repetition, and **transition words** such as *next* and *then*.

Prompt 1 Write an interpretative response comparing and contrasting two characters from two different books or short stories. Support your ideas and opinions with specific details and examples from the texts.

SAT®/PSAT PREP ACT

Spiral Review: Persuasive Respond to Prompt 2 by writing an **argumentative essay**. Make sure your argumentative essay reflects all of the characteristics described on page 172, including:

- A clear **thesis** or position based on logical reasons
- Precise and relevant **supporting evidence**
- **Consideration** of the whole range of information and views on the topic, and accurate and honest **representation** of these views
- **Counter-arguments** based on evidence to anticipate and address objections
- An **organizing structure** appropriate to the purpose, audience, and context
- An **analysis** of the relative value of specific data, facts, and ideas

Prompt 2 Write an essay persuading people to buy locally grown food. Include details to address others' views and to support your own.

WRITING COACH Online

www.phwritingcoach.com

Interactive Writing Coach™

Plan your response to the prompt. If you are using the prompt for practice, write one paragraph at a time or your entire draft and then submit it for feedback. If you are using the prompt as a timed test, write your entire draft and then submit it for feedback.

Remember **ABCD**

Attack the prompt

Brainstorm possible answers

Choose the order of your response

Detect errors before turning in the draft

CHAPTER 11

RESEARCH WRITING

What Do You Want To Know?

How do people find out more information about interesting topics? They do research to gather, organize, and present information.

One of the first steps of research writing is to identify a topic that interests you and then formulate open-ended research questions. Open-ended research questions ask what you want to find out about the topic. For example, if you want to find out more about the machine in the photograph, you would first decide what you want to know about it.

Try It! Take a few minutes to list some things you might want to know about this machine. Consider these questions as you participate in an extended discussion with a partner. Take turns expressing your ideas.

- What could I ask about the machine and the industry in which it is used?
- What could I ask about related careers?
- What could I ask about safety or innovation?
- What else might I want to learn about this?

Review your list of questions with a partner. Compare lists to determine which ideas overlap, or how you might build off each other's ideas. Then, discuss where you would go to research answers to your questions.

What's Ahead

In this chapter, you will review a strong example of an informational research report. Then, using the examples as guidance, you will develop your own research plan and write your own informational research report.

WRITING COACH Online

www.phwritingcoach.com

Online Journal

Try It! Record your answers and ideas in the online journal.

You can also record and save your answers and ideas on pop-up sticky notes in the eText.

Connect to the Big Questions

Discuss these questions with your partner:

1 What do you think? How does technology affect our lives?

2 Why write? Do you understand a subject well enough to write about it? How will you find at what the facts are?

RESEARCH WRITING

Research writing is a way to gather information from various sources, and then evaluate, organize, and synthesize that information into a report for others to read. In this chapter, you will write an informational research report that conveys what you have learned about a topic that interests you. Before you write, you will search for information about your topic in different kinds of sources. You will evaluate the information you find, choose the best facts and details for your report, and organize your ideas so that you can clearly communicate them to your audience.

You will develop your informational research report by taking it through each of the steps of the writing process: prewriting, drafting, revising, editing, and publishing. You will also have an opportunity to use your informational research report in an oral or multimedia presentation that uses photos, charts, graphs, and other visuals to share what you have learned. To preview the criteria for how your research report will be evaluated, see the rubric on page 247.

FEATURE ASSIGNMENT

Research Writing: Informational Research Report

An effective informational research report has these characteristics:

- A specific **thesis statement** that states the report's main ideas
- **Evidence,** such as facts and the opinions of experts, to support the thesis
- An **analysis** of the topic that is organized in a **logical progression,** or order, with a clearly stated **point of view**
- **Graphics** and **illustrations** that help explain important ideas when appropriate
- Proper **documentation of sources** to show where the author found information
- Correct **formatting,** or presentation, of written materials according to a style manual
- **Effective sentence structure** and correct spelling, grammar, and usage

Other Forms of Research Writing

In addition to an informational research report, there are other forms of research writing, including:

Annotated bibliographies list sources of information about a topic and provide a summary or evaluation of the main ideas in each source. Full publication information is given, including the title, author, date, and publisher of each source.

Biographical profiles give specific details about the life and work of a real person. The person may be living or dead, someone famous, or someone familiar to the writer.

Documentaries are filmed reports that focus on a specific topic or issue. These multimedia presentations use spoken and written text as well as photographs, videos, music, and other sound effects.

Health reports present the latest information, data, and research about a specific disease or health-related issue.

Historical reports give in-depth information about a past event or situation. These kinds of reports focus on a narrow topic and may discuss causes and effects.

Scientific reports analyze information and data concerning a current, past, or future scientific issue or problem. A **lab report** describes a scientific experiment, including observations and conclusions.

Try It! For each research report described, brainstorm for possible topics with others. Then, consult with others to decide on and write an open-ended research question for each topic. As you write, keep your audience and purpose in mind.

- A biographical profile of someone you admire
- A lab report about the results of a scientific experiment
- A documentary to raise money for a local cause

WRITING COACH Online

www.phwritingcoach.com

Resource

Word Bank Listen to English and Spanish pronunciations of new words in the eText glossary.

Online Journal

Try It! Record your answers and ideas in the online journal.

WORD BANK

People use these words when they talk about writing that reports information. Work with a partner. Take turns using each word in a sentence. If you are unsure of the meaning of a word, use the Glossary or a dictionary to check the definition.

cite	relevant
expert	research
quote	resource

STUDENT MODEL Informational Research Report

Use a Reader's Eye

Read the Student Model on pages 226–229. Then, use the symbols to react to what you've read.

Reader's Response Symbols

- √ **OK. I understand this. It's very clearly explained.**
- ? **I don't follow what the writer is saying here.**
- + **I think the writer needs more details here.**
- – **This information doesn't seem relevant.**
- ! **Wow! That is cool/weird/interesting.**

Learn From Experience

Read the numbered notes in the margins as you reread the Student Model to learn about how the writer presented her ideas.

Analyze, infer, or draw conclusions to answer the *Try It!* questions online or in your notebook.

❶ The report uses **proper formatting** and style for heads and pagination.

❷ The **thesis statement** of a research paper explains the idea or reason for the research and how it will be supported with evidence.

❸ This **analysis** of when solar eclipses occur is one type of **evidence** used to support the thesis.

Try It! Read the thesis statement in the report. What is the main idea? What supporting evidence do you expect to find? Make a list of your expectations.

❶ Kwang 1

❶ Soo Mee Kwang
Ms. S. R. Mansfield
Science, First Period
15 February 2010

❶ Solar Eclipses: Why They Occur and What They Teach Us

Imagine that it is a clear, sunny morning. Suddenly the sky starts to grow dark. The sun is disappearing bit by bit, and no one knows why. To anyone who does not understand this rare solar occurrence, a solar eclipse is a terrifying experience. Ancient people all over the world created myths to explain why the sun disappeared in this way. In ancient China, for example, people believed that a dragon was swallowing the sun. The ancient Norse people thought that Sköll, a huge wolf, was devouring their sun (Harrington 2). ❷ Modern scientists called astronomers have studied solar eclipses with a more analytical approach. Through careful scientific analyses, astronomers have taken the mystery out of solar eclipses by applying an understanding of how, when, where, and why they occur, as well as learning much about the sun itself in the process.

Everyone knows that our moon orbits Earth in 28 days and that Earth travels around the sun in a year—365 ¼ days. As it revolves around Earth, the moon goes through different phases. It changes from a thin crescent to a full moon and then decreases until it becomes a totally dark new moon. ❸ Solar eclipses occur only when the new moon lines up exactly with the sun and Earth, blocking our view of the sun. According to physicist Paul Doherty, solar eclipses don't happen every month because "the orbit of the moon is actually tilted a little bit so that most of the

Kwang 2

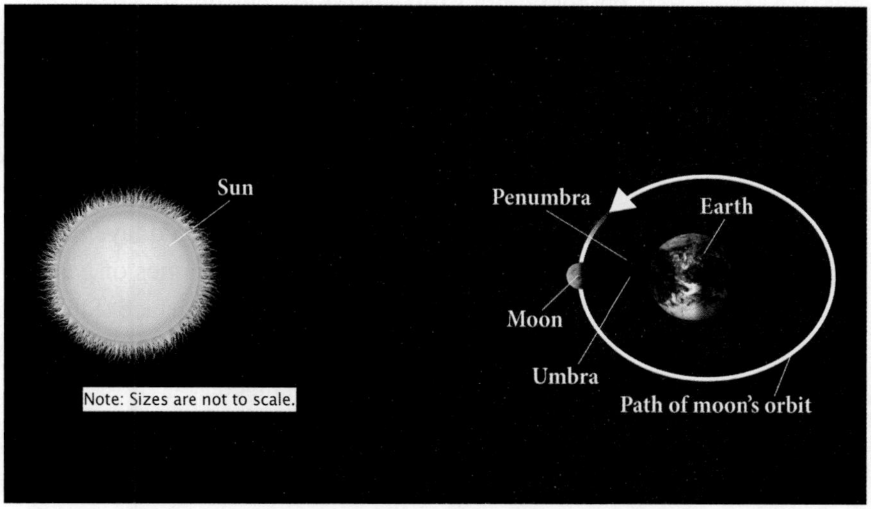

❹ Figure 1. Anatomy of a Solar Eclipse, adapted from Geoff Gaherty, "Darkness at Noon," *Starry Night Education,* Mar. 2006 (Edina, MN: Imaginova, 2006). Web. 7 Nov. 2010.

time the moon passes above the sun or below the sun" (*Eclipse Chasers*).

Maybe the easiest way to understand what happens during a solar eclipse is to study a graphic of it. Look at the diagram of a solar eclipse ❹ (see figure 1). Notice that the moon casts a cone-shaped shadow on Earth. The darkest part of that shadow, the umbra, is 60 to 100 miles wide and marks the *path of totality* ❺ (Steel 4).

On a clear day, viewers in the path of totality see a total solar eclipse, while viewers in the *penumbra* shadow see a partial eclipse. During a partial eclipse, the sun is partially, not totally, blocked.

❻ Scientists can predict solar eclipses with great accuracy. You can find an amazing interactive chart, the Javascript Solar Eclipse Explorer, on the NASA Eclipse Web site (Espenak and O'Byrne). Choose a city anywhere in the world. Then, choose a 100-year period anywhere from 2000 B.C.E. to the year 3000 C.E. That's 5,000 years! Hit a button, and you will get a list of every partial and total eclipse visible in that city during that century.

WRITING COACH Online

www.phwritingcoach.com

Interactive Model

Listen to an audio recording of the Student Model in the eText. You can refer back to the Student Model notes whenever you need support in developing your own writing. Use the Reader's and Writer's Response Symbols with the eText tools to note what you read.

Online Journal

Try It! Record your answers and ideas in the online journal.

❹ This **graphic** is relevant to the written explanation of what happens during a solar eclipse.

Try It! How does the diagram of an eclipse help clarify the written explanation?

❺ **Proper documentation** shows where the student writer found information. The name and page number in parentheses refer to a source on the Works Cited list.

❻ The report is written with a clear **point of view.**

Try It! Summarize lines 34–40. Determine what facts and opinions are presented. What conclusions can you draw about the writer's point of view of the interactive chart?

STUDENT MODEL Informational Research Report *(continued)*

(7) The paragraph first describes past methods of learning about the sun, then describes present methods. This is a **logical progression** of ideas.

Try It! Why is it helpful to readers to put events in the order in which they happened?

(8) Long **quotations** (4 lines or more) are set off and indented without quotation marks.

Try It! Why is it a good idea to set off long quotes so they are separate from the rest of the text?

(9) **Evidence** is provided to support the idea that solar eclipses help prove part of Einstein's General Theory of Relativity.

Try It! Do you think photographs are convincing proof? Explain.

(10) The Works Cited list provides proper **documentation** by listing publication information for each source used to write the report. The **formatting** of the list follows the MLA style manual.

Try It! Study the Works Cited list on page 229.

- Why is it helpful to readers to list sources in alphabetical order?
- Why might readers want to know what types of resources—print, Web, and so on—were used?

Extension Locate one of the sources from the Works Cited page, and write a brief synopsis of it in your own words.

Kwang 3

(7) In the past, astronomers learned about the sun by observing and photographing total eclipses. During an interview, Nancy Adams-Wolk, an IT Specialist/Scientist at Harvard-Smithsonian Center for Astrophysics, explains why: "We learned that the sun extends far past the visible surface." For example, during a total solar eclipse astronomers can see the sun's *corona*, a white crown of light that extends millions of miles into space. Beneath the corona is the *chromosphere*, a thin red-edged layer of gas. Total eclipses also reveal *prominence*s, huge plumes of gas that shoot as much as 100,000 miles from the sun's surface (Steel 436–437, 439). (7) For 21st century astronomers, the value of eclipses as a means for studying the sun has changed:

> (8) Today astronomers learn very little about the sun and moon during solar eclipses. Instead of waiting for eclipses to occur, we have space-based telescopes to observe the sun and moon up close (Adams-Wolk).

(9) Scientists even used photographs like the one shown (see figure 2) of total solar eclipses to prove part of Albert Einstein's General Theory of Relativity. In 1915 Einstein proposed that the pull of gravity of a huge object like the sun would bend light rays

Figure 2. The diamond ring effect appears just before totality of a solar eclipse; courtesy of NASA.

Kwang 4

coming from distant stars toward the sun. Photographs taken during a total solar eclipse in May 1919 proved that Einstein was right ("Einstein's General Theory").

Solar eclipses are one of our universe's strangest, most awesome sights. Don't miss a chance to see a nearby eclipse in person, but be sure to follow the safety precautions for viewing an eclipse. Looking directly at the sun during an eclipse can burn the retina, which will cause partial or even total blindness.

Anyone with access to the Internet can safely witness a total solar eclipse while viewing videos posted by eclipse watchers all over the world. There are eclipses of the moon, too. Do some online exploring to learn more about these strange, awe-inspiring—but no longer terrifying—solar and lunar eclipses.

---

10 Works Cited

Adams-Wolk, Nancy. Telephone interview. 10 Jan. 2010.

"Eclipse Chasers." KQED. 12 Nov. 2008 *QUEST.*

"Einstein's General Theory of Relativity" Celebrating the 20th Century's Most Important Experiment." *Science Daily.* Royal Astronomical Society. 2 June 2009. Web. 12 Jan. 2010.

Espenak, Fred and Chris O'Byrne. "Solar Eclipse Explorer." *NASA Eclipse Web Site.* GSFC Solar System Exploration Division. 17 Apr. 2007. Web. 16 Jan. 2010.

Harrington, Philip S. *Eclipse! The What, Where, When, Why, and How Guide to Watching Solar and Lunar Eclipses.* New York: Wiley, 1997. Print.

Steel, Duncan. *Eclipse.* Washington, DC: Joseph Henry Press, 2001. Print.

WRITING COACH Online

www.phwritingcoach.com

Interactive Model

Listen to an audio recording of the Student Model in the eText. You can refer back to the Student Model whenever you need support in developing your own writing. Use the Reader's and Writer's Response Symbols with the eText tools to note what you read.

Use a Writer's Eye

Now go back to the beginning of the Student Model and evaluate the piece as a writer. On your copy of the Student Model, use the Writer's Response Symbols to react to what you read. Identify places where the student writer uses characteristics of an effective informational research report.

Writer's Response Symbols

T.S.	Clear thesis statement
S.E.	Supporting evidence
R.G.	Relevant graphic
D.S.	Proper documentation of sources

Your Turn Feature Assignment: Informational Research Report

Prewriting

Begin to plan a first draft of your research report by determining an appropriate topic. You can select from the Topic Bank or come up with an idea of your own.

Choose From the Topic Bank

TOPIC BANK

Pandemic What is a pandemic? Research a pandemic of the recent past, such as polio, measles, or smallpox. How many people were affected? How did the pandemic end? As an alternative, find out what governments and health officials do to control pandemics today.

EcoIntruders What are the effects of introducing a non-indigenous species, such as the mongoose, the zebra mussel, or Andean pampas grass, into a U.S. ecosystem? Why and how was the species brought here? Did it serve its purpose? What problems has it caused?

Communicating in the 21st Century Cell phones, instant messaging, e-mail, and video conferencing are examples of communications technology in use today. How do these devices work, and who invented them? What are the best improvements to communicating today?

Choose Your Own Topic

Determine an appropriate topic of your own by using use the following **range of strategies** to generate ideas.

Brainstorm and Browse

- **Consult** with a partner to **brainstorm** for and decide upon a list of topics that interest you.
- **Formulate open-ended research questions** about your topics. Circle key words and phrases in your questions.
- Use your key words to browse your library's research resources. Note what sparks your curiosity and may make a good research topic. Search the Internet, using the same key words and phrases. Decide which topics provide results that interest you most.
- Review your work and choose a topic.

Formulate Your Research Question

A broad, general topic is almost impossible to research well and cover thoroughly. Plan to do some preliminary research in order to narrow your topic and then formulate your research question.

Apply It! Use an online or printed graphic organizer like the one shown to narrow your topic.

- Write your general topic in the top box, and keep narrowing your topic with research questions as you move down the chart.
- Your last box should hold your narrowest or "smallest" research question. This will be the focus of your informational research report.

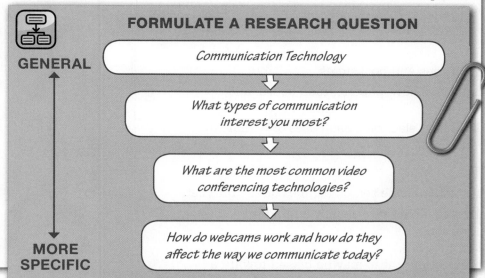

FORMULATE A RESEARCH QUESTION

GENERAL

Communication Technology

↓

What types of communication interest you most?

↓

What are the most common video conferencing technologies?

↓

How do webcams work and how do they affect the way we communicate today?

MORE SPECIFIC

Consider Multiple Audiences and Purposes

Before you start researching, think about your audiences and purposes. Then, think about the kinds of information you'll look for in order to meet your audiences' needs and your purpose.

Questions About Audiences	Questions About Purposes
• Who are my audiences: My teacher? My classmates? Someone else? • What do my audiences need and want to know about the topic for my research report? • What technical terms will I need to explain to my audiences?	• Why am I writing the report: To inform? To make my audiences want to learn more about the topic? • How do I want my audiences to react to my report as they read it? • What is my point of view, or attitude, toward my topic?

Record your answers in your writing journal.

WRITING COACH Online

www.phwritingcoach.com

Interactive Writing Coach™

- Choosing from the Topic Bank gives you access to the Interactive Writing Coach™.
- Submit your writing paragraph by paragraph and receive detailed feedback and guidance as you draft, revise, and edit your writing.

Interactive Graphic Organizers

Use the interactive graphic organizers to help you narrow your topic.

Online Journal

Try It! Record your answers and ideas in the online journal.

Make a Research Plan

Once you have written your major research question, you are ready to make a research plan. As part of your plan, you will create a timeline for finishing your report. You also will find and evaluate sources of information.

Find Authoritative, Objective Sources For your report, you will need to **compile data,** or gather information, from a variety of sources. Make sure the sources you plan to use are **authoritative**—written or put together by experts on your topic. For example, they should **identify major issues and debates,** including points about which experts may disagree. Also look to see that your sources are **objective** and unbiased, or fair. For most topics, there are a variety of resources from which to choose. Consider these tips:

Print Resources

- Find print resources in libraries and bookstores.
- Use encyclopedias, magazines, newspapers, trade books, and textbooks.
- Search for print resources using electronic databases or with help from a reference librarian.

Electronic Resources

- Find electronic resources using online search engines on the Internet.
- Choose only authoritative, reliable sites, usually ending in:
  .edu (educational institution)
  .gov (government group)
  .org (not-for-profit organization; these may be biased toward a specific goal)
- If you are not sure that a site is reliable and unbiased, do not use it.

Interviews With Experts

- Ask questions of an expert on your topic.
- Set up a short in-person, e-mail, or telephone interview.
- Record the interview and take good notes.

Multimedia Resources

- Watch movies about your topic.
- Listen to podcasts or seminars related to the topic.
- Search for relevant photos, diagrams, charts, and graphs.

Evaluate Your Sources Do not assume that all sources of information on your topic are useful, good, or trustworthy. Use the checklist on page 233 to evaluate sources of information you find. The more questions that you can answer with a yes, the more likely you should use the source.

Checklist for Evaluating Sources

Does the source of information:

- ❑ Contain **relevant** information that answers your research questions?
- ❑ Provide **facts** and not just **subjective** opinions unsupported by facts?
- ❑ Give **valid** facts and details at a level you can understand?
- ❑ Tell all sides of a story, including opposing viewpoints, so that it is **objective and unbiased**?
- ❑ Provide **authoritative, reliable, and accurate** information written or compiled by experts?
- ❑ Have a recent **publication date,** indicating it is up-to-date?

WRITING COACH Online

www.phwritingcoach.com

Online Journal

Record your answers and ideas in the online journal.

Distinguish Between Types of Sources As you research, you will discover two kinds of sources: primary sources and secondary sources. Your teacher may require that you use both kinds of sources.

- A **primary source** is an original document, or **text itself** without any interpretation by another person. For example, the text of the Declaration of Independence and a page from the census of 1910 are primary sources.
- A **secondary source** is a source that provides an **interpretation** or understanding of a primary source. For example, a book about the Declaration of Independence is a secondary source. Be aware that secondary sources are a writer's interpretation of a subject. You may find conflicting information in secondary sources (such as reports of a news event). If you do, try to find a primary source (such as an eyewitness account).

Apply It! Devise a **research plan** and timeline for finishing your report, and list at least four sources of information that you plan to use when writing your report.

- Work with your teacher to determine the dates by which you need to finish your research, thesis statement, drafting, and final report.
- As you compile data from authoritative sources be sure to examine any **major issues** or **debates.**
- For each source you plan to use, give full publication information.
- Organize the data from all your sources and create needed **charts, graphs, or forms** to best share main ideas.
- Identify whether each source is primary or secondary.
- Show that you have evaluated whether each source is authoritative and objective by using the Checklist for Evaluating Sources.

Modify Your Plan After you begin to research a topic, you may find that you need to **modify**, or change, **your research questions**. If you cannot find answers to a research question, you may decide to **refocus,** or change the emphasis of, your topic. **Critique** your research plan at each step to evaluate it and make changes as the need occurs.

Collect and Organize Your Data

For your informational research report, you will need to use **multiple sources** of information. Notes will help you remember and keep track of your sources and information. Different forms of notes include handwritten notes on note cards, typed notes in an electronic document, and a learning log summarizing what you know and still need to know about your topic.

Keep Track of Multiple Sources You can create a card for each source and give each its own number. Write the full publishing information for the source, including the author, title, city of publication, publisher, and copyright date. The example shown is from the Student Model. It matches the MLA style used in the Works Cited on page 229.

> *Source 1*
>
> *Steel, Duncan. Eclipse. Washington, DC: Joseph Henry Press, 2001. Print.*

Take Notes When you take notes from a source, follow these guidelines.

- Note only facts and details you might use.
- To help you access information later, organize the notes using headings that sum up the main ideas of each group of notes.
- Be very careful to use your own words. You can also use abbreviations.
- If you want to quote someone, enclose the exact words in large quotation marks. The quotes will remind you that these are someone else's words—not your own.

> *Notes From Source 1*
>
> *Chart of Eclipses*
>
> - *Javascript solar eclipse explorer*
> - *Choose city: tells latitude, longitude, altitude*
> - *Choose any 100 years list of all eclipses that can be seen from that city*
> - *Lists total, partial, solar, and lunar*

Apply It! As you conduct research on your topic, take notes on information that is relevant to your research questions. Effectively **organize the information** from different sources on note cards. **Paraphrase** the information, or **summarize** it your own words. If you want to **quote,** copy the original, using quotation marks. Be sure to **accurately cite sources** using a standard format, such as MLA style.

Avoid Plagiarism

Plagiarism is using someone else's words or ideas as your own, without documenting the source of the information. Plagiarism is a serious error with severe consequences. Do not plagiarize. Teachers know when a paper you turn in isn't yours. They know your "voice."

Careful Note-taking Matters You can accidentally set yourself up to plagiarize by not taking good notes. The student who wrote this note card made two mistakes. She followed the original source too closely, and she did not include correct publication information. Even though she changed the sentence structure, she essentially used another writer's ideas without crediting her source.

The sun is a gigantic nuclear reactor, fusing hydrogen nuclei together to produce helium and liberating vast amounts of energy in consequence.

Original Source

Notes From Source 5

About the Sun

Our sun is a gigantic nuclear reactor. It fuses hydrogen nuclei together to produce helium. It also liberates huge amounts of energy in consequence.

from Eclipse by Duncan Searl, p. 5

Plagiarized Notes

Use these strategies to avoid plagiarism.

- **Paraphrase** When you paraphrase information from a source, state the writer's idea in your own words. Read a passage, think about what it means, then write it as you might explain it to someone else.
- **Summarize** Use your own words to state the most important ideas in a long passage. A summary should be shorter than the original passage.
- Use a **direct quotation,** and **identify the source**. Enclose the writer's exact words in quotation marks, and give credit to the person who said it. (See page 247.)

Try It! Look at the Notes From Source 5 in the example. Highlight the parts that are plagiarizing the original. Now, write a new note based on the original source. Be sure to avoid plagiarizing the content.

WRITING COACH Online

www.phwritingcoach.com

Online Journal

Record your answers and ideas in the online journal.

Partner Talk

Review taking notes with a partner. Explain why each of these is essential:

- A source card for each source
- A source card number on each note card
- Your own words to paraphrase or summarize ideas
- Large quotation marks for direct quotations

Document Your Sources

When you write a research report, you have to use a standard style to tell your readers where you found information. You need to cite all **researched information** that is not common knowledge, and cite it **according to a standard format**.

Works Cited On the Works Cited page at the end of your report, list all the sources that you used to write your report. Do not include sources you looked into but did not use. Follow the format shown in a standard style manual, such as that of the Modern Language Association (MLA) or American Psychological Association (APA). Your teacher will tell you which standard format style to use.

Look at the example citations shown. Use these and the MLA Style for Listing Sources on page R16 as a guide for writing your citations. Pay attention to formatting, especially italics, abbreviations, and punctuation.

Book

Author's last name, author's first name followed by the author's middle name or initial (if given). *Full title of book.* City where book was published: Name of publisher, date of publication. Medium of publication.

Harrington, Philip S. *Eclipse! The What, Where, When, Why and How Guide to Watching Solar and Lunar Eclipses.* New York: Wiley, 1997. Print.

Magazine Article

Author's last name, author's first name followed by the author's middle name or initial (if given). "Title of article." *Title of magazine.* Date of magazine issue: page numbers on which article appears OR plus sign (+) if the article does not appear on consecutive pages. Medium of publication.

Burgess, Nate. "Solar Eclipse 'Proves' Relativity." *Earth.* June 2009: 52–53. Print.

Web Page

Author/editor last name, first name, OR group name. "Name of page." *Name of the site.* Publisher or N.p. if none provided. Date page was posted or n.d. if none provided. Medium of publication. Date on which you accessed the page.

Espenak, Fred and Chris O'Byrne. "Solar Eclipse Explorer." *NASA Eclipse Web Site.* GSFC Solar System Exploration. 17 Apr. 2007. Web. 16 Nov. 2011.

Parenthetical Citations A parenthetical citation is a quick reference to a source listed on the Works Cited page. These citations give the author's last name or a book or article title and the page number on which the information is located. Look at this sample citation from the Student Model.

STUDENT MODEL from **"Solar Eclipses: Why They Occur and What They Teach Us"**
page 227; lines 29–30

The darkest part of that shadow, the umbra, is 60 to 100 miles wide and marks the *path of totality* (Steel 4).

If the author is mentioned in the sentence, only the page number is given in parentheses. For more on proper documentation, see Grammar Game Plan Error 3, page 275.

> According to Steel, the darkest part of that shadow, the umbra, is 60–100 miles wide and marks the path of totality (4).

When an author's name is not available, use a title or a word from the title:

> "the orbit of the moon is actually tilted a little bit so . . . the moon passes above the sun or below the sun" ("Eclipse Chasers").

Try It! Use MLA style to create a short Works Cited page based on the sources described.

- A book by Billy Aronson titled *Eclipses: Nature's Blackouts.* It was published in 1996 by the publisher Franklin Watts in New York City.
- A Web page called "More sun and eclipse mythology." The site is *Sunstopper.* No author is shown. The writer looked at the page on November 20, 2009.
- The answer by Raymond Shubinski to a reader's question about solar eclipses in a magazine article called "Ask Astro." The article appeared in *Astronomy* magazine in Sept. of 2009 on pages 54–55.

Critique Your Research Process

At every step in the research process, be prepared to modify or change your research plan. If you can't find enough information to write your thesis statement, try rewording your research question. Some writers get bogged down in the research step, wanting to search for more. It's essential to stick to your **timeline**. You're ready to wrap up the prewriting part of your research paper and start drafting your paper.

Apply It! Write an entry on your Works Cited page for every source you have consulted for your informational research report. To format and document your sources accurately, use MLA style or the style your teacher has directed you to use. After confirming that you have researched enough information to begin writing your draft, write a clear thesis statement for your research report in your writing journal.

WRITING COACH Online
www.phwritingcoach.com

Interactive Model
Refer back to the Student Model as you document your sources.

Online Journal
Record your answers and ideas in the online journal.

Partner Talk

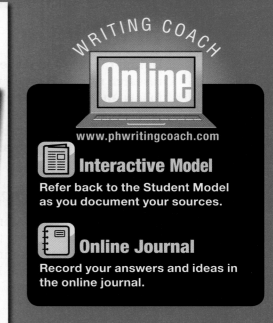

Get together with a partner to discuss research sources. Where have you looked for information on your topic? What sources do you like? What hasn't been reliable? How have you been keeping track of them?

Drafting

During the drafting stage, you will start to write your ideas for your research report. You will write a clear thesis statement. You will follow an outline that provides an organizational strategy that will help you write a focused, organized, and coherent research report. As you write your draft or prepare your notes for an oral presentation, remember to keep your audience in mind.

The Organization of an Informational Research Report

The chart shows an organizational strategy for a research report. Look back at how the Student Model follows this same strategy. Then, create a detailed outline for your informational research report. Use the outline template shown on page R26 to guide development of your outline. Also refer to the Outline for Success as you work.

Outline for Success

I. Introduction

See Student Model, p. 226.

- Attention-grabbing introduction
- Clear thesis statement

II. Body

See Student Model, pp. 227–229.

- Synthesis of information from multiple sources presented as a logical progression of ideas
- Evidence that supports the thesis statement
- Graphics and illustrations to explain concepts

III. Conclusion

See Student Model, p. 229.

- Summary of findings and final conclusions
- Memorable ending with a final thought or conclusion

Introduce Your Thesis Statement

- A quotation, story, question, or interesting fact that relates to the thesis will grab the reader's attention.
- A **clear thesis statement** is often the last sentence in the introduction and answers your research question.

Support Your Thesis Statement

- This is where the data is synthesized from various notes.
- The headings on researched notes have been grouped, and similar ideas that support your thesis are put into a logical order.
- Each paragraph states a major idea and supports it with evidence, such as facts, examples, and quotations. Relevant photos, charts, or other visuals are included to help convey complicated information.

Add a Final Thought

- A conclusion pulls all the details together, reminding us of the importance of the thesis.
- The writer's point of view about the topic is revealed or restated in the final paragraph.
- The reader may be asked to do something as a follow-up to the report.

Start Your Draft

Use the checklist below to help complete your draft. Use your specific thesis statement; your detailed outline that lists your supporting evidence; logical progression of ideas; and graphics and illustrations; and the Outline for Success as guides.

While drafting, aim at writing your ideas, not on making your writing perfect. Remember, you will have the chance to improve your draft when you revise and edit.

√ Start your **introduction** by drafting attention-getting sentences.

√ End with a clearly worded **thesis statement** that is based on your research question. Your thesis should be the roadmap for your report.

√ Develop the **body** one paragraph at a time. Organize and present your ideas to suit the purpose of your report and your specific audience. Choose only the strongest **supporting evidence** for each major idea.

√ For each paragraph, draft a **topic sentence** that states its main idea. This will help you choose the best supporting evidence.

√ Each paragraph should use the **marshalled**—collected and organized—evidence to support the thesis statement and any other related claims your report is making.

√ Provide an **analysis of the evidence** that builds on your ideas in a logical progression and states a clear point of view.

√ Draft a **concluding paragraph** that sums up, restates, and adds a final thought.

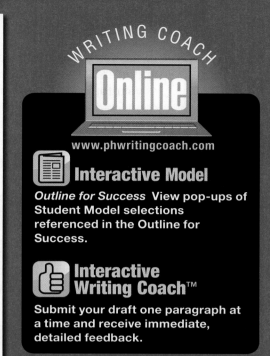

WRITING COACH **Online**

www.phwritingcoach.com

Interactive Model

Outline for Success **View pop-ups of Student Model selections referenced in the Outline for Success.**

Interactive Writing Coach™

Submit your draft one paragraph at a time and receive immediate, detailed feedback.

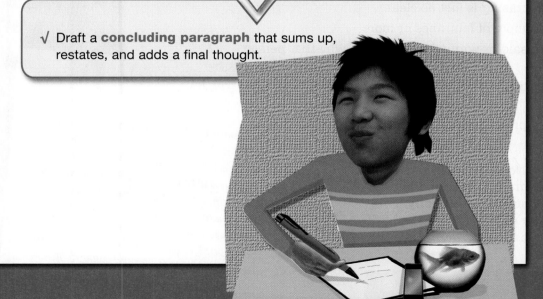

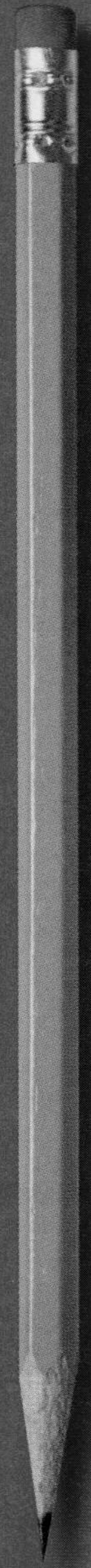

Provide and Document Evidence

While you are drafting, you will provide **evidence** to support your thesis and related claims. Your **claims** are an important part of your **analysis** of your topic. They are your opinions or understanding of information connected to your thesis, stated from your **point of view**. Be careful to differentiate between your opinions and ideas and those of other people. **Document** the words and ideas of other people when you provide evidence.

Give Facts and Statistics Facts are convincing evidence because they can be proven true. Statistics, or facts stated in numbers, are also convincing when they come from authoritative and up-to-date sources. Remember to document facts and statistics that are not common knowledge or that could not be found in most sources about a topic.

Give Examples Make abstract or complicated ideas easier to understand by providing examples. You do not need to document examples from personal experience, but you do need to document examples from a particular source as shown in the example from the Student Model.

STUDENT MODEL from **"Solar Eclipses: Why They Occur and What They Teach Us"**
page 226; lines 7–9

The ancient Norse people thought that Sköll, a huge wolf, was devouring their sun (Harrington 2).

Quote Authorities Direct quotations from experts are also convincing evidence. Make sure a quotation fits smoothly into your paragraph, and use your own words to identify the expert.

Remember to follow these guidelines:

- Only quote if you must use an expert's exact words.
- Do not quote if paraphrasing is just as clear.
- Separate and inset a quote of four lines or more.
- Always indicate who said or wrote the quote and why that person is an expert.
- Be sure to punctuate quotes correctly. (See page 247.)
- Follow quotes with a proper parenthetical citation.

Try It! Use the Notes From Source 5 to write a paragraph that supports this thesis: **It is dangerous to look directly at the sun during a solar eclipse.** Your paragraph should include facts, examples, a quotation, and citation.

Notes From Source 5
Viewing Eclipses

Looking at the sun is unsafe. Why? "Not only does the Sun radiate visible light, but its photosphere also emits intense infrared (IR) and ultraviolet (UV) radiation." UV radiation is bad. "Just as ultraviolet radiation causes sunburn to exposed skin, so too will it damage your eyes' retinas—and at a much faster rate." It only takes a few seconds to cause damage or blindness.—p. 25 of Philip S. Harrington's book Eclipse! The What, Where, When, Why, and How Guide to Watching Solar and Lunar Eclipses.

Use Graphics and Illustrations

You can present evidence in graphics and other visuals as well as in words. While you are drafting, consider how you can create a diagram or other types of graphics to help your audience understand your ideas and analysis in your report. Be sure to refer to the figure in your text. Then, label your visuals with a figure or table number, caption, and source citations for the data. Use caution when copying an existing graphic because you will need permission from the copyright holder if you publish your work for use outside school.

- **Photographs** Use a photograph to help your audience picture how something looks. If you insert a photograph in your report, include a caption, or brief sentence explaining what the photo shows.
- **Maps** Maps can provide geographical information visually. Be sure to include a legend and a compass with your map, in addition to the figure number, caption, and source.
- **Charts, Tables, and Graphs** Create a chart, table, or graph to provide information in a more visual or organized way. Give each a title that tells what it shows. If you include more than one, number them in numerical order. Include a complete citation for the source of information you used to create the chart, table, or graph. Put it below after the word *Source* and a colon.

Table 1. Defining Eclipse Contacts—Used for Timing

C1	1st Contact	moon first appears in front of sun
C2	2nd Contact	diamond ring effect; sun totally covered
C3	3rd Contact	diamond ring effect; totality ends
C4	Last Contact	moon disappears from in front of sun

Apply It! Brainstorm for two graphics that you might use in your informational research report. Be sure to identify the type of information each graphic would explain, find or create the two graphics, and add them to your report. Remember to give your graphics titles. Use a style manual to format graphics and to document your sources. Use peer, teacher, or family feedback to check that the quality of your created and researched visuals is appropriate for your report.

WRITING COACH Online

www.phwritingcoach.com

Interactive Model

Refer back to the Student Model as you draft your writing.

Online Journal

Record your ideas in the online journal.

Partner Talk

Get together with a partner to evaluate each graphic that you are considering using. Explain to your partner why you have chosen each one, and discuss the reliability, validity, and accuracy of each source.

Revising: Making It Better

Now that you have finished your draft, you are ready to revise. Think about the "big picture" of audience, purpose, and genre. You can use the Revision RADaR strategy as a guide for making changes to improve your draft. Revision RADaR provides four major ways to improve your writing: (R) replace, (A) add, (D) delete, and (R) reorder.

Kelly Gallagher, M. Ed.

KEEP REVISION ON YOUR RADaR

Read part of the first draft of the Student Model "Solar Eclipses: Why They Occur and What They Teach Us." Then, look at questions the writer asked herself as she thought about how well her draft addressed issues of audience, purpose, and genre.

from Solar Eclipses: Why They Occur and What They Teach Us

1ST DRAFT

Everyone knows that our moon orbits Earth in 28 days and that Earth travels around the sun in a year—365 ¼ days. We add an extra day to the calendar every fourth year, which is leap year with 366 days. As it moves around Earth, the moon goes through different changes. It changes from a thin sliver to a full moon and then decreases until it becomes a new moon. Solar eclipses occur only when the totally dark new moon lines up exactly with the sun and Earth, blocking our view of the sun.

On a clear day, viewers in the path of totality see a total solar eclipse, while viewers in the penumbra nearby see a partial eclipse. During a solar eclipse, the moon casts a cone-shaped shadow on Earth. The darkest part of that shadow, the umbra, is 60–100 miles wide and marks the *path of totality.*

*Have I provided enough **evidence** to support my **thesis statement?** Is all of the information **relevant?***

*Have I explained solar eclipses clearly enough? Do I need to **define terms** or add more information?*

*Is the information **clearly** and **logically presented?** Have I **documented** my sources according to a style manual?*

Now, look at how the writer applied Revision RADaR to write an improved second draft.

2ND DRAFT

from Solar Eclipses: Why They Occur and What They Teach Us

Everyone knows that our moon orbits Earth in 28 days and that Earth travels around the sun in a year—365 ¼ days. As it revolves around Earth, the moon goes through different phases. It changes from a thin crescent to a full moon and then decreases until it becomes a totally dark new moon. Solar eclipses occur only when the new moon lines up exactly with the sun and Earth, blocking our view of the sun. According to physicist Paul Doherty, solar eclipses don't happen every month because "the orbit of the moon is actually tilted a little bit so that most of the time the moon passes above the sun or below the sun" ("Eclipse Chasers").

Maybe the easiest way to understand what happens during a solar eclipse is to study a graphic of it. Look at the diagram of a solar eclipse (see figure 1). Notice that the moon casts a cone-shaped shadow on Earth. The darkest part of that shadow, the umbra, is 60 to 100 miles wide and marks the *path of totality* (Steel 4). On a clear day, viewers in the path of totality see a total solar eclipse, while viewers in the *penumbra* shadow see a partial eclipse. During a partial eclipse, the sun is partially, not totally, blocked.

D *Deleted the sentence about leap year because it isn't relevant to the explanation of solar eclipses*

R *Replaced general, vague words with scientific terms*

A *Added a quotation from an expert that explains why solar eclipses don't occur every month*

A *Added proper documentation of the source*

R *Reordered the sentences to define the path of totality and umbra at the beginning of the paragraph, not at the end*

A *Added definition of term partial eclipse, which audience might not know*

Apply It! Use your Revision RADaR to revise your draft.

- First, determine if you have addressed the needs of your audience, explained your purpose, and met the expectations of the research genre.
- Then, apply Revision RADaR to make needed changes. Remember—you can use the steps in the strategy in any order.

WRITING COACH Online

www.phwritingcoach.com

Video

Learn more strategies for effective writing from program author Kelly Gallagher.

Interactive Writing Coach™

Use the Revision RADaR strategy in your own writing. Then submit your draft paragraph by paragraph for feedback.

Look at the Big Picture

Use the chart and your analytical skills to evaluate how well each section of your informational research report addresses **purpose, audience, and genre**. When necessary, use the suggestions in the chart to revise your piece.

Section	Evaluate	Revise
Introduction	• Check that the **opening paragraphs** grab your reader's attention. They should make the reader want to learn the answers to your research question.	• Add a quotation, anecdote, or brief story to help build interest in your topic and make your point of view clear.
	• Make sure you have a **clear thesis statement** that indicates the major ideas your report will explore.	• Clarify your thesis statement to be sure it answers your research question and identifies the key points of your report.
Body	• Make sure each body paragraph clearly develops one **major idea**.	• Add a topic sentence to each paragraph. Use marshalled evidence to support the thesis and any related claims.
	• Check that you use **graphics and illustrations** to help explain complex ideas.	• Review the research and look for data that can best be shared visually. Then, correctly format it for the report.
	• Check that your information and analysis are **logically presented** and progress in a way that the audience can understand.	• Reorder words, sentences, and paragraphs in a logical order. Add transitions—as words, phrases, or even sentences or paragraphs—to guide.
	• Make sure quotations and facts that are not common knowledge are **documented** and **formatted** according to a style manual.	• Review your note cards and source cards to confirm the source of each quotation. Add parenthetical citations, following the style specified in a style manual.
Conclusion	• Check that your conclusion reveals or restates your **point of view** about your topic.	• Add a statement of what you learned and how you feel about what you learned.
	• Make sure your research report ends with a new **insight** that leaves the reader with a final thought.	• Add a quotation or fact that brings your report to a definite end and helps your reader to understand your purpose.
Works Cited/ Bibliography	• Complete your **reference list** using a style manual.	• Add all documented sources you used in your paper to the Works Cited page or bibliography.

Focus on Craft: Subtlety of Meaning

Many English words have **synonyms**—words that have the same or almost the same meaning. The differences in meaning can be subtle. *Thin* and *slim,* for example, are synonyms with slightly different meanings. When you write a research report, keep your audience and purpose in mind. You will want to use the most accurate words, but avoid repeating the same words over and over again.

Think about subtlety of meaning as you read these sentences from the Student Model.

STUDENT MODEL from **"Solar Eclipses: Why They Occur and What They Teach Us"**
page 226; lines 16–19

As it revolves around Earth, the moon goes through different phases. It changes from a thin crescent to a full moon and then decreases until it becomes a totally dark new moon.

Try It! Now, ask yourself this question. Record your answer in your journal.

- Why does the student writer use scientific terms for more general words: *revolves* for *moves; phases* for *changes; crescent* for *sliver*?

Fine-Tune Your Draft

Apply It! Use the revision suggestions to prepare your final draft. Make sure you keep your audience and purpose in mind as you focus on choosing words to express exactly what you mean.

- **Focus on Subtlety of Meaning** Focus on the key words that communicate essential information related to your topic. To avoid repeating the same vocabulary, choose the word that best fits the context and expresses the idea most precisely.
- **Define Terms** Clearly define terms and explain concepts that will be unfamiliar to your audience. If you add a quotation in order to provide a definition, be sure to document your source properly.
- **Improve Sentence Variety** Add, delete, or combine sentences to keep your writing engaging and interesting.

Teacher and Family Feedback Share your draft with your teacher or a family member. Ask for feedback on the quality of your research. Carefully review the comments you receive and revise your final draft as needed.

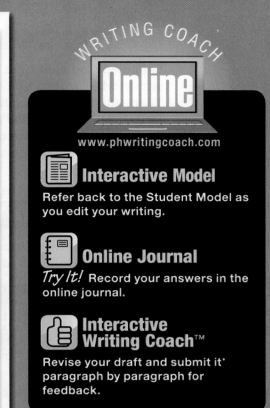

WRITING COACH **Online**

www.phwritingcoach.com

Interactive Model

Refer back to the Student Model as you edit your writing.

Online Journal

Try It! Record your answers in the online journal.

Interactive Writing Coach™

Revise your draft and submit it paragraph by paragraph for feedback.

Editing: Making It Correct

Before editing your final draft, think about how you will paraphrase, summarize, quote, and accurately cite all researched information. Then, edit your draft using a style manual, such as *MLA Handbook for Writers of Research Papers,* to document sources and format the materials, including quotations. Finally, edit your final draft for errors in grammar, mechanics and spelling.

WRITE GUY *Jeff Anderson, M. Ed.*

WHAT DO YOU NOTICE?

Zoom in on Conventions Focus on quotations as you zoom in on these lines from the Student Model.

STUDENT MODEL from **"Solar Eclipses: Why They Occur and What They Teach Us"**
pages 226–227; lines 19–25

> Solar eclipses occur only when the new moon lines up exactly with the sun and Earth, blocking our view of the sun. According to physicist Paul Doherty, solar eclipses don't happen every month because "the orbit of the moon is actually tilted a little bit so that most of the time the moon passes above the sun or below the sun" ("Eclipse Chasers").

To learn more about integrating quotations, see Grammar Game Plan, Error 18, page 290.

Now, ask yourself this question: *What techniques has the writer used to help integrate the quotation?*

Perhaps you noted the writer used these helpful techniques to surround the quotation.

- Part of the introductory phrase identifies the quote's author or speaker.
- The writer prepares the reader for the information in the quote by using **an introductory phrase.**
- The writer used quotation marks at the beginning and at the end of the quotation.
- The writer has properly cited the source, using correct format and punctuation.

Partner Talk Discuss this question with a partner: *How does the writer ensure that the quotation flows smoothly with the sentences that surround it?*

Grammar Mini-Lesson: Punctuation

To learn more, see Chapter 23.

Punctuating Quotations With Citations Quotations follow specific rules for punctuation. For example, parenthetical citations occur after the quote but before the period. See Grammar Game Plan, Error 6, on page 278 for more examples. Study these sentences from the Student Model. Notice how the writer punctuated the quotation with a citation.

STUDENT MODEL from **"Solar Eclipses: Why They Occur and What They Teach Us"** page 228; lines 42–45

During an interview, Nancy Adams-Wolk, an IT Specialist/Scientist at Harvard-Smithsonian Center for Astrophysics, explains why: "We learned that the sun extends far past the visible surface."

Try It! Determine whether these quotations are punctuated properly and have correct citation formatting. Correct the punctuation where necessary. Write the answers in your journal.

1. In a speech, the astronomer Saji Patel stated, "We have a greater ability to study space today because of the Hubble, one of many technological advances in telescopes (Patel 2009).
2. During a solar eclipse, a tourist was overheard asking, Why is it getting dark in the middle of the day?"

Apply It! Edit your draft for grammar, mechanics, and spelling. If necessary, rewrite sentences with quotations to ensure you've integrated them properly, as well as punctuated and cited them correctly. Use a style manual to check your formatting and documentation of sources.

Use the rubric to evaluate your piece. If necessary, rethink, rewrite, or revise.

Rubric for Informational Research Report	Rating Scale
Ideas: How clearly have you expressed and developed your thesis statement?	Not very Very 1 2 3 4 5 6
Organization: How logical is the progression of your ideas?	1 2 3 4 5 6
Voice: How effectively have you developed an authoritative voice?	1 2 3 4 5 6
Word Choice: How clearly have you expressed your point of view?	1 2 3 4 5 6
Sentence Fluency: How well have you used sentence variety in your report?	1 2 3 4 5 6
Conventions: How correct is the formatting of the sources that you used?	1 2 3 4 5 6

WRITING COACH **Online**

www.phwritingcoach.com

Video

Learn effective editing techniques from program author Jeff Anderson.

Interactive Model

Refer back to the Student Model as you edit your writing.

Online Journal

Try It! Record your answers in the online journal.

Interactive Writing Coach™

Edit your draft and check it against the rubric. Submit it paragraph by paragraph for feedback.

Publishing

Now that you worked through the writing process to create your report, find a way to share your knowledge. When you've finished your final draft, publish it for an appropriate audience.

Wrap Up Your Presentation

Is your piece handwritten or written on a computer? Your teacher may require a word-processed final report. If your piece is handwritten, you may need to make a new, clean copy. If so, be sure to **write legibly.** Follow the guidelines provided—create a cover sheet, table of contents, and a Works Cited list.

Publish Your Piece

Use the chart to identify a way to publish your informational research report for the appropriate audience.

If your audience is...	...then publish it by...
Students or adults at school	• Displaying your written report in the school library or media center • Presenting your research at an assembly or to another English class
A local group or club with a special interest in your topic	• Presenting an oral or multimedia report at a club meeting; answering questions about your research • Posting your report online and inviting comments

Reflect on Your Writing

Now that you are done with your informational research report, read it over and use your writing journal to answer these questions.

- Which parts of your research report are the strongest? Which parts could be better?
- What will you do differently the next time you are assigned a research report?
- What are the most important things you learned about the research process?

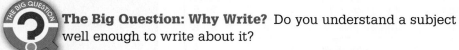

The Big Question: Why Write? Do you understand a subject well enough to write about it?

Manage Your Portfolio You may wish to include your published informational research report in your writing portfolio. If so, consider what this piece reveals about your writing and your growth as a writer.

21st Century Learning

MAKE YOUR WRITING COUNT

Present a Research-Based Documentary

Research reports answer questions about the world by providing evidence from solid sources. Help your schoolmates learn about a topic from one of your research reports by producing a **documentary**.

A documentary is a film that uses text, images, and interviews to share information about a specific topic. Work in groups to produce a **multimedia presentation** of a documentary. You can present your documentary as a storyboard to make a video. Your presentation should include text, graphics, images, and sound.

Here's your action plan.

1. Meet with your group. Choose roles such as director, storyboard artist, and videographer.
2. Select a peer's research report that will interest your schoolmates and fit the documentary format.
3. View online documentaries for inspiration.
4. Find appropriate images and sounds, on the Internet or in other sources.
5. Create a storyboard that:
   - Presents information from the same objective and distinctive point of view as the research report
   - Includes notes about text, images, sounds, and graphics
   - Appeals to your specific audience
   - Includes plans for scripted voice-overs or interviews
6. Rehearse your presentation, keeping your audience in mind.
7. Present your storyboard, or record and edit your video documentary.

Listening and Speaking Meet with your group to discuss how to present your storyboard or video to your schoolmates. Then, practice your multimedia presentation, tying in images, sounds, and graphics. During rehearsals, listeners should provide feedback about segments that might confuse your audience. During the presentation or recording of the video, the director and speakers should keep the listeners' feedback in mind.

WRITING COACH Online

www.phwritingcoach.com

Online Journal

Reflect on your writing. Record your answers and ideas in the online journal.

Resource

Link to resources on 21st Century Learning for help in creating a group project.

Your Turn

Writing for Media: Online Travel Report

21st Century Learning

Online Travel Report

Why are the Egyptian pyramids such a magnificent sight? What is it like to sail through the Panama Canal? You can find answers to all your travel questions by searching the Internet. In this assignment, you will create your own **online travel report** about a place you would like to visit someday. You'll follow a research plan as you gather information from multiple sources. Make your citations Web links to a References, or Works Cited, page. Then, you'll put it all together to inform your audience and to entice them to visit the place you are writing about.

Try It! Study the excerpt from this sample online travel report. Then, answer these questions. Record your answers in your journal.

1. What place or **destination** is the writer describing? Where exactly is it located?
2. What do you think is the writer's **purpose?** Who do you think is the intended **audience?**
3. An online travel report gives **essential information** about visiting a specific place. What information is shown here?
4. What other information do you want to know? What **subheadings** would you expect this travel report to include?
5. Is the writing **subjective** (presenting the writer's personal opinion) or **objective** (presenting only factual information)? How can you tell?
6. What effect does the **photograph** have? What other kinds of **visuals** would be helpful in this report?
7. What suggestions would you give the writer for **improving** this travel report?

Figure 1. Lava flow crossing road; courtesy of Jupiter Images.

Danger: Volcano Crossing!

Mt. Kilauea is an active volcano in Hawaii Volcanoes National Park on the Big Island. From deep inside the earth, red-hot molten lava flows through vents down to the sea. Huge plumes of steam mark the spot where lava plunges into the ocean, actually building new land. *(GeoResources)*

You can see this fantastic phenomenon every day and night. Start at the Visitor Center, and watch the 25-minute movie "Born of Fire...Born of the Sea." Then, drive the 11-mile Chain of Craters Road until you reach the place where hardened lava blocks the road (see figure 1). You can hike over cooled lava to where the bubbling lava is flowing. Be sure to wear hiking boots and bring water and binoculars. nps.gov/havo

What Else Can You Do?

- Go on a ranger-led hike.
- Attend a lecture by a geologist.
- Visit the park's tropical rain forest.
- Walk through a lava tube.
- Stay at Volcano House, built in 1846.

Create an Online Travel Report

Follow these steps to create your own **online travel report**. To plan your online travel report, review the graphic organizers on pages R24–R27 to select one best suited to your needs.

Prewriting

- **Brainstorm** for a list of places anywhere in the world that you would really like to visit someday. Consult with others and consider cities, states, countries, historic places, natural features, and ecosystems. When you've finished, circle the topic you've decided on.
- Be sure to identify the target **audience** for your online report. Are you writing to **inform** teenagers? Families? Single adults?
- It's important to formulate a **research plan** and critique it at each step. What specific **research question** will you try to answer? You'll need to **compile information** from **multiple sources.** As you research, you may find you need to modify the research question and refocus your plan in order to produce better results.
- **Evaluate** every source you consider using. Decide whether a source is **authoritative and objective** by checking that its information is **reliable, valid,** and **accurate.** Reject any sources that seem **subjective** or biased. Be sure to examine any major issues or debates related to your topic.
- Record information systematically on note cards, or on the computer. Document your **sources.** Make a note card for each source using a standard format for citations.
- As you take notes, **paraphrase** or **summarize** information. If you use a **direct quotation,** enclose it in big quotation marks.
- Organize the data you've collected from all your sources to help you see big ideas. Think of **graphics, forms,** and **illustrations** you can add to your report. Be sure to record source information for any graphics you intend to use.

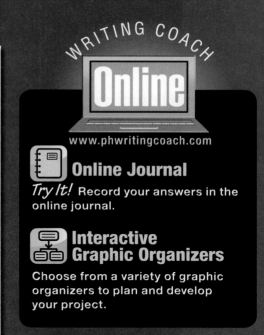

Notes From Source 2

Daily update on action at Mt. Kilauea by US Geological Survey (USGS) Web site

Includes information releases, status reports, hazard alerts, Webcams, and movies

WRITING COACH **Online**

www.phwritingcoach.com

Online Journal

Try It! Record your answers in the online journal.

Interactive Graphic Organizers

Choose from a variety of graphic organizers to plan and develop your project.

Partner Talk

Ask a partner to critique your research plan. Does your partner have questions you haven't thought about asking? Modify your research questions to refocus your research plan.

Your Turn Writing for Media: Online Travel Report *(continued)*

21st Century Learning

Drafting

- **Organize** your notes by subject heading, such as *Important Sights, How to Get There,* and *Where to Stay.* Then, start drafting.
- Whatever you do, avoid plagiarizing. Use your own words, or enclose direct quotations in quotation marks.
- A good travel report entices the reader. Begin with an attention-grabbing opening that contains a **thesis statement** and clearly reveals your **point of view** about your subject.
- Marshall your evidence by collecting and organizing ideas and details to support the thesis and any related claims you include.
- Sensory details help the reader visualize a place. Describe what your reader will see and do in the place you're writing about. Use eye-catching **graphics** and **illustrations** to show readers what to expect.
- Present your analysis in a **logical progression** that the audience can easily follow. Lively **subheadings** will organize your report and help readers find information.
- Acknowledge your **sources** in context or in a credits section.

Revising

Use Revision RADaR techniques as you review your draft carefully.

- **Replace** general terms with vivid details and unclear explanations with precise ideas.
- **Add** specific details or missing information to support your argument.
- **Delete** information that does not support your thesis or develop your argument.
- **Reorder** sentences and paragraphs to present ideas clearly and logically.
- Use an **evaluative tool,** such as a rubric or teacher feedback, to check the quality of your research report.

Extension Find another example of an online travel report and compare it with the one you are writing.

Editing

Now take the time to check your Online Travel Report carefully before you post it online. Focus on each sentence and then on each word. Look for these common kinds of errors:

- Errors in subject-verb agreement
- Errors in pronoun usage
- Run-on sentences and sentence fragments
- Spelling and capitalization mistakes
- Omitted punctuation marks
- Problem with proper citations and quotations

Publishing

- If your school newspaper is published online, submit your online travel report to the newspaper editor.
- Search for online forums run by travel guide book publishers, and submit your report as a comment.
- Post your travel report as a blog entry. To help you, search for one of the Web sites that allow you to create a free blog.
- With your classmates, create an anthology of your online travel reports. Print it for classroom display or for your school library.
- Publish your online travel report on a social networking site.
- Post your travel report as a comment or in a forum on a travel Web site.
- Post your report as a comment on an online newspaper article about the place you have researched.
- Print your report for friends and relatives.

WRITING COACH **Online**

www.phwritingcoach.com

Online Journal

Record your answers in the online journal.

Interactive Graphic Organizers

Choose from a variety of graphic organizers to plan and develop your project.

Partner Talk

Before you post your travel report online, ask a partner to check it carefully. Proofread each other's reports for errors.

Writing for Assessment

Many standardized tests include a prompt that asks you to write or critique a research plan. Use these prompts to practice. Respond using the characteristics of your informational research report. (See page 224.)

Try It! Read the prompt, and write a **research plan**. List all of the actions you will take to research this topic. Tell where you will look for sources, and how you will evaluate them. Be as specific as you can.

Format

Write your *research plan* in the form of an outline. List everything you would do in the order you would do it. Under some main headings, you may have subheadings. (For example, what types of sources would you look for?)

Research Plan Prompt

Write a research plan for an informational report that discusses one of the latest teenage fashions. Your plan should include: a research topic and question, a list of potential sources, the audience, and the steps you'll take following a timeline. [30 minutes]

Academic Vocabulary

Potential sources are those resources you might use if you were to develop a research report based on this plan. In your response, list reliable sources you might use. For example, consider information that is accurate (without errors), authoritative (from an expert you can trust), relevant (directly related to your research question), objective (without bias), and valid (true).

The ABCDs of On-Demand Writing

Use the following ABCDs to help you respond to the prompt.

Before you write your draft:

Attack the prompt [1 MINUTE]

- Circle or highlight important verbs in the prompt. Draw a line from the verb to what it refers to.
- Rewrite the prompt in your own words.

Brainstorm possible answers [4 MINUTES]

- Create a graphic organizer to generate ideas.
- Use one for each part of the prompt if necessary.

Choose the order of your response [1 MINUTE]

- Think about the best way to organize your ideas.
- Number your ideas in the order you will write about them. Cross out ideas you will not be using.

After you write your draft:

Detect errors before turning in the draft [1 MINUTE]

- Carefully reread your writing.
- Make sure that your response makes sense and is complete.
- Look for spelling, punctuation, and grammar errors.

More Prompts for Practice

Apply It! Work with a partner to **critique the research plan** in Prompt 1. Make specific suggestions to improve the research plan. Consider these:

- Is there a limited topic? Is it appropriate for the **audience and purpose**?
- Is the writer planning to find **reliable** sources? Are the sources varied?
- Does the writer plan to include **graphics**?
- Does the research plan say anything about **evaluating sources**?

Prompt 1 Jamie wrote the following research plan. Explain what he did well and what needs improvement.

> *My Topic:* I'm going to research sky diving because I'd like to try it someday. I think my friends would like it too.
> *My Research:* I'll interview my uncle, who almost tried it once. I'll search the Internet to see what's listed there. Maybe I can find an advertisement from a company that takes people sky diving.
> *My Writing:* After a week of searching, I'll use my notes to write a draft. Then, I'll show my teacher before revising it.

Spiral Review: Narrative If you choose to respond to Prompt 2, write a **personal narrative**. Make sure your story reflects the characteristics described on page 66.

Prompt 2 Write a personal narrative about a time you went someplace you had never been. Include details about how you felt and what you heard and saw. Were there surprises? Disappointments? Would you recommend that someone else go there?

Spiral Review: Response to Literature For Prompt 3, write an **interpretative response.** Make sure your response reflects all of the characteristics described on page 198, including: **extending beyond a summary and literal analysis; addressing the writing skills for an analytical essay** (see page 146); **providing evidence from the text using embedded quotations;** and **analyzing the aesthetic effects of the author's use of stylistic or rhetorical devices.**

Prompt 3 Choose an expository or literary text that you feel has an interesting setting or location. Write an interpretative response about how the writer described that place. Include information about word choice, vivid imagery, and sensory details, as well as an analysis of how the location is important to the writing.

WRITING COACH Online

www.phwritingcoach.com

Interactive Writing Coach™

Plan your response to the prompt. If you are using the prompt for practice, write one paragraph at a time or your entire draft and then submit it for feedback. If you are using the prompt as a timed test, write your entire draft and then submit it for feedback.

Remember ABCD

- **A**ttack the prompt
- **B**rainstorm possible answers
- **C**hoose the order of your response
- **D**etect errors before turning in the draft

CHAPTER 12

WORKPLACE WRITING

What's Ahead

In this chapter, you will learn how you can write workplace and procedural documents, which explain how something works or is done. You will also learn how to write other practical forms of communicating, including letters and various work-related documents. All of these functional documents should present organized information that is accurately conveyed, or written, and presented in a reader-friendly format.

CHARACTERISTICS OF WRITING

Effective workplace and procedural writing has these characteristics:

- **Information** that is well-organized and accurate
- A **clear purpose** and intended **audience**
- Detailed and clear language that is **formal, polite**
- **Reader-friendly formatting techniques,** such as sufficient white or blank space and clearly defined sections
- Correct **grammar, punctuation, and spelling** appropriate to the form of writing

Forms of Writing

Forms of workplace writing that you will learn are:

Business letters are formal correspondence written to, from, or within a business. They can be written for various reasons, including to make requests and to express concerns or approval.

Business e-mails are an electronic form of correspondence used for less formal communication.

Instructions explain how to complete a task or procedure. These procedural texts are written in a step-by-step format.

Other forms of workplace writing include:

Memos are short documents usually written from one member of an organization to another or to a group. They assume some background knowledge of the topic.

Project plans usually divide a project into steps or stages and outline what will be accomplished in each stage.

Try It! For each audience and purpose described, select the correct form, such as a business letter or procedural document, that is appropriate. Explain your choices, evaluating the different forms of text according to the way each one presents information.

- To express your feelings about a product to a company
- To tell your grandparent how to access your school's Web page

WRITING COACH **Online**

www.phwritingcoach.com

Resource

Word Bank Use the eText glossary to learn more about these words.

Online Journal

Try It! Record your answers and ideas in the online journal.

THE BIG QUESTION

Connect to the Big Questions

Discuss these questions with your partner:

1 **What do you think?** When is accuracy most important in writing?

2 **Why write?** What do daily workplace communications require of format, content, and style?

WORD BANK

These vocabulary words are often used with workplace writing. Use the Glossary or a dictionary to check the definitions.

document	procedure
instructions	task

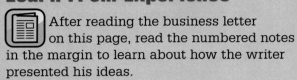

STUDENT MODEL Business Letter

Learn From Experience

After reading the business letter on this page, read the numbered notes in the margin to learn about how the writer presented his ideas.

Try It! Record your answers and ideas in the online journal.

---

1 The letter begins with the proper **business letter** requirements:

- Writer's return address including street, town, state, and zip code
- Date of letter including month, day, and year
- Recipient's name and complete address
- Formal greeting with correct punctuation of a colon

2 In the first paragraph, the writer sets a business-like tone **and conveys the purpose** of the letter.

3 Here and elsewhere in the **body** of the letter, the writer **conveys ideas** that help fulfill the letter's purpose.

4 The writer signs his letter. It is important to include your **signature** when you write a letter on paper.

Try It!

- Why is it important to include a return address on work-related documents, such as business letters?
- What is the purpose of the letter?
- In your opinion, does the letter fulfill its purpose? Why or why not?

Extension Write an e-mail in response to the sender as if you are the recipient.

1 Tony Gazana
606 Main Street
Tyler, TX 75702

1 March 6, 2010

1 Dr. Emily Solon
Riverside Thoroughbred Care
5678 Countyline Road
Tyler, TX 75702

1 Dear Dr. Solon:

My name is Tony Gazana. I am a ninth-grader in the Tyler Youth Group. Each year, our school holds a career fair where people come to speak about their work. 2 We would like you to come this year to talk about your work caring for thoroughbred horses.

The fair will take place on Tuesday, April 7th from 7–9 pm. 3 We would like you to speak for about 15 minutes about the reasons you chose this field, the education required, and the tasks you perform in your everyday work-life. After you speak, we would like you to answer questions from a group of interested young people. The question period will take about ten minutes.

Please contact the youth group director, Mrs. Smith, by e-mail or phone (dsmith@example.edu or 555-555-5555) to let us know whether you will be able to attend the Career Fair. We hope to see you then.

4 Sincerely,

Tony Gazana

Tony Gazana

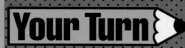

Your Turn — Feature Assignment: Business Letter

Prewriting

- Plan a first draft of your **business letter.** You can select from the Topic Bank or come up with an idea of your own.

TOPIC BANK

Career Exploration Think of a career or job you might be interested in pursuing. Write a letter to a local professional to ask for an interview that will help you to learn more about what the job demands.

Animal Adoption Write a letter to a local animal shelter inquiring about the requirements for adopting a cat or dog.

- Think about your purpose for writing and brainstorm for a list of things that your letter's recipient will need to know about you.
- Use a telephone directory or online resources to find the accurate contact information for the letter's recipient.

Drafting

- Use **reader-friendly formatting techniques,** including all of the features of business letters.
- **Organize the information** so that the purpose is clearly stated early in the letter and so that each paragraph has a clear focus.
- **Accurately convey information** by double-checking your facts.

Revising and Editing

Before you revise, review your draft to ensure that information is presented accurately and concisely. Ask yourself if the purpose and audience for your letter are clearly identified and addressed. Then, revise the draft to **improve your style**—check that you have used precise words and used a variety of sentence lengths.

Publishing

- If you plan to mail the letter, print it on paper that is suitable for business correspondence.
- Address an envelope, accurately including your return address and the recipient's address. Then, stamp and mail the letter.
- If you plan to e-mail the letter, confirm the e-mail address and attach your letter to a message as a Portable Document Format (PDF).

WRITING COACH Online

www.phwritingcoach.com

Interactive Model

Listen to an audio recording of the Student Model.

Online Journal

Try It! Record your answers and ideas in the online journal.

Interactive Writing Coach™

Submit your writing and receive personalized feedback and support as you draft, revise, and edit.

Video

Learn strategies for effective revising and editing from program authors Jeff Anderson and Kelly Gallagher.

Partner Talk

Work with a partner to edit your letter. Ask if your purpose is clear. As you work, practice newly acquired vocabulary by correctly producing the word's sound.

STUDENT MODEL Business E-mail

Learn From Experience

After reading the business e-mail on this page, read the numbered notes in the margin to learn about how the writer presented her ideas.

Try It! Record your answers and ideas in the online journal.

1 An informative subject line is a **reader-friendly formatting technique** that saves time for busy workers.

2 The writer has appropriately **copied** her immediate supervisor and no one else in the CC.

3 A semi-formal, friendly **greeting** is used here because the writer knows the recipient but not well. In some business situations—for example, when you work closely with a colleague—a less formal greeting could be used, such as "Hello, Mark" or just "Mark."

4 The e-mail is short and concise, with **well-organized information.** This writer includes some information about how much she enjoyed the event, but her suggestion for improvement is clearly the focus of the e-mail.

Try It!

- Develop an outline of this e-mail that notes the important features to be included.
- Why is it important for a work-related document such as a business e-mail to be well organized and reader-friendly?
- Where do you expect to locate the sender's return information in a business e-mail?

---

1 **Subject:** Idea for Next Labor Day Party
From: Mercedes Rios <m.rios@example.com>
Sent: September 12, 2010
To: Markus Jones, President <markus.jones@example.com>
2 **CC:** Rita Esposito, Supervisor <rita.esposito@example.com>

---

3 Dear Markus:

I am a high school student who works part time for your company. I'm writing to thank you for organizing the Labor Day celebration in Oak Park for all employees. My family had a great time celebrating with other people from work, playing games at the booths, and riding the rides.

The only problem was that my brother lost his wallet. We went back to the booths we had visited, and one of the workers gave us directions to Lost and Found. But we could not find the Lost and Found booth. On Monday, I came to your office where someone, thankfully, was able to return the wallet to me.

4 My suggestion is that next year you could have signs that have maps showing where you are and where other things are. Another possibility would be to have volunteers pass out paper maps to visitors.

If you use this suggestion, your event will be even better for families who will be able to arrange to meet at specific places in the park without fear of getting lost.

Thank you for your consideration,
Mercedes Rios

Your Turn Feature Assignment: Business E-mail

Prewriting

- Plan a first draft of your **business e-mail.** You can select from the Topic Bank or come up with an idea of your own.

TOPIC BANK

Request for Product Information Write an e-mail to a company, requesting information about a game or piece of sports equipment.

Express an Opinion Write an e-mail to a political representative, expressing an opinion about a local issue.

- Brainstorm for a list of things that your audience will need to know about your purpose for writing.
- Use the organization's Web site to find accurate contact information for the individual who can address your concern.
- Carefully consider whom you will copy because e-mail creates a permanent record that can be easily forwarded to others.

Drafting

- Use **reader-friendly formatting techniques,** such as including an appropriate greeting for the recipient and a clear signature at the end of the message.
- Include **organized information** that clearly states your purpose in the subject line and restates it in the e-mail.
- **Accurately convey information** by double-checking your facts.

Revising and Editing

Before you revise, review your draft to ensure that information is presented accurately and concisely. Ask yourself if the **purpose and audience** for your e-mail are clearly identified and addressed. Then, revise the draft to **improve your word choice.** For example, confirm that you have used precise words in your message.

Publishing

- Review the list of recipients and your overall message. If the information is sensitive, consider making a phone call instead.
- Confirm that you have the correct e-mail address, and send the e-mail.

WRITING COACH Online

www.phwritingcoach.com

Interactive Model

Listen to an audio recording of the Student Model.

Online Journal

Try It! Record your answers and ideas in the online journal.

Interactive Writing Coach™

Submit your writing and receive personalized feedback and support as you draft, revise, and edit.

Video

Learn strategies for effective revising and editing from program authors Jeff Anderson and Kelly Gallagher.

Partner Talk

Work with a partner to revise your e-mail. Ask if your purpose and language are clear.

STUDENT MODEL Procedural Text

Learn From Experience

After reading the procedural text on this page, read the numbered notes in the margin to learn about how the writer presented his ideas. As you read, take notes to develop your understanding of basic sight and English vocabulary.

Try It! Record your answers and ideas in the online journal.

---

1 The descriptive name for the recipe is a **reader-friendly formatting technique** that will help the reader when scanning for a particular instruction.

2 An introductory description of the juice and its uses addresses the needs of the **audience** by providing additional information for the reader.

3 Accurate lists of the ingredients and tools help the reader know whether he or she has everything needed to make the juice.

4 The writer lists the steps in the order they should be performed. This is an essential feature of **procedural text,** and it is an important reader-friendly formatting technique.

Try It!

- Why is it important for a procedural document, such as a recipe, to list the ingredients and tools needed, and the steps in the order they should be performed?
- What might happen if the steps are out of order?
- What might happen if the wrong amount of an ingredient is listed?

1 Zingy Carrot-Apple Ginger Juice

by Sean O'Brien

2 This spicy juice is a zingy way to start your day or to get a bit of energy when your reserves are low. Also, the juice's zip will make your cheeks pink and give you a healthy glow. Serves: 2

3 **Ingredients:**

4-5 Carrots
2 Apples
1/2–1 inch ginger root (according to taste)

3 **Tools:**

Small knife for peeling and coring
Juicer
Glasses
Ice

4
1. Wash and peel the carrots.
2. Wash and core the apples.
3. Wash and peel the ginger.
4. Send all ingredients through the juicer. (Make sure your pitcher or glass is properly placed to catch the juice or you will have a sticky mess!)
5. Stir the juice.
6. Pour over ice.
7. Serve.

A note about clean-up: Rinse your juicer right away. If you don't, the pulp will dry and may be very hard to clean later. Between uses, take the juicer apart and clean each piece thoroughly. This prevents the growth of bacteria.

Your Turn

Feature Assignment: Procedural Text

Prewriting

- Plan a first draft of your **procedural text.** You can select from the Topic Bank or come up with an idea of your own.

TOPIC BANK

Operating an Electronic Device Write a how-to essay in which you provide step-by-step directions for operating a household appliance. Include adequate detail and description so that a person who is totally unfamiliar with the product will be able to safely use it.

Writing a Favorite Recipe Write a recipe for making a favorite dish. Use terms and lists to make it possible for someone who is not familiar with the dish to follow the recipe.

- Make a list of the tools, ingredients, and other items necessary for the procedure you are explaining.
- Think about your audience, so you know how much detail to include. For example, someone unfamiliar with DVD players may also need an explanation of what these machines do.

Drafting

- Use **reader-friendly formatting techniques.** Provide a descriptive title and a clear purpose. Include boldfacing to help set off sections of the document.
- **Organize the information** by writing steps in a logical order.
- **Accurately convey information** by double-checking the process. Try following the process yourself or have somebody else do so.

Revising and Editing

Before you revise, review your draft to ensure that all of the necessary tools and steps are thoroughly explained. Ask for **feedback** from your **peers and teacher.** Revise your final draft in response to this feedback.

Publishing

Consider posting your instructions online or combining your documents with others to create a class booklet or online collection.

WRITING COACH Online

www.phwritingcoach.com

Interactive Model

Listen to an audio recording of the Student Model.

Online Journal

Try It! Record your answers and ideas in the online journal.

Interactive Writing Coach™

Submit your writing and receive personalized feedback and support as you draft, revise, and edit.

Video

Learn strategies for effective revising and editing from program authors Jeff Anderson and Kelly Gallagher.

Partner Talk

Read your final draft to a partner. Ask if he or she would be able to follow the steps as you have written them. What might you need to change?

21st Century Learning

MAKE YOUR WRITING COUNT

Present a Research Report on Career Day

Business letters, e-mails, and instructions help people communicate important information to specific audiences. These documents may involve the seeds for activities or ideas that will help classmates learn more. Make a **research report** and presentation to share.

With a group, **brainstorm** for several topics from the workplace documents that you can explore further. Have a discussion with others to **decide upon a topic** that will be helpful to someone thinking about future career options. Work together to formulate **an open-ended research question** that will help you produce a research report about the topic. Consider topics like careers in science, educational requirements for a career in media, or ways to find internships.

As you develop your report, you may need to **modify research questions** and **evaluate collected information**. Group members should **consult** one another to **critique the process** as you work. Be prepared to refocus and implement changes as needed. Focus on researching information related to the workplace and careers. Remember that a research report should:

- State a clear thesis
- Consider audience and purpose
- Express a clear point of view
- Provide supporting evidence
- Present ideas in a logical way
- Document sources properly

Organize a Career Day to present your research results to students in your school. Share the information you have gathered in a **multimedia presentation** that uses graphics, images, and sound.

21st Century Learning

Here's your action plan.

1. Research takes time. In a group, make a plan for several group meetings. Set objectives and choose roles for each member.
2. Work together to develop a **research plan.** Each team member should help gather initial research and take notes. A research plan involves:
   - **Marshalling**—collecting and organizing—**evidence** from authoritative sources to support a clear thesis statement and related claims
   - Identifying any **major issues or debates** related to your topic
   - Checking the **authority and objectivity** of your sources to determine if they are relevant, reliable, valid, and accurate
3. Discuss your findings. Use **an evaluative tool**, such as the group's feedback, to check the quality of the research and make adjustments. Then, work together to create a clear **thesis statement**.
4. Outline the content of the report. Assign sections of the outline to each group member. You may need to research further before you write a draft based on your notes. Be sure to **paraphrase, summarize, quote,** and **accurately cite sources** according to a standard format, such as MLA style.
5. Work together to **compile data** and write a rough draft. As you write, analyze data in a way that allows the audience to follow the **logical progression** of your ideas and clearly reflects your **point of view** on the topic. Where needed, organize the information from all your sources to create appropriate **illustrations, graphics, and forms** that help explain the topic. Use a style manual to check that you have properly **documented sources** and **formatted materials.**
6. Revise and edit your writing to ensure that the thesis is well-supported, the analysis is logical and easy to follow, and that you communicate a **clear point of view.**
7. Finally, include **audio-visual support,** such as music, recorded interviews, sound effects, and video clips in your final product.
8. Present your report to interested students, counselors, and teachers.

Listening and Speaking Practice the presentation in front of another group or each other, and request feedback to make improvements. On Career Day, speak clearly and confidently to your audience. Be prepared for questions that may need to be researched further and answered later.

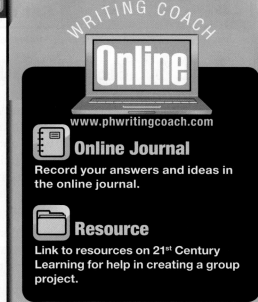

WRITING COACH Online

www.phwritingcoach.com

Online Journal

Record your answers and ideas in the online journal.

Resource

Link to resources on 21st Century Learning for help in creating a group project.

Your Turn | **Writing for Media: Set of Instructions**

21st Century Learning

Set of Instructions

Multimedia presentations are frequently used in schools, in the workplace, at conferences, and online because they are an effective way to present information to a wide audience. Multimedia presentations use a combination of text, images, music, charts, graphics, and animations to allow people to share information on a variety of topics. Slideshows allow the presenter to share only key points in text, supported or elaborated by an oral presentation.

A multimedia presentation is well-suited to sharing a **set of instructions** because the presenter can pace the information, discussing one point fully before exposing the audience to the next part of the presentation.

Try It! Study the slides on this page. Then, answer these questions. Record your answers in your journal.

- How does the **title slide** help to communicate the purpose of the multimedia presentation?
- How do the **numbered steps** help the reader to follow along?
- How do the **images** used on the slides help show the presenter's point of view? How do they appeal to the specific **audience**?
- Is the amount of **text** per slide reader-friendly?

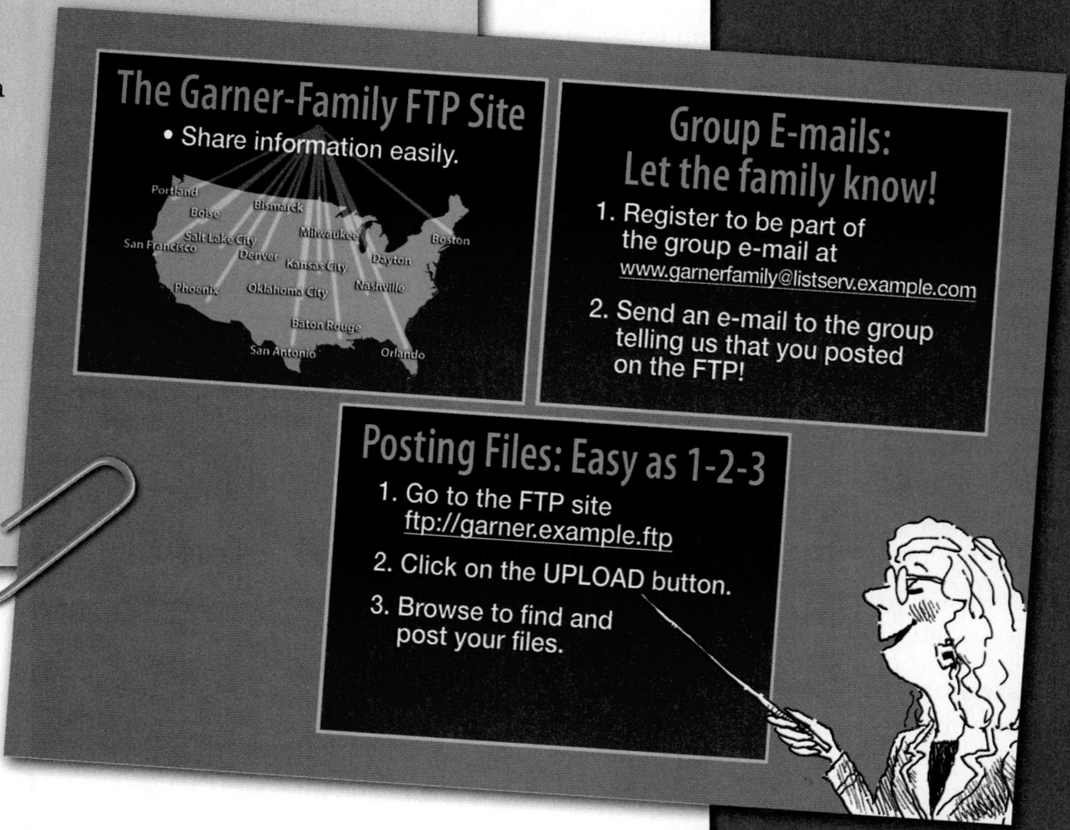

The Garner-Family FTP Site
• Share information easily.
Portland
Boise
Bismarck
Salt Lake City
San Francisco
Milwaukee
Boston
Denver
Kansas City
Dayton
Phoenix
Oklahoma City
Nashville
Baton Rouge
San Antonio
Orlando
Group E-mails: Let the family know!
1. Register to be part of the group e-mail at www.garnerfamily@listserv.example.com
2. Send an e-mail to the group telling us that you posted on the FTP!
Posting Files: Easy as 1-2-3
1. Go to the FTP site ftp://garner.example.ftp
2. Click on the UPLOAD button.
3. Browse to find and post your files.

Extension Find another example of a multimedia presentation of instructions, and compare it with this one.

Create a Set of Instructions

Follow these steps to create your own **multimedia presentation** slide show that features a **set of instructions.** Review the graphic organizers on pages R24–R27 to select one best suited to your needs.

Prewriting

- Brainstorm for a list of instructions for a procedure that you could present using a slide show. Choose the one you think is best.
- Make a detailed list of the steps involved in the procedure.
- Consider the needs of your specific audience. What does your audience already know about the procedure? What does the audience need to know?

Drafting

- To ensure that you use **reader-friendly formatting techniques** for the information text, divide your procedure into slides. Each slide should contain only a small amount of text. This will allow your audience to focus on the details of your oral presentation without getting confused or overwhelmed.
- Number the steps of the procedure and order them according to what is done first, second, next, and so on.
- Plan to share details to explain the reason for a step when needed. However, do not put too much text on each slide.
- Choose **graphics, images, and sound** that convey your distinctive point of view. Be sure that your content appeals to your specific audience.
- Write a script for the oral presentation. **Organize** the information to support the content of each slide.

Revising and Editing

As you revise, review each slide to be sure that its content correctly matches each section of your oral presentation. Check that the design of your slides makes them easy to read. Is your point of view coming across? Double-check the **accuracy** of the information conveyed on your slides. Remember to check your spelling and grammar.

Publishing

- Present your slide show to the class or to another audience.
- Speak clearly and allow time for your audience to ask questions.

WRITING COACH Online

www.phwritingcoach.com

Online Journal

Try It! Record your answers and ideas in the online journal.

Interactive Graphic Organizers

Use the graphic organizers to plan your multimedia presentation.

Partner Talk

Before publishing, practice your presentation with a partner. Listen critically and evaluate each other's presentations. Monitor your partner's spoken language by asking follow-up questions to confirm your understanding.

Writing for Assessment

Many tests include a prompt that asks you to write a procedural text. Your response should include most of the same characteristics of your procedural text. (See pages 262–263.)

Try It! Read the **procedural text** prompt and the information on the format and academic vocabulary. Use the ABCDs of On-Demand Writing to help you plan and write your procedural text.

Format
Describe the purpose of the *procedural text* in the first section. Be sure to include steps that organize information using reader-friendly formatting techniques such as a numbered list or materials lists.

Procedural Text Prompt

Your grandfather wants to use the texting feature on his cell phone. He needs to have written instructions to get started. Write a procedural text that includes stepped-out instructions on how to use texting on his phone.

Academic Vocabulary
A procedural text is a kind of text that tells somebody how to perform a task. *Stepped-out instructions* have numbered lists that provide details in the order they are used.

The ABCDs of On-Demand Writing

Use the following ABCDs to help you respond to the prompt.

Before you write your draft:

Attack the prompt [1 MINUTE]

- Circle or highlight important verbs in the prompt. Draw a line from the verb to what it refers to.
- Rewrite the prompt in your own words.

Brainstorm possible answers [4 MINUTES]

- Create a graphic organizer to generate ideas.
- Use one for each part of the prompt if necessary.

Choose the order of your response [1 MINUTE]

- Think about the best way to organize your ideas.
- Number your ideas in the order you will write about them. Cross out ideas you will not be using.

After you write your draft:

Detect errors before turning in the draft [1 MINUTE]

- Carefully reread your writing.
- Look for spelling, punctuation, and grammar errors.
- Make sure that your response makes sense and is complete.

More Prompts for Practice

Apply It! Respond to Prompt 1 in a timed or open-ended situation by writing a **procedural text** that **organizes information, accurately conveys information, and includes reader-friendly formatting techniques.** As you write, be sure to:

- Consider what your **audience** knows and needs to know about the procedure
- Clearly state the **purpose** of the text you are writing
- **Organize information** into steps or paragraphs that have a clear purpose
- **Define** any terms that your audience may not know
- Develop a draft with **transitions** that clearly **convey meaning**

Prompt 1 A visiting relative needs walking directions from your house to a local store. Write a procedural text that includes stepped-out instructions for making the trip.

Spiral Review: Research Respond to Prompt 2 by writing a **critique of the research process**. Your critique should determine if the research plan:

- Addresses a major topic and **research question**
- Sets up to do research on a complex, **multifaceted topic**
- Contains plans for **compiling data** from **reliable sources**
- Mentions **organizing information** to include graphics and forms
- References using a **standard format** from an appropriate **style manual**

Prompt 2 Evelyn wrote this research plan. Explain what she did well and what needs improvement.

My Topic: I'm interested in researching the first detective stories.

My Research: I'm going to search the Internet, talk to the reference librarian, and look for print sources. Maybe I can find information to make a timeline of the most popular stories.

My Writing: I know that Edgar Allan Poe's "The Murders in the Rue Morgue" is one of the first detective stories. As I reread it, I'll start to write my report using notes about that book.

WRITING COACH **Online**

www.phwritingcoach.com

Interactive Writing Coach™

Plan your response to the prompt. If you are writing the prompt for practice, write one paragraph at a time or your entire draft and submit it for feedback. If you are using the prompt for a timed test, write your entire draft and submit it for feedback.

Remember **ABCD**

- **A**ttack the prompt
- **B**rainstorm possible answers
- **C**hoose the order of your response
- **D**etect errors before turning in the draft

HE PARTS OF SPEECH *Nouns and Pronouns* BASIC SENTENCE PARTS *Subj*
our Functions of a Sentence VERB USAGE *Verb Tenses* PRONOUN USAGE *C*
ouns BASIC SENTENCE PARTS *Subjects and Predicates* PHRASES AND CL
SAGE *Verb Tenses* PRONOUN USAGE *Case* AGREEMENT *Subject-Verb Agr*
ects and Predicates PHRASES AND CLAUSES *Phrases* EFFECTIVE SENTEN
ase AGREEMENT *Subject-Verb Agreement* THE PARTS OF SPEECH *Nouns*
LAUSES *Phrases* EFFECTIVE SENTENCES *The Four Functions of a Sentence*
greement THE PARTS OF SPEECH *Nouns and Pronouns* BASIC SENTENCE
ENCES *The Four Functions of a Sentence* VERB USAGE *Verb Tenses* PRONC

[redacted]

and Predicates PHRASES AND CLAUSES Phrases EFFECTIVE SENTENCES
AGREEMENT Subject-Verb Agreement THE PARTS OF SPEECH Nouns and
S Phrases EFFECTIVE SENTENCES The Four Functions of a Sentence VERB
ent THE PARTS OF SPEECH Nouns and Pronouns BASIC SENTENCE PARTS
The Four Functions of a Sentence VERB USAGE Verb Tenses PRONOUN USA
Prono   SES AND
RB US   E Ve   ject-Verb
TS Su   nd Predic   FECTIVE S
USAG   REE   ARTS OF SPEEC

Grammar

Find It FIX IT

Grammar Game Plan

20 Major Grammatical Errors and How to Fix Them

This handy guide will help you find and fix errors in your writing!

Find It/FIX IT

1 Using the Wrong Word

GAME PLAN **Use the right words to add clarity and authority to your writing. Make sure your words say exactly what you mean them to say.**

CLARIFY MEANING Do not confuse the meanings of words with similar spellings. Also, words with similar definitions can have important shades of meaning. Check that words you found in a thesaurus are used correctly.

Find It FIX IT

We collected ~~precedes~~ ^ proceeds for the fundraiser.

Aunt Sally is ~~infamous~~ ^ famous for her cookies.

SPELL-CHECK ERRORS Computer spell-checkers often correct a misspelling with a different, similarly spelled word. Be sure to proofread your work carefully to catch these errors.

Find It FIX IT

The novel's ~~begging~~ ^ beginning introduces the setting and characters.

A new ~~vision~~ ^ version of the computer is due out shortly.

Check It

Use a current or completed draft of your work to practice using words correctly.

- ✓ **READ carefully.** Take the time to read your draft closely. For a double-check, have someone else read your work.
- ✓ **IDENTIFY possible mistakes.** Mark any difficult or commonly misused words in your draft.
- ✓ **USE a dictionary.** If you are not sure of a word's meaning, consult a dictionary.

Tech Tip

Be your own "spell-checker"! Proofread! Your computer's spell-checker will not identify every misspelling or incorrectly used word.

LEARN MORE

- See Chapter 21, Miscellaneous Problems in Usage, pages 528–542
- See Writing Coach Online

Find It/FIX IT

2 Missing Comma After Introductory Element

Tech Tip

Remember to add commas to introductory elements that you cut and paste from different parts of a sentence or paragraph.

LEARN MORE

- See Chapter 23, Punctuation, pages 576–581
- See Writing Coach Online

GAME PLAN Place a comma after the following introductory elements in your work.

WORDS Place a comma after introductory words of direct address, words of permission, and interjections.

Find It FIX IT

Rita, where is your homework?

Yes, we have time to stop at the library.

Wow, what a lot of rain.

PHRASES Place a comma after introductory prepositional, participial, and infinitive phrases.

Find It FIX IT

In case of fire, please exit the building.

Writing quickly, Tricia finished her draft.

To save your file, click "enter" now.

CLAUSES Introductory adverbial clauses should be followed by a comma.

Find It FIX IT

After the rain stops, we will play soccer.

Check It

Use a current or completed draft of your work to practice placing commas after introductory elements.

- ✓ **SCAN your draft.** Look for introductory words, phrases, and clauses.
- ✓ **IDENTIFY missing commas.** Mark sentence starters that might need a comma.
- ✓ **USE your textbook.** Consult the grammar section of your textbook if you are not sure whether or not to use a comma.

GAME PLAN Provide complete citations for borrowed words and ideas. Use the citation style (such as MLA) that your teacher recommends.

MISSING CITATIONS Cite sources of direct quotes and statistics. Remember—when in doubt, cite the source.

Find It FIX IT

As the senator stated, "The price of failure now is tyranny later"^(Phillips 123).

Fuller reported a thirty percent drop in production over ten years^(9).

INCOMPLETE CITATIONS Make sure your citations include complete source information. This information will vary depending on the source and the citation style, but it may include the author's name, the source's title, and the page number or other location information.

Find It FIX IT

The new text has been called "a genuine improvement" (Singh^12).

More than two-thirds of all teenagers now own cellular phones (Babbit^87).

Check It

Use a current or completed draft of your work to practice documenting your sources.

- **REVIEW your notes.** Look for introductory words, phrases, and clauses.
- **USE a style guide.** Check the appropriate format and contents for your citations in the style guide your teacher recommends.

Find It/FIX IT

3

Incomplete or Missing Documentation

Tech Tip

Be sure to include the citations attached to sentences when you cut and paste text.

LEARN MORE

- See Chapter 11, Research Writing, pages 234–237
- See Writing Coach Online

Find It/FIX IT

4

Vague Pronoun Reference

Tech Tip

It is important to proofread your work after you cut and paste text to form new sentences or paragraphs. You may have inserted vague pronoun references while restructuring.

LEARN MORE

- **See Chapter 19, Agreement, pages 502–506**
- **See Writing Coach Online**

GAME PLAN Create clear pronoun-antecedent relationships to make your writing more accurate and powerful.

VAGUE IDEA Pronouns such as *which, this, that,* and *these* should refer to a specific idea. Sometimes, changing a pronoun to an adjective that modifies a specific noun can avoid a vague reference.

Find It FIX IT

Gov. Murphy gave a compelling speech yesterday to a large crowd. That ^speech might be responsible for her reelection.

UNCLEAR USE OF *IT, THEY,* AND *YOU* Be sure that the pronouns *it, they,* and *you* have a clearly stated antecedent. Replacing the personal pronoun with a specific noun can make a sentence clearer.

Find It FIX IT

The governor is speaking at the university next week. ~~It~~ ^The speech should be informative.

The teachers ~~told~~ ^congratulated the students ~~that they were~~ ^on doing a great job!

In order to do well on the history test, ~~you~~ ^students need to remember the important dates.

Check It

Use a current or completed draft of your work to practice identifying vague pronoun references.

- **READ** carefully. Read your draft slowly to locate pronouns.
- **IDENTIFY** possible errors. Mark any vague pronoun references.
- **REVISE** your draft. Rewrite sentences with vague pronoun-antecedent relationships.

5

Spelling Error

GAME PLAN Spelling errors can change the meaning of a sentence. Proofread your work after spell-checking to be sure you have used the correct words.

SPELL-CHECK ERRORS Computer spell-checkers often replace misspelled words with others close in spelling but different in meaning. Proofread your work carefully to correct these errors.

Find It FIX IT

Even ~~thought~~ ^though it was raining, I decided to leave my umbrella at home.

The queen gave her ~~degree~~ ^decree to the crowd of people gathered to hear her speak.

HOMOPHONES Words that are pronounced the same but have different spellings and meanings are called homophones. Check that you have used the correct homophones to convey your intended meaning.

Find It FIX IT

I saw a black ~~bare~~ ^bear when I was hiking in Canada.

Sara had to slam on the car's ~~break~~ ^brake.

Check It

Use a current or completed draft of your work to practice spelling words correctly.

- ✓ **READ** carefully. Read your draft word by word looking for spelling errors.
- ✓ **IDENTIFY** possible mistakes. Mark any incorrect words or words that are misspelled.
- ✓ **USE** a dictionary. If you are not certain how to spell a word or think a homophone has been used incorrectly, consult a dictionary.

Tech Tip

Proper nouns are not checked by a computer spell-checker. Proofread to make sure that you have spelled people's names correctly.

LEARN MORE

- See Chapter 21, Miscellaneous Problems in Usage, pages 528–542
- See Writing Coach Online

Find It/FIX IT

6

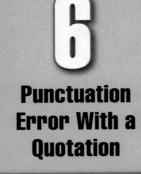

Punctuation Error With a Quotation

GAME PLAN Quotation marks are used to identify direct quotations. Proper punctuation helps to identify quotations and relate them to your work.

DIRECT AND INDIRECT QUOTATIONS A direct quotation is enclosed in quotation marks. Indirect quotations do not need quotation marks.

Find It FIX IT

The mayor said, **"**Today, our city begins its road to recovery.**"**

The mayor said that today our city is on the road to recovery.

QUOTATION MARKS WITH OTHER PUNCTUATION When commas or periods end a quotation, the punctuation goes inside the quotation marks. Question marks and exclamation marks go either inside or outside the quotation marks, depending on the sentence structure. Colons and semicolons used after quoted material should be placed outside the quotation marks.

Find It FIX IT

The principal said, **"**We have secured the funds to build our new basketball court**.""**

"We will be able to host sectionals at our school**!"** the team captain said.

Did the coach say, **"**The team has practice today**"?**

The coach said, **"**The new basketball court will have hardwood floors**";** we were all excited.

Check It

Use a current or completed draft of your work to practice punctuating quotations correctly.

- ✓ **READ** carefully. If you used indirect quotations, make sure that they are not set in quotation marks.
- ✓ **IDENTIFY** direct quotations. Mark each direct quotation in your work. Is each quotation punctuated correctly?
- ✓ **REVISE** your sentences. Correct all punctuation errors in your quotations.

Tech Tip

If you cut and paste quotations, remember to copy the taglines to make sure you have included all of the correct punctuation marks that accompany direct quotations.

LEARN MORE

- See Chapter 23, Punctuation, pages 595–599
- See Writing Coach Online

GAME PLAN Before you insert a comma, think about how your ideas relate to one another. Make sure the comma is necessary.

ESSENTIAL ELEMENTS Appositives, participial phrases, and adjectival clauses that are essential to the meaning of a sentence are not set off by commas.

Find It FIX IT

My friend, Carla, went to auditions for the play.

The student, playing the lead female role, is out sick.

The play, that everyone is talking about, opens in two weeks.

COMPOUND PREDICATE Commas should not break apart a compound predicate.

Find It FIX IT

He lived in France, and was born in America.

The director wrote student plays, and directed community theater.

Check It

Use a current or completed draft of your work to practice correctly punctuating essential elements.

- **SCAN** Mentor Texts. Notice how professional writers use commas.
- **IDENTIFY** essential elements. Did you use commas to indicate these elements?
- **REVISE** your sentences. Delete any commas that set off essential elements.

Find It/FIX IT

7

Unnecessary Comma

Tech Tip

As you restructure sentences by cutting and pasting from different parts of a sentence or paragraph, remember to add or delete commas.

LEARN MORE

- See Chapter 23, Punctuation, pages 578–580, 587–588
- See Writing Coach Online

Find It/FIX IT

8 Unnecessary or Missing Capitalization

GAME PLAN Follow the rules of capitalization, such as capitalizing proper nouns, the first word of a sentence, and titles of works of art.

PROPER NOUNS Names, geographical locations, and organizations are examples of nouns that should be capitalized.

Find It FIX IT

William Shakespeare is a famous playwright from England whose plays are performed around the world.

I attended the Shakespeare Club meeting.

TITLES OF WORKS OF ART The first word and all other key words in the titles of books, poems, stories, plays, paintings, and other works of art are capitalized.

Find It FIX IT

Shakespeare wrote *Romeo and Juliet.*

The *Mona Lisa* is one of Leonardo da Vinci's most famous paintings.

Check It

Use a current or completed draft of your work to practice correctly capitalizing words.

- **SCAN** your draft. Look for words that are capitalized.
- **IDENTIFY** incorrect capitalization. Mark words that might be capitalized incorrectly.
- **USE** your textbook. Consult the grammar section of your textbook if you are not sure if a word should be capitalized.

Tech Tip

Sometimes word processors will automatically capitalize any word that follows a period, even if the period is part of an abbreviation. Proofread carefully for incorrectly capitalized words.

LEARN MORE

- See Chapter 22, Capitalization, pages 546–564
- See Writing Coach Online

9 Missing Word

GAME PLAN **Make sure there are no missing words in a text. This allows ideas to flow smoothly and will help readers understand the text.**

ARTICLES In order to make sure that ideas flow smoothly and sentences are coherent, you must proofread your work. A missing word, even a missing article (*a, an, the*), is enough to confuse a reader.

Find It FIX IT

The school board held ^a meeting to discuss the increase in teachers' salaries.

KEY IDEAS When copying and pasting text, you might miss moving a word in a sentence. If that word is central to the main idea of the sentence, the intended meaning could be lost.

Find It FIX IT

After careful deliberation, the school board voted to ^reject the salary increase.

Many teachers were ^disappointed but understood the budget limitations.

Check It

Use a current or completed draft of your work to practice proofreading.

- **READ** carefully. Read your draft word by word to make sure that you did not omit a word.
- **IDENTIFY** unclear sentences. Mark any sentences you find that do not make sense. Are they unclear because of a missing word?
- **REVISE** your sentences. Add words to your sentences to make the meaning clear.

Tech Tip

When cutting and pasting sentences, you may accidentally insert the same word twice, one right after the other. While spell-checkers generally highlight duplicate words, proofread to be sure the sentence reads as you intended.

LEARN MORE

- See Editing sections in the Writing Chapters
- See Writing Coach Online

Find It/FIX IT

10

Faulty Sentence Structure

Tech Tip

When you cut one part of a sentence and paste it in another, remember to check that the new sentence structure is correct.

LEARN MORE

- See Chapter 16, Effective Sentences, pages 415–421
- See Writing Coach Online

GAME PLAN Sentences should express complex ideas using consistent tenses and similar structures.

FAULTY PARALLELISM When you express complex ideas, it is important that you use parallel grammatical structures to express ideas in phrases, clauses, or sentences of similar types.

Find It FIX IT

Alice uses her new computer to play games, to e-mail friends, and ~~writes~~ ^to write stories.

The computer that he bought and ^that I want is on sale today only!

FAULTY COORDINATION Ideas that are not of equal importance should not be connected with *and.* Instead, use multiple sentences or turn one idea into a subordinate clause.

Find It FIX IT

When the pitcher was up to bat, he hit a homerun.^ ~~and the~~ ^The fans were surprised ~~and~~ ^because they knew his record did not include many homeruns.

I did well on my math test~~, and~~ ^although everyone said it was hard.

Check It

Use a current or corrected draft of your work to practice correctly structuring sentences.

- **SCAN** Mentor Texts. Notice how professional writers present complex ideas.
- **IDENTIFY** possible mistakes. Mark any sentences that have faulty parallelism or faulty coordination.
- **REVISE** your sentences. Rewrite any sentences that do not have correct sentence structure.

GAME PLAN Use commas to set off nonessential elements of sentences.

APPOSITIVE If an appositive is not essential to the meaning of a sentence, it should be set off by commas.

Find It FIX IT Abraham Lincoln, an American, was a United States president.

PARTICIPIAL PHRASE A participial phrase not essential to the meaning of a sentence is set off by commas.

Find It FIX IT Lincoln, elected to office in 1860, was president during the American Civil War.

ADJECTIVAL CLAUSE Use commas to set off an adjectival clause if it is not essential to the meaning of a sentence.

Find It FIX IT Lincoln, who was born in Kentucky, moved with his family to Illinois.

Check It

Use a current or completed draft of your work to practice using commas correctly with nonessential elements.

- ✓ **SCAN** Mentor Texts. Notice how professional writers use commas to set off nonessential elements.
- ✓ **IDENTIFY** nonessential elements. Did you use commas to indicate these words, phrases, or clauses?
- ✓ **REVISE** your sentences. Use commas to set off nonessential elements.

Find It/FIX IT

11

Missing Comma With a Nonessential Element

Tech Tip

When you cut part of a sentence and paste it to another, be sure to include the correct punctuation. Proofread these sentences carefully.

LEARN MORE

- See Chapter 23, Punctuation, pages 578–580
- See Writing Coach Online

Find It/FIX IT

12

Unnecessary Shift in Verb Tense

Tech Tip

When you cut text from one section to paste to another, the new sentence may have verbs that are not consistent in tense. Proofread revised sentences to make sure they use consistent tenses.

LEARN MORE

- See Chapter 17, Verb Usage, pages 446–452
- See Writing Coach Online

GAME PLAN Use consistent verb tenses in your work. Shift tenses only to show that one event comes before or after another.

SEQUENCE OF EVENTS Do not shift tenses unnecessarily when showing a sequence of events.

Find It FIX IT

We will walk to the stadium, and then we ~~bought~~ ^will buy our tickets.

He stood in left field for six innings and ~~stands~~ ^stood in center field for three innings.

SUBORDINATE CLAUSE The verb in the subordinate clause should follow logically from the tense of the main verb. The verbs require a shift in tense if one event happens before or after another.

Find It FIX IT

He wishes that he ~~plays~~ ^had played baseball when he was a child.

Jonathan knows that we ~~went~~ ^will go to the city tomorrow.

Check It

Use a current or completed draft of your work to practice using consistent tenses.

- ✓ **SCAN** Mentor Texts. Notice how professional writers use consistent tenses within a sentence.
- ✓ **IDENTIFY** possible mistakes. Mark any shift in verb tense within a sentence.
- ✓ **USE** your textbook. Consult the grammar section of your textbook if you are not sure that you have used consistent tenses.

Find It/FIX IT

13

Missing Comma in a Compound Sentence

GAME PLAN Use a comma before a coordinating conjunction to separate two or more main clauses in a compound sentence.

MAIN CLAUSES Place a comma before a coordinating conjunction (e.g. *and, but, or, nor, yet, so, for*) in a compound sentence.

Find It FIX IT Alyssa is on vacation at the beach, but the weather forecast predicted rain all week.

BRIEF CLAUSES The main clauses in some compound sentences are brief and do not need a comma if the meaning is clear.

Find It FIX IT The rain stopped and the sun shone.

COMPOUND SUBJECTS AND VERBS Commas should *not* be used to separate compound subjects and compound verbs in a sentence.

Find It FIX IT The trees, and flowers received a healthy dose of water from the rain.

She drove to the airport, and flew home in time for dinner.

Check It

Use a current or completed draft of your work to practice using commas in compound sentences.

- ✓ **SCAN** your draft. Look for compound sentences.
- ✓ **IDENTIFY** missing commas. Mark any compound sentences that should be punctuated with a comma.
- ✓ **REVISE** your sentences. Add commas before coordinating conjunctions to separate main clauses.

Tech Tip

Be careful when you create a compound sentence by cutting and pasting from different parts of a sentence or paragraph. Remember to include a comma to separate the main clauses.

LEARN MORE

- See Chapter 23, Punctuation, pages 571–575
- See Writing Coach Online

Find It/FIX IT

14

Unnecessary or Missing Apostrophe

Tech Tip

Proofread your draft carefully. Not all computer grammar checkers will point out incorrect uses of apostrophes.

LEARN MORE

- See Chapter 18, Pronoun Usage, pages 471–473
- See Chapter 23, Punctuation, pages 614–619
- See Writing Coach Online

GAME PLAN Use apostrophes correctly to show possession.

SINGULAR NOUNS To show the possessive case of most singular nouns, add an apostrophe and *-s.*

Find It FIX IT The maple tree near the pond's bank is bright orange.

PLURAL NOUNS Add an apostrophe to show the possessive case for most plural nouns ending in *-s* or *-es.* For plural nouns that do not end in *-s* or *-es,* add an apostrophe and *-s.*

Find It FIX IT The leaves' color is brilliant in autumn.

The firemen's gear is all stored in one place.

POSSESSIVE PRONOUNS Possessive pronouns (e.g. *his, hers, its, our, their*) show possession without the use of an apostrophe. Remember that the word *it's* means "it is" while *its* shows possession.

Find It FIX IT His favorite vehicle is the fire engine because of its red color.

Check It

Use a current or completed draft of your work to practice showing possession.

- **SCAN** Mentor Texts. Notice when professional writers use apostrophes to indicate possession.
- **IDENTIFY** possible mistakes. Mark each apostrophe in your draft. Did you use them correctly to show possession?
- **REVISE** your sentences. Make sure to delete any apostrophes you used with possessive pronouns.

GAME PLAN Use correct punctuation to avoid run-on sentences, which are two or more sentences punctuated as if they were a single sentence.

FUSED SENTENCE A fused sentence contains two or more sentences joined with no punctuation. To correct a fused sentence, place a period (and capitalize the following word) or a semicolon between the main clauses.

Find It FIX IT

When the mayor began campaigning, he was certain he would be reelected ~~his~~ ^. His opponent was not well known.

The debate showed that the opponents had different points of view; ^ the challenger gained support.

RUN-ON SENTENCE Make sure you place a comma before coordinating conjunctions that join main clauses to avoid run-on sentences.

Find It FIX IT

The votes were tallied after the polls closed, ^ and the mayor won by a narrow margin.

Check It

Use a current or completed draft of your work to practice correcting run-on sentences.

- ✓ **SCAN** your draft. Look for run-on sentences.
- ✓ **IDENTIFY** missing punctuation. Mark sentences that might need a period or a semicolon to separate main clauses.
- ✓ **REVISE** your sentences. When correcting fused sentences, vary your sentence structure.

Find It/FIX IT

15

Run-on Sentence

Tech Tip

Remember to proofread your work. Not all grammar checkers identify run-on sentences.

LEARN MORE

- See Chapter 16, Effective Sentences, pages 410–411
- See Writing Coach Online

Find It/FIX IT

16

Comma Splice

Tech Tip

Some grammar checkers will not catch comma splices. Proofread your work carefully to avoid comma splices.

LEARN MORE

- See Chapter 16, Effective Sentences, pages 410–411
- See Chapter 23, Punctuation, page 572
- See Writing Coach Online

GAME PLAN Use correct punctuation to avoid comma splices. A comma splice happens when two or more complete sentences are joined only with a comma.

PERIOD Replace the comma with a period (and capitalize the following word) to separate two complete thoughts.

Find It FIX IT The snow plows worked all day and all night, ~~it~~ . It was still snowing in the morning.

SEMICOLON Replace the comma with a semicolon if the ideas are similar.

Find It FIX IT Six inches of snow accumulated overnight, ; the forecast called for six more inches by noon.

COORDINATING CONJUNCTION A comma splice can be corrected by placing a coordinating conjunction (e.g., *and, or, but, yet, nor*) after the comma.

Find It FIX IT The temperature rose to 38 degrees, and the snow started to melt.

Check It

Use a current or completed draft of your work to practice correcting comma splices.

- ✓ **READ** carefully. Take time to read your draft carefully. Have someone else read your work for a double-check.
- ✓ **IDENTIFY** possible mistakes. Mark any comma splices you find.
- ✓ **REVISE** your sentences. Fix comma splices in different ways to vary your sentence structure.

Find It/FIX IT

17 Lack of Pronoun-Antecedent Agreement

GAME PLAN Check that pronouns agree with their antecedents in number, person, and gender. When the gender is not specified, the pronoun must still agree in number.

GENDER NEUTRAL ANTECEDENTS When gender is not specific, use *his or her* to refer to the singular antecedent.

Find It FIX IT

<u>Each</u> student must turn in ~~their~~ ^ his or her essay contest piece by the end of the week.

OR, NOR, AND When two or more singular antecedents are joined by *or* or *nor,* use a singular personal pronoun. Use a plural personal pronoun when two or more antecedents are joined by *and.*

Find It FIX IT

Neither Megan <u>nor</u> Emily will learn how to ride ~~their~~ ^ her bike.

Tegan <u>and</u> Amanda are practicing for ~~her~~ ^ their dance recital.

INDEFINITE PRONOUNS A plural indefinite pronoun must agree with a plural personal pronoun. A singular indefinite pronoun must agree with a singular personal pronoun.

Find It FIX IT

<u>Both</u> of the boys wanted to get ~~his~~ ^ their own copy of the comic book released today.

<u>One</u> of the teachers waited for ~~their~~ ^ her students to get on the bus after school.

Check It

Use a current or completed draft of your work to practice pronoun-antecedent agreement.

- ✓ **READ** carefully. Take time to read your draft carefully. For a double-check, have someone else read your work.
- ✓ **IDENTIFY** possible mistakes. Mark any pronouns that do not agree with their antecedents in a sentence.
- ✓ **USE** your textbook. Consult the grammar section of your textbook if you are not sure whether your pronouns and antecedents agree.

Tech Tip

When you cut and paste text from one sentence to another, check that the pronouns agree with the antecedent in the new sentence you create.

LEARN MORE

- See Chapter 19, Agreement, pages 495–501
- See Writing Coach Online

Find It/FIX IT

18 Poorly Integrated Quotation

Tech Tip

When you cut a quote from one sentence and paste it in another, remember to revise the surrounding sentence to integrate the quote into the text.

LEARN MORE

- See Chapter 23, Punctuation, pages 595–599
- See Writing Coach Online

GAME PLAN Quotations should flow smoothly into the sentences that surround them. Add explanatory information to link quotes to the rest of your work.

QUOTE IN A SENTENCE Prepare the reader for the information contained in the quote by introducing the quote's idea.

Find It FIX IT

LaPorte in his autobiography ^ spoke about the importance of his life experience: "My art cannot be seen as separate from my life" (14).

Taylor says ^ that first steps toward a new law are badly needed: "We have to start sometime, and that time is now."

QUOTE AS A SENTENCE Place an introductory phrase before or after a quotation that stands alone. In most cases, this phrase should identify the quote's author or speaker.

Find It FIX IT

^ According to Cass Bergman, "Funds for the building project were misspent" (Stills 4). Other resources were simply missing.

Check It

Use a current or completed draft of your work to practice integrating quotations.

- ✓ **SCAN Mentor Texts.** Notice how professional writers integrate quotations into their work.
- ✓ **IDENTIFY quotes.** Mark each quote in your work. Does each quote flow smoothly with the surrounding sentence?
- ✓ **REVISE your sentences.** Add explanatory information and introductions as needed.

Find It/FIX IT

19

Unnecessary or Missing Hyphen

GAME PLAN Use hyphens correctly in your writing, including with compound words and compound adjectives.

COMPOUND WORDS Hyphens can connect two or more words that are used as one compound word. Some compound words do not require a hyphen. Check a current dictionary if you are unsure about hyphenating a word.

Find It FIX IT

The ~~editorinchief~~ ^ editor-in-chief is in charge of a large staff at the ~~news-paper~~ ^ newspaper.

The ~~motherinlaw~~ ^ mother-in-law took care of her ~~grand-children~~ ^ grandchildren on Wednesday night.

COMPOUND ADJECTIVES A compound adjective that appears before a noun should be hyphenated. Remember, do not hyphenate a compound proper noun acting as an adjective.

Find It FIX IT

The left-^handed quarterback was the best the fans had seen in years.

European settlers met the Native American people.

Check It

Use a current or completed draft of your work to practice hyphenating words.

- ✓ **IDENTIFY** possible errors. Mark any compound adjectives before a noun that are not hyphenated.
- ✓ **REVISE** your sentences. Add a hyphen to words that should be hyphenated.
- ✓ **USE** a dictionary. Consult a dictionary if you are not sure if a word should be hyphenated.

Tech Tip

The automatic hyphenation setting in word processors causes words at the end of a line of text to hyphenate automatically. Be sure to turn off this setting when you are writing a standard essay.

LEARN MORE

- See Chapter 23, Punctuation, pages 607–610
- See Writing Coach Online

Find It/FIX IT

20

Sentence Fragment

Tech Tip

Sometimes, when you cut text from a sentence and paste it to another, you may miss cutting the whole sentence. Make sure you have both a subject and a verb in the new sentences.

LEARN MORE

- See Chapter 14, Basic Sentence Parts, pages 339–342
- See Chapter 16, Effective Sentences, pages 407–411
- See Writing Coach Online

GAME PLAN Use complete sentences when writing. Make sure you have a subject and a complete verb in each and that each sentence expresses a complete thought.

LACKING A SUBJECT OR VERB A complete sentence must have a subject and a verb.

Find It FIX IT

The librarian was in charge of collecting fines for overdue books. ~~And~~ ^She was always kept busy!

The polar bear ^was sliding on the ice.

SUBORDINATE CLAUSE A subordinate clause cannot stand on its own as a complete sentence because it does not express a complete thought.

Find It FIX IT

Ari took all five of his history books home to study for the test~~. Even~~ ^even though he only needed one.

Ms. Clark quizzed the students about the Roman Empire~~. Because~~ ^because that was the subject of tomorrow's test.

Check It

Use a current or completed draft of your work to practice writing complete sentences.

- ✓ **SCAN** your draft. Look for incomplete sentences.
- ✓ **IDENTIFY** missing words. Mark sentences that have missing subjects or verbs.
- ✓ **REVISE** your sentences. Rewrite any sentences that are missing subjects or verbs or that are subordinate clauses standing on their own.

CHAPTER 13

THE PARTS *of* SPEECH

Use the various parts of speech to form sentences that are strong in structure and meaning.

WRITE GUY *Jeff Anderson, M.Ed.*

WHAT DO YOU NOTICE?

Notice different parts of speech as you zoom in on this sentence from "Uncle Marcos," an excerpt from *The House of the Spirits* by Isabel Allende.

MENTOR TEXT

All that remained on earth were the comments of the amazed crowd below and a multitude of experts, who attempted to provide a reasonable explanation of the miracle.

Now, ask yourself the following questions:

- What is the function of the verb *were* in the sentence?
- Which words are adjectives, and which nouns do they modify?

The verb *were* functions as a linking verb that connects the subject *all* to the nouns *comments* and *multitude.* Linking verbs serve to connect the subject of a sentence to words that identify or describe it. The word *amazed* is used as an adjective modifying the noun *crowd*, and the adjective *reasonable* modifies the noun *explanation.*

Grammar for Writers Each part of speech plays an important role in crafting clear and meaningful sentences. Use each part of speech to its best advantage to improve the quality of your writing.

Do you think the word cool is a good adjective?
I'm pretty lukewarm about it.
IDEAS
A- Essay

13.1 Nouns and Pronouns

Nouns and pronouns make it possible for people to label everything around them.

WRITING COACH **Online**

www.phwritingcoach.com

Grammar Tutorials

Brush up on your Grammar skills with these animated videos.

Grammar Practice

Practice your grammar skills with Writing Coach Online.

Grammar Games

Test your knowledge of grammar in this fast-paced interactive video game.

Nouns

The word *noun* comes from the Latin word *nomen*, which means "name."

RULE 13.1.1

A noun is the part of speech that names a person, place, thing, or idea.

Nouns that name a *person* or *place* are easy to identify.

PERSON	Uncle Mike, neighbor, girls, Bob, swimmer, Ms. Yang, Captain Smith
PLACE	library, Dallas, garden, city, kitchen, James River, canyon, Oklahoma

The category *thing* includes visible things, ideas, actions, conditions, and qualities.

VISIBLE THINGS	chair, pencil, school, duck, daffodil, fort
IDEAS	independence, democracy, militarism, capitalism, recession, freedom
ACTIONS	work, research, exploration, competition, exercise, labor
CONDITIONS	sadness, illness, excitement, joy, health, happiness
QUALITIES	kindness, patience, ability, compassion, intelligence, drive

Concrete and Abstract Nouns

Nouns can also be grouped as *concrete* or *abstract.* A **concrete noun** names something you can see, touch, taste, hear, or smell. An **abstract noun** names something you cannot perceive through any of your five senses.

CONCRETE NOUNS	person, cannon, road, city, music
ABSTRACT NOUNS	hope, improvement, independence, desperation, cooperation

See Practice 13.1A

Collective Nouns

A **collective noun** names a *group* of people or things. A collective noun looks singular, but its meaning may be singular or plural, depending on how it is used in a sentence.

COLLECTIVE NOUNS			
army	choir	troop	faculty
cast	class	crew	legislature

Do not confuse collective nouns—nouns that name a collection of people or things acting as a unit—with plural nouns.

Compound Nouns

A **compound noun** is a noun made up of two or more words acting as a single unit. Compound nouns may be written as separate words, hyphenated words, or combined words.

COMPOUND NOUNS	
Separate	life preserver coffee table bird dog
Hyphenated	sergeant-at-arms self-rule daughter-in-law
Combined	battlefield dreamland porthole

Check a dictionary if you are not sure how to write a compound noun.

Common and Proper Nouns

Any noun may be categorized as either *common* or *proper*. A **common noun** names any one of a class of people, places, or things. A **proper noun** names a specific person, place, or thing. Proper nouns are capitalized, but common nouns are not. (See Chapter 22 for rules of capitalization.)

COMMON NOUNS	building, writer, nation, month, leader, place, book, war
PROPER NOUNS	Jones, Virginia, *Leaves of Grass,* Revolutionary War, White House, Mark Twain, France, June

A noun of direct address—the name of a person to whom you are directly speaking—is always a proper noun, as is a family title before a name. In the examples below, common nouns are highlighted in yellow, and proper nouns are highlighted in orange.

COMMON NOUNS

My **aunt** is a **pilot**.

Our **coach** is never late.

My favorite person is my **uncle**.

DIRECT ADDRESS

Please, **Dad**, tell us about your trip.

Mom, can you pick me up?

Jake, please bring your fruit salad when you come to the party.

FAMILY TITLE

Aunt Sarah works for **NASA**.

Grandma makes great pies, but her blueberry pie is my favorite.

My favorite person is **Uncle Barry**.

See Practice 13.1B

PRACTICE 13.1A Identifying and Labeling Nouns as Concrete or Abstract

Read each sentence. Then, write the noun or nouns in each sentence, and label them *concrete* or *abstract*.

EXAMPLE No one knows the identity of the robber.

ANSWER *identity — abstract*
robber — concrete

1. It seems very few mosquitoes display much intelligence.
2. Her loyalty always impresses her friends.
3. Very few visitors understand the culture.
4. Rarely does Martha miss the bus.
5. Strangely, nobody saw the dog in the backyard.
6. After a long time, Franco finally appeared.
7. All the volunteers developed strong friendships.
8. If it is not too much trouble, can you help Max?
9. His cat was known for its curiosity.
10. Brent called me twice about his excitement.

PRACTICE 13.1B Recognizing Kinds of Nouns (Collective, Compound, Proper)

Read each sentence. Then, write whether the underlined noun is *collective*, *compound*, or *proper*.

EXAMPLE Cars were moving along the freeway.

ANSWER *compound*

11. My family was late for the awards show.
12. The weather becomes warmer in April.
13. Many of the speakers were early for the fundraiser.
14. One team flew across the country for the tournament.
15. After two hours, he finally received his suitcase.
16. At the end of the summer, I'm going to Virginia.
17. Sheila had meatloaf for dinner.
18. Does anyone know who wrote *To Kill A Mockingbird*?
19. A crowd gathered near the entrance.
20. They scored a touchdown to win the game.

SPEAKING APPLICATION

Take turns with a partner. Tell about what you did over the weekend, using both concrete and abstract nouns. Your partner should listen for and name each type of noun that you use.

WRITING APPLICATION

Write four sentences. Each sentence should have a collective, compound, proper, or common noun.

Pronouns

Pronouns help writers and speakers avoid awkward repetition of nouns.

RULE 13.1.2

Pronouns are words that stand for nouns or for words that take the place of nouns.

Antecedents of Pronouns Pronouns get their meaning from the words they stand for. These words are called **antecedents.**

RULE 13.1.3

Antecedents are nouns or words that take the place of nouns to which pronouns refer.

The arrows point from pronouns to their antecedents.

EXAMPLES **Michael** said **he** lost **his** watch at the fair.

When the **Lees** moved, **they** gave **their** pets to me.

Attending the state fair is tiring, but **it** is fun!

Antecedents do not always appear before their pronouns, however. Sometimes an antecedent follows its pronoun.

EXAMPLE Because of **its** carnival, **Rottweil**, Germany, is my favorite city.

There are several kinds of pronouns. Most of them have specific antecedents, but a few do not.

See Practice 13.1C

Personal Pronouns The most common pronouns are the **personal pronouns.**

Personal pronouns refer to the person speaking (first person), the person spoken to (second person), or the person, place, or thing spoken about (third person).

RULE 13.1.4

PERSONAL PRONOUNS		
	SINGULAR	PLURAL
First Person	I, me my, mine	we, us our, ours
Second Person	you your, yours	you your, yours
Third Person	he, him, his she, her, hers it, its	they, them their, theirs

In the first example below, the antecedent of the personal pronoun is the person speaking. In the second, the antecedent of the personal pronoun is the person being spoken to. In the last example, the antecedent of the personal pronoun is the thing spoken about.

FIRST PERSON — **My** name is not Jorge.

SECOND PERSON — When **you** left, **you** forgot **your** coat.

THIRD PERSON — Don't judge a book by **its** cover.

Reflexive and Intensive Pronouns These two types of pronouns look the same, but they function differently in sentences.

A reflexive pronoun ends in *-self* or *-selves* and indicates that someone or something in the sentence acts for or on itself. A reflexive pronoun is essential to the meaning of a sentence. An intensive pronoun ends in *-self* or *-selves* and simply adds emphasis to a noun or pronoun in the sentence.

RULE 13.1.5

REFLEXIVE AND INTENSIVE PRONOUNS		
	SINGULAR	**PLURAL**
First Person	myself	ourselves
Second Person	yourself	yourselves
Third Person	himself, herself, itself	themselves

REFLEXIVE The settlers prepared **themselves** for a feast.

INTENSIVE The leader **himself** cooked the turkey.

See Practice 13.1D

Reciprocal Pronouns **Reciprocal pronouns** show a mutual action or relationship.

RULE 13.1.6

The reciprocal pronouns *each other* and *one another* refer to a plural antecedent. They express a mutual action or relationship.

EXAMPLES The two dogs shook water all over **each other**.

The class collected books from **one another**.

See Practice 13.1E
See Practice 13.1F

Demonstrative Pronouns **Demonstrative pronouns** are used to point out one or more nouns.

RULE 13.1.7

A demonstrative pronoun directs attention to a specific person, place, or thing.

There are four demonstrative pronouns.

DEMONSTRATIVE PRONOUNS	
SINGULAR	**PLURAL**
this, that	these, those

Demonstrative pronouns may come before or after their antecedents.

BEFORE **That** is the **ranch** I would like to own.

AFTER I hope to visit **Butte** and **Helena**. **Those** are my first choices.

One of the demonstrative pronouns, *that*, can also be used as a relative pronoun.

Relative Pronouns

Relative pronouns are used to relate one idea in a sentence to another. There are five relative pronouns.

A relative pronoun introduces an adjective clause and connects it to the word that the clause modifies.

RULE 13.1.8

RELATIVE PRONOUNS				
that	which	who	whom	whose

EXAMPLES We read a **book** **that** contained an account of the settlers' experiences.

The **settlers** **who** had written it described their hardships.

The **winter**, **which** they knew would be harsh, was fast approaching.

See Practice 13.1G
See Practice 13.1H

PRACTICE 13.1C Identifying Pronouns and Antecedents

Read each sentence. Then, write the pronoun in each sentence and its antecedent.

EXAMPLE Did Julie forget to bring her lunch?

ANSWER *her, Julie*

1. Jonathan asked his father for help.
2. This is not the movie that Alicia ordered.
3. The pig has broken out of its sty.
4. The Smiths enjoyed themselves at the concert.
5. The boat with its sail spread wide won the race.
6. The twins rented a video game with their money.
7. The princess wore a pink dress to her ceremony.
8. Lauren bought herself a new comic book at the store.
9. The girls said they would be early.
10. The choir just sang its final song.

PRACTICE 13.1D Identifying Personal, Reflexive, and Intensive Pronouns

Read each sentence. Then, write the pronoun in each sentence, and label it *personal, reflexive,* or *intensive*.

EXAMPLE Lance promised himself to work harder next summer.

ANSWER *himself— reflexive*

11. It is time to make myself some lunch.
12. Students, just keep telling yourselves that learning is fun!
13. Franklin finished his homework before watching the game.
14. The host herself showed up late to the party.
15. Terrance forgot his books on the bus.
16. The defensive player scored a touchdown himself.
17. The thirsty actors poured themselves some water.
18. The coach was ready with her whistle and clipboard.
19. I mowed the lawn myself.
20. The students congratulated themselves on performing so well.

SPEAKING APPLICATION

Take turns with a partner. Tell about your favorite character in a movie, using at least two pronouns that refer to that character. Your partner should identify both the pronouns you used and their antecedents.

WRITING APPLICATION

Write a brief paragraph about something you've done on a holiday. Use a personal, a reflexive, and an intensive pronoun in your paragraph.

PRACTICE 13.1E Identifying Reciprocal Pronouns

Read each sentence. Then, write the reciprocal pronoun in each sentence.

EXAMPLE The students congratulated each other.

ANSWER *each other*

1. The committee members complimented one another.
2. Tammy and William respect each other.
3. After a long summer, they kept in touch with each other.
4. Don and Chung greeted each other.
5. Betsy, Carmen, and Helen were embarrassed that they had forgotten one another's names.
6. The toddlers played with one another at daycare.
7. They see each other often.
8. We gave presents to one another.
9. They don't speak to each other often because they are both very busy.
10. Barbara, Julian, and Caitlin always greet one another.

PRACTICE 13.1F Writing Sentences With Reciprocal Pronouns

Read each item. Then, write a sentence to summarize each item, using a reciprocal pronoun. Read your sentences to a partner, who will tell you if you have used the reciprocal pronoun correctly.

EXAMPLE Stella sent cards to her classmates. They sent cards to Stella.

ANSWER *Stella and her classmates sent cards to one another.*

11. Rami lives near Nina. Nina lives near Rami.
12. George eats lunch with Dylan. Dylan eats lunch with George.
13. Celina cheered for her teammates. Her teammates cheered for Celina.
14. Harriet waves to her friends. Her friends wave to Harriet.
15. Cody visits Dan. Dan visits Cody.
16. Jared e-mails his cousins every day. His cousins e-mail Jared every day.
17. Carlos was chatting with Olga. Olga was chatting with Carlos.
18. Muna helps her brother do the dishes. Her brother helps Muna do the dishes.
19. Jin practices basketball with her neighbors. Her neighbors practice basketball with Jin.
20. Ivana shares toys with Sara. Sara shares toys with Ivana.

SPEAKING APPLICATION

Describe a family event to a partner. Show that you understand reciprocal pronouns by using several in your description. Your partner should listen for and identify the reciprocal pronouns that you use.

WRITING APPLICATION

Use Practice 13.1F as a model to write three more items. Read your items to a partner. Your partner should say a sentence using the correct reciprocal pronoun to summarize each item.

Test Warm-Up

DIRECTIONS
Read the introduction and the passage that follows. Then, answer the questions to show that you can use and understand the function of reciprocal pronouns in reading and writing.

Marie wrote this paragraph about chimpanzees. Read the paragraph and think about the changes you would suggest as a peer editor. When you finish reading, answer the questions that follow.

Chimpanzee Party

(1) Chimpanzees love company, which is why they live in groups. (2) They use sounds, facial expressions, hand gestures, and body postures to communicate with them. (3) Even the way chimps touch sends a message. (4) When a chimp needs something, it may hold out a hand to beg. (5) One chimp may greet another with a wave. (6) The other chimp may wave back. (7) Grooming is one way chimps show they are feeling friendly. (8) Chimps make different calls to represent food, danger, and play. (9) The chimpanzee's ability to communicate creates a strong social bond within their group.

---

1 What change should be made in sentence 2?

A Replace ***them*** with **they**

B Replace ***them*** with **one another**

C Replace ***them*** with **each of them**

D Replace ***them*** with **those others**

2 What is the most effective way to add a reciprocal pronoun to sentence 3?

F Even the way chimps touch each other sends a message.

G Even the way chimps touch sends a message to each other.

H Even the way each other touches sends a message.

J Even the way chimps touch sends to each other a message.

3 What is the most effective way to combine sentences 5 and 6?

A When greeting each other, chimps may wave.

B Two chimps may wave as a form of greeting to each other.

C One chimp may greet another with a wave, and the other chimp may wave, too.

D If one chimp waves to greet another chimp, the other chimp may wave back.

4 How should sentence 7 be revised?

F To show they are feeling friendly, some chimps may groom.

G Grooming each other is one way chimps show they are feeling friendly.

H Grooming chimps are feeling friendly.

J Chimps groom to show they are feeling friendly.

PRACTICE 13.1G Writing Demonstrative and Relative Pronouns

Read each sentence. Then, write a demonstrative or relative pronoun to complete each sentence. Label the pronoun *demonstrative* or *relative*.

EXAMPLE We watched a movie _____ was filmed in black-and-white.

ANSWER *that — relative*

1. _____ is an exciting football game.
2. Raul stepped gingerly onto the sand, _____ was hot from sun.
3. The author _____ wrote that book won an award.
4. Carter is the student _____ painting was displayed in the community center.
5. Of all the songs on the list, _____ are the ones I like best.
6. Kalya and Mario went to a movie _____ friends had recommended.
7. _____ shoes in the corner belong to Jody.
8. The business owners _____ I interviewed were very helpful.
9. Janell is sure _____ is the right street.
10. After finishing the book, Petro thought, "_____ was not the ending I expected!"

PRACTICE 13.1H Recognizing Demonstrative and Relative Pronouns

Read each sentence. Then, write the pronoun or pronouns in each sentence, and label them *demonstrative* or *relative*.

EXAMPLE The man who goes by the name of Bobby owns this building.

ANSWER *who — relative*
this — demonstrative

11. That is Emmett's favorite song.
12. These certainly will increase in value.
13. That man whose name was picked won a prize.
14. Local vendors brought jewelry and displayed these at the fair.
15. Janice was the person who told Maria about the sale.
16. The ten guests whom I invited came and brought presents.
17. Julio has a cousin who lives in New Hampshire.
18. This is a perfect example of why you shouldn't watch television while doing your homework.
19. The pieces that covered the playing board fell onto this pillow.
20. Sandy's neighbor borrowed those serving dishes a few weeks ago.

SPEAKING APPLICATION

Take turns with a partner. Using demonstrative and relative pronouns, describe a black-and-white movie that you have seen. Your partner should listen for and identify the demonstrative and relative pronouns that you use.

WRITING APPLICATION

Using sentence 18 as your first sentence, write a short paragraph about what you think happened, using a demonstrative and a relative pronoun in your paragraph.

Interrogative Pronouns

Interrogative pronouns are used to ask questions.

RULE 13.1.9

An interrogative pronoun is used to begin a question.

The five interrogative pronouns are *what*, *which*, *who*, *whom*, and *whose*. Sometimes the antecedent of an interrogative pronoun is not known.

EXAMPLE **Who** picked up the children?

See Practice 13.1I

Indefinite Pronouns

Indefinite pronouns sometimes lack specific antecedents.

RULE 13.1.10

An indefinite pronoun refers to a person, place, or thing that may or may not be specifically named.

INDEFINITE PRONOUNS				
SINGULAR			PLURAL	BOTH
another	everyone	nothing	both	all
anybody	everything	one	few	any
anyone	little	other	many	more
anything	much	somebody	others	most
each	neither	someone	several	none
either	nobody	something		some
everybody	no one			

Indefinite pronouns sometimes have specific antecedents.

NO SPECIFIC ANTECEDENT **Many** have visited Gettysburg.

SPECIFIC ANTECEDENTS **One** of the **students** sang.

Some indefinite pronouns can also function as adjectives.

ADJECTIVE **Few** orchestras are as famous as this one.

See Practice 13.1J

PRACTICE 13.1I **Recognizing Interrogative Pronouns**

Read each sentence. Then, write the correct interrogative pronoun needed in each sentence.

EXAMPLE _____ will happen next?

ANSWER *What*

1. _____ of the candidates is leading in the polls?
2. _____ was chosen as team captain?
3. _____ is Diane making for the bake-off?
4. _____ child is causing all that commotion?
5. _____ of these colors do you think works the best?
6. With _____ did Malik go to the dance?
7. _____ is your favorite topping on a pizza?
8. _____ will start in the big game tonight?
9. To _____ does this bag belong?
10. _____ of these hats did your sister knit?

PRACTICE 13.1J **Identifying Indefinite Pronouns**

Read each sentence. Then, write the indefinite pronoun in each sentence.

EXAMPLE Did anyone remember to bring a radio?

ANSWER *anyone*

11. Some of the players refused to leave the field.
12. My teacher knows everything about current events.
13. None of the answers were obvious.
14. Tiffany is always thinking of others.
15. Both of my friends promised to keep things a secret.
16. My uncle will worry about anything.
17. Most of the fans were cheering.
18. Two weeks before the debate, most of the tickets had been sold.
19. She can do little in this situation.
20. Has anyone seen this movie lately?

SPEAKING APPLICATION

With a partner, take turns interviewing each other. Ask at least five questions that begin with interrogative pronouns.

WRITING APPLICATION

Replace the indefinite pronouns in sentences 12, 13, and 16 with different indefinite pronouns.

13.2 Verbs

Every complete sentence must have at least one **verb**, which may consist of as many as four words.

WRITING COACH Online
www.phwritingcoach.com

Grammar Practice
Practice your grammar skills with Writing Coach Online.

Grammar Games
Test your knowledge of grammar in this fast-paced interactive video game.

RULE 13.2.1

A verb is a word or group of words that expresses time while showing an action, a condition, or the fact that something exists.

Action Verbs and Linking Verbs

Action verbs express action. They are used to tell what someone or something does, did, or will do. **Linking verbs** express a condition or show that something exists.

RULE 13.2.2

An action verb tells what action someone or something is performing.

ACTION VERBS

Mia **learned** about winter sports.

The radio **blared** the broadcast of the hockey game.

We **chose** two books about Texas.

They **remember** the film about China.

The action expressed by a verb does not have to be visible. Words expressing mental activities—such as *learn, think*, or *decide*—are also considered action verbs.

The person or thing that performs the action is called the *subject* of the verb. In the examples above, *Mia, radio, we,* and *they* are the subjects of *learned, blared, chose,* and *remember.*

13.2.3 RULE

A linking verb is a verb that connects its subject with a noun, pronoun, or adjective that identifies or describes the subject.

LINKING VERBS The man **is** a famous hockey player.

The ice surface **seems** smooth.

The verb *be* is the most common linking verb.

THE FORMS OF *BE*			
am	am being	can be	have been
are	are being	could be	has been
is	is being	may be	had been
was	was being	might be	could have been
were	were being	must be	may have been
		shall be	might have been
		should be	shall have been
		will be	should have been
		would be	will have been
			would have been

Most often, the forms of *be* that function as linking verbs express the condition of the subject. Occasionally, however, they may merely express existence, usually by showing, with other words, where the subject is located.

EXAMPLE The skater **is** on the rink.

Other Linking Verbs A few other verbs can also serve as linking verbs.

OTHER LINKING VERBS		
appear	look	sound
become	remain	stay
feel	seem	taste
grow	smell	turn

EXAMPLES

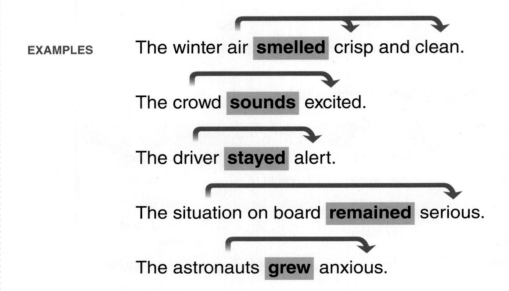

The winter air **smelled** crisp and clean.

The crowd **sounds** excited.

The driver **stayed** alert.

The situation on board **remained** serious.

The astronauts **grew** anxious.

Some of these verbs may also act as action—not linking—verbs. To determine whether the word is functioning as an action verb or as a linking verb, insert *am*, *are*, or *is* in place of the verb. If the substitute makes sense while connecting two words, then the original verb is a linking verb.

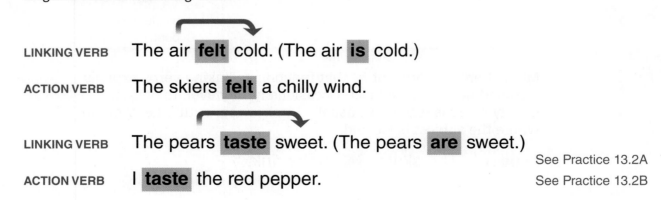

LINKING VERB The air **felt** cold. (The air **is** cold.)

ACTION VERB The skiers **felt** a chilly wind.

LINKING VERB The pears **taste** sweet. (The pears **are** sweet.)

ACTION VERB I **taste** the red pepper.

See Practice 13.2A
See Practice 13.2B

PRACTICE 13.2A Identifying Action and Linking Verbs

Read each sentence. Write the action verb in each sentence.

EXAMPLE I tasted squid for the first time.

ANSWER *tasted*

1. The bus turned left into the service area.
2. Our neighbor grows beautiful roses.
3. Dad played with the children.
4. The detective looked at the clues.
5. They wandered through the forest.

Read each sentence. Write the linking verb in each sentence.

EXAMPLE Cold water is refreshing.

ANSWER *is*

6. The crowd became restless.
7. I grew interested in coins a year ago.
8. The two remained friends all year.
9. We all felt cooler after a dip in the ocean.
10. Each bird's call sounds different.

PRACTICE 13.2B Distinguishing Between Action and Linking Verbs

Read each sentence. Then, write the verb in each sentence, and label it *action* or *linking*.

EXAMPLE The vegetables tasted salty.

ANSWER *tasted — linking*

11. Fred smelled the bouquet of flowers.
12. The bridge looked sturdy enough.
13. The guard sounded the alarm.
14. The candidate appeared confident.
15. The farmer grows wheat in these fields.
16. Levi tasted the sweet and sour pork at the Chinese restaurant.
17. The skunk smelled awful.
18. She performs at the music fair each summer.
19. I turned the volume down on the television.
20. Aunt Judy feels fine after her illness last week.

SPEAKING APPLICATION

Take turns with a partner. Tell about something fun you did recently, using both action verbs and linking verbs. Your partner should listen for and name three verbs that you use.

WRITING APPLICATION

Use sentences 17 and 20 as models to write sentences of your own. Replace the verb in each sentence with another action verb or linking verb.

Transitive and Intransitive Verbs

All verbs are either **transitive** or **intransitive,** depending on whether or not they transfer action to another word in a sentence.

RULE 13.2.4

A transitive verb directs action toward someone or something named in the same sentence. An intransitive verb does not direct action toward anyone or anything named in the same sentence.

The word toward which a transitive verb directs its action is called the *object* of the verb. Intransitive verbs never have objects. You can determine whether a verb has an object by asking *whom* or *what* after the verb.

TRANSITIVE — Jack **shot** the puck.
(Shot what? puck)

We **ate** the chicken.
(Ate what? chicken)

INTRANSITIVE — The team **practiced** on the outdoor field.
(Practiced what? [no answer])

The fan **shouted** loudly.
(Shouted what? [no answer])

RULE 13.2.5

Because linking verbs do not express action, they are always intransitive. Most action verbs can be either transitive or intransitive, depending on the sentence. However, some action verbs can only be transitive, and others can only be intransitive.

TRANSITIVE — I **wrote** a letter from New Mexico.

INTRANSITIVE — The secretary **wrote** quickly.

ALWAYS TRANSITIVE California grapes **rival** those of France.

ALWAYS INTRANSITIVE She **winced** at the sound of his voice.

See Practice 13.2C

Verb Phrases

A verb that has more than one word is a **verb phrase.**

RULE 13.2.6

A verb phrase consists of a main verb and one or more helping verbs.

Helping verbs are often called auxiliary verbs. One or more helping verbs may precede the main verb in a verb phrase.

VERB PHRASES I **will be taking** a horse-and-carriage ride.

I **should have been watching** when I crossed the road.

All the forms of *be* listed in this chapter can be used as helping verbs. The following verbs can also be helping verbs.

OTHER HELPING VERBS			
do	have	shall	can
does	has	should	could
did	had	will	may
		would	might
			must

A verb phrase is often interrupted by other words in a sentence.

INTERRUPTED VERB PHRASE I **will** definitely **be taking** a horse-and-carriage ride through the snow.

Should I **take** a horse-and-carriage ride through the snow?

See Practice 13.2D

PRACTICE 13.2C Distinguishing Between Transitive and Intransitive Verbs

Read each sentence. Then, write the action verb in each sentence, and label it *transitive* or *intransitive*.

EXAMPLE Dana entered her poem in the contest.

ANSWER *entered — transitive*

1. The chef prepared spectacular desserts.
2. The monkeys swung from tree to tree.
3. We divided the rest of the sandwich among us.
4. Mr. Anderson lives alone.
5. Icicles hung from the roof.
6. We saw Grandma last night.
7. The fans cheered from the bleachers.
8. We crawled carefully to the fence.
9. A stray dog followed us home from the park.
10. The quarterback ran down the field.

PRACTICE 13.2D Recognizing Verb Phrases

Read each sentence. Then, write the verb phrase in each sentence.

EXAMPLE I have been studying for hours.

ANSWER *have been studying*

11. You should have come with us.
12. We are going to Arizona this summer.
13. David could not see his brother in the fog.
14. Nguyen does know the words to the song.
15. Cameron might come to the party after all.
16. Basketball was invented in 1891.
17. This sewing machine does work.
18. I have seen that portrait before.
19. Elise will perform a solo at the recital.
20. I am talking on my cellphone.

SPEAKING APPLICATION

Take turns with a partner. Tell about what you did last summer, using both transitive and intransitive verbs. Your partner should listen for and name three transitive or intransitive verbs that you use.

WRITING APPLICATION

Write three sentences with verb phrases. The first sentence should have one helping verb. The second sentence should have two helping verbs. The third should have three helping verbs.

13.3 Adjectives and Adverbs

Adjectives and **adverbs** are the two parts of speech known as *modifiers*—that is, they slightly change the meaning of other words by adding description or making them more precise.

WRITING COACH
Online
www.phwritingcoach.com

Grammar Tutorials
Brush up on your Grammar skills with these animated videos.

Grammar Practice
Practice your grammar skills with Writing Coach Online.

Grammar Games
Test your knowledge of grammar in this fast-paced interactive video game.

Adjectives

An **adjective** clarifies the meaning of a noun or pronoun by providing information about its appearance, location, and so on.

An adjective is a word used to describe a noun or pronoun or to give it a more specific meaning.

13.3.1 RULE

An adjective answers one of four questions about a noun or pronoun: *What kind? Which one? How many? How much?*

EXAMPLES **green** fields (What kind of fields?)

that garden (Which garden?)

six roses (How many roses?)

extensive rainfall (How much rainfall?)

When an adjective modifies a noun, it usually precedes the noun. Occasionally, the adjective may follow the noun.

EXAMPLES The expert was **tactful** about my limited knowledge.

I considered the expert **tactful**.

An adjective that modifies a pronoun usually follows it. Sometimes, however, the adjective precedes the pronoun as it does in the example on the next page.

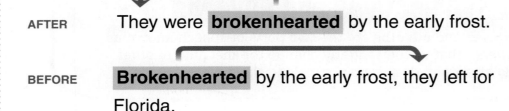

AFTER They were **brokenhearted** by the early frost.

BEFORE **Brokenhearted** by the early frost, they left for Florida.

More than one adjective may modify a single noun or pronoun.

EXAMPLE We hired a **competent, enthusiastic** gardener.

Articles Three common adjectives—*a, an*, and *the*—are known as **articles.** *A* and *an* are called **indefinite articles** because they refer to any one of a class of nouns. *The* refers to a specific noun and, therefore, is called the **definite article.**

INDEFINITE EXAMPLES	DEFINITE EXAMPLES
a daisy	the stem
an orchid	the mask

Remember that *an* is used before a vowel sound; *a* is used before a consonant sound.

EXAMPLES **a** one-horse town (*w* sound)

a union (*y* sound)

an honest man (no *h* sound)

See Practice 13.3A

Nouns Used as Adjectives Words that are usually nouns sometimes act as adjectives. In this case, the noun answers the questions *What kind?* or *Which one?* about another noun.

NOUNS USED AS ADJECTIVES	
flower	flower garden
lawn	lawn mower

See Practice 13.3B

Proper Adjectives Adjectives can also be proper. **Proper adjectives** are proper nouns used as adjectives or adjectives formed from proper nouns. They usually begin with capital letters.

PROPER NOUNS	PROPER ADJECTIVES
Monday	Monday morning
San Francisco	San Francisco streets
Europe	European roses
Rome	Roman hyacinth

Compound Adjectives Adjectives can be compound. Most are hyphenated; others are combined or are separate words.

HYPHENATED **rain-forest** plants

water-soluble pigments

COMBINED **airborne** pollen

evergreen shrubs

See Practice 13.3C

SEPARATE **North American** rhododendrons

Pronouns Used as Adjectives Certain pronouns can also function as adjectives. The seven personal pronouns, known as either **possessive adjectives** or **possessive pronouns,** do double duty in a sentence. They act as pronouns because they have antecedents. They also act as adjectives because they modify nouns by answering *Which one?* The other pronouns become adjectives instead of pronouns when they stand before nouns and answer the question *Which one?*

A pronoun is used as an adjective if it modifies a noun.

RULE 13.3.2

Possessive pronouns, demonstrative pronouns, interrogative pronouns, and indefinite pronouns can all function as adjectives when they modify nouns.

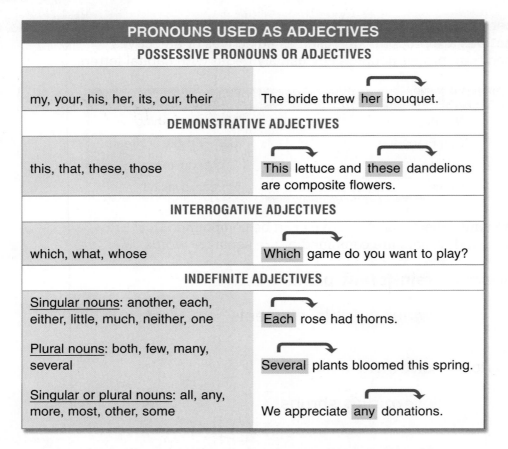

PRONOUNS USED AS ADJECTIVES	
POSSESSIVE PRONOUNS OR ADJECTIVES	
my, your, his, her, its, our, their	The bride threw her bouquet.
DEMONSTRATIVE ADJECTIVES	
this, that, these, those	This lettuce and these dandelions are composite flowers.
INTERROGATIVE ADJECTIVES	
which, what, whose	Which game do you want to play?
INDEFINITE ADJECTIVES	
Singular nouns: another, each, either, little, much, neither, one	Each rose had thorns.
Plural nouns: both, few, many, several	Several plants bloomed this spring.
Singular or plural nouns: all, any, more, most, other, some	We appreciate any donations.

Verb Forms Used as Adjectives Verb forms used as adjectives usually end in *-ing* or *-ed* and are called **participles.**

EXAMPLE I pruned the **wilting** flowers.

Nouns, pronouns, and verb forms function as adjectives only when they modify other nouns or pronouns. The following examples show how their function in a sentence can change.

	REGULAR FUNCTION	AS AN ADJECTIVE
Noun	The deck was slippery.	I sat in the deck chair.
Pronoun	This was an idyllic life.	This life was idyllic.
Verb	The ice melted in the sun.	The melted ice made a puddle.

See Practice 13.3D

PRACTICE 13.3A **Recognizing Adjectives and Articles**

Read each sentence. Then, write the adjective in each sentence.

EXAMPLE Dad baked an apple pie.
ANSWER *apple*

1. The runner set a new record.
2. The passenger remained calm.
3. The house floods during heavy rains.
4. No one knew the answer to the last question.
5. The speaker raised an interesting point.

Read each sentence. Then, write the article(s) in each sentence.

EXAMPLE I saw an ostrich and a penguin.
ANSWER *an, a*

6. The students were eager to volunteer.
7. The lifeguard raised a white flag.
8. The dog came to the woman.
9. The wicker basket contained an apple.
10. Uncle Harry gave Erin a present.

PRACTICE 13.3B **Identifying Nouns Used as Adjectives**

Read each sentence. Then, write the noun that is used as an adjective in each sentence.

EXAMPLE She is running for a town office.
ANSWER *town*

11. Dairy products can be good for you.
12. Each camper had insect repellent.
13. We have a birdbath in our rose garden.
14. Melissa had a delicious lettuce salad for lunch.
15. The apartment building is very high.
16. We put the breakfast dishes away.
17. Emma missed her ballet class last week.
18. Rocco is a player on the football team.
19. The television show has too many commercials.
20. My sister is going to day camp this summer.

SPEAKING APPLICATION

Take turns with a partner. Tell about your favorite movie. Your partner should listen for and name four adjectives and four articles that you use.

WRITING APPLICATION

Write three sentences that contain nouns used as adjectives.

PRACTICE 13.3C Recognizing Proper and Compound Adjectives

Read each sentence. Then, write the adjective in each sentence, and label it as either *proper* or *compound*.

EXAMPLE The decision had far-reaching effects.

ANSWER *far-reaching — compound*

1. My mother grows African violets.
2. She is very closemouthed about her life.
3. The restaurant serves soft-shell crab.
4. Emily took a ride on her Shetland pony.
5. The program was started by a farsighted group.
6. We shared a triple-decker sandwich.
7. The Italian restaurant makes lasagna.
8. Do not turn onto the one-way street.
9. England flourished during the Elizabethan period.
10. He is my next-door neighbor.

PRACTICE 13.3D Recognizing Pronouns and Verbs Used as Adjectives

Read each sentence. Then, write the pronoun or verb used as an adjective in each sentence.

EXAMPLE Some students still have tickets for the game.

ANSWER *some*

11. All citizens have a duty to vote.
12. The sinking ship was lost at sea.
13. We visited several natural history museums.
14. Please mail those letters.
15. The boiling water was ready.
16. A bouncing bunny hopped through the field.
17. Several teachers attended the game.
18. That movie was so funny!
19. We camped in a few parks during the trip.
20. The spoiled food was thrown into the garbage.

SPEAKING APPLICATION

With a partner, name four adjectives that are proper or compound. Then, each of you should use one of the adjectives in a sentence.

WRITING APPLICATION

Write four sentences that use pronouns as adjectives. Then, write four sentences that use verbs as adjectives.

Adverbs

Adverbs, like adjectives, describe other words or make other words more specific.

An adverb is a word that modifies a verb, an adjective, or another adverb.

13.3.3 RULE

When an adverb modifies a verb, it will answer any of the following questions: *Where? When? In what way? To what extent?*

An adverb answers only one question when modifying an adjective or another adverb: *To what extent?* Because it specifies the degree or intensity of the modified adjective or adverb, such an adverb is often called an **intensifier.**

The position of an adverb in relation to the word it modifies can vary in a sentence. If the adverb modifies a verb, it may precede or follow it or even interrupt a verb phrase. Normally, adverbs modifying adjectives and adverbs will immediately precede the words they modify.

ADVERBS MODIFYING VERBS	
Where?	**When?**
The plant grew here.	She never raked the leaves.
The bushes were planted there.	Later, we toured the greenhouses.
The snake slid underground.	The boat sails daily to the city.
In what way?	**To what extent?**
He officially announced it.	The bees were still buzzing loudly.
She was graciously helping.	He always did it right.
Jeff left quickly after the party.	Be sure to wash completely after painting.

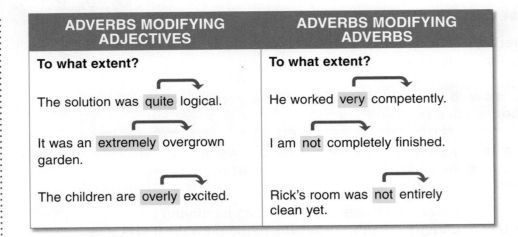

ADVERBS MODIFYING ADJECTIVES	ADVERBS MODIFYING ADVERBS
To what extent?	**To what extent?**
The solution was quite logical.	He worked very competently.
It was an extremely overgrown garden.	I am not completely finished.
The children are overly excited.	Rick's room was not entirely clean yet.

Adverbs as Parts of Verbs Some verbs require an adverb to complete their meaning. Adverbs used this way are considered part of the verb. An adverb functioning as part of a verb does not answer the usual questions for adverbs.

EXAMPLES The tractor **backed up** alongside the field.

Please **point out** which band instrument is yours.

Jennifer had to **run out** at lunch to pick up her car.

See Practice 13.3E

Nouns Functioning as Adverbs

Several nouns can function as adverbs that answer the questions *Where?* or *When?* Some of these words are *home*, *yesterday*, *today*, *tomorrow*, *mornings*, *afternoons*, *evenings*, *nights*, *week*, *month*, and *year*.

NOUNS USED AS ADVERBS	
NOUNS	**AS ADVERBS**
Evenings are restful times.	I work evenings.
My home is miles from here.	Let's head home.
Yesterday was a lovely day.	I saw them yesterday at the show.

Adverb or Adjective?

Adverbs usually have different forms from adjectives and thus are easily identified. Many adverbs are formed by the addition of *-ly* to an adjective.

ADJECTIVES Our professor looked **pensive**.

Teri walked through the **open** door.

ADVERBS The professor looked at her notes **pensively**.

We discussed the matter **openly**.

Some adjectives, however, also end in *-ly*. Therefore, you cannot assume that every word ending in *-ly* is an adverb.

ADJECTIVES an **ugly** scene

a **nightly** bloom

a **lovely** shell

curly edges

Some adjectives and adverbs share the same form. You can determine the part of speech of such words by checking their function in the sentence. An adverb will modify a verb, adjective, or adverb; an adjective will modify a noun or pronoun.

ADVERB The concert ran **late**.

ADJECTIVE We enjoyed the **late** dinners in Spain.

ADVERB The fish swam **straight** through the channel.

See Practice 13.3F ADJECTIVE The path was **straight**.

PRACTICE 13.3E Recognizing Adverbs

Read each sentence. Then, write the adverb in each sentence.

EXAMPLE The snow completely covered our car.

ANSWER *completely*

1. The play began promptly.
2. A new mall is nearby.
3. Let's stop here and rest.
4. I opened the door cautiously.
5. The woman put her packages down.
6. We threw away our trash.
7. That was an extremely funny comedian.
8. Juan was somewhat tired after the game.
9. Hardly any students bought tickets for the play.
10. The actor was extraordinarily talented.

PRACTICE 13.3F Identifying Adverbs and the Words They Modify

Read each sentence. Then, write the adverb in each sentence and the word it modifies.

EXAMPLE I am going home.

ANSWER *home, going*

11. The baseball season starts tomorrow.
12. Sarah took the test early.
13. Who finished first in the contest?
14. My grandparents arrived yesterday from Florida.
15. I ran fast and scored a run.
16. Please go downstairs and feed the cat.
17. We arrived later than our friends.
18. My dad works nights at the factory.
19. We have only one chance to pass the test.
20. Tim worked hard to finish his project.

SPEAKING APPLICATION

Take turns with a partner. Tell about something that you enjoy doing. Your partner should name adverbs that you use to describe where, when, in what way, and to what extent you do the activity.

WRITING APPLICATION

Use sentence 12 as a model to write three sentences of your own. Replace the adverb in sentence 12 with other adverbs.

13.4 Prepositions, Conjunctions, and Interjections

Prepositions and conjunctions function in sentences as connectors. **Prepositions** express relationships between words or ideas, whereas **conjunctions** join words, groups of words, or even entire sentences. **Interjections** function by themselves and are independent of other words in a sentence.

WRITING COACH Online

@www.phwritingcoach.com

Grammar Tutorials

Brush up on your Grammar skills with these animated videos.

Grammar Practice

Practice your grammar skills with Writing Coach Online.

Grammar Games

Test your knowledge of grammar in this fast-paced interactive video game.

Prepositions and Prepositional Phrases

Prepositions make it possible to show relationships between words. The relationships may involve, for example, location, direction, time, cause, or possession. A preposition may consist of one word or multiple words. (See the chart on the next page.)

A preposition relates the noun or pronoun that appears with it to another word in the sentence.

RULE 13.4.1

Notice how the prepositions below, highlighted in pink, relate to the words highlighted in yellow.

LOCATION Inventions **are made** **around** the **world**.

TIME Some inventions **last** **for** **centuries**.

CAUSE Tina is **late** **because of** the **train**.

A prepositional phrase is a group of words that includes a preposition and a noun or pronoun.

RULE 13.4.2

The noun or pronoun with a preposition is called the **object of the preposition.** Objects may have one or more modifiers. A prepositional phrase may also have more than one object. In the example below, the objects of the prepositions are highlighted in blue, and the prepositions are in pink.

EXAMPLE Eric and Alisha applied **for** **jobs** **on** **Tuesday**.

PREPOSITIONS			
aboard	before	in front of	over
about	behind	in place of	owing to
above	below	in regard to	past
according to	beneath	inside	prior to
across	beside	in spite of	regarding
across from	besides	instead of	round
after	between	into	since
against	beyond	in view of	through
ahead of	but	like	throughout
along	by	near	till
alongside	by means of	nearby	to
along with	concerning	next to	together with
amid	considering	of	toward
among	despite	off	under
apart from	down	on	underneath
around	during	on account of	until
aside from	except	onto	unto
as of	for	on top of	up
as	from	opposite	upon
atop	in	out	with
barring	in addition to	out of	within
because of	in back of	outside	without

See Practice 13.4A

Preposition or Adverb?

Many words may be used either as prepositions or adverbs. Words that can function in either role include *around, before, behind, down, in, off, on, out, over,* and *up*. If an object accompanies the word, the word is used as a preposition.

PREPOSITION The Machine Age developed **around** a group of inventions.

ADVERB My thoughts went **around and around**.

See Practice 13.4B

PRACTICE 13.4A Identifying Prepositions and Prepositional Phrases

Read each sentence. Then, write the prepositional phrase in each sentence, and underline the preposition.

EXAMPLE The girls are playing in the back yard.

ANSWER *in the back yard*

1. Most players on our team practice every day.
2. Each boy told a story about his pet.
3. Trish made a gift for Michelle.
4. Our neighbors have friends from many different states.
5. The computer I saw in the catalog was the newest model.
6. The main difference between my brother and me is that I am taller.
7. My aunt and uncle live above a restaurant.
8. Sanjay painted a picture of a beach.
9. We climbed aboard the sailboat.
10. We visited their fishing cabin at the lake.

PRACTICE 13.4B Distinguishing Between Prepositions and Adverbs

Read each sentence. Then, label each underlined word as a *preposition* or an *adverb.*

EXAMPLE We planted flowers around the fountain.

ANSWER *preposition*

11. I like to work outside.
12. Palm trees swayed outside the hotel.
13. Two eager fans ran past the guard.
14. As we cheered, the runners raced past.
15. Skyscrapers towered above.
16. The jet roared above the clouds.
17. We put our boots on quickly.
18. A small boat floated on the lake.
19. The catcher crouched behind home plate.
20. Carla went home and left her sweater behind.

SPEAKING APPLICATION

Take turns with a partner. Describe the locations of different objects in the room. Your partner should listen for and identify three prepositional phrases that you use and the preposition in each phrase.

WRITING APPLICATION

Write a sentence using the word *off* as a preposition. Then, write another sentence using *off* as an adverb.

Conjunctions

There are three main kinds of conjunctions: **coordinating, correlative,** and **subordinating.** Sometimes a type of adverb, the **conjunctive adverb,** is also considered a conjunction.

RULE 13.4.3

A conjunction is a word used to connect other words or groups of words.

Coordinating Conjunctions The seven coordinating conjunctions are used to connect similar parts of speech or groups of words of equal grammatical weight.

COORDINATING CONJUNCTIONS						
and	but	for	nor	or	so	yet

EXAMPLES My sister **and** brother ran the program.

Bob left early, **so** I left with him.

Correlative Conjunctions The five paired correlative conjunctions join elements of equal grammatical weight.

CORRELATIVE CONJUNCTIONS		
both . . . and	either . . . or	neither . . . nor
not only . . . but also	whether . . . or	

EXAMPLES He saw **both** lions **and** tigers.

Neither John **nor** Joan came to the picnic.

I don't know **whether** to go to the movies **or** see a play.

Subordinating Conjunctions Subordinating conjunctions join two complete ideas by making one of the ideas subordinate to, or dependent upon, the other.

SUBORDINATING CONJUNCTIONS			
after	because	lest	till
although	before	now that	unless
as	even if	provided	until
as if	even though	since	when
as long as	how	so that	whenever
as much as	if	than	where
as soon as	inasmuch as	that	wherever
as though	in order that	though	while

The subordinate idea in a sentence always begins with a subordinating conjunction and makes up what is known as a subordinate clause. A subordinate clause may either follow or precede the main idea in a sentence.

EXAMPLES We protect the wetlands **because** they are important to the ecosystem.

As soon as the volunteers arrived, the cleanup work began.

Conjunctive Adverbs Conjunctive adverbs act as transitions between complete ideas by indicating comparisons, contrasts, results, and other relationships. The chart below lists the most common conjunctive adverbs.

CONJUNCTIVE ADVERBS		
accordingly	finally	nevertheless
again	furthermore	otherwise
also	however	then
besides	indeed	therefore
consequently	moreover	thus

Punctuation With Conjunctive Adverbs Punctuation is usually required both before and after conjunctive adverbs.

EXAMPLES The team was very successful. **Nevertheless**, they continued to practice very hard.

Sophia played several instruments well; **however**, her favorite is the piano.

I arrived late; **furthermore**, I forgot my books.

See Practice 13.4C

Interjections

Interjections express emotion. Unlike most words, they have no grammatical connection to other words in a sentence.

RULE 13.4.4

An interjection is a word that expresses feeling or emotion and functions independently of a sentence.

Interjections can express a variety of sentiments, such as happiness, fear, anger, pain, surprise, sorrow, exhaustion, or hesitation.

SOME COMMON INTERJECTIONS				
ah	dear	hey	ouch	well
aha	goodness	hurray	psst	whew
alas	gracious	oh	tsk	wow

EXAMPLES **Ouch**! That machine is very hot.

Wow! This is great!

Oh! Go away.

Whew! We worked hard cleaning the mountain trail.

See Practice 13.4D

PRACTICE 13.4C Identifying Different Conjunctions

Read each sentence. Then, write the conjunction in each sentence, and label it as *coordinating*, *correlative*, *subordinating*, or *conjunctive adverb*.

EXAMPLE After walking home in the rain, we were not only wet but also tired.

ANSWER *not only . . . but also* — correlative

1. A package arrived while we were out.
2. Jake said he would be here, yet he didn't show up.
3. The coach was kind but firm.
4. Jen likes her new school; besides, she was ready for a change.
5. The team needs both a pitcher and an outfielder.
6. I did my homework while they watched television.
7. Kevin sleeps later than I do.
8. Neither Jamal nor Keisha knows where Trina is.
9. Tran won the race; therefore, he will go to the state track meet.
10. Class will begin as soon as the teacher arrives.

PRACTICE 13.4D Supplying Interjections

Read each sentence. Then, write an interjection that shows the feeling expressed in the sentence.

EXAMPLE _____! This soup is awful!

ANSWER *Eek*

11. _____, we never found the ball.
12. _____! I hurt my knee!
13. _____, isn't that Marcy over there?
14. _____! I've been hoping for a new baseball mitt!
15. _____! That was the best concert I've ever been to.
16. _____! I'm stuck!
17. _____, I knew I wouldn't get the part.
18. _____, I can't believe it's raining again.
19. _____! Our team won the game!
20. _____! I'm really tired!

SPEAKING APPLICATION

Take turns with a partner. Tell about something that you did with a friend. Your partner should name conjunctions that you use and identify the kind of conjunction.

WRITING APPLICATION

Write three sentences using interjections.

13.5 Words as Different Parts of Speech

Words are flexible, often serving as one part of speech in one sentence and as another part of speech in another.

WRITING COACH Online

www.phwritingcoach.com

Grammar Practice

Practice your grammar skills with Writing Coach Online.

Grammar Games

Test your knowledge of grammar in this fast-paced interactive video game.

Identifying Parts of Speech

To *function* means "to serve in a particular capacity." The function of a word may change from one sentence to another.

RULE 13.5.1

The way a word is used in a sentence determines its part of speech.

The word *well* has different meanings in the following sentences.

As a Noun	Our well ran dry.
As a Verb	After falling off her bicycle, tears welled in Jill's eyes.
As an Adjective	She does not feel well today.

Nouns, Pronouns, and Verbs A **noun** names a person, place, or thing. A **pronoun** stands for a noun. A **verb** shows action, condition, or existence.

The chart below reviews the definition of each part of speech.

PARTS OF SPEECH	QUESTIONS TO ASK YOURSELF	EXAMPLES
Noun	Does the word name a person, place, or thing?	Our visit to the Grand Canyon delighted Rosa.
Pronoun	Does the word stand for a noun?	They gave some to him.

PARTS OF SPEECH	QUESTIONS TO ASK YOURSELF	EXAMPLES
Verb	Does the word tell what someone or something did? Does the word link one word with another word that identifies or describes it? Does the word show that something exists?	We played baseball. The woman was a lawyer. Mother appeared happy. The family is here.

See Practice 13.5A

The Other Parts of Speech An **adjective** modifies a noun or pronoun. An **adverb** modifies a verb, an adjective, or another adverb. A **preposition** relates a noun or pronoun that appears with it to another word. A **conjunction** connects words or groups of words. An **interjection** expresses emotion.

PARTS OF SPEECH	QUESTIONS TO ASK YOURSELF	EXAMPLES
Adjective	Does the word tell *what kind, which one, how many, or how much?*	Those three apples are an unusual color.
Adverb	Does the word tell *where, when, in what way,* or *to what extent?*	Go home. Leave now. Drive very slowly. I am thoroughly tired.
Preposition	Is the word part of a phrase that includes a noun or pronoun?	Near our house, the carnival was in full swing.
Conjunction	Does the word connect other words in the sentence or connect clauses?	Both you and I will go because they need more people; besides, it will be fun.
Interjection	Does the word express feeling or emotion and function independently of the sentence?	Hey, give me that! Wow! That's amazing!

See Practice 13.5B

PRACTICE 13.5A Identifying Nouns, Pronouns, and Verbs

Read each sentence. Then, label the underlined word in each sentence as a *noun*, *pronoun*, or *verb*.

EXAMPLE We visited a sheep ranch.

ANSWER *pronoun*

1. Our school's new library is a big hit with students.
2. Lightning hit the tree and caused a fire.
3. Jared asked for a computer for his birthday.
4. She asked the teacher a question.
5. I hope no one spots the stain on my shirt.
6. The puppies have spots on their backs.
7. Did you see our car in the parking lot?
8. The team is practicing at the park.
9. Mom parks her car in the driveway.
10. Will you help Sean take out the trash?

PRACTICE 13.5B Recognizing All the Parts of Speech

Read each sentence. Then, for each sentence, write the part of speech of the underlined word.

EXAMPLE Nobody is absent today but Erin.

ANSWER *preposition*

11. Pedro plays baseball, but I don't.
12. Since it's raining, let's watch a movie.
13. Hey, why didn't I see you at lunch?
14. I lost my notebook yesterday, and it's been missing ever since.
15. I ate a late dinner and went to bed.
16. William arrived late again.
17. After school we played basketball.
18. Fireworks are set off after a player hits a home run.
19. We have an early test tomorrow.
20. Did you find your locker yet?

SPEAKING APPLICATION

Take turns with a partner. Tell about something that you did earlier today. Your partner should identify the nouns, pronouns, and verbs that you use.

WRITING APPLICATION

Write the part of speech of each word in sentence 18.

CHAPTER 14

BASIC SENTENCE PARTS

Use strong subjects and verbs in your writing, and use vivid complements to add description.

WRITE GUY *Jeff Anderson, M.Ed.*

WHAT DO YOU NOTICE?

Uncover different sentence parts as you zoom in on this sentence from the essay "Single Room, Earth View" by Sally Ride.

MENTOR TEXT

Spectacular as the view is from 200 miles up, the Earth is not the awe-inspiring "blue marble" made famous by the photos from the moon.

Now, ask yourself the following questions:

- What is the simple subject of the sentence?
- Which noun in the sentence further explains the word *Earth*?

Earth is the simple subject of the sentence. A complement is a group of words that helps complete the meaning of a sentence. The noun *marble* helps explain what the Earth is *not* like and serves as a complement called a predicate nominative, which is a noun or pronoun that gives more detail about the subject.

Grammar for Writers Think of complements as adding details that perfect, or complement, your sentences. Use complements to add clarity and variety to your writing.

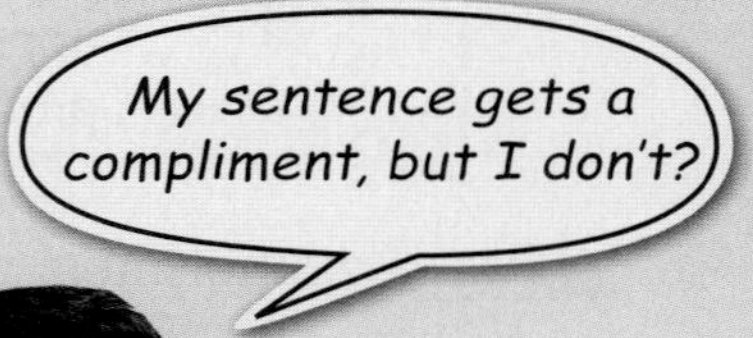

My sentence gets a compliment, but I don't?

Your sentence needs a complement to complete the meaning.
SMART

14.1 Subjects and Predicates

A **sentence** is a group of words that expresses a complete unit of thought. *The cereal in the bowl* is not a complete unit of thought because you probably wonder what the writer wanted to say about the cereal. *The cereal in the bowl is soggy,* however, does express a complete unit of thought.

WRITING COACH Online

www.phwritingcoach.com

Grammar Tutorials

Brush up on your Grammar skills with these animated videos.

Grammar Practice

Practice your grammar skills with Writing Coach Online.

Grammar Games

Test your knowledge of grammar in this fast-paced interactive video game.

RULE 14.1.1

A sentence is a group of words that has two main parts: a complete subject and a complete predicate. Together, these parts express a complete thought or paint a complete picture.

The **complete subject** contains a noun, pronoun, or group of words acting as a noun, plus its modifiers. These words tell *who* or *what* the sentence is about. The **complete predicate** consists of the verb or verb phrase, plus its modifiers. These words tell what the complete subject is or does.

COMPLETE SUBJECTS	COMPLETE PREDICATES
Snakes	slither.
A bell-clanging streetcar	moved through the turn.
Wood or cellulose	makes a delicious meal for a termite.
The candidate's approach to fiscal problems	impressed the voters attending the rally.

Sometimes, part of the predicate precedes the complete subject.

EXAMPLES **At midnight** (complete), **the cluster of spiders** (complete subject) **spun webs** (predicate).

Yesterday (complete) **my social studies class** (complete subject) **visited a Wild West exhibit** (predicate).

See Practice 14.1A

Simple Subjects and Predicates

The most essential parts of a sentence are the **simple subject** and the **simple predicate.** These words tell you the basics of what you need to know about the topic of the sentence. All of the other words in the sentence give you information about the simple subject and simple predicate.

The simple subject is the essential noun, pronoun, or group of words that acts as a noun in a complete subject. The simple predicate is the essential verb or verb phrase in a complete predicate.

RULE 14.1.2

Note: When sentences are discussed in this chapter, the term *subject* will refer to a simple subject, and the term *verb* will refer to a simple predicate.

SUBJECTS	VERBS
Small mice	fit nicely into coat pockets.
Many horror films	have used bugs to terrifying effect.
Jugs of sweet cider	were covering the table.
A colorful flag	hung above the porch.
The writer's children	published all of his early poetry.
Studies of insects	have certainly revealed much about their behavior.

In the last example, the simple subject is *studies,* not *insects; insects* is the object of the preposition *of.* Objects of prepositions never function as simple subjects. In this same example, the simple predicate is a verb phrase. In addition, the word *certainly* is not part of the simple predicate because it does not provide essential information.

See Practice 14 .1B

PRACTICE 14.1A Recognizing Complete Subjects and Predicates

Read each sentence. Then, write whether the underlined word or group of words in each sentence is the *complete subject* or the *complete predicate*.

EXAMPLE The shoes with the green laces are mine.

ANSWER *complete predicate*

1. Roses are the most popular flower.
2. The first talent show performer was really funny.
3. Most of the dogs on our block are friendly.
4. The person who collects the most newspapers wins.
5. The coaches expect another tough game from Harrison High.
6. The first spelling bee champion from our school was a sophomore.
7. Thomas Delgado used to be a teacher here.
8. Many wild animals become dependent on food provided by people.
9. We may need to call the librarian for help.
10. Who sells tickets to the play?

PRACTICE 14.1B Identifying Simple Subjects and Predicates

Read each sentence. The complete subject is underlined. The rest of the sentence is the complete predicate. Write the simple subject and simple predicate in each sentence.

EXAMPLE That tall boy in math class is on the basketball team.

ANSWER *boy, is*

11. That book that we both liked was made into a movie.
12. Kyle nominated me for class president.
13. The second Saturday of each month is when our club meets.
14. The speaker arrived on time.
15. Coyotes often howl from the hilltops.
16. Exchange students from all over the world have come to our school.
17. Our huge, fancy tower of blocks fell.
18. Pies are popular Thanksgiving desserts.
19. Several teachers from my school are going to New York City.
20. The quiet stranger from abroad participated in the fundraiser.

SPEAKING APPLICATION

Take turns with a partner. Tell about something interesting that happened to you. Your partner should tell the complete subject and complete predicate in each of your sentences.

WRITING APPLICATION

Write a paragraph about a favorite place. In each sentence, underline the simple subject, and double underline the simple predicate.

Fragments

Find It/FIX IT 20 Grammar Game Plan

A **fragment** is a group of words that does not contain either a complete subject or a complete predicate, or both. Fragments are usually not used in formal writing. You can correct a fragment by adding the parts needed to complete the thought.

RULE 14.1.3

A fragment is a group of words that lacks a subject or a predicate, or both. It does not express a complete unit of thought.

FRAGMENTS	COMPLETE SENTENCES
the basket of apples (complete predicate missing)	The basket of apples was eaten quickly. (complete predicate added)
thrive in the rain forests (complete subject missing)	Tarantulas thrive in the rain forests. (complete subject added)
from the barn (complete subject and predicate missing)	Flies from the barn swarmed into the house. (subject and complete predicate added)

In conversations, fragments usually do not present a problem because tone of voice, gestures, and facial expressions can add the missing information. A reader, however, cannot ask a writer for clarification.

Fragments are sometimes acceptable in writing that represents speech, such as the dialogue in a play or short story. Fragments are also sometimes acceptable in elliptical sentences.

RULE 14.1.4

An elliptical sentence is one in which the missing word or words can be easily understood.

EXAMPLES Until later.

Why such a sad face?

Don't be late!

Locating Subjects and Verbs

To avoid writing a fragment, look for the subject and verb in a sentence. To find the subject, ask, "Which word tells *what* or *who* this sentence is about?" Once you have the answer (the subject), then ask, "What does the subject do?" or "What is being done to the subject?" This will help you locate the verb.

In some sentences, it's easier to find the verb first. In this case, ask, "Which word states the action or condition in this sentence?" This question should help you locate the verb. Then ask, "*Who* or *what* is involved in the action of the verb?" The resulting word or words will be the subject.

EXAMPLE Grasshoppers often feed on corn and grass.

To find the subject first, ask, "Which word or words tell what or whom this sentence is about?"

ANSWER Grasshoppers (*Grasshoppers* is the subject.)

Then ask, "What do grasshoppers do?"

ANSWER feed (*Feed* is the verb.)

To find the verb first, ask, "Which word or words state the action or condition in the sentence?"

ANSWER feed (*Feed* states the action, so it is the verb.)

Then ask, "Who or what feeds?"

ANSWER Grasshoppers (*Grasshoppers* is the subject.)

To easily locate the subject and verb, mentally cross out any adjectives, adverbs, and prepositional phrases you see. These words add information, but they are usually less important than the simple subject and verb.

EXAMPLE ~~Green~~ **technology** **should grow** ~~rapidly in the next ten years.~~

simple subject (technology) — verb phrase (should grow)

Sentences With More Than One Subject or Verb

Some sentences contain a **compound subject** or a **compound verb,** or a subject or verb with more than one part.

A compound subject consists of two or more subjects. These subjects may be joined by a conjunction such as *and* or *or*.

RULE 14.1.5

EXAMPLES The **campers** and **hikers** repelled the mosquitoes with insect spray.

Flies, **gnats**, and **bees** are always buzzing around the garbage can.

Neither the **horse** nor the **driver** looked tired.

A compound verb consists of two or more verbs. These verbs may be joined by a conjunction such as *and, but, or,* or *nor*.

RULE 14.1.6

EXAMPLES I neither **saw** them nor **heard** them.

Randy **left** school and **ran** to the gym.

She **sneezed** and **coughed** all day.

Some sentences contain both a compound subject and a compound verb.

EXAMPLES My **father** and **brother** **swatted** at the fly but **smacked** each other in the head instead.

The **dog** and **cat** **eyed** each other, **circled** warily, and then **advanced** into combat.

See Practice 14.1C
See Practice 14.1D

PRACTICE 14.1C Locating Subjects and Verbs

Read each sentence. Then, write the subject and the verb in each sentence. Underline the subject.

EXAMPLE A fifteen-year-old boy from our state entered and won the poetry contest.

ANSWER *boy; entered, won*

1. The curious horse in the stable sniffed and nibbled at Jan's popcorn.
2. Will and Ken showed me how to solve the problem.
3. The beautiful geese were honking as they flew overhead.
4. The girl and boy with the best voices got the solo parts.
5. The classrooms on the first floor are all dark.
6. The frightened fawn ran when we approached.
7. The tour guide lost his boot in the deep snow.
8. All of the musicians in the concert arrived and began rehearsing.
9. The new player from Hilton High hit a home run and stole a base.
10. Stargazers in our club saw several shooting stars.

PRACTICE 14.1D Fixing Sentence Errors

Read each fragment. Then, use each fragment in a sentence.

EXAMPLE swimming in the lake

ANSWER *Josie went swimming in the lake.*

11. to meet the president
12. which my uncle brought from Turkey
13. who left
14. the student
15. likes getting up early in the morning
16. went to the park
17. the taste of fresh-baked bread
18. the most frightening thing about earthquakes
19. playing my favorite song
20. our car

SPEAKING APPLICATION

Take turns with a partner. Tell about your favorite possessions. Your partner should name the subject and verb in each of your sentences.

WRITING APPLICATION

Write three original fragments. Exchange papers with a partner. Your partner should turn your fragments into sentences.

14.2 Hard-to-Find Subjects

While most sentences have subjects that are easy to find, some present a challenge.

WRITING COACH Online
www.phwritingcoach.com

Grammar Practice
Practice your grammar skills with Writing Coach Online.

Grammar Games
Test your knowledge of grammar in this fast-paced interactive video game.

Subjects in Declarative Sentences Beginning With *Here* or *There*

When the word *here* or *there* begins a declarative sentence, it is often mistaken for the subject.

RULE 14.2.1 ***Here* and *there* are never the subject of a sentence.**

Here and *there* are usually adverbs that modify the verb by pointing out *where* something is located. However, *there* may occasionally begin a sentence simply as an introductory word.

In some sentences beginning with *here* or *there*, the subject appears before the verb. However, many sentences beginning with *here* or *there* are **inverted.** In an inverted sentence, the subject follows the verb. If you rearrange such a sentence in subject–verb order, you can identify the subject more easily.

INVERTED There **are** the **buses**. (verb–subject order)

REARRANGED The **buses** **are** there. (subject–verb order)

SENTENCES BEGINNING WITH *HERE* OR *THERE*	SENTENCES REARRANGED IN SUBJECT–VERB ORDER
There are the downtown buildings.	The downtown buildings are there.
Here is the ticket for your trip.	The ticket for your trip is here.
There is money in the cash register.	Money is in the cash register there.

RULE 14.2.2 **In some declarative sentences, the subject is placed after the verb in order to give the subject greater emphasis.**

Because most sentences are written in subject–verb order, changing that order makes readers stop and think. Inverted sentences often begin with prepositional phrases.

SENTENCES INVERTED FOR EMPHASIS	SENTENCES REARRANGED IN SUBJECT–VERB ORDER
Toward the elevated train rushed the evening commuters.	The evening commuters rushed toward the elevated train.
Around the corner careened the speeding car.	The speeding car careened around the corner.

Subjects in Interrogative Sentences

Some interrogative sentences use subject–verb order. Often, however, the word order of an interrogative sentence is verb–subject.

EXAMPLES Which **car** **gets** the best mileage?
(subject–verb order)

Where **are** **we** going?
(verb–subject order)

RULE 14.2.3

In interrogative sentences, the subject often follows the verb.

An inverted interrogative sentence can begin with an action verb, a helping verb, or one of the following words: *how, what, when, where, which, who, whose,* or *why*. Some interrogative sentences divide the helping verb from the main verb. To help locate the subject, mentally rearrange the sentence into subject–verb order.

INTERROGATIVE SENTENCES	REARRANGED IN SUBJECT–VERB ORDER
Is the City Zoo open in the morning?	The City Zoo is open in the morning.
Do they own that house?	They do own that house.
Where will the dance be held?	The dance will be held where?

Subjects in Imperative Sentences

The subject of an imperative sentence is usually implied rather than specifically stated.

RULE 14.2.4

In imperative sentences, the subject is understood to be *you*.

IMPERATIVE SENTENCES	SENTENCES WITH *YOU* ADDED
First, visit the Sears Tower.	First, [you] visit the Sears Tower.
After the tour, come home right away.	After the tour, [you] come home right away.
Mia, show me the map.	Mia, [you] show me the map.

In the last example, the name of the person being addressed, *Mia*, is not the subject of the imperative sentence. Instead, the subject is still understood to be *you*.

Subjects in Exclamatory Sentences

In some **exclamatory sentences,** the subject appears before the verb. In others, the verb appears first. To find the subject, rearrange the sentence in subject–verb order.

RULE 14.2.5

In exclamatory sentences, the subject often appears after the verb, or it may be understood.

EXAMPLES What **does he know**!
(He does know what.)

Go now!
(Subject understood: [You] go now!)

In other exclamatory sentences, both the subject and verb may be unstated.

See Practice 14.2A
See Practice 14.2B

EXAMPLES Fire! ([**You watch** out for the] fire!)
Snakes! ([I see] snakes!)

PRACTICE 14.2A **Identifying Hard-to-Find Subjects**

Read each sentence. Then, write the subject of each sentence.

EXAMPLE How far does this path go?
ANSWER *path*

1. Do you know the phone number of the restaurant?
2. Has your teacher asked you to turn in your report?
3. There is the new principal.
4. Here are the documents you asked for.
5. How were the pyramids built?
6. There has never been a hotter summer.
7. What instrument do you play in the band?
8. There are few places available to rent at this time of year.
9. Here comes the nurse with your medicine.
10. How fast was the train traveling?

PRACTICE 14.2B **Locating Hard-to-Find Verbs**

Read each sentence. Then, write the verb in each sentence.

EXAMPLE Eat at the restaurant I told you about.
ANSWER *Eat*

11. Do you believe what you're seeing?
12. How could you do such a thing!
13. In the woods are many brooks and streams.
14. Before the game, tell me about yourself.
15. Leave us alone, please.
16. Is that a tarantula?
17. Hey, give that back!
18. Where is my hat?
19. Can you tell me where the elevator is?
20. Come inside right away.

SPEAKING APPLICATION

With a partner, take turns asking questions. Your partner should name the subject in each of your responses.

WRITING APPLICATION

Write three exclamatory sentences. Underline the subject, and double underline the verb in each sentence.

14.3 Complements

Some sentences are complete with just a subject and a verb or with a subject, verb, and modifiers: *The crowd cheered.* Other sentences need more information to be complete.

WRITING COACH Online

www.phwritingcoach.com

Grammar Tutorials
Brush up on your Grammar skills with these animated videos.

Grammar Practice
Practice your grammar skills with Writing Coach Online.

Grammar Games
Test your knowledge of grammar in this fast-paced interactive video game.

The meaning of many sentences, however, depends on additional words that add information to the subject and verb. For example, although *The satellite continually sends* has a subject and verb, it is an incomplete sentence. To complete the meaning of the predicate—in this case, to tell *what* a satellite sends—a writer must add a **complement.**

A complement is a word or group of words that completes the meaning of the predicate of a sentence.

RULE 14.3.1

There are five kinds of complements in English: **direct objects, indirect objects, object complements, predicate nominatives,** and **predicate adjectives.** The first three occur in sentences that have transitive verbs. The last two are often called **subject complements.** Subject complements are found only with linking verbs. (See Chapter 13 for more information about action and linking verbs.)

Direct Objects

Direct objects are the most common of the five types of complements. They complete the meaning of action verbs by telling *who* or *what* receives the action.

A direct object is a noun, pronoun, or group of words acting as a noun that receives the action of a transitive verb.

RULE 14.3.2

EXAMPLES I visited the Air and Space Museum.
(Air and Space Museum: direct object)

Sticks and leaves clogged the gutters.
(gutters: direct object)

Direct Objects and Action Verbs The direct object answers the question *Whom?* or *What?* about the action verb. If you cannot answer the question *Whom?* or *What?* the verb may be intransitive, and there is no direct object in the sentence.

EXAMPLES Owls **can see** in the dark.
(Ask, "Owls can see *what*?" No answer; the verb is intransitive.)

The satellite **spun** beyond the atmosphere.
(Ask, "The satellite spun *what*?" No answer; the verb is intransitive.)

See Practice 14.3A

RULE 14.3.3

In some inverted questions, the direct object may appear before the verb. To find the direct object easily, rearrange inverted questions in subject–verb order.

INVERTED QUESTION Which **books** (direct object) **did they read**?

REARRANGED IN SUBJECT–VERB ORDER **They did read** which **books** (direct object)?

Some sentences have more than one direct object, known as a **compound direct object.** If a sentence contains a compound direct object, asking *Whom?* or *What?* after the action verb will yield two or more answers.

EXAMPLES The astronauts **wore** **helmets** (direct object) and **spacesuits** (direct object).

The band **has played** **fairs** (direct object) and **concerts** (direct object) over the last four months.

In the last example, *months* is the object of the preposition *over*. The object of a preposition is never a direct object.

See Practice 14.3B

Indirect Objects

Indirect objects appear only in sentences that contain transitive verbs and direct objects. Indirect objects are common with such verbs as *ask, bring, buy, give, lend, make, show, teach, tell,* and *write*. Some sentences may contain a compound indirect object.

RULE 14.3.4

An indirect object is a noun or pronoun that appears with a direct object. It often names the person or thing that something is given to or done for.

EXAMPLES **NASA** **gave** the **astronauts** (indirect object) a course **correction** (direct object).

I **showed** my **mom** and **dad** (compound indirect object) the tennis **poster** (direct object).

To locate an indirect object, make sure the sentence contains a direct object. Then, ask one of these questions after the verb and direct object: *To* or *for whom?* or *To* or *for what?*

EXAMPLES The **teacher** **taught** our **class** **music**.
(The teacher taught music *to whom*? ANSWER: our class)

We **made** our **dog** a **raincoat**.
(Made a raincoat *for what*? ANSWER: our dog)

An indirect object almost always appears between the verb and the direct object. In a sentence with subject–verb order, the indirect object never follows the direct object, nor will it ever be the object of the preposition *to* or *for*.

EXAMPLES **Paul** **sent** the **poster** (direct object) to **me** (object of preposition).

Paul **sent** **me** (indirect object) the **poster** (direct object).

Paul **gave** **Doug** (indirect object) a **review** (direct object) of the movie.

See Practice 14.3C

Object Complements

While an indirect object almost always comes *before* a direct object, an **object complement** almost always *follows* a direct object. The object complement completes the meaning of the direct object.

RULE 14.3.5

An object complement is an adjective or noun that appears with a direct object and describes or renames it.

A sentence that contains an object complement may seem to have two direct objects. However, object complements occur only with such verbs as *appoint, call, consider, declare, elect, judge, label, make, name, select,* and *think*. The words *to be* are often understood before an object complement.

EXAMPLES

The **organizers** of the dance **declared** **it** (direct object) **successful** (object complement).

The **president** **appointed** **him** (direct object) **ambassador** (object complement) to China.

I **consider** **Dave** (direct object) a strong **swimmer** (object complement) and a graceful **diver** (object complement).

Subject Complements

Linking verbs require **subject complements** to complete their meaning.

RULE 14.3.6

A subject complement is a noun, pronoun, or adjective that appears with a linking verb and gives more information about the subject.

There are two kinds of subject complements: **predicate nominatives** and **predicate adjectives.**

Predicate Nominatives

The **predicate nominative** refers to the same person, place, or thing as the subject of the sentence.

> **A predicate nominative is a noun or pronoun that appears with a linking verb and renames, identifies, or explains the subject. Some sentences may contain a compound predicate nominative.**

RULE 14.3.7

EXAMPLES **Ann Pace** **is** a **scientist** with NASA.
predicate nominative

The **winner** **will be** **you**.
predicate nominative

John Glenn **was** a former **senator** and former **astronaut**.
compound predicate nominative

Predicate Adjectives

A **predicate adjective** is an adjective that appears with a linking verb. It describes the subject in much the same way that an adjective modifies a noun or pronoun. Some sentences may contain a compound predicate adjective.

> **A predicate adjective is an adjective that appears with a linking verb and describes the subject of the sentence.**

RULE 14.3.8

EXAMPLES Your **reasoning** **seems** **logical**.
predicate adjective

The **swimmer** **was** **fast**.
predicate adjective

The **storm** **sounded** **loud** and **thunderous**.
compound predicate adjective

See Practice 14.3D

The **uniforms** **are** **green** and **white**.
compound predicate adjective

PRACTICE 14.3A Identifying Direct Objects

Read each sentence. Then, write the direct object in each sentence. If a sentence does not have a direct object, write *The verb is intransitive.*

EXAMPLE The kite is soaring in the sky.

ANSWER *The verb is intransitive.*

1. The tree shaded the old barn.
2. Train tracks cross the intersection near my home.
3. The programs crashed their computers.
4. Fans cheered loudly as the ball flew out of the stadium.
5. The actors rehearsed until past ten o'clock.
6. Chipmunks and squirrels ate the birdseed.
7. The technology students downloaded several new programs.
8. Several charities are participating in a food drive.
9. The Historical Railways Association invites schools to bring students on field trips.
10. Amazingly, one tiny mouse shredded a large cardboard box.

PRACTICE 14.3B Rearranging Inverted Questions to Subject-Verb Order

Read each question. Then, write a sentence that rearranges the question to subject-verb order.

EXAMPLE Which train will you be taking?

ANSWER *You will be taking which train?*

11. Which part did Helen play in the school musical?
12. What subject did you choose for your research project?
13. Which Lewis and Clark documentary did you watch?
14. What sights at the Grand Canyon National Park has Carmen seen?
15. Which bracelet did Samantha lose?
16. Which beaches on Galveston Island has Joshua visited?
17. Which Langston Hughes poems have you read?
18. What exhibits are featured at the National Cowgirl Museum and Hall of Fame?
19. Which magazine does Ms. Ortiz read?
20. Which musical instrument does Andy play?

SPEAKING APPLICATION

Take turns with a partner. Say sentences that contain direct objects and sentences that contain intransitive verbs. Your partner should identify the direct objects and the sentences that have intransitive verbs.

WRITING APPLICATION

Review the sentences you wrote for Practice 14.3B. For each sentence, write the direct object.

PRACTICE 14.3C Identifying Indirect Objects

Read each sentence. Then, write the indirect object in each sentence.

EXAMPLE Sandra gave me the math book.
ANSWER *me*

1. The coach gave the team a pep talk.
2. Mrs. Haus offered Stephanie a ride.
3. Gregory gave his parents a gift.
4. The waitress brought Donna and Serge pizza and salad.
5. Patrick bought his dog a purple sweater.
6. The company offered unsatisfied customers a refund.
7. At the banquet, the superintendent gave each honors student an award.
8. Jordan brought the librarian a stack of books.
9. Her grandfather sent Liza tickets to the championship volleyball game.
10. The parent-teacher organization gave the students daily planners.

PRACTICE 14.3D Locating Object and Subject Complements

Read each sentence. Then, write the complement in each sentence, and label it as an *object complement* or a *subject complement*.

EXAMPLE The victory left us joyful.
ANSWER *joyful— object complement*

11. That has always been my favorite song.
12. The tea made me sleepy.
13. Everest is the mountain to climb.
14. Caryn thinks tennis and baseball are the hardest sports.
15. Ed became a teacher in order to work with children.
16. The mayor appointed Mr. Zaragosa constable.
17. The principal found the student believable.
18. We call our lake cabin "The Castle."
19. The elderly actor is still a fan favorite.
20. My grandmother's special dish is beef stew.

SPEAKING APPLICATION

Take turns with a partner. Say sentences that contain direct objects and indirect objects. Your partner should identify each direct object and each indirect object.

WRITING APPLICATION

Use sentences 11 and 12 as models to write sentences of your own. Underline and label the complement in each sentence.

Test Warm-Up

DIRECTIONS

Read the introduction and the passage that follows. Then, answer the questions to show that you can use and understand the function of subject complements in reading and writing.

Willie wrote this paragraph about marine mammals. Read the paragraph and think about the changes you would suggest as a peer editor. When you finish reading, answer the questions that follow.

Surf or Turf

(1) Most mammals, like humans, live on land. (2) However, some mammals spend some or all of their time in water. (3) While they look like fish, whales are mammals. (4) Another marine mammal is the porpoise. (5) Also a marine mammal is the walrus. (6) Pinnepeds, which have four flippers, live both on land and in the sea. (7) Some types of pinnepeds are walruses, seals, and sea lions. (8) Marine mammals have warm blood and breathe oxygen.

---

1 What is the most effective way to revise sentence 3 to include a predicate adjective?

A While looking like fish, whales are not fish.

B While they live among fish, whales are mammals.

C Though they appear fish-like, whales are mammals.

D While they share certain traits with fish, whales are mammals.

2 What is the most effective way to combine sentences 4 and 5 to include a compound predicate nominative?

F The porpoise is a marine mammal, and so is the walrus.

G The porpoise is a marine mammal, and the walrus is a marine mammal.

H Another marine mammal is the porpoise, and the walrus is one, too.

J Other marine mammals are the porpoise and the walrus.

3 How should sentence 6 be revised to include a predicate nominative?

A Pinnepeds, which have four flippers, are happy both on land and in the sea.

B Pinnepeds, which have four flippers, are creatures of both land and sea.

C Pinnepeds, which have four flippers, have dual habitats, both on land and in the sea.

D Pinnepeds, which have four flippers, move about both on land and in the sea.

4 What is the most effective way to revise sentence 8 to include a compound predicate adjective?

F Marine mammals are warm-blooded and breathe oxygen.

G Marine mammals have warm blood and are oxygen-breathing.

H Marine mammals are warm-blooded and oxygen-breathing.

J Marine mammals breathe oxygen and have warm blood.

CHAPTER 15

PHRASES and CLAUSES

Use phrases and clauses to make your sentences more descriptive and dynamic.

WRITE GUY *Jeff Anderson, M.Ed.*

WHAT DO YOU NOTICE?

Seek out phrases as you zoom in on these lines from the play *The Tragedy of Romeo and Juliet* by William Shakespeare.

MENTOR TEXT

The boy gives warning something doth approach.
What cursèd foot wanders this way tonight…?

Now, ask yourself the following questions:

- Which phrase in the sentence contains a form of a verb that functions as a noun?
- Which phrase includes a form of a verb that acts as an adjective?

The phrase *gives warning* contains the gerund *warning*. A gerund is a form of a verb that functions as a noun and ends in *-ing*. Because the phrase *gives warning* includes a gerund, it is a gerund phrase. *Cursèd* is a participle that acts as an adjective modifying the noun *foot*. A participle is a form of a verb ending in *-ing* or *-ed* that acts as an adjective. Since the phrase *cursèd foot* contains a participle, it is a participial phrase.

Grammar for Writers Phrases and clauses allow a writer to expand on meaning. See if there are sentences in your writing that could benefit from adding a phrase or clause.

Phrases get to have all the fun.
This phrase adds humor, and this one adds suspense.
Phrases and Clauses
Phrases and Clauses

15.1 Phrases

When one adjective or adverb cannot convey enough information, a phrase can contribute more detail to a sentence. A **phrase** is a group of words that does not include a subject and verb and cannot stand alone as a sentence.

WRITING COACH Online
www.phwritingcoach.com

Grammar Tutorials
Brush up on your Grammar skills with these animated videos.

Grammar Practice
Practice your grammar skills with Writing Coach Online.

Grammar Games
Test your knowledge of grammar in this fast-paced interactive video game.

There are several kinds of phrases, including **prepositional phrases, appositive phrases, participial phrases, gerund phrases,** and **infinitive phrases.**

Prepositional Phrases

A **prepositional phrase** consists of a preposition and a noun or pronoun, called the object of the preposition. *Over their heads, until dark,* and *after the baseball game* are all prepositional phrases. Prepositional phrases often modify other words by functioning as adjectives or adverbs.

Sometimes, a single prepositional phrase may include two or more objects joined by a conjunction.

EXAMPLES

between (preposition) the **window** (object) and the **wall** (object)

with (preposition) the **wind** (object) and the freezing **rain** (object)

beside (preposition) the underground **stream** (object) and **rocks** (object)

See Practice 15.1A

Adjectival Phrases

A prepositional phrase that acts as an adjective is called an **adjectival phrase.**

RULE 15.1.1

An adjectival phrase is a prepositional phrase that modifies a noun or pronoun by telling *what kind* or *which one*.

ADJECTIVES	ADJECTIVAL PHRASES
A beautiful painting hung in the palace.	A painting of great beauty hung in the palace. *(What kind of painting?)*
Mary had a paperbag lunch.	Mary had lunch from a paperbag. *(What kind of lunch?)*

Like one-word adjectives, adjectival phrases can modify subjects, direct objects, indirect objects, or predicate nominatives.

MODIFYING A SUBJECT — The mansion **across the road** has been abandoned.

MODIFYING A DIRECT OBJECT — Let's take a picture **of the Eiffel Tower**.

MODIFYING AN INDIRECT OBJECT — I gave the people **on the bus** a tour.

MODIFYING A PREDICATE NOMINATIVE — France is a country **with many charms**.

A sentence may contain two or more **adjectival phrases.** In some cases, one phrase may modify a noun in the preceding phrase. In others, two phrases may modify the same word.

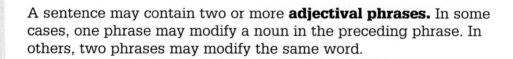

EXAMPLES — We bought tickets **for the trip** **to Paris**. (MODIFIES, MODIFIES)

The painting **of the zoo** **in the museum** is old. (MODIFIES)

Adverbial Phrases

RULE 15.1.2

An adverbial phrase is a prepositional phrase that modifies a verb, an adjective, or an adverb by pointing out *where, why, when, in what way,* or *to what extent.*

ADVERBS	ADVERBIAL PHRASES
She ran swiftly. (Ran *in what way?*)	She ran with speed.
I was frightened then. (Frightened *when?*)	I was frightened at the time.
The birds flew overhead. (Flew *where?*)	The birds flew over our house.

Adverbial phrases can modify verbs, adjectives, or adverbs.

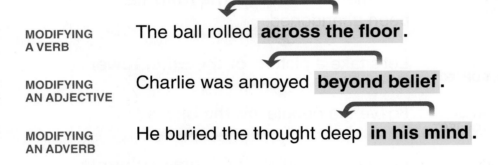

MODIFYING A VERB — The ball rolled **across the floor**.

MODIFYING AN ADJECTIVE — Charlie was annoyed **beyond belief**.

MODIFYING AN ADVERB — He buried the thought deep **in his mind**.

An adverbial phrase may either follow the word it modifies or be located elsewhere in the sentence. Often, two adverbs in different parts of a sentence can modify the same word.

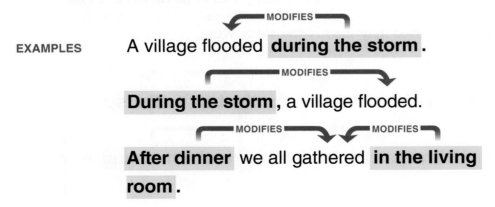

EXAMPLES

A village flooded **during the storm**. (MODIFIES)

During the storm, a village flooded. (MODIFIES)

After dinner we all gathered **in the living room**. (MODIFIES, MODIFIES)

See Practice 15.1B

PRACTICE 15.1A Identifying Prepositional Phrases

Read each sentence. Write the prepositional phrase in each sentence, and underline the preposition.

EXAMPLE The flowering plants in the front yard need water.

ANSWER *in the front yard*

1. Only one of us can play the guitar.
2. Several houses on our street have pools.
3. Each student will write a story about a different city.
4. My mother collects teapots from different places.
5. The dress in the shop window is very pretty.
6. There is a difference between right and wrong.
7. Someone just sold the house down the street.
8. Emma made a statue of a bird.
9. The top of the wall is concrete.
10. Their house on the beach is amazing.

PRACTICE 15.1B Identifying Adjectival and Adverbial Phrases

Read each sentence. Write the adjectival or adverbial phrase. Then, identify each phrase as *adjectival* or *adverbial*.

EXAMPLE The price of the guitar was much too high.

ANSWER *of the guitar* — adjectival

11. You can put that box of magazines down here.
12. The house on the corner is haunted.
13. The shapes of the objects are very different.
14. This coupon is valid for another year.
15. Did you close the window in the bedroom?
16. You deserve a vacation for all the hours that you've worked.
17. We arrived at the theater late.
18. I enjoyed your story about your vacation.
19. Something moved down the hall.
20. We sometimes drive far beyond the city limits.

SPEAKING APPLICATION

Take turns with a partner. Describe the classroom. Your partner should listen for and identify three prepositions that you use.

WRITING APPLICATION

Using sentences 11, 14, and 18 as models, write three sentences of your own. Use the same prepositions, but change the other words.

Appositives and Appositive Phrases

The term *appositive* comes from a Latin verb that means "to put near or next to."

Appositives Using **appositives** in your writing is an easy way to give additional meaning to a noun or pronoun.

RULE 15.1.3

An appositive is a group of words that identifies, renames, or explains a noun or pronoun.

As the examples below show, appositives usually follow immediately after the words they explain.

EXAMPLES Some villagers, **the old-timers**, prefer to travel the dirt roads.

The home team, **the Cougars**, won the season title.

Notice that commas are used in the examples above because these appositives are **nonessential.** In other words, the appositives could be omitted from the sentences without altering the basic meaning of the sentences.

Some appositives, however, are not set off by any punctuation because they are **essential** to the meaning of the sentence.

EXAMPLES The artist **Monet** was a French painter.
(The appositive is essential because it identifies which specific artist.)

My brother **Hermando** is a graceful dancer.
(The appositive is essential because you might have several brothers.)

Note About Terms: Sometimes, the terms *nonrestrictive* and *restrictive* are used in place of *nonessential* and *essential.*

Appositive Phrases When an appositive is accompanied by its own modifiers, it is called an **appositive phrase.**

RULE 15.1.4

An appositive phrase is a noun or pronoun with modifiers that adds information by identifying, renaming, or explaining a noun or pronoun.

Appositives and appositive phrases may follow nouns or pronouns used in almost any role within a sentence. The modifiers within an appositive phrase can be adjectives, adjective phrases, or other groups of words functioning as adjectives.

EXAMPLES Ms. James, **my English teacher**, assigned an essay.

Fred explained numismatics, **the hobby of coin collecting**.

ROLES OF APPOSITIVE PHRASES IN SENTENCES	
Identifying a Subject	Ernest Hemingway, a famous author, wrote in a terse style.
Identifying a Direct Object	The chef prepared lasagna, an Italian dish.
Identifying an Indirect Object	I brought my brother, a boy of six, a souvenir from my trip.
Identifying an Object Complement	I chose the color purple, an unusual color for a house.
Identifying a Predicate Nominative	My favorite food is cassoulet, a hearty stew.
Identifying the Object of a Preposition	Store the onions in the cellar, a cool, dry place.

Compound Appositives Appositives and appositive phrases can also be compound.

EXAMPLES The entire team—**guards**, **forwards**, and **centers**—practiced together.

All computers, **desktops** and **laptops**, are on sale this month.

I used my favorite colors, **pink**, **lavender**, and **green**, to make the quilt.

See Practice 15.1C

Grammar and Style Tip When **appositives** or **appositive phrases** are used to combine sentences, they help to eliminate unnecessary words. One way to streamline your writing is to combine sentences by using an appositive phrase.

TWO SENTENCES	COMBINED SENTENCE
Marseilles is located on the Mediterranean Sea. The city is an important French seaport.	Marseilles, an important French seaport, is located on the Mediterranean Sea.
The minuet was danced in the seventeenth century. The dance includes many intricate steps and turns.	The minuet, a seventeenth-century dance, includes many intricate steps and turns.
California is on the West Coast. It is one of our largest states.	California, one of our largest states, is on the West Coast.

Read aloud the pairs of sentences in the chart. Notice how the combined sentences, which began as two choppy sentences, include the same information. However, they flow much more smoothly once the information in both sentences is clearly linked.

See Practice 15.1D

PRACTICE 15.1C Identifying Appositives and Appositive Phrases

Read each sentence. Then, write the appositive or appositive phrase in each sentence.

EXAMPLE Michael, my brother, is very kind.

ANSWER *my brother*

1. Anna Maria, a new student from Nicaragua, likes science class.
2. The Hays High Steppers, our school dance team, will be holding auditions this afternoon.
3. My sister Mona deserves a second chance.
4. My friend Johnna just got a new car.
5. Our neighbor Mr. Brodie planted a new garden.
6. Her brother Kenny is learning how to play the piano.
7. Nigel, her cousin, will be attending veterinary school in the spring.
8. Her parents are sending her on a European trip, a generous gift.
9. Our teacher, Mrs. Wu, is teaching the class about gerunds.
10. She is practicing calligraphy, a form of writing.

PRACTICE 15.1D Using Appositives and Appositive Phrases to Combine Sentences

Read each pair of sentences. Then, combine the sentences using an appositive or an appositive phrase.

EXAMPLE The book is a novel. The book is an extremely slow read.

ANSWER *The book, a novel, is an extremely slow read.*

11. Lin is a writer. Lin wrote the story.
12. My favorite teacher is Mrs. Ladner. She will retire next year.
13. The mechanic drove my car into the garage. The car is a sporty model.
14. The newspaper had an ad about a part-time job. The newspaper is a big-city daily.
15. Dad's specialty is chili. It won a blue ribbon.
16. Edward ordered his favorite dinner. His favorite dinner is enchiladas.
17. The new bicycle path is near the lake. The bicycle path is four feet wide.
18. The marching band performed on the field. The marching band is made up of all seniors.
19. The centerpiece was beautiful. It was an arrangement of roses.
20. The unicorn is a mythical animal. It is a strange creature with one horn.

SPEAKING APPLICATION

Take turns with a partner. Tell about your favorite book or story. Use three appositives or appositive phrases in your sentences. Your partner should identify the appositives or appositive phrases that you use.

WRITING APPLICATION

Write two pairs of sentences with the same subject. Then, combine each pair with an appositive or an appositive phrase.

Verbal Phrases

When a verb is used as a noun, an adjective, or an adverb, it is called a **verbal.** Although a verbal does not function as a verb, it retains two characteristics of verbs: It can be modified in different ways, and it can have one or more complements. A verbal with modifiers or complements is called a **verbal phrase.**

Participles

Many of the adjectives you use are actually verbals known as **participles.**

RULE 15.1.5

A participle is a form of a verb that can act as an adjective.

The most common kinds of participles are **present participles** and **past participles.** These two participles can be distinguished from one another by their endings. Present participles usually end in *-ing (frightening, entertaining).* Past participles usually end in *-ed (frightened, entertained),* but many have irregular endings, such as *-t* or *-en (burnt, written).*

PRESENT PARTICIPLES	PAST PARTICIPLES
The limping hiker favored his aching ankle.	Confused, Nan returned to her interrupted work.

Like other adjectives, participles answer the question *What kind?* or *Which one?* about the nouns or pronouns they modify.

EXAMPLES Irma's **shining** eyes betrayed her excitement.
(*What kind* of eyes? Answer: *shining* eyes)

The **shattered** window needs replacement.
(*Which* window? Answer: *shattered* window)

Participles may also have a **present perfect** form.

EXAMPLES **Having decided,** Madeleine acted quickly.

Having arrived at last, François shakes hands all around.

Verb or Participle? Because **verbs** often have endings such as *-ing* and *-ed*, you may confuse them with **participles.** If a word ending in *-ed* or *-ing* expresses the action of the sentence, it is a verb or part of a verb phrase. If it describes a noun or pronoun, it is a participle.

A verb shows an action, a condition, or the fact that something exists. A participle acting as an adjective modifies a noun or a pronoun.

RULE 15.1.6

ACTING AS VERBS	ACTING AS ADJECTIVES
The dog is snarling at the plumber. (What is the dog doing?)	The snarling dog attacked the plumber. (Which dog?)
The mimes delighted the kids. (What did the mimes do?)	Delighted, the kids applauded the mimes. (What kind of kids?)

See Practice 15.1E

Participial Phrases

A participle can be expanded by adding modifiers and complements to form a **participial phrase.**

A participial phrase is a participle modified by an adverb or adverbial phrase or accompanied by a complement. The entire participial phrase acts as an adjective.

RULE 15.1.7

WITH AN ADVERB — **Traveling quickly**, we completed the trip in two hours.

WITH AN ADVERB PHRASE — **Traveling at breakneck speed**, we completed the trip in two hours.

WITH A COMPLEMENT — **Avoiding stops**, we completed the trip in two hours.

A participial phrase that is nonessential to the basic meaning of a sentence is set off by commas or other forms of punctuation. A participial phrase that is essential is not set off by punctuation.

NONESSENTIAL PHRASES	ESSENTIAL PHRASES
There is Craig, standing at the bus stop.	The boy standing at the bus stop is Craig.
Painted in 1497, the mural is Leonardo's masterpiece.	The mural painted in 1497 is the one that needs the most repair.

In the first sentence on the left side of the chart above, *standing by the bus stop* merely adds information about Craig, so it is nonessential. In the sentence on the right, however, the same phrase is essential because many different boys might be in view.

In the second sentence on the left, *Painted in 1497* is an additional description of *mural,* so it is nonessential. In the sentence on the right, however, the phrase is essential because it identifies the specific mural that is being discussed.

RULE 15.1.8

Participial phrases **can often be used to combine information from two sentences into one.**

TWO SENTENCES We were exhausted by the climb up Mont Blanc. We rested by the side of the trail.

COMBINED **Exhausted by the climb up Mont Blanc**, we rested by the side of the trail.

TWO SENTENCES We ate sandwiches. We shared stories about our adventure.

COMBINED **Eating sandwiches**, we shared stories about our adventure.

Notice how part of the verb in one sentence is changed into a participle in the combined sentence.

See Practice 15.1F

PRACTICE 15.1E Identifying Participles

Read each sentence. Show that you understand verbals (participles) by writing whether the underlined word is a *verb* or a *participle*. If the word is a participle, write whether it is a *present* or a *past* participle. Use the word in a new sentence. Read your sentences to a partner. Your partner should tell if the word is a verb or a participle.

EXAMPLE The annoyed customer spoke loudly to the manager.

ANSWER *participle, past; The annoyed driver beeped his car horn.*

1. The plane has been delayed by snow.
2. A growing child needs a healthy diet.
3. You can find what you need on the following pages.
4. Brilliant red roses were growing by the fence.
5. The white car was following too closely.
6. Some spots in the grass are becoming dry.
7. This restaurant has a wide but unappealing menu.
8. The plane is arriving at gate 20.
9. The painted house looked wonderful.
10. The home team was winning at halftime.

PRACTICE 15.1F Recognizing Participial Phrases

Read each sentence. Write the participial phrase in each sentence. Then, write *E* for *essential* or *N* for *nonessential.*

EXAMPLE The train arriving on track 13 is two hours late.

ANSWER *arriving on track 13— E*

11. All the food cooked in that restaurant is homemade.
12. Found at a garage sale, the statue was in good shape.
13. Looking worn out, the football players rested.
14. Katie is the girl sweeping the floor.
15. Excited by the flashing lights, the dog began to bark.
16. The tree growing beside the back door is a maple.
17. The cat, rubbing against the chair leg, purred contentedly.
18. Our house, shaded by trees, stays cool in the summer.
19. They boarded the bus packed with tourists.
20. Having spotted a wave, the surfers began paddling.

SPEAKING APPLICATION

Tell a partner about movies that you have seen recently. Use participles as you speak. Your partner should write each participle that you use. After you finish speaking, your partner should read aloud each participle, and tell whether it is past or present.

WRITING APPLICATION

Write three sentences, using one of the following participial phrases in each sentence: *waking up late this morning; baked in a brick oven; spotting a friend.*

Gerunds

Many nouns that end in *-ing* are actually **verbals** known as **gerunds.** Gerunds are not difficult to recognize: They always end in *-ing,* and they always function as **nouns.**

RULE 15.1.9

A gerund is a form of a verb that ends in *-ing* and acts as a noun.

FUNCTIONS OF GERUNDS	
Subject	Skiing is my favorite pastime.
Direct Object	The French people make visiting France a pleasure.
Indirect Object	Mr. Mendoza's lecture gave traveling a new dimension.
Predicate Nominative	My dad's favorite activity is fishing.
Object of a Preposition	His dog showed signs of careful training.
Appositive	Brady's profession, advertising, is very competitive.

Verb, Participle, or Gerund? Words ending in *-ing* may be parts of verb phrases, participles acting as adjectives, or gerunds.

RULE 15.1.10

Words ending in *-ing* that act as nouns are called gerunds. Unlike verbs ending in *-ing,* gerunds do not have helping verbs. Unlike participles ending in *-ing,* they do not act as adjectives.

VERB Kevin is **yawning** at his desk.

PARTICIPLE The **yawning** boy was very tired.

GERUND **Yawning** is contagious.

VERB My sister was **sighing**, and that upset me.

PARTICIPLE **Sighing**, my sister upset me.

GERUND My sister's **sighing** upset me.

See Practice 15.1G

Gerund Phrases Like participles, gerunds may be joined by other words to make **gerund phrases.**

A gerund phrase consists of a gerund and one or more modifiers or a complement. These phrases act together as a noun.

15.1.11 RULE

GERUND PHRASES	
With Adjectives	Solo flying is not for beginners.
With an Adverb	Answering quickly is not always a good idea.
With a Prepositional Phrase	Many places in the city prohibit walking on the grass.
With a Direct Object	Pierre was incapable of reciting the poem.
With an Indirect and a Direct Object	The algebra teacher tried giving her students praise.

Note About Gerunds and Possessive Pronouns: Always use the possessive form of a personal pronoun in front of a gerund.

INCORRECT We never listen to **him** boasting.

CORRECT We never listen to **his** boasting.

INCORRECT **Them** refusing to wear helmets is dangerous.

CORRECT **Their** refusing to wear helmets is dangerous.

See Practice 15.1H
See Practice 15.1I

Infinitives

The third kind of verbal is the **infinitive.** Infinitives have many different uses. They can act as nouns, adjectives, or adverbs.

An infinitive is a form of a verb that generally appears with the word *to* in front of it and acts as a noun, an adjective, or an adverb.

15.1.12 RULE

EXAMPLE The teacher asked the students **to read quietly**.

INFINITIVES USED AS NOUNS	
Subject	To understand life requires maturity and acceptance.
Direct Object	The peasants decided to rebel.
Predicate Nominative	The soldier's only hope was to surrender.
Object of a Preposition	I have no goal except to finish school.
Appositive	You have only one choice, to stay.

Unlike gerunds, infinitives can also act as adjectives and adverbs.

INFINITIVES USED AS MODIFIERS	
Adjective	The children showed a willingness to cooperate.
Adverb	Some people were unable to fight.

See Practice 15.1J

Prepositional Phrase or Infinitive? Although both **prepositional phrases** and **infinitives** often begin with *to,* you can tell the difference between them by analyzing the words that follow *to.*

RULE 15.1.13

A prepositional phrase always ends with a noun or pronoun that acts as the object of the preposition. An infinitive always ends with a verb.

PREPOSITIONAL PHRASE	INFINITIVE
The soldier listened to the command.	A general's role in the army is to command.
We took the computer to the back of the room.	Make sure to back up your computer so you won't lose data.

Note About Infinitives Without *to*: Sometimes infinitives do not include the word *to.* When an infinitive follows one of the eight verbs listed below, the *to* is generally omitted. However, it may be understood.

VERBS THAT PRECEDE INFINITIVES WITHOUT *TO*			
dare	help	make	see
hear	let	please	watch

EXAMPLES She doesn't dare **[to] go** without permission.

Please help me **[to] leave** this place now!

Juan helped Sam **[to] extinguish** the fire.

Infinitive Phrases Infinitives also can be joined with other words to form phrases.

An infinitive phrase consists of an infinitive and its modifiers, complements, or subject, all acting together as a single part of speech.

RULE 15.1.14

INFINITIVE PHRASES	
With an Adverb	Jeffrey's family likes to eat early.
With an Adverb Phrase	To skate on the ice is not easy.
With a Direct Object	He hated to leave New York City.
With an Indirect and a Direct Object	They promised to show (direct object) us (indirect object) the pictures (direct object) from their trip.
With a Subject and a Complement	I want her (subject) to determine her own goals (complement).

See Practice 15.1K
See Practice 15.1L

PRACTICE 15.1G Writing Gerunds

Read each item. Then, for each item, write a sentence using the function of the gerund indicated in parentheses.

EXAMPLE spelling (predicate nominative)

ANSWER *My best subject is spelling.*

1. exercising (subject)
2. painting (appositive)
3. bowling (direct object)
4. grooming (object of preposition)
5. bicycling (predicate nominative)
6. dancing (indirect object)
7. acting (object of preposition)
8. cooking (direct object)
9. skating (predicate nominative)
10. studying (indirect object)

PRACTICE 15.1H Writing Gerund Phrases

Read each item. Then, write a sentence using each gerund phrase as indicated in parentheses. Read your sentences to a partner, who will tell you if your sentences are correct.

EXAMPLE giving the man his money (with an indirect and a direct object)

ANSWER *Giving the man his money was gratifying.*

11. the calm, gentle rocking (with adjectives)
12. following closely (with an adverb)
13. jumping in the lake (with a prepositional phrase)
14. finishing the race (with a direct object)
15. asking the policeman a question (with an indirect and direct object)
16. fishing without a permit (with a prepositional phrase)
17. talking loudly (with an adverb)
18. lifting the gate (with a direct object)
19. her silly, good-natured teasing (with adjectives)
20. showing Jason the new locker room (with an indirect and direct object)

WRITING APPLICATION

Write a sentence for each of the six functions of gerunds. Be sure to mix up the order. Then, read your sentences to a partner, who should identify the function of each gerund in your sentences.

SPEAKING APPLICATION

Take turns with a partner. Choose one of the five functions of gerund phrases. Your partner should write a sentence, using a gerund phrase in the function that you've indicated. Your partner should read his or her sentence aloud. Together, discuss if the sentence is correct.

PRACTICE 15.1I **Identifying Gerunds and Gerund Phrases**

Read each sentence. Then, write the gerund or gerund phrase, and use it in a new sentence. Read your sentences to a partner who will tell you if your sentences are correct.

EXAMPLE Bertha enjoys hiking.

ANSWER *hiking; We go hiking in the mountains.*

1. Jogging is a healthy activity.
2. The criminal went to court for stealing.
3. Keith's hobby, painting, keeps him busy.
4. Running across a busy street can be dangerous.
5. Vijay loves seeing good movies.
6. Driving through Texas will be the longest part of our trip.
7. Sarah was awarded a medal after winning the race.
8. Watching airplanes take off is fun.
9. Hitting a homerun is a baseball player's goal.
10. Brushing your teeth twice daily is what most dentists recommend.

PRACTICE 15.1J **Identifying the Function of Infinitives**

Read each sentence. Then, write the infinitive and tell if it acts as a *noun*, an *adjective*, or an *adverb*. Discuss your answers with a partner. Determine if your answers are correct.

EXAMPLE He made his final decision, to compete.

ANSWER *to compete—noun*

11. On Saturday mornings, I have one goal, to sleep late.
12. The students who were causing the ruckus were asked to leave.
13. The protestors were determined to speak.
14. I have no warm sweaters to wear.
15. To have close friends is important to me.
16. Sandra's deepest desire was to perform.
17. Mrs. Assad wants to swim.
18. When Carla's arms got tired, Tomas decided to row.
19. The clowns for the party were beginning to arrive.
20. Janine, the star runner of the track team, was eager to compete.

SPEAKING APPLICATION

Use gerunds in sentences to tell a partner about your favorite activities. Ask your partner to identify the gerunds as you speak.

WRITING APPLICATION

Write three different sentences that use infinitives as a noun, adjective, or adverb. Read your sentences to a partner. Your partner should identify each infinitive and tell how it acts.

PRACTICE 15.2C Writing Independent Clauses

Read each item. Then, write a sentence using each item in an independent clause.

EXAMPLE the neighbor's cat

ANSWER *I heard the neighbor's cat screech.*

1. the trolley car
2. the aging tiger
3. Carlotta's kitchen table
4. the black-and-white photograph
5. my favorite video game
6. a wooden swing
7. tenor saxophone
8. his latest CD
9. the rodeo
10. a Roman soldier

PRACTICE 15.2D Writing Subordinate Clauses

Read each item. Then, write a sentence using each item in a subordinate clause.

EXAMPLE squeaky door

ANSWER *We heard the noise that came from the squeaky door.*

11. tattered book
12. old maple tree
13. my brother's cell phone
14. her red pen
15. wet floor
16. wind
17. parents
18. Libby
19. broken gate
20. computer keyboard

SPEAKING APPLICATION

Take turns with a partner. Read your sentences for Practice 15.2C to each other. Compare your sentences and decide if they are independent clauses.

WRITING APPLICATION

Write a few paragraphs about your favorite holiday. Be sure to include independent clauses and subordinate clauses. Exchange papers with a partner. Your partner should underline the independent clauses and circle the subordinate clauses in your paragraphs.

PRACTICE 15.2E Identifying Restrictive and Nonrestrictive Relative Clauses

Read each sentence. Write each clause, and identify it as *restrictive* or *nonrestrictive*. Discuss your answers with a partner. Determine if your answers are correct.

EXAMPLE The house, which is owned by Mr. Hunter, is for sale.

ANSWER *which is owned by Mr. Hunter— nonrestrictive*

1. I remember that I picked out our first kitten.
2. Josie knows the boy whose bike was stolen.
3. Mount Rushmore, which honors four presidents, is located in South Dakota.
4. Judith Ortiz Coffer is the author who wrote *Call Me Maria*.
5. This restaurant, whose chef was featured on television, is Mom's favorite.
6. The design that Maya Lin proposed for the Vietnam Memorial won the competition.
7. The rain, which was heavy, caused flooding.
8. Despite many sightings of Bigfoot that have been reported, no one has proven its existence.
9. Author Tamora Pierce, who visited our school, started writing in sixth grade.
10. Joe owns a car that is run by batteries.

PRACTICE 15.2F Writing Restrictive and Nonrestrictive Relative Clauses

Read each sentence. If the sentence contains a restrictive relative clause, rewrite it to contain a nonrestrictive relative clause. If the sentence contains a nonrestrictive relative clause, rewrite it to contain a restrictive relative clause. Read your sentences to a partner to check if they are correct.

EXAMPLE The story, which I wrote, won a prize.

ANSWER *The story that I wrote won a prize.*

11. A layer of blubber, which is under their skin, keeps seals warm.
12. The sweater that was found is mine.
13. Ivan went on a vacation, which was disrupted by storms.
14. A farmer who discovered a rare dinosaur bone was in the news.
15. The clown camp, which is in Buffalo, is fun.
16. My sister, who wrote an essay, won the contest.
17. E-books, which can be read on the computer, are becoming quite popular.
18. The costume that Neil wore fooled everyone.
19. The North Star that guided Harriet Tubman was the subject of songs.
20. The battery, which fell out of my camera, rolled under the desk.

WRITING APPLICATION

Write an article about an event that has occurred, using restrictive and nonrestrictive relative clauses. Exchange papers with a partner. Your partner should read your article and underline all the restrictive relative clauses and circle all the nonrestrictive relative clauses.

SPEAKING APPLICATION

With a partner, discuss the difference in meaning between the example and answer in Practice 15.2F. Explain the function of the commas in the example.

Test Warm-Up

DIRECTIONS
Read the introduction and the passage that follows. Then, answer the questions to show that you can use and understand the function of restrictive and nonrestrictive relative clauses in reading and writing.

Faith wrote a paragraph about interesting foods from around the world. Read the paragraph and think about the changes you would suggest as a peer editor. When you finish reading, answer the questions that follow.

Spicy Adventures

(1) My family and I like to try new things, especially when it comes to food. (2) Each week, we agree on a recipe for an ethnic dish, that we haven't eaten before, and prepare it together. (3) As a result, we have eaten foods, whose origins are scattered across the world. (4) Friends never know what we will serve them when they visit us on ethnic night. (5) There is one rule: everyone must at least try each of the courses of which we serve. (6) We literally have added some spice to our lives!

1 What change should be made in sentence 2?

- **A** Replace the comma after ***dish*** with a semicolon
- **B** Delete the comma after ***dish***
- **C** Delete the commas after ***dish*** and ***before***
- **D** Delete the comma after ***before***

2 What change, if any, should be made in sentence 3?

- **F** Replace the comma after ***result*** with a colon
- **G** Delete the comma after ***foods***
- **H** Add a comma after ***scattered***
- **J** Make no change

3 How should sentence 4 be revised to include a restrictive relative clause?

- **A** Friends, who visit us on ethnic night, never know what we will serve them.
- **B** When they visit us, friends never know what we will serve them on ethnic night.
- **C** Friends who visit us on ethnic night never know what we will serve them.
- **D** On ethnic night, friends never know what we will serve them when they visit us.

4 What is the most effective way to rewrite the ideas in sentence 5?

- **F** There is one rule: everyone must try at least the courses, which we serve.
- **G** There is one rule: the courses of which we serve, everyone at least must try.
- **H** There is one rule: of the courses that we serve, everyone at least must try some of each.
- **J** There is one rule: everyone must at least try each of the courses that we serve.

Relative Pronouns **Relative pronouns** help link a subordinate clause to another part of a sentence. They also have a function in the subordinate clause.

> **Relative pronouns** **connect adjectival clauses to the words they modify and act as subjects, direct objects, objects of prepositions, or adjectives in the subordinate clauses.**

RULE 15.2.8

To tell how a relative pronoun is used within a clause, separate the clause from the rest of the sentence, and find the subject and verb in the clause.

FUNCTIONS OF RELATIVE PRONOUNS IN CLAUSES	
As a Subject	A house that is built on a good foundation (subject) is built to last.
As a Direct Object	Mario, whom my sister met at college (direct object), is a poet. (Reworded clause: my sister met *whom* at college)
As an Object of a Preposition	This is the book about which I read great reviews (object of preposition). (Reworded clause: I read great reviews about *which*)
As an Adjective	The senator whose opinion was in question (adjective) spoke to the press.

Sometimes in writing and in speech, a relative pronoun is left out of an adjectival clause. However, the missing word, though simply understood, still functions in the sentence.

EXAMPLES The heroes [**whom**] we studied were great women.

The suggestions [**that**] they made were ignored.

Relative Adverbs Like relative pronouns, **relative adverbs** help link the subordinate clause to another part of a sentence. However, they have only one use within a subordinate clause.

See Practice 15.2E

RULE 15.2.9

Relative adverbs connect adjectival clauses to the words they modify and act as adverbs in the clauses.

EXAMPLE Pat yearned for the day **when** she could walk without crutches.

In the example, the adjectival clause is *when she could walk without crutches.* Reword the clause this way to see that *when* functions as an adverb: *she could walk without crutches when.*

Adverbial Clauses

Subordinate clauses may also serve as adverbs in sentences. They are introduced by subordinating conjunctions. Like adverbs, **adverbial clauses** modify verbs, adjectives, or other adverbs.

RULE 15.2.10

Subordinate adverbial clauses modify verbs, adjectives, adverbs, or verbals by telling *where, when, in what way, to what extent, under what condition,* or *why.*

An adverbial clause begins with a subordinating conjunction and contains a subject and a verb, although they are not the main subject and verb in the sentence. In the chart that follows, the adverbial clauses are highlighted in orange. Arrows point to the words they modify.

ADVERBIAL CLAUSES	
Modifying a Verb	After you read about Rome, you should begin your report. (Begin *when?*)
Modifying an Adjective	Tricia seemed happy wherever she was. (Happy *where?*)
Modifying a Gerund	Driving a car if you do not have a license is illegal. (Driving *under what condition?*)

Adverbial clauses begin with **subordinating conjunctions** and contain subjects and verbs.

15.2.11 RULE

EXAMPLE **Although** it rained, the game was still played.
subordinating conjunction

Recognizing the subordinating conjunctions will help you identify adverbial clauses. The following chart shows some of the most common subordinating conjunctions.

SUBORDINATING CONJUNCTIONS			
after	because	so that	when
although	before	than	whenever
as	even though	though	where
as if	if	unless	wherever
as long as	since	until	while

Whether an adverbial clause appears at the beginning, middle, or end of a sentence can sometimes affect the sentence meaning.

EXAMPLE **Before the year was over**, Joel made plans to visit Rome.

Joel made plans to visit Rome **before the year was over**.

Like adjectival clauses, adverbial clauses can be used to combine the information from two sentences into one. The combined sentence shows a close relationship between the ideas.

TWO SENTENCES **It rained**. They did not go out.

See Practice 15.2F

COMBINED **Because** it rained, they did not go out.
subordinating conjunction

PRACTICE 15.2G Identifying Relative Pronouns and Adjectival Clauses

Read each sentence. Then, write the adjectival clause in each sentence, and underline the relative pronoun that introduces the clause.

EXAMPLE The only student who could complete the race was Sophia.

ANSWER *who could complete the race*

1. Lilacs, which are known for their scent, grow best in cold climates.
2. The new teacher, whom I have not met, starts tomorrow.
3. The store, which just opened to the public, once sold products to wholesalers.
4. My aunt, who is a substitute teacher, worked at my school Monday.
5. Miguel tried the window, which wouldn't open.
6. The snow that fell last night has melted.
7. The rain, which had been falling all morning, finally stopped.
8. The park where I play basketball has put in new courts.
9. The cat that I found is a stray.
10. Sophia, whose father plays drums in a jazz band, is very musical.

PRACTICE 15.2H Recognizing Adverbial Clauses

Read each sentence. Then, write the adverbial clause in each sentence.

EXAMPLE That's the place where we first met.

ANSWER *where we first met*

11. Your little sister cried when you started school.
12. Pluto is not a planet, although it was considered one for many years.
13. Although we were late, we still found good seats.
14. Dad waited while I ran into the store.
15. We ate dinner after the movie.
16. Mario wouldn't have changed his seat unless he couldn't see the screen.
17. Jane goes wherever Mary goes.
18. My dog barks if he sees a cat.
19. I always stretch before I exercise.
20. Her dog went where she went.

SPEAKING APPLICATION

With a partner, take turns telling each other about your favorite holiday. Use relative pronouns to introduce adjectival clauses in your description. Your partner should listen for and identify the relative pronouns.

WRITING APPLICATION

Write a sentence using the following adverbial clauses: *while I slept*; *because it was raining*; *after the show.*

Elliptical Adverbial Clauses Sometimes, words are omitted in adverbial clauses, especially in those clauses that begin with *as* or *than* and are used to express comparisons. Such clauses are said to be *elliptical.*

An elliptical clause is a clause in which the verb or the subject and verb are understood but not actually stated.

15.2.12 RULE

Even though the subject or the verb (or both) may not appear in an elliptical clause, they make the clause express a complete thought.

In the following examples, the understood words appear in brackets. The sentences are alike, except for the words *he* and *him*. In the first sentence, *he* is a subject of the adverbial clause. In the second sentence, *him* functions as a direct object of the adverbial clause.

VERB UNDERSTOOD	His sister resembles their father more **than he [does]**.
SUBJECT AND VERB UNDERSTOOD	His sister resembles their father more **than [she resembles] him**.

When you read or write elliptical clauses, mentally include the omitted words to clarify the intended meaning.

See Practice 15.2G

Noun Clauses

Subordinate clauses can also act as nouns in sentences.

A noun clause is a subordinate clause that acts as a noun.

15.2.13 RULE

A noun clause acts in almost the same way a one-word noun does in a sentence: It tells what or whom the sentence is about.

RULE 15.2.14

In a sentence, a noun clause may act as a subject, direct object, indirect object, predicate nominative, object of a preposition, or appositive.

EXAMPLES **Whatever you lost** (subject) can be found in the office.

My father remembered **what I wanted for my birthday** (direct object).

The chart on the next page contains more examples of the functions of noun clauses.

Introductory Words

Noun clauses frequently begin with the words *that, which, who, whom,* or *whose*—the same words that are used to begin adjective clauses. *Whichever, whoever,* or *whomever* may also be used as introductory words in noun clauses. Other noun clauses begin with the words *how, if, what, whatever, where, when, whether,* or *why.*

RULE 15.2.15

Introductory words may act as subjects, direct objects, objects of prepositions, adjectives, or adverbs in noun clauses, or they may simply introduce the clauses.

SOME USES OF INTRODUCTORY WORDS IN NOUN CLAUSES

FUNCTIONS IN CLAUSES	EXAMPLES
Adjective	She could not decide which kitten was her favorite.
Adverb	We want to know how we should dress.
Subject	I want the recipe from whoever made that delicious casserole.
Direct Object	Whatever my supervisor advised, I did.
No Function	The doctor determined that he had the flu.

Note that in the following chart the introductory word *that* in the last example has no function except to introduce the clause.

FUNCTIONS OF NOUN CLAUSES IN SENTENCES	
Acting as a Subject	Whoever is last must pay the penalty.
Acting as a Direct Object	Please invite whomever you want to the party.
Acting as an Indirect Object	His manner gave whomever met him a shock.
Acting as a Predicate Nominative	Our problem is whether we should stay or go.
Acting as an Object of a Preposition	Use the money for whatever purpose you choose.
Acting as an Appositive	The occupied country rejected our plea that orphans be cared for by the Red Cross.

Some words that introduce noun clauses also introduce adjectival and adverbial clauses. It is necessary to check the function of the clause in the sentence to determine its type. To check the function, try substituting the words *it, you, fact,* or *thing* for the clause. If the sentence retains its smoothness, you probably replaced a noun clause.

NOUN CLAUSE — I knew **that she would be late**.

SUBSTITUTION — I knew it.

In the following examples, all three subordinating clauses begin with *where,* but only the first is a noun clause because it functions in the sentence as a direct object.

NOUN CLAUSE — Mr. Wong told his students **where they would gather for the tour**.
(Told the students *what?*)

ADJECTIVAL CLAUSE — They took the soldier to a tent, **where a doctor examined his wound**.
(*Which* tent?)

ADVERBIAL CLAUSE — She lives **where the weather is warm all year**.
(Lives *where*?)

Note About Introductory Words: The introductory word *that* is often omitted from a noun clause. In the following examples, the understood word *that* is in brackets.

EXAMPLES — The assistant suggested **[that] you leave your name**.

After the coach chose her for the team, Ling knew **[that] she was going to have a very busy year**.

We remember **[that] you wanted to raise the flag in the morning**.

See Practice 15.2H

PRACTICE 15.2I **Identifying Elliptical Adverbial Clauses**

Read each sentence. Then, write the adverbial clause in each sentence. For the adverbial clauses that are elliptical, add the understood words in parentheses.

EXAMPLE My essay received a higher grade than his essay.

ANSWER *than his essay (did)*

1. My cousin is as tall as I.
2. A spider's silk is as strong as steel.
3. Bill is always as late as Nina.
4. Gillian's cousin is as smart as Gillian.
5. Stephen enjoys science class more than math class.
6. That monkey is as small as a mouse.
7. Aaron knows Dee better than I.
8. Vinnie spoke to Lauren more than to Daniel.
9. This restaurant has better food than that restaurant.
10. Nadia can run faster than Craig.

PRACTICE 15.2J **Recognizing Noun Clauses**

Read each sentence. Then, write the noun clause, and label it as a *subject, direct object, indirect object, predicate nominative,* or *object of a preposition.*

EXAMPLE We were concerned about what we should perform next.

ANSWER *what we should perform next — object of a preposition*

11. When the next showing will be held has only appeared online.
12. Tony sheepishly admitted that he had scored the winning touchdown.
13. Mrs. Baksh's one wish was that she could have a house of her own.
14. All of Kristen's classmates understood what she said.
15. The witnesses disagreed about how old the defendant had been.
16. What happened next made even me a believer.
17. The weatherman predicted that the storm would hit around midnight.
18. Do you know if our team won last night?
19. Mr. Newman explained why an owl is a symbol of wisdom.
20. Kemal wished that they would stay longer.

SPEAKING APPLICATION

Take turns with a partner. Say four elliptical clauses. Your partner should repeat your clauses, filling in the missing words.

WRITING APPLICATION

Using sentence 16 as your first sentence, write a paragraph about what happened next using at least three noun clauses in your paragraph. Underline the noun clauses in your sentences.

15.3 The Four Structures of Sentences

Independent and subordinate clauses are the building blocks of sentences. These clauses can be combined in an endless number of ways to form the four basic sentence structures: **simple, compound, complex,** and **compound-complex.**

WRITING COACH **Online**
www.phwritingcoach.com

Grammar Tutorials
Brush up on your Grammar skills with these animated videos.

Grammar Practice
Practice your grammar skills with Writing Coach Online.

Grammar Games
Test your knowledge of grammar in this fast-paced interactive video game.

RULE 15.3.1

A simple sentence contains a single independent or main clause.

Although a simple sentence contains only one main or independent clause, its subject, verb, or both may be compound. A simple sentence may also have modifying phrases and complements. However, it cannot have a subordinate clause.

In the following simple sentences, the subjects are highlighted in yellow, and the verbs are highlighted in orange.

ONE SUBJECT AND VERB — The **snow** **melted**.

COMPOUND SUBJECT — **Ed** and **I** **checked** our answers.

COMPOUND VERB — The **tree** **rotted** and **died**.

COMPOUND SUBJECT AND VERB — Neither the **driver** nor the **skier** **heard** or **saw** the other boat.

RULE 15.3.2

A compound sentence contains two or more main clauses.

The main clauses in a compound sentence can be joined by a comma and a coordinating conjunction *(and, but, for, nor, or, so, yet)* or by a semicolon (;). Like a simple sentence, a compound sentence contains no subordinate clauses.

EXAMPLE — A Sotho **bride** **carries** a beaded doll at her wedding, and **she** **keeps** the doll for a year.

See Practice 15.3A

A complex sentence consists of one independent or main clause and one or more subordinate clauses.

RULE 15.3.3

The independent clause in a complex sentence is often called the main clause to distinguish it from the subordinate clause or clauses. The subject and verb in the independent clause are called the subject of the sentence and the main verb. A subordinate clause may fall between the parts of a main clause. In the examples below, the main clauses are highlighted in blue, and the subordinate clauses are highlighted in pink.

EXAMPLES **No one answered the phone when she called us.**

The bouquet of flowers that the bride carried didn't have any roses.

Note on Complex Sentences With Noun Clauses: The subject of the main clause may sometimes be the subordinate clause itself.

EXAMPLE **That I wanted to go bothered them.**

A compound-complex sentence consists of two or more independent clauses and one or more subordinate clauses.

RULE 15.3.4

In the example below, the independent clauses are highlighted in blue, and the subordinate clauses are highlighted in pink.

EXAMPLE **The roof leaks when it rains heavily, and we have to repaint the ceilings so that we cover any water stains.**

See Practice 15.3B

PRACTICE 15.3A Distinguishing Between the Four Structures of Sentences

Read each sentence. Then, label each sentence as either *simple, compound, complex,* or *compound-complex.*

EXAMPLE The horse stomped the ground and kicked.

ANSWER *simple*

1. Sharks and marlin are fish, but whales are not.
2. The contestants were in their spots, and the game was about to begin.
3. Mr. Thomas and Mrs. Chin are my favorite teachers.
4. Lorraine lifted herself off the couch and walked gingerly.
5. Jackson took the wrong route.
6. They learned a song with a number of verses.
7. The tremor from the earthquake caused the bed to shake.
8. The paint got onto his face and looked like a bruise.
9. Margo wore a new jacket, but her pants were worn and old.
10. As the scene opens, a portrait hangs over a fireplace and the main characters are arguing.

PRACTICE 15.3B Writing the Four Structures of Sentences

Read the words in each item. Then, use each group of words to write the type of sentence indicated in parentheses. Read your sentences to a partner. Discuss if your sentences are correct.

EXAMPLE chicken and pasta (simple)

ANSWER Chicken and pasta are my favorite foods.

11. exit sign (compound)
12. ball, hit, bounced (simple)
13. cowboys and field hands (simple)
14. refrigerator, because (complex)
15. Allison, party, Juan (compound-complex)
16. committee, meeting (complex)
17. Professor Mailer (simple)
18. earlier flight, arrive (compound-complex)
19. members, oath (compound)
20. travel, money (compound)

SPEAKING APPLICATION

With a partner, take turns describing the longest trip you have ever taken. Use simple, compound, complex, and compound-complex sentences. Your partner should listen for and identify each type of sentence in your description.

WRITING APPLICATION

Write a brief paragraph about your morning, using a variety of correctly structured sentences: simple, compound, complex, and compound-complex.

Cumulative Review Chapters 13–15

PRACTICE 1 Identifying Nouns

Read the sentences. Then, label each underlined noun as *concrete* or *abstract*. If the noun is concrete, label it *collective*, *compound*, or *proper*.

1. The committee decided to push the agenda until next week.
2. Passersby stopped to look at Tim's artwork.
3. Daniel exhibited much bravery rescuing the kitten.
4. The team enjoyed much success in the playoffs.
5. My dream is to work in the White House.

PRACTICE 2 Identifying Pronouns

Read the sentences. Then, label each underlined pronoun as *reciprocal, demonstrative*, *relative*, *interrogative*, or *indefinite*.

1. Does Frankie know who owns that house?
2. Is that the guy whom you took to the dance?
3. Gerald and Carlos greeted each other.
4. Which of the contestants won the prize?
5. Some of the students left early.

PRACTICE 3 Classifying Verbs and Verb Phrases

Read the sentences. Then, write the verb or verb phrase in each sentence. Label each as *action verb* or *linking verb*, and *transitive* or *intransitive*.

1. Nat remained under the shade of the tree.
2. Thomas will carry the box for me.
3. Out in the field, the corn grows quickly.
4. This perfume smells like lilacs.
5. Every day, Les drives me home.

PRACTICE 4 Identifying Adjectives and Adverbs

Read the sentences. Then, label the underlined word as an *adverb* or *adjective*. Write the word that is modified.

1. Weston is noticeably stronger than I.
2. A healthy portion of fruit will keep you fit.
3. You were helpful this morning at practice.
4. The theater is regularly full on weekends.
5. Samuel ordered an enormous salad.

PRACTICE 5 Using Conjunctions and Interjections

Read the sentences. Then, write the conjunction or interjection. Label conjunctions as *coordinating*, *correlative*, or *subordinating*.

1. Both my brother and I play tennis.
2. While I was standing in line, I read my book.
3. My word! Did you see that?
4. Neither the team nor the coach wanted to lose.
5. Nancy will buy either a dress or shoes.
6. Jared wants to stop at a restaurant, and he wants to see a movie.
7. The gym not only has a trainer but it also has a pool.
8. I wanted front row seats, so I ordered my tickets online.
9. Yikes! I can't eat all that cake.
10. Indeed! Of course I will go.

Continued on next page ▶

Cumulative Review Chapters 13–15

PRACTICE 6 Recognizing Direct and Indirect Objects and Object of a Preposition

Identify the underlined items as *direct object, indirect object*, or *object of a preposition*.

1. Has your teacher given you the assignment?
2. Running around the pool will not be allowed.
3. Has Kyle shown Jason his new car?
4. Jimmy told us his plans for the summer.
5. Mr. Williams told the audience some jokes.
6. The new owner offered Louis a higher salary.
7. Was Frank waiting around the corner?
8. I loaned Stanley and Jim my football.
9. Haley got us tickets to the movie.
10. Did someone put milk in my tea?

PRACTICE 7 Identifying Phrases

Write the phrases, and label them *prepositional, appositive, participial, gerund*, or *infinitive*.

1. A wonderful golden retriever, Bobo was my favorite.
2. I finally arrived home at midnight.
3. Sitting behind his desk, the teacher scanned the class.
4. I am hopeful that you appreciate my giving you this chance.
5. Joe has sworn never to ask for directions.
6. Being the class president made Stan feel proud.
7. Tom Benson, my next-door neighbor, borrowed my lawn mower.
8. Waiting near the train station, Courtney noticed her bag was missing.
9. That dress, to be perfectly honest, is so beautiful.
10. My legs cramped during the race.

PRACTICE 8 Recognizing Clauses

Label the underlined clauses in the following sentences *independent* or *subordinate*. Identify any subordinate clause as *adjectival*, *adverbial*, or *noun clause*. Then, label any adjectival clause *essential* or *nonessential*.

1. The new student who sits in the front always participates.
2. Danny waited in the airport for his brother's arrival.
3. When the next audition will be held has not been posted.
4. Gordon plays guitar whenever he finds the time.
5. I want to be an astronaut, but I need to improve my grades.
6. My cat will jump out if the window is open.
7. Maria, who was dressed in a black gown, waved from the balcony.
8. Harold enjoyed his trip to the zoo even though the gorilla exhibit was closed.
9. The real tragedy is how the story ends.
10. My best friend, Wendy, who lives in Galveston, visited me this weekend.

CHAPTER 16

EFFECTIVE SENTENCES

Use a combination of simple, compound, and complex sentences to add interest to your writing.

WRITE GUY *Jeff Anderson, M.Ed.*

WHAT DO YOU NOTICE?

Notice the complexity of this sentence as you zoom in on these lines from the epic poem the *Odyssey* by Homer.

MENTOR TEXT

I might have made it safely home, that time,
but as I came around Malea the current
took me out to sea, and from the north
a fresh gale drove me on, past Cythera.

Now, ask yourself the following questions:

- What are the main or independent clauses in this compound sentence?
- How does the poet combine these clauses into a single compound sentence?

The poet uses three main or independent clauses, groups of words that can stand alone as their own sentences. The first main clause is *I might have made it safely home, that time*, the second is *as I came around Malea the current took me out to sea*, and the third is *from the north a fresh gale drove me on, past Cythera.* The poet combines these clauses into one compound sentence using commas and the conjunctions *but* and *and*.

Grammar for Writers Writers craft sentences that work well together by varying the length and complexity of their sentences. Evaluate your sentences to see if they would be more effective if they were shorter or longer.

Are they having trouble sharing one sentence?
My main clauses are too independent.

16.1 The Four Functions of a Sentence

Sentences can be classified according to what they do—that is, whether they state ideas, ask questions, give orders, or express strong emotions.

WRITING COACH Online

www.phwritingcoach.com

Grammar Practice

Practice your grammar skills with Writing Coach Online.

Grammar Games

Test your knowledge of grammar in this fast-paced interactive video game.

Declarative sentences are used to declare, or state, facts.

RULE 16.1.1

A declarative sentence states an idea and ends with a period.

DECLARATIVE London is a city in England.

To *interrogate* means "to ask." An **interrogative sentence** is a question.

RULE 16.1.2

An interrogative sentence asks a question and ends with a question mark.

INTERROGATIVE In which countries do tigers live?

Imperative sentences give commands or directions.

RULE 16.1.3

An imperative sentence gives an order or a direction and ends with either a period or an exclamation mark.

Most imperative sentences start with a verb. In this type of imperative sentence, the subject is understood to be *you.*

IMPERATIVE Follow the directions carefully.

Exclamatory sentences are used to express emotions.

RULE 16.1.4

An exclamatory sentence conveys strong emotion and ends with an exclamation mark.

EXCLAMATORY This is an outrage!

See Practice 16.1A
See Practice 16.1B

PRACTICE 16.1A Identifying the Four Types of Sentences

Read each sentence. Then, label each sentence *declarative, interrogative, imperative,* or *exclamatory.*

EXAMPLE Stop in your tracks.
ANSWER *imperative*

1. Has anyone here ever recorded a song in a studio?
2. Toast the bread until it is golden-brown.
3. Make sure you keep the receipt.
4. Which is harder to complete, a marathon or a triathlon?
5. The whale and the dolphin are both mammals.
6. Apply the bracket before hanging the painting.
7. What a horrible program that was!
8. Do NOT pass go.
9. Some Native Americans used smoke signals to communicate with one another.
10. Eating eggs provides you with protein.

PRACTICE 16.1B Punctuating the Four Types of Sentences

Read each sentence. Then, label each sentence *declarative, interrogative, imperative,* or *exclamatory.* In parentheses, write the correct end mark.

EXAMPLE Have you finished your work
ANSWER *interrogative (?)*

11. What a great time this is
12. Did you see your schedule
13. Take a taxi toward downtown
14. Do you plan to travel
15. Phoenix has many interesting sights to see
16. Please take out the trash before it is too late
17. What a terrible day it was
18. This coffee shop has the best bagels
19. Who is the mayor of this city
20. My brother sometimes plays soccer at this venue

SPEAKING APPLICATION

Take turns with a partner. Say sentences that are declarative, interrogative, imperative, and exclamatory. Your partner should identify each type of sentence.

WRITING APPLICATION

Write a scripted dialogue between two people in an airport. Include declarative, interrogative, imperative, and exclamatory sentences in the script.

16.2 Sentence Combining

Too many short sentences can make your writing choppy and disconnected.

WRITING COACH **Online**

www.phwritingcoach.com

Grammar Tutorials
Brush up on your Grammar skills with these animated videos.

Grammar Practice
Practice your grammar skills with Writing Coach Online.

Grammar Games
Test your knowledge of grammar in this fast-paced interactive video game.

One way to avoid the excessive use of short sentences and to achieve variety is to combine sentences.

RULE 16.2.1

Sentences can be combined by using a compound subject, a compound verb, or a compound object.

TWO SENTENCES	Moira enjoyed watching the lions. Jon enjoyed watching the lions.
COMPOUND SUBJECT	Moira and Jon enjoyed watching the lions.
TWO SENTENCES	Lisa played the game. Lisa won a prize.
COMPOUND VERB	Lisa played the game and won a prize.
TWO SENTENCES	Scott saw the cheetah. Scott saw the hyena.
COMPOUND OBJECT	Scott saw the cheetah and the hyena.

See Practice 16.2A

RULE 16.2.2

Sentences can be combined by joining two main or independent clauses to create a compound sentence.

Use a compound sentence when combining ideas that are related but independent. To join main clauses, use a comma and a coordinating conjunction (*for, and, but, or, nor, yet,* or *so*) or a semicolon.

EXAMPLE	The antelope was looking for enemies. It did not notice the lion.
COMPOUND SENTENCE	The antelope was looking for enemies, but it did not notice the lion.

Sentences can be combined by changing one into a subordinate clause to create a complex sentence.

RULE 16.2.3

To show the relationship between ideas in which one depends on the other, use a **complex sentence.** The subordinating conjunction will help readers understand the relationship. Some common subordinating conjunctions are *after, although, because, if, since, when,* and *while.*

EXAMPLE	We were frightened. We thought the lion we saw was hungry.
COMBINED WITH A SUBORDINATE CLAUSE	We were frightened **because we thought the lion was hungry**.

Sentences can be combined by changing one of them into a phrase.

RULE 16.2.4

EXAMPLE	My team plays tomorrow. We play the Cougars.
COMBINED WITH PREPOSITIONAL PHRASE	My team plays **against the Cougars** tomorrow.
EXAMPLE	My team will play against the Cougars. They are an undefeated team.
COMBINED WITH APPOSITIVE PHRASE	My team will play against the Cougars, **an undefeated team**.

See Practice 16.2B
See Practice 16.2C

PRACTICE 16.2A Combining Sentences Using Compound Subjects, Verbs, and Objects

Read each set of sentences. Then, write one sentence that combines each set of sentences.

EXAMPLE The player scored a basket in overtime. She won the game.

ANSWER *The player scored a basket in overtime and won the game.*

1. Tom Mays went to law school. My mother went to law school.
2. The bald eagle symbolizes our country. The bird also symbolizes independence.
3. Dale will choose a ham sandwich. He will choose cole slaw.
4. Westlake is a neighborhood school. Loyola is a neighborhood school.
5. While on vacation, Jules visited a museum. Jules also visited an aquarium.
6. Wally wrote his essay over the weekend. Wally handed in his essay on Monday.
7. His manuscript was published last year. His manuscript was well–received by critics.
8. Brandon sprained his knee. Brandon sprained his ankle.
9. The diamond was stolen from the museum. The diamond was never recovered.
10. A small girl sits on the dock. A small girl fishes.

PRACTICE 16.2B Combining Sentences Using Phrases

Read each set of sentences. Combine each set by turning one sentence into a phrase—prepositional, participial, or appositive—that adds detail to the other.

EXAMPLE The women stand at the box office. They wait to buy tickets.

ANSWER *The women standing at the box office wait to buy tickets.*

11. The sun rises between the trees. It is a breathtaking view.
12. Many movies have been made by that director. He is a hard-working man.
13. Mrs. Campbell approached the podium. Mrs. Campbell appeared excited.
14. The audience clapped for the actors. The actors were still wearing costumes.
15. The flames bend in the breeze. They look like tongues.
16. The ox pulls the cart. The ox works hard.
17. The wind blows. It makes leaves float down.
18. Tabitha lined up her shot carefully. She is the best player on the team.
19. The wooden fence was shattered by the storm. The storm was a real downpour.
20. The boat sprayed water onto the beach. The beach was crowded with sunbathers.

SPEAKING APPLICATION

Take turns with a partner. Tell two related sentences. Your partner should combine these two sentences to make one logical sentence.

WRITING APPLICATION

Write two sentences that relate to each other. Then, exchange papers with a partner. Your partner should combine the two sentences into one by turning one sentence into a phrase.

PRACTICE 16.2C Combining Sentences by Forming Compound or Complex Sentences

Read each pair of sentences. Then, combine the sentences to form compound, complex sentences using the coordinating or subordinating conjunction indicated in parentheses.

EXAMPLE I stay active. I jog every day. (because)

ANSWER *I stay active because I jog every day.*

1. The team won the game. They didn't practice all week. (although)
2. I cleaned the closet. Boxes spilled out. (after)
3. We called for room service. No one responded. (but)
4. The pathway was slick. We could not keep our footing. (and)
5. Paul insisted on seeing the movie. He doesn't like westerns. (even though)
6. We could come back. We could stay here for the night. (or)
7. I couldn't say no. Who could resist the chance to meet a famous artist? (for)
8. I could read a suspense novel. I could read a magazine. (or)
9. Some of us study music. Others just enjoy listening to the radio. (but)
10. Planets are not stars. They can appear bright in the night sky. (yet)

SPEAKING APPLICATION

Take turns with a partner. Tell about a famous person whom you would like to meet, and explain why. Use at least three compound, complex, or compound–complex sentences along with three coordinating or subordinating conjunctions in your description. Your partner should identify which of your sentences are compound or complex, as well as the types of conjunctions that you use.

WRITING APPLICATION

Write a paragraph about what makes you different from either your friends or your classmates. Use at least three compound, complex, or compound–complex sentences, along with three coordinating or subordinating conjunctions.

16.3 Varying Sentences

Vary your sentences to develop a rhythm, to achieve an effect, or to emphasize the connections between ideas. There are several ways you can vary your sentences.

WRITING COACH **Online**
www.phwritingcoach.com

Grammar Practice
Practice your grammar skills with Writing Coach Online.

Grammar Games
Test your knowledge of grammar in this fast-paced interactive video game.

Varying Sentence Length

To emphasize a point or surprise a reader, include a short, direct sentence to interrupt the flow of long sentences. Notice the effect of the last sentence in the following paragraph.

EXAMPLE The Jacobites derived their name from *Jacobus,* the Latin name for King James II of England, who was dethroned in 1688 by William of Orange during the Glorious Revolution. Unpopular because of his Catholicism and autocratic ruling style, James fled to France to seek the aid of King Louis XIV. In 1690, James, along with a small body of French troops, landed in Ireland in an attempt to regain his throne. His hopes ended at the Battle of the Boyne.

Some sentences contain only one idea and can't be broken. It may be possible, however, to state the idea in a shorter sentence. Other sentences contain two or more ideas and might be shortened by breaking up the ideas.

LONGER SENTENCE Many of James II's predecessors were able to avoid major economic problems, but James had serious economic problems.

MORE DIRECT Unlike many of his predecessors, James II was unable to avoid major economic problems.

LONGER SENTENCE James tried to work with Parliament to develop a plan of taxation that would be fair and reasonable, but members of Parliament rejected his efforts, and James dissolved the Parliament.

SHORTER SENTENCES James tried to work with Parliament to develop a fair and reasonable taxation plan. However, because members of Parliament rejected his efforts, James dissolved the Parliament.

Varying Sentence Beginnings

Another way to create sentence variety is to start sentences with different parts of speech.

WAYS TO VARY SENTENCE BEGINNINGS	
Start With a Noun	Bicycles are difficult to build.
Start With an Adverb	Naturally, bicycles are difficult to build.
Start With an Adverbial Phrase	Because of their complexity, bicycles are difficult to build.
Start With a Participial Phrase	Having tried to build several bicycles, I know how hard it is.
Start With a Prepositional Phrase	For the average person, bicycles are very difficult to build.
Start With an Infinitive Phrase	To build a high-performance bicycle was my goal.

See Practice 16.3A

Using Inverted Word Order

You can also vary sentence beginnings by reversing the traditional subject–verb order to create verb–subject order. You can reverse order by starting the sentence with a **participial phrase** or a **prepositional phrase.** You can also move a complement to the beginning of the sentence.

SUBJECT–VERB ORDER

The navy waited for the attack.

The royal armada sailed into the bay.

The booming of cannon fire filled the air.

The sound was deafening.

VERB–SUBJECT ORDER

Waiting for the attack was the navy.
participial phrase

Into the bay sailed the royal armada.
prepositional phrase

Filling the air was the booming of cannon fire.
participial phrase

Deafening was the sound.
predicate adjective

See Practice 16.3B

PRACTICE 16.3A Revising to Vary Sentence Beginnings

Read each sentence. Rewrite each sentence to begin with the part of speech or phrase indicated in parentheses. You may need to add a word or phrase.

EXAMPLE The teller counted five-dollar bills. (adverbs)

ANSWER *Slowly and carefully, the teller counted the five-dollar bills.*

1. I haven't seen her since lunch. (preposition)
2. Mrs. Rosenthal watered her garden after sunset. (prepositional phrase)
3. The magnolia tree will be blooming soon. (adverb)
4. The river flooded the streets. (participial phrase)
5. My antique watch broke. (adverb)
6. The bicycle rider made it across the finish line. (participial phrase)
7. We will meet you at the park. (prepositional phrase)
8. We walked instead of driving. (infinitive phrase)
9. New condominiums will be built nearby. (adverb)
10. We watched fireflies. (adverb)

PRACTICE 16.3B Inverting Sentences to Vary Subject–Verb Order

Read each sentence. Rewrite each sentence by inverting subject-verb order to verb-subject order.

EXAMPLE The Memorial Day parade is coming.

ANSWER *Here comes the Memorial Day parade.*

11. The new mayor is watching by the stands.
12. We had never heard such noise.
13. Four laughing children ran ahead of the couple.
14. A lush meadow stretches between the creek and the dirt road.
15. The ingredients are listed on the back.
16. A story about the student of the year appeared on the front page.
17. The Statue of Liberty stands in New York harbor.
18. Restored colonial houses stood along the streets.
19. A beautiful rainbow appeared after the rain.
20. The call of a bird came out of the stillness of dusk.

SPEAKING APPLICATION

Take turns with a partner. Say the following phrases: *if you review your notes, when the storm ended, you need good balance.* Your partner should add words to the beginning of each phrase to form a sentence.

WRITING APPLICATION

Write three original sentences about something fun you did recently. Then, exchange papers with a partner. Your partner should invert the order of your sentences to vary their beginnings.

16.4 Avoid Fragments and Run-ons

Hasty writers sometimes omit crucial words, punctuate awkwardly, or leave their thoughts unfinished, causing two common sentence errors: **fragments** and **run-ons.**

Find It/FIX IT 20 Grammar Game Plan

WRITING COACH Online

www.phwritingcoach.com

Grammar Practice

Practice your grammar skills with Writing Coach Online.

Grammar Games

Test your knowledge of grammar in this fast-paced interactive video game.

Recognizing Fragments

Although some writers use them for stylistic effect, **fragments** are generally considered errors in standard English.

Do not capitalize and punctuate phrases, subordinate clauses, or words in a series as if they were complete sentences.

RULE 16.4.1

Reading your work aloud to listen for natural pauses and stops should help you avoid fragments. Sometimes, you can repair a fragment by connecting it to words that come before or after it.

One way to correct a fragment is to connect it to the words in a nearby sentence.

RULE 16.4.2

PARTICIPIAL FRAGMENT	inspired by the grace of the dancer
ADDED TO A NEARBY SENTENCE	**Inspired by the grace of the dancer**, Linda saw the performance again.
PREPOSITIONAL FRAGMENT	before her partner
ADDED TO A NEARBY SENTENCE	The ballerina came on stage **before her partner**.
PRONOUN AND PARTICIPIAL FRAGMENT	the one hanging in the closet
ADDED TO NEARBY SENTENCE	The leotard I like is **the one hanging in the closet**.

RULE 16.4.3

Another way to correct a fragment is to add any sentence part that is needed to make the fragment a complete sentence.

Remember that every complete sentence must have both a subject and a verb and express a complete thought. Check to see that each of your sentences contains all of the parts necessary to be complete.

NOUN FRAGMENT **the troupe of lively young dancers**

COMPLETED SENTENCES **The troupe of lively young dancers** (subject) **moved** (verb) **across the stage.**

We (subject) **excitedly watched** (verb) **the troupe of lively young dancers** (direct object)**.**

Notice what missing sentence parts must be added to the following types of phrase fragments to make them complete.

	FRAGMENTS	COMPLETED SENTENCES
Noun Fragment With Participial Phrase	the food eaten by us	The food was eaten by us.
Verb Fragment	will be at the rehearsal today	I will be at the rehearsal today.
Prepositional Fragment	in the hall closet	I put the shoes in the hall closet.
Participial Fragment	found under the desk	The books found under the desk are mine.
Gerund Fragment	teaching children to dance	Teaching children to dance is rewarding.
Infinitive Fragment	to see the new ballet	I expect to see the new ballet.

RULE 16.4.4

You may need to attach a subordinate clause to a main clause to correct a fragment.

A **subordinate clause** contains a subject and a verb but does not express a complete thought and cannot stand alone as a sentence. Link it to a main clause to make the sentence complete.

ADJECTIVAL CLAUSE FRAGMENT	which was being performed outdoors
COMPLETED SENTENCE	I enjoyed watching the dance rehearsal, **which was being performed outdoors**.
ADVERBIAL CLAUSE FRAGMENT	after she practiced the new dance routine
COMPLETED SENTENCE	**After she practiced the new dance routine**, she was ready for the show.
NOUN CLAUSE FRAGMENT	whatever ballet we see in this theater
COMPLETED SENTENCE	We always enjoy **whatever ballet we see in this theater**.

Series Fragments A fragment is not always short. A long series of words still needs to have a subject and a verb and express a complete thought. It may be a long fragment masquerading as a sentence.

SERIES FRAGMENT	COMPLETE SENTENCE
after reading Steinbeck's novel, with its probing look at poverty and greed, in the style so typical of this master storyteller	After reading Steinbeck's novel, with its probing look at poverty and greed, in the style so typical of this master storyteller, I was able to prepare an interesting oral presentation.

See Practice 16.4A

Find It/FIX IT 15 Grammar Game Plan

Avoiding Run-on Sentences

A **run-on** sentence is two or more sentences capitalized and punctuated as if they were a single sentence.

RULE 16.4.5

Use punctuation and conjunctions to correctly join or separate parts of a run-on sentence.

Find It/FIX IT 16 Grammar Game Plan

There are two kinds of **run-ons: fused sentences,** which are two or more sentences joined with no punctuation, and **comma splices,** which have two or more sentences separated only by commas rather than by commas and conjunctions.

FUSED SENTENCE The dancers practiced every day they were soon the best in the state.

COMMA SPLICE Only one package arrived in the mail, the other items never came.

As with fragments, proofreading or reading your work aloud will help you find run-ons. Once found, they can be corrected by adding punctuation and conjunctions or by rewording the sentences.

FOUR WAYS TO CORRECT RUN-ONS

	RUN-ON	CORRECTION
With End Marks and Capitals	The dance was in full swing in the gym people crowded together.	The dance was in full swing. In the gym, people crowded together.
With Commas and Conjunctions	The paper needed cutting we could not locate the scissors.	The paper needed cutting, but we could not locate the scissors.
With Semicolons	Our city has many cultural activities, for example it hosts the National Ballet.	Our city has many cultural activities; for example, it hosts the National Ballet.
By Rewriting	The horse show began late, someone had misplaced the registration forms.	The horse show began late because someone had misplaced the registration forms.

See Practice 16.4B

PRACTICE 16.4A Identifying and Correcting Fragments

Read each item. If an item contains a fragment, rewrite it to make a complete sentence. If an item is a complete sentence, write *correct*.

EXAMPLE Riding on the *Orient Express*.

ANSWER *Riding on the Orient Express would be thrilling.*

1. To see the new airplane.
2. Which Cindy received for her birthday.
3. Who won the contest?
4. Enjoys riding her bike.
5. The smell of freshly mowed grass.
6. My notebook is missing.
7. What time is the party?
8. After searching high and low.
9. The play is so funny.
10. Known for its quick service and friendly atmosphere.

PRACTICE 16.4B Revising to Eliminate Run-on Sentences

Read each sentence. Correct each run-on by correctly joining or separating the sentence parts.

EXAMPLE The children played in the backyard, the swing amused them.

ANSWER *The children played in the backyard. The swing amused them.*

11. We made three easy outs it was our team's turn at bat.
12. Laila did a wonderful job, we knew she would.
13. Hector wanted to be an actor, acting jobs were hard to get.
14. Math is easy for me I also do well in science.
15. The beach is very pretty, you can see into tide pools at low tide.
16. Shrimp eggs can survive for more than one year in the desert, rainwater brings them to life.
17. The trick amazed the group they had never seen anything like it.
18. Senator Gonzalez was the speaker he talked about citizenship.
19. Several committee members opposed the increase, they voted against it.
20. Many cactuses are odd-looking plants they have beautiful blossoms.

SPEAKING APPLICATION

Take turns with a partner. Say sentence fragments. Your partner should turn each fragment into a complete sentence.

WRITING APPLICATION

Rewrite the following run-on sentences as complete sentences:
The explorer followed the map he found the treasure.
We rounded the bend the castle came into view.

16.5 Misplaced and Dangling Modifiers

Careful writers put modifiers as close as possible to the words they modify. When modifiers are misplaced or left dangling in a sentence, the result may be illogical or confusing.

WRITING COACH **Online**

www.phwritingcoach.com

Grammar Practice

Practice your grammar skills with Writing Coach Online.

Grammar Games

Test your knowledge of grammar in this fast-paced interactive video game.

Recognizing Misplaced Modifiers

A **misplaced modifier** is placed too far from the modified word and appears to modify the wrong word or words.

RULE 16.5.1

A misplaced modifier seems to modify the wrong word in the sentence.

MISPLACED MODIFIER	The man fell over a rock **running on the road**.
CORRECTION	The man **running on the road** fell over a rock.
MISPLACED MODIFIER	We heard the telephone ring **while watching television**.
CORRECTION	**While watching television**, we heard the telephone ring.

Recognizing Dangling Modifiers

With **dangling modifiers,** the word that should be modified is missing from the sentence. Dangling modifiers usually come at the beginning of a sentence and are followed by a comma. The subject being modified should come right after the comma.

RULE 16.5.2

A dangling modifier seems to modify the wrong word or no word at all because the word it should modify has been omitted from the sentence.

See Practice 16.5A

DANGLING PARTICIPIAL PHRASE	Measuring carefully, the span over the river was closed accurately. (*Who* did the measuring?)
CORRECTED SENTENCE	Measuring carefully, **the engineer** accurately closed the span over the river.

Dangling participial phrases are corrected by adding missing words and making other needed changes.

Dangling infinitive phrases and elliptical clauses can be corrected in the same way. First, identify the subject of the sentence. Then, make sure each subject is clearly stated. You may also need to change the form of the verb.

DANGLING INFINITIVE PHRASE	To cross the river, the bridge toll must be paid. (*Who* is crossing and must pay?)
CORRECTED SENTENCE	To cross the river, **drivers** must pay the bridge toll.
DANGLING ELLIPTICAL CLAUSE	While sailing under the bridge, a school of porpoises was sighted. (*Who* was sailing and sighted the porpoises?)
CORRECTED SENTENCE	While sailing under the bridge, **we** saw a school of porpoises.

A dangling adverbial clause may also occur when the antecedent of a pronoun is not clear.

DANGLING ADVERBIAL CLAUSE	When she was ninety years old, Mrs. Smith's granddaughter planned a picnic near the bridge. (*Who* is ninety, Mrs. Smith or her granddaughter?)
CORRECTED SENTENCE	**When Mrs. Smith was ninety years old**, her granddaughter planned a picnic near the bridge.

See Practice 16.5B

PRACTICE 16.5A Identifying and Correcting Misplaced Modifiers

Read each sentence. Then, rewrite each sentence, putting the misplaced modifiers closer to the words they should modify. If a sentence is correct, write *correct*.

EXAMPLE We pitched our tent in the mountains with a view of the lake.

ANSWER *In the mountains, we pitched our tent with a view of the lake.*

1. Rafael waved at me walking from the car.
2. Mom came by while I was washing the windows with a casserole.
3. Please give the pizza to my brother with extra anchovies.
4. Maggie picked up the heavy package left by the delivery man with a groan.
5. Roger accidentally spent the rare coins on gasoline that his grandfather gave him.
6. Tim saw a bird soar in the sky while jogging.
7. Anita designs delightful clothing for children in prints and plaids.
8. Trying to avoid a tie score, the player made a desperate shot at the basket.
9. Earth revolves around the sun once a year.
10. Crossing the ford is easy on horseback.

PRACTICE 16.5B Identifying and Correcting Dangling Modifiers

Read each sentence. Then, rewrite each sentence, correcting any dangling modifiers by supplying missing words or ideas.

EXAMPLE Hiking through the woods at night, many animal sounds were heard.

ANSWER *Hiking through the woods at night, I heard many animal sounds.*

11. Born in Uganda, America seemed like a dream.
12. Running down the hallway, the elevator door closed.
13. After mopping the floor, the dog tracked mud through the kitchen.
14. To get the job, a test must be passed.
15. While climbing the mountain, a herd of goats was spotted.
16. Remaining calm, the entire building was evacuated.
17. When she was asleep, the babysitter carried the infant to her crib.
18. To reach the bottom of the canyon, safety must be considered.
19. Feeling exhausted, the road seemed to go on forever.
20. When he was three, Paul's father got a new job.

SPEAKING APPLICATION

Take turns with a partner. Tell about something interesting that you have done. Use modifiers in your sentences. Your partner should name the modifiers in your description, and tell whether they are correctly placed.

WRITING APPLICATION

Rewrite sentences 12, 15, and 18, replacing the verbs. Then, rewrite each sentence to correct the dangling modifier.

16.6 Faulty Parallelism

Good writers try to present a series of ideas in similar grammatical structures so the ideas will read smoothly. If one element in a series is not parallel with the others, the result may be jarring or confusing.

Find It/FIX IT
10
Grammar Game Plan

WRITING COACH Online
www.phwritingcoach.com

Grammar Practice
Practice your grammar skills with Writing Coach Online.

Grammar Games
Test your knowledge of grammar in this fast-paced interactive video game.

Recognizing the Correct Use of Parallelism

To present a series of ideas of equal importance, you should use parallel grammatical structures.

Parallelism involves presenting equal ideas in words, phrases, clauses, or sentences of similar types.

RULE 16.6.1

PARALLEL WORDS: The surfer looked **strong**, **fit**, and **agile**.

PARALLEL PHRASES: The greatest feeling I know is **to ride a giant wave flawlessly** and **to have all my friends watch me enviously**.

PARALLEL CLAUSES: The surfboard **that you recommended** and **that my brother wants** is on sale.

PARALLEL SENTENCES: **It couldn't be**, of course. **It could never, never be**. –Dorothy Parker

Correcting Faulty Parallelism

Faulty parallelism occurs when a writer uses unequal grammatical structures to express related ideas.

Correct a sentence containing faulty parallelism by rewriting it so that each parallel idea is expressed in the same grammatical structure.

RULE 16.6.2

Faulty parallelism can involve words, phrases, and clauses in a series or in comparisons.

Nonparallel Words, Phrases, and Clauses in a Series
Always check for parallelism when your writing contains items in a series.

Correcting Faulty Parallelism in a Series

NONPARALLEL STRUCTURES	**Planning** (gerund), **drafting** (gerund), and **revision** (noun) are three steps in the writing process.
CORRECTION	**Planning** (gerund), **drafting** (gerund), and **revising** (gerund) are three steps in the writing process.
NONPARALLEL STRUCTURES	**I could not wait to try my new surfboard** (infinitive phrase), **to catch some waves** (infinitive phrase), and **visiting the beach** (participial phrase).
CORRECTION	**I could not wait to try my new surfboard** (infinitive phrase), **to catch some waves** (infinitive phrase), and **to visit the beach** (infinitive phrase).
NONPARALLEL STRUCTURE	**Some experts feel that surfing is not a sport** (noun clause), **but it requires athleticism** (independent clause).
CORRECTION	**Some experts feel that surfing is not a sport** (noun clause) **but that it requires athleticism** (noun clause).

Another potential problem involves correlative conjunctions, such as *both ... and* or *not only ... but also.* Though these conjunctions connect two related items, writers sometimes misplace or split the first part of the conjunction. The result is faulty parallelism.

NONPARALLEL	Pia **not only** won the local surfing championship **but also** the state title.
PARALLEL	Pia won **not only** the local surfing championship **but also** the state title.

Nonparallel Words, Phrases, and Clauses in Comparisons

As the saying goes, you cannot compare apples with oranges. In writing comparisons, you generally should compare a phrase with the same type of phrase and a clause with the same type of clause.

Correcting Faulty Parallelism in Comparisons

NONPARALLEL STRUCTURES	**Most people prefer corn (noun) to eating beets (gerund phrase).**
CORRECTION	**Most people prefer corn (noun) to beets (noun).**
NONPARALLEL STRUCTURES	**I left my job at 7:00 P.M. (prepositional phrase) rather than stopping work at 5:00 P.M. (participial phrase)**
CORRECTION	**I left my job at 7:00 P.M. (prepositional phrase) rather than at the usual 5:00 P.M. (prepositional phrase)**
NONPARALLEL STRUCTURES	**Jaime (subject) delights in foggy days (prepositional phrase) as much as sunny days (subject) delight other people (direct object).**
CORRECTION	**Jaime (subject) delights in foggy days (prepositional phrase) as much as other people (subject) delight in sunny days (prepositional phrase).**

See Practice 16.6A
See Practice 16.6B

Find It/FIX IT
10
Grammar Game Plan

16.7 Faulty Coordination

When two or more independent clauses of unequal importance are joined by *and*, the result can be faulty **coordination**.

WRITING COACH Online
www.phwritingcoach.com

Grammar Practice
Practice your grammar skills with Writing Coach Online.

Grammar Games
Test your knowledge of grammar in this fast-paced interactive video game.

Recognizing Faulty Coordination

To *coordinate* means to "place side by side in equal rank." Two independent clauses that are joined by the coordinating conjunction *and*, therefore, should have equal rank.

RULE 16.7.1

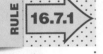

Use *and* or other coordinating conjunctions only to connect ideas of equal importance.

CORRECT COORDINATION: Otis designed an airplane, **and** Oliver built it.

Sometimes, however, writers carelessly use *and* to join main clauses that either should not be joined or should be joined in another way so that the real relationship between the clauses is clear. Faulty coordination puts all the ideas on the same level of importance, even though logically they should not be.

FAULTY COORDINATION: Production of aircraft accelerated in World War II, **and** aircraft became a decisive factor in the war.

I didn't do well, **and** the race was very easy.

The dog looked ferocious, **and** it was snarling and snapping at me.

Occasionally, writers will also string together so many ideas with *and's* that the reader is left breathless.

STRINGY SENTENCE: The plane that flew over the field did a few dips and turns, **and** the people on the ground craned their necks to watch, **and** everyone laughed and cheered.

Correcting Faulty Coordination

Faulty coordination can be corrected in several ways.

One way to correct faulty coordination is to put unrelated ideas into separate sentences.

RULE 16.7.2

When faulty coordination occurs in a sentence in which the main clauses are not closely related, separate the clauses and omit the coordinating conjunction.

FAULTY COORDINATION	Production of aircraft accelerated in World War II, **and** aircraft became a decisive factor in the war.
CORRECTION	Production of aircraft accelerated in World War II. Aircraft became a decisive factor in the war.

You can correct faulty coordination by putting less important ideas into subordinate clauses or phrases.

RULE 16.7.3

If one main clause is less important than, or subordinate to, the other, turn it into a subordinate clause. You can also reduce a less important idea to a phrase.

FAULTY COORDINATION	I didn't do well, **and** the race was easy.
CORRECTION	I didn't do well, **even though** the race was easy.
FAULTY COORDINATION	The dog looked angry, **and** it was snarling at me.
CORRECTION	Snarling at me, the dog looked angry.

Stringy sentences should be broken up and revised using any of the three methods just described. Following is one way that the stringy sentence on the previous page can be revised.

REVISION OF A STRINGY SENTENCE	The plane that flew over the field did a few dips and turns. Craning their necks to watch, the people on the ground laughed and cheered.

See Practice 16.6C
See Practice 16.6D

PRACTICE 16.6A Revising to Eliminate Faulty Parallelism

Read each sentence. Then, rewrite the sentence to correct any nonparallel structures.

EXAMPLE I was wet, cold, and needing sleep.

ANSWER *I was wet, cold, and tired.*

1. This weekend we have a paper to write, a cake to bake, and a birthday party.
2. I like my school because the teachers are good, the students are nice, and I play on the football team.
3. Tell me about the students in your classes and your soccer team.
4. I did a poor job painting more because I was rushed than that I did not know how to do it.
5. If my parents give permission and I can get a ride with my cousin, I'll go.
6. I did not buy the car because it needs brakes, and I would have to get new tires.
7. The book was funny, fast-paced, and kept us interested.
8. I had a hamburger, Kim had a salad, but coffee was all that Jon ordered.
9. The mayor proposed cutting library hours, recycling pickup, and to cut other services.
10. Mom washed both the car and the windows.

PRACTICE 16.6B Writing Parallelisms in Comparisons

Read each item. Then, rewrite each item, completing the comparison using correct parallelism.

EXAMPLE Mother knits scarves as well as _____.

ANSWER *Mother knits scarves as well as she knits hats.*

11. Elias did his homework at his desk rather than _____.
12. The ceremony was long, but the party afterward _____.
13. The drama club meets after school, but the art club _____.
14. Salina likes to bowl as much as _____.
15. I usually bring my lunch instead of _____.
16. Darnell rides a skateboard as well as _____.
17. Mrs. Downing arrived at 10:00 A.M. rather than _____.
18. Shelly draws landscapes as well as Damien _____.
19. Jonah prefers dogs to _____.
20. Ms. Gibbs administered the test in place of _____.

SPEAKING APPLICATION

Take turns with a partner. Tell about something unusual that has happened to you or to someone you know. Your partner should point out and correct any faulty parallelism in your description.

WRITING APPLICATION

Use Practice 16.6B as a model to write five additional items. Exchange papers with a partner. Your partner should complete each comparison using correct parallelism.

PRACTICE 16.6C Rewriting to Correct Faulty Coordination

Read each sentence. Then, correct the faulty coordination in each sentence by reducing a less important idea to a phrase.

EXAMPLE The soup was served, and it was steaming hot.

ANSWER *Steaming hot, the soup was served.*

1. Ms. Rasha gave a quiz, and it was at the end of the class.
2. A robin perched on the branch, and it was chirping loudly.
3. I like naan; naan is an Asian bread.
4. The snake lifted its head; it was preparing to strike.
5. The video store has a great selection, and the store is across the street.
6. Jack London wrote *The Call of the Wild,* and he is a famous author.
7. David was ready to play, and he was seated at the piano.
8. The truck driver ran the light, and he was driving fast.
9. Sonya struggled to tell Joe the truth, and she was avoiding his eyes.
10. Harvey served the people their food, and the people were sitting by the window.

PRACTICE 16.6D Revising to Eliminate Faulty Coordination

Read each sentence. Then, rewrite the sentence to correct the faulty coordination.

EXAMPLE I chose our new pet, and it's a puppy.

ANSWER *I chose our new pet, a puppy.*

11. The rose is one of the most popular flowers, and it has a lovely scent.
12. We drove to the stadium, and crowds filled the stands.
13. The Canadian forests stretch for miles, and they provide a home for many kinds of wildlife.
14. There's a tree house, and it has running water!
15. The picnic basket was stuffed with food, and they headed for the park.
16. I was so tired that I went to bed at 7:00, and it was still light.
17. Jay is having his car fixed, and he was in a fender bender last week.
18. We were going to practice on Saturday, but some players couldn't make it, so we switched to Sunday, but that didn't work either, so now we have practice on Monday.
19. Kristen's favorite book is *Huckleberry Finn,* and she reads it over and over.
20. The bus arrived ten minutes late, and it arrived at its next stop on time.

SPEAKING APPLICATION

Take turns with a partner. Use Practice 16.6C to say similar sentences. Your partner should correct the faulty coordination by reducing a less important idea to a phrase.

WRITING APPLICATION

Write three sentences with faulty coordination. Exchange papers with a partner and correct each other's work.

Test Warm-Up

DIRECTIONS
Read the introduction and the passage that follows. Then, answer the questions to show that you can identify and correct faulty parallelism and faulty coordination in reading and writing.

Ella wrote this paragraph about her favorite season. Read the paragraph and think about the changes you would suggest as a peer editor. When you finish reading, answer the questions that follow.

An Autumn Frolic

(1) Autumn has always been my favorite season. (2) I prefer the crisp air to sweating in the summer heat. (3) I love looking at the colorful leaves but not to rake them. (4) I raked leaves for three hours yesterday, and I was grumbling. (5) I looked at my huge pile and when I was looking at it, I had a silly idea. (6) I invited Tina to come over, and what happened next was a return to younger days. (7) Tina and I played in the leaves like little kids. (8) Autumn really is my favorite season, but I had forgotten its simpler pleasures!

1 What change, if any, should be made in sentence 2?

A Replace ***sweating*** with **being baked**

B Delete the words ***sweating in***

C Replace ***crisp*** with **bracing**

D Make no change

2 What change, if any, should be made in sentence 3?

F Replace ***to rake*** with **raking**

G Replace the words ***but not*** with **rather than**

H Replace ***at*** with **to**

J Make no change

3 How should sentence 4 be revised?

A I raked leaves and grumbled for three hours yesterday.

B I spent three hours grumbling about raking leaves yesterday.

C I raked for three hours yesterday and was grumbling.

D Grumbling, I did rake leaves for three hours yesterday.

4 What is the most effective way to rewrite the ideas in sentence 5?

F I looked at my huge pile and, looking at it, I had a silly idea.

G I looked at my huge pile and had a silly idea.

H While looking at it, I had a silly idea about my huge pile.

J I looked at my huge pile and I had a silly idea when I was looking at it.

CHAPTER 17

VERB USAGE

Using the correct verb tenses will help you present the timing of actions accurately in your writing.

WRITE GUY *Jeff Anderson, M.Ed.*

WHAT DO YOU NOTICE?

Spot the verbs as you zoom in on these sentences from the story "The Interlopers" by Saki.

MENTOR TEXT

"I'm caught in my own forest land," retorted Ulrich. "When my men come to release us you will wish, perhaps, that you were in a better plight than caught poaching on a neighbor's land, shame on you."

Now, ask yourself the following questions:

- Which verb tense did the author use in the clause *I'm caught* in the first sentence? (Remember that the word *I'm* in the first sentence is the shortened form of *I am*.)
- Which verb tense did the author use in the phrase *will wish* in the second sentence?

The author used present tense in *I'm caught*. The clause shows what is happening now to the subject of the sentence. In *will wish*, the author uses *will* before *wish* to create the future tense form. The narrator follows the phrase *will wish* with *perhaps*, showing that this might happen.

Grammar for Writers Verbs are tools that writers use to show action and to link important ideas within sentences. To help your readers follow the action in your writing, use verb tenses that accurately describe the timing of events.

How about using some action on this assignment in the present?
Using this verb will put my action in the future.

17.1 Verb Tenses

Besides expressing actions or conditions, verbs have different **tenses** to indicate when the action or condition occurred.

WRITING COACH Online
www.phwritingcoach.com

Grammar Tutorials
Brush up on your Grammar skills with these animated videos.

Grammar Practice
Practice your grammar skills with Writing Coach Online.

Dimension G
Test your knowledge of grammar in this fast-paced interactive video game.

RULE 17.1.1

A tense is the form of a verb that shows the time of an action or a condition.

The Six Verb Tenses

There are six tenses that indicate when an action or a condition of a verb is, was, or will be in effect. Each of these six tenses has at least two forms.

RULE 17.1.2

Each tense has a basic and a progressive form.

The chart that follows shows examples of the six tenses.

THE BASIC FORMS OF THE SIX TENSES	
Present	I visit the Statue of Liberty.
Past	I visited Ellis Island last Sunday.
Future	I will visit Washington, D.C.
Present Perfect	I have visited children at the hospital for almost a year now.
Past Perfect	I had visited my grandmother every weekend until this past month.
Future Perfect	I will have visited Dallas three times a week by the end of May.
Present	Tim runs for fun.
Past	Tim ran every day during the summer.
Future	Tim will run a race next week.
Present Perfect	Tim has run in many races.
Past Perfect	Tim had run his first race by age five.
Future Perfect	Tim will have run in ten races by June.

See Practice 17.1A

Basic Verb Forms or Tenses

Verb tenses are identified simply by their tense names. The **progressive tenses,** however, are identified by their tense names plus the word *progressive.* Progressive tenses show that an action is or was happening for a period of time.

The chart below shows examples of the six tenses in their progressive form or tense. Note that all of these progressive tenses end in *-ing.* (See the section on verb conjugation later in this chapter for more about the progressive tense.)

THE PROGRESSIVE TENSES	
Present Progressive	I am drawing right now.
Past Progressive	I was drawing when you called.
Future Progressive	I will be drawing all weekend.
Present Perfect Progressive	I have been drawing more than usual lately.
Past Perfect Progressive	I had been drawing apples until the art teacher suggested that I draw boats.
Future Perfect Progressive	I will have been drawing for two years by the end of March.

The Emphatic Form

There is also a third form or tense, the **emphatic,** which exists only for the present and past tenses. The **present emphatic** is formed with the helping verbs *do* or *does,* depending on the subject. The **past emphatic** is formed with *did.* The purpose of the emphatic tense is to put more emphasis on, or to stress, the action of the verb.

THE EMPHATIC TENSES OF THE PRESENT AND THE PAST	
Present Emphatic	I do exercise more frequently than you. Sally does practice piano more often than I do.
Past Emphatic	I did exercise last night to work on my form. Jerome did work later than Alia did.

See Practice 17.1B

PRACTICE 17.1A Identifying Verb Tenses

Read each sentence. Write the tense (*present, past, future, present perfect, past perfect,* or *future perfect*) of the underlined verb or verbs in each sentence.

EXAMPLE The runner sprinted across the finish line and smiled.

ANSWER *past, past*

1. After he had taken a nap, the pilot felt much more awake.
2. My family will drive to the beach on Saturday.
3. The circus will have traveled 3,000 miles by the time it ends its tour.
4. This play has interested many drama students.
5. Joe enjoys playing basketball outdoors.
6. After she passed her test, Lisa worked even harder.
7. People of all ages have participated in fund-raising events.
8. The girl answered when her mother called her.
9. Once he had received his allowance, the boy bought a baseball mitt.
10. When I am older, I will go to college.

PRACTICE 17.1B Recognizing Tenses or Forms of Verbs

Read each sentence. Rewrite each sentence and the underlined verb, using the verb tense or form shown in parentheses.

EXAMPLE I finished my homework after school. (past emphatic)

ANSWER *I did finish my homework after school.*

11. The home team won the game by the tenth inning. (future perfect)
12. The violin instructor plays beautifully. (present emphatic)
13. The baby sucked his thumb until today. (past perfect progressive)
14. The athlete planned to run a marathon. (past emphatic)
15. The zookeeper attends a month-long conference. (future progressive)
16. The appetizers taste delicious! (present emphatic)
17. My friend saw the play. (future perfect)
18. I tried to win the game. (past progressive)
19. The traffic gets worse every day. (present perfect progressive)
20. The family will have lived here for ten years. (past perfect progressive)

SPEAKING APPLICATION

Take turns with a partner. Tell about your favorite after-school activity. Say a sentence with each of the six verb tenses in your description.

WRITING APPLICATION

Write a paragraph about a good friend. Use at least eight different verb forms or tenses in your paragraph.

The Four Principal Parts of Verbs

Every verb in the English language has four **principal parts** from which all of the tenses are formed.

A verb has four principal parts: the present, the present participle, the past, and the past participle.

RULE 17.1.3

The chart below shows the principal parts of the verbs *talk, draw,* and *run.*

THE FOUR PRINCIPAL PARTS			
PRESENT	PRESENT PARTICIPLE	PAST	PAST PARTICIPLE
talk	talking	talked	(have) talked
draw	drawing	drew	(have) drawn
run	running	ran	(have) run

The first principal part, the present, is used for the basic forms of the present and future tenses, as well as for the emphatic forms or tenses. The present tense is formed by adding an *-s* or *-es* when the subject is *he, she, it,* or a singular noun. The future tense is formed with the helping verb *will. (I will talk. Mary will draw. Carl will run.)* The present emphatic is formed with the helping verb *do* or *does. (I do talk. Mary does draw. Carl does run.)* The past emphatic is formed with the helping verb *did. (I did talk. Mary did draw. Carl did run.)*

The second principal part, the present participle, is used with helping verbs for all of the progressive forms. *(I am talking. Mary is drawing. Carl is running.)*

The third principal part, the past, is used to form the past tense. *(I talked. Mary drew. Carl ran.)* As in the example *ran,* the past tense of a verb can change its spelling. (See the next section for more information.)

The fourth principal part, the past participle, is used with helping verbs to create the perfect tenses. *(I have talked. Mary had drawn. Carl had run.)*

See Practice 17.1C
See Practice 17.1D

PRACTICE 17.1C Recognizing the Four Principal Parts of Verbs

Read each set of words. Find the verb that is in the form indicated in parentheses. Write the word and its present tense.

EXAMPLE jumping, fly, swoop (present participle)

ANSWER *jumping, jump*

1. shrinking, like, said (past)
2. worked, trying, listen (past)
3. smile, (have) grinned, winking (past participle)
4. scribble, typed, studying (present participle)
5. coloring, sketch, (have) painted (present participle)
6. whistle, (have) played, strumming (past participle)
7. close, shutting, slammed (past)
8. (have) cried, leap, laughing (past participle)
9. bowed, surprise, sighing (past)
10. dancing, performed, trip (present participle)

PRACTICE 17.1D Identifying the Four Principal Parts of Verbs

Read each sentence. Rewrite each sentence by replacing the underlined verb with the verb form indicated in parentheses.

EXAMPLE The actress wishes for a quieter life. (present participle)

ANSWER *The actress is wishing for a quieter life.*

11. The doctor was explaining why the patient's arm hurt. (past participle)
12. On her birthday, the girl had wanted a horse. (present)
13. I have liked picking apples off of trees. (past)
14. The students were singing well. (present)
15. After the dam broke, the water was flowing through the street. (past)
16. The boy pedals his bike quickly through the park. (past participle)
17. My father has driven past the house. (present participle)
18. Uncle Berto raked the leaves. (present)
19. The dog was barking loudly in the kennel. (present participle)
20. I went fishing down by the lake. (past)

SPEAKING APPLICATION

Take turns with a partner. Tell a fictional story, using many verbs in your story. Your partner should listen for and identify the principal parts of the verbs that you use.

WRITING APPLICATION

Write a paragraph that uses sentence 19 as the beginning of an interesting story, and underline all of the past participles.

Regular and Irregular Verbs

The way the past and past participle forms of a verb are formed determines whether the verb is **regular** or **irregular.**

Regular Verbs The majority of verbs are regular. Regular verbs form their past and past participles according to a predictable pattern.

A regular verb is one for which the past and past participle are formed by adding *-ed* or *-d* to the present form.

RULE 17.1.4

In the chart below, notice that a final consonant is sometimes doubled to form the present participle, the past, and the past participle. A final *e* may also be dropped to form the participle.

PRINCIPAL PARTS OF REGULAR VERBS			
PRESENT	PRESENT PARTICIPLE	PAST	PAST PARTICIPLE
contend	contending	contended	(have) contended
manage	managing	managed	(have) managed
stop	stopping	stopped	(have) stopped

See Practice 17.1E
See Practice 17.1F

Irregular Verbs Although most verbs are regular, many of the most common verbs are irregular. Irregular verbs do not use a predictable pattern to form their past and past participles.

An irregular verb is one whose past and past participle are *not* formed by adding *-ed* or *-d* to the present form.

RULE 17.1.5

Usage Problems Remembering the principal parts of irregular verbs can help you avoid usage problems. One common usage problem is using a principal part that is not standard.

INCORRECT They **knowed** about the Jefferson Memorial.

CORRECT They **knew** about the Jefferson Memorial.

A second usage problem is confusing the past and past participle when they have different forms.

INCORRECT She **done** the right thing.

CORRECT She **did** the right thing.

Some common irregular verbs are shown in the charts that follow. Use a dictionary if you are not sure how to form the principal parts of an irregular verb.

IRREGULAR VERBS WITH THE SAME PRESENT, PAST, AND PAST PARTICIPLE			
PRESENT	PRESENT PARTICIPLE	PAST	PAST PARTICIPLE
burst	bursting	burst	(have) burst
cost	costing	cost	(have) cost
cut	cutting	cut	(have) cut
hit	hitting	hit	(have) hit
hurt	hurting	hurt	(have) hurt
let	letting	let	(have) let
put	putting	put	(have) put
set	setting	set	(have) set
shut	shutting	shut	(have) shut
split	splitting	split	(have) split
spread	spreading	spread	(have) spread

Note About *Be*: *Be* is one of the most irregular of all of the verbs. The present participle of *be* is *being*. The past participle is *been*. The present and the past depend on the subject and tense of the verb.

CONJUGATION OF *BE*		
	SINGULAR	PLURAL
Present	I am. You are. He, she, or it is.	We are. You are. They are.
Past	I was. You were. He, she, or it was.	We were. You were. They were.
Future	I will be. You will be. He, she, or it will be.	We will be. You will be. They will be.

IRREGULAR VERBS WITH THE SAME PAST AND PAST PARTICIPLE			
PRESENT	PRESENT PARTICIPLE	PAST	PAST PARTICIPLE
bring	bringing	brought	(have) brought
build	building	built	(have) built
buy	buying	bought	(have) bought
catch	catching	caught	(have) caught
fight	fighting	fought	(have) fought
find	finding	found	(have) found
get	getting	got	(have) got or (have) gotten
hold	holding	held	(have) held
keep	keeping	kept	(have) kept
lay	laying	laid	(have) laid
lead	leading	led	(have) led
leave	leaving	left	(have) left
lose	losing	lost	(have) lost
pay	paying	paid	(have) paid
say	saying	said	(have) said
sell	selling	sold	(have) sold
send	sending	sent	(have) sent
shine	shining	shone or shined	(have) shone or (have) shined
sit	sitting	sat	(have) sat
sleep	sleeping	slept	(have) slept
spend	spending	spent	(have) spent
stand	standing	stood	(have) stood
stick	sticking	stuck	(have) stuck
sting	stinging	stung	(have) stung
strike	striking	struck	(have) struck
swing	swinging	swung	(have) swung
teach	teaching	taught	(have) taught
win	winning	won	(have) won
wind	winding	wound	(have) wound

IRREGULAR VERBS THAT CHANGE IN OTHER WAYS			
PRESENT	PRESENT PARTICIPLE	PAST	PAST PARTICIPLE
arise	arising	arose	(have) arisen
become	becoming	became	(have) become
begin	beginning	began	(have) begun
bite	biting	bit	(have) bitten
break	breaking	broke	(have) broken
choose	choosing	chose	(have) chosen
come	coming	came	(have) come
do	doing	did	(have) done
draw	drawing	drew	(have) drawn
drink	drinking	drank	(have) drunk
drive	driving	drove	(have) driven
eat	eating	ate	(have) eaten
fall	falling	fell	(have) fallen
fly	flying	flew	(have) flown
give	giving	gave	(have) given
go	going	went	(have) gone
grow	growing	grew	(have) grown
know	knowing	knew	(have) known
lie	lying	lay	(have) lain
ride	riding	rode	(have) ridden
ring	ringing	rang	(have) rung
rise	rising	rose	(have) risen
run	running	ran	(have) run
see	seeing	saw	(have) seen
sing	singing	sang	(have) sung
sink	sinking	sank	(have) sunk
speak	speaking	spoke	(have) spoken
swim	swimming	swam	(have) swum
take	taking	took	(have) taken
tear	tearing	tore	(have) torn
throw	throwing	threw	(have) thrown
wear	wearing	wore	(have) worn
write	writing	wrote	(have) written

See Practice 17.1G
See Practice 17.1H

PRACTICE 17.1E Recognizing Principal Parts of Regular Verbs

Read each set of verbs. Write the missing principal part of the verb indicated in parentheses.

EXAMPLE slump, slumping, slumped (past participle)

ANSWER *(have) slumped*

1. peering, peered, (have) peered (present)
2. cough, coughed, (have) coughed (present participle)
3. fear, fearing, (have) feared (past)
4. discuss, discussing, discussed (past participle)
5. pretend, pretending, (have) pretended (past)
6. need, needed, (have) needed (present participle)
7. polishing, polished, (have) polished (present)
8. restore, restoring, restored (past participle)
9. grab, grabbed, (have) grabbed (present participle)
10. train, training, (have) trained (past)

PRACTICE 17.1F Using the Correct Form of Regular Verbs

Read each sentence. Then, write a correct form of the verb in parentheses to complete each sentence, and write the principal part of the verb.

EXAMPLE The mouse is (run) quickly through the maze.

ANSWER *running — present participle*

11. Students who graduated from high school (receive) a diploma.
12. The water (flow) down the hill.
13. I (pause) for a break.
14. If you had hurried, you could (reach) the bus on time.
15. Classical music (help) me feel relaxed.
16. I (hope) that I could learn to waltz easily.
17. The jury members (prepare) for the trial.
18. After losing the game, the players (vow) to practice more.
19. The moon looks as though it (float) in the sky.
20. John joined me as I (travel) through Timbuktu.

SPEAKING APPLICATION

Take turns with a partner. Tell about your last summer vacation. Use as many principal parts of verbs as you can in your description.

WRITING APPLICATION

Write a letter to a friend that describes a day in your life, using principal verb forms from Practice 17.1F.

PRACTICE 17.1G Recognizing Principal Parts of Irregular Verbs

Read each group of words. Write the two words in each group that are correct forms of the same verb.

EXAMPLE set, setted, setting

ANSWER *set, setting*

1. sit, sitted, sat
2. ground, grinded, grinding
3. crepted, creep, crept
4. lending, lended, lent
5. sing, sang, singed
6. fell, falled, fallen
7. written, writed, wrote
8. flying, flied, flew
9. swung, swinged, swing
10. shut, shutted, shutting

PRACTICE 17.1H Supplying the Correct Form of Irregular Verbs

Read each sentence. The underlined verb has been written incorrectly in each sentence. Write the correct form of the verb and its present form.

EXAMPLE The chef will spreaded jam on the cake.

ANSWER *will spread, spread*

11. The woman has drawed a beautiful portrait.
12. After a long time, he swimming across the English Channel.
13. My grandfather was happy that he has finded his missing hat.
14. The corn grown until it was eight feet tall!
15. Tracy hitted a home run!
16. The plane has flew high into the sky.
17. I am slept on the top bunk bed.
18. The *Titanic* sunk after it hit an iceberg.
19. After school, a group of students seen their teacher at the library.
20. Each student has chose a different research topic.

SPEAKING APPLICATION

Take turns with a partner. Say sentences with irregular verbs. Your partner should listen for and identify the form of the verbs that you use.

WRITING APPLICATION

Use irregular verbs to write a short story about an animal that goes on an adventure. Be sure to use correct verb forms.

Verb Conjugation

The **conjugation** of a verb displays all of its different forms.

A conjugation is a complete list of the singular and plural forms of a verb in a particular tense.

17.1.6 RULE

The singular forms of a verb correspond to the singular personal pronouns (*I, you, he, she, it*), and the plural forms correspond to the plural personal pronouns (*we, you, they*).

To conjugate a verb, you need the four principal parts: the present (*go*), the present participle (*going*), the past (*went*), and the past participle (*gone*). You also need various helping verbs, such as *has, have,* or *will.*

Notice that only three principal parts—the present, the past, and the past participle—are used to conjugate all six of the basic forms.

CONJUGATION OF THE BASIC FORMS OF *GO*

		SINGULAR	PLURAL
Present	First Person Second Person Third Person	I go. You go. He, she, or it goes.	We go. You go. They go.
Past	First Person Second Person Third Person	I went. You went. He, she, or it went.	We went. You went. They went.
Future	First Person Second Person Third Person	I will go. You will go. He, she, or it will go.	We will go. You will go. They will go.
Present Perfect	First Person Second Person Third Person	I have gone. You have gone. He, she, or it has gone.	We have gone. You have gone. They have gone.
Past Perfect	First Person Second Person Third Person	I had gone. You had gone. He, she, or it had gone.	We had gone. You had gone. They had gone.
Future Perfect	First Person Second Person Third Person	I will have gone. You will have gone. He, she, or it will have gone.	We will have gone. You will have gone. They will have gone.

See Practice 17.1I

Conjugating the Progressive Tense With *Be*

As you learned earlier, the **progressive tense** shows an ongoing action or condition. To form the progressive tense, use the present participle form of the verb (the *-ing* form) with a form of the verb *be*.

CONJUGATION OF THE PROGRESSIVE FORMS OF *GO*			
		SINGULAR	PLURAL
Present Progressive	First Person Second Person Third Person	I am going. You are going. He, she, or it is going.	We are going. You are going. They are going.
Past Progressive	First Person Second Person Third Person	I was going. You were going. He, she, or it was going.	We were going. You were going. They were going.
Future Progressive	First Person Second Person Third Person	I will be going. You will be going. He, she, or it will be going.	We will be going. You will be going. They will be going.
Present Perfect Progressive	First Person Second Person Third Person	I have been going. You have been going. He, she, or it has been going.	We have been going. You have been going. They have been going.
Past Perfect Progressive	First Person Second Person Third Person	I had been going. You had been going. He, she, or it had been going.	We had been going. You had been going. They had been going.
Future Perfect Progressive	First Person Second Person Third Person	I will have been going. You will have been going. He, she, or it will have been going.	We will have been going. You will have been going. They will have been going.

See Practice 17.1J

PRACTICE 17.1I Conjugating the Basic Forms of Verbs

Read each group of words. Then, write the words in each group that are missing from the verb conjugation. Use the verb and tense shown in parentheses.

EXAMPLE I _____, you _____, he _____ (buy; present perfect)

ANSWER *have bought, have bought, has bought*

1. we _____, you _____, it _____ (care; future)
2. I _____, she _____, they _____ (give; past perfect)
3. he _____, we _____, you _____ (think; past)
4. you _____, we _____, she _____ (work; future perfect)
5. I _____, we _____, you _____ (begin; present perfect)
6. I _____, you _____, it _____ (bat; future)
7. we _____, you _____, they _____ (test; past perfect)
8. I _____, she _____, they _____ (run; past)
9. it _____, we _____, you _____ (kick; present)
10. you _____, we _____, she _____ (see; present perfect)

PRACTICE 17.1J Conjugating the Progressive Forms of Verbs

Read each sentence. Rewrite each sentence, using the form of the verb that is indicated in parentheses.

EXAMPLE I bake. (present perfect progressive)

ANSWER *I have been baking.*

11. He throws. (future progressive)
12. They train. (past perfect progressive)
13. We laugh. (present progressive)
14. It cries. (past progressive)
15. You see. (present perfect progressive)
16. I jog. (present progressive)
17. You make. (future progressive)
18. We cook. (past progressive)
19. They speak. (present progressive)
20. She looks. (past perfect progressive)

SPEAKING APPLICATION

Challenge a partner. Give your partner a verb, such as *write*. Your partner should conjugate the verb in all the singular and plural forms for all six tenses.

WRITING APPLICATION

Use the conjugated verb forms from at least two of the items in Practice 17.1J to write a humorous paragraph.

17.2 The Correct Use of Tenses

The basic, progressive, and emphatic forms of the six tenses show time within one of three general categories: **present, past, and future.** This section will explain how each verb form has a specific use that distinguishes it from the other forms.

WRITING COACH Online

www.phwritingcoach.com

Grammar Practice

Practice your grammar skills with Writing Coach Online.

Dimension G

Test your knowledge of grammar in this fast-paced interactive video game.

Present, Past, and Future Tense

Good usage depends on an understanding of how each form works within its general category of time to express meaning.

Uses of Tense in Present Time

Three different forms can be used to express present time.

RULE 17.2.1

The three forms of the present tense show present actions or conditions as well as various continuing actions or conditions.

EXPRESSING PRESENT TENSE	
Present	I paint.
Present Progressive	I am painting.
Present Emphatic	I do paint.

The main uses of the basic form of the present tense are shown in the chart below.

EXPRESSING PRESENT TENSE	
Present Action	The shopper strolls down the aisle.
Present Condition	My head is aching.
Regularly Occurring Action	They frequently drive to Maine.
Regularly Occurring Condition	This road is slippery in winter.
Constant Action	Fish breathe through gills.
Constant Condition	Human beings are primates.

See Practice 17.2A

Historical Present The present tense may also be used to express historical events. This use of the present, called the **historical present tense,** is occasionally used in narration to make past actions or conditions sound more lively.

THE HISTORICAL PRESENT TENSE	
Past Actions Expressed in Historical Present Tense	In the late 1800s, thousands of immigrants are passing through Ellis Island.
Past Condition Expressed in Historical Present Tense	The exodus of middle-class people from the cities in the 1960s is one of the factors in the decline of urban areas.

The **critical present tense** is most often used to discuss deceased authors and their literary achievements.

THE CRITICAL PRESENT TENSE	
Action Expressed in Critical Present	Dame Agatha Christie writes with a skill that makes her stories classics.
Condition Expressed in Critical Present	In addition to his novels, Thomas Hardy is the author of several volumes of poetry.

The **present progressive tense** is used to show a continuing action or condition of a long or short duration.

USES OF THE PRESENT PROGRESSIVE TENSE	
Long Continuing Action	I am working at the park this summer.
Short Continuing Action	I am watering the plants this week.
Continuing Condition	Julio is being very helpful.

USES OF THE PRESENT EMPHATIC TENSE	
Emphasizing a Statement	I do intend to meet her at the airport.
Denying a Contrary Assertion	No, he does not have the answer.
Asking a Question	Do you guide tours of the parks?
Making a Sentence Negative	She does not have our blessing.

See Practice 17.2B

PRACTICE 17.2A Identifying Tense in Present Time

Read each sentence. For the underlined verb in each sentence, write the form of the present tense that is used.

EXAMPLE All living things digest food.

ANSWER *present*

1. The crickets do chirp, but not very loudly.
2. Robots are making life easier for some people.
3. My friend is traveling to Italy with her parents.
4. I do attend dance classes.
5. The bridge freezes before the road freezes.
6. Piers Anthony writes fantasy novels to entertain readers.
7. The hockey team is hoping for a victory this weekend.
8. Labrador retrievers are good family pets.
9. I am eating dinner.
10. The manager asks employees to arrive on time.

PRACTICE 17.2B Supplying Verbs in Present Time

Read each sentence. Rewrite each sentence, changing the underlined verb according to the verb tense indicated in parentheses.

EXAMPLE The seamstress makes hats. (present progressive)

ANSWER *The seamstress is making hats.*

11. The family will travel to Asia. (present progressive)
12. The girl is wearing a jacket. (present)
13. People in the early 1900s had electricity. (historical present)
14. Mozart composed piano and symphonic music. (historical present)
15. With a glass of milk, the sandwich tastes wonderful. (present emphatic)
16. Students often wrote with quills and ink in a one-room schoolhouse. (historical present)
17. Students at the school support their student government. (present emphatic)
18. Joblessness was a common problem during the 1930s. (historical present)
19. After the play closes, I will move to New York. (present progressive)
20. The main characters in Jane Austen's books were often women. (critical present)

SPEAKING APPLICATION

Take turns with a partner. Describe a normal day in your life. Use the present progressive, present emphatic, and present tenses in your description. Your partner should listen for and identify each present tense form.

WRITING APPLICATION

Write about your favorite day of the year. Using the present progressive tense, describe what you will do on that day the next time it comes around. Using the present emphatic tense, tell the best features of the day.

Uses of Tense in Past Time

There are seven verb forms that express past actions or conditions.

The seven forms that express past tense show actions and conditions that began at some time in the past.

RULE 17.2.2

FORMS EXPRESSING PAST TENSE	
Past	I drew.
Present Perfect	I have drawn.
Past Perfect	I had drawn.
Past Progressive	I was drawing.
Present Perfect Progressive	I have been drawing.
Past Perfect Progressive	I had been drawing.
Past Emphatic	I did draw.

The uses of the most common form, the past, are shown below.

USES OF THE PAST TENSE	
Completed Action	They halted work on the bridge.
Completed Condition	Several apartments were empty.

See Practice 17.2C

Notice in the chart above that the time of the action or the condition could be changed from indefinite to definite if such words as *last week* or *yesterday* were added to the sentences.

Present Perfect The **present perfect tense** always expresses indefinite time. Use it to show actions or conditions continuing from the past to the present.

USES OF THE PRESENT PERFECT TENSE	
Completed Action (Indefinite Time)	They have invited us to the party.
Completed Condition (Indefinite Time)	I have been here before.
Action Continuing to Present	It has rained intermittently for days.
Condition Continuing to Present	I have felt sluggish all day.

Past Perfect The **past perfect tense** expresses an action that took place before another action.

USES OF THE PAST PERFECT TENSE	
Action Completed Before Another Action	Perhaps the nomadic hunters had drawn on the ground before they drew on the cave walls.
Condition Completed Before Another Condition	Rhoda had been a photographer until she became ill.

These charts show the **past progressive** and **emphatic tenses.**

USES OF THE PROGRESSIVE TENSE TO EXPRESS PAST TIME	
Past Progressive	**LONG CONTINUING ACTION** She was going to China that year. **SHORT CONTINUING ACTION** I was talking to Mary when you tried to call. **CONTINUOUS CONDITION** I was being honest when I said I was sorry about the incident.
Present Perfect Progressive	**CONTINUING ACTION** Edith has been touring the Southwest all summer.
Past Perfect Progressive	**CONTINUING ACTION INTERRUPTED** He had been dreaming of victory until reality interrupted that dream.

USES OF THE PAST EMPHATIC TENSE	
Emphasizing a Statement	The cactus did grow without any water.
Denying a Contrary Assertion	But I did hike to the ancient ruins!
Asking a Question	When did the United States add Alaska as a state?
Making a Sentence Negative	He did not appreciate her hard work.

See Practice 17.2D

PRACTICE 17.2C Identifying Tense in Past Time

Read each sentence. Then, write the tense of the underlined verb in each sentence.

EXAMPLE The captain had pulled up the anchor.

ANSWER *past perfect*

1. After writing his paper, the boy gave himself a break.
2. The couples were dancing until the music stopped.
3. Although she had been planning to leave, she stayed.
4. I got overly tired, but I did enjoy the hike.
5. The tourist had wanted to see Rome, but she changed her mind.
6. After school, the students rode the bus home.
7. Sometimes it had been too hot to sleep.
8. The barber was thinking about becoming a butcher.
9. The stars have been twinkling for many nights.
10. Asking lots of questions did not get him into trouble.

PRACTICE 17.2D Supplying Verbs in Past Time

Read each sentence. For the underlined verb in each sentence, write the past tense indicated in parentheses.

EXAMPLE Long ago, people drew on stones. (past emphatic)

ANSWER *did draw*

11. The boy gave his friend a drink of water. (past perfect progressive)
12. I had a flu vaccination seven years in a row. (past emphatic)
13. The girl had left her purse on the coffee table. (past perfect progressive)
14. I accidentally ground dirt into the carpet. (past progressive)
15. The teacher shut the door when it became too noisy outside. (past perfect)
16. The poster stuck to the wall. (past perfect progressive)
17. Nancy slept late yesterday. (past progressive)
18. He tasted each type of cheese. (past perfect progressive)
19. The objects cast strange shadows on the wall. (past progressive)
20. After dinner, the young couple paid the bill. (past perfect progressive)

SPEAKING APPLICATION

Take turns with a partner. Tell about something interesting you did after school last week. Use as many different forms of the past tense as possible. Your partner should listen for and identify the tenses you use.

WRITING APPLICATION

Write a paragraph about a time when you forgot to do something. Use four different forms of the past tense in your paragraph.

Uses of Tense in Future Time

The **future tense** shows actions or conditions that will happen at a later date.

RULE 17.2.3 **The future tense expresses actions or conditions that have not yet occurred.**

FORMS EXPRESSING FUTURE TENSE	
Future	I will walk.
Future Perfect	I will have walked.
Future Progressive	I will be walking.
Future Perfect Progressive	I will have been walking.

USES OF THE FUTURE AND THE FUTURE PERFECT TENSE	
Future	I will jog in the morning. I will be late for the meeting.
Future Perfect	I will have run a mile by the time you arrive. The orchestra will have toured for a month before the new concert season begins.

Notice in the next chart that the **future progressive** and the **future perfect progressive tenses** express only future actions.

USES OF THE PROGRESSIVE TENSE TO EXPRESS FUTURE TIME	
Future Progressive	Rita will be studying all weekend.
Future Perfect Progressive	Sharon will have been preparing for ten years before she embarks on her trip around the world.

The basic forms of the present and the present progressive tense are often used with other words to express future time.

EXAMPLES The new store **opens** next weekend.

My family **is leaving** next month for Hawaii.

See Practice 17.2E
See Practice 17.2F

PRACTICE 17.2E Identifying Tense in Future Time

Read each sentence. Then, write the future-tense verb and the form of the tense in each sentence.

EXAMPLE Mary will be working on Friday night.

ANSWER *will be working — future progressive*

1. In January, Mom will have been playing piano for twenty years.
2. Grandpa will visit us next month.
3. The bus will have left without us.
4. I will be cleaning the garage all day.
5. Crista will help us prepare for the recital.
6. You will have gone home by then.
7. New islands will have been forming by volcanic eruptions.
8. Tomorrow, our class will take a trip to the park.
9. After you arrive, we will discuss our plans.
10. The reporter will have written four articles by next week.

PRACTICE 17.2F Supplying Verbs in Future Time

Read each sentence. Then, rewrite each sentence, filling in the blank with the future-tense form of the verb indicated in parentheses.

EXAMPLE The train _____ soon. (arrive, future)

ANSWER *The train will arrive soon.*

11. Aunt Elaine _____ us next week. (visit, future progressive)
12. I _____ decorations for the party by tomorrow. (make, future perfect)
13. On June 1, the event _____. (occur, future)
14. When you receive your money, the bank _____. (call, future progressive)
15. Next year, my parents _____ their 25th wedding anniversary. (celebrate, future progressive)
16. By tonight, we _____ at baby pictures for six hours. (look, future perfect progressive)
17. The glass _____ if dropped. (break, future)
18. If the wind blows too hard, the leaves _____ off the trees. (fall, future progressive)
19. By Saturday, the teacher _____ all the essays. (grade, future perfect)
20. At the end of the race, I _____ over ten miles. (run, future perfect)

SPEAKING APPLICATION

Take turns with a partner. Tell about what you hope to be doing in five years. Use future-tense verbs in your sentences. Your partner should listen for and identify the future-tense verbs that you use.

WRITING APPLICATION

Rewrite your corrections of sentences 11, 12, and 13, changing the verbs to include other future-tense verbs. Make sure your sentences still make sense.

Find It/ FIX IT

12

Grammar Game Plan

Sequence of Tenses

A sentence with more than one verb must be consistent in its time sequence.

RULE 17.2.4

When showing a sequence of events, do not shift tenses unnecessarily.

EXAMPLES Joe **will go** to school, then he **will go** to practice.

Maria **has walked** her dog, and she **has fed** her three cats.

Liz **skied** all day and **danced** all night.

Sometimes, however, it is necessary to shift tenses, especially when a sentence is complex or compound-complex. The tense of the main verb often determines the tense of the verb in the subordinate clause. Moreover, the form of the participle or infinitive often depends on the tense of the verb in the main clause.

Verbs in Subordinate Clauses It is frequently necessary to look at the tense of the main verb in a sentence before choosing the tense of the verb in the subordinate clause.

RULE 17.2.5

The tense of a verb in a subordinate clause should follow logically from the tense of the main verb.

INCORRECT I **will understand** that Paul **wrote** a play.

CORRECT I **understand** that Paul **wrote** a play.

As you study the combinations of tenses in the charts on the next pages, notice that the choice of tenses affects the logical relationship between the events being expressed. Some combinations indicate that the events are **simultaneous**—meaning that they occur at the same time. Other combinations indicate that the events are **sequential**—meaning that one event occurs before or after the other.

SEQUENCE OF EVENTS		
MAIN VERB	**SUBORDINATE VERB**	**MEANING**
MAIN VERB IN PRESENT TENSE		
I understand…	**PRESENT** that he writes novels. **PRESENT PROGRESSIVE** that he is writing a novel. **PRESENT EMPHATIC** that he does write novels.	Simultaneous events: All events occur in present time.
I understand…	**PAST** that he wrote a novel. **PRESENT PERFECT** that he has written a novel. **PAST PERFECT** that he had written a novel. **PAST PROGRESSIVE** that he was writing a novel. **PRESENT PERFECT PROGRESSIVE** that he has been writing a novel. **PAST PERFECT PROGRESSIVE** that he had been writing a novel. **PAST EMPHATIC** that he did write a novel.	Sequential events: The writing comes before the understanding.
I understand…	**FUTURE** that he will write a novel. **FUTURE PERFECT** that he will have written a novel. **FUTURE PROGRESSIVE** that he will be writing a novel. **FUTURE PERFECT PROGRESSIVE** that he will have been writing a novel.	Sequential events: The understanding comes before the writing.

SEQUENCE OF EVENTS		
MAIN VERB	**SUBORDINATE VERB**	**MEANING**
MAIN VERB IN PAST TENSE		
I understood...	**PAST** that he wrote a novel. **PAST PROGRESSIVE** that he was writing a novel. **PAST EMPHATIC** that he did write a novel.	Simultaneous events: All events take place in the past.
I understood...	**PAST PERFECT** that he had written a novel. **PAST PERFECT PROGRESSIVE** that he had been writing a novel.	Sequential events: The writing came before the understanding.
MAIN VERB IN FUTURE TENSE		
I will understand...	**PRESENT** if he writes a novel. **PRESENT PROGRESSIVE** if he is writing a novel. **PRESENT EMPHATIC** if he does write a novel.	Simultaneous events: All events take place in future time.
I will understand...	**PAST** if he wrote a novel. **PRESENT PERFECT** if he has written a novel. **PRESENT PERFECT PROGRESSIVE** if he has been writing a novel. **PAST EMPHATIC** if he did write a novel.	Sequential events: The writing comes before the understanding.

See Practice 17.2G
See Practice 17.2H
See Practice 17.2I
See Practice 17.2J

Time Sequence With Participles and Infinitives Frequently, the form of a participle or infinitive determines whether the events are simultaneous or sequential. Participles can be present (*seeing*), past (*seen*), or perfect (*having seen*). Infinitives can be present (*to see*) or perfect (*to have seen*).

The form of a participle or an infinitive should logically relate to the verb in the same clause or sentence.

RULE 17.2.6

To show simultaneous events, you will generally need to use the present participle or the present infinitive, whether the main verb is present, past, or future.

Simultaneous Events

IN PRESENT TIME **Seeing** (present) the results, she **laughs** (present).

IN PAST TIME **Seeing** (present) the results, she **laughed** (past).

IN FUTURE TIME **Seeing** (present) the results, she **will laugh** (future).

To show sequential events, use the perfect form of the participle and infinitive, regardless of the tense of the main verb.

Sequential Events

IN PRESENT TIME **Having seen** (perfect) the results, she **is laughing** (present progressive).
(She saw *before* she laughed.)

IN PAST TIME **Having seen** (perfect) the results, she **laughed** (past).
(She saw *before* she laughed.)

SPANNING PAST AND FUTURE TIME **Having seen** (perfect) her work, I **will recommend** (future) her.
(Someone recommended her *after* seeing her work.)

See Practice 17.2K
See Practice 17.2L

PRACTICE 17.2G Identifying the Time Sequence in Sentences With More Than One Verb

Read each sentence. Then, write the verb of the event that happens second in each sentence.

EXAMPLE Having read the viewers' letters, the network will cancel the program.

ANSWER *will cancel*

1. I am lucky that I will be studying French this year.
2. Worried about missing her flight, Carol left an hour early.
3. Having failed to hail a cab, I rode a bus instead.
4. I was happy that Janelle had been gracious.
5. He was told that the team will be practicing every Saturday afternoon.
6. I was thrilled that my sister arrived.
7. Having survived the long winter, our trees have been growing at an amazing rate.
8. Having taken a new job, my aunt will be traveling in Brazil for a month.
9. After milking the cows, the farmer's wife began to feed the chickens.
10. I was told that the Bergers will be traveling to Texas this summer.

PRACTICE 17.2H Recognizing and Correcting Errors in Tense Sequence

Read each sentence. Then, if a sentence has an error in tense sequence, rewrite it to correct the error. If a sentence is correct, write *correct*.

EXAMPLE Lea knocks and waited patiently at the door.

ANSWER *Lea knocked and waited patiently at the door.*

11. I picked up the telephone receiver quickly, but the line is still dead.
12. When we go shopping, we bought shoes.
13. My uncle comes back to visit us, and he drives his vintage sports car.
14. Ava finished her assignment, but she forgets to include a title page.
15. The stages of the rocket dropped away as the space shuttle climbed into the sky.
16. Aunt Maureen jumped to her feet and cheers when Mia makes the winning basket.
17. When George presents his science fair project, all the judges were very impressed.
18. Every time Roger comes to visit me, he brought his dog with him.
19. Randy has played drums before, but now he plays the guitar.
20. After the bell rang, we left the building.

SPEAKING APPLICATION

Take turns with a partner. Tell about something fun that you like to do. Use two verbs in your sentences. Your partner should listen for and identify the sequence of events in your sentences.

WRITING APPLICATION

Use sentences 16, 17, and 18 as models to write your own sentences with incorrect tense sequence. Then, exchange papers with a partner. Your partner should rewrite your sentences, using the correct sequence in tense.

PRACTICE 17.2I Writing Sentences to Be Consistent When the Main Verbs Are Present Tense

Read each sentence. Then, rewrite each sentence to change the verb in the subordinate clause to the tense indicated in parentheses.

EXAMPLE I hope that he votes for me. (present progressive)

ANSWER *I hope that he is voting for me.*

1. I believe that Tim left. (past progressive)
2. Marissa knows that her brother left for school. (future progressive)
3. Kelly hopes that her friend finishes her homework. (present perfect).
4. I see that Malik is waiting for his ride. (present perfect progressive)
5. Do you know that Kordell has been studying French? (past emphatic)
6. I hear that Shannon plans to apologize to you. (past perfect)
7. The doctor says that I have had chicken pox. (present emphatic)
8. My parents feel that Shawn will be learning a lesson. (future perfect)
9. Nikita thinks that her sister used her perfume. (past perfect progressive)
10. I hope that Angelo already has studied for his test. (future perfect progressive)

PRACTICE 17.2J Writing Sentences to Be Consistent When the Main Verbs Are Past and Future Tense

Read each sentence. Then, rewrite each sentence to change the verb in the subordinate clause to the tense indicated in parentheses.

EXAMPLE He felt that it was boring. (past perfect)

ANSWER *He felt that it had been boring.*

11. Jake saw that his cat scratched the table. (past perfect progressive)
12. I will ask if the bus stops here. (present progressive)
13. Aldo knew that Katherine was performing her solo tonight. (past perfect)
14. Becky hoped that John had fixed the flat tire. (past progressive)
15. He saw that she had been there. (past)
16. You will find that Brandon has been creating a Web site. (present perfect)
17. The coach will understand if he quits the team to improve his grades. (present emphatic)
18. I felt that I worked hard. (past emphatic)
19. He will not be surprised if Haley did forget his name. (present perfect)
20. The janitor will know who is using the classroom. (present perfect progressive)

WRITING APPLICATION

Review the sentences in Practice 17.2I. Then, rewrite each sentence, keeping the main clause but changing the tense of the verb in the subordinate clause. In parentheses, identify the new tense.

SPEAKING APPLICATION

Review the sentences in Practice 17.2J and your answers. Discuss with a partner how changing the tense in the subordinate clause changes the meaning of the sentence.

PRACTICE 17.2K **Supplying Participles in Simultaneous Events**

Read each sentence. Then, supply a participle to complete the sentence and to show a simultaneous event.

EXAMPLE _____ her skirt, Terry concentrates.

ANSWER *Sewing her skirt, Terry concentrates.*

1. _____ a loud noise, Anik stops.
2. _____ the curb, Sasha swerves.
3. _____ his cue, Daniel entered.
4. _____ the comics, Jen will laugh.
5. _____ the treats, the walrus will clap.
6. _____ her alarm, Sherisse awakens.
7. _____ Jeremy's name, Anita blushes.
8. _____ his password, Sammy logged on.
9. _____ the way, André will lead.
10. _____ the mountain, Devon struggled.

PRACTICE 17.2L **Supplying Participles in Sequential Events**

Read each sentence. Then, supply a participle to complete the sentence and to show a sequential event.

EXAMPLE _____ the meal, she is satisfied.

ANSWER *Having eaten the meal, she is satisfied.*

11. _____ the answer, I am confident.
12. _____ ten laps, Bailey was tired.
13. _____ the news, he is celebrating.
14. _____ his scores, Dante had been relieved.
15. _____ the latest model, I will be buying the phone.
16. _____ the dog, Christopher was wet.
17. _____ her coat, Elise was borrowing mine.
18. _____ early, I will find a good seat.
19. _____ his chores, Philip went out with his friends.
20. _____ the letter, she has written a response.

SPEAKING APPLICATION

Take turns with a partner. Say each sentence in Practice 17.2K, providing a new participle or participial phrase to complete each sentence.

WRITING APPLICATION

Review your sentences for Practice 17.2L. Rewrite each sentence, changing the main verb to another tense. In parentheses, identify the new tense.

Modifiers That Help Clarify Tense

The time expressed by a verb can often be clarified by adverbs such as *often, sometimes, always,* or *frequently* and phrases such as *once in a while, within a week, last week,* or *now and then.*

Use modifiers when they can help clarify tense.

17.2.7 RULE

In the examples below, the modifiers that help clarify the tense of the verb are highlighted in orange. Think about how the sentences would read without the modifiers. Modifiers help to make your writing more precise and interesting.

EXAMPLES We **read** the sports scores **every weekend**.

My brother **practices** his saxophone **once a day**.

My brother **practices** his saxophone **now and then**.

(These two sentences have very different meanings.)

Occasionally, I **enjoy** playing volleyball at the beach.

Susan **always** **swims** with her goggles on.

By next year, Walter **will have fished** in every river in Colorado.

I **swim** 40 laps **once a week**.

Water-skiing **is** **now** one of my favorite water sports.

Sometimes, people **attempt** to swim across large bodies of water.

I **always** **visit** my grandfather on weekends.

See Practice 17.2M
See Practice 17.2N

PRACTICE 17.2M Identifying Modifiers That Help Clarify Tense

Read each sentence. Then, write the modifier in each sentence that helps clarify the verb tense.

EXAMPLE Suddenly, the balloon burst.

ANSWER *Suddenly*

1. The clothes sometimes shrink in the dryer.
2. All at once, the computers and printers shut down.
3. He always brings all of his books to class.
4. One at a time, the pitcher threw the balls high and outside.
5. Steve drives me home once a week.
6. He never wants to walk home in the rain.
7. Frequently, we pay our bills early.
8. Quickly, I laid the dishes on the table.
9. I always see the same television commercials.
10. We sometimes see the sunrise over the mountains.

PRACTICE 17.2N Supplying Modifiers to Clarify Meaning

Read each sentence. Then, fill in the blank in each sentence with a modifier that will clarify the meaning of the sentence.

EXAMPLE _____, the writer worked on the revisions.

ANSWER *Recently, the writer worked on the revisions.*

11. The musicians will _____ perform for an audience.
12. _____, our flight from Chicago arrived.
13. My grandfather _____ works on the Sunday crossword puzzle.
14. _____, a news station crew arrived.
15. Our neighbors will be moving away _____.
16. I returned the call _____.
17. He is _____ polite.
18. The guests arrived _____.
19. _____, we finished our work.
20. Eliana can _____ answer the teacher's questions.

SPEAKING APPLICATION

Take turns with a partner. Tell about a trip that you have taken. Use modifiers that help clarify tense in your sentences. Your partner should listen for and identify the modifiers in your sentences.

WRITING APPLICATION

Use your corrections of sentences 13, 16, and 19 as models to write your own sentences. Rewrite the sentences to include different modifiers that clarify the meaning of each sentence.

17.3 The Subjunctive Mood

There are three **moods,** or ways in which a verb can express an action or condition: **indicative, imperative,** and **subjunctive.** The **indicative** mood, which is the most common, is used to make factual statements (*Karl is helpful.*) and to ask questions (*Is Karl helpful?*). The **imperative** mood is used to give orders or directions (*Be helpful.*).

WRITING COACH Online

www.phwritingcoach.com

Grammar Practice

Practice your grammar skills with Writing Coach Online.

Dimension G

Test your knowledge of grammar in this fast-paced interactive video game.

Using the Subjunctive Mood

There are two important differences between verbs in the **subjunctive** mood and those in the indicative mood. First, in the present tense, third-person singular verbs in the subjunctive mood do not have the usual *-s* or *-es* ending. Second, the subjunctive mood of *be* in the present tense is *be;* in the past tense, it is *were,* regardless of the subject.

INDICATIVE MOOD	SUBJUNCTIVE MOOD
He listens to me.	I suggest that he listen to me.
They are ready.	He insists that they be ready.
She was impatient.	If she were impatient, she could not do this work.

Use the subjunctive mood (1) in clauses beginning with *if* or *that* to express an idea that is contrary to fact or (2) in clauses beginning with *that* to express a request, a demand, or a proposal.

RULE 17.3.1

Expressing Ideas Contrary to Fact Ideas that are contrary to fact are commonly expressed as wishes, doubts, possibilities, or conditions. Using the subjunctive mood in these situations shows that the idea expressed is not true now and may never be true.

EXAMPLES He wishes that the climate **were** milder.

Brett wished that he **were** a better driver.

If he **were** coming, he would be here by now.

RULE 17.3.2

Some *if* clauses do not take a subjunctive verb. If the idea expressed may be true, an indicative form is used.

EXAMPLES I said that **if** the weather **was** bad, we'd leave early, so let's go.

If I **want** to ski, I'll have to get up early.

Expressing Requests, Demands, and Proposals Verbs that request, demand, or propose are often followed by a *that* clause containing a verb in the subjunctive mood.

REQUEST She requests that we **be** on time for the trip.

DEMAND It is required that each student **wear** a uniform.

PROPOSAL He proposed that a motion **be** made to adjourn.

See Practice 17.3A
See Practice 17.3B

Auxiliary Verbs That Express the Subjunctive Mood

Because certain helping verbs suggest conditions contrary to fact, they can often be used in place of the subjunctive mood.

RULE 17.3.3

***Could, would,* or *should* can be used with a verb to express the subjunctive mood.**

The sentences on the left in the chart below have the usual subjunctive form of the verb *be: were.* The sentences on the right have been reworded with *could, would,* and *should.*

THE SUBJUNCTIVE MOOD WITH AUXILIARY VERBS	
WITH FORMS OF *BE*	WITH *COULD, WOULD,* OR *SHOULD*
If the future were clear, we'd act.	If the future could be clear, we'd act.
If someone were to escort her, she would go.	If someone would escort her, she would go.
If you were to move, would you write to me?	If you should move, would you write to me?

See Practice 17.3C
See Practice 17.3D

PRACTICE 17.3A **Identifying Mood (Indicative, Imperative, Subjunctive)**

With a partner, take turns reading each sentence aloud. Then, identify whether each sentence expresses the *indicative, imperative,* or *subjunctive* mood. For each sentence that expresses the subjunctive mood, discuss whether the verb is used to express doubts, wishes, and possibilities. Then, use the verb in a new sentence that also expresses the subjunctive mood.

EXAMPLE If the principal were to request it, Hal would drop by the office.

ANSWER *subjunctive; If Tom were to request it, Meg would drop by the game.*

1. If it were urgent, he would take the next plane.
2. Get your homework done early.
3. If it were possible, I would do it myself.
4. He treats me as if I were one of his friends.
5. The writer sat at the computer all day.
6. Include a cash payment with your order form.
7. I wish that I were back in my warm bed.
8. Please leave!
9. If the judge were to order it, the defendant would pay a fine.
10. Did the dog bark nonstop in the yard?

PRACTICE 17.3B **Writing the Subjunctive Mood**

Read each sentence. Then, rewrite each sentence so that it uses the subjunctive mood to express doubts, wishes, and possibilities. Read your sentences to a partner. Together, discuss if your sentences are correct.

EXAMPLE Cate feeds the dog.

ANSWER *If it were possible, Cate would feed the dog.*

11. Kelly opens the window.
12. They are on time.
13. She runs faster.
14. Each person brings a calculator.
15. The door was left open.
16. Isobel goes straight home.
17. He is the group leader.
18. Rob calls her by her first name.
19. Tobias does his homework immediately after school.
20. You are eighteen.

SPEAKING APPLICATION

Take turns with a partner. Say sentences that express doubts, wishes, and possibilities. Use the subjunctive mood in your sentences. Your partner should identify the subjunctive mood that identifies wishes, doubts, and possibilities in your sentences.

WRITING APPLICATION

Use the sentences in Practice 17.3B as a model to write similar sentences. Exchange papers with a partner. Your partner should rewrite your sentences so that they use the subjunctive mood to express doubts, wishes, and possibilities.

PRACTICE 17.3C **Supplying Auxiliary Verbs to Express the Subjunctive Mood**

Read each sentence. Then, rewrite each sentence, and complete it by supplying an auxiliary verb.

EXAMPLE I _____ leave tomorrow if I could.

ANSWER *I would leave tomorrow if I could.*

1. If I _____ insist, he might finish his homework.
2. If it _____ be better, she would go with us.
3. If we _____ demand it, they might listen to what we have to say.
4. I _____ be glad if he _____ give me the paper.
5. If you _____ clean your room, it would make me happy.
6. If it seems necessary, we _____ work together.
7. If Mary _____ want good advice, she might try listening to her mother.
8. If we _____ only ask him, he might be more generous.
9. If it _____ be convenient, you _____ help us this weekend.
10. You might be happier if you _____ go home.

PRACTICE 17.3D **Writing Sentences With Auxiliary Verbs**

Read each sentence. Then, rewrite each sentence using auxiliary verbs.

EXAMPLE If my class were canceled, I'd go home.

ANSWER *If my class should be canceled, I'd go home.*

11. If Joey's bike were fixed in time, he'd join us on our ride.
12. If the rain were to stop, we'd have a picnic.
13. If Stephen were to miss class, I would let him copy my notes.
14. If the old maple were to fall down, it would land on the driveway.
15. If you were to have any birthday cake, what kind would it be?
16. If someone were to wash the dishes, I would put them away.
17. If the movie were to run late, Jolleen will miss the bus.
18. If the fire were to go out, the cabin would be cold.
19. If Jim were to set the table, we could eat.
20. If you were to adopt a pet, what kind would you want?

SPEAKING APPLICATION

With a partner, take turns reading your sentences for Practice 17.3C. Your partner should tell you if your sentences correctly use auxiliary verbs and the subjunctive mood to express doubts, wishes, and possibilities.

WRITING APPLICATION

Use auxiliary verbs to write your own subjunctive mood sentences that express doubts, wishes, and possibilities. Then, exchange papers with a partner. Your partner should underline all the auxiliary verbs in your sentences.

Test Warm-Up

DIRECTIONS
Read the introduction and the passage that follows. Then, answer the questions to show that you can use and understand the function of the subjunctive mood to express doubts, wishes, and possibilities in reading and writing.

This paragraph is about the relationship between two brothers. Read the paragraph and think about the changes you would suggest as a peer editor. When you finish reading, answer the questions that follow.

Asking My Brother

(1) Danny needed a ride to the movies, and he was certain his brother would say no. (2) Last time, Kevin said that if he was to give Danny a ride, he would get his clean car muddy. (3) Danny imagined Kevin's excuses. (4) "My insurance rates should increase if I were in an accident." (5) "I don't want to run into heavy traffic that could make me miss the football game." (6) When Danny got up his courage to ask, he was stunned by Kevin's response. (7) "If I were to say no again, I would feel guilty like I did last time. (8) Of course, I'll take you!"

---

1 What change, if any, should be made in sentence 2?

- **A** Change ***would*** to **should**
- **B** Add **going** after ***was***
- **C** Change ***was*** to **were**
- **D** Make no change

2 How should sentence 4 be revised?

- **F** "My insurance rates would increase if I were in an accident."
- **G** "My insurance rates would increase if I might be in an accident."
- **H** "My insurance rates should increase if I could be in an accident."
- **J** "My insurance rates were to increase if I should be in an accident."

3 What is the most effective way to rewrite the ideas in sentence 5?

- **A** "When there is a heavy traffic, I am going to miss the football game."
- **B** "If there were heavy traffic, I won't want to miss the football game."
- **C** "Being in heavy traffic will make me miss the football game."
- **D** "If there should be heavy traffic, I could miss the football game."

4 What change, if any, should be made in sentence 7?

- **F** Change ***were to*** to **could**
- **G** Change ***would*** to **will**
- **H** Change ***If*** to **When**
- **J** Make no change

17.4 Voice

This section discusses a characteristic of verbs called **voice.**

WRITING COACH **Online**

www.phwritingcoach.com

Grammar Tutorials
Brush up on your Grammar skills with these animated videos.

Grammar Practice
Practice your grammar skills with Writing Coach Online.

Dimension G
Test your knowledge of grammar in this fast-paced interactive video game.

RULE 17.4.1 **Voice or tense is the form of a verb that shows whether the subject is performing the action or is being acted upon.**

In English, there are two voices: **active** and **passive.** Only action verbs can indicate the active voice; linking verbs cannot.

Active and Passive Voice or Tense

If the subject of a verb performs the action, the verb is active; if the subject receives the action, the verb is passive.

Active Voice Any action verb can be used in the active voice. The action verb may be transitive (that is, it may have a direct object) or intransitive (without a direct object).

RULE 17.4.2 **A verb is active if its subject performs the action.**

In the examples below, the subject performs the action. In the first example, the verb *telephoned* is transitive; *team* is the direct object, which receives the action. In the second example, the verb *developed* is transitive; *pictures* is the direct object. In the third example, the verb *gathered* is intransitive; it has no direct object. In the last example, the verb *worked* is intransitive and has no direct object.

ACTIVE VOICE

The captain **telephoned** (transitive verb) the **team** (direct object).

Bill **developed** (transitive verb) twenty-five **pictures** (direct object) of the ocean.

Telephone messages **gathered** (intransitive verb) on the desk while she was away.

Bill **worked** (intransitive verb) quickly.

See Practice 17.4A
See Practice 17.4B

Passive Voice Most action verbs can also be used in the passive voice.

A verb is passive if its action is performed upon the subject.

RULE 17.4.3

In the following examples, the subjects are the receivers of the action. The first example names the performer, the captain, as the object of the preposition *by* instead of the subject. In the second example, no performer of the action is mentioned.

PASSIVE VOICE

The **team** (receiver of action) **was telephoned** (verb) by the captain.

The **messages** (receiver of action) **were gathered** (verb) into neat piles.

A passive verb is always a verb phrase made from a form of *be* plus the past participle of a verb. The tense of the helping verb *be* determines the tense of the passive verb.

RULE 17.4.4

The chart below provides a conjugation in the passive voice of the verb *believe* in the three moods. Notice that there are only two progressive forms and no emphatic form.

See Practice 17.4C

THE VERB *BELIEVE* IN THE PASSIVE VOICE	
Present Indicative	He is believed.
Past Indicative	He was believed.
Future Indicative	He will be believed.
Present Perfect Indicative	He has been believed.
Past Perfect Indicative	He had been believed.
Future Perfect Indicative	He will have been believed.
Present Progressive Indicative	He is being believed.
Past Progressive Indicative	He was being believed.
Present Imperative	(You) be believed.
Present Subjunctive	(if) he be believed
Past Subjunctive	(if) he were believed

Using Active and Passive Voice

Writing that uses the active voice tends to be much more lively than writing that uses the passive voice. The active voice is usually more direct and economical. That is because active voice shows someone doing something.

RULE 17.4.5 **Use the active voice whenever possible.**

ACTIVE VOICE Finally, Debbie **repaired** the telephone.

PASSIVE VOICE Finally, the telephone **was repaired** by Debbie.

The passive voice has two uses in English.

RULE 17.4.6 **Use the passive voice when you want to emphasize the receiver of an action rather than the performer of an action.**

EXAMPLE My best friend **was awarded** a medal.

RULE 17.4.7 **Use the passive voice to point out the receiver of an action whenever the performer is not important or not easily identified.**

EXAMPLE At noon, the doors to the tomb **were unlocked**, and the archaeologists entered it.

The active voice lends more excitement to writing, making it more interesting to readers. In the example below, notice how the sentence you just read has been revised to show someone doing something, rather than something just happening.

EXAMPLE At noon, the archaeologists **unlocked** the doors to the tomb and entered it.
(*Who* unlocked the doors and entered the tomb?)

See Practice 17.4D

PRACTICE 17.4A Recognizing Active Voice (Active Tense)

Read each sentence. Then, write the active verb in each sentence and use it in a new sentence.

EXAMPLE Sally added fresh cucumbers to the salad.

ANSWER *added; I added both numbers to get the answer.*

1. The team selected a new member.
2. Linda talked with us this week.
3. Robert picked his tennis partner.
4. We each bought several notebooks.
5. Later, the student wrote an essay.
6. Many wild animals live in the forest.
7. Amy grew her own vegetables this summer.
8. In the winter, snow covers the ground.
9. The train reached Baton Rouge in three hours.
10. He always reads the morning paper before breakfast.

PRACTICE 17.4B Using Active Verbs

Read each item. Then, write different sentences, using each item as an active verb.

EXAMPLE signed

ANSWER *The author signed the book.*

11. identifies
12. played
13. ask
14. nest
15. elect
16. performed
17. eaten
18. skips
19. cooked
20. slept

SPEAKING APPLICATION

Take turns with a partner. Give directions on how to do something, such as how to perform a search using the Internet. Your partner should listen for and identify the active verbs in your directions.

WRITING APPLICATION

Write a paragraph about yourself and the activities that you enjoy doing. Underline all the active verbs in your paragraph.

PRACTICE 17.4C Forming the Tenses of Passive Verbs

Read each verb. Then, using the subject indicated in parentheses, conjugate each verb in the passive voice for the present indicative, past indicative, future indicative, present perfect indicative, past perfect indicative, and future perfect indicative. Read your conjugated verbs to a partner and discuss if your answers are correct.

EXAMPLE say (it)

ANSWER *it is said, it was said, it will be said, it has been said, it had been said, it will have been said*

1. drive (they)
2. tell (you)
3. ask (we)
4. mow (it)
5. forgive (we)
6. move (it)
7. alert (they)
8. instruct (we)
9. play (it)
10. create (it)

PRACTICE 17.4D Supplying Verbs in the Active Voice (Active Tense)

Read each sentence. Then, complete each sentence by supplying a verb in the active voice. Read your sentences to a partner and discuss if your sentences are correct.

EXAMPLE A little boy ____ the door.

ANSWER *opened*

11. Reporters ____ the president.
12. Thomas ____ the podium on the stage.
13. Miss Van Patten ____ the bird calls.
14. That college ____ advanced algebra to undergraduate students.
15. Renoir ____ the portrait.
16. They ____ the posters.
17. The lost dog ____ us home.
18. The magazine ____ my first story.
19. Eduardo ____ the phone.
20. Rachel ____ the new computer system.

SPEAKING APPLICATION

Take turns with a partner. Exchange a list of five verbs. Your partner should say the conjugation of each verb in the passive voice for the present indicative, past indicative, and future indicative.

WRITING APPLICATION

Show that you understand active and passive tenses by writing four sentences, using active tenses twice and passive tenses twice. Read your sentences to a partner who should tell if the sentence is active tense or passive tense as you speak.

CHAPTER 18

PRONOUN USAGE

Knowing how to use pronouns correctly will help you write clear sentences that flow.

WRITE GUY *Jeff Anderson, M.Ed.*

WHAT DO YOU NOTICE?

Stay on the lookout for pronouns as you zoom in on this sentence from "My English," an excerpt from *Something to Declare* by Julia Alvarez.

MENTOR TEXT

> Mami and Papi used to speak it when they had a secret they wanted to keep from us children.

Now, ask yourself the following questions:

- Which words do the pronouns *it* and *they* refer to?
- Why does the author use the pronoun *us* instead of *we* in the phrase *us children*?

The pronoun *it* is the object of the verb *speak*, so *it* refers to the language used by the subjects of the sentence. The pronoun *they* renames the subjects *Mami* and *Papi* both times it appears. The author uses the pronoun *us* instead of *we* because *us* is the object of the preposition in the prepositional phrase *from us children*.

Grammar for Writers Understanding the uses of pronouns helps writers to craft sentences that convey the meaning that is intended. As you edit your writing, check that your readers will be able to tell to whom or what your pronouns refer.

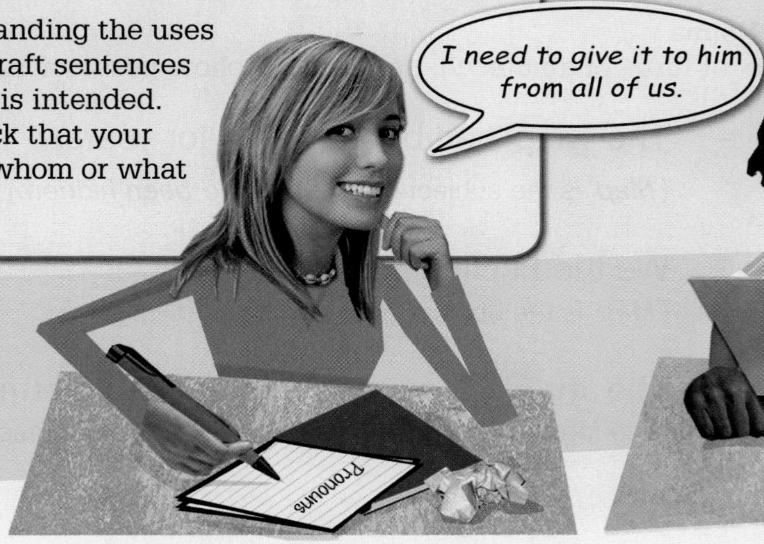
I need to give it to him from all of us.
Pronouns

Wow! You're a pronoun pro this morning.

18.1 Case

Nouns and pronouns are the only parts of speech that have **case.**

RULE 18.1.1

Case is the form of a noun or a pronoun that shows how it is used in a sentence.

WRITING COACH Online

www.phwritingcoach.com

Grammar Practice

Practice your grammar skills with Writing Coach Online.

Grammar Games

Test your knowledge of grammar in this fast-paced interactive video game.

The Three Cases

Nouns and pronouns have three cases, each of which has its own distinctive uses.

RULE 18.1.2

The three cases of nouns and pronouns are the nominative, the objective, and the possessive.

CASE	USE IN SENTENCE
Nominative	As the Subject of a Verb, Predicate Nominative, or Nominative Absolute
Objective	As the Direct Object, Indirect Object, Object of a Preposition, Object of a Verbal, or Subject of an Infinitive
Possessive	To Show Ownership

Case in Nouns

The case, or form, of a noun changes only to show possession.

NOMINATIVE The **map** had been hidden for years.

(*Map* is the subject of the verb *had been hidden*.)

OBJECTIVE We tried to find the **map**.

(***Map*** is the object of the infinitive *to find.*)

POSSESSIVE The **map's** location could not be determined.

(The form changes when *'s* is added to show possession.)

Case in Pronouns

Personal pronouns often have different forms for all three cases. The pronoun that you use depends on its function in a sentence.

NOMINATIVE	OBJECTIVE	POSSESSIVE
I *you* *he, she, it* *we, they*	*me* *you* *him, her, it* *us, them*	*my, mine* *your, yours* *his, her, hers, its* *our, ours* *their, theirs*

EXAMPLES **I** read the book about space.

Jerome sent the book to **me**.

The book about space is **mine**.

See Practice 18.1A

The Nominative Case in Pronouns

The **nominative case** is used when a personal pronoun acts in one of three ways.

RULE 18.1.3

Use the nominative case when a pronoun is the subject of a verb, a predicate nominative, or in a nominative absolute.

A **nominative absolute** consists of a noun or nominative pronoun followed by a participial phrase. It functions independently from the rest of the sentence.

EXAMPLE **We having opened our textbooks,** the geography teacher pointed out the map on page 435.

NOMINATIVE PRONOUNS	
As the Subject of a Verb	I will consult the map while she asks for directions.
As a Predicate Nominative	The finalists were he and she.
In a Nominative Absolute	We having finished the meal, the waiter cleared our table.

Nominative Pronouns in Compounds

When you use a pronoun in a compound subject or predicate nominative, check the case either by mentally crossing out the other part of the compound or by inverting the sentence.

COMPOUND SUBJECT The teacher and **I** inspected the map.
(**I** inspected the map.)

She and her father sailed the boat.
(**She** sailed the boat.)

COMPOUND PREDICATE NOMINATIVE The fastest sailors were Jody and **he**.
(Jody and **he** were the fastest sailors.)

The surveyors were Lin and **I**.
(Lin and **I** were the surveyors.)

Nominative Pronouns With Appositives

When an appositive follows a pronoun that is being used as a subject or predicate nominative, the pronoun should stay in the nominative case. To check that you have used the correct case, either mentally cross out the appositive or isolate the subject and verb.

SUBJECT **We** mapmakers use technology.
(**We** use technology.)

PREDICATE NOMINATIVE The winners were **we** seniors.
(**We** were the winners.)

APPOSITIVE AFTER NOUN The nominees, **she** and **I**, ran for class president.
(**She** and **I** ran for class president.)

See Practice 18.1B

PRACTICE 18.1A Identifying Case

Read each sentence. Then, label the underlined pronoun in each sentence *nominative, objective,* or *possessive.*

EXAMPLE Within an hour of leaving, we had a flat tire.

ANSWER *nominative*

1. The realtor will not meet with you until next Tuesday.
2. Amanda has lost her sunglasses.
3. Choi dropped his glove in the snow.
4. The Foresters brought their cat with them to their summer house.
5. There is no doubt that this scarf is yours.
6. I appreciate a helping hand.
7. Stella mentioned that someone requested her presence at the meeting.
8. The car showed dents and scratches on its roof.
9. You asked us for the homework assignment.
10. It was a moment of complete tranquility.

PRACTICE 18.1B Supplying Pronouns in the Nominative Case

Read each sentence. Then, supply a nominative pronoun to complete each sentence.

EXAMPLE Sophia and _____ worked overtime.

ANSWER *she*

11. Marica and _____ are looking for him at the library.
12. _____ is a warm and beautiful evening.
13. Are _____ sincere in your apology?
14. _____ are longing for a phone call from Jill.
15. The solution to the problem is that she and _____ need to deposit money into the account.
16. _____ is the teacher that I highly respect.
17. You understand that _____ is absent today.
18. My closest friend is _____.
19. I know that _____ will travel with me.
20. The leaders of the band are he and _____.

SPEAKING APPLICATION

Take turns with a partner. Describe a class that you have really enjoyed. Use at least one example of a pronoun in each of the three cases. Your partner should listen for and identify your use of pronouns as nominative, objective, and possessive.

WRITING APPLICATION

Write a paragraph describing an event you have attended. Use at least three nominative pronouns in your paragraph.

The Objective Case

Objective pronouns are used for any kind of object in a sentence as well as for the subject of an infinitive.

RULE 18.1.4

Use the objective case for the object of any verb, preposition, or verbal or for the subject of an infinitive.

OBJECTIVE PRONOUNS	
Direct Object	A basketball hit him in the head.
Indirect Object	My uncle sent me a lace fan from Hong Kong.
Object of Preposition	Three very tall men sat in front of us in the movie theater.
Object of Participle	The sharks following them were very hungry.
Object of Gerund	Meeting them will be a great pleasure.
Object of Infinitive	I am obligated to help her move this Saturday.
Subject of Infinitive	The firm wanted her to work the night shift.

Objective Pronouns in Compounds

As with the nominative case, errors with objective pronouns most often occur in compounds. To find the correct case, mentally cross out the other part of the compound.

EXAMPLES Cracking ice floes alarmed Burt and **him**.
(Cracking ice floes alarmed **him**.)

Sally drew Laurie and **me** a map to her house.
(Sally drew **me** a map.)

Note About *Between:* Be sure to use the objective case after the preposition *between*.

INCORRECT This argument is between you and **I**.

CORRECT This argument is between you and **me**.

See Practice 18.1C

Objective Pronouns With Appositives

Use the objective case when a pronoun that is used as an object or as the subject of an infinitive is followed by an appositive.

EXAMPLES
The mapmaking quiz intimidated **us** students.
My aunt brought **us** nieces an iguana.
The guide asked **us** stragglers to hurry.

The Possessive Case

One use for the **possessive case** is before gerunds. A **gerund** is a verbal form ending in *-ing* that is used as a noun.

RULE 18.1.5 Use the **possessive case** before gerunds.

EXAMPLES
Your tracing of the map was sloppy.
We objected to **his** insinuating that we were lazy.
Sarah insists on **our** attending the dance.

Common Errors in the Possessive Case

Be sure not to use an apostrophe with a possessive pronoun because possessives already show ownership. Spellings such as *her's, our's, their's,* and *your's* are incorrect.

In addition, be sure not to confuse possessive pronouns and contractions that sound alike. *It's* (with an apostrophe) is the contraction for *it is* or *it has*. *Its* (without the apostrophe) is a possessive pronoun that means "belonging to it." *You're* is a contraction of *you are*; the possessive form of *you* is *your*.

Find It/FIX IT 14 Grammar Game Plan

POSSESSIVE PRONOUNS
The map had served **its** purpose.
Don't forget **your** map.

CONTRACTIONS
It's not likely you will become lost.
You're the only ones who wouldn't use the map.

See Practice 18.1D
See Practice 18.1E
See Practice 18.1F

PRACTICE 18.1C Supplying Pronouns in the Objective Case

Read each sentence. Then, supply an objective pronoun to complete each sentence.

EXAMPLE I applauded _____ and the other cast members.

ANSWER *them*

1. Emily offered _____ her prom dress.
2. Abigail gave Jessie and _____ lots of unwanted attention.
3. The children waved at _____ mothers.
4. My boss advanced _____ a week's pay.
5. Our coaches bought _____ brand new basketballs after our trip to the finals.
6. The secret is between you and _____ .
7. The incident gave _____ a new perspective.
8. Ask for Wai and _____ when you arrive.
9. I gave _____ new books to read.
10. The teacher asked _____ to answer the question.

PRACTICE 18.1D Recognizing Pronouns in the Possessive Case

Read each sentence. Then, select the correct pronoun from the choices in parentheses to complete each sentence.

EXAMPLE That pig has (it's, its) own pen to play in.

ANSWER *its*

11. (Him, His) endless kindness is extremely thoughtful.
12. None of the books on this shelf are (mine, my).
13. I'm positive Mrs. Landry appreciated (our, us) assisting her.
14. These are Christopher's pencils, but where are (your's, yours)?
15. Jhanna remembered (her, hers) appointment.
16. Did you confront Joshua about (him, his) playing his radio too loudly?
17. The Thompsons told us that these garden supplies are (their's, theirs).
18. (Me, My) teaching piano lessons helped pay my tuition.
19. After you have looked through it, put the comic book back into (it's, its) original plastic sleeve.
20. No one appreciated (them, their) cheerful attitude.

SPEAKING APPLICATION

Take turns with a partner. Describe a kind act that you have witnessed. Include at least three objective pronouns in your description.

WRITING APPLICATION

Write a paragraph about the type of person who inspires you, and explain why. Use at least three pronouns in the possessive case in your paragraph.

PRACTICE 18.1E Writing Possessive Pronouns Before Gerunds

Read each sentence. Then, rewrite each sentence and include a correct possessive pronoun. Read your sentences to a partner and discuss if your sentences are correct.

EXAMPLE Lauren was happy with _____ praising of her work.

ANSWER *Lauren was happy with **his** praising of her work.*

1. _____ stopping alerted us that the light had changed.
2. She knew the cat was hurt by _____ limping.
3. _____ laughing broke the tension.
4. I hoped _____ yawning wasn't obvious.
5. The baby was startled by _____ clapping.
6. He insisted on _____ participating in the meeting.
7. Bradley was offended by _____ insisting that he was wrong.
8. Mitch knew _____ playing was improving.
9. _____ leaving gave Chad the impression we were angry.
10. I admire _____ working so hard to raise your grades.

PRACTICE 18.1F Correcting Common Errors in the Possessive Case

Read each sentence. Then, rewrite each sentence and correct the error. If the pronouns in possessive case and the contractions are written correctly, write *correct*.

EXAMPLE I think its your turn to wash the dishes.

ANSWER *I think **it's** your turn to wash the dishes.*

11. Its time for my favorite TV show.
12. You left your coat at my house.
13. When are we celebrating you're birthday?
14. Our car has a dent in it's hood.
15. So your the one who sent the letter!
16. The tree has shed its leaves.
17. When its time to go, please call me.
18. If your not busy, can you wash the car?
19. It's purpose is to prevent infection.
20. You have to wait your turn.

WRITING APPLICATION

Review Practice 18.1E. For each item, write an additional sentence using another correct possessive pronoun.

SPEAKING APPLICATION

With a partner, take turns reading aloud the sentences in Practice 18.1F. Together, discuss whether the sentences use the possessive case. Then, take turns saying similar sentences. Your partner should indicate if your sentences use the possessive case.

Test Warm-Up

DIRECTIONS
Read the introduction and the passage that follows. Then, answer the questions to show that you can use and understand the function of pronouns in the objective and possessive cases in reading and writing.

Betsy wrote this paragraph to offer classmates tips about delivering a speech. Read the paragraph and think about the changes you would suggest as a peer editor. When you finish reading, answer the questions that follow.

Speak Up

(1) Don't freeze up when your teacher gives you an assignment to deliver a speech. (2) Use note cards to organize what you will say. (3) You planning will be well worth the effort. (4) Practicing before an audience, like family members or friends, will help you be more at ease when you present you're speech. (5) Its finally your turn. (6) Look straight at your classmates as you talk. (7) You will impress your teacher with their confidence. (8) You will impress your classmates, too.

---

1 What change, if any, should be made in sentence 3?

- **A** Change ***the*** to **its**
- **B** Change ***You*** to **Your**
- **C** Change ***planning*** to **plan**
- **D** Make no change

2 What change should be made in sentence 4?

- **F** Change ***members*** to **member's**
- **G** Change ***help you*** to **help your**
- **H** Replace ***you're*** with **your**
- **J** Insert **to** after ***will***

3 What change, if any, should be made in sentence 5?

- **A** Change ***Its*** to **It's**
- **B** Delete ***your***
- **C** Change ***your*** to **you're**
- **D** Make no change

4 What is the most effective way to combine sentences 7 and 8?

- **F** You will impress your teacher with their confidence along with those.
- **G** You will impress your teacher, as you will impress them, with your confidence.
- **H** You will impress them and your teacher with your confidence.
- **J** You will impress your teacher and they with your confidence.

18.2 Special Problems With Pronouns

Choosing the correct case is not always a matter of choosing the form that "sounds correct," because writing is usually more formal than speech. For example, it would be incorrect to say, "John is smarter than *me*," because the verb is understood in the sentence: "John is smarter than *I [am]*."

WRITING COACH Online

www.phwritingcoach.com

Grammar Practice

Practice your grammar skills with Writing Coach Online.

Grammar Games

Test your knowledge of grammar in this fast-paced interactive video game.

Using *Who* and *Whom* Correctly

In order to decide when to use *who* or *whom* and the related forms *whoever* and *whomever*, you need to know how the pronoun is used in a sentence and what case is appropriate.

RULE 18.2.1 ***Who*** **is used for the nominative case.** ***Whom*** **is used for the objective case.**

CASE	PRONOUNS	USE IN SENTENCES
Nominative	*who* *whoever*	As the Subject of a Verb or Predicate Nominative
Objective	*whom* *whomever*	As the Direct Object, Object of a Verbal, Object of a Preposition, or Subject of an Infinitive
Possessive	*whose* *whosever*	To Show Ownership

EXAMPLES I know **who** has a new car.

Tippy brought **whoever** was sitting down her chew toy.

Jake did not know **whom** Tim chose.

Whose car is in front of the store?

The nominative and objective cases are the source of certain problems. Pronoun problems can appear in two kinds of sentences: direct questions and complex sentences.

In Direct Questions

Who is the correct form when the pronoun is the subject of a simple question. *Whom* is the correct form when the pronoun is the direct object, object of a verbal, or object of a preposition.

Questions in subject–verb word order always begin with *who*. However, questions in inverted order never correctly begin with *who*. To see if you should use *who* or *whom*, reword the question as a statement in subject–verb word order.

EXAMPLES **Who** wants a free ticket to the movies?

Whom did you take with you?

(You did take **whom** with you.)

In Complex Sentences

Follow these steps to see if the case of a pronoun in a subordinate clause is correct. First, find the subordinate clause. If the complex sentence is a question, rearrange it in subject–verb order. Second, if the subordinate clause is inverted, rearrange the words in subject–verb word order. Finally, determine how the pronoun is used in the subordinate clause.

EXAMPLE **Who**, may I ask, has seen a whale?

REARRANGED I may ask **who** has seen a whale.

USE OF PRONOUN (subject of the verb *has seen*)

EXAMPLE Is Jake the one **whom** they chose to leave?

REARRANGED They chose **whom** to leave.

USE OF PRONOUN (object of the verb *chose*)

Note About *Whose:* The word *whose* is a possessive pronoun; the contraction *who's* means "who is" or "who has."

POSSESSIVE PRONOUN **Whose** umbrella is this?

CONTRACTION **Who's** [who has] taken my umbrella?

See Practice 18.2A

Pronouns in Elliptical Clauses

An **elliptical clause** is one in which some words are omitted but still understood. Errors in pronoun usage can easily be made when an elliptical clause that begins with *than* or *as* is used to make a comparison.

In elliptical clauses beginning with *than* or *as*, use the form of the pronoun that you would use if the clause were fully stated.

RULE 18.2.2

The case of the pronoun is determined by whether the omitted words fall before or after the pronoun. The omitted words in the examples below are shown in brackets.

WORDS OMITTED BEFORE PRONOUN

You gave Lewis more than **me**.

(You gave Lewis more than [you gave] **me**.)

WORDS OMITTED AFTER PRONOUN

Ray is as dedicated as **he**.

(Ray is as dedicated as **he** [is].)

Mentally add the missing words. If they come *before* the pronoun, choose the objective case. If they come *after* the pronoun, choose the nominative case.

CHOOSING A PRONOUN IN ELLIPTICAL CLAUSES
1. Consider the choices of pronouns: nominative or objective.
2. Mentally complete the elliptical clause.
3. Base your choice on what you find.

The case of the pronoun can sometimes change the entire meaning of the sentence.

NOMINATIVE PRONOUN

He liked whales more than **I**.

He liked whales more than **I** [did].

OBJECTIVE PRONOUN

He liked whales more than **me**.

He liked whales more than [he liked] **me**.

See Practice 18.2B

PRACTICE 18.2A Choosing *Who* or *Whom* Correctly

Read each sentence. Then, write *who* or *whom* to complete the sentence.

EXAMPLE _____ will start for the Houston Astros tomorrow?

ANSWER *Who*

1. _____ is the best student in the class?
2. For _____ did you vote?
3. He is a talented singer _____ is destined for great things.
4. The woman on the phone was not _____ he had anticipated.
5. To _____ did you speak about the charity event?
6. _____ was at the dance last weekend?
7. Ada knows _____ made the mistake.
8. Do you know _____ wrote that song?
9. With _____ did you drive?
10. _____ should I ask about the return policy?

PRACTICE 18.2B Identifying the Correct Pronoun in Elliptical Clauses

Read each sentence. Then, select the correct pronoun from the choices in parentheses to complete each elliptical clause.

EXAMPLE Grant is much stronger than _____. (me, I)

ANSWER *I*

11. He is taller than _____. (her, she)
12. Penny sends e-mails to others more often than to _____. (I, me)
13. Tim and Ronan speak better Spanish than _____. (he, him)
14. I am not as well prepared as _____. (her, she)
15. Edith is a lot funnier than _____. (I, me)
16. Mr. Qin does not visit a doctor as often as _____. (I, me)
17. She can write faster than _____. (I, me)
18. Harold always thought he was more outgoing than _____. (her, she)
19. You offered more of your advice to Gia than _____. (I, me)
20. Abdel is as misunderstood as _____. (him, he)

SPEAKING APPLICATION

Take turns with a partner. Ask questions using both *who* and *whom*. Your partner should respond by also using *who* and *whom* correctly in his or her response.

WRITING APPLICATION

Write a paragraph describing a funny scene from a movie. Use two elliptical clauses in your paragraph.

CHAPTER 19

AGREEMENT

Making subjects agree with verbs and pronouns agree with their antecedents, or the words they refer to, will help you write clear, meaningful sentences.

WRITE GUY *Jeff Anderson, M.Ed.*

WHAT DO YOU NOTICE?

Look out for examples of agreement as you zoom in on these sentences from "My English," an excerpt from *Something to Declare* by Julia Alvarez.

MENTOR TEXT

One Sunday at our extended family dinner, my grandfather sat down at the children's table to chat with us. He was famous, in fact, for the way he could carry on adult conversations with his grandchildren.

Now, ask yourself the following questions:

- In the context of both sentences, whom does the pronoun *us* refer to?
- In the second sentence, how do the pronouns *he* and *his* relate to their antecedent?

When using the plural pronoun *us*, the author is referring to herself and other children. In the second sentence, *grandchildren* clarifies to whom *us* refers. Both *he* and *his* are third-person pronouns that are singular in number and masculine in gender; they relate to the singular, masculine antecedent, *grandfather*.

Grammar for Writers Writers can avoid repetition of nouns by using pronouns. By checking that pronouns agree in number, person, and gender with their antecedents, you can craft sentences that are clear in meaning.

Check with the nouns.
Whom does this pronoun belong to?

19.1 Subject–Verb Agreement

For a subject and a verb to agree, both must be singular, or both must be plural. In this section, you will learn how to make sure singular and plural subjects and verbs agree.

WRITING COACH **Online**

www.phwritingcoach.com

Grammar Practice

Practice your grammar skills with Writing Coach Online.

Grammar Games

Test your knowledge of grammar in this fast-paced interactive video game.

Number in Nouns, Pronouns, and Verbs

In grammar, **number** indicates whether a word is singular or plural. Only three parts of speech have different forms that indicate number: nouns, pronouns, and verbs.

RULE 19.1.1

Number shows whether a noun, pronoun, or verb is singular or plural.

Recognizing the number of most nouns is seldom a problem because most form their plurals by adding *-s* or *-es.* Some, such as *mouse* or *ox,* form their plurals irregularly: *mice, oxen.*

Pronouns, however, have different forms to indicate their number. The chart below shows the different forms of personal pronouns in the nominative case, the case that is used for subjects.

PERSONAL PRONOUNS		
SINGULAR	PLURAL	SINGULAR OR PLURAL
I	*we*	*you*
he, she, it	*they*	

The grammatical number of verbs is sometimes difficult to determine. That is because the form of many verbs can be either singular or plural, and they may form plurals in different ways.

SINGULAR She **sees**.

She **has seen**.

PLURAL We **see**.

We **have seen**.

Some verb forms can be only singular. The personal pronouns *he, she,* and *it* and all singular nouns call for singular verbs in the present and the present perfect tense.

ALWAYS SINGULAR

He **sees**.

He **has seen**.

Pat **runs**.

Chris **has run**.

She **jumps**.

She **has jumped**.

The verb *be* in the present tense has special forms to agree with singular subjects. The pronoun *I* has its own singular form of *be*; so do *he, she, it,* and singular nouns.

ALWAYS SINGULAR

I **am** hungry.

He **is** tall.

Jody **is** late.

She **is** ready.

All singular subjects except *you* share the same past tense verb form of *be*.

ALWAYS SINGULAR

I **was** going home.

He **was** team captain.

Carolyn **was** early to practice.

She **was** getting on the bus.

See Practice 19.1A

A verb form will always be singular if it has had an *-s* or *-es* added to it or if it includes the words *has, am, is,* or *was*. The number of any other verb depends on its subject.

The chart on the next page shows verb forms that are always singular and those that can be singular or plural.

VERBS THAT ARE ALWAYS SINGULAR	VERBS THAT CAN BE SINGULAR OR PLURAL
(he, she, Jane) sees (he, she, Jane) has seen (I) am (he, she, Jane) is (I, he, she, Jane) was	(I, you, we, they) see (I, you, we, they) have seen (you, we, they) are (you, we, they) were

Singular and Plural Subjects

When making a verb agree with its subject, be sure to identify the subject and determine its number.

RULE 19.1.2

A singular subject must have a singular verb. A plural subject must have a plural verb.

SINGULAR SUBJECT AND VERB	PLURAL SUBJECT AND VERB
The archaeologist works in Egypt.	These archaeologists work in Egypt.
She was being mysterious about the dig's location.	They were being mysterious about the dig's location.
Roni looks through an encyclopedia for information about China.	Mike and Sam look through an encyclopedia for information about China.
China is a large country in Asia.	China and India are large countries in Asia.
Chris takes organic chemistry.	Annie and Kelly take organic chemistry.
Rhonda is planning a vacation to Yellowstone National Park.	Our neighbors are planning a vacation to Yellowstone National Park.
Sasha plays forward on the basketball team.	Julio and Jim play on the soccer team.
He looks through the telescope.	They look through the telescope.
Elizabeth has been studying the solar system.	We have been studying the solar system.

See Practice 19.1B

PRACTICE 19.1A Identifying Number in Nouns, Pronouns, and Verbs

Read each word or group of words. Then, write whether the word or words are *singular, plural,* or *both*.

EXAMPLE toes
ANSWER *plural*

1. men
2. listens
3. you
4. musical note
5. sneakers
6. should
7. we
8. is
9. he
10. have seen

PRACTICE 19.1B Identifying Singular and Plural Subjects and Verbs

Read each sentence. Write the correct verb form from the choices in parentheses. Then, label the verb *singular* or *plural*.

EXAMPLE That song (has, have) become a classic.

ANSWER *has become— singular*

11. Vacations (is, are) often very expensive.
12. In the morning, the ships (sails, sail) out to sea.
13. The twins (wash, washes) the dishes.
14. Meshaun's brother (likes, like) to play baseball.
15. The chairs (is, are) made of pine.
16. The people on the talk show sometimes (disagrees, disagree).
17. The students (listens, listen) to the speech.
18. (Does, Do) lions live in this area?
19. She told us that English literature (was, were) her best class.
20. (There's, There are) the leaders of both groups.

SPEAKING APPLICATION

Take turns with a partner. Tell about your favorite subject in school. Your partner should listen for and name the singular and plural nouns and verbs that you use.

WRITING APPLICATION

Write three sentences about your favorite season. Use singular and plural subjects and verbs in your sentences. Make sure that there is subject-and-verb agreement in your sentences.

Intervening Phrases and Clauses

When you check for agreement, mentally cross out any words that separate the subject and verb.

RULE 19.1.3

A phrase or clause that interrupts a subject and its verb does not affect subject–verb agreement.

In the first example below, the singular subject *discovery* agrees with the singular verb *interests* despite the intervening prepositional phrase *of mummies,* which contains a plural noun.

EXAMPLES The **discovery** of mummies **interests** many people.

The **archaeologists**, whose work is nearly complete, **require** more funding.

Intervening parenthetical expressions—such as those beginning with *as well as, in addition to, in spite of,* or *including*—also have no effect on the agreement of the subject and verb.

EXAMPLES Your **information**, in addition to the data gathered by those working at the site, **is helping** to solve the mystery.

Jonathan's **trip**, including visits to Germany and France, **is lasting** four months.

See Practice 19.1C

Relative Pronouns as Subjects

When *who, which,* or *that* acts as a subject of a subordinate clause, its verb will be singular or plural depending on the number of the antecedent.

RULE 19.1.4

The antecedent of a relative pronoun determines its agreement with a verb.

EXAMPLES He is the only **one** of the students **who has** prior experience working in a chemistry lab.

(The antecedent of *who* is *one*.)

He is the only one of several **students who have** prior experience working in chemistry labs.

(The antecedent of *who* is *students*.)

Compound Subjects

A **compound subject** has two or more simple subjects, which are usually joined by *or* or *and*. Use the following rules when making compound subjects agree with verbs.

Subjects Joined by *And*

Only one rule applies to compound subjects connected by *and:* The verb is usually plural, whether the parts of the compound subject are all singular, all plural, or mixed.

A compound subject joined by *and* is generally plural and must have a plural verb.

RULE 19.1.5

TWO SINGULAR SUBJECTS A **thunderstorm** and a **tornado hit** the town.

TWO PLURAL SUBJECTS **Thunderstorms** and **tornadoes appear** on the radar screen.

A SINGULAR SUBJECT AND A PLURAL SUBJECT Luckily, a **tornado** and the **winds** it brings often **miss** our area.

There are two exceptions to this rule. The verb is singular if the parts of a compound subject are thought of as one item or if the word *every* or *each* precedes the compound subject.

EXAMPLES **Bread and butter was** all they served for snack.

Every weather center and emergency network issues warnings for severe weather.

Singular Subjects Joined by *Or* or *Nor*

When both parts of a compound subject connected by *or* or *nor* are singular, a singular verb is required.

RULE 19.1.6

Two or more singular subjects joined by *or* or *nor* must have a singular verb.

EXAMPLE A **tornado** or **windstorm causes** damage.

Plural Subjects Joined by *Or* or *Nor*

When both parts of a compound subject connected by *or* or *nor* are plural, a plural verb is required.

RULE 19.1.7

Two or more plural subjects joined by *or* or *nor* must have a plural verb.

EXAMPLE Either **grapes** or **raisins make** a nice dessert for lunch.

Subjects of Mixed Number Joined by *Or* or *Nor*

If one part of a compound subject is singular and the other is plural, the verb agrees with the subject that is closer to it.

RULE 19.1.8

If one or more singular subjects are joined to one or more plural subjects by *or* or *nor*, the subject closest to the verb determines agreement.

EXAMPLES Neither **David** nor my **parents are frightened**.

Neither my **parents** nor **David is frightened**.

See Practice 19.1D

PRACTICE 19.1C Identifying Intervening Phrases and Clauses

Read each sentence. Then, underline the intervening phrase or clause between the subject and verb in each sentence.

EXAMPLE My painting for the art show was not quite finished.

ANSWER *My painting for the art show was not quite finished.*

1. The planting of the new trees took place yesterday.
2. The singers as well as the dancers worked very hard on the show.
3. Math, like history, is an interesting subject.
4. The neighbor across the street grows roses.
5. Two students in my school wrote a play.
6. New York, despite its crowded streets, is fun to visit.
7. Her team, including the coaches, had pizza after the game.
8. My sisters, who live all over the country, get together once a year.
9. The rehearsals for the concert began at eight o'clock.
10. The picnic feast that we brought tasted delicious.

PRACTICE 19.1D Making Verbs Agree With Singular and Compound Subjects

Read each sentence. Then, fill in the blank with the form of a verb that agrees with the singular or compound subject in each sentence.

EXAMPLE Amy and Sarah _____ next door to each other.

ANSWER *live*

11. Either chicken or fish _____ good.
12. Neither hats nor phones _____ allowed in school.
13. My mom _____ me run at the track meet.
14. Mary, Casey, and I _____ to the music.
15. Aunts, uncles, cousins, and grandparents _____ all at the reunion.
16. After the game, Melinda and Juanita _____ shopping.
17. Swimming _____ fun to do in the summer.
18. Seagulls _____ around the beach in search of food.
19. Both Jim and Dasai _____ mountain climbing.
20. Neither Ken nor his brother _____ home.

SPEAKING APPLICATION

Take turns with a partner. Say sentences with intervening clauses to tell about a trip you once took. Your partner should listen for and identify the intervening clauses in your sentences.

WRITING APPLICATION

Use sentences 13, 14, 19, and 20 as models to write similar sentences. Exchange papers with a partner. Your partner should complete the sentences with the correct form of a verb that agrees with the subject.

Confusing Subjects

Some kinds of subjects have special agreement problems.

Hard-to-Find Subjects and Inverted Sentences

Subjects that appear after verbs are said to be **inverted.** Subject–verb order is usually inverted in questions. To find out whether to use a singular or plural verb, mentally rearrange the sentence into subject–verb order.

RULE **19.1.9** **A verb must still agree in number with a subject that comes after it.**

EXAMPLE	On the roof **are** two lightning **rods**.
REARRANGED IN SUBJECT–VERB ORDER	Two lightning **rods are** on the roof.

The words *there* and *here* often signal an inverted sentence. These words never function as the subject of a sentence.

EXAMPLES	There **are** the satellite **photos**.
	Here **is** the revised **information**.

Note About *There's* and *Here's*: Both of these contractions contain the singular verb *is: there is* and *here is.* They should be used only with singular subjects.

CORRECT	**There's** only one **class** expected.
	Here's a blue **dress** to try on.

See Practice 19.1E

Subjects With Linking Verbs

Subjects with linking verbs may also cause agreement problems.

RULE **19.1.10** **A linking verb must agree with its subject, regardless of the number of its predicate nominative.**

EXAMPLES **Tulips are** my favorite flower.

One **reason** we expect a tornado **is** that strong winds are forecast.

In the first example, the plural verb *are* agrees with the plural subject *tulips*. In the next example, the singular subject *reason* takes the singular verb *is*.

See Practice 19.1F

Collective Nouns

Collective nouns name groups of people or things. Examples include *audience, class, club,* and *committee.*

A collective noun takes a singular verb when the group it names acts as a single unit. A collective noun takes a plural verb when the group acts as individuals.

RULE 19.1.11

SINGULAR The senior **class graduates** on Wednesday.

(The members act as a unit.)

PLURAL The senior **class were going** on separate trips.

(The members act individually.)

See Practice 19.1G

Nouns That Look Like Plurals

Some nouns that end in *-s* are actually singular. For example, nouns that name branches of knowledge, such as *civics,* and those that name illnesses, such as *mumps,* take singular verbs.

Use singular verbs to agree with nouns that are plural in form but singular in meaning.

RULE 19.1.12

SINGULAR **Physics is** a lot of fun.

When words such as *ethics* and *politics* do not name branches of knowledge but indicate characteristics, their meanings are plural. Similarly, such words as *eyeglasses, pants,* and *scissors* generally take plural verbs.

PLURAL Only my green **pants are** in the laundry.

Indefinite Pronouns

Some indefinite pronouns are always singular, some are always plural, and some may be either singular or plural. Prepositional phrases do not affect subject–verb agreement.

RULE 19.1.13

Singular indefinite pronouns take singular verbs. Plural indefinite pronouns take plural verbs.

SINGULAR *anybody, anyone, anything, each, either, everybody, everyone, everything, neither, nobody, no one, nothing, somebody, someone, something*

PLURAL *both, few, many, others, several*

SINGULAR **Everyone** on the rescue squad **has left**.

PLURAL **Many** of the houses **were repaired**.

RULE 19.1.14

The pronouns *all, any, more, most, none,* and *some* usually take a singular verb if the antecedent is singular, and a plural verb if it is plural.

SINGULAR **Some** of the area **was ruined** by the hurricane.

PLURAL **Some** of the damaged cars **are** beyond repair.

See Practice 19.1H

Titles of Creative Works and Names of Organizations

Plural words in the title of a creative work or in the name of an organization do not affect subject–verb agreement.

RULE 19.1.15

A title of a creative work or name of an organization is singular and must have a singular verb.

EXAMPLES **The National Institutes of Health is** a helpful agency.
(organization)

Sunflowers by Vincent Van Gogh **is** a famous painting.
(creative work)

Amounts and Measurements

Although they appear to be plural, most amounts and measurements actually express single units or ideas.

A noun expressing an amount or measurement is usually singular and requires a singular verb.

RULE 19.1.16

EXAMPLES **Two hundred million dollars is** the cost in property damage from the snowstorm.
(*Two hundred million dollars* is one sum of money.)

Two miles was our distance from the nearest food store.
(*Two miles* is a single distance.)

Three quarters of the class **attends** the big game.
(*Three quarters* is one part of the class.)

Half of the trees **were uprooted**.

(*Half* refers to a number of individual trees, and not part of an individual tree, so it is plural.)

PRACTICE 19.1E Identifying Subjects and Verbs in Inverted Sentences

Read each sentence. Then, identify the subject and verb in each sentence.

EXAMPLE Outside our kitchen window blooms a beautiful rosebush.

ANSWER *subject:* ***rosebush****; verb:* ***blooms***

1. Between the street and our house is a small creek.
2. Here is your copy of the rehearsal schedule.
3. Into the mall file the many eager shoppers.
4. All around the teacher sit the quiet students.
5. Here comes the marching band.
6. Ahead of Efrem runs his dog.
7. Next to the school was a new playground.
8. Here are the best movies of the year.
9. There is no doubt about who will win.
10. To the south stretches a shimmering lake.

PRACTICE 19.1F Making Linking Verbs Agree With Subjects

Read each sentence. Then, rewrite each sentence to make the linking verb agree with the subject. If the sentence is correct, write *correct*.

EXAMPLE The room, decorated with posters, are on the left.

ANSWER *The room, decorated with posters,* ***is*** *on the left.*

11. In the refrigerator are two cheese sandwiches in plastic baggies.
12. There are the photo of my sand sculptures.
13. Here are the last plate of spaghetti.
14. Strawberries is an excellent source of vitamin C.
15. Our bikes, stored in the garage, is in good shape.
16. See if there's a hammer on the shelf.
17. One of the ways to get to my house are to turn on Gibson Road.
18. Civics are offered to all high school students.
19. Another problem we discovered were that the computer had a virus.
20. In the trees are a wild turkey.

SPEAKING APPLICATION

Take turns with a partner. Tell about your summer plans, using four inverted sentences. Your partner should listen for and identify the subject and verb in each of your sentences.

WRITING APPLICATION

Write a paragraph describing your home. Be sure to write some sentences where the linking verb does not agree with the subject. Exchange papers with a partner. Your partner should correct the subject-verb errors.

PRACTICE 19.1G Making Verbs Agree With Collective Nouns

Read each sentence. Then, choose the correct verb that agrees with the collective noun.

EXAMPLE The colony of ants (are being, is being) observed.

ANSWER *is being*

1. The drama club (is performing, are performing) individual skits.
2. The marching band (practices, practice) on the football field.
3. Our American government class (is going, are going) to visit the courthouse.
4. The film crew (uses, use) the studio every afternoon.
5. The crowd (is choosing, are choosing) their own seats.
6. The group of friends (goes, go) to separate classrooms.
7. The art club (gives, give) out free brushes.
8. The audience of fans (is, are) disappointed in the performance.
9. The Gorman family (travels, travel) to visit friends in Oregon each year.
10. The band of musicians (sing, sings) well.

PRACTICE 19.1H Making Verbs Agree With Indefinite Pronouns

Read each sentence. Then, complete each sentence by supplying a verb that agrees with the subject.

EXAMPLE None of the students _____ absent today.

ANSWER *None of the students **is** absent today.*

11. Nobody _____ my tennis racket.
12. Only a few people _____ the meeting.
13. Everyone _____ to order tacos.
14. Not many students _____ the answer.
15. All of the food _____ organically grown.
16. Either movie _____ fine with me.
17. More of the kittens _____ been adopted.
18. Somebody _____ to wait for Fatima.
19. Something _____ on the carpet.
20. Each of the bags _____ packed with canned goods.

WRITING APPLICATION

Research on the Internet five unusual collective nouns that refer to groups of animals, such as *plague of locusts*. Write a sentence for each collective noun. Make sure that the verb in each of your sentences agrees with the collective noun.

SPEAKING APPLICATION

Take turns with a partner. Use sentences in Practice 19.1H as models to say similar sentences. Your partner should supply a verb that agrees with each of your subjects.

Test Warm-Up

DIRECTIONS
Read the introduction and the passage that follows. Then, answer the questions to show that you can use and understand the function of subject-verb agreement in reading and writing.

Devoted to exercise, Leia wrote this paragraph about aerobics. Read the paragraph and think about the changes you would suggest as a peer editor. When you finish reading, answer the questions that follow.

Aerobically Speaking

(1) Aerobics is a great form of exercise. (2) The National Institutes of Health are an organization that recognizes the many benefits of aerobic exercise. (3) In fact, everyone in the different branches of medicine agree that working out improves health. (4) Two benefits are a stronger heart and an improved mood. (5) Another benefit is a longer life. (6) Aerobics has many health benefits, and they are an important reason to work out, but I do aerobics because it is fun.

---

1 What change, if any, should be made in sentence 2?

A Change ***many*** to **most**

B Change ***are*** to **were**

C Change ***are*** to **is**

D Make no change

2 What change, if any, should be made in sentence 3?

F Change ***Everyone*** to **Everybody**

G Change ***agree*** to **agrees**

H Change ***branches*** to **branch**

J Make no change

3 What is the most effective way to combine sentences 4 and 5?

A Some benefits is a stronger heart, an improved mood and a longer life.

B Some benefits are a stronger heart, an improved mood, and a longer life.

C Each benefit are a stronger heart, an improved mood, and a longer life.

D A stronger heart, an improved mood, and a longer life is each benefits.

4 What is the most effective way to rewrite the ideas in sentence 6?

F The health benefits of aerobics is an important reason to work out.

G Aerobics have many health benefits and are an important reason to work out, and I do it because it is fun.

H While health benefits is an important reason to work out, I do aerobics for fun.

J While health benefits are an important reason to work out, I do aerobics because they are fun.

19.2 Pronoun–Antecedent Agreement

Like a subject and its verb, a pronoun and its antecedent must agree. An **antecedent** is the word or group of words for which the pronoun stands.

Find It/FIX IT
17
Grammar Game Plan

WRITING COACH Online
www.phwritingcoach.com

Grammar Practice
Practice your grammar skills with Writing Coach Online.

Grammar Games
Test your knowledge of grammar in this fast-paced interactive video game.

Agreement Between Personal Pronouns and Antecedents

While a subject and verb must agree only in number, a personal pronoun and its antecedent must agree in three ways.

A personal pronoun must agree with its antecedent in number, person, and gender.

RULE 19.2.1

The **number** of a pronoun indicates whether it is singular or plural. **Person** refers to a pronoun's ability to indicate either the person speaking (first person), the person spoken to (second person), or the person, place, or thing spoken about (third person). **Gender** is the characteristic of nouns and pronouns that indicates whether the word is *masculine* (referring to males), *feminine* (referring to females), or *neuter* (referring to neither males nor females).

The only pronouns that indicate gender are third-person singular personal pronouns.

GENDER OF THIRD-PERSON SINGULAR PRONOUNS	
Masculine	*he, him, his*
Feminine	*she, her, hers*
Neuter	*it, its*

In the example below, the pronoun *her* agrees with the antecedent *actress* in number (both are singular), in person (both are third person), and in gender (both are feminine).

EXAMPLE The actress has opened **her** home to the public.

Agreement in Number

There are three rules to keep in mind to determine the number of compound antecedents.

RULE 19.2.2

Use a singular personal pronoun when two or more singular antecedents are joined by *or* or *nor*.

EXAMPLES Either Craig **or** Todd will bring **his** model of a castle to class.

Neither Charlie **nor** Pepper will eat **his** new dog food.

RULE 19.2.3

Use a plural personal pronoun when two or more antecedents are joined by *and*.

EXAMPLE Melissa **and** I are studying for **our** exams.

An exception occurs when a distinction must be made between individual and joint ownership. If individual ownership is intended, use a singular pronoun to refer to a compound antecedent. If joint ownership is intended, use a plural pronoun.

SINGULAR **Thomas and Cecily** played **her** guitar.

PLURAL **Thomas and Cecily** paid for **their** guitar.

SINGULAR Neither **Tim nor Kevin** let me ride **his** horse.

PLURAL Neither **Tim nor Kevin** let me ride **their** horse.

The third rule applies to compound antecedents whose parts are mixed in number.

RULE 19.2.4

Use a plural personal pronoun if any part of a compound antecedent joined by *or* or *nor* is plural.

EXAMPLE If either the **teacher** or the **students** arrive, take **them** to the cafeteria.

See Practice 19.2A

Agreement in Person and Gender Avoid shifts in person or gender of pronouns.

As part of pronoun–antecedent agreement, take care not to shift either person or gender.

19.2.5 RULE

SHIFT IN PERSON **Mike** is planning to visit Windsor Castle because **you** can see how royalty lives.

CORRECT **Mike** is planning to visit Windsor Castle because **he** wants to see how royalty lives.

SHIFT IN GENDER The **horse** threw **its** head back and stood on **his** hind legs.

CORRECT The **horse** threw **its** head back and stood on **its** hind legs.

Generic Masculine Pronouns Traditionally, a masculine pronoun has been used to refer to a singular antecedent whose gender is unknown. Such use is called *generic* because it applies to both masculine and feminine genders. Many writers now prefer to use *his or her, he or she, him or her,* or to rephrase a sentence to eliminate the situation.

When gender is not specified, either use *his or her* or rewrite the sentence.

19.2.6 RULE

EXAMPLES Each **student** found a useful Web site on which to research **his or her report** on castles.

Students found useful Web sites on which to research **their reports** on castles.

See Practice 19.2B

PRACTICE 19.2A Making Personal Pronouns Agree With Their Antecedents

Read each sentence. Then, rewrite each sentence to include the correct personal pronoun.

EXAMPLE My sister and I visited _____ aunt and uncle.

ANSWER *My sister and I visited our aunt and uncle.*

1. Jim and Doreen called loudly from the cave, but nobody heard _____.
2. Annie will read _____ report to the class.
3. The president and the Congress announced _____ new ideas.
4. Either Ryan or Cal will drive _____ truck.
5. Neither Heather nor Celia had a pencil with _____.
6. Antonio said he had done _____ homework.
7. One of the girls has lost _____ backpack.
8. When my brothers or my sister celebrates a birthday, _____ always request cupcakes.
9. Either the boy or his brothers spoke to _____ parents.
10. Neither puppy will thrive if _____ is not well cared for.

PRACTICE 19.2B Revising for Agreement in Person and Gender

Read each sentence. Then, revise each sentence so that the personal pronoun agrees with the antecedent.

EXAMPLE All of the boys lost his money.

ANSWER *All of the boys lost their money.*

11. One of the managers gave his approval.
12. Every one of the girls has their assignments.
13. The hikers realized that you can't explore the Grand Canyon in just one day.
14. Neither of the students agreed to ask their parents.
15. One of the men will have to volunteer their time.
16. One of the monkeys had her tail wrapped around a tree limb.
17. Each of the women was given their award.
18. All of the parents refused to give her consent.
19. Both of my relatives sent her congratulations.
20. None of the men had lost their maps.

SPEAKING APPLICATION

Take turns with a partner. Tell about members of your family. Use several different personal pronouns in your sentences. Your partner should listen for and name the personal pronouns you use and tell whether they agree with their antecedents.

WRITING APPLICATION

Use sentences 14, 15, and 16 as models to write similar sentences. Then, exchange papers with a partner. Your partner should revise each sentence to make the personal pronoun agree with the antecedent.

Agreement With Indefinite Pronouns

When an indefinite pronoun, such as *each, all,* or *most,* is used with a personal pronoun, the pronouns must agree.

Use a plural personal pronoun when the antecedent is a plural indefinite pronoun. RULE 19.2.7

EXAMPLES **Many** of the children were excited about **their** music lessons.

All of the boys forgot to bring **their** books.

When both pronouns are singular, a similar rule applies.

Use a singular personal pronoun when the antecedent is a singular indefinite pronoun. RULE 19.2.8

In the first example, the personal pronoun *his* agrees in number with the singular indefinite pronoun *one.* The gender (masculine) is determined by the word *boys.*

EXAMPLES Only **one** of the boys practiced **his** trumpet.

One of the girls remembered to bring **her** music.

If other words in the sentence do not indicate a gender, you may use *him or her, he or she, his or her,* or rephrase the sentence.

EXAMPLES **Each** of the musicians wore **his or her** new band uniform.

The **musicians** wore **their** new band uniforms.

For indefinite pronouns that can be either singular or plural, such as *all, any, more, most, none,* and *some,* agreement depends on the antecedent of the indefinite pronoun.

EXAMPLES **Most** of the music had lost **its** appeal.
(The antecedent of *most* is *music,* which is singular.)

Most of the listeners wanted **their** money back.
(The antecedent of *most* is *listeners,* which is plural.)

Some of the food **was** cold.
(The antecedent of *some* is *food,* which is singular.)

All of the documents **were** on the table.
(The antecedent of *all* is *documents,* which is plural.)

In some situations, strict grammatical agreement may be illogical. In these situations, either let the meaning of the sentence determine the number of the personal pronoun, or reword the sentence.

ILLOGICAL When **each of the telephones** rang, I answered **it** as quickly as possible.

MORE LOGICAL When **each of the telephones** rang, I answered **them** as quickly as possible.

MORE LOGICAL When **all of the telephones** rang, I answered **them** as quickly as possible.

See Practice 19.2C

Agreement With Reflexive Pronouns

Reflexive pronouns, which end in *-self* or *-selves,* should only refer to a word earlier in the same sentence.

RULE 19.2.9

A reflexive pronoun must agree with an antecedent that is clearly stated.

EXAMPLES **Frank** made dinner for **himself**.

You should consider **yourself** lucky.

Class **clowns** enjoy making fools of **themselves**.

See Practice 19.2D

PRACTICE 19.2C Making Personal and Indefinite Pronouns Agree

Read each sentence. Then, rewrite each sentence, filling in the blank with an appropriate personal pronoun that agrees with the indefinite pronoun.

EXAMPLE Each of the students presented _____ project.

ANSWER *Each of the students presented his or her project.*

1. Each of the women wanted _____ turn to speak.
2. Every student in our class finished _____ paper on time.
3. Many students in the class already paid _____ share of the party expenses.
4. All of the artists displayed _____ paintings at the art show.
5. One of the tigers in the zoo hurt _____ paw.
6. A few of the dancers brought _____ shoes.
7. Each of the male leads remembered _____ lines.
8. Anyone who needs help with a particular scene may review _____ script.
9. Several of the cats had _____ claws clipped.
10. Most of the girls' softball team members brought _____ rule book.

PRACTICE 19.2D Supplying Reflexive Pronouns

Read each sentence. Then, write the correct reflexive pronoun that agrees with the antecedent in each sentence.

EXAMPLE We told _____ to keep working.

ANSWER *ourselves*

11. Gina, please help _____ to some pizza.
12. The musicians amused _____ by playing different musical selections.
13. Louie and I will take the dogs to the park by _____.
14. Amanda and Wilson kept _____ busy by playing a board game.
15. She found _____ reading another chapter before she went to sleep.
16. Jason wrote the entire play by _____.
17. I made _____ a salad for lunch.
18. Sal was worried that he might hurt _____ while running the obstacle course.
19. All of you should be proud of _____ for the improvements you have made in your writing.
20. Deb gave _____ a manicure before her sister's wedding.

SPEAKING APPLICATION

Take turns with a partner. Choose three indefinite pronouns. Your partner should say sentences, using a personal pronoun that agrees with each indefinite pronoun.

WRITING APPLICATION

Use sentences 11, 12, and 15 as models to write similar sentences. Then, exchange papers with a partner. Your partner should rewrite each sentence, using the correct reflexive pronoun that agrees with the antecedent.

Find It/FIX IT
4
Grammar Game Plan

19.3 Special Problems With Pronoun Agreement

This section will show you how to avoid some common errors that can obscure the meaning of your sentences.

WRITING COACH Online
www.phwritingcoach.com

Grammar Practice
Practice your grammar skills with Writing Coach Online.

Grammar Games
Test your knowledge of grammar in this fast-paced interactive video game.

Vague Pronoun References

One basic rule governs all of the rules for pronoun reference.

RULE 19.3.1

To avoid confusion, a pronoun requires an antecedent that is either stated or clearly understood.

The pronouns *which, this, that,* and *these* should not be used to refer to a vague or overly general idea.

In the following example, it is impossible to determine exactly what the pronoun *these* stands for because it may refer to three different groups of words.

VAGUE REFERENCE Jay was carsick, the dog was restless, and the air conditioner was broken. **These** made our trip to the aquarium unpleasant.

This vague reference can be corrected in two ways. One way is to change the pronoun to an adjective that modifies a specific noun. The second way is to revise the sentence so that the pronoun *these* is eliminated.

CORRECT Jay was carsick, the dog was restless, and the air conditioner was broken. **These misfortunes** made our trip to the aquarium unpleasant.

CORRECT Jay's carsickness, the dog's restlessness, and the air conditioner's breakdown made our trip to the aquarium unpleasant.

RULE 19.3.2

The personal pronouns *it, they,* and *you* should always have a clear antecedent.

In the next example, the pronoun *it* has no clearly stated antecedent.

VAGUE REFERENCE Marge is studying marine mammals next year. **It** should be very educational.

Again, there are two methods of correction. The first method is to replace the personal pronoun with a specific noun. The second method is to revise the sentence entirely in order to make the whole idea clear.

CORRECT Marge is studying marine mammals next year. **The experience** should be very educational.

CORRECT **Marge's study** of marine mammals next year should be very educational.

In the next example, the pronoun *they* is used without an accurate antecedent.

VAGUE REFERENCE I enjoyed reading *Moby-Dick*, but **they** never explained what the whale symbolized.

CORRECT I enjoyed reading *Moby-Dick*, but **the author** never explained what the whale symbolized.

VAGUE REFERENCE When we arrived at the aquarium, **they** told us that the whale show was about to start.

CORRECT When we arrived at the aquarium, **the ticket taker** told us that the whale show was about to start.

RULE 19.3.3

Use *you* only when the reference is truly to the reader or listener.

VAGUE REFERENCE **You** couldn't understand a word Jim said.

CORRECT **We** couldn't understand a word Jim said.

VAGUE REFERENCE In the school my great-aunt attended, **you** were expected to stand up when addressed.

CORRECT In the school my great-aunt attended, **students** were expected to stand up when addressed.

Note About *It:* In many idiomatic expressions, the personal pronoun *it* has no specific antecedent. In statements such as "It is late," *it* is an idiom that is accepted as standard English.

See Practice 19.3A

Ambiguous Pronoun References

A pronoun is **ambiguous** if it can refer to more than one antecedent.

RULE 19.3.4

A pronoun should never refer to more than one antecedent.

In the following sentence, *he* is confusing because it can refer to either *Joe* or *Walt*. Revise such a sentence by changing the pronoun to a noun or rephrasing the sentence entirely.

AMBIGUOUS REFERENCE Joe told Walt about the whales **he** observed.

CORRECT Joe told Walt about the whales **Walt** observed.

(Joe knew about the whales.)

RULE 19.3.5

Do not repeat a personal pronoun in a sentence if it can refer to a different antecedent each time.

AMBIGUOUS REPETITION	When Jon asked his father if **he** could borrow the car, **he** said that **he** needed it.
CLEAR	When Jon asked his father if **he** could borrow the car, **Jon** said that **he** needed it.
CLEAR	When Jon asked his father if **he** could borrow the car, his **father** said that **he** needed it **himself**.

Notice that in the first sentence above, it is unclear whether *he* is referring to Jon or to his father. To eliminate the confusion, Jon's name was used in the second sentence. In the third sentence, the reflexive pronoun *himself* helps to clarify the meaning.

Avoiding Distant Pronoun References

A pronoun should be placed close to its antecedent.

A personal pronoun should always be close enough to its antecedent to prevent confusion.

RULE 19.3.6

A distant pronoun reference can be corrected by moving the pronoun closer to its antecedent or by changing the pronoun to a noun. In the example below, *it* is too far from the antecedent *leg*.

DISTANT REFERENCE	Molly shifted her weight from her injured leg. Two days ago she had fallen, cutting herself on the glass in the street. Now **it** was swathed in bandages.
CORRECT	Molly shifted her weight from her injured leg. Two days ago she had fallen, cutting herself on the glass in the street. Now her **leg** was swathed in bandages. (*Leg* replaces the pronoun *it*.)

See Practice 19.3B

PRACTICE 19.3A Correcting Vague Pronouns

Read each sentence. Then, rewrite each sentence to avoid the use of vague pronouns.

EXAMPLE At the end of the play, they bow to the audience.

ANSWER *At the end of the play, the actors bow to the audience.*

1. They predict that this summer will be very hot.
2. On the news, it mentioned that people are saving more money.
3. The road was dangerous because they had not yet cleared the snow.
4. The flyer says that you must be eighteen to enter.
5. To learn to play an instrument, you must practice often.
6. After forgetting her lines in the play, my sister did not want to try it again.
7. This is the movie that they have raved about in all the papers.
8. You have to pass a swimming test in order to become a lifeguard.
9. During the basketball game, they called a lot of fouls on both teams.
10. In the club, you have to pay dues every six months.

PRACTICE 19.3B Recognizing Ambiguous Pronouns

Read each sentence. Then, rewrite each sentence to avoid the use of ambiguous pronouns.

EXAMPLE Tasha told Annie that she must not be late for the party.

ANSWER *Tasha told Annie that Annie must not be late for the party.*

11. Sammie left the car in the garage without locking it.
12. Mike told Ethan that his bicycle had a flat tire.
13. When Mother shops for my sister, she is usually distracted.
14. Take the shoes out of the bags and throw them away.
15. Whenever Andrea talks to Evita, she enjoys the conversation.
16. Aunt Mary fed Kirsten before she took a nap.
17. Take the curtain off the window and wash it.
18. The polls said that our choices for city council would lose, but they are often wrong.
19. Whenever Serena calls Karen, she never gets a chance to say much.
20. When Andrew invites Omar to go to the movies, he is always late.

SPEAKING APPLICATION

Take turns with a partner. Use sentences from Practice 19.3A as models to say similar sentences that contain vague pronoun references. Your partner should reword each sentence to make it clearer.

WRITING APPLICATION

Use sentences 11, 12, and 15 as models to write similar sentences. Then, exchange papers with a partner. Your partner should rewrite each sentence, correcting the ambiguous pronoun references.

CHAPTER 20

USING MODIFIERS

Understanding how to use different degrees of adjectives and adverbs as modifiers will help you to write logical comparisons.

WRITE GUY *Jeff Anderson, M.Ed.*

WHAT DO YOU NOTICE?

Hunt for degrees of comparison as you zoom in on this sentence from the first inaugural address by President Franklin Delano Roosevelt.

MENTOR TEXT

> That is why our constitutional system has proved itself the most superbly enduring political mechanism the modern world has produced.

Now, ask yourself the following questions:

- What modifier does the speaker use to make a comparison in this sentence?
- What is being compared in the sentence?

The speaker uses the modifier *most* to form the superlative degree of the adverb *superbly.* The superlative degree is used to compare three or more things. The speaker uses the adverbial phrase *most superbly* to describe *enduring.* He is comparing our constitutional system to *all* other political mechanisms in the modern world by saying that no other can match its endurance.

Grammar for Writers Using modifiers is an effective way for writers to demonstrate their viewpoints. Check your modifiers to be sure you have used the appropriate degrees of comparison.

Your penmanship is much better than mine.
I agree. In this case, there's no comparison.

20.1 Degrees of Comparison

In the English language, there are three degrees, or forms, of most adjectives and adverbs that are used in comparisons.

WRITING COACH **Online**
www.phwritingcoach.com

Grammar Tutorials
Brush up on your Grammar skills with these animated videos.

Grammar Practice
Practice your grammar skills with Writing Coach Online.

Grammar Games
Test your knowledge of grammar in this fast-paced interactive video game.

Recognizing Degrees of Comparison

In order to write effective comparisons, you first need to know the three degrees.

RULE 20.1.1

The three degrees of comparison are the positive, the comparative, and the superlative.

The following chart shows adjectives and adverbs in each of the three degrees. Notice the three different ways that modifiers are changed to show degree: (1) by adding *-er* or *-est*, (2) by adding *more* or *most*, and (3) by using entirely different words.

DEGREES OF ADJECTIVES		
POSITIVE	COMPARATIVE	SUPERLATIVE
slow	slower	slowest
disagreeable	more disagreeable	most disagreeable
good	better	best
DEGREES OF ADVERBS		
slowly	more slowly	most slowly
disagreeably	more disagreeably	most disagreeably
well	better	best

See Practice 20.1A

Regular Forms

Adjectives and adverbs can be either **regular** or **irregular,** depending on how their comparative and superlative degrees are formed. The degrees of most adjectives and adverbs are formed regularly. The number of syllables in regular modifiers determines how their degrees are formed.

RULE 20.1.2

Use *-er* or *more* to form the comparative degree and *-est* or *most* to form the superlative degree of most one- and two-syllable modifiers.

EXAMPLES	smart	smarter	smartest
	harmful	more harmful	most harmful

RULE 20.1.3

All adverbs that end in *-ly* form their comparative and superlative degrees with *more* and *most*.

EXAMPLES	curtly	more curtly	most curtly
	shrewdly	more shrewdly	most shrewdly

RULE 20.1.4

Use *more* and *most* to form the comparative and superlative degrees of all modifiers with three or more syllables.

EXAMPLES	beautiful	more beautiful	most beautiful
	generous	more generous	most generous

Note About Comparisons With *Less* and *Least*: *Less* and *least* can be used to form another version of the comparative and superlative degrees of most modifiers.

EXAMPLES	soft	less soft	least soft
	appetizing	less appetizing	least appetizing

See Practice 20.1B

Irregular Forms

The comparative and superlative degrees of a few commonly used adjectives and adverbs are formed in unpredictable ways.

RULE 20.1.5

The irregular comparative and superlative forms of certain adjectives and adverbs must be memorized.

In the chart on the following page, the form of some irregular modifiers differs only in the positive degree. The modifiers *bad, badly,* and *ill*, for example, all have the same comparative and superlative degrees *(worse, worst)*.

PRACTICE 20.1C Supplying Irregular Comparative and Superlative Forms

Read each modifier. Then, write its irregular comparative and superlative forms.

EXAMPLE good
ANSWER *better, best*

1. little (amount)
2. much
3. bad
4. many
5. far (distance)
6. far (extent)
7. well
8. badly
9. late
10. ill

PRACTICE 20.1D Supplying Irregular Modifiers

Read each sentence. Then, fill in the blank with the form of the modifier indicated in parentheses that best completes each sentence.

EXAMPLE I performed the clarinet solo _____ than I ever had before. (good)
ANSWER *better*

11. During the track meet, I threw the javelin the _____. (far)
12. _____ students ride the bus to school than walk. (many)
13. Because I practiced every day, I was able to perform at my _____. (good)
14. Before I begin writing my paper, I plan to research the topic _____. (far)
15. Because my alarm didn't go off, I was the _____ student on the bus. (late)
16. To help control blood pressure, patients should try to use _____ salt in their cooking. (little)
17. I sometimes hum off-key, but I sing _____. (badly)
18. The _____ I can do is buy her lunch. (little)
19. When I sprained my ankle, the pain was always the _____ at night. (bad)
20. According to our records, the _____ people attended the fair on Saturday. (many)

SPEAKING APPLICATION

Take turns with a partner. Say sentences with irregular comparative and superlative forms. Your partner should indicate if incorrect comparisons have been used and suggest corrections.

WRITING APPLICATION

Write pairs of sentences in which you use *farther* and *further*, *worse* and *worst*, and *more* and *most* correctly.

20.2 Making Clear Comparisons

The comparative and superlative degrees help you make comparisons that are clear and logical.

WRITING COACH Online

www.phwritingcoach.com

Grammar Practice

Practice your grammar skills with Writing Coach Online.

Grammar Games

Test your knowledge of grammar in this fast-paced interactive video game.

Using Comparative and Superlative Degrees

One basic rule that has two parts covers the correct use of comparative and superlative forms.

RULE 20.2.1 Use the **comparative degree** to compare two persons, places, or things. Use the **superlative degree** to compare three or more persons, places, or things.

The context of a sentence should indicate whether two items or more than two items are being compared.

COMPARATIVE My calculator is **more dependable** than Troy's.

My dog is **larger** than his.

He requires **less money** than she does.

SUPERLATIVE Emily is the **most dependable** friend I have.

This is the **largest** gym I have ever seen.

He is the **least materialistic** person I know.

See Practice 20.2A

In informal writing, the superlative degree is sometimes used just for emphasis, without any specific comparison.

EXAMPLE He is the **greatest**!

Note About Double Comparisons: A double comparison is caused by using both *-er* and *more* or both *-est* and *most* to form a regular modifier or by adding an extra comparison form to an irregular modifier.

See Practice 20.2B
See Practice 20.2C
See Practice 20.2D

INCORRECT Your workload is **more heavier** than mine.

CORRECT Your workload is **heavier** than mine.

PRACTICE 20.2A Recognizing When to Use Comparative and Superlative Degrees

Read each set of items. Then, tell if the comparative or superlative degree would be used to compare the items within each set.

EXAMPLE cars, buses, trains

ANSWER *superlative*

1. barns, silos
2. chickadees, finches, wrens
3. a refreshing nap, a deep sleep
4. ravioli, dumplings
5. the film studio, the director's office, the dressing room
6. geometry, algebra
7. Jason's Auto Repair, Car Crash Headquarters
8. your navy shirt, your lilac sweater, your pink cardigan
9. my car collection, Dad's stamp collection
10. a wintry evening, a sunny afternoon, a beautiful sunset

PRACTICE 20.2B Identifying Comparative and Superlative Forms

Read each sentence. Then, identify each sentence as using the *comparative* degree or *superlative* degree.

EXAMPLE The blue van is better on gas mileage than the red pick-up truck.

ANSWER *comparative*

11. The white picket fence is closer to the house than the split-rail fence.
12. My Junior Achievement meetings last longer than my chess club meetings.
13. Gregory is the most muscular person at the gym.
14. The Burj Dubai is the tallest building in the world.
15. The cherries we picked from our tree are sweeter than those from the store.
16. This is the least realistic sketch in the exhibit.
17. Pine Creek Park is farther from school than Timberland Park.
18. Border collies are the greatest!
19. The Northern Lights are the most beautiful sight I have ever seen.
20. The yellow crate holds more than the blue one.

SPEAKING APPLICATION

Take turns with a partner. Choose two sets of items from Practice 20.2A and say sentences using the comparative or superlative degree to compare the items within each set.

WRITING APPLICATION

Review Practice 20.2B. For every sentence that uses the comparative degree, write a similar sentence that contains the superlative degree.

PRACTICE 20.2C Supplying the Comparative and Superlative Degrees of Modifiers

Read each sentence. Then, fill in the blank with the correct form of the underlined modifier.

EXAMPLE I may have little money, but he has _____ than I do.

ANSWER *less*

1. Salmon tastes good, but trout tastes _____.
2. Tanya is late, but Nellie is usually _____.
3. James danced better than Kerri did, but Sam danced the _____.
4. Brian is funny, but of all the students, Steve is the _____.
5. Many of the books are suspenseful, but this one is _____.
6. Today, the weather is warm, but the weather will be _____ tomorrow.
7. Kara is sad that the class trip is over, but Paula is the _____ in the group.
8. Eduardo's house is far from town, but Hannah's house is even _____.
9. All of my friends are fun, but Mandy is _____. (fun)
10. Dallas is farther from Houston than Austin is, but Amarillo is the _____ from Houston.

PRACTICE 20.2D Revising Sentences to Correct Errors in Modifier Usage

Read each sentence. Then, rewrite each sentence, correcting any errors in the usage of modifiers to make comparisons. If a sentence contains no errors, write *correct*.

EXAMPLE The patient seems somewhat best today.

ANSWER *The patient seems somewhat better today.*

11. Mom's health is most robust than it was last year.
12. Your memory is more best than mine.
13. The tractor moved more slower across the field than on the road.
14. This sculpture is the better artwork I have ever created.
15. I thought the movie was more interesting than the book.
16. She is best in biology than she is in reading.
17. We arrived more earlier than Tiffany.
18. The young tiger roared most ferociously.
19. Didn't the juggler in the red cape perform more better than the other juggler?
20. Of those three dancers, the third one dances the most skillfully.

SPEAKING APPLICATION

Take turns with a partner comparing two movies. Your partner should listen for and identify the comparisons in your sentences.

WRITING APPLICATION

Write three sentences with errors in modifier usage. Then, exchange papers with a partner. Your partner should correct your sentences.

Test Warm-Up

DIRECTIONS
Read the introduction and the passage that follows. Then, answer the questions to show that you can use and understand the function of using comparative and superlative degrees in reading and writing.

Bev wrote this paragraph about her family's ideas for a vacation. Read the paragraph and think about the changes you would suggest as a peer editor. When you finish reading, answer the questions that follow.

Destination Undetermined

(1) I like all three places our family is considering for vacation. (2) Cedar Point, the roller coaster capital of the world, would be the more thrilling to visit. (3) It is on Lake Erie, so we could boat, fish, and swim. (4) Niagara Falls is the second larger falls in the world! (5) This natural wonder would be spectacular, and Colonial Williamsburg would not be as spectacular. (6) However, Colonial Williamsburg has a historic village and theme parks, Busch Gardens Williamsburg and Water Country USA, offering least variety in activities than Niagara Falls. (7) This decision is tough!

1 What change, if any, should be made in sentence 2?

A Change ***more*** to **most**

B Change ***thrilling*** to **thrillingest**

C Change ***more thrilling*** to **thrillinger**

D Make no change

2 What change, if any, should be made in sentence 4?

F Change ***larger*** to **more large**

G Change ***larger*** to **most large**

H Change ***larger*** to **largest**

J Make no change

3 What is the most effective way to rewrite the ideas in sentence 5?

A This natural wonder would be spectacular, but not Colonial Williamsburg.

B This natural wonder would be spectacular more than Colonial Williamsburg would be.

C Colonial Williamsburg would be more spectacular than this natural wonder.

D Colonial Williamsburg would be less spectacular than this natural wonder.

4 The meaning of sentence 6 can be clarified by changing the word ***least*** to —

F **most**

G **even less**

H **worst**

J **greater**

Using Logical Comparisons

Two common usage problems are the comparison of unrelated items and the comparison of something with itself.

Balanced Comparisons

Be certain that things being compared in a sentence are similar.

Your sentences should only compare items of a similar kind.

RULE 20.2.2

The following unbalanced sentences illogically compare dissimilar things.

UNBALANCED **Jim's play** is better written than **Ray**.

CORRECT **Jim's play** is better written than **Ray's**.

UNBALANCED The **height of the bookcase** is greater than the **wall**.

CORRECT The **height of the bookcase** is greater than the **height of the wall**.

Note About *Other* and *Else* in Comparisons

Another illogical comparison results when something is inadvertently compared with itself.

When comparing one of a group with the rest of the group, make sure that your sentence contains the word *other* or the word *else*.

RULE 20.2.3

Adding *other* or *else* when comparing one person or thing with a group will make the comparison clear and logical.

ILLOGICAL John was busier than any clerk on the floor. (John cannot be busier than himself.)

LOGICAL John was busier than any **other** clerk on the floor.

See Practice 20.2E
See Practice 20.2F

PRACTICE 20.2E **Revising to Make Comparisons Balanced and Logical**

Read each sentence. Then, rewrite each sentence, correcting the unbalanced or illogical comparison.

EXAMPLE Jana's skating ability is better than Sara.

ANSWER *Jana's skating ability is better than Sara's.*

1. Carol's watch is smaller than Shaun.
2. Anna travels more than anyone in her family.
3. Steve's suitcase is newer than Molly.
4. Mark's parrot talks more cheerfully than Albert.
5. The Panthers have won more state championships than any football team.
6. Rob's skateboard is in better condition than Mike.
7. The student who answered the question speaks French better than anyone in our class.
8. Carolyn runs faster than any athlete on the track team.
9. Kevin's backpack is larger than Dan.
10. The length of Madison's desk is shorter than Jill.

PRACTICE 20.2F **Writing Clear Comparisons**

Read each sentence. Then, rewrite each sentence, filling in the blanks to make a comparison that is clear and logical.

EXAMPLE Joe's painting is better than ____.

ANSWER *Joe's painting is better than Rose's painting.*

11. Caroline is more talented than ____ in her class.
12. The size of Jupiter is larger than ____.
13. Felix's cat is more playful than ____.
14. That flower is brighter than ____ flower in the yard.
15. Margarita's guitar is better tuned than ____.
16. The smell of a rose is stronger than ____.
17. My foot is bigger than ____.
18. Sherilyn's photographs of mountains are more impressive than ____.
19. I prefer the color blue more than ____ color.
20. Thomas Edison is more famous than ____ scientist.

SPEAKING APPLICATION

Take turns with a partner. Say sentences that have unbalanced or illogical comparisons. Your partner should restate the sentences, using balanced and logical comparisons.

WRITING APPLICATION

Use sentences 12, 13, and 20 as models to write similar sentences. Then, exchange papers with a partner. Your partner should fill in the blanks to make the comparison in each sentence clear and logical.

Avoiding Comparisons With Absolute Modifiers

Some modifiers cannot be used logically to make comparisons because their meanings are *absolute*—that is, their meanings are entirely contained in the positive degree. For example, if a line is *vertical*, another line cannot be *more* vertical. Some other common absolute modifiers are *dead, entirely, fatal, final, identical, infinite, opposite, perfect, right, straight*, and *unique*.

Avoid using absolute modifiers illogically in comparisons.

RULE 20.2.4

INCORRECT The color pattern he chose was **most unique**.

CORRECT The color pattern he chose was **unique**.

Often, it is not only the word *more* or *most* that makes an absolute modifier illogical; sometimes it is best to replace the absolute modifier with one that expresses the intended meaning more precisely.

ILLOGICAL The color pattern he chose was **more unique** than Sandor's choice.

CORRECT The color pattern he chose was **more distinctive** than Sandor's choice.

Sometimes an absolute modifier may overstate the meaning that you want.

ILLOGICAL This hockey loss was the **most fatal**.

CORRECT This hockey loss was the **most severe**.

See Practice 20.2G
See Practice 20.2H

In the preceding example, *most fatal* is illogical because something is either fatal or it is not. However, even *fatal* is an overstatement. *Most severe* better conveys the intended meaning.

PRACTICE 20.2G **Revising Sentences to Correct Comparisons Using Absolute Modifiers**

Read each sentence. Then, correct each illogical comparison by replacing the absolute modifier with more precise words.

EXAMPLE The new painting she chose was most unique.

ANSWER *The new painting she chose was unique.*

1. The story he told was most entirely untrue.
2. The accident yesterday was more fatal.
3. The competition results were most final.
4. Her two brothers are more identical.
5. Scientists think that the realm of space is most infinite.
6. My two best friends are the most opposite in personality.
7. The color of the house is more perfect.
8. Sandy drew two most right angles in geometry.
9. For many, bubonic plague was severely fatal.
10. My mom's rosebush is more dead.

PRACTICE 20.2H **Revising Overstated Absolute Modifiers**

Read each sentence. Then, rewrite each sentence, revising the overstated absolute modifier.

EXAMPLE The plastic flowers are not quite real.

ANSWER *The plastic flowers are not real.*

11. The plan to build a new stadium is completely dead.
12. Maya's hypothesis was very wrong.
13. The dancer performed a very perfect leap into her partner's arms.
14. Maria was committed to singing her very absolute best in the musical.
15. Derrick treated all his friends more equally.
16. My decision to run in the marathon is extremely final.
17. The testimony of the witness was most entirely true.
18. Eva created a most unique design for a wedding gown.
19. The party last year was the most supremely fun event.
20. People and all other living things are most mortal.

SPEAKING APPLICATION

Take turns with a partner. Say sentences that incorrectly use absolute modifiers. Your partner should restate your sentences correctly.

WRITING APPLICATION

Write three sentences with overstated absolute modifiers. Then, exchange papers with a partner. Your partner should revise the overstated absolute modifiers in your sentences.

CHAPTER 21

MISCELLANEOUS PROBLEMS *in* USAGE

Knowing the rules of correct usage will help you construct sentences that communicate clearly.

WRITE GUY *Jeff Anderson, M.Ed.*

WHAT DO YOU NOTICE?

Note how prepositions are used as you zoom in on lines from the poem "Dream Deferred" by Langston Hughes.

MENTOR TEXT

What happens to a dream deferred?
Does it dry up
Like a raisin in the sun?
Or fester like a sore . . . ?

Now, ask yourself the following questions:

- How is the preposition *like* used in these lines?
- Could you use the preposition *as* in the same way? Why or why not?

Prepositions show the relationship of a noun or a pronoun to another word in a sentence. In the poem, *like* is used to mean "similar to" or "such as." While the phrase *as if* is similar in meaning to *like*, the preposition *as* cannot be used alone as a substitute for *like*.

Grammar for Writers Writers use prepositions to show relationships. Check how you use prepositions in order to clearly express what you mean in your writing.

I want to make fewer mistakes in usage.
Fewer is all right with me!
12

21.1 Negative Sentences

In English, only one *no* is needed in a sentence to deny or refuse something. You can express a negative idea with words such as *not* or *never* or with contractions such as *can't, couldn't,* and *wasn't.* (The ending *-n't* in a contraction is an abbreviation of *not.*)

WRITING COACH Online

www.phwritingcoach.com

Grammar Practice

Practice your grammar skills with Writing Coach Online.

Grammar Games

Test your knowledge of grammar in this fast-paced interactive video game.

Recognizing Double Negatives

Using two negative words in a sentence when one is sufficient is called a **double negative.** While double negatives may sometimes be used in informal speech, they should be avoided in formal English speech and writing.

RULE 21.1.1

Do not use **double negatives** in formal writing.

The following chart provides examples of double negatives and two ways each can be corrected.

DOUBLE NEGATIVE	CORRECTIONS
Starfish don't bother no one.	Starfish don't bother anyone. Starfish bother no one.
I haven't seen no whales.	I haven't seen any whales. I have seen no whales.
Tom never said nothing.	Tom never said anything. Tom said nothing.

Sentences that contain more than one clause can correctly contain more than one negative word. Each clause, however, should contain only one negative word.

EXAMPLES The fish **did not** survive because the tank **was not** properly aerated.

Even if you **don't** know an answer, you **shouldn't** leave a space blank.

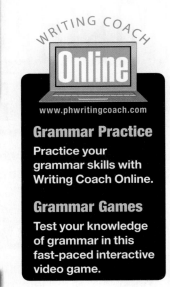

See Practice 21.1A

Forming Negative Sentences Correctly

There are three common ways to form negative sentences.

Using One Negative Word The most common ways to make a statement negative are to use one **negative word,** such as *never, no,* or *none,* or to add the contraction *-n't* to a helping verb.

Use only one negative word in each clause.

RULE 21.1.2

DOUBLE NEGATIVE We **don't** want **no** help from you.

PREFERRED We **don't** want **any** help from you.

We want **no** help from you.

Using *But* in a Negative Sense When *but* means "only," it usually acts as a negative. Do not use it with another negative word.

DOUBLE NEGATIVE There **wasn't but** one whale in the inlet.

PREFERRED There was **but** one whale in the inlet.

There was **only** one whale in the inlet.

Using *Barely, Hardly,* and *Scarcely* Each of these words is negative. If you use one of these words with another negative word, you create a double negative.

Do not use *barely, hardly,* or *scarcely* with another negative word.

RULE 21.1.3

DOUBLE NEGATIVE The tree **wasn't barely** visible in the dim light.

PREFERRED The tree was **barely** visible in the dim light.

DOUBLE NEGATIVE We **didn't scarcely** recognize you.

PREFERRED We **scarcely** recognized you.

DOUBLE NEGATIVE I **couldn't hardly** stop laughing.

PREFERRED I could **hardly** stop laughing.

See Practice 21.1B
See Practice 21.1C

Using Negatives to Create Understatement

Sometimes a writer wants to express an idea indirectly, either to minimize the importance of the idea or to draw attention to it. One such technique is called **understatement.**

RULE 21.1.4

Understatement can be achieved by using a negative word and a word with a negative prefix, such as *un-, in-, im-, dis-,* and *under-*.

EXAMPLES Keisha was **hardly inexperienced** at baking.

The home team did **not underestimate** its opponent.

The moon's light **isn't** completely **unromantic**.

These examples show that the writer is praising the people or things he or she is discussing. In the first example, the writer states that Keisha is actually quite experienced at baking. In the second example, the writer states that the home team understood the challenge they would face when they played the opposing team. In the third example, the writer states that the moon's light is romantic.

If you choose to use understatement, be sure to use it carefully so that you do not sound critical when you wish to praise.

EXAMPLES Malia does **not dislike** Sara's fruit pies and muffins.

Even though they were on sale, the jeans were **not inexpensive**.

In both examples above, the writer is actually making a negative statement. In the first example, although the writer "does not dislike" Sara's pies and muffins, he or she clearly doesn't like them very much, either. In the second example, the writer seems to think that, although the jeans were on sale, they were still expensive.

See Practice 21.1D

PRACTICE 21.1A Recognizing Sentences With Double Negatives

Read each sentence. Then, if the sentence contains a double negative, write the double negative. If the sentence is correct, write *correct*.

EXAMPLE The bird doesn't have no bright feathers.

ANSWER *doesn't, no*

1. Rashad didn't wake up in time, so she won't be on the bus.
2. I don't have no idea where the museum is.
3. Denzel hasn't had no dinner yet.
4. If you don't hurry, we won't see Chico's performance.
5. There weren't no people at the park yesterday.
6. Harvey hasn't started the book, so he knows nothing about the plot.
7. It wasn't nobody's fault.
8. There isn't no more room at the table.
9. Ellie never heard nothing about the bookstore's grand opening plans.
10. Jack hasn't never been to New York City.

PRACTICE 21.1B Revising Sentences to Avoid Double Negatives

Read each sentence. Then, rewrite each sentence to correct the double negative.

EXAMPLE The stranded explorers hadn't had no food for days.

ANSWER *The stranded explorers hadn't had any food for days.*

11. You shouldn't have said nothing about our trip.
12. We couldn't hardly stand the suspense toward the end of the movie.
13. Are you sure I can't bring no book?
14. The missing cat wasn't nowhere in sight.
15. You can be sure Sam won't eat none of those desserts.
16. Mrs. Fernandez didn't say nothing about her vacation.
17. We don't need no more players.
18. They can't never get cell phone reception there.
19. There wasn't barely an inch of snow by morning.
20. He couldn't find none of the lost jewelry.

SPEAKING APPLICATION

Take turns with a partner. Say sentences that contain double negatives. Your partner should listen to and correct your sentences to avoid the double negatives.

WRITING APPLICATION

In Practice 21.1A, you decided which sentences contained double negatives. Rewrite each of those sentences to eliminate the double negative. Read your sentences to a partner. Your partner should tell if you corrected the double negatives.

PRACTICE 21.1C Rewriting Sentences to Avoid Double Negatives

Read each sentence. Then, rewrite each sentence to correct the double negative.

EXAMPLE Jim hadn't but one assignment to complete.

ANSWER *Jim had but one assignment to complete.*

1. Mona doesn't want no more chicken.
2. There wasn't but one pitchfork in the barn.
3. I hadn't scarcely fallen asleep when my alarm went off.
4. You don't hardly ever see her room this tidy.
5. The dog doesn't never sit when I give him the command.
6. I haven't barely started my geometry assignment.
7. You couldn't hardly see the dent in Joy's car.
8. There wasn't but one clean shirt in the closet.
9. Michael hasn't scarcely any paper left in this notebook.
10. I haven't seen no finches at the bird feeder lately.

PRACTICE 21.1D Recognizing Understatement

Read each sentence. Then, if the sentence expresses understatement, write *understatement* and the words that create the understatement. If the sentence does not express understatement, write *No understatement expressed.*

EXAMPLE Jorge doesn't seem unenthusiastic about running for student council.

ANSWER *understatement; doesn't, unenthusiastic*

11. Cara does not understand the directions.
12. She did not overestimate how long it would take to get here.
13. Paulo is not the most insensitive person.
14. Mary doesn't think Mike is very imaginative.
15. My coach was hardly disappointed with the score.
16. I don't find the juggler impressive.
17. I was not entirely disenchanted with the holiday display.
18. The invitation wasn't impersonal.
19. Your explanation isn't completely unbelievable.
20. Hester can't run a very long distance.

SPEAKING APPLICATION

Take turns with a partner. Use sentences from Practice 21.1C to say similar sentences with double negatives. Your partner should repeat your sentences, correcting the double negatives.

WRITING APPLICATION

Use Practice 21.1D to write similar sentences, some that contain understatement and some that don't. Exchange papers with a partner. In the sentences that use understatement, your partner should underline the words that express the understatement.

Test Warm-Up

DIRECTIONS
Read the introduction and the passage that follows. Then, answer the questions to show that you can use and understand the function of negatives to create understatement in reading and writing.

Belinda wrote this paragraph after her visit to Niagara Falls. Read the paragraph and think about the changes you would suggest as a peer editor. When you finish reading, answer the questions that follow.

Fabulous Falls

(1) Niagara Falls is not the least impressive natural wonder. (2) The sheer force of the water is so incredible, it is scarcely unimaginable. (3) An average of 56 semi-truck trailers full of water goes over the falls every second. (4) You will not be delighted if you visit this amazing waterfall system. (5) The majesty and beauty of Niagara Falls are not estimated above what they deserve.

---

1 What is the most effective way to rewrite the ideas in sentence 1 to create understatement?

A Niagara Falls is the most impressive natural wonder.

B Niagara Falls is one of the most impressive natural wonders.

C Niagara Falls is not underrated as a natural wonder.

D Niagara Falls is not a natural wonder.

2 What is the most effective way to rewrite the ideas in sentence 2?

F It is so incredible that the sheer force of the water is not unimaginable.

G The sheer force of the water is imaginable in its incredibleness.

H The sheer force of the water is so incredible that it is scarcely imaginable.

J The sheer force of the water, so incredible, it is not unimaginable.

3 What change, if any, should be made in sentence 4?

A Change ***will not*** to **won't**

B Change ***delighted*** to **disappointed**

C Insert **totally** after ***be***

D Make no change

4 What is the most effective way to rewrite the ideas in sentence 5 to include understatement?

F The majesty and beauty of Niagara Falls are overestimated.

G The majesty and beauty of Niagara Falls are not underestimated.

H The majesty and beauty of Niagara Falls are underestimated.

J The majesty and beauty of Niagara Falls are underrated.

21.2 Common Usage Problems

Find It/FIX IT 1
Grammar Game Plan

Find It/FIX IT 5
Grammar Game Plan

WRITING COACH Online
www.phwritingcoach.com

Grammar Practice
Practice your grammar skills with Writing Coach Online.

Grammar Games
Test your knowledge of grammar in this fast-paced interactive video game.

(1) a, an The use of the article *a* or *an* is determined by the sound of the word that follows it. *A* is used before consonant sounds, while *an* is used before vowel sounds. Words beginning with *hon-*, *o-*, or *u-* may have either a consonant or a vowel sound.

EXAMPLES **a** honeybee (*h* sound)
a one-day excursion (*w* sound)
an honest merchant (no *h* sound)
an omen (*o* sound)
an urgent message (*u* sound)

(2) accept, except *Accept,* a verb, means "to receive." *Except,* a preposition, means "to leave out" or "other than."

VERB We must all **accept** responsibility for pollution.
PREPOSITION Everyone joined in the cleanup **except** Jermaine.

(3) adapt, adopt *Adapt* means "to change." *Adopt* means "to take as one's own."

EXAMPLES The Puritans had to **adapt** to the harsh weather.
Newcomers often **adopt** new customs.

(4) affect, effect *Affect* is almost always a verb meaning "to influence." *Effect,* usually a noun, means "a result." Sometimes, *effect* is a verb meaning "to bring about" or "to cause."

VERB An increase in prices **affects** everyone.
NOUN Economists study the **effect** of increased prices.
VERB The council **effected** many changes in tax policies.

(5) aggravate *Aggravate* means "to make worse." Avoid using this word to mean "annoy."

INCORRECT The chirping of the birds at 6:00 A.M. **aggravated** me.
PREFERRED The drought is **aggravating** the risk of forest fires.

(6) ain't *Ain't,* which was originally a contraction for *am not,* is no longer considered acceptable in standard English. Always use *am not,* and never use *ain't.* The exception is in certain instances of dialogue.

(7) all ready, already *All ready,* which consists of two separate words used as an adjective, means "ready." *Already,* which is an adverb, means "by or before this time" or "even now."

ADJECTIVE	The cowboys were **all ready** for the cattle drive.
ADVERB	My brother had **already** eaten breakfast.

(8) all right, alright *Alright* is a nonstandard spelling. Make sure you use the two-word form.

INCORRECT	The coach said it was **alright** for me to come to practice late.
PREFERRED	The coach said it was **all right** for me to come to practice late.

(9) all together, altogether *All together* means "together as a single group." *Altogether* means "completely" or "in all."

EXAMPLES	The birds flew **all together** in a chevron pattern.
	The old television set finally broke **altogether**.

(10) among, between Both of these words are prepositions. *Among* shows a connection between three or more items. *Between* generally shows a connection between two items.

EXAMPLES	The teacher divided the tasks **among** all the members of the class.
	It was difficult for voters to choose **between** Sammi and Len.

See Practice 21.2A

(11) anxious This adjective implies uneasiness, worry, or fear. Do not use it as a substitute for *eager.*

INCORRECT	The ranchers were **anxious** to start the cattle drive.
PREFERRED	The ranchers were **anxious** about cattle thieves.

(12) anyone, any one, everyone, every one *Anyone* and *everyone* mean "any person" or "every person." *Any one* means "any single person (or thing)"; *every one* means "every single person (or thing)."

EXAMPLES **Anyone** is eligible to try out for the chorus.

Any one of the singers may be chosen to perform a solo.

Everyone enjoys beautiful harmonies.

Every one of the singers can read music.

(13) anyway, anywhere, everywhere, nowhere, somewhere These adverbs should never end in *-s.*

INCORRECT There is a treasure hidden **somewheres** on this island.

PREFERRED There is a treasure hidden **somewhere** on this island.

(14) as Do not use the conjunction *as* to mean "because" or "since."

INCORRECT There are few plants growing in this area **as** there is very little sunlight.

PREFERRED There are few plants growing in this area **because** there is very little sunlight.

(15) as to *As to* is awkward. Replace it with *about.*

INCORRECT There is some doubt **as to** the effectiveness of this home remedy.

PREFERRED There is some doubt **about** the effectiveness of this home remedy.

(16) at Do not use *at* after *where.* Simply eliminate *at.*

INCORRECT We weren't sure **where** the town was **at** on the map.

PREFERRED We weren't sure **where** the town was on the map.

(17) at, about Avoid using *at* with *about*. Simply eliminate *at* or *about*.

INCORRECT	The city is located **at about** sea level.
PREFERRED	The city is located **at** sea level.

(18) awful, awfully *Awful* is used informally to mean that something is "extremely bad." *Awfully* is used informally to mean "very." Both words are overused and should be replaced with more descriptive words. In standard English speech and writing, *awful* should only be used to mean "inspiring fear or awe in someone."

OVERUSED	The heat is **awful**.
PREFERRED	The heat is **oppressive**.
OVERUSED	It can get **awfully** hot in equatorial countries.
PREFERRED	It can get **extremely** hot in equatorial countries.
OVERUSED	The weather report was **awful**.
PREFERRED	The weather report was **dreadful**.

(19) awhile, a while *Awhile* is an adverb that means "for a short time." *A while,* which is a noun, means "a period of time." It is usually used after the preposition *for* or *after.*

ADVERB	Let's wait **awhile** and play ball when it's cooler.
	Jake blew on his soup **awhile** so that it cooled more quickly.
NOUN	We remained in the meeting room for quite **a while**.
	It will take **a while** for me to learn the new guitar solo.

(20) beat, win When you *win*, you "achieve a victory in something." When you *beat* someone or something, you "overcome an opponent."

INCORRECT	Ellen **won** her sister playing checkers.
PREFERRED	Ellen **beat** her sister playing checkers.
	I hope I **win** the game.

See Practice 21.2B

PRACTICE 21.2A Recognizing Usage Problems 1–10

Read each sentence. Then, choose the correct item to complete each sentence.

EXAMPLE The drawing has (already, all ready) been held.

ANSWER *already*

1. What is (a, an) honorary degree?
2. Air pollution (affects, effects) bodies of water, monuments, statues, and buildings.
3. My cousins and I had only three dollars (among, between) us.
4. Amusement parks (ain't, aren't) my favorite places to visit.
5. Adding more lanes to the highways is (annoying, aggravating) the delays at the toll booths.
6. Are you (all ready, already) to go?
7. Everyone visited the museum (accept, except) my father.
8. Is everything (all right, alright) in the office?
9. The horses were standing (all together, altogether).
10. Carmen (adapted, adopted) the customs of each country that she lived in.

PRACTICE 21.2B Recognizing Usage Problems 11–20

Read each sentence. Then, choose the correct item to complete each sentence.

EXAMPLE Will (anyone, any one) of these toys appeal to a four-year-old?

ANSWER *any one*

11. They had plenty of suggestions (as to, about) how to spend the prize money.
12. Todd was so (anxious, eager) about the play that he couldn't sleep last night.
13. Our new kitten is (awfully, extremely) playful.
14. My new sweater is hanging (somewhere, somewheres) in the closet.
15. We need directions to determine where the new store (is at, is located).
16. The students are well prepared (as, because) they have studied hard.
17. (Everyone, Every one) in the class wants to participate in the science fair.
18. We hiked for (a while, awhile).
19. We will start the cleanup (at about, at) 2:00 P.M.
20. Tanisha (won, beat) all of her opponents in the chess tournament.

SPEAKING APPLICATION

Take turns with a partner. Choose any pair of words from Practice 21.2A (except from #4 or #8), and tell your partner your choices. Your partner should say two sentences, using both words correctly.

WRITING APPLICATION

Write two sentences that include usage problems. Exchange papers with a partner. Your partner should correct your sentences.

(21) because Do not use *because* after the phrase *the reason*. Say "The reason is that" or reword the sentence.

INCORRECT One **reason** to preserve the environment **is because** it will benefit humans.

PREFERRED One **reason** to preserve the environment **is that** it will benefit humans.

(22) being as, being that Avoid using either of these expressions. Use *because* instead.

INCORRECT **Being as** (or **that**) we were late, we decided to skip lunch.

PREFERRED **Because** we were late, we decided to skip lunch.

(23) beside, besides *Beside* means "at the side of" or "close to." *Besides* means "in addition to."

EXAMPLES Zebras often live **beside** gnus on the African plains.

Other animals **besides** zebras can be found nearby.

(24) bring, take *Bring* means "to carry from a distant place to a nearer one." *Take* means "to carry from a near place to a far one."

EXAMPLES Please **bring** your gym clothes home today so I can wash them.

You can **take** your clean clothes back tomorrow.

(25) can, may Use *can* to mean "have the ability to." Use *may* to mean "have permission to" or "to be likely to."

ABILITY Helene **can** spell many difficult words.

PERMISSION The teacher said we **may** use dictionaries to help correct our spelling.

POSSIBILITY I **may** need to look up these words in the dictionary.

(26) clipped words Avoid using clipped or shortened words, such as *gym* and *photo* in formal writing.

INFORMAL The basketball team posed for a **photo**.

FORMAL The basketball team posed for a **photograph**.

(27) different from, different than *Different from* is preferred in standard English.

INCORRECT Monday's menu is **different than** Tuesday's.

PREFERRED Monday's menu is **different from** Tuesday's.

(28) doesn't, don't Do not use *don't* with third-person singular subjects. Instead, use *doesn't*.

INCORRECT This cactus **don't** need to be watered each week.

PREFERRED This cactus **doesn't** need to be watered each week.

(29) done *Done* is the past participle of the verb *do*. It should always take a helping verb.

INCORRECT We **done** what we could to help.

PREFERRED We **have done** what we could to help.

(30) due to *Due to* means "caused by" and should be used only when the words *caused by* can be logically substituted.

INCORRECT The plant didn't grow **due to** lack of sunlight.

PREFERRED The plant's stunted growth was **due to** lack of sunlight.

See Practice 21.2C

(31) each other, one another These expressions usually are interchangeable. At times, however, *each other* is more logically used in reference to only two and *one another* in reference to more than two.

EXAMPLES The relay team must rely on **one another's** motivation to win.

The composer and lyricist appreciated **each other's** skills.

(32) farther, further *Farther* refers to distance. *Further* means "additional" or "to a greater degree or extent."

EXAMPLES Our art teacher showed us how to make some objects appear **farther** away than others.

Sharon's art skills are **further** developed than mine are.

(33) fewer, less Use *fewer* with things that can be counted. Use *less* with qualities and quantities that cannot be counted.

EXAMPLES **fewer** resources, **less** space

(34) get, got, gotten These forms of the verb *get* are acceptable in standard English, but a more specific word is preferable.

INCORRECT **get** a new suit, **got** a job, **have gotten** awards
PREFERRED **buy** a new suit, **found** a job, **have received** awards

(35) gone, went *Gone* is the past participle of the verb *go* and is used only with a helping verb. *Went* is the past tense of *go* and is never used with a helping verb.

INCORRECT Craig and Louise **gone** to the movies.
You really should **have went** to the game.
PREFERRED Craig and Louise **went** to the movies.
You really should **have gone** to the game.

(36) good, lovely, nice Replace these overused words with a more specific adjective.

WEAK **good** example, **lovely** painting, **nice** aroma
BETTER **fitting** example, **evocative** painting, **delicious** aroma

(37) in, into *In* refers to position. *Into* suggests motion.

EXAMPLES A wide variety of plants grew **in** the garden.
Plants absorb nutrients **into** their roots.

(38) irregardless Avoid this word in formal speech and writing. Instead, use *regardless*.

(39) just When you use *just* as an adverb to mean "no more than," place it immediately before the word it modifies.

INCORRECT She **just** received one letter.
PREFERRED She received **just** one letter.

(40) kind of, sort of Do not use these phrases in formal speech. Instead, use *rather* or *somewhat*.

See Practice 21.2D

PRACTICE 21.2C **Recognizing Usage Problems 21–30**

Read each sentence. Then, choose the correct item to complete each sentence.

EXAMPLE Did Timothy (bring, take) a book from the shelf?

ANSWER *take*

1. The man with a beard stood (beside, besides) the oak tree.
2. This lawn mower (don't, doesn't) work very well.
3. Practice is canceled (being as, because) the coach is out of town.
4. This movie is very (different from, different than) the one we saw last week.
5. The trains are running today; therefore, we (may, can) take the subway.
6. (Because, Being as) I broke the eggs, I had to return to the store.
7. The games are scheduled to be played in the middle school (gym, gymnasium).
8. The reason we got lost is (because, that) Joey gave us the wrong directions.
9. Tyrone (done, has done) so much work for the senior class.
10. The lateness of the bus was (because of, due to) mechanical problems.

PRACTICE 21.2D **Revising Sentences to Correct Usage Problems 31–40**

Read each sentence. Then, rewrite each sentence, correcting the errors in usage.

EXAMPLE The carnival will take place irregardless of the weather conditions.

ANSWER *The carnival will take place regardless of the weather conditions.*

11. After farther consideration, we realized that changes needed to be made to the proposal.
12. Customers with less than ten items may use the express line.
13. Mr. Lee had went to visit his daughter.
14. Let's go in the lobby to wait for them.
15. He just brought a single change of clothing.
16. Cherise was acting kind of mysterious.
17. Jermaine has got all *A*'s on his report card.
18. How much further do we have to go before we get to the Grand Canyon?
19. That color looks nice on you.
20. I had just gotten home when the telephone rang.

SPEAKING APPLICATION

Take turns with a partner. Say sentences with usage problems. Your partner should correct each of your sentences.

WRITING APPLICATION

Write a paragraph about a topic of your choice. Include sentences that contain usage problems. Exchange papers with a partner. Your partner should correct the usage problems in your paragraph.

(41) lay, lie The verb *lay* means "to put or set (something) down." Its principal parts—*lay, laying, laid, laid*—are followed by a direct object. The verb *lie* means "to recline." Its principal parts—*lie, lying, lay, lain*—are not followed by a direct object.

LAY	Please **lay** the basket on the counter.
	Those turtles are **laying** their eggs on the beach.
	When she arrived, she **laid** her keys on the table.
	The masons **have laid** three layers of bricks.
LIE	If you are sick, you should **lie** down in bed.
	The sunbathers **are lying** on lounges.
	Last week, many of them **lay** in hammocks.
	My brother **has lain** in bed all morning.

(42) learn, teach *Learn* means "to receive knowledge." *Teach* means "to give knowledge."

EXAMPLES	Dolphins can **learn** to follow commands.
	The trainer **taught** the killer whale a new trick.

(43) leave, let *Leave* means "to allow to remain." *Let* means "to permit."

INCORRECT	**Let** the snake alone, and it won't bother you.
PREFERRED	**Leave** the snake alone, and it won't bother you.

(44) like, as *Like* is a preposition meaning "similar to" or "such as." It should not be used in place of the conjunction *as*.

INCORRECT	She acted **like** she was nervous.
PREFERRED	She acted **as if** she was nervous.
	She acted **like** a nervous person.

(45) loose, lose *Loose* is usually an adjective or part of such idioms as *cut loose, turn loose,* or *break loose. Lose* is always a verb and usually means "to miss from one's possession."

EXAMPLES	The shelf is **loose**, and it may fall.
	Take care, so you don't **lose** your place in line.

(46) maybe, may be *Maybe* is an adverb meaning "perhaps." *May be* is a helping verb connected to a main verb.

ADVERB **Maybe** we can preserve the marshland.

VERB It **may be** too late to save the marshland.

(47) of Do not use *of* after a helping verb such as *should, would, could,* or *must.* Use *have* instead. Do not use *of* after *outside, inside, off,* and *atop.* Simply eliminate *of.*

INCORRECT If she had scored, Stella **would of** set a new record.

PREFERRED If she had scored, Stella **would have** set a new record.

(48) OK, O.K., okay In informal writing, *OK, O.K.,* and *okay* are acceptably used to mean "all right." Do not use them in standard English speech or writing, however.

INFORMAL The mayor said the new ruling was **okay**.

PREFERRED The mayor **approved** the new ruling.

(49) only *Only* should be placed immediately before the word it modifies. Placing it elsewhere can lead to confusion.

EXAMPLES **Only** Rita wanted to go bowling.
(No one else wanted to go bowling.)
Rita **only** wanted to go bowling.
(She didn't want to do anything else.)

(50) ought Do not use *ought* with *have* or *had.*

INCORRECT The settlers **hadn't ought** to have planted beans.

PREFERRED The settlers **ought not** to have planted beans.

See Practice 21.2E

(51) outside of Do not use this expression to mean "besides" or "except."

INCORRECT We couldn't name any desert **outside of** the Mojave.

PREFERRED We couldn't name any desert **except** the Mojave.

(52) plurals that do not end in *-s* The English plurals of certain nouns from Greek and Latin are formed as they were in their original language. Words such as *criteria, media,* and *phenomena* are plural. Their singular forms are *criterion, medium,* and *phenomenon.*

INCORRECT	The teacher explained the single most important **criteria** for the experiment.
PREFERRED	The teacher explained the single most important **criterion** for the experiment.
	The teacher explained the three most important **criteria** for the experiment.

(53) precede, proceed *Precede* means "to go before." *Proceed* means "to move or go forward."

EXAMPLES	Pasteur's research **preceded** Lister's by five years.
	Both men **proceeded** to investigate germ theory.

(54) principal, principle As an adjective, *principal* means "most important" or "chief." As a noun, it means "a person who has controlling authority," as in a school. *Principle* is always a noun that means "a fundamental law."

ADJECTIVE	The aorta is the **principal** artery in the body.
NOUN	Mr. Saunders is a **principal** in the new business.
NOUN	The company agreed to follow the **principles** of proper waste disposal.

(55) real *Real* means "authentic." In formal writing, avoid using *real* to mean "very" or "really."

INCORRECT	The crowd was **real** disappointed with the outcome.
PREFERRED	The crowd was **deeply** disappointed with the outcome.

(56) says *Says* should not be used as a substitute for *said.*

INCORRECT	Then the emperor **says**, "Let the games begin!"
PREFERRED	Then the emperor **said**, "Let the games begin!"

(57) seen *Seen* is a past participle and must be used with a helping verb.

INCORRECT	Stephon **seen** his brother in the crowd.
PREFERRED	Stephon **had seen** his brother in the crowd.

(58) set, sit *Set* means "to put (something) in a certain place." Its principal parts—*set, setting, set, set*—are usually followed by a direct object. *Sit* means "to be seated." Its principal parts—*sit, sitting, sat, sat*—are never followed by a direct object.

SET	She **set** the peaches carefully in the bowl.
	Stanley **is setting** the basket in the corner.
	They **set** the television on the new table.
	I **have set** the alarm to ring at six.
SIT	I **will sit** in my dad's chair tonight.
	You must **have been sitting** there for hours.
	She **sat** quietly at her desk and daydreamed.
	We **have sat** in these same seats at every game.

(59) so Avoid using *so* when you mean "so that."

INCORRECT	Sponges use filters **so** they can eat.
PREFERRED	Sponges use filters **so that** they can eat.

(60) than, then Use *than* in comparisons. Use *then* as an adverb to refer to time.

EXAMPLES	Danielle is more graceful **than** her sister.
	First, she studied ballet; **then**, she took jazz classes.

(61) that, which, who Use these relative pronouns in the following ways: *that* and *which* refer to things; *who* refers only to people.

EXAMPLES	I went to the exhibit **that** you told me to see.
	The walls, **which** were painted bright white, contrasted well with the paintings.
	I admire the artist **who** painted the works.

(62) their, there, they're *Their,* a possessive pronoun, always modifies a noun. *There* can be used either as an expletive at the beginning of a sentence or as an adverb showing place or direction. *They're* is a contraction of *they are.*

PRONOUN	Farmers spent all **their** time preparing **their** fields for the spring planting.
EXPLETIVE	**There** are so many problems for farmers to overcome to have a successful crop yield.
ADVERB	The fields over **there** will be planted with a different crop this year.
CONTRACTION	**They're** going to help us do the planting this year.

(63) them Do not use *them* as a substitute for *those.*

INCORRECT	**Them** horses are extremely fast.
PREFERRED	**Those** horses are extremely fast.

(64) to, too, two To begins a prepositional phrase or an infinitive. *Too,* an adverb, modifies adjectives and other adverbs and means "very" or "also." *Two* is a number.

PREPOSITION	**to** the ocean floor, **to** the shore
INFINITIVE	**to** swim, **to** fly
ADVERB	**too** tall, **too** quickly
NUMBER	**two** fins, **two** schools of fish

(65) when, where Do not use *when* or *where* immediately after a linking verb. Do not use *where* in place of *that.*

INCORRECT	Night is **when** you can watch fish feed. On the beach is **where** turtles lay eggs.
PREFERRED	Night is **the time** you can watch fish feed. On the beach is **the place** turtles lay eggs.

See Practice 21.2F

PRACTICE 21.2E Recognizing Usage Problems 41–50

Read each sentence. Then, choose the correct item to complete each sentence.

EXAMPLE The dog loves (lying, laying) in the sun.

ANSWER *lying*

1. (Let, Leave) your homework on top of your desk.
2. The (loose, lose) knot became untied.
3. Please (lie, lay) the bat on the ground.
4. Will the instructor (learn, teach) us the backstroke?
5. The girl (ought to have, should have) worn warmer clothes.
6. The cause of the leak (maybe, may be) a corroding pipe.
7. He ran (like, as if) he was being chased by wild animals.
8. The judge said that parking in front of the courthouse is (okay, permissible).
9. The flowers were placed (atop, atop of) the cake.
10. Of the group, (only Michelle, Michelle only) wanted to go fishing.

PRACTICE 21.2F Revising Sentences to Correct Usage Problems 51–65

Read each sentence. Then, rewrite each sentence, correcting the errors in usage.

EXAMPLE Them apples are ripening fast.

ANSWER *Those apples are ripening fast.*

11. In the oak tree is where we will build the treehouse.
12. I'm afraid their not home right now.
13. Two reveal a meteor, the night sky has to be cloudless.
14. Noon is when the sun is highest in the sky.
15. The students voted for the candidate that gave the best speech.
16. After I seen who was at the door, I smoothed my hair.
17. I have spent more time training mynah birds then training parrots.
18. The speeches proceeded the fireworks display.
19. Only a few fans set in the bleachers, waiting for the game to begin.
20. I believe that keeping one's promises is an important principal to live by.

SPEAKING APPLICATION

Reread each sentence in Practice 21.2E. Discuss with a partner which usage errors you've made in past writing assignments.

WRITING APPLICATION

Write four sentences that include usage problems. Exchange papers with a partner. Your partner should correct your sentences.

Cumulative Review Chapters 16–21

PRACTICE 1 Combining and Varying Sentences

Read the sentences. Then, rewrite each sentence according to the instructions in parentheses.

1. The fire alarm went off in the middle of second period. (Start with a prepositional phrase.)
2. The squirrel hid in the basement. (Invert the subject-verb order.)
3. Mike played hockey. He also played basketball to prove his athleticism. (Create a compound direct object; start with an infinitive.)
4. Texas is the second largest state in the United States. It is also known as the Lone Star State. Austin is the capital of Texas. (Create a compound sentence; include an appositive.)
5. Some students become nervous around new technology. Other students seem to enjoy the challenges. (Create a compound sentence; include a semicolon.)
6. Nell had been nervous about her solo. She sang beautifully. (Create a compound sentence; include a conjunction.)
7. We've had record high winds this summer. We've also had record rainfalls. (Create a compound sentence; start with a phrase.)
8. Mrs. Johnson's missing cat was in the tree. (Invert the subject-verb order.)
9. Meghan wanted to surprise her sister. She bought a special gift. She bought a cake. (Create a compound direct object; start with an infinitive.)
10. Mr. Yen is a great teacher. He is my mathematics teacher. He has taught for ten years. (Create a compound sentence; include an appositive.)

PRACTICE 2 Revising Pronoun and Verb Usage

Read the sentences. Then, revise them to eliminate problems in pronoun and verb usage. You may need to reorder, add, or eliminate words in a sentence.

1. Only someone who likes heights will enjoy their trip to the top of the tower.
2. Whom is the best singer in the chorus?
3. Anna and Jen decides to join the club.
4. He and his sister returned them life jackets to the rack in the boathouse.
5. My dad left the car for him and I.
6. A student who commits to excellence should have no fears about their future.
7. To who did you give the key?
8. Neither Tom nor me are responsible for that.
9. Everybody on the team have new uniforms.
10. Aunt Jo gave gifts to my sister and I.

PRACTICE 3 Revising for Correct Use of Active and Passive Voice

Read the sentences. Then, revise each sentence to be in the active voice. You may reorder, add, or delete words.

1. People in the audience were blinded by the bright lights onstage.
2. The homework assignment will be finished by Jeannie before bedtime.
3. The bake sale will be organized by Sara.
4. A time-out was called by one of the coaches.
5. The employees were informed of the pay raise.
6. The rules were changed by the chairman.

Continued on next page ▶

7. Charlie was home-schooled by his mother.
8. Roller coasters were avoided by Angela because of her weak stomach.
9. Grapes are grown in the valley.
10. The door was opened by Mike.

PRACTICE 4 Correcting Errors in Pronoun and Verb Usage

Read the sentences. Then, revise each sentence to correct errors in agreement, verb usage, and pronoun usage. Write *correct* if a sentence contains no errors.

1. Michael and his dad gave the dog a bath.
2. Neither Laura nor Lisa remembered their locker combination.
3. Pam noticed an old man who is sitting on a bench next to the post office.
4. Some of the flowers had lost its petals.
5. Neither of the boys brought their ticket.

PRACTICE 5 Using Comparative and Superlative Forms Correctly

Read the sentences. Then, write the appropriate comparative or superlative degree of the modifier in parentheses.

1. This box is the (heavy) of the two.
2. Today is (cold) than yesterday.
3. I had a (good) time than I thought I would.
4. That was the (fancy) restaurant I have ever been to.
5. The Louvre has the (fine) art collection in Europe, in my opinion.

PRACTICE 6 Avoiding Double Negatives

Read the sentences. Then, choose the word in parentheses that makes each sentence negative without forming a double negative.

1. I would not want to be (anywhere, nowhere) but here right now.
2. I am not going to buy (no, any) more DVDs.
3. Khadija hasn't met (no one, anyone) who can beat her at chess.
4. The accident wasn't (nobody's, anybody's) fault.
5. Maxine hasn't (never, ever) ridden in an airplane.

PRACTICE 7 Avoiding Usage Problems

Read the sentences. Then, rewrite each sentence using the appropriate word in the parentheses.

1. The musicians were (all ready, already) for the concert.
2. (Lay, Lie) the papers on the table.
3. Flowers, (like, as if) roses, lilies, and tulips, are a popular gift on Valentine's Day.
4. The Sanchez family had to (adapt, adopt) to the cold weather when they moved from California to Alaska.
5. Mr. Carlos will not (accept, except) term papers written in pencil.
6. Volunteering at the animal shelter had a profound (affect, effect) on Miguel.
7. (Can, May) I help you find that book?
8. Ned found it difficult to (except, accept) the coach's decision to forfeit the game.
9. It's usually hotter (then, than) this in August.
10. (There, Their) are many possible answers to your question.

CHAPTER 22

CAPITALIZATION

Knowing the rules of capitalization will help you identify and highlight names of people, places, and things in your writing.

WRITE GUY *Jeff Anderson, M.Ed.*

WHAT DO YOU NOTICE?

Look for the capitals as you zoom in on a sentence from "New Directions," an excerpt from *Wouldn't Take Nothing for My Journey Now* by Maya Angelou.

MENTOR TEXT

In 1903 the late Mrs. Annie Johnson of Arkansas found herself with two toddling sons, very little money, a slight ability to read and add simple numbers.

Now, ask yourself the following questions:

- What do the capitalized words in the sentence indicate?
- Why is *Mrs.* capitalized?

The word *In* is capitalized to signal the start of the sentence. *Annie Johnson* and *Arkansas* indicate a person's name and a specific place, so they are capitalized as proper nouns. *Mrs.* is capitalized because it is the abbreviation of the title *Mistress*, which is used to show that a woman is married.

Grammar for Writers Writers use capitalization for many purposes, including starting sentences and quotations and identifying proper nouns and proper adjectives. Think of capital letters as signals that help readers navigate your writing.

What is the capital of our country?
It's W for Washington, as in Washington, D.C.

Find It/ FIX IT
8
Grammar Game Plan

22.1 Capitalization in Sentences

Just as road signs help to guide people through a town, capital letters help to guide readers through sentences and paragraphs. Capitalization signals the start of a new sentence or points out certain words within a sentence to give readers visual clues that aid in their understanding.

WRITING COACH Online
www.phwritingcoach.com

Grammar Practice
Practice your grammar skills with Writing Coach Online.

Grammar Games
Test your knowledge of grammar in this fast-paced interactive video game.

Using Capitals for First Words

Always capitalize the first word in a sentence.

RULE 22.1.1

Capitalize the first word in **declarative, interrogative, imperative,** and **exclamatory** sentences.

DECLARATIVE	**K**atie visited the Grand Canyon.
INTERROGATIVE	**W**here will the dance be held?
IMPERATIVE	**W**atch out for icy sidewalks.
EXCLAMATORY	**W**hat an astounding turn of events!

RULE 22.1.2

Capitalize the first word in **interjections** and **incomplete questions.**

INTERJECTIONS	**O**h! Wonderful!
INCOMPLETE QUESTIONS	**W**here? **W**hat time?

The word *I* is always capitalized, whether it is the first word in a sentence or not.

RULE 22.1.3

Always capitalize the pronoun ***I***.

EXAMPLE Troy and **I** ran the race.

Capitalize the first word after a colon only if the word begins a complete sentence. Do not capitalize the word if it begins a list of words or phrases.

RULE 22.1.4

SENTENCE FOLLOWING A COLON He repeated his comment breathlessly: **H**e was unable to continue running.

LIST FOLLOWING A COLON The campers packed the following equipment: **b**ackpacks, tents, and blankets.

Capitalize the first word in each line of traditional poetry, even if the line does not start a new sentence.

RULE 22.1.5

See Practice 22.1A
See Practice 22.1B
See Practice 22.1C

EXAMPLE **I** think that I shall never see
A poem lovely as a tree. – Joyce Kilmer

Using Capitals With Quotations

There are special rules for using capitalization with **quotations.**

Capitalize the first word of a quotation. However, do not capitalize the first word of a continuing sentence when a quotation is interrupted by identifying words or when the first word of a quotation is the continuation of a speaker's sentence.

RULE 22.1.6

EXAMPLES Joe said, "**T**he dog is loose on the ball field!"

"**A**s the ship came plowing through the water," he said, "**t**he crowd cheered."

Grant remarked that this was "**t**he noisiest concert I have ever attended."

See Practice 22.1D

PRACTICE 22.1A Capitalizing Words

Read each sentence. Then, write the word or words that should be capitalized in each sentence.

EXAMPLE will you be around after school today?

ANSWER *Will*

1. how excited were we to get front-row tickets?
2. the teacher read the directions: fill in the blanks for each item.
3. doing too many things causes me to get confused.
4. i wondered if i prepared enough food for the party.
5. we packed the picnic basket for the trip: sandwiches, fruit, and drinks.
6. what? where did you say you were going?
7. wow! what a discovery!
8. they were very happy: their new house was a lot bigger than their old house.
9. will you be going to the town library this weekend?
10. roses are red
violets are blue.

PRACTICE 22.1B Using Capital Words in Sentences

Read each item. Write a sentence using each item according to the directions in parentheses.

EXAMPLE she (after a colon)

ANSWER *He repeated his statement: She is running late.*

11. the sun (the first word in a line of traditional poetry)
12. wow (in an interjection)
13. where (the first word in a sentence)
14. bikes (after a colon)
15. how (in an incomplete question)
16. i (a pronoun in a sentence)
17. no (in an interjection)
18. they (after a colon)
19. computers (the first word in a sentence)
20. a branch (the first word in a line of traditional poetry)

SPEAKING APPLICATION

Take turns with a partner. Say a variety of sentences, describing yourself in the first person. Your partner should indicate, with a nod of his or her head, each time you use a word that should be capitalized.

WRITING APPLICATION

Use the items in Practice 22.1B to create additional items. Exchange papers with a partner. Your partner should write sentences for each of your items.

PRACTICE 22.1C Using Correct Capitalization in Sentences

Read each sentence. Rewrite each sentence, correcting capitalization errors.

EXAMPLE oh, no! it's going to rain.

ANSWER *Oh, no! It's going to rain.*

1. What time do i need to arrive?
2. She remembered the rule: always call home if you will be late.
3. you were great!
4. sign on the dotted line.
5. no! i don't want to stay.
6. pumpkin bread is his favorite.
7. Kim was asked to bring these party supplies: Cups, napkins, and paper plates.
8. why not?
9. her hope perched like a nightingale in a tree, its song as eloquent as could be
10. amazing! how do you figure?

PRACTICE 22.1D Using Capitals With Quotations

Read each sentence. Then, write the word or words in each sentence that should be capitalized.

EXAMPLE monica asked, "are you going out to lunch today?"

ANSWER *Monica, Are*

11. the coach said, "run ten laps and then take a break."
12. "ask what you can do for your country!" exclaimed President John F. Kennedy.
13. my mother cautioned, "don't answer too quickly."
14. "if i had wanted to go to the party," Christina said, "i would have asked for a ride."
15. "please talk quietly," the librarian requested.
16. "stop! don't move." Jacob continued, "you're standing on thin ice."
17. the director shouted, "places, everyone!"
18. my grandfather loved to say, "a quiet man can be heard better than anyone else."
19. one of my favorite sayings is "everywhere I go, there I am."
20. "as the car appeared around the corner," he said, "i could see the driver."

SPEAKING APPLICATION

Take turns with a partner saying sentences with interjections and incomplete questions. Use Practice 22.1C as a model. Your partner should indicate when he or she thinks a word should be capitalized.

WRITING APPLICATION

Write five quotations with a variety of capitalization errors. Exchange papers with a partner. Your partner should rewrite each sentence using capitalization correctly.

Test Warm-Up

DIRECTIONS
Read the introduction and the passage that follows. Then, answer the questions to show that you can use the conventions of capitalization in reading and writing.

Oliver wrote this paragraph about his pet's fear of thunder. Read the paragraph and think about the changes you would suggest as a peer editor. When you finish reading, answer the questions that follow.

Thundered Over

(1) We were shopping when we heard the first roll of thunder and headed home. (2) "oh no!" (3) Dad's exasperated voice indicated that we were too late. (4) When our dog hears thunder, she runs and knocks over anything in her way. (5) This time Zozo toppled the following: Two lamps, a table, and several kitchen chairs. (6) I snapped, "look at this mess!" (7) When I saw poor Zozo trembling, I regretted scolding her. (8) As I comforted our dog, Dad made a comment. (9) He said, "This is part of owning a pet."

---

1 What change, if any, should be made in sentence 2?

A Change ***oh*** to **Oh**

B Change ***no*** to **No**

C Change ***oh no!*** to **Oh No!**

D Make no change

2 What change, if any, should be made in sentence 5?

F Replace the colon with a period

G Change ***This*** to **this**

H Change ***Two*** to **two**

J Make no change

3 How should sentence 6 be revised?

A I snapped, "look at this Mess!"

B I snapped, "Look at This Mess!"

C i snapped, "look at this mess!"

D I snapped, "Look at this mess!"

4 What is the most effective way to combine sentences 8 and 9?

F Dad made a comment while I comforted our dog, saying "this is part of owning a pet."

G As I comforted our dog, dad made a comment about owning a pet: this is part of it.

H I comforted our dog and Dad commented, "this is part of owning a pet."

J As I comforted our dog, Dad commented, "This is part of owning a pet."

22.2 Proper Nouns

Capitalization makes important words stand out in your writing, such as the names of people, places, countries, book titles, and other proper names. Sometimes proper names are used as nouns and sometimes as adjectives modifying nouns or pronouns.

Find It/FIX IT 8 Grammar Game Plan

WRITING COACH Online

www.phwritingcoach.com

Grammar Practice

Practice your grammar skills with Writing Coach Online.

Grammar Games

Test your knowledge of grammar in this fast-paced interactive video game.

Using Capitals for Proper Nouns

Nouns, as you may remember, are either **common** or **proper.**

Common nouns, such as *sailor, brother, city,* and *ocean,* identify classes of people, places, or things and are not capitalized.

Proper nouns name specific examples of people, places, or things and should be capitalized.

Capitalize all proper nouns.

RULE 22.2.1

EXAMPLES Jennifer Professor Wilkens Governor Percy

Chicago Main Street Halloran House

The Red Badge of Courage USS *Monitor*

Names

Each part of a person's name—the given name, the middle name or initial standing for that name, and the surname—should be capitalized. If a surname begins with *Mc* or *O',* the letter following it is capitalized (McAdams, O'Reilly).

Capitalize each part of a person's name even when the full name is not used.

RULE 22.2.2

EXAMPLES Jean Grog R. R. Brig Erin H. Sands

Capitalize the proper names that are given to animals.

EXAMPLES Flipper Traveler Rin Tin Tin

Geographical and Place Names

If a place can be found on a map, it should generally be capitalized.

RULE 22.2.3

Capitalize geographical and place names.

Examples of different kinds of geographical and place names are listed in the following chart.

GEOGRAPHICAL AND PLACE NAMES	
Streets	Madison Avenue, First Street, Green Valley Road
Towns and Cities	Dallas, Oakdale, New York City
Counties, States, and Provinces	Champlain County, Texas, Quebec
Nations and Continents	Austria, Kenya, the United States of America, Asia, Mexico, Europe
Mountains	the Adirondack Mountains, Mount Washington
Valleys and Deserts	the San Fernando Valley, the Mojave Desert, the Gobi
Islands and Peninsulas	Aruba, the Faroe Islands, Cape York Peninsula
Sections of a Country	the Northeast, Siberia, the Great Plains
Scenic Spots	Gateway National Park, Carlsbad Caverns
Rivers and Falls	the Missouri River, Victoria Falls
Lakes and Bays	Lake Cayuga, Gulf of Mexico, the Bay of Biscayne
Seas and Oceans	the Sargasso Sea, the Indian Ocean
Celestial Bodies and Constellations	Mars, the Big Dipper, moon, Venus
Monuments and Memorials	the Tomb of the Unknown Soldier, Kennedy Memorial Library, the Washington Monument
Buildings	Madison Square Garden, Fort Hood, the Astrodome, the White House
School and Meeting Rooms	Room 6, Laboratory 3B, the Red Room, Conference Room C

Capitalizing Directions

Words indicating direction are capitalized only when they refer to a section of a country.

EXAMPLES The courier made his way through the **S**outh.

The train stops two miles **e**ast of the city.

Capitalizing Names of Celestial Bodies

Capitalize the names of celestial bodies except *moon* and *sun*.

EXAMPLE When the **m**oon passes between the **s**un and **E**arth, a solar eclipse occurs.

Capitalizing Buildings and Places

Do not capitalize words such as *theater, hotel, university,* and *park*, unless the word is part of a proper name.

EXAMPLES We visited Stone Mountain **P**ark.

I will meet you at the **p**ark.

Events and Times

Capitalize references to historic events, periods, and documents as well as dates and holidays. Use a dictionary to check capitalization.

Capitalize the names of specific events and periods in history.

RULE 22.2.4

SPECIAL EVENTS AND TIMES	
Historic Events	the Battle of Waterloo, World War I
Historical Periods	the Manchu Dynasty, Reconstruction
Documents	the Bill of Rights, the Magna Carta
Days and Months	Monday, June 22, the third week in May
Holidays	Labor Day, Memorial Day, Veterans Day
Religious Holidays	Rosh Hashanah, Christmas, Easter
Special Events	the World Series, the Holiday Antiques Show

Capitalizing Seasons
Do not capitalize seasons unless the name of the season is being used as a proper noun or adjective.

EXAMPLES My cousins spent their **s**ummer vacation in Florida.
The **A**utumn Harvest Dance is next week.

RULE 22.2.5

Capitalize the names of organizations, government bodies, political parties, races, nationalities, languages, and religions.

VARIOUS GROUPS	
Clubs and Organizations	Rotary, Knights of Columbus, the Red Cross, National Organization for Women
Institutions	the Museum of Fine Arts, the Mayo Clinic
Schools	Kennedy High School, University of Texas
Businesses	General Motors, Prentice Hall
Government Bodies	Department of State, Federal Trade Commission, House of Representatives
Political Parties	Republicans, the Democratic party
Nationalities	American, Mexican, Chinese, Israeli, Canadian
Languages	English, Italian, Polish, Swahili
Religions and Religious References	Christianity: God, the Holy Spirit, the Bible Judaism: the Lord, the Prophets, the Torah Islam: Allah, the Prophets, the Qur'an, Mohammed Hinduism: Brahma, the Bhagavad Gita, the Vedas Buddhism: the Buddha, Mahayana, Hinayana

References to Mythological Gods When referring to mythology, do not capitalize the word *god* (the *gods* of Olympus).

RULE 22.2.6

Capitalize the names of awards; the names of specific types of air, sea, and spacecraft; and brand names.

EXAMPLES the **P**ulitzer **P**rize the **M**edal of **H**onor
Biska **T**reats **A**pollo **V**

See Practice 22.2A
See Practice 22.2B

PRACTICE 22.2A **Identifying Proper Nouns**

Read each sentence. Then, write the proper noun or nouns in each sentence.

EXAMPLE I went to Lake Michigan last winter.

ANSWER *Lake Michigan*

1. I know that George Washington was the first president of the United States.
2. My friends and I always go to the same chain of movie theaters, MovieForU.
3. The Musicians for the Environment Board of Trustees meets twice a month.
4. After the moon rises, Mars can be seen in the east.
5. Both the Cherokee and Sioux live in the West.
6. Jonas Salk developed the polio vaccine.
7. The Daytona 500 takes place every year in Florida.
8. Clara Barton organized the American Red Cross.
9. The Oval Office is where the president works in the White House.
10. The Great Depression lasted for over a decade.

PRACTICE 22.2B **Capitalizing Proper Nouns**

Read each sentence. Then, write the word or words in each sentence that should be capitalized.

EXAMPLE While in south america, we went to peru and argentina.

ANSWER *South America, Peru, Argentina*

11. We have tickets to see the joffrey ballet.
12. The empire state building is in new york city.
13. abraham lincoln's birthday is on february 12.
14. The southwest is very hot and dry.
15. Every february, we celebrate african american history month.
16. The environmental protection agency helps reduce pollution in our world.
17. My best friend anna is european and asian.
18. The colorado river lies at the bottom of the grand canyon.
19. In greek mythology, zeus is the leader of the gods.
20. The uss *south dakota* was stationed in the pacific ocean during world war II.

SPEAKING APPLICATION

Take turns with a partner. Tell about an important period in history. Your partner should identify the proper nouns that you use.

WRITING APPLICATION

Use sentence 12 as a model to write three similar sentences. Replace the proper nouns in sentence 12 with other proper nouns.

Using Capitals for Proper Adjectives

A **proper adjective** is either an adjective formed from a proper noun or a proper noun used as an adjective.

RULE 22.2.7 **Capitalize most proper adjectives.**

PROPER ADJECTIVES FORMED FROM PROPER NOUNS	**A**ustralian kangaroo	**S**hakespearean play
	Afghan hound	**E**uropean settlers
	Spanish ambassador	**I**talian food
PROPER NOUNS USED AS ADJECTIVES	the **S**enate floor	the **R**iley speeches
	Shakespeare festival	a **B**ible class
	the **B**rowns' house	**C**hicago pizza

Some proper adjectives have become so commonly used that they are no longer capitalized.

EXAMPLES	**h**erculean effort	**f**rench fries
	pasteurized milk	**q**uixotic hope
	venetian blinds	**t**eddy bear

Brand names are often used as proper adjectives.

RULE 22.2.8 **Capitalize a brand name when it is used as an adjective, but do not capitalize the common noun it modifies.**

EXAMPLES	**T**imo **w**atches	**S**witzles **c**hocolate
	Super **C**ool **j**eans	**L**onglasting **r**efrigerator

Multiple Proper Adjectives

When you have two or more proper adjectives used together, do not capitalize the associated common nouns.

Do not capitalize a common noun used with two proper adjectives.

RULE 22.2.9

ONE PROPER ADJECTIVE	TWO PROPER ADJECTIVES
Mississippi River	Ohio and Mississippi rivers
Washington Street	Washington, Madison, and Lincoln streets
Suez Canal	Suez and Panama canals
Banking Act	Banking and Taxing acts
Atlantic Ocean	Atlantic and Pacific oceans
Bergen County	Bergen and Morris counties
Fiji Islands	Fiji and Canary islands

Prefixes and Hyphenated Adjectives

Prefixes and hyphenated adjectives cause special problems. Prefixes used with proper adjectives should be capitalized only if they refer to a nationality.

Do not capitalize prefixes attached to proper adjectives unless the prefix refers to a nationality. In a hyphenated adjective, capitalize only the proper adjective.

RULE 22.2.10

EXAMPLES all-American Anglo-American
Spanish-speaking pro-English
American Korean-language newspaper
pre-Renaissance Sino-Russian
pre-Mayan architecture Indo-European

See Practice 22.2C
See Practice 22.2D

PRACTICE 22.2C Capitalizing Proper Adjectives

Read each sentence. Then, write the word or words in each sentence that should be capitalized.

EXAMPLE Terrance and Carol were late for english class.

ANSWER *English*

1. I have never been to a spanish-speaking country.
2. Steamed dumplings is my favorite chinese dish.
3. We live near an indian grocery store.
4. My mother reads a hebrew-language newspaper every morning.
5. The florida panther is on the endangered species list.
6. Pro-american sentiments were felt during the president's african tour.
7. The excavated pottery is pre-colombian.
8. The russo-japanese war lasted one year.
9. In 1916, irish patriots proclaimed independence from England on o'connell street.
10. Marla has an english bulldog and a french poodle.

PRACTICE 22.2D Revising Sentences to Correct Capitalization Errors

Read each sentence. Then, rewrite each sentence using the conventions of capitalization.

EXAMPLE Dov thinks our greek tragedy is fine, but I think it could be improved.

ANSWER *Dov thinks our Greek tragedy is fine, but I think it could be improved.*

11. The national football league has many teams.
12. Many businesspeople have been lobbying in congress.
13. My ecuadorian sweater is very warm.
14. Sam Houston, a virginia-born statesman, was the governor of both tennessee and texas.
15. I cannot decide if I should open an account at money bank, american money, or j.t.t. bank.
16. In british history, Elizabeth I was admired both during and after her time.
17. The dallas cowboys play at texas stadium.
18. My grandparents drink english tea every afternoon.
19. Essex and ocean counties are located in New Jersey.
20. The monarch butterfly migrates to mexico before winter sets in.

SPEAKING APPLICATION

Discuss with a partner the importance of capitals. Suggest three ways capitalization makes reading and comprehension easier.

WRITING APPLICATION

Write a brief paragraph that contains proper adjectives. Be sure to use conventions of capitalization.

22.3 Other Uses of Capitals

Find It/FIX IT
8
Grammar Game Plan

Even though the purpose of using capital letters is to make writing clearer, some rules for capitalization can be confusing. For example, it may be difficult to remember which words in a letter you write need to start with a capital, which words in a book title should be capitalized, or when a person's title—such as Senator or Reverend—needs to start with a capital. The rules and examples that follow should clear up the confusion.

WRITING COACH Online
www.phwritingcoach.com

Grammar Practice
Practice your grammar skills with Writing Coach Online.

Grammar Games
Test your knowledge of grammar in this fast-paced interactive video game.

Using Capitals in Letters

Capitalization is required in parts of personal letters and business letters.

Capitalize the first word and all nouns in letter salutations and the first word in letter closings.

RULE 22.3.1

SALUTATIONS
Dear Eric,
Dear Sirs:
Dear Mr. Levitt:
My Dear Cousin,

CLOSINGS
With love,
Yours truly,
Sincerely yours,
Best regards,

Using Capitals for Titles

Capitals are used for titles of people and titles of literary and artistic works. The charts and rules on the following pages will guide you in capitalizing titles correctly.

RULE 22.3.2

Capitalize a person's title only when it is used with the person's name or when it is used as a proper name by itself.

WITH A PROPER NAME	Yesterday, **G**overnor **W**ilson signed the bill.
AS A PROPER NAME	I'm glad you can join us, **G**randma.
IN A GENERAL REFERENCE	The **s**enator followed the progress of the debate.

The following chart illustrates the correct form for a variety of titles. Study the chart, paying particular attention to compound titles and titles with prefixes or suffixes.

SOCIAL, BUSINESS, RELIGIOUS, MILITARY, AND GOVERNMENT TITLES	
Commonly Used Titles	Sir, Madam, Miss, Professor, Doctor, Reverend, Bishop, Sister, Father, Rabbi, Corporal, Major, Admiral, Mayor, Governor, Ambassador
Abbreviated Titles	*Before names*: Mr., Mrs., Ms., Dr., Hon. *After names*: Jr., Sr., Ph.D., M.D., D.D.S., Esq.
Compound Titles	Vice President, Secretary of State, Lieutenant Governor, Commander in Chief
Titles With Prefixes or Suffixes	ex-Congressman Randolph, Governor-elect Loughman

Some honorary titles are capitalized. These include First Lady of the United States, Speaker of the House of Representatives, Queen Mother of England, and the Prince of Wales.

Capitalize certain honorary titles even when the titles are not followed by a proper name.

RULE 22.3.3

EXAMPLE The **p**resident and **F**irst **L**ady visited with the **q**ueen of England.

Occasionally, the titles of other government officials may be capitalized as a sign of respect when referring to a specific person whose name is not given. However, you usually do not capitalize titles when they stand alone unless they are used as nouns of direct address.

EXAMPLES We thank you, **G**overnor, for taking time to meet with us.

Fourteen **s**enators voted against the bill.

Relatives are often referred to by titles. These references should be capitalized when used with or as the person's name.

RULE 22.3.4

WITH THE PERSON'S NAME In the summer, **U**ncle **T**ed enjoys gardening.

AS A NAME He says that **G**randmother enjoys gardening, too.

Do not capitalize titles showing family relationships when they are preceded by a possessive noun or pronoun.

RULE 22.3.5

EXAMPLES my **a**unt her **f**ather Jeff's **m**other

RULE 22.3.6

Capitalize the first word and all other key words in the titles of books, periodicals, poems, stories, plays, paintings, and other works of art.

The following chart lists examples to guide you in capitalizing titles and subtitles of various works. Note that the articles (*a, an,* and *the*) are not capitalized unless they are used as the first word of a title or subtitle. Conjunctions and prepositions are also left uncapitalized unless they are the first or last word in a title or subtitle or contain four letters or more. Note also that verbs, no matter how short, are always capitalized.

TITLES OF WORKS	
Books	*The Red Badge of Courage* *Profiles in Courage* *All Through the Night* *John Ford: The Man and His Films* *Heart of Darkness*
Periodicals	*International Wildlife, Allure,* *Better Homes and Gardens*
Poems	"The Raven" "The Rime of the Ancient Mariner" "Flower in the Crannied Wall"
Stories and Articles	"Editha" "The Fall of the House of Usher" "Here Is New York"
Plays and Musicals	*The Tragedy of Macbeth* *Our Town* *West Side Story*
Paintings	*Starry Night* *Mona Lisa* *The Artist's Daughter With a Cat*
Music	*The Unfinished Symphony* "Heartbreak Hotel" "This Land Is Your Land"

Capitalize titles of educational courses when they are language courses or when they are followed by a number or preceded by a proper noun or adjective. Do not capitalize school subjects discussed in a general manner.

RULE 22.3.7

WITH CAPITALS	Latin	Honors Biology
	History 105	Math 4
	Economics 313	French
WITHOUT CAPITALS	geology	psychology
	woodworking	history
	biology	math

EXAMPLES

This year, I will be taking algebra, English, Honors Chemistry, and world history.

Catherine's favorite classes are art history, Italian, and biology.

She does not like physical education and math as much.

After English class, I have to rush across the building to chemistry.

See Practice 22.3A
See Practice 22.3B

PRACTICE 22.3A Capitalizing Titles

Read each sentence. Then, write the word or words in each sentence that should be capitalized.

EXAMPLE Tyrone Plunkett sr. is here to see you.

ANSWER *Sr.*

1. Did you see the latest copy of *the new york times*?
2. I think lieutenant bell has some urgent news.
3. Last night, Thomas read "politics in the english language" by George Orwell.
4. In 1991, Colin Powell became chairman of the joint chiefs of staff.
5. At the vote, senator wellington was noticeably absent.
6. *Beautiful world* is a painting by grandma moses.
7. I just finished reading the novel *cold mountain*.
8. DaVinci's *mona lisa* is still the pride of the Louvre in Paris.
9. "Excuse me, mr. lopes. I would like to introduce you to ms. carlton."
10. Thomas Hardy's "hap" is one of the most emotionally charged poems I've read in class.

PRACTICE 22.3B Using All of the Rules of Capitalization

Read each sentence. Then, rewrite each sentence, using the conventions of capitalization.

EXAMPLE t.j. thinks we should drive along st. lawrence avenue.

ANSWER *T.J. thinks we should drive along St. Lawrence Avenue.*

11. The class will have to read Gustave Flaubert's *madame bovary*.
12. The jackson years were some of the most controversial in american history.
13. Ironically, hamburgers are not named for hamburg, germany.
14. Fans applauded sir elton john as he strolled down the red carpet.
15. It is rare that mr. and mrs. singh are late.
16. kirsten is no longer the company's liaison to japan.
17. The average new yorker walks five miles every day.
18. Pardon me, miss, but where is the nearest ATM?
19. Even the civilians saluted vice-admiral salva for his brilliant strategy.
20. A french-canadian man asked berta to dance.

SPEAKING APPLICATION

Discuss with a partner the importance of capitals in names and titles. Together, answer the following question: How does capitalizing a title show respect?

WRITING APPLICATION

Pick a personal title, such as "captain" or "doctor," and write four sentences. Two should demonstrate when the title is capitalized, and two should demonstrate when it is not capitalized.

CHAPTER 23

PUNCTUATION

Using punctuation correctly will help you to organize and clarify your writing.

WRITE GUY *Jeff Anderson, M.Ed.*

WHAT DO YOU NOTICE?

Notice how punctuation is used as you zoom in on these sentences from the story "The Red-Headed League" by Sir Arthur Conan Doyle.

MENTOR TEXT

> "You may place considerable confidence in Mr. Holmes, sir," said the police agent loftily. "He has his own little methods, which are, if he won't mind my saying so, just a little too theoretical and fantastic, but he has the makings of a detective in him."

Now, ask yourself the following questions:

- Why is the word *sir* set off by commas?
- How are commas used in the second sentence?

The word *sir* is set off by commas to show that the speaker is addressing someone directly. The second comma serves to separate *sir* from the tag line *said the police agent loftily.* In the second sentence, commas set off nonrestrictive phrases, those not needed to complete the meaning of the sentence but that add extra detail. The author uses the comma before the conjunction *but* to separate the main, or independent, clauses.

Grammar for Writers Text would be difficult to read and understand without punctuation because it shows readers how to group words. Writers have a variety of punctuation marks available to make their writing clear.

Commas are such useful things.
I, always, have, extra, if, you, need, one.

23.1 End Marks

End marks tell readers when to pause and for how long. They signal the end or conclusion of a sentence, word, or phrase. There are three end marks: the **period (.)**, the **question mark (?)**, and the **exclamation mark (!)**.

WRITING COACH **Online**

www.phwritingcoach.com

Grammar Practice

Practice your grammar skills with Writing Coach Online.

Grammar Games

Test your knowledge of grammar in this fast-paced interactive video game.

Using Periods

A **period** indicates the end of a declarative or imperative sentence, an indirect question, or an abbreviation. The period is the most common end mark.

RULE 23.1.1

Use a period to end a declarative sentence, a mild imperative sentence, and an indirect question.

A **declarative sentence** is a statement of fact or opinion.

DECLARATIVE SENTENCE — This is a beautiful park.

An **imperative sentence** gives a direction or command. Often, the first word of an imperative sentence is a verb.

MILD IMPERATIVE SENTENCE — Finish reading the chapter.

An **indirect question** restates a question in a declarative sentence. It does not give the speaker's exact words.

INDIRECT QUESTION — Mae asked me whether I could stay.

Other Uses of Periods

In addition to signaling the end of a statement, periods can also signal that words have been shortened, or abbreviated.

RULE 23.1.2

Use a period after most abbreviations and after initials.

PERIODS IN ABBREVIATIONS	
Titles	Dr., Sr., Mrs., Mr., Gov., Maj., Rev., Prof.
Place Names	Ave., Bldg., Blvd., Mt., Dr., St., Ter., Rd.
Times and Dates	Sun., Dec., sec., min., hr., yr., A.M.
Initials	E. B. White, Robin F. Brancato, R. Brett

Some abbreviations do not end with periods. Metric measurements, state abbreviations used with ZIP Codes, and most standard measurements do not need periods. The abbreviation for inch, *in.,* is the exception.

EXAMPLES mm, cm, kg, L, C, CA, TX, ft, gal

The following chart lists some abbreviations with and without periods.

ABBREVIATIONS WITH AND WITHOUT END MARKS	
approx. = approximately	misc. = miscellaneous
COD = cash on delivery	mph = miles per hour
dept. = department	No. = number
doz. = dozen(s)	p. or pg. = page; pp. = pages
EST = Eastern Standard Time	POW = prisoner of war
FM = frequency modulation	pub. = published, publisher
gov. or govt. = government	pvt. = private
ht. = height	rpm = revolutions per minute
incl. = including	R.S.V.P. = please reply
ital = italics	sp. = spelling
kt. = karat or carat	SRO = standing room only
meas. = measure	vol. = volume
mfg. = manufacturing	wt. = weight

Sentences Ending With Abbreviations When a sentence ends with an abbreviation that uses a period, do not put a second period at the end. If an end mark other than a period is required, add the end mark.

EXAMPLES Be sure to call Jack Jenkins Jr.

Is that Adam Martin Jr.?

See Practice 23.1A

RULE 23.1.3

Do not use periods with acronyms, words formed with the first or first few letters of a series of words.

ACRONYMS NASA (National Aeronautics and Space Administration)

RADAR (Radio Detecting and Range)

RULE 23.1.4

Use a period after numbers and letters in outlines.

EXAMPLE

I. Maintaining your pet's health
  A. Diet
    1. For a puppy
    2. For a mature dog
  B. Exercise

Using Question Marks

A **question mark** follows a word, phrase, or sentence that asks a question. A question is often in inverted word order.

RULE 23.1.5

Use a question mark to end an interrogative sentence, an incomplete question, or a statement intended as a question.

INTERROGATIVE SENTENCE Do snakes hatch from eggs?

What time do you want me to pick you up?

INCOMPLETE QUESTION Many small birds build false nests. Why?

I'll leave you money. How much?

Use care, however, in ending statements with question marks. It is better to rephrase the statement as a direct question.

STATEMENT WITH A QUESTION MARK	The geese haven't migrated yet?
	We are having spaghetti for dinner?
REVISED INTO A DIRECT QUESTION	Haven't the geese migrated yet?
	Are we having spaghetti for dinner?

Use a period instead of a question mark with an **indirect question**—a question that is restated as a declarative sentence.

EXAMPLES	Ted wanted to know which bus to take.
	He wondered if he would be on time.

Using Exclamation Marks

An **exclamation mark** signals an exclamatory sentence, an imperative sentence, or an interjection. It indicates strong emotion and should be used sparingly.

Use an exclamation mark to end an exclamatory sentence, a forceful imperative sentence, or an interjection expressing strong emotion.

RULE 23.1.6

EXCLAMATORY SENTENCE	Look at that huge vulture!
FORCEFUL IMPERATIVE SENTENCE	Don't spill the water!

An interjection can be used with a comma or an exclamation mark. An exclamation mark increases the emphasis.

EXAMPLES	Wow! That was a great throw.
	Oh! Look what I found.
WITH A COMMA	Wow, that was a great throw.

See Practice 23.1B

PRACTICE 23.1A Using Periods Correctly in Sentences

Read each sentence. Then, rewrite each sentence, adding periods where they are needed.

EXAMPLE Michael C Young published that famous book

ANSWER *Michael C. Young published that famous book.*

1. I asked Mrs Robinson to watch my cats
2. The bus leaves promptly at 7:15 AM
3. S E Hinton wrote *The Outsiders*
4. Send the letter to Dr Paul K Wright
5. One of the candidates was a POW
6. Nellie asked me if I saw her cellphone
7. This is 18 mm of copper wiring
8. Deanna asked me if I wanted to bring my sweater
9. The forty-fourth president of the United States is Barack H Obama
10. The high-speed train can travel over 300 mph

PRACTICE 23.1B Using Question Marks and Exclamation Marks Correctly in Sentences

Read each sentence. Then, write the correct end mark for each item.

EXAMPLE What a great new hat

ANSWER *!*

11. How many sweaters does she have
12. How many books did Ernest Hemingway write
13. Did you wipe your muddy shoes on the mat
14. Surprise
15. When will Dean arrive
16. Watch out
17. What a beautiful symphony
18. What time are we eating dinner
19. Do you know where Plano, Texas, is
20. Be careful with that vase

SPEAKING APPLICATION

Take turns with a partner. Say declarative sentences, imperative sentences, and indirect questions. Your partner should listen for and identify each sentence type.

WRITING APPLICATION

Write two sentences that use question marks and two sentences that use exclamation marks.

23.2 Commas

A **comma** tells the reader to pause briefly before continuing a sentence. Commas may be used to separate elements in a sentence or to set off part of a sentence.

Commas are used more than any other internal punctuation mark. To check for correct comma use, read a sentence aloud and note where a pause helps you to group your ideas. Commas signal to readers that they should take a short breath.

Find It/FIX IT
13
Grammar Game Plan

WRITING COACH Online
www.phwritingcoach.com

Grammar Tutorials
Brush up on your Grammar skills with these animated videos.

Grammar Practice
Practice your grammar skills with Writing Coach Online.

Grammar Games
Test your knowledge of grammar in this fast-paced interactive video game.

Using Commas With Compound Sentences

A **compound sentence** consists of two or more main or independent clauses that are joined by a coordinating conjunction, such as *and, but, for, nor, or, so,* or *yet.*

Use a comma before a conjunction to separate two or more independent or main clauses in a compound sentence.

RULE 23.2.1

Use a comma before a conjunction when there are complete sentences on both sides of the conjunction.

EXAMPLE Joe is getting married this summer, but I won't be able to attend the wedding.
(independent clause: Joe is getting married this summer; independent clause: I won't be able to attend the wedding.)

In some compound sentences, the main or independent clauses are very brief, and the meaning is clear. When this occurs, the comma before the conjunction may be omitted.

EXAMPLES Jonathan listened carefully but he heard nothing.

Mira would like to visit in June but she is too busy.

In other sentences, conjunctions are used to join compound subjects, objects, appositives, or verbs, prepositional phrases, or subordinate clauses. When the conjunction joins only two of these elements, the sentence does not take a comma before the conjunction.

CONJUNCTIONS WITHOUT COMMAS	
Compound Subject	Diana and Jill met for lunch at the mall.
Compound Verb	The friends chatted and laughed as they ate lunch.
Two Prepositional Phrases	My cat flew through the living room and up the stairs.
Two Subordinate Clauses	I enjoy shopping trips only if they are short and if I find what I need.

A **nominative absolute** is a noun or pronoun followed by a participle or participial phrase that functions independently of the rest of the sentence.

RULE 23.2.2

Use a comma after a nominative absolute.

The following example shows a comma with a nominative absolute.

EXAMPLE Precious minutes having been lost, I decided to call the fire department.

Find It/FIX IT 16 Grammar Game Plan

Avoiding Comma Splices

Remember to use both a comma and a coordinating conjunction in a compound sentence. Using only a comma can result in a **run-on sentence** or a **comma splice.** A **comma splice** occurs when two or more complete sentences have been joined with only a comma. Either punctuate separate sentences with an end mark or a semicolon, or find a way to join the sentences. (See Section 23.3 for more information on semicolons.)

RULE 23.2.3

Avoid comma splices.

INCORRECT The snow clumped on the trees, many branches snapped under the weight.

CORRECT The snow clumped on the trees. Many branches snapped under the weight.

Using Commas in a Series

A **series** consists of three or more words, phrases, or subordinate clauses of a similar kind. A series can occur in any part of a sentence.

Use commas to separate three or more words, phrases, or clauses in a series.

RULE 23.2.4

Notice that a comma follows each of the items except the last one in these series. The conjunction *and* or *or* is added after the last comma.

SERIES OF WORDS	The desert animals included camels, toads, gerbils, and insects.
SERIES OF PREPOSITIONAL PHRASES	The treasure map directed them over the dunes, into the oasis, and past the palm trees.
SUBORDINATE CLAUSES IN A SERIES	The newspapers reported that the service was flawless, that the dinner was impeccable, and that the band played remarkably well.

If each item (except for the last one) in a series is followed by a conjunction, do not use commas.

EXAMPLE I visited castles and museums and forts.

A second exception to this rule concerns items such as *salt and pepper*, which are paired so often that they are considered a single item.

EXAMPLES Every table in the diner was set with a knife and fork, a cup and saucer, and salt and pepper.

Dave's favorite dinners are macaroni and cheese, spaghetti and meatballs, and franks and beans.

Using Commas Between Adjectives

Sometimes, two or more adjectives are placed before the noun they describe.

RULE 23.2.5

Use commas to separate coordinate adjectives, also called independent modifiers, or adjectives of equal rank.

EXAMPLES a tasteless, boring show

a raucous, festive, thrilling occasion

An adjective is equal in rank to another if the word *and* can be inserted between them without changing the meaning of the sentence. Another way to test whether or not adjectives are equal is to reverse their order. If the sentence still sounds correct, they are of equal rank. In the first example, *a boring, tasteless show* still makes sense.

If you cannot place the word *and* between adjectives or reverse their order without changing the meaning of the sentence, they are called **cumulative adjectives.**

RULE 23.2.6

Do not use a comma between cumulative adjectives.

EXAMPLES a new dinner jacket
(*a dinner new jacket* does not make sense)

many unusual T-shirts
(*unusual many T-shirts* does not make sense)

RULE 23.2.7

Do not use a comma to separate the last adjective in a series from the noun it modifies.

INCORRECT A tall, majestic, building rose above the skyline.

CORRECT A tall, majestic building rose above the skyline.

See Practice 23.2A
See Practice 23.2B

PRACTICE 23.2A Using Commas Correctly in Sentences

Read each sentence. Then, rewrite each sentence, adding commas where they are needed.

EXAMPLE It snowed last night but it was all melted by this morning.

ANSWER *It snowed last night, but it was all melted by this morning.*

1. The thunderclap startled my brother and he jumped up from the chair.
2. I washed the dishes swept the floor and put away the groceries.
3. David must have arrived on time or we would have received a phone call from the school.
4. The tubas stopped playing but the drum line continued the song.
5. The proud happy contest winner celebrated with her parents.
6. Devon bought canned peaches pears and plums.
7. I called Jake but he didn't answer.
8. She sang the anthem in a soft sweet voice.
9. Tears glistening in her eyes she clapped louder for her son than anyone else.
10. His face red with embarrassment Doug picked up the scattered papers.

PRACTICE 23.2B Revising to Correct Errors in Comma Use

Read each sentence. Then, rewrite each sentence, adding or deleting commas as necessary.

EXAMPLE We took sandwiches, apples, and, juice for lunch.

ANSWER *We took sandwiches, apples, and juice for lunch.*

11. I took an umbrella but Joe left it at Anita's house.
12. With trumpet lessons, baseball practice and play rehearsal I have no time to join that club.
13. The bus driver was running behind schedule and then the bus broke down.
14. I'm tired yet I can't fall asleep.
15. Laura can't find her homework her lunch or her new, field-hockey stick.
16. We sat around the campfire and John told a gruesome scary story.
17. Stella ate strawberries, and blueberries, and raspberries.
18. We watched the movie, and cheered at every victorious part.
19. The bread was moist chewy, and delicious.
20. Their faces glowing the bride and groom greeted their guests.

SPEAKING APPLICATION

Take turns with a partner. Say compound sentences. Your partner should tell where a comma would go if your sentences were written.

WRITING APPLICATION

Write four sentences that use commas incorrectly. Exchange papers with a partner. Your partner should rewrite each sentence correctly.

Find It/ FIX IT

2

Grammar Game Plan

Using Commas After Introductory Material

Most material that introduces a sentence should be set off with a comma.

RULE 23.2.8

Use a comma after an introductory word, phrase, or clause.

KINDS OF INTRODUCTORY MATERIAL	
Introductory Words	Yes, we do expect to hear from them soon. No, there has been no response. Well, I was definitely surprised by her question.
Nouns of Direct Address	Joe, will you attend?
Introductory Adverbs	Hurriedly, they gathered up their equipment. Patiently, the children's mother explained it to them again.
Participial Phrases	Moving quickly, she averted a potential social disaster. Marching next to each other in the parade, we introduced ourselves and started to chat.
Prepositional Phrases	In the shade of the maple tree, a family spread a picnic blanket. After lengthy festivities, we were all exhausted.
Infinitive Phrases	To choose the right gift, I consulted the bridal registry. To finish my speech on time, I will have to cut some examples.
Adverbial Clauses	When she asked for a permit for the fair, she was sure it would be denied. If you compete in marathons, you may be interested in this one.

Commas and Prepositional Phrases Only one comma should be used after two prepositional phrases or a compound participial or infinitive phrase.

EXAMPLES In the pocket of his vest, he found the ring.

Lost in the crowd of people, the children asked a police officer for help.

It is not necessary to set off short prepositional phrases. However, a comma can help avoid confusion.

CONFUSING In the rain water stained the silk tablecloth.

CLEAR In the rain, water stained the silk tablecloth.

Using Commas With Parenthetical Expressions

A **parenthetical expression** is a word or phrase that interrupts the flow of the sentence.

Use commas to set off parenthetical expressions from the rest of the sentence.

RULE 23.2.9

Parenthetical expressions may come in the middle or at the end of a sentence. A parenthetical expression in the middle of a sentence needs two commas—one on each side; it needs only one comma if it appears at the end of a sentence.

KINDS OF PARENTHETICAL EXPRESSIONS	
Nouns of Direct Address	Will you have lunch with us, Ted? I wonder, Mr. Green, where Lee is.
Conjunctive Adverbs	Someone had already bought them towels, however. We could not, therefore, buy those.
Common Expressions	I listened to Jack's directions as carefully as you did, I think.
Contrasting Expressions	Tom is seventeen, not eighteen. These books, not those, are yours.

Find It/FIX IT 7
Grammar Game Plan

Find It/FIX IT 11
Grammar Game Plan

Using Commas With Nonessential Expressions

To determine when a phrase or clause should be set off with commas, decide whether the phrase or clause is *essential* or *nonessential* to the meaning of the sentence. The terms *restrictive* and *nonrestrictive* may also be used.

An **essential,** or **restrictive, phrase** or **clause** is necessary to the meaning of the sentence. **Nonessential,** or **nonrestrictive, expressions** can be left out without changing the meaning of the sentence. Although the nonessential material may be interesting, the sentence can be read without it and still make sense. Depending on their importance in a sentence, appositives, participial phrases, and adjectival clauses can be either essential or nonessential. Only nonessential expressions should be set off with commas.

See Practice 23.2C
See Practice 23.2D
See Practice 23.2E
See Practice 23.2F

NONESSENTIAL APPOSITIVE	The part was played by Henry Fonda, the famous actor.
NONESSENTIAL PARTICIPIAL PHRASE	The graceful bridge, built in the 1800s, spans a lake in Central Park.
NONESSENTIAL ADJECTIVAL CLAUSE	The lake, which freezes in winter, is popular with swimmers in summer.

Do not use commas to set off essential expressions.

ESSENTIAL APPOSITIVE	The part was played by the famous actor Henry Fonda.
ESSENTIAL PARTICIPIAL PHRASE	The man wearing the white cap is my uncle.
ESSENTIAL ADJECTIVAL CLAUSE	The paragraph that Juan suggested would change the paper's thesis.

PRACTICE 23.2C Identifying Comma Use

Read each sentence. Then, for each sentence, tell what kind of introductory material is set off with a comma.

EXAMPLE To pay for her new car, Miranda started babysitting.

ANSWER *infinitive phrase*

1. To make the choice simpler, Ida gave us only three options.
2. Quickly, I added up the total sale.
3. Actually, the library is not open on Mondays.
4. Sleeping deeply, I didn't hear the train pass.
5. Yes, I'd like to enter the book fair.
6. Unless it rains, I plan to go swimming.
7. Mr. Casale, may I go to the nurse's office?
8. Walking to the counter, Brenda noticed the list of daily specials.
9. Although Miranda prefers burritos, she decided to order tamales.
10. From under the table, the cat batted at the wad of paper.

PRACTICE 23.2D Using Commas With Prepositional Phrases

Read each sentence. Rewrite each sentence, inserting a comma to set off prepositional phrases.

EXAMPLE Across the lake Jordan could see the camp.

ANSWER *Across the lake, Jordan could see the camp.*

11. Until evening Carol will be volunteering at the hospital.
12. Throughout the story the dragon tried to help the main character.
13. At the third stop sign turn left.
14. Within five minutes Ty spotted the missing puzzle piece.
15. Under the bridge next to the boathouse the canoe drifted to shore.
16. On a table in the science lab there are two empty beakers.
17. After the dance buses will take students home.
18. Near the shed and fence a fawn stood feeding.
19. In spite of the cold weather we plan to walk to the store.
20. Since she was alone Hattie turned up the volume.

SPEAKING APPLICATION

Take turns with a partner. Say sentences with different kinds of introductory material. Your partner should write each of your sentences, using a comma to set off the introductory material.

WRITING APPLICATION

Use the sentences in Practice 23.2D as a model to write similar sentences. Exchange papers with a partner. Your partner should insert commas to set off prepositional phrases.

PRACTICE 23.2E Placing Commas Correctly in Sentences

Read each sentence. Then, rewrite each sentence, adding commas where they are needed. Explain whether you used the commas in introductory material, nonrestrictive expressions, contrasting expressions, or other parenthetical expressions.

EXAMPLE No she doesn't like the painting.

ANSWER *No, she doesn't like the painting.*

1. Yes he came with us to the meeting.
2. After the previews ended the audience became quiet.
3. Mom what should I do with these old books?
4. When he's happy Alberto is very funny.
5. The plant the one sitting on the sill is growing healthy because it receives a lot of sunlight.
6. To arrive early for the performance we'll need to leave within ten minutes.
7. Louis Pasteur who was French was a famous scientist.
8. Waiting impatiently the man paced the hallways.
9. My little brother whose name is Kyle is in first grade not second grade.
10. Tell me what happened Marcos.

PRACTICE 23.2F Revising Sentences for Proper Comma Use

Read each sentence. Then, rewrite each sentence, adding or deleting commas as necessary. Discuss with a partner why you added or deleted each comma (include comma placement in introductory material, nonrestrictive expressions, contrasting expressions, and other parenthetical expressions).

EXAMPLE Mickey Mantle who was a Yankee was inducted to the National Baseball Hall of Fame, in 1974.

ANSWER *Mickey Mantle, who was a Yankee, was inducted to the National Baseball Hall of Fame in 1974.*

11. We had already paid for the tickets however.
12. Ed met us, before school not after school.
13. Slowly we opened the door.
14. Grinning, broadly, Warren accepted the science award.
15. My neighbor who is a chef, told us about the new restaurant.
16. Amanda please pass out these papers.
17. She was therefore chosen for the starring role.
18. The lamp which was an antique was broken in two pieces.
19. Yes Ted I heard the noise.
20. That scarf is mine I believe.

SPEAKING APPLICATION

Discuss with a partner the difference between the necessity of a comma in sentence 1 and the necessity of a comma in sentence 7. Tell what the purpose of the comma is in both sentences.

WRITING APPLICATION

Write a funny short story. Be sure to use correct punctuation marks, including comma placement in clauses, nonrestrictive phrases, contrasting expressions, introductory material, and parenthetical expressions.

Test Warm-Up

DIRECTIONS

Read the introduction and the passage that follows. Then, answer the questions to show that you can use correct punctuation marks including comma placement in nonrestrictive phrases, clauses, and contrasting expressions in reading and writing.

Jordan wrote this paragraph about his family reunion. Read the paragraph and think about the changes you would suggest as a peer editor. When you finish reading, answer the questions that follow.

Three Hundred Costas

(1) Attending our family reunion is quite an experience. (2) Around 300 of my relatives proud to be part of the Costas family, meet every two years. (3) Last year's gathering which was in Dallas was convenient. (4) The older relatives are the ones who try to remember who belongs to whom and play guessing games with the kids. (5) I say, "I'm Jack's son." (6) Then I'd have to add, "I'm not Jerry's son."

---

1 What change, if any, should be made in sentence 2?

- **A** Add a comma after ***Around***
- **B** Add a comma after ***relatives***
- **C** Change the comma after ***family*** to a semicolon
- **D** Make no change

2 What is the most effective way to revise the ideas in sentence 3?

- **F** Last year's gathering, which was in Dallas, was convenient.
- **G** Last year's gathering, which was in Dallas was convenient.
- **H** Last year's gathering was in Dallas and was convenient.
- **J** Last year's gathering which was in Dallas, was convenient.

3 How should sentence 4 be revised?

- **A** The older relatives, the ones who try to remember who belongs to whom, play guessing games with the kids.
- **B** As older relatives, ones who remember who belongs to whom, play games.
- **C** The older relatives play guessing games with the kids, who try to remember who belongs to whom.
- **D** The older relatives, who try to remember who belongs to whom, play guessing games with the kids.

4 What is the most effective way to combine sentences 5 and 6?

- **F** I say, "Yes, I'm Jack's son, but I'm not Jerry's son."
- **G** I say, "I'm Jack's son, not Jerry's son."
- **H** I say, "I'm Jack's son," adding that I'm not Jerry's son.
- **J** I say, "I'm Jack's son, and I'm adding that I'm not Jerry's son."

Using Commas With Dates, Geographical Names, and Titles

Dates usually have several parts, including months, days, and years. Commas separate these elements for easier reading.

RULE 23.2.10

When a date is made up of two or more parts, use a comma after each item, except in the case of a month followed by a day.

EXAMPLES The wedding took place on June 16, 2005, and their son was born on June 16, 2006.

The show opened on June 16 and closed two days later.
(no comma needed after the day of the month)

Commas are also used when the month and the day are used as an appositive to rename a day of the week.

EXAMPLES Friday, August 23, was the first day of the fair.

Craig will arrive on Wednesday, May 14, and will stay until Friday.

When a date contains only a month and a year, commas are unnecessary.

EXAMPLES I will graduate in June 2015.

Joy will visit Europe in August 2011.

If the parts of a date have already been joined by prepositions, no comma is needed.

EXAMPLE The city's new subway system ran its first train in June of 1890.

When a geographical name is made up of two or more parts, use a comma after each item.

23.2.11 RULE

EXAMPLES My cousin who lives in Santa Fe, New Mexico, is cutting the ribbon for the grand opening.

They're going to Toronto, Ontario, Canada, for their winter vacation.

See Practice 23.2G

When a name is followed by one or more titles, use a comma after the name and after each title.

23.2.12 RULE

EXAMPLE I see that Jeremy McGuire, Ph.D., works here.

A similar rule applies with some business abbreviations.

EXAMPLE BookWright, Inc., published a book about food.

Using Commas in Numbers

Commas make large numbers easier to read by grouping them.

With large numbers of more than three digits, use a comma after every third digit starting from the right.

23.2.13 RULE

EXAMPLES 3,823 books, 205,000 gallons, 2,674,970 tons

Do not use a comma in ZIP Codes, telephone numbers, page numbers, years, serial numbers, or house numbers.

23.2.14 RULE

ZIP CODE	07632	YEAR NUMBER	2004
TELEPHONE NUMBER	(805) 555-6224	SERIAL NUMBER	602 988 6768
PAGE NUMBER	Page 1258	HOUSE NUMBER	18436 Lamson Road

See Practice 23.2H

PRACTICE 23.2G Using Commas With Dates and Geographical Names

Read each sentence. Then, rewrite each sentence to show where to correctly place commas in dates and geographical names.

EXAMPLE It takes fourteen hours to drive from Nashville Tennessee to Austin Texas.

ANSWER *It takes fourteen hours to drive from Nashville, Tennessee, to Austin, Texas.*

1. On December 7 1941, Japanese bombers attacked Pearl Harbor.
2. On February 2 2009, we visited San Antonio Texas.
3. The hospital is located in Newark New Jersey.
4. My cousin got married in Vail Colorado on August 30 2008.
5. The new girl in our class is from Nice France.
6. In July 2008, we took a cruise that left from Miami Florida.
7. Sally was born in Oklahoma City Oklahoma.
8. The test will be on Monday October 12.
9. On April 30 1803, the United States purchased the Louisiana Territory.
10. My uncle took me to see the Houston Texans play on Sunday November 23.

PRACTICE 23.2H Editing Sentences for Proper Comma Usage

Read each sentence. Then, rewrite each sentence, deleting or adding commas where they are needed.

EXAMPLE This Sunday March, 1 I'm going to New York.

ANSWER *This Sunday, March 1, I'm going to New York.*

11. Jillian Polk M.D. spoke at the medical conference.
12. Did you drive from Atlanta, Georgia to Seattle, Washington, last summer?
13. Flora estimated that the box contained 5822 marbles.
14. Have you ever visited Madrid Spain?
15. Randall Tilde Ph.D. attended the meeting.
16. We will be on vacation from Friday September 9, to Wednesday September 14.
17. The plane had a layover in Salt Lake City Utah on its way to Sacramento California.
18. Unabridged Books Ltd. opens for business at 8:00 A.M.
19. The lawyer signed her name "Ingrid Blush J.D."
20. On March 4 1789 the U.S. Constitution went into effect.

SPEAKING APPLICATION

Take turns with a partner. Use sentences 2 and 6 as models to say similar sentences. Your partner should tell which sentence needs a comma in the date.

WRITING APPLICATION

Write four sentences that contain dates, geographical names, and large numbers, but omit all commas. Exchange papers with a partner. Your partner should add commas where necessary.

Using Commas With Addresses and in Letters

Commas are also used in addresses, salutations of friendly letters, and closings of friendly or business letters.

Use a comma after each item in an address made up of two or more parts.

23.2.15 RULE

Commas are placed after the name, street, and city. No comma separates the state from the ZIP Code. Instead, insert an extra space between them.

EXAMPLE Send an invitation to Mrs. Robert Brooks, 145 River Road, Jacksonville, Florida 32211.

Fewer commas are needed when an address is written in a letter or on an envelope.

EXAMPLE Mrs. Robert Brooks
145 River Road
Jacksonville, FL 32211

Use a comma after the salutation in a personal letter and after the closing in all letters.

23.2.16 RULE

SALUTATIONS Dear Emily, Dear Uncle Frank,

CLOSINGS Yours truly, Sincerely,

See Practice 23.2I

Using Commas in Elliptical Sentences

In **elliptical sentences,** words that are understood are left out. Commas make these sentences easier to read.

Use a comma to indicate the words left out of an elliptical sentence.

23.2.17 RULE

EXAMPLE Alan celebrates his birthday formally; Fred, casually.

The words *celebrates his birthday* have been omitted from the second clause of the sentence. The comma has been inserted in their place so the meaning is still clear. The sentence could be restated in this way: *Alan celebrates his birthday formally; Fred celebrates his birthday casually.*

Using Commas With Direct Quotations

Commas are also used to indicate where **direct quotations** begin and end. (See Section 23.4 for more information on punctuating quotations.)

RULE 23.2.18

Use commas to set off a direct quotation from the rest of a sentence.

EXAMPLES "You came home late," commented Bill's mother.

He said, "The rehearsal ran longer than expected."

"I hope," Bill's mother said, "the leading man doesn't forget his lines."

Using Commas for Clarity

Commas help you group words that belong together.

RULE 23.2.19

Use a comma to prevent a sentence from being misunderstood.

UNCLEAR Near the highway developers were building a shopping mall.

CLEAR Near the highway, developers were building a shopping mall.

Misuses of Commas

Because commas appear so frequently in writing, some people are tempted to use them where they are not needed. Before you insert a comma, think about how your ideas relate to one another.

Find It/FIX IT
7
Grammar Game Plan

MISUSED WITH AN ADJECTIVE AND A NOUN	After a dance, I enjoy a cool, refreshing, drink.
CORRECT	After a dance, I enjoy a cool, refreshing drink.
MISUSED WITH A COMPOUND SUBJECT	After the election, my friend Nancy, and her sister Julia, were invited to the inaugural ball.
CORRECT	After the election, my friend Nancy and her sister Julia were invited to the inaugural ball.
MISUSED WITH A COMPOUND VERB	He looked into her eyes, and spoke from his heart.
CORRECT	He looked into her eyes and spoke from his heart.
MISUSED WITH A COMPOUND OBJECT	She chose a dress with long sleeves, and a train.
CORRECT	She chose a dress with long sleeves and a train.
MISUSED WITH PHRASES	Reading the invitation, and wondering who sent it, Brian did not hear the phone ring.
CORRECT	Reading the invitation and wondering who sent it, Brian did not hear the phone ring.
MISUSED WITH CLAUSES	He discussed what elements are crucial to a party, and which caterers are most reliable.
CORRECT	He discussed what elements are crucial to a party and which caterers are most reliable.

See Practice 23.2J

PRACTICE 23.2I Adding Commas to Addresses and Letters

Read each item. Then, add commas where needed.

EXAMPLE To my sweet little angel

ANSWER *To my sweet little angel,*

1. Dear Aunt Carol
2. Yours truly
   Uncle Arnie
3. Send an invitation to Kate Myer 15 Blauvelt Avenue Rockland Maine 04841.
4. My best friend moved to Tasmania Australia.
5. Sincerely
   Tim Jones
6. Dear Amanda Sophia and Isabella
7. My pen pal lives at 1025 Willow Street San Francisco California 94102.
8. Dear Mom and Dad
9. With all our love
   Kate and Sam
10. John Barrett
    802 Main Street
    Portland OR 97222

PRACTICE 23.2J Revising Sentences With Misused Commas

Read each sentence. Then, if a sentence contains a misused comma, rewrite the sentence to show correct comma usage.

EXAMPLE Sally likes roses but, Lily likes tulips.

ANSWER *Sally likes roses, but Lily likes tulips.*

11. Hey, I found my mitt, in the yard.
12. The new teacher, seemed, excited, and shy.
13. Running, swimming, and, cycling are all part of a triathlon.
14. Alan's address is 1,491 Crescent Drive Chinook MT 5,9523.
15. Brian, Forrester Ph.D. is a genius.
16. My cousin Julia visited Rome, Italy in July 2009.
17. I want to stop in Little, Rock on our way to Montgomery Alabama.
18. Klever Designs, Inc. gives its employees a bonus every year.
19. To run, in a marathon takes a lot of training.
20. On March, 4 1893, Grover Cleveland became the first president to serve two, nonconsecutive, terms.

SPEAKING APPLICATION

Discuss with a partner the necessity of placing commas in addresses.

WRITING APPLICATION

Write five compound sentences with dates, lists, or multiple adjectives. Be sure to use commas properly.

23.3 Semicolons and Colons

The **semicolon (;)** is used to join related independent clauses. Semicolons can also help you avoid confusion in sentences with other internal punctuation. The **colon (:)** is used to introduce lists of items and in other special situations.

WRITING COACH Online

www.phwritingcoach.com

Grammar Tutorials

Brush up on your Grammar skills with these animated videos.

Grammar Practice

Practice your grammar skills with Writing Coach Online.

Grammar Games

Test your knowledge of grammar in this fast-paced interactive video game.

Using Semicolons to Join Independent Clauses

Semicolons establish relationships between two independent clauses that are closely connected in thought and structure. A semicolon can also be used to separate independent clauses or items in a series that already contain a number of commas.

Use a semicolon to join related independent clauses that are not already joined by the conjunctions *and, but, for, nor, or, so,* or *yet.*

RULE 23.3.1

EXAMPLE We explored the attic together; we were amazed at all the useless junk we found there.

Do not use a semicolon to join two unrelated independent clauses. If the clauses are not related, they should be written as separate sentences with a period or another end mark to separate them.

Note that when a sentence contains three or more related independent clauses, they may still be separated with semicolons.

EXAMPLE The birds vanished; the sky grew dark; the little pond was still.

Semicolons Join Clauses Separated by Conjunctive Adverbs or Transitional Expressions

Conjunctive adverbs are adverbs that are used as conjunctions to join independent clauses. **Transitional expressions** are expressions that connect one independent clause with another one.

Use a semicolon to join independent clauses separated by either a conjunctive adverb or a transitional expression.

RULE 23.3.2

CONJUNCTIVE ADVERBS	*also, besides, consequently, first, furthermore, however, indeed, instead, moreover, nevertheless, otherwise, second, then, therefore, thus*
TRANSITIONAL EXPRESSIONS	*as a result, at this time, for instance, in fact, on the other hand, that is*

Place a semicolon *before* a conjunctive adverb or a transitional expression, and place a comma *after* a conjunctive adverb or transitional expression. The comma sets off the conjunctive adverb or transitional expression, which introduces the second clause.

EXAMPLE She never found the shipwreck; in fact, she really had no interest in scuba diving.

Because words used as conjunctive adverbs and transitions can also interrupt one continuous sentence, use a semicolon only when there is an independent clause on each side of the conjunctive adverb or transitional expression.

EXAMPLES We visited antique shops in eight counties in only two days; consequently, we had no time for sightseeing.

We were very impressed, however, with Amy's knowledge of history.

Using Semicolons to Avoid Confusion

Sometimes, semicolons are used to separate items in a series.

RULE 23.3.3

Use semicolons to avoid confusion when independent clauses or items in a series already contain commas.

When the items in a series already contain several commas, semicolons can be used to group items that belong together. Semicolons are placed at the end of all but the last complete item in the series.

INDEPENDENT CLAUSES The city, supposedly filled with gold, was a fable; and the hungry, tired explorers would only find it in their dreams.

ITEMS IN A SERIES On their trip, my parents visited my aunt, who lives in Grand Rapids; my brother, who lives in Indianapolis; and our former neighbors, the Garcias, who live in Chicago.

Semicolons appear most commonly in a series that contains either nonessential appositives, participial phrases, or adjectival clauses. Commas should separate the nonessential material from the word or words they modify; semicolons should separate the complete items in the series.

APPOSITIVES I sent notes to Mr. Nielson, my science teacher; Mrs. Jensen, my history instructor; and Mrs. Seltz, the librarian.

PARTICIPIAL PHRASES I developed a fascination with space travel from television, watching live rocket launches; from school, learning about astronomy; and from movies, watching science-fiction adventures.

ADJECTIVAL CLAUSES The toy police car that I bought has spare tires, which are brand new; a siren, which has just been installed; and flashing lights, which have new bulbs.

Using Colons

The **colon (:)** is used to introduce lists of items and in certain special situations.

RULE 23.3.4

Use a colon after an independent clause to introduce a list of items. Use commas to separate three or more items.

Independent clauses that appear before a colon often include the words *the following, as follows, these,* or *those.*

EXAMPLES For our class, we had to interview the following experts: an economist, a scientist, and a doctor.

RULE 23.3.5

Do not use a colon after a verb or a preposition.

INCORRECT Veronica always orders: soup, salad, and dessert.

CORRECT Veronica always orders soup, salad, and dessert.

RULE 23.3.6

Use a colon to introduce a quotation that is formal or lengthy or a quotation that does not contain a "he said/she said" expression.

EXAMPLE Oliver Wendell Holmes Jr. wrote this about freedom: "It is only through free debate and free exchange of ideas that government remains responsive to the will of the people and peaceful change is effected."

Even if it is lengthy, dialogue or a casual remark should be introduced by a comma. Use the colon if the quotation is formal or has no tagline.

A colon may also be used to introduce a sentence that explains the sentence that precedes it.

Use a colon to introduce a sentence that summarizes or explains the sentence before it.

RULE 23.3.7

EXAMPLE His explanation for being late was believable: He had had a flat tire on the way.

Notice that the complete sentence introduced by the colon starts with a capital letter.

Use a colon to introduce a formal appositive that follows an independent clause.

RULE 23.3.8

EXAMPLE I had finally decided on a career: nursing.

The colon is a stronger punctuation mark than a comma. Using the colon gives more emphasis to the appositive it introduces.

Use a colon in a number of special writing situations.

RULE 23.3.9

SPECIAL SITUATIONS REQUIRING COLONS	
Numerals Giving the Time	1:30 A.M. 9:15 P.M.
References to Periodicals (Volume Number: Page Number)	*Scientific American* 74:12 *Sports Illustrated* 53:15
Biblical References (Chapter Number: Verse Number)	1 Corinthians 13:13
Subtitles for Books and Magazines	*A Field Guide to the Birds: Eastern Land and Water Birds*
Salutations in Business Letters	Dear Mr. Gordon: Dear Sir:
Labels Used to Signal Important Ideas	**Danger**: High-voltage wires

See Practice 23.3A
See Practice 23.3B

PRACTICE 23.3A Adding Semicolons and Colons to Sentences

Read each sentence. Then, rewrite each sentence, inserting a semicolon or colon where needed.

EXAMPLE Belle and Jessica see each other a lot they are good friends.

ANSWER *Belle and Jessica see each other a lot; they are good friends.*

1. Jeff woke up early otherwise, he would have missed the bus.
2. I only like three toppings on my pizza mushrooms, tomatoes, and peppers.
3. Janine, do your homework it won't take long.
4. Exercise is good for you however, remember to stretch before you start.
5. Dee only drinks one type of juice apple juice.
6. It's a pleasure to see the club's oldest member Robert Shaw.
7. Brush your teeth also, remember to floss.
8. Delivering papers, Aaron earned fifty dollars it was enough to buy the new shoes he wanted.
9. At our picnic, we had three kinds of sandwiches ham, peanut butter, and turkey.
10. I sent letters to Alex, my friend from camp Alana, my pen pal, and Naomi, my cousin.

PRACTICE 23.3B Using Semicolons and Colons

Read each item. Then, for each item, write a complete sentence, using the item, the punctuation indicated in parentheses, and additional words.

EXAMPLE I have two tests next week (colon)

ANSWER *I have two tests next week: one in math and one in science.*

11. broccoli or spinach (colon)
12. There were all sorts of activities at camp (colon)
13. The boy began to laugh (semicolon)
14. I started reading a book by my favorite author (colon)
15. We drilled, sprinted, and ran (semicolon)
16. My dog knows three tricks (colon)
17. Joseph likes to swim (semicolon)
18. Three people attended the show (colon)
19. *The Washington Post and The New York Times* (colon)
20. Phillip, don't forget the juice (semicolon)

SPEAKING APPLICATION

Discuss with a partner the similarities between your corrections for sentences 5 and 6. Explain how the sentences would be different if commas were used instead.

WRITING APPLICATION

Write instructions for completing a task. Use at least one semicolon and two colons correctly.

23.4 Quotation Marks, Underlining, and Italics

Quotation marks (" ") set off direct quotations, dialogue, and certain types of titles. Other titles are **underlined** or set in *italics,* a slanted type style.

Find It/FIX IT
6
Grammar Game Plan

Find It/FIX IT
18
Grammar Game Plan

WRITING COACH Online
www.phwritingcoach.com

Grammar Practice
Practice your grammar skills with Writing Coach Online.

Grammar Games
Test your knowledge of grammar in this fast-paced interactive video game.

Using Quotation Marks With Quotations

Quotation marks identify spoken or written words that you are including in your writing. A **direct quotation** represents a person's exact speech or thoughts. An **indirect quotation** reports the general meaning of what a person said or thought.

A **direct quotation** is enclosed in quotation marks.

RULE 23.4.1

DIRECT QUOTATION "When I learn to ride," said the student, "I'll use the bridle path every day."

An **indirect quotation** does not require quotation marks.

RULE 23.4.2

INDIRECT QUOTATION The student said that when she learns to ride, she plans to use the bridle path every day.

Both types of quotations are acceptable when you write. Direct quotations, however, generally result in a livelier writing style.

Using Direct Quotations With Introductory, Concluding, and Interrupting Expressions

A writer will generally identify a speaker by using words such as *he asked* or *she said* with a quotation. These expressions, called **conversational taglines** or **tags,** can introduce, conclude, or interrupt a quotation.

Direct Quotations With Introductory Expressions

Commas help you set off introductory information so that your reader understands who is speaking.

RULE 23.4.3

Use a comma after short introductory expressions that precede direct quotations.

EXAMPLE My mother warned, "If you get a horse, you'll be responsible for taking care of it."

If the introductory conversational tagline is very long or formal in tone, set it off with a colon instead of a comma.

EXAMPLE At the end of the meeting, Marge spoke of her dreams: "I hope to advance the cause of women jockeys everywhere."

Direct Quotations With Concluding Expressions

Conversational taglines may also act as concluding expressions.

RULE 23.4.4

Use a comma, question mark, or exclamation mark after a direct quotation followed by a concluding expression.

EXAMPLE "If you get a horse, you'll be responsible for taking care of it," my mother warned.

Concluding expressions are not complete sentences; therefore, they do not begin with capital letters. Closing quotation marks are always placed outside the punctuation at the end of direct quotations. Concluding expressions generally end with a period.

Divided Quotations With Interrupting Expressions

You may use a conversational tagline to interrupt the words of a direct quotation, which is also called a **divided quotation.**

Use a comma after the part of a quoted sentence followed by an interrupting conversational tagline. Use another comma after the tagline. Do not capitalize the first word of the rest of the sentence. Use quotation marks to enclose the quotation. End punctuation should be inside the last quotation mark.

RULE 23.4.5

EXAMPLE "If you get a horse," my mother warned, "you'll be responsible for taking care of it."

Use a comma, question mark, or exclamation mark after a quoted sentence that comes before an interrupting conversational tagline. Use a period after the tagline.

RULE 23.4.6

EXAMPLE "You own a horse now," stated my mother. "You are responsible for taking care of it."

Quotation Marks With Other Punctuation Marks

Quotation marks are used with commas, semicolons, colons, and all of the end marks. However, the location of the quotation marks in relation to the punctuation marks varies.

Place a comma or a period *inside* the final quotation mark. Place a semicolon or colon *outside* the final quotation mark.

RULE 23.4.7

EXAMPLES "Secretariat was a great horse," sighed Mother.

We were just informed about his "earth-shaking discovery"; we are very pleased.

Place a question mark or an exclamation mark inside the final quotation mark if the end mark is part of the quotation. Do not use an additional end mark.

RULE 23.4.8

EXAMPLE Larry wondered, "How could I lose the race?"

RULE 23.4.9

Place a question mark or exclamation mark outside the final quotation mark if the end mark is part of the entire sentence, not part of the quotation.

EXAMPLE We were shocked when he said, "Yes" !

Using Single Quotation Marks for Quotations Within Quotations

As you have learned, double quotation marks **(" ")** should enclose the main quotation in a sentence. The rules for using commas and end marks with double quotation marks also apply to **single quotation marks.**

RULE 23.4.10

Use single quotation marks (' ') to set off a quotation within a quotation.

EXAMPLES "I remember Ali quoting Shelley, 'If winter comes, can spring be far behind?' " Mike said.

"The doctor said, 'Good news!' " Lainie explained.

Punctuating Explanatory Material Within Quotations

Explanatory material within quotations should be placed in brackets. (See Section 23.7 for more information on brackets.)

RULE 23.4.11

Use brackets to enclose an explanation located within a quotation. The brackets show that the explanation is not part of the original quotation.

EXAMPLE The mayor said, "This bridge is a link between two communities [Dover and Flint]."

See Practice 23.4A
See Practice 23.4B

PRACTICE 23.4A **Using Quotation Marks**

Read each sentence. Then, rewrite each sentence, inserting quotation marks where needed.

EXAMPLE This cannot be right, he said.

ANSWER *"This cannot be right," he said.*

1. Karen asked, Have you studied for the test?
2. Throughout the movie, the actor repeated the same line: Be patient.
3. Darren borrowed my book, said Amanda.
4. This is my favorite song! exclaimed Mia.
5. I am not sure, said Jeff, where I put my scarf.
6. I didn't know for sure until Eric said, Let's go. Then, I knew, Cameron stated.
7. Did you see a movie last night? asked Dominic.
8. Is it possible that there is life on Mars? asked Alex.
9. Yes, I have read that book, replied Thomas.
10. Don't miss the bus! Dad warned.

PRACTICE 23.4B **Revising for the Correct Use of Quotation Marks**

Read each sentence. Then, rewrite each sentence, correcting the misuse of quotation marks.

EXAMPLE "I can't believe that happened, said Chris."

ANSWER *"I can't believe that happened," said Chris.*

11. "I thought the chapter assigned for homework was really interesting, observed Bella."
12. "Martin said, I need a ride to work."
13. "Do you have *The New York Times* delivered" every morning? asked Carrie.
14. "Is it time to leave for the market"? Tom asked.
15. "The book I am reading is fantastic! said Claire."
16. "What time," asked Hilary, will we be leaving for the airport?
17. Jamie asked "to borrow a pencil," and I said, Sure.
18. "Mom said, "Come straight home after school!" Jesse explained."
19. "Nancy gave it to her, said" Andrea.
20. "I can see the car from here, Steve informed us."

SPEAKING APPLICATION

Take turns with a partner. Say some sentences with direct quotes. Your partner should tell where quotation marks would be inserted if your sentences were written.

WRITING APPLICATION

Write three sentences: one direct quotation with any introductory expression, one direct quotation with a concluding expression, and one divided quotation with an interrupting expression.

Using Quotation Marks for Dialogue

A conversation between two or more people is called a **dialogue.**

RULE 23.4.12

When writing a dialogue, begin a new paragraph with each change of speaker.

The sun slowly set over the western edge of the windswept beach as the waves lapped the shore.

Charlie sat in the cooling sand and talked with his brother about his plans.

"I'm going south," said Charlie. "I think I'll like the climate better; you know I don't like the cold."

"Have you packed yet?" asked Roy. "Can I have your snow boots?"

"They are all yours," said Charlie. "If I never see them again, it is fine with me."

RULE 23.4.13

For quotations longer than a paragraph, put quotation marks at the beginning of each paragraph and at the end of the final paragraph.

John McPhee wrote an essay about a canoe trip on the St. John River in northern Maine. He introduces his readers to the river in the following way:

"We have been out here four days now and rain has been falling three. The rain appears to be ending. Breaks of blue are opening in the sky. Sunlight is coming through, and a wind is rising.

"I was not prepared for the St. John River, did not anticipate its size. I saw it as a narrow trail flowing north, twisting through balsam and spruce—a small and intimate forest river, something like the Allagash. . . ."

Using Quotation Marks in Titles

Generally, quotation marks are used around the titles of shorter works.

Use quotation marks to enclose the titles of short written works.

RULE 23.4.14

WRITTEN WORKS THAT USE QUOTATION MARKS	
Title of a Short Story	"The Jockey" by Carson McCullers "The Tell-Tale Heart" by Edgar Allan Poe
Chapter From a Book	"Dynamic Democracy" in *Freedom's Ferment* "Railroads in America" in *Travel West*
Title of a Short Poem	"Boy Breaking Glass" by Gwendolyn Brooks
Essay Title	"Self-Reliance" by Ralph Waldo Emerson
Title of an Article	"The Benefits of Train Travel" by Raul Jones

Use quotation marks around the titles of episodes in a television or radio series, songs, and parts of a long musical composition.

RULE 23.4.15

ARTISTIC WORK TITLES THAT USE QUOTATION MARKS	
Episode	"The Iran File" from *60 Minutes*
Song Title	"Something" by the Beatles
Part of a Long Musical Composition	"Spring" from *The Four Seasons* "E.T. Phone Home" from the *E.T. The Extra-Terrestrial* soundtrack

Use quotation marks around the title of a work that is mentioned as part of a collection.

RULE 23.4.16

The title *Plato* would normally be underlined or italicized. In the example below, however, the title is placed in quotation marks because it is cited as part of a larger work.

EXAMPLE "Plato" from *Great Books of the Western World*

Using Underlining and Italics in Titles and Other Special Words

Underlining and **italics** help make titles and other special words and names stand out in your writing. Underlining is used only in handwritten or typewritten material. In printed material, italic (slanted) print is generally used instead of underlining.

RULE 23.4.17

Underline or italicize the titles of long written works and the titles of publications that are published as a single work.

WRITTEN WORKS THAT ARE UNDERLINED OR ITALICIZED	
Title of a Book	*War and Peace* *To Kill a Mockingbird*
Title of a Newspaper	*The New York Times*
Title of a Play	*The Glass Menagerie* *Long Day's Journey Into Night*
Title of a Long Poem	*Paradise Lost*
Title of a Magazine	*Newsweek*

The portion of a newspaper title that should be italicized or underlined will vary from newspaper to newspaper. *The New York Times* should always be fully capitalized and italicized or underlined. Other papers, however, can be treated in one of two ways: the *Los Angeles Times* or the Los Angeles *Times*. You may want to check the paper's Web site for correct formatting.

RULE 23.4.18

Underline or italicize the titles of movies, television and radio series, long works of music, and works of art.

ARTISTIC WORKS THAT ARE UNDERLINED OR ITALICIZED	
Title of a Movie	*Titanic, It's a Wonderful Life*
Title of a Television Series	*Friends, Nova*
Title of a Long Work of Music	*Surprise Symphony*
Title of an Album (on any media)	*TJ's Greatest Hits*
Title of a Painting	*Mona Lisa, The River*
Title of a Sculpture	*The Thinker, The Minute Man*

Do not underline, italicize, or place in quotation marks the name of the Bible, its books and divisions, or other holy scriptures, such as the Torah and the Qu'ran.

RULE 23.4.19

EXAMPLE Adam read from Genesis in the Old Testament.

Government documents should also not be underlined or enclosed in quotation marks.

Do not underline, italicize, or place in quotation marks the titles of government charters, alliances, treaties, acts, statutes, speeches, or reports.

RULE 23.4.20

EXAMPLE The Taft-Hartley Labor Act was passed in 1947.

Underline or italicize the names of air, sea, and space craft.

RULE 23.4.21

EXAMPLE Were there horses aboard the *Santa Maria*?

Underline or italicize words, letters, or numbers (figures) used as names for themselves.

RULE 23.4.22

EXAMPLES Her *i's* and her *l's* look too much like *1's*.

Avoid sprinkling your speech with *you know*.

Underline or italicize foreign words and phrases not yet accepted into English.

RULE 23.4.23

EXAMPLE "*Bonne nuit*," she said, meaning "goodnight" in French.

See Practice 23.4C
See Practice 23.4D

Using Quotation Marks to Indicate Sarcasm or Irony

Quotation marks are also used to set off words intended as sarcasm or irony. **Sarcasm** and **irony** use words to express the opposite of their literal meaning. Both literary devices are often meant to be humorous, but can also express anger or frustration. Irony often describes situations, whereas sarcasm is speech that expresses mockery or criticism.

Writers may use quotation marks to indicate sarcasm or irony. In the following examples, quotation marks create distance between the author's perspective and the words.

SARCASM Dana "forgot" her wallet, so Rita had to pay.

IRONY The ferocious dog is named "Fluffy."

Words that indicate sarcasm or irony often are not set off by quotation marks. Use quotation marks only to avoid sarcasm or irony being missed or lost altogether, as overuse may dilute their effect.

RULE 23.4.24

Do not overuse quotation marks. They should be used only when you want to emphasize sarcasm or irony.

Also, the reader may confuse the words within quotation marks as dialogue, clouding the writer's intent. Instead, make the sarcasm or irony clear by choosing your words carefully or using adjectives like *so-called, alleged,* or *supposed* to show the logic of the sentence.

EXAMPLE The **so-called** breakfast was dry toast and stale juice.

See Practice 23.4E
See Practice 23.4F

PRACTICE 23.4C Using Punctuation in Titles and Dialogue

Read each sentence. Then, rewrite each sentence, adding correct punctuation where needed. If any words need to be italicized, underline those words.

EXAMPLE Maria asked, Have you read The Scarlet Letter?

ANSWER *Maria asked, "Have you read The Scarlet Letter?"*

1. What time is the movie? asked Nathan.
2. The movie is at 7:00 P.M. replied Juan.
3. Great, said Nathan, I'll meet you at the theater at 6:45 P.M.
4. My favorite short story is Aaron's Gift.
5. My mother reads The New York Times every day.
6. The chapter titled Cells should help you with your assignment.
7. Anne said, I just read Walker Percy's book The Moviegoer.
8. Have you read the short story The Necklace? asked Gloria.
9. Is your science project almost finished? asked John.
10. Yes, answered Heather, my project will be ready for the science fair tomorrow.

PRACTICE 23.4D Revising Punctuation in Titles and Dialogue

Read each sentence. Then, rewrite each sentence, using correct punctuation. If any words need to be italicized, underline those words.

EXAMPLE My favorite song by the Beatles is Hey Jude.

ANSWER *My favorite song by the Beatles is "Hey Jude."*

11. "Did you read the essay Melting Glaciers for class asked Gregory."
12. "Yes, replied Angel, I read it last night."
13. "At the end of the movie Mr. Franks forewarned is a surprising twist."
14. "I think the movie Citizen Kane has a great ending chimed Ricky."
15. "My favorite black-and-white movie is Lifeboat directed by Alfred Hitchcock," said Jordan.
16. "Alfred Hitchcock wrote an interesting book titled The Murder of Monty Woolley, Mr. Franks informed the class.
17. "That painting said our teacher is by a very famous artist."
18. "It's The Starry Night a painting by van Gogh, replied Joe."
19. "I just read the short story titled Quail Seed.
20. Do you have the current issue of Science?

SPEAKING APPLICATION

Take turns with a partner. Say sentences that contain both dialogue and titles. For each sentence, your partner should indicate which words should be put in quotation marks and/or italicized.

WRITING APPLICATION

Write a short dialogue between two characters who are discussing a book. Include incorrect usage of quotation marks, underlining, and italics. Exchange papers with a partner. Your partner should rewrite your dialogue and correct punctuation errors.

PRACTICE 23.4E **Using Quotation Marks, Underlining, and Italics**

Read each sentence. Then, rewrite each sentence, adding quotation marks, underlining, and italics where necessary.

EXAMPLE You did such a wonderful job that I had to redo it later.

ANSWER *You did such a "wonderful" job that I had to redo it later.*

1. Michaela missed the history test because she had the flu again.
2. Travis and Louise went to hear Beethoven's Pastoral Symphony.
3. Our science club's trusted treasurer misplaced some of our funds.
4. My sister watches the movie The Sound of Music at least once a week.
5. She supposedly went to the library.
6. Mr. Mathers gets his political news from The Washington Post.
7. Antoine was too busy to join our study group.
8. To help her father with his diet, Sally ate the rest of his dessert.
9. Ray plays his favorite song, Lean On Me, over and over again.
10. Homer's The Iliad is required reading in our Greek class.

PRACTICE 23.4F **Using Quotation Marks to Indicate Sarcasm or Irony**

Read each sentence. Then, rewrite each sentence using quotation marks to indicate sarcasm or irony.

EXAMPLE Your pessimism is such an endearing quality.

ANSWER *Your pessimism is such an "endearing" quality.*

11. It was considerate of you to return my sweater after six months.
12. Who was the wise person who told my little sister scary stories at bedtime?
13. Reggie claimed that he just happened to show up at dinnertime.
14. The light winds the weather service predicted resulted in a huge power outage.
15. Staying up until 3:00 A.M. on a school night sounds like a terrific idea.
16. Mr. Levine believes it is reasonable for us to read 60 pages by tomorrow.
17. Your frown is reassuring.
18. Leslie said she couldn't help out because she lost the directions.
19. The training session consisted of a quick tour of the restaurant's kitchen.
20. Billy went to a rock concert to do research for an assignment.

SPEAKING APPLICATION

Take turns with a partner. Say sentences that require quotation marks, italics, or words that should be underlined. Your partner should listen for and identify the words that should receive special punctuation.

WRITING APPLICATION

Create a sarcastic character or an event that expresses irony. Write an essay that describes your creation. Be sure to use correct punctuation marks, including quotation marks to indicate sarcasm or irony.

23.5 Hyphens

The **hyphen (-)** is used to combine words, spell some numbers and words, and show a connection between the syllables of words that are broken at the ends of lines.

Find It/FIX IT 19 Grammar Game Plan

WRITING COACH Online
www.phwritingcoach.com

Grammar Practice
Practice your grammar skills with Writing Coach Online.

Grammar Games
Test your knowledge of grammar in this fast-paced interactive video game.

Using Hyphens in Numbers

Hyphens are used to join compound numbers and fractions.

Use a hyphen when you spell out two-word numbers from twenty-one through ninety-nine. RULE 23.5.1

EXAMPLES thirty-three inches forty-seven acres

Use a hyphen when you use a fraction as an adjective but not when you use a fraction as a noun. RULE 23.5.2

ADJECTIVE The recipe calls for one-half cup of mushrooms.

NOUN Three quarters of the report on Japan is complete.

Use a hyphen between a number and a word when they are combined as modifiers. Do not use a hyphen if the word in the modifier is possessive. RULE 23.5.3

EXAMPLES The team members took a 15-minute break.

The students put 12 weeks' work into their projects.

If a series of consecutive, hyphenated modifiers ends with the same word, do not repeat the modified word each time. Instead, use a suspended hyphen (also called a dangling hyphen) and the modified word only at the end of the series. RULE 23.5.4

EXAMPLE The eighth- and ninth-grade students came.

Using Hyphens With Prefixes and Suffixes

Hyphens help your reader easily see the parts of a long word.

RULE 23.5.5

Use a hyphen after a prefix that is followed by a proper noun or proper adjective.

The following prefixes are often used before proper nouns: *ante-*, *anti-*, *mid-*, *post-*, *pre-*, *pro-*, and *un-*.

EXAMPLES pre-Renaissance mid-February

RULE 23.5.6

Use a hyphen in words with the prefixes *all-*, *ex-*, and *self-* and words with the suffix *-elect*.

EXAMPLES all-powerful senator-elect

Many words with common prefixes are no longer hyphenated. Check a dictionary if you are unsure whether to use a hyphen.

Using Hyphens With Compound Words

Hyphens help preserve the units of meaning in compound words.

RULE 23.5.7

Use a hyphen to connect two or more words that are used as one compound word, unless your dictionary gives a different spelling.

EXAMPLES merry-go-round off-season
sister-in-law six-year-old

RULE 23.5.8

Use a hyphen to connect a compound modifier that appears before a noun. The exceptions to this rule include adverbs ending in *-ly* and compound proper adjectives or compound proper nouns that are acting as an adjective.

EXAMPLES WITH HYPHENS	EXAMPLES WITHOUT HYPHENS
a well-made pair of jeans	widely distributed information
the bright-eyed children	Native American people
an up-to-date decision	Red River valley

When compound modifiers follow a noun, they generally do not require the use of hyphens.

EXAMPLE The jeans were **well made.**

However, if a dictionary spells a word with a hyphen, the word must always be hyphenated, even when it follows a noun.

EXAMPLE The news was up-to-date.

Using Hyphens for Clarity

Some words or group of words can be misread if a hyphen is not used.

Use a hyphen within a word when a combination of letters might otherwise be confusing. RULE 23.5.9

EXAMPLES semi-independent, co-op, re-cede

Use a hyphen between words to keep readers from combining them incorrectly. RULE 23.5.10

See Practice 23.5A
See Practice 23.5B

INCORRECT the special delivery-carrier

CORRECT the special-delivery carrier

PRACTICE 23.5A **Using Hyphens Correctly**

Read each sentence. Then, write the words that need hyphenation, adding hyphens where necessary.

EXAMPLE The glass is one third full.

ANSWER *one-third*

1. Is that your new brother in law?
2. That was a thought provoking speech.
3. Heather thought it was a well conducted presentation.
4. Jones Road is a one way street.
5. Elizabeth watched the interview with the mayor elect.
6. Please measure three quarters cup of flour.
7. We were surprised by the mid April snowstorm.
8. Please make sure your information is up to date.
9. The ninth grade students performed the play.
10. By the time he is twenty one, William wants to graduate from college.

PRACTICE 23.5B **Revising Sentences With Hyphens**

Read each sentence. Then, rewrite the sentence, correcting any error in hyphen usage. If the punctuation is correct, write *correct*.

EXAMPLE He was a well known writer and poet.

ANSWER *He was a well-known writer and poet.*

11. Tanya's sister-in law is flying into town tomorrow.
12. My coworker always has lunch at noon.
13. I suppose I was mis-informed on the subject.
14. My sister plans to open a shoe store by the time she is twenty eight.
15. The six-year-old's new toy is well-made.
16. Two thirds of the students attended the game.
17. Tony will be in charge of publishing the bimonthly newsletter.
18. My grandfather is semiretired.
19. My doctor recommended an X ray.
20. The well-known actor accepted the hotly-contested award.

SPEAKING APPLICATION

Take turns with a partner. Use hyphenated words in sentences about your family and friends. Your partner should listen for and identify which words need hyphens.

WRITING APPLICATION

Write a paragraph about an event at your school. Use at least three hyphenated words.

Using Hyphens at the Ends of Lines

Hyphens help you keep the lines in your paragraphs more even, making your work easier to read.

Dividing Words at the End of a Line

Although you should try to avoid dividing a word at the end of a line, if a word must be broken, use a hyphen to show the division.

If a word must be divided at the end of a line, always divide it between syllables.

RULE 23.5.11

EXAMPLE The lonely children had been sending letters describing their adventures at camp.

A hyphen used to divide a word should never be placed at the beginning of the second line. It must be placed at the end of the first line.

RULE 23.5.12

INCORRECT The fans and players will continue to sup
-port this coach as long as he wins.

CORRECT The fans and players will continue to support this coach as long as he wins.

Using Hyphens Correctly to Divide Words

One-syllable words cannot be divided.

Do not divide one-syllable words even if they seem long or sound like words with two syllables.

RULE 23.5.13

INCORRECT	lod-ge	clo-thes	thro-ugh
CORRECT	lodge	clothes	through

RULE 23.5.14

Do not divide a word so that a single letter or the letters *-ed* stand alone.

INCORRECT	a-ble	stead-y	e-vict	scream-ed
CORRECT	able	steady	evict	screamed

RULE 23.5.15

Avoid dividing proper nouns and proper adjectives.

INCORRECT	Fe-licia	Amer-ican
CORRECT	Felicia	American

RULE 23.5.16

Divide a hyphenated word only after the hyphen.

INCORRECT We are going with my sister and my bro-
ther-in-law to visit the museum.

CORRECT We are going with my sister and my brother-
in-law to visit the museum.

RULE 23.5.17

Avoid dividing a word so that part of the word is on one page and the remainder is on the next page.

Often, chopping up a word in this way will confuse your readers or cause them to lose their train of thought. If this happens, rewrite the sentence or move the entire word to the next page.

See Practice 23.5C
See Practice 23.5D

PRACTICE 23.5C Writing Correctly Divided Words

Read each group of divided words. Identify the word that is not correctly divided. Then, rewrite the word, putting the hyphen(s) in the correct place, or writing it as one word if it cannot be divided.

EXAMPLE	circ-le	fol-low	sub-stitute
ANSWER	*cir-cle*		
1.	mu-sic	boa-rd	hap-py
2.	mir-ror	fever-ish	camer-a
3.	fo-olish	sup-port	fan-tasy
4.	sharp-ened	fold-ed	merry-go-round
5.	auto-mobile	break-fast	serio-us
6.	Camer-on	vol-ume	cush-ion
7.	pluck-y	fam-ished	favor-ite
8.	shak-en	thou-ght	smel-ling
9.	fla-vorful	comput-er	a-long
10.	for-ever	fore-leg	forl-orn

PRACTICE 23.5D Using Hyphens to Divide Words

Read each sentence. If the word at the end of line has been incorrectly divided, then correctly divide the word, or write it as one word.

EXAMPLE Is Ethan planning to compet-
e in the tournament next week?

ANSWER *com-pete*

11. The teacher had us complete a self-evaluation.

12. My favorite sandwich is peanut butter and jelly.

13. My father wants to put a billiards table into our basement.

14. Yesterday, my mom checked the smoke det-
ectors in our house.

15. We're all going to a wedding in New Mexico next month.

16. My parents looked so graceful walt-
zing across the dance floor.

17. After the play ended, we walked through the park.

18. My brother and I took our niece Dakota to see a movie.

19. The light in this room is perfect for painting.

20. My father's business partner, Mr. Whitehall, is coming for dinner.

SPEAKING APPLICATION

Take turns with a partner. Say five words. Your partner should tell where each word can be divided.

WRITING APPLICATION

Write five sentences that include an incorrectly divided word at the end of a line. Exchange papers with a partner. Your partner should correct your sentences so that the words are divided correctly.

Find It/FIX IT 14 Grammar Game Plan

23.6 Apostrophes

The **apostrophe (')** is used to form possessives, contractions, and a few special plurals.

WRITING COACH Online
www.phwritingcoach.com

Grammar Practice
Practice your grammar skills with Writing Coach Online.

Grammar Games
Test your knowledge of grammar in this fast-paced interactive video game.

Using Apostrophes to Form Possessive Nouns

Apostrophes are used with nouns to show ownership or possession.

RULE 23.6.1 **Add an apostrophe and *-s* to show the possessive case of most singular nouns.**

EXAMPLES the wallet of the woman — the woman's wallet

the wings of the insect — the insect's wings

Even when a singular noun already ends in *-s*, you can usually add an apostrophe and *-s* to show possession. However, names that end in the *eez* sound get an apostrophe, but no *-s.*

EXAMPLE The Ganges' source is in the Himalayas.

For classical references that end in *-s*, only an apostrophe is used.

EXAMPLES Confucius' teachings — Zeus' thunderbolt

RULE 23.6.2 **Add an apostrophe to show the possessive case of plural nouns ending in *-s* or *-es*.**

EXAMPLE the color of the leaves — the leaves' color

RULE 23.6.3 **Add an apostrophe and an *-s* to show the possessive case of plural nouns that do not end in *-s* or *-es*.**

EXAMPLE the songs of the people

the people's songs

Add an apostrophe and *-s* (or just an apostrophe if the word is a plural ending in *-s*) to the last word of a compound noun to form the possessive.

23.6.4 RULE

APOSTROPHES THAT SHOW POSSESSION	
Names of Businesses and Organizations	the Salvation Army's headquarters the Department of the Interior's budget the Johnson Associates' clients
Titles of Rulers or Leaders	Catherine the Great's victories Louis XVI's palace the chairperson of the board's decision
Hyphenated Compound Nouns Used to Describe People	my sister-in-law's car the secretary-treasurer's idea the nurse-practitioner's patient

To form possessives involving time, amounts, or the word *sake,* use an apostrophe and an *-s* or just an apostrophe if the possessive is plural.

23.6.5 RULE

APOSTROPHES WITH POSSESSIVES	
Time	a month's vacation three days' vacation a half-hour's time
Amount	one quarter's worth two cents' worth
Sake	for Marjorie's sake

RULE 23.6.6

To show joint ownership, make the final noun possessive. To show individual ownership, make each noun possessive.

JOINT OWNERSHIP	I enjoyed Bob and Ray's radio show.
INDIVIDUAL OWNERSHIP	Liz's and Meg's coats are hanging here.

Use the owner's complete name before the apostrophe to form the possessive case.

INCORRECT SINGULAR	Jame's idea
CORRECT SINGULAR	James's idea
INCORRECT PLURAL	two girl's books
CORRECT PLURAL	two girls' books

Using Apostrophes With Pronouns

Both indefinite and personal pronouns can show possession.

RULE 23.6.7

Use an apostrophe and *-s* with indefinite pronouns to show possession.

EXAMPLES somebody's umbrella

each other's homework

RULE 23.6.8

Do not use an apostrophe with possessive personal pronouns; their form already shows ownership.

EXAMPLES			
	his jazz records	our house	her blue sweater
	its tires	their party	whose paper

Be careful not to confuse the contractions *who's, it's,* and *they're* with possessive pronouns. They are contractions for *who is, it is* or *it has,* and *they are*. Remember also that *whose, its,* and *their* show possession.

PRONOUNS	CONTRACTIONS
Whose homework is this?	*Who's* at the door?
Its tires were all flat.	*It's* going to rain.
Their dinner is ready.	*They're* going to the beach.

Using Apostrophes to Form Contractions

Contractions are used in informal speech and writing. You can often find contractions in the dialogue of stories and plays; they often create the sound of real speech.

Use an apostrophe in a contraction to show the position of the missing letter or letters.

RULE 23.6.9

COMMON CONTRACTIONS				
Verb + *not*	cannot could not	can't couldn't	are not will not	aren't won't
Pronoun + *will*	he will you will she will	he'll you'll she'll	I will we will they will	I'll we'll they'll
Pronoun + *would*	she would he would you would	she'd he'd you'd	I would we would they would	I'd we'd they'd
Noun or Pronoun + *be*	you are she is they are	you're she's they're	I am Jane is dog is	I'm Jane's dog's

Still another type of contraction is found in poetry.

EXAMPLES e'en *(even)* o'er *(over)*

Other contractions represent the abbreviated form of *of the* and *the* as they are written in several different languages. These letters are most often combined with surnames.

EXAMPLES O'Hare

d'Lorenzo

o'clock

l'Abbé

Using Contractions to Represent Speaking Styles

A final use of contractions is for representing individual speaking styles in dialogue. As noted previously, you will often want to use contractions with verbs in dialogue. You may also want to approximate a regional dialect or a foreign accent, which may include nonstandard pronunciations of words or omitted letters. However, you should avoid overusing contractions in dialogue. Overuse reduces the effectiveness of the apostrophe.

EXAMPLES "Hey, ol' buddy. How you feelin'?"

"Don' you be foolin' me."

Using Apostrophes to Create Special Plurals

Apostrophes can help avoid confusion with special plurals.

RULE 23.6.10

Use an apostrophe and *-s* to create the plural form of a letter, numeral, symbol, or a word that is used as a name for itself.

EXAMPLES *A*'s and *an*'s cause confusion.

There are two *8*'s in that number.

I don't like to hear *if*'s or *maybe*'s.

Form groups of 2's or *3*'s.

You need two more *?*'s.

See Practice 23.6A
See Practice 23.6B

PRACTICE 23.6A Identifying the Use of Apostrophes

Read each sentence. Then, tell if each apostrophe is used to form a *possessive*, a *contraction*, or a *special plural*.

EXAMPLE The dog's bed is next to the fireplace.

ANSWER *possessive*

1. The lesson plan involved reviewing for Friday's test.
2. If he does not hurry, he'll miss the bus.
3. Ben's brother was the star of his college lacrosse team.
4. My aunt's house is one of my favorite places to visit.
5. My sister received all A's on her report card.
6. Wasn't that performance amazing?
7. Molly's brother has great taste in music.
8. Please arrive by eight o'clock.
9. Our new phone number contains two *8*'s.
10. Have you seen Andy's new car?

PRACTICE 23.6B Revising to Add Apostrophes

Read each sentence. Then, rewrite each sentence, adding apostrophes as needed.

EXAMPLE Most of the students received As and Bs.

ANSWER *Most of the students received A's and B's.*

11. Whos coming to Sunday dinner?
12. I put *6*s, *7*s, and *8*s on the doors of the middle school classrooms.
13. Have you seen Jackies coat?
14. The neighbors cats are in our yard.
15. I had to write hundreds of cursive *z*s before I got the hang of them.
16. Our teacher gave us three weeks worth of homework.
17. Fidos puppies are named Moe, Larry, and Curly.
18. Cals and Drews bikes are chained to the fence post.
19. My sisters photograph is in the 2009 yearbook.
20. Shell be back with an extra blanket for the baby.

SPEAKING APPLICATION

Take turns with a partner. Say sentences with words that indicate possession, contractions, or special plurals. Your partner should identify how each word uses an apostrophe.

WRITING APPLICATION

Write five sentences that contain words with missing apostrophes. Exchange papers with a partner. Your partner should add the missing apostrophes.

23.7 Parentheses and Brackets

Parentheses enclose explanations or other information that may be omitted from the rest of the sentence without changing its basic meaning or construction. Using parentheses is a stronger, more noticeable way to set off a parenthetical expression than using commas. **Brackets** are used to enclose a word or phrase added by a writer to the words of another.

WRITING COACH Online

www.phwritingcoach.com

Grammar Practice

Practice your grammar skills with Writing Coach Online.

Grammar Games

Test your knowledge of grammar in this fast-paced interactive video game.

Parentheses

Parentheses help you group material within a sentence.

RULE 23.7.1 **Use parentheses to set off information when the material is not essential or when it consists of one or more sentences.**

EXAMPLE The task of cleaning the mansion (as she learned within the month) was far greater than she had believed.

RULE 23.7.2 **Use parentheses to set off numerical explanations such as dates of a person's birth and death and around numbers and letters marking a series.**

EXAMPLES James Naismith invented the game of basketball at the request of his employer, Luther H. Gulick (1865–1918).

Go to the store and pick up these items: (1) basketball, (2) water bottle, and (3) towels.

Who played in the NBA first: (a) Larry Bird, (b) Nate Archibald, or (c) Shaquille O'Neal?

Although material enclosed in parentheses is not essential to the meaning of the sentence, a writer indicates that the material is important and calls attention to it by using parentheses.

When a phrase or declarative sentence interrupts another sentence, do not use an initial capital letter or end mark inside the parentheses.

RULE 23.7.3

EXAMPLE Bill Frazier finally sold his vacation home (we used to love to visit) to a young couple.

When a question or exclamation interrupts another sentence, use both an initial capital letter and an end mark inside the parentheses.

RULE 23.7.4

EXAMPLE Bruce (He is a fabulous chef!) cooked our dinner.

When you place a sentence in parentheses between two other sentences, use both an initial capital letter and an end mark inside the parentheses.

RULE 23.7.5

EXAMPLE Newport is known for its incredible mansions. (See the Vanderbilt home as an example.) The excesses of wealth are staggering to behold.

In a sentence that includes parentheses, place any punctuation belonging to the main sentence after the final parenthesis.

RULE 23.7.6

EXAMPLE The town council approved the construction (after some deliberations), and they explained the new zoning laws to the public (with some doubts about how the changes would be received).

Special Uses of Parentheses

Parentheses are also used to set off numerical explanations such as dates of a person's birth and death and numbers or letters marking a series.

EXAMPLES Frank Lloyd Wright (1867–1959) was an innovative American architect.

Mike's phone number is (303) 555-4211.

Her research will take her to (1) Portugal, (2) Canada, and (3) Romania.

Brackets

Brackets are used to enclose a word or phrase added by a writer to the words of another writer.

RULE 23.7.7 **Use brackets to enclose words you insert in quotations when quoting someone else.**

EXAMPLES Cooper noted: "And with [*E.T.'s*] success, 'Phone home' is certain to become one of the most often repeated phrases of the year [1982]."

"The results of this vote [98–2] indicate overwhelming support for our proposal," he stated.

The Latin expression *sic* (meaning "thus") is sometimes enclosed in brackets to show that the author of the quoted material has misspelled or mispronounced a word or phrase.

EXAMPLE Michaelson, citing Dorothy's signature line from *The Wizard of Oz,* wrote, "Theirs [sic] no place like home."

See Practice 23.7A
See Practice 23.7B

PRACTICE 23.7A **Using Parentheses and Brackets Correctly**

Read each item. Then, rewrite each sentence, adding the items indicated in parentheses. The items can be placed in parentheses or brackets.

EXAMPLE The boat tied to the dock will be sailing tomorrow. (*Lucky Seven*)

ANSWER *The boat (Lucky Seven) tied to the dock will be sailing tomorrow.*

1. I helped Ryan with his chores. (washing the dishes and taking out the garbage)
2. The deed was filed away. (signed and)
3. I appreciate it, but I must refuse. (the offer)
4. That dancer is the best in the class. (the one in the purple leotard)
5. That little boy can name all fifty states. (Can you believe he's only seven years old?)
6. That tree is more than 15 feet tall. (a hemlock)
7. Allie wrote "That movie is fantastic!" (*A Hopeful Heart*)
8. Mrs. Avery drew this picture. (she is the art teacher)
9. Go to the grocery store and pick up these items: milk, eggs, and bread. (1) (2) (3)
10. During the performance, Nadia commented, "That dancer is so talented!" (Anna Willis)

PRACTICE 23.7B **Revising to Add Parentheses or Brackets**

Read each sentence. Then, rewrite each sentence, adding parentheses or brackets where needed.

EXAMPLE My sister the one who's an artist won an award.

ANSWER *My sister (the one who's an artist) won an award.*

11. "We have created a new product a frictionless bike," said the CEO.
12. Reba is in Atlanta visiting her aunt.
13. "All seaven sic of the men were rescued."
14. The department anticipates reductions in the budget for the coming year 2010.
15. Dana's new phone number is 212 555-0808.
16. I met Bret my best friend at camp last summer.
17. Sean and Avery visited several cities Rome, Venice, and Florence during their vacation.
18. Please read this information Attachment B.
19. Mrs. Po my neighbor has a dog named Albie.
20. Tom broke the lamp he was painting the wall behind the lamp.

SPEAKING APPLICATION

Say a sentence that includes information that could be placed in parentheses if the sentence was written. Your partner should identify where the parentheses would go.

WRITING APPLICATION

Write five sentences. Then, have a partner tell you some additional information to add to each sentence. Rewrite each sentence, including the additional information in parentheses or brackets.

23.8 Ellipses, Dashes, and Slashes

An **ellipsis (. . .)** shows where words have been omitted from a quoted passage. It can also mark a pause or interruption in dialogue. A **dash (—)** shows a strong, sudden break in thought or speech. A **slash (/)** separates numbers in dates and fractions, shows line breaks in quoted poetry, and represents *or.* A slash is also used to separate the parts of a Web address.

WRITING COACH **Online**

www.phwritingcoach.com

Grammar Tutorials

Brush up on your Grammar skills with these animated videos.

Grammar Practice

Practice your grammar skills with Writing Coach Online.

Grammar Games

Test your knowledge of grammar in this fast-paced interactive video game.

Using the Ellipsis

An **ellipsis** is three evenly spaced periods, or ellipsis points, in a row. Always include a space before the first ellipsis point, between ellipsis points, and after the last ellipsis point. (The plural of *ellipsis* is *ellipses.*)

RULE 23.8.1

Use an ellipsis to show where words have been omitted from a quoted passage.

ELLIPSES IN QUOTATIONS	
The Entire Quotation	"The Black River, which cuts a winding course through southern Missouri's rugged Ozark highlands, lends its name to an area of great natural beauty. Within this expanse are old mines and quarries to explore, fast-running waters to canoe, and wooded trails to ride."—Suzanne Charle
At the Beginning	Suzanne Charle described the Black River area in Missouri as having ". . . old mines and quarries to explore, fast-running waters to canoe, and wooded trails to ride."
In the Middle	Suzanne Charle wrote, "The Black River . . . lends its name to an area of great natural beauty. Within this expanse are old mines and quarries to explore, fast-running waters to canoe, and wooded trails to ride."
At the End	Suzanne Charle wrote, "The Black River, which cuts a winding course through southern Missouri's rugged Ozark highlands, lends its name to an area of great natural beauty . . . ."

Use an ellipsis to mark a pause in a dialogue or speech.

RULE 23.8.2

EXAMPLE The coach shouted "Ready . . . set . . . go!"

Dashes

A **dash** signals a stronger, more sudden interruption in thought or speech than commas or parentheses. A dash may also take the place of certain words before an explanation. Overuse of the dash diminishes its effectiveness. Consider the proper use of the dash in the rule below.

Use dashes to indicate an abrupt change of thought, a dramatic interrupting idea, or a summary statement.

RULE 23.8.3

USING DASHES IN WRITING	
To indicate an abrupt change of thought	The article doesn't provide enough information on Japan—by the way, where did you find the article? I cannot believe how many free throws my brother missed—oh, I don't even want to think about it.
To set off interrupting ideas dramatically	The pagoda was built—you may find this hard to believe—in one month. The pagoda was built—Where did they get the money?—in one month.
To set off a summary statement	A good scholastic record and good political connections—if you have these, you may be able to get a job in a congressional office. To see his jersey hanging from the rafters—this was his greatest dream.

RULE 23.8.4

Use dashes to set off a nonessential appositive or modifier when it is long, when it is already punctuated, or when you want to be dramatic.

APPOSITIVE The cause of the damage to the porch and the roof—a rare species of termite—went undiscovered for years.

MODIFIER The home-improvement editor—bored with writing about cement and grout—quit the next day.

Dashes may be used to set off one other special type of sentence interrupter—the parenthetical expression.

RULE 23.8.5

Use dashes to set off a parenthetical expression when it is long, already punctuated, or especially dramatic.

EXAMPLE We visited a castle—what an amazing place!—set on a lake out in the country.

Slashes

A **slash** is used to separate numbers in dates and fractions, lines of quoted poetry, or options. Slashes are also used to separate parts of a Web address.

RULE 23.8.6

Use slashes to separate the day, month, and year in dates and to separate the numerator and denominator in numerical fractions.

DATE She listed her birth date as 5/12/71.

FRACTIONS 3/4 1/2 1/4

Use slashes to indicate line breaks in up to three lines of quoted poetry in continuous text. Insert a space on each side of the slash.

RULE 23.8.7

EXAMPLE I used a quote from William Blake, "Tyger! Tyger! burning bright. / In the forests of the night," to begin my paper.

Use slashes to separate choices or options and to represent the words *and* and *or*.

RULE 23.8.8

EXAMPLES Choose your topping: ketchup/mustard/relish.

Each student should bring a book and pen/pencil.

You can walk and/or run the last leg of the race.

Use slashes to separate parts of a Web address.

RULE 23.8.9

EXAMPLES http://www.fafsa.ed.gov/
(for financial aid for students)

http://www.whitehouse.gov/
(the White House)

http://www.si.edu/
(the Smithsonian Institution)

See Practice 23.8A
See Practice 23.8B

PRACTICE 23.8A **Using Ellipses, Dashes, and Slashes Correctly**

Read each sentence. Then, rewrite each sentence, adding dashes to emphasize parenthetical information, slashes, or ellipses where appropriate. Explain the function of the dashes, slashes, and ellipses you added.

EXAMPLE Molly my best friend is sleeping over tonight.

ANSWER *Molly—my best friend—is sleeping over tonight.*

1. "I think uh I'm not sure," said Sam.
2. The view from the top of the mountain What a hike that was! is magnificent.
3. The backyard is 34 of an acre.
4. Wait you forgot your sweatshirt!
5. Jen or Brendan will be asked to moderate lead the debate next week.
6. She wrote the date 5/10 09 at the top of her paper.
7. The boys Jim, John, and Jeff left the party early.
8. Everyone must have his or her passport to leave enter the country.
9. Please measure 1 2 of an inch of that string.
10. There was only one thing left to do apologize.

PRACTICE 23.8B **Revising Sentences With Ellipses, Dashes, and Slashes**

Read each sentence. Then, rewrite each sentence, using the appropriate punctuation to add or delete the information in parentheses to or from each sentence. Be sure to include dashes that emphasize parenthetical information.

EXAMPLE "Well, I'm not sure about that," Mark said. (Delete *about that.*)

ANSWER *"Well, I'm not sure..." Mark said.*

11. Susan and Becky will help you. (Add *or*)
12. Mrs. Johnson's dogs are going to a vet tomorrow. (Add *Max and Casey*)
13. Several sports are offered in the fall. (Add *volleyball, field hockey, and swimming.*)
14. "Julie is a kind, generous, and funny person." (Delete *kind, generous, and*)
15. Some people are allergic to wheat. (Add *including my two best friends*)
16. Some of Mrs. Nelson's students play on the school soccer team. (Add *Jim, Bill, and Ming*)
17. Alexandra is coming to visit next week. (Add *my cousin*)
18. "This movie is funny, exciting, and full of action," said the reviewer. (Delete *funny, exciting, and*)
19. Jen and Nate will be here after school. (Add *or*)
20. After talking it over, I still can't decide. (Add *but I hope to make a decision soon.*)

SPEAKING APPLICATION

Take turns with a partner. Say a sentence to your partner. Then, have your partner add additional information to the sentence. Discuss which punctuation mark would be used if you were to write the modified sentence and why.

WRITING APPLICATION

Use sentences 12, 14, and 16 as models to write similar sentences. Exchange papers with a partner. Your partner should correctly use dashes to emphasize parenthetical information.

Cumulative Review Chapters 22–23

PRACTICE 1 **Using Periods, Question Marks, and Exclamation Marks**

Read each sentence. Rewrite each sentence, adding question marks, periods, and exclamation marks where needed.

1. Can I lend a hand
2. Eek I saw a mouse
3. John Jr lives on W Main Street
4. Wow David almost set a new track record
5. Sit here, close to the window
6. The train leaves from Kensington Rd Station
7. How much does that shirt cost
8. My uncle asked me if I enjoyed the class trip
9. Don't touch the wet paint
10. The umpire called a time out Why

PRACTICE 2 **Using Commas Correctly**

Read each sentence. Rewrite each sentence, adding commas where needed. If a sentence is correct as is, write *correct*.

1. Sheila's house the one with green shutters is the oldest on the block.
2. Mia called but Ted wasn't home yet.
3. We bought apples pears oranges and lemons.
4. The dinner was an elegant fancy event
5. No Harry didn't answer his cellphone.
6. There are 1524 names on the list.
7. Katrina lives in Galveston Texas.
8. "I couldn't find my shoe" said Joe "because the dog buried it somewhere."
9. The fair starts on Thursday, August 23.
10. Tina Smith Ph.D. is a neurosurgeon.

PRACTICE 3 **Using Colons, Semicolons, and Quotation Marks**

Read each sentence. Rewrite each sentence, using colons, semicolons, and quotation marks where needed. If a sentence is correct as is, write *correct*.

1. My father received a promotion consequently, he'll be managing more people.
2. He had an excuse: His laptop isn't working.
3. Who wrote the poem The Raven?
4. The train departs at 1145 A.M.
5. The sky darkened the waves grew choppy.
6. Jim asked, Whose car is parked in the lot?
7. There's one thing I forgot the gift.
8. Warning Keep Out!
9. My tooth, said young Bobby, just fell out.
10. Ash finished first therefore, he won.

Continued on next page ▶

Cumulative Review Chapters 22–23

PRACTICE 4 Using Apostrophes

Read each sentence. Rewrite each sentence, using apostrophes where needed. If a sentence is correct as is, write *correct*.

1. The dog wags its tail when its happy.
2. Rons listening to music so he cant hear us.
3. Ginny received three Bs on her report card.
4. The Mackenzies' house is for sale.
5. Thats my locker, not someone elses.
6. About the furniture, whats not ours, you may keep.
7. Its five oclock and somebodys knocking on the door.
8. Theirs is the best restaurant in town.
9. Hes not my partner because he wont dance.
10. Lets listen to the bands new CD.

PRACTICE 5 Using Underlining (or Italics), Hyphens, Dashes, Parentheses, Brackets, and Ellipses

Read each sentence. Rewrite each sentence, adding underlining (or italics), hyphens, dashes, brackets, parentheses, and ellipses. If a sentence is correct as is, write *correct*.

1. Our winter vacation starts in midFebruary.
2. Gary Paulsen wrote the novel Hatchet.
3. The article stated, "The school Elm Elementary will host the celebration."
4. My Aunt Lucy is thirty two years old.
5. Natalie's goal to come in first at the swimming finals is becoming a reality.
6. I read the Houston Chronicle every morning.
7. The poem *Paul Revere's Ride* starts with "Listen my children and you shall hear of the midnight ride of Paul Revere."
8. My mother she's an artist has her own studio.
9. The list contains three items: 1 shoes, 2 gloves, and 3 sunglasses.
10. The song—it was written by my music teacher—is about summer vacations.

PRACTICE 6 Using Capital Letters Correctly

Read each sentence. Rewrite each sentence, using capital letters where they are needed.

1. planet earth is the only planet not named after a greek or roman god or goddess.
2. i plan to go to the american history museum on saturday.
3. Did o. henry write the "gift of the magi"?
4. cindy's birthday is thursday, december 12.
5. british troops were sent to capture american soldiers during the revolutionary war.
6. mrs. grady lives on lake michigan.
7. wow! what an intricate persian rug.
8. melanie asked, "is it my turn, yet?"
9. governor hill is retiring soon.
10. i went on a tour of the white house.

RESOURCES FOR Writing COACH

WRITING IN THE *Content Areas*

Writing in the content areas—math, social studies, science, the arts, and various career and technical studies—is an important tool for learning. The following pages give examples of content area writing along with strategies.

FORMS OF MATH WRITING

Written Estimate An estimate, or informed idea, of the size, cost, time, or other measure of a thing, based on given information.

Analysis of a Problem A description of a problem, such as figuring out how long a trip will take, along with an explanation of the mathematical formulas or equations you can use to solve the problem.

Response to an Open-Ended Math Prompt A response to a question or writing assignment involving math, such as a word problem or a question about a graph or a mathematical concept.

Writing in Math

Prewriting

- **Choosing a Topic** If you have a choice of topics, review your textbook and class notes for ideas, and choose one that interests you.
- **Responding to a Prompt** If you are responding to a prompt, read and then reread the instructions, ensuring that you understand all of the requirements of the assignment.

Drafting

- **State Problems Clearly** Be clear, complete, and accurate in your description of the problem you are analyzing or reporting on. Make sure that you have used technical terms, such as *ratio*, *area*, and *factor*, accurately.
- **Explain Your Solution** Tell readers exactly which mathematical rules or formulas you use in your analysis and why they apply. Clearly spell out each step you take in your reasoning.
- **Use Graphics** By presenting quantitative information in a graph, table, or chart, you make it easier for readers to absorb information. Choose the format appropriate to the material, as follows:
  - ✔ **Line Graphs** Use a line graph to show the relationship between two variables, such as time and speed in a problem about a moving object. Clearly label the x- and y-axis with the variable each represents and with the units you are using. Choose units appropriately to make the graph manageable. For example, do not try to represent time in years if you are plotting changes for an entire century; instead, use units of ten years each.
  - ✔ **Other Graphs** Use a pie chart to analyze facts about a group, such as the percentage of students who walk to school, the percentage who drive, and the percentage who take the bus. Use a bar graph to compare two or more things at different times or in different categories. Assign a single color to each thing, and use that color consistently for all the bars representing data about that thing.
  - ✔ **Tables** Use a table to help readers look up specific values quickly, such as the time the sun sets in each month of the year. Label each column and row with terms that clearly identify the data you are presenting, including the units you are using.

Revising

- **Ensure Accuracy** For accuracy, double-check the formulas you use and the calculations you make.
- **Revise for Traits of Good Writing** Ask yourself the following questions: *How well have I applied mathematical ideas? Does my organizational plan help readers follow my reasoning? Is my voice suitable to my audience and purpose? Have I chosen precise words and used mathematical terms accurately? Are my sentences well constructed and varied? Have I made any errors in grammar, usage, mechanics, and spelling?* Use your answers to help you revise and edit your work.

Writing in Science

Prewriting

- **Choosing a Topic** If you have a choice of topics, look through class notes and your textbook, or conduct a "media flip-through," browsing online articles, or watching television news and documentaries to find a science-related topic.
- **Responding to a Prompt** If you are responding to a prompt, read the instructions carefully, analyzing the requirements and parts of the assignment. Identify key direction words in the prompt or assignment, such as *explain* and *predict*.
- **Gathering Details**
  - ✔ If your assignment requires you to conduct research, search for credible and current sources. Examples of strong sources may include articles in recent issues of science magazines or recently published books. Confirm key facts in more than one source.
  - ✔ If your assignment requires you to conduct an experiment, make sure you follow the guidelines for the experiment accurately. Carefully record the steps you take and the observations you make, and date your notes. Repeat the experiment to confirm results.

Drafting

- **Focus and Elaborate** In your introduction, clearly state your topic. Make sure you tell readers why your topic matters. As you draft, give sufficient details, including background, facts, and examples, to help your readers understand your topic. Summarize your findings and insights in your conclusion.
- **Organize** As you draft, follow a suitable organizational pattern. If you are telling the story of an important scientific breakthrough, consider telling events in chronological order. If you are explaining a natural process, consider discussing causes and the effects that follow from them. If you are defending a solution to a problem, you might give pros and cons, answering each counterargument in turn.
- **Present Data Visually** Consider presenting quantitative information, such as statistics or measurements, in a graph, table, or chart. Choose the format appropriate to the material. (Consult the guidance on visual displays of data under "Use Graphics" on page R2.)

Revising

- **Meet Your Audience's Needs** Identify places in your draft where your audience may need more information, such as additional background, more explanation, or the definition of a technical term. Add the information required.
- **Revise for Traits of Good Writing** Ask yourself the following questions: *How clearly have I presented scientific ideas? Will my organization help a reader see the connections I am making? Is my voice suitable to my audience and purpose? Have I chosen precise words and used technical terms accurately? Are my sentences well constructed and varied? Have I made any errors in grammar, usage, mechanics, and spelling?* Use your answers to revise and edit your work.

FORMS OF SCIENCE WRITING

Lab Report A firsthand report of a scientific experiment, following an appropriate format. A standard lab report includes a statement of the hypothesis, or prediction, that the experiment is designed to test; a list of the materials used; an account of the steps performed; a report of the results observed; and the experimenter's conclusions.

Cause-and-Effect Essay A scientific explanation of the causes and effects involved in natural or technical phenomena, such as solar flares, the digestion of food, or the response of metal to stress.

Technical Procedure Document A step-by-step guide to performing a scientific experiment or performing a technical task involving science. A well-written technical procedure document presents the steps of the procedure in clear order. It breaks steps into substeps and prepares readers by explaining what materials they will need and the time they can expect each step to take.

Response to an Open-Ended Science Prompt A response to a question or writing assignment about science.

Summary of a Science-Related Article A retelling of the main ideas in an article that concerns science or technology, such as an article on a new medical procedure.

Writing in Social Studies

FORMS OF SOCIAL STUDIES WRITING

Social Studies Research Report An informative paper, based on research, about a historical period or event or about a specific place or culture. A well-written research report draws on a variety of sources to develop and support a thoughtful point of view on the topic. It cites those sources accurately, following an accepted format.

Biographical Essay An overview of the life of a historically important person. A well-written biographical essay reports the life of its subject accurately and clearly explains the importance of his or her contributions.

Historical Overview A survey, or general picture, of a historical period or development, such as the struggle for women's right to vote. A successful historical overview presents the "big picture," covering major events and important aspects of the topic without getting lost in details.

Historical Cause-and-Effect Essay An analysis of the causes and effects of a historical event. A well-written historical explanation makes clear connections between events to help readers follow the explanation.

Prewriting

- **Choosing a Topic** If you have a choice of topics, find a suitable topic by looking through class notes and your textbook. Make a quick list of topics in history, politics, or geography that interest you and choose a topic based on your list.
- **Responding to a Prompt** If you are responding to a prompt, read the instructions carefully, analyzing the requirements and parts of the assignment. Identify key direction words in the prompt or assignment, such as *compare*, *describe*, and *argue*.
- **Gathering Details** If your assignment requires you to conduct research, consult a variety of credible sources. For in-depth research, review both primary sources (documents from the time you are investigating) and secondary sources (accounts by those who analyze or report on the information). If you find contradictions, evaluate the likely reasons for the differences.

Drafting

- **Establish a Thesis or Theme** If you are writing a research report or other informative piece, state your main point about your topic in a thesis statement. Include your thesis statement in your introduction. If you are writing a creative piece, such as a historical skit or short story, identify the theme, or main message, you wish to convey.
- **Support Your Thesis or Theme** Organize your work around your main idea.
  - ✔ In a research report, support and develop your thesis with well-chosen, relevant details. First, provide background information your readers will need, and then discuss different subtopics in different sections of the body of your report. Clearly connect each subtopic to your main thesis.
  - ✔ In a creative work, develop your theme through the conflict between characters. For example, a conflict between two brothers during the Civil War over which side to fight on might dramatize the theme of divided loyalties. Organize events to build to a climax, or point of greatest excitement, that clearly conveys your message.

Revising

- **Sharpen Your Focus** Review your draft for sections that do not clearly support your thesis or theme, and consider eliminating them. Revise unnecessary repetition of ideas. Ensure that the sequence of ideas or events will help reader comprehension.
- **Revise for Traits of Good Writing** Ask yourself the following questions: *How clearly have I developed my thesis or my theme? Will my organization help a reader follow my development of my thesis or theme? Is my voice suitable to my audience and purpose? Have I chosen precise and vivid words, accurately using terms from the period or place about which I am writing? Are my sentences well constructed and varied? Have I made any errors in grammar, usage, mechanics, and spelling?* Use your answers to revise and edit your work.

Writing About the Arts

Prewriting

Experience the Work Take notes on the subject of each work you will discuss. Consider its mood, or general feeling, and its theme, or insight into life.

- ✔ For visual arts, consider the use of color, light, line (sharp or smooth, smudged or definite), mass (heavy or light), and composition (the arrangement and balance of forms).
- ✔ For music, consider the use of melody, rhythm, harmony, and instrumentation. Also, consider the performers' interpretation of the work.

Drafting

Develop Your Ideas As you draft, support your main ideas, including your insights into or feelings about a work, with relevant details.

Revising

Revise for Traits of Good Writing Ask yourself the following questions: *How clearly do I present my ideas? Will my organization help a reader follow my points? Is my voice suitable to my audience and purpose? Have I chosen precise and vivid words, to describe the works? Are my sentences varied? Have I made any errors in grammar, usage, and mechanics?* Use your answers to revise and edit your work.

Writing in Career and Technical Studies

Prewriting

Choosing a Topic If you have a choice of topics, find a suitable one by looking through class notes and your textbook or by listing your own related projects or experiences.

Drafting

Organize Information As you draft, follow a logical organization. If you are explaining a procedure, list steps in the order that your readers should follow. If they need information about the materials and preparation required, provide that information first. Use formatting (such as headings, numbered steps, and bullet points), graphics (such as diagrams), and transitional words and phrases (such as *first*, *next*, and *if… then*).

Revising

Revise for Traits of Good Writing Ask yourself the following questions: *Have I given readers all the information they will need? Will my organization help a reader follow my points? Is my voice suitable to my audience and purpose? Have I chosen precise words, using technical terms accurately? Are my sentences well constructed? Have I made errors in grammar, usage, and mechanics?* Use your answers to revise and edit your work.

FORMS OF WRITING ABOUT THE ARTS

Research Report on a Trend or Style in Art An informative paper, based on research, about a specific group of artists or trend in the arts.

Biographical Essay An overview of the life of an artist or performer.

Analysis of a Work A detailed description of a work offering insights into its meaning and importance.

Review of a Performance or Exhibit An evaluation of an artistic performance or exhibit.

FORMS OF CAREER AND TECHNICAL WRITING

Technical Procedure Document A step-by-step guide to performing a specialized task, such as wiring a circuit or providing first aid.

Response to an Open-Ended Practical Studies Prompt A response to a question or writing assignment about a task or concept in a specialized field.

Technical Research Report An informative paper, based on research, about a specific topic in a practical field, such as a report on balanced diet in the field of health.

Analysis of a Career An informative paper explaining the requirements for a particular job, along with the responsibilities, salary, benefits, and job opportunities.

WRITING FOR *Media*

New technology has created many new ways to communicate. Today, it is easy to contribute information to the Internet and send a variety of messages to friends far and near. You can also share your ideas through photos, illustrations, video, and sound recordings.

Writing for Media gives you an overview of some ways you can use today's technology to create, share, and find information. **Here are the topics you will find in this section:**

- **Blogs**
- **Social Networking**
- **Widgets and Feeds**
- **Multimedia Elements**
- **Podcasts**
- **Wikis**

Blogs

A **blog** is a common form of online writing. The word *blog* is a contraction of *Web log*. Most blogs include a series of entries known as posts. The posts appear in a single column and are displayed in reverse chronological order. That means that the most recent post is at the top of the page. As you scroll down, you will find earlier posts.

Blogs have become increasingly popular. Researchers estimate that 75,000 new blogs are launched every day. Blog authors are often called bloggers. They can use their personal sites to share ideas, songs, videos, photos, and other media. People who read blogs can often post their responses with a comments feature found in each new post.

Because blogs are designed so that they are easy to update, bloggers can post new messages as often as they like, often daily. For some people blogs become a public journal or diary in which they share their thoughts about daily events.

Types of Blogs

Not all blogs are the same. Many blogs have a single author, but others are group projects. These are some common types of blog:

- **Personal blogs** often have a general focus. Bloggers post their thoughts on any topic they find interesting in their daily lives.
- **Topical blogs** focus on a specific theme, such as movie reviews, political news, class assignments, or health-care opportunities.

WEB SAFETY Using the Internet safely means keeping personal information personal. Never include your address (e-mail or physical), last name, or telephone numbers. Avoid mentioning places you go to often.

Never give out passwords you use to access other Web sites and do not respond to e-mails from people you do not know.
Hello,
How ar

Anatomy of a Blog

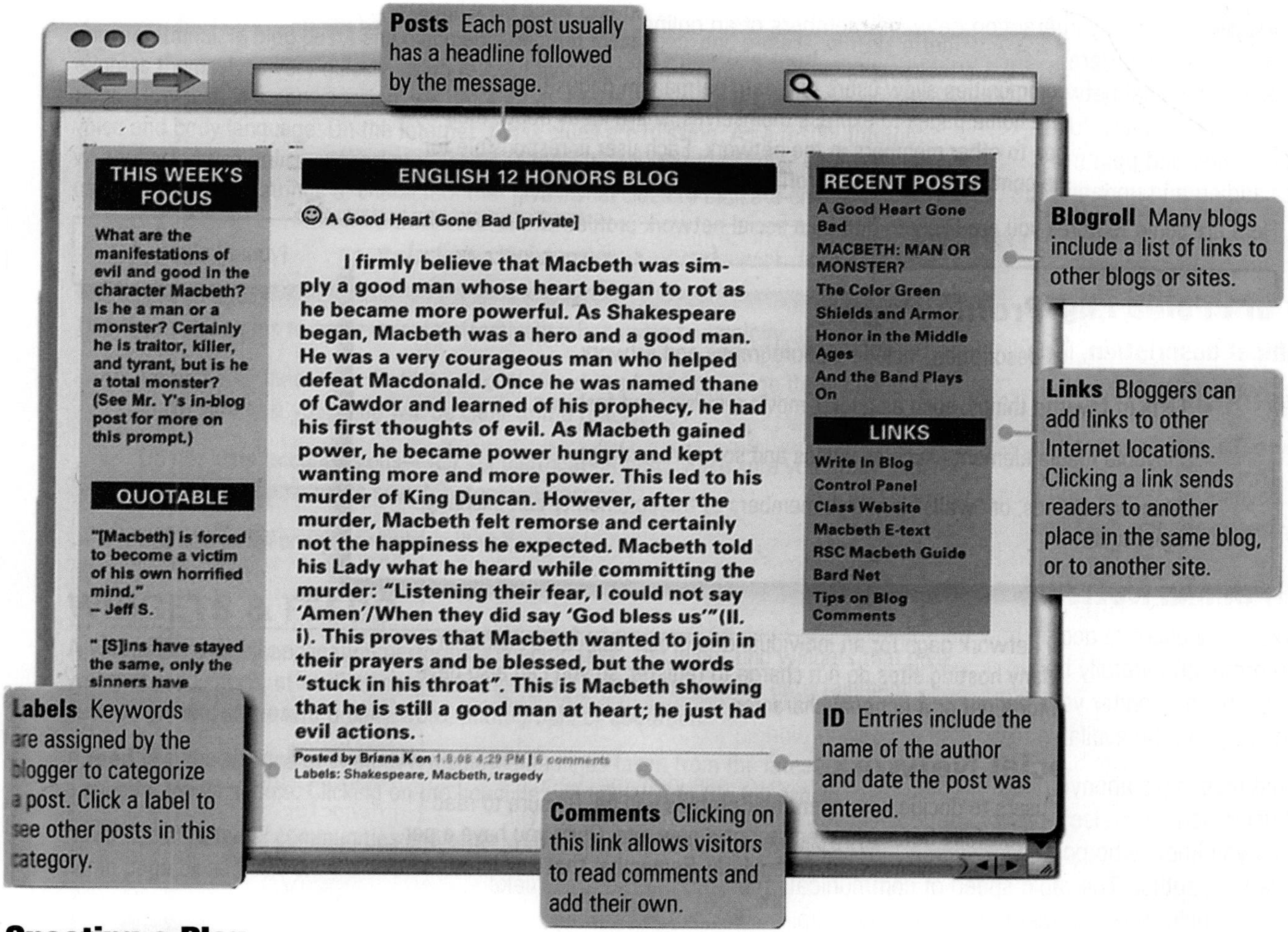
Posts Each post usually has a headline followed by the message.
THIS WEEK'S FOCUS
What are the manifestations of evil and good in the character Macbeth? Is he a man or a monster? Certainly he is traitor, killer, and tyrant, but is he a total monster? (See Mr. Y's in-blog post for more on this prompt.)
QUOTABLE
"[Macbeth] is forced to become a victim of his own horrified mind." – Jeff S.
" [S]ins have stayed the same, only the sinners have
ENGLISH 12 HONORS BLOG
A Good Heart Gone Bad [private]
I firmly believe that Macbeth was simply a good man whose heart began to rot as he became more powerful. As Shakespeare began, Macbeth was a hero and a good man. He was a very courageous man who helped defeat Macdonald. Once he was named thane of Cawdor and learned of his prophecy, he had his first thoughts of evil. As Macbeth gained power, he became power hungry and kept wanting more and more power. This led to his murder of King Duncan. However, after the murder, Macbeth felt remorse and certainly not the happiness he expected. Macbeth told his Lady what he heard while committing the murder: "Listening their fear, I could not say 'Amen'/When they did say 'God bless us'" (II. i). This proves that Macbeth wanted to join in their prayers and be blessed, but the words "stuck in his throat". This is Macbeth showing that he is still a good man at heart; he just had evil actions.
Posted by Briana K on 1.8.08 4:29 PM | 6 comments
Labels: Shakespeare, Macbeth, tragedy
RECENT POSTS
A Good Heart Gone Bad
MACBETH: MAN OR MONSTER?
The Color Green
Shields and Armor
Honor in the Middle Ages
And the Band Plays On
LINKS
Write in Blog
Control Panel
Class Website
Macbeth E-text
RSC Macbeth Guide
Bard Net
Tips on Blog Comments
Blogroll Many blogs include a list of links to other blogs or sites.
Links Bloggers can add links to other Internet locations. Clicking a link sends readers to another place in the same blog, or to another site.
Labels Keywords are assigned by the blogger to categorize a post. Click a label to see other posts in this category.
Comments Clicking on this link allows visitors to read comments and add their own.
ID Entries include the name of the author and date the post was entered.

Creating a Blog

Keep these hints and strategies in mind to help you create an interesting and fair blog:

- Focus each blog entry on a single topic.
- Vary the length of your posts. Sometimes, all you need is a line or two to share a quick thought. Other posts will be much longer.
- Choose font colors and styles that can be read easily.
- Many people scan blogs rather than read them closely. You can make your main ideas pop out by using clear or clever headlines and boldfacing key terms.
- Give credit to other people's work and ideas. State the names of people whose ideas you are quoting or add a link to take readers to that person's blog or site.
- If you post comments, try to make them brief and polite.

Social Networking

Social networking means any interaction between members of an online community. People can exchange many different kinds of information, from text and voice messages to video images. Many social network communities allow users to create permanent pages that describe themselves. Users create home pages to express themselves, share ideas about their lives, and post messages to other members in the network. Each user is responsible for adding and updating the content on his or her profile page.

Here are some features you are likely to find on a social network profile:

Features of Profile Pages

- A **biographical description**, including photographs and artwork
- **Lists of favorite things**, such as books, movies, music, and fashions
- **Playable media** elements such as videos and sound recordings
- **Message boards**, or "walls," on which members of the community can exchange messages

Privacy in Social Networks

Social networks allow users to decide how open their profiles will be. Be sure to read introductory information carefully before you register at a new site. Once you have a personal profile page, monitor your privacy settings regularly. Remember that any information you post will be available to anyone in your network.

Users often post messages anonymously or using false names, or pseudonyms. People can also post using someone else's name. Judge all information on the net critically. Do not assume that you know who posted some information simply because you recognize the name of the post author. The rapid speed of communication on the Internet can make it easy to jump to conclusions—be careful to avoid this trap.

You can create a social network page for an individual or a group, such as a school or special interest club. Many hosting sites do not charge to register, so you can also have fun by creating a page for a pet or a fictional character.

Tips for Sending Effective Messages

Technology makes it easy to share ideas quickly, but writing for the Internet poses some special challenges. The writing style for blogs and social networks is often very conversational. In blog posts and comments, instant messages, and e-mails, writers often express themselves very quickly, using relaxed language, short sentences, and abbreviations. However in a face-to-face conversation, we get a lot of information from a speaker's tone of voice and body language. On the Internet, those clues are missing. As a result, Internet writers often use italics or bracketed labels to indicate emotions. Another alternative is using emoticons—strings of characters that give visual clues to indicate emotion.

:-) **smile** *(happy)* :-(**frown** *(unhappy)* ;-) **wink** *(light sarcasm)*

Use these strategies to communicate effectively when using technology:

- ✔ *Before you click Send,* ***reread your message*** *to make sure that your tone is clear.*
- ✔ ***Do not jump to conclusions****—ask for clarification first. Make sure you really understand what someone is saying before you respond.*
- ✔ ***Use abbreviations*** *your reader will understand.*

Widgets and Feeds

A **widget** is a small application that performs a specific task. You might find widgets that give weather predictions, offer dictionary definitions or translations, provide entertainment such as games, or present a daily word, photograph, or quotation.

A **feed** is a special kind of widget. It displays headlines taken from the latest content on a specific media source. Clicking on the headline will take you to the full article. Many social network communities and other Web sites allow you to personalize your home page by adding widgets and feeds.

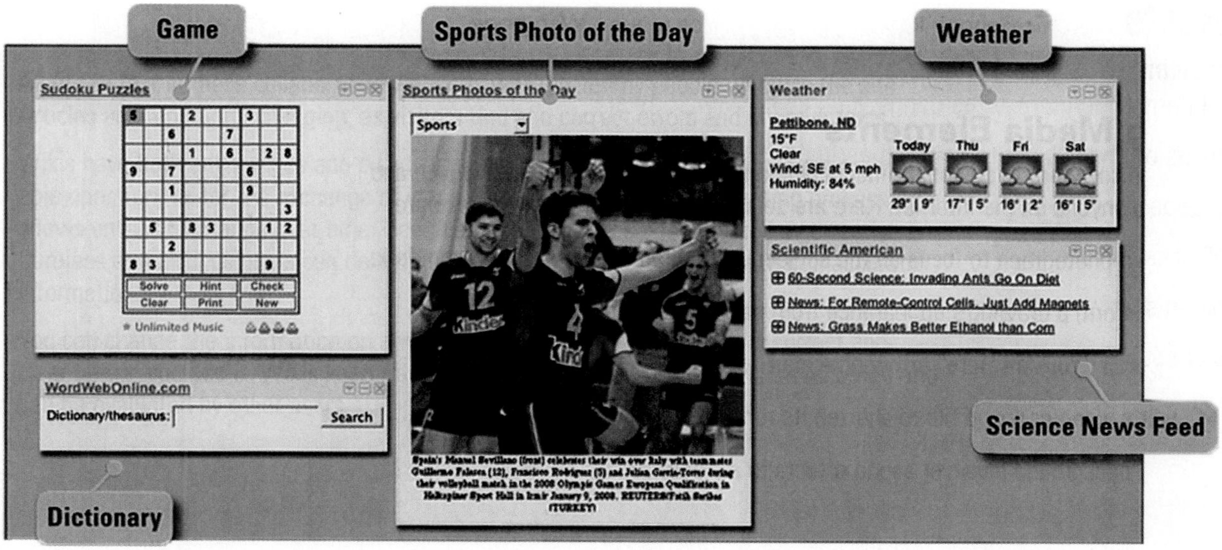

Multimedia Elements

One of the great advantages of communicating on the Internet is that you are not limited to using text only. When you create a Web profile or blog, you can share your ideas using a wide variety of media. In addition to widgets and feeds (see page R9), these media elements can make your Internet communication more entertaining and useful.

GRAPHICS	
Photographs	You can post photographs taken by digital cameras or scanned as files.
Illustrations	Artwork can be created using computer software. You can also use a scanner to post a digital image of a drawing or sketch.
Charts, Graphs, and Maps	Charts and graphs can make statistical information clear. Use spreadsheet software to create these elements. Use Internet sites to find maps of specific places.

VIDEO	
Live Action	Digital video can be recorded by a camera or recorded from another media source.
Animation	Animated videos can also be created using software.

AUDIO	
Music	Many social network communities make it easy to share your favorite music with people who visit your page.
Voice	Use a microphone to add your own voice to your Web page.

Editing Media Elements

You can use software to customize media elements. Open source software is free and available to anyone on the Internet. Here are some things you can do with software:

- **Crop** a photograph to focus on the subject or brighten an image that is too dark.
- **Transform** a drawing's appearance from flat to three-dimensional.
- **Insert** a "You Are Here" arrow on a map.
- **Edit** a video or sound file to shorten its running time.
- **Add** background music or sound effects to a video.

Podcasts

A **podcast** is a digital audio or video recording of a program that is made available on the Internet. Users can replay the podcast on a computer, or download it and replay it on a personal audio player. You might think of podcasts as radio or television programs that you create yourself. They can be embedded on a Web site or fed to a Web page through a podcast widget.

Creating an Effective Podcast

To make a podcast, you will need a recording device, such as a microphone or digital video camera, as well as editing software. Open source editing software is widely available and free of charge. Most audio podcasts are converted into the MP3 format. Here are some tips for creating a podcast that is clear and entertaining:

- **Listen to several podcasts by different authors** to get a feeling for the medium.
- **Make a list** of features and styles you like and also those you want to avoid.
- **Test your microphone** to find the best recording distance. Stand close enough to the microphone so that your voice sounds full, but not so close that you create an echo.
- **Create an outline** that shows your estimated timing for each element.
- **Be prepared** before you record. Rehearse, but do not create a script. Podcasts are best when they have a natural, easy flow.
- **Talk directly to your listeners**. Slow down enough so they can understand you.
- Use software to **edit your podcast before publishing it**. You can edit out mistakes or add additional elements.

Wikis

A **wiki** is a collaborative Web site that lets visitors create, add, remove, and edit content. The term comes from the Hawaiian phrase *wikiwiki*, which means "quick." Web users of a wiki are both the readers and the writers of the site. Some wikis are open to contributions from anyone. Others require visitors to register before they can edit the content. All of the text in these collaborative Web sites was written by people who use the site. Articles are constantly changing, as visitors find and correct errors and improve texts.

Wikis have both advantages and disadvantages as sources of information. They are valuable open forums for the exchange of ideas. The unique collaborative writing process allows entries to change over time. However, entries can also be modified incorrectly. Careless or malicious users can delete good content and add inappropriate or inaccurate information. Wikis may be useful for gathering background information, but should not be used as research resources.

You can change the information on a wiki, but be sure your information is correct and clear before you add it. Wikis keep track of all changes, so your work will be recorded and can be evaluated by other users.

WRITING FOR THE
Workplace

Writing is something many people do every day at work, school, or home. They write letters and reports, do research, plan meetings, and keep track of information in notes.

Writing for the Workplace shows you some models of the following forms of writing:

- **Note Cards**
- **Meeting Agenda**
- **Business Letter**
- **Friendly Letter**

Creating Note Cards

Whether you are working on a research report or gathering information for another purpose, it is helpful to keep your notes on individual cards or in note files on a computer. You will need to make sure that you note your sources on your cards. You can organize information many different ways, but it is most helpful to keep notes of one kind together.

You can name the **source**, as shown here, or refer to the source by number (e.g., Source 3) if you are using source cards.

The **topic** is the main focus of the notes.

Topic: Octopus

Source: PBS Web site Accessed 10/15/2010

http://www.pbs.org/wnet/nature/episodes/ the-octopus-show/ a-legend-of-the-deep/2014/

- Acrobatic and shy animals
- Can squeeze into very small spaces to hide or catch food
- Talented swimmers
- Can change color
- Live in all kinds of environments

In the notes section focus on the ideas that are most important to your research. Note that these ideas may not always be the main ideas of the selection you are reading. You do not need to write in full sentences. However, you may want to use bullets to make your notes easier to read.

Writing a Meeting Agenda

When you have a meeting, it is helpful to use an agenda. An agenda tells what will be discussed in the meeting. It tells who is responsible for which topic. It also provides a guide for the amount of time to be spent on each topic.

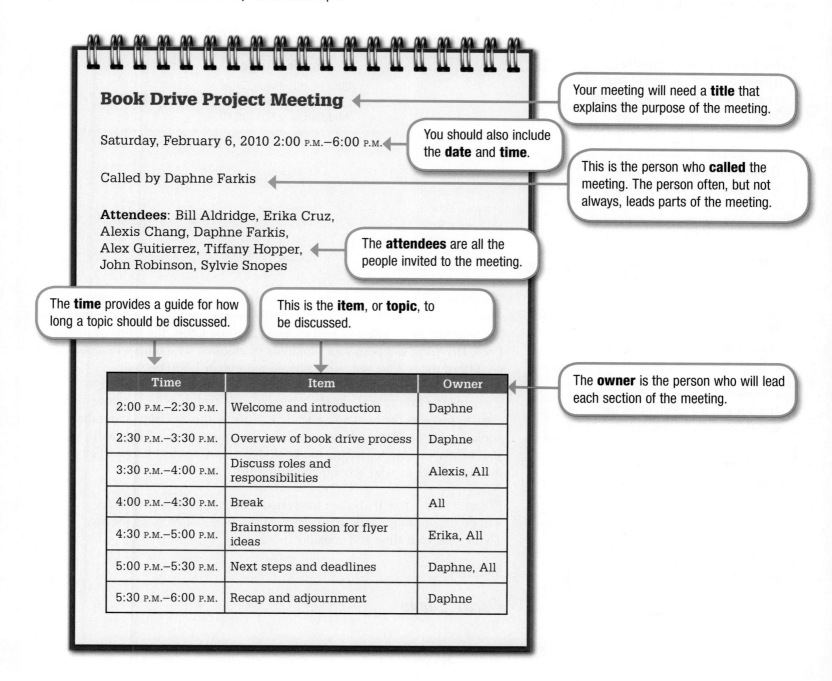

Book Drive Project Meeting

Your meeting will need a **title** that explains the purpose of the meeting.

Saturday, February 6, 2010 2:00 P.M.–6:00 P.M.

You should also include the **date** and **time**.

Called by Daphne Farkis

This is the person who **called** the meeting. The person often, but not always, leads parts of the meeting.

Attendees: Bill Aldridge, Erika Cruz, Alexis Chang, Daphne Farkis, Alex Guitierrez, Tiffany Hopper, John Robinson, Sylvie Snopes

The **attendees** are all the people invited to the meeting.

The **time** provides a guide for how long a topic should be discussed.

This is the **item**, or **topic**, to be discussed.

The **owner** is the person who will lead each section of the meeting.

Time	Item	Owner
2:00 P.M.–2:30 P.M.	Welcome and introduction	Daphne
2:30 P.M.–3:30 P.M.	Overview of book drive process	Daphne
3:30 P.M.–4:00 P.M.	Discuss roles and responsibilities	Alexis, All
4:00 P.M.–4:30 P.M.	Break	All
4:30 P.M.–5:00 P.M.	Brainstorm session for flyer ideas	Erika, All
5:00 P.M.–5:30 P.M.	Next steps and deadlines	Daphne, All
5:30 P.M.–6:00 P.M.	Recap and adjournment	Daphne

Writing Business Letters

Business letters are often formal in tone and written for a specific business purpose. They generally follow one of several acceptable formats. In block format, all parts of the letter are at the left margin. All business letters, however, have the same parts: heading, inside address, salutation, body, closing, and signature.

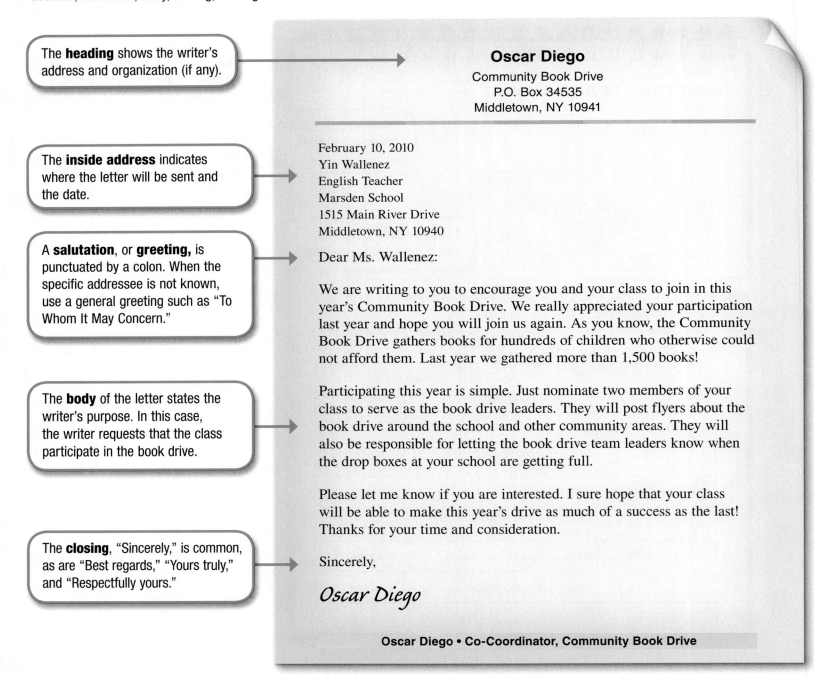

The **heading** shows the writer's address and organization (if any).

The **inside address** indicates where the letter will be sent and the date.

A **salutation**, or **greeting,** is punctuated by a colon. When the specific addressee is not known, use a general greeting such as "To Whom It May Concern."

The **body** of the letter states the writer's purpose. In this case, the writer requests that the class participate in the book drive.

The **closing**, "Sincerely," is common, as are "Best regards," "Yours truly," and "Respectfully yours."

Oscar Diego
Community Book Drive
P.O. Box 34535
Middletown, NY 10941

February 10, 2010
Yin Wallenez
English Teacher
Marsden School
1515 Main River Drive
Middletown, NY 10940

Dear Ms. Wallenez:

We are writing to you to encourage you and your class to join in this year's Community Book Drive. We really appreciated your participation last year and hope you will join us again. As you know, the Community Book Drive gathers books for hundreds of children who otherwise could not afford them. Last year we gathered more than 1,500 books!

Participating this year is simple. Just nominate two members of your class to serve as the book drive leaders. They will post flyers about the book drive around the school and other community areas. They will also be responsible for letting the book drive team leaders know when the drop boxes at your school are getting full.

Please let me know if you are interested. I sure hope that your class will be able to make this year's drive as much of a success as the last! Thanks for your time and consideration.

Sincerely,

Oscar Diego

Oscar Diego • Co-Coordinator, Community Book Drive

Writing Friendly Letters

Friendly letters are less formal than business letters. You can use this form to write to a friend, a family member, or anyone with whom you'd like to communicate in a personal, friendly way. Like business letters, friendly letters have the following parts: heading, inside address, salutation, body, closing, and signature. The purpose of a friendly letter might be:

- to share news and feelings
- to send or answer an invitation
- to express thanks

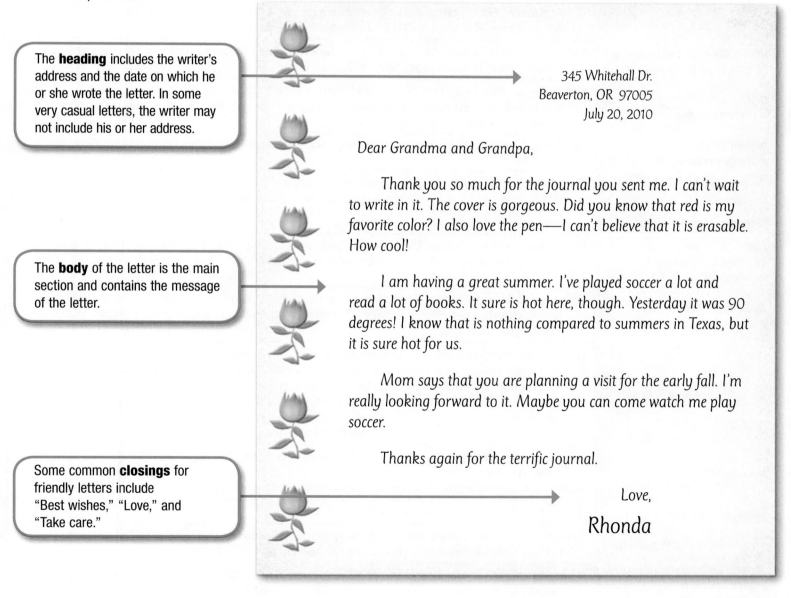

The **heading** includes the writer's address and the date on which he or she wrote the letter. In some very casual letters, the writer may not include his or her address.

345 Whitehall Dr.
Beaverton, OR 97005
July 20, 2010

Dear Grandma and Grandpa,

Thank you so much for the journal you sent me. I can't wait to write in it. The cover is gorgeous. Did you know that red is my favorite color? I also love the pen—I can't believe that it is erasable. How cool!

The **body** of the letter is the main section and contains the message of the letter.

I am having a great summer. I've played soccer a lot and read a lot of books. It sure is hot here, though. Yesterday it was 90 degrees! I know that is nothing compared to summers in Texas, but it is sure hot for us.

Mom says that you are planning a visit for the early fall. I'm really looking forward to it. Maybe you can come watch me play soccer.

Thanks again for the terrific journal.

Some common **closings** for friendly letters include "Best wishes," "Love," and "Take care."

Love,

Rhonda

MLA Style for Listing Sources

Book with one author	London, Jack. *White Fang.* Clayton, DE: Prestwick House, 2007. Print.
Book with two or three authors	Veit, Richard, and Christopher Gould. *Writing, Reading, and Research.* 8th ed. Boston: Wadsworth Cengage, 2009. Print.
Book prepared by an editor	Twain, Mark. *The Complete Essays of Mark Twain.* Ed. Charles Neider. New York: Da Capo, 2000. Print.
Book with more than three authors or editors	Donald, Robert B., et al. *Writing Clear Essays.* 3rd ed. Upper Saddle River, NJ: Prentice Hall, Inc., 1996. Print.
A single work from an anthology	Poe, Edgar Allan. "The Fall of the House of Usher." *American Literature: A Chronological Approach.* Ed. Edgar H. Schuster, Anthony Tovatt, and Patricia O. Tovatt. New York City, NY: McGraw-Hill, 1985. 233–247. Print. [Indicate pages for the entire selection.]
Introduction, foreward, preface, or afterward in a book	Vidal, Gore. Introduction. *Abraham Lincoln: Selected Speeches and Writings.* By Abraham Lincoln. New York: Vintage, 1992. xxi–xxvii. Print.
Signed article in a weekly magazine	Walsh, Brian. "Greening This Old House." *Time* 4 May 2009: 45–47. Print. [For a multi-page article that does not appear on consecutive pages, write only the first page number on which it appears, followed by a plus sign.]
Signed article in a monthly magazine	Fischman, Josh. "A Better Life with Bionics." *National Geographic* Jan. 2010: 34–53. Print.
Unsigned editorial or story	"Wind Power." Editorial. *New York Times* 9 January 2010: A18. Print. [If the editorial or story is signed, begin with the author's name.]
Signed pamphlet	[Treat the pamphlet as though it were a book.]
Audiovisual media, such as films, slide programs, videocassettes, DVDs	*Where the Red Fern Grows.* Dir. Norman Toker. Perf. James Whitmore, Beverly Garland, and Stewart Peterson. 1974. Sterling Entertainment, 1997. DVD.
Radio or TV broadcast transcript	"Texas High School Football Titans Ready for Clash." *Weekend Edition Sunday.* Host Melissa Block. Guests Mike Pesca and Tom Goldman. Natl. Public Radio. KUHF, Houston, 18 Dec. 2009. Print. Transcript.
A single page on a Web site	U.S. Census Bureau: Customer Liaison and Marketing Services Office. "State Facts for Students: Texas." *U.S. Census Bureau.* U.S. Census Bureau, 15 October 2009. Web. 1 November 2009. [Indicate the date of last update if known or use n.d. if not known. After the medium of publication, include the date you accessed the information. You do not need the URL unless it is the only way to find the page. If needed, include it in angled brackets at the end, i.e. <http://www.census.gov/schools/facts/texas.html >.]
Newspaper	Yardley, Jim. "Hurricane Sweeps into Rural Texas; Cities Are Spared." *New York Times* 23 Aug. 1999: A1. Print. [For a multipage article that does not appear on consecutive pages, write only the first page number on which it appears, followed by a plus sign.]
Personal interview	Jones, Robert. Personal interview. 4 Sept. 2006.
Audio with multiple publishers	Simms, James, ed. *Romeo and Juliet.* By William Shakespeare. Oxford: Attica Cybernetics; London: BBC Education; London: HarperCollins, 1995. CD-ROM.
Signed article from an encyclopedia	Askeland, Donald R. "Welding." *World Book Encyclopedia.* 1991 ed. Print. [For a well-known reference, you do not need to include the publisher information, only the edition and year, followed by the medium used.]

Commonly Misspelled Words

The list on this page presents words that cause problems for many people. Some of these words are spelled according to set rules, but others follow no specific rules. As you review this list, check to see how many of the words give you trouble in your own writing.

absence
absolutely
accidentally
accurate
achievement
affect
agreeable
aisle
all right
allowance
analysis
analyze
ancient
anniversary
answer
anticipate
anxiety
apologize
appearance
appreciate
appropriate
argument
athletic
attendance
awkward
bargain
battery
beautiful
beginning
believe
benefit
bicycle
bought
brief
brilliant
bulletin
bury
buses
business
cafeteria
calendar
campaign
canceled
candidate
capital
capitol
career
cashier
category
ceiling
certain
changeable
characteristic
clothes
colonel
column
commercial
commitment
condemn
congratulate
conscience
conscientious
conscious
continuous
convenience
coolly
cooperate
correspondence
courageous
courteous
criticism
curiosity
deceive
decision
defendant
definitely
dependent
description
desert
dessert
dining
disappointed
distinguish
effect
eighth
embarrass
enthusiastic
envelope
environment
especially
excellent
exercise
experience
explanation
extension
extraordinary
familiar
fascinating
February
fiery
financial
foreign
fourth
generally
genuine
government
grammar
guidance
height
humorous
immediately
immigrant
independence
independent
individual
intelligence
judgment
knowledge
lawyer
legible
library
license
lightning
likable
literature
mathematics
maximum
minimum
misspell
naturally
necessary
neighbor
niece
ninety
noticeable
occasion
occasionally
occur
occurred
occurrence
opinion
opportunity
parallel
particularly
personally
persuade
physician
possibility
precede
preferable
prejudice
previous
probably
procedure
proceed
pronunciation
realize
really
receipt
receive
recognize
recommend
rehearse
repetition
restaurant
rhythm
sandwich
schedule
scissors
theater
truly
usage
valuable
various
vegetable
weight
weird
whale
yield

A

accurate (ak´yər it) *adj.* without errors; true

aesthetic (es thet´ik) *adj.* relating to beauty; artistic; pleasing to the senses

agree (ə grē´) *v.* to have the same opinion

analysis (ə nal´ə sis) *n.* the process of looking at something closely in order to understand its meaning, structure, or parts

analytical (an´ə lit´ik əl) *adj.* relating to, or using, logical reasoning

analyze (an´ə līz) *v.* to look at something carefully to understand its meaning or structure

anticipate (an tis´ə pāt´) *v.* to expect or predict; to be prepared for something to happen

assertion (ə sʉr´shən) *n.* a strong statement of fact or belief about a subject

audience (ô´dē əns) *n.* the readers of a book or other piece of writing; a group of listeners or viewers

autobiographical (ôt´ō bī´ə graf´i kəl) *adj.* of, or relating to, an author's writings about his or her own life

B

ballad (bal´əd) *n.* a song-like poem that tells a story, often of love and adventure

biographical (bī´ə graf´i kəl) *adj.* of, or relating to, an author's writing about the life of a real person (but not about the writer's own life)

C

challenge (chal´ənj) *n.* a task or situation which tests a person's abilities; something new and difficult which requires effort, determination, or skill

character (kar´ik tər) *n.* a person (or animal) who plays a part in the action of a story, play, or movie

characterization (kar´ik tər i zā´shən) *n.* the act of creating and developing a character in a story

cite (sīt) *v.* to give credit when referring to a source of information

concern (kən sʉrn´) *n.* a matter of interest; a worry

concluding paragraph (kən klüd´ing par´ə graf´) *n.* the closing paragraph at the end of a piece of writing; the paragraph that sums up and puts forward a conclusion

conflict (kän´flikt´) *n.* the struggle between people or opposing forces which creates the dramatic action in a play or story

consequences (kän´si kwens´ez) *n.* what happens because of something else; the outcome of a previous action

context (kän´tekst´) *n.* the part of a sentence which surrounds a word and which can be used to shed light on the word's meaning; the situation in which something occurs which can help that thing to be fully understood; the setting or environment

counter-argument (kount´ər är´gyü mənt) *n.* a reason against the original argument

D

demonstrate (dem´ən strāt´) *v.* to make a fact clear by giving proof or evidence

describe (di skrīb´) *v.* to say what something is like

device (di vīs´) *n.* the use of words to gain a particular effect in a piece of writing

dialogue (dī´ə lôg´) *n.* a conversation between two or more people in a book, play, or movie

diction (dik´shən) *n.* a writer's choice of words

document (däk´yü mənt) *n.* anything printed or written that gives information; *v.* to support ideas with information from sources

documentation (däk´yü mən tā´shən) *n.* the noting of sources to back up an idea or opinion

E

element (el´ə mənt) *n.* one of several parts that make up a whole

e-mail (ē´māl) *n.* a message sent from one person to another by computer

embedded (em bed´id) *adj.* placed firmly in the middle of something; (of a quotation) placed inside a sentence, not set apart from the rest of the text

emotion (ē mō´shən) n. a feeling, such as love or joy; feelings generally, as opposed to reason and logic

engaging (en gāj´ing) *adj.* something which draws in and interests (engages) the reader; charming, interesting

essay (es´ā) *n.* a short piece of nonfiction writing on a particular subject

establish (ə stab´lish) *v.* to show or prove with facts and evidence; to set up, start, or create

evidence (ev´ə dəns) *n.* anything that gives proof or shows something to be true

example (eg zam´pəl) *n.* something typical of a particular group which can be used to represent or explain

expert (eks´pərt) *n.* a person who has a special knowledge on a subject

F

fact (fakt) *n.* a piece of information that can be shown to be true

feeling (fēl´ing) *n.* an opinion or belief; an emotion or emotional state; a physical sensation (touch, heat, cold); a sense or perception

figurative (fig´yər ə tiv´) *adj.* (of language) writing that is full of metaphors and images, where the words are very descriptive but not meant to be taken literally

formal (fôr´məl) *adj.* reflecting language that is traditional and correct, not casual

formatting (fôr´mat´ing) *adj.* related to the arrangement of text, images, and graphics on a page

G

goal (gōl) *n.* the end point of a person's effort or ambition; an objective

I

imagery (im´ij rē) *n.* descriptive language that paints pictures in the mind or appeals to the senses

improve (im prüv´) *v.* to make better

infer (in fʉr´) *v.* to conclude or figure out based on available facts; to make an educated guess

inference (in´fər əns) *n.* a conclusion drawn from available information; the act of drawing this kind of conclusion

instructions (in struk´shənz) *n.* steps to be followed to accomplish something

interpret (in tʉr´prət) *v.* to decide on and explain the meaning of something

introductory paragraph (in´trə duk´tə rē par´ə graf´) *n.* in a piece of writing, the beginning or opening paragraph which often gives both the topic and thesis

L

letter (let´ər) *n.* a written or printed message

literal (lit´ər əl) *adj.* the most basic meaning of a word or words, without metaphor or other figurative language; without any exaggeration or distortion

literary (lit´ər er´ē) *adj.* of or relating to books or other written material

logical (läj´i kəl) *adj.* based on logic; clear and reasonable

M

mood (müd) n. the atmosphere or overall feeling of a piece of writing as created by the author

O

objection (əb jek´shən) *n.* a reason for disagreeing; an argument put forward to go against an idea or theory

opinion (ə pin´yən) *n.* a belief or view that is not necessarily based on facts

P

plot (plät) *n.* the sequence of events in a story

poetic (pō et´ik) *adj.* beautiful, expressive, sensitive, or imaginative; like a poem

precise (prē cīs´) *adj.* exact, accurate; careful about details

problem (präb´ləm) *n.* a difficulty; a question to be examined and discussed

procedure (prō sē´jər) *n.* the way a task or other work is done

progression (prō gresh´ən) *n.* a natural series of events; a moving forward

purpose (pʉr´pəs) *n.* the reason something exists, is done, or is created; the aim or goal of an activity or piece of writing

Q

quotation (kwō tā´shən) *n.* a group of words copied exactly from a speech or piece of writing

quote (kwōt) *v.* to write or say a group of words copied exactly from a piece of writing or someone's spoken words

R

reader-friendly (rēd´ər frend´lē) *adj.* easy for an audience to read and understand

reasonable (rē´zən ə bəl) *adj.* fair and sensible; the result of good sense, reason, and logic; moderate, not extreme, neither very good not very bad; inexpensive

relevant (rel´ə vənt) *adj.* closely connected, important, or significant to the matter at hand

research (rē´sʉrch´) *v.* to carefully study information on a topic; *n.* the careful study of information on a topic

resolution (rez´ə lü´shən) *n.* what happens to resolve the conflict in the plot of a story

resource (rē´sôrs) *n.* (in research) a book or document that can be used as evidence in research, or when making an argument and trying to prove a point; a place, person, or thing which supplies information or other things; the place something begins, the origin

rhetorical devices (ri tôr´i kəl di vī´səz) *n.* strategies and techniques, for example metaphor and hyperbole, used by writers to create an effect or achieve a purpose

rhyme (rīme) *n.* the repetition of the same sounds at the ends of words, especially in poetry

rhythm (rith´əm) *n.* the pattern of stressed and unstressed syllables in spoken or written language, particularly in poetry

S

sense (sens) *n.* one of the five abilities of sight, touch, taste, hearing, and smell

sensory (sen´sər ē) *adj.* relating to the senses

setting (set´ing) *n.* the time and place of the action in a story or other piece of writing

solution (sə lü´shən) *n.* the answer to a problem

sonnet (sän´it) *n.* a poem of fourteen lines, often with a set pattern of rhymes

statement (stāt´mənt) *n.* something written or said which presents information in a clear and definite way

strategies (strat´ə jēz) *n.* in a piece of writing, literary tactics or methods (such as flashback or foreshadowing) used by the writer to achieve certain goals or effects

structural (struk´chər əl) *adj.* having to do with the form an object takes or the way an object appears

style (stīl) *n.* a way of doing something; a way of writing, composing, or painting, etc. special to a period in history, a group of artists, or a particular person

support (sə pôrt´) *v.* to back up ideas with evidence

suspense (sə spens´) *n.* a feeling of anxiety and uncertainty about what will happen in a story or other piece of writing

T

task (task) *n.* a piece of work to be done

technique (tek nēk´) *n.* a method of doing an activity or carrying out a task, often involving skill

theme (thēm) *n.* a central message, concern, or purpose in a literary work

thesis (thē´sis) *n.* an idea or theory that is stated and then discussed in a logical way

transition (tran zish´ən) *n.* the change from one part, place, or idea to another

V

valid (val´id) *adj.* reasonable and logical, and therefore worth taking seriously; acceptable as true and correct

Spanish Glossary

A

accurate / **correcto** *s.* el estado de no tener errores

aesthetic / **estético** *adj.* perteneciente a la belleza; artístico; agradable a los sentidos

agree / **estar de acuerdo** *v.* tener la misma opinión

analysis / **análisis** *s.* el proceso de examinar algo detenidamente para entender su significado, su estructura o sus partes

analytical / **analítico** *adj.* perteneciente a o utilizando el razonamiento lógico

analyze / **analizar** *v.* examinar algo detenidamente para entender su significado o estructura

anticipate / **anticipar** *v.* esperar o predecir; prever y estar preparado para tratar con algo

assertion / **aseveración** *s.* una declaración fuerte de un hecho o creencia sobre un tema

audience / **audiencia, público** *s.* los lectores de un libro u otra obra escrita; un grupo de oyentes o espectadores

autobiographical / **autobiográfico** *adj.* perteneciente o relativo a la escritura de un autor sobre su propia vida

B

ballad / **balada** *s.* una canción poética que cuenta una historia, muchas veces del amor y la aventura

biographical / **biográfico** *adj.* perteneciente o relativo a la escritura de un autor sobre la vida de una persona real (pero no sobre la vida del autor mismo)

C

challenge / **reto** *s.* una tarea o situación que pone a prueba las habilidades de una persona; algo nuevo y difícil que requiere el esfuerzo, la determinación o la aptitud

character / **personaje** *s.* un individuo (humano o animal) que tiene un papel en la acción de un cuento, una obra de teatro o una película

characterization / **caracterización** *s.* el acto de crear y desarrollar un personaje en un cuento

cite / **citar** *v.* dar crédito cuando uno se refiere a una fuente de información

concern / **asunto, preocupación** *s.* una cuestión de interés; una inquietud

concluding paragraph / **párrafo conclusivo** *s.* el párrafo final de una obra escrita; el párrafo que resume y concluye

conflict / **conflicto** *s.* la lucha entre personas o fuerzas opuestas que crea la acción dramática en una obra de teatro o un cuento

consequences / **consecuencias** *s.* lo que ocurre a causa de otra cosa; el resultado de una acción previa

context / **contexto** *s.* la parte de una oración que rodea una palabra y que se puede usar para sacar el significado de la palabra; la situación en la que algo ocurre que puede facilitar la comprensión de la cosa; el escenario o el entorno

counter-argument / **contraargumento** *s.* una razón contra el argumento original

D

demonstrate / **demostrar** *v.* aclarar un hecho por dar pruebas o evidencia

describe / **describir** *v.* decir cómo es algo

device / **técnica (literaria)** *s.* el uso de palabras para tener un efecto específico en una obra escrita

dialogue / **diálogo** *s.* una conversación entre dos personajes o más en un libro, obra de teatro o película

diction / **dicción** *s.* la selección de palabras de un escritor

document / **documento** *s.* cualquier cosa impresa o escrita que aporta información; **documentar** *v.* apoyar las ideas con información de fuentes

documentation / **documentación** *s.* la anotación de fuentes para apoyar una idea u opinión

E

e-mail / **correo electrónico** *s.* un mensaje que una persona envía a otra por computadora

element / **elemento** *s.* una de varias partes que forman parte de una totalidad

embedded / **colocado** *adj.* metido firmemente en medio de algo; (de una cita) insertada dentro de una oración, no separada del resto del texto

emotion / **sentimiento** s. una sensación emotiva, como el amor o la alegría; los sentimientos en general, opuestos al razonamiento y la lógica

engaging / **interesante** *adj.* algo que le atrae y le interesa al lector; encantador, interesante

essay / **ensayo** *s.* una obra escrita breve de no ficción sobre un tema particular

establish / **establecer** *v.* demostrar o probar con hechos y evidencia; armar, empezar o crear

evidence / **pruebas** *s.* cualquier cosa que demuestre o indique que algo es verdadero

example / **ejemplo** *s.* algo típico de un grupo particular que se puede usar para representar o aclarar

expert / **experto(a)** *s.* una persona que sabe mucho de un tema en particular

F

fact / **hecho** *s.* un dato que se puede verificar

feeling / **impresión, sentimiento, sensación** *s.* una opinión o creencia; un estado emocional; una sensación física (tacto, calor, frío); un sentido de percepción

figurative / **figurado** *adj.* (de lenguaje) escritura que está repleta de metáforas e imágenes, donde las palabras son muy descriptivas pero su significado no debe ser interpretado literalmente

formal / **formal** *adj.* que refleja lenguaje tradicional y correcto, no informal

formatting / **formateo** *s.* la colocación de texto, imágenes y gráficos en una página

G

goal / **meta** *s.* el punto final del esfuerzo o ambición de una persona; un objetivo

I

imagery / **vimágenes** *s.* lenguaje descriptivo que crea dibujos en la mente o que atrae los sentidos

improve / **mejorar** *v.* hacer mejor

infer / **inferir** *v.* concluir o sacar conclusiones basadas en los hechos disponibles; hacer una estimación razonada

inference / **inferencia** *s.* una conclusión sacada de la información disponible; el acto de llegar a este tipo de conclusión

instructions / **instrucciones** *s.* los pasos que hay que seguir para realizar algo

interpret / **interpretar** *v.* determinar y explicar el significado de algo

introductory paragraph / **párrafo introductorio** *s.* en una obra escrita, el párrafo al principio que muchas veces expone tanto el tema como la tesis

L

letter / **carta** *s.* un mensaje escrito o impreso

literal / **literal** *adj.* el significado más básico de una palabra o palabras, sin metáfora u otro lenguaje figurado; sin exageración o distorsión

literary / **literario** *adj.* perteneciente o relativo a los libros u otros materiales escritos

logical / **lógico** *adj.* claro y razonable; basado en la lógica

M

mood / **ambiente, tono** *s.* el ambiente o sentimiento general de una obra escrita creado por el autor

O

objection / **objeción** *s.* una razón por no estar de acuerdo; un argumento para estar en contra de una idea o teoría

opinion / **opinión** *s.* una creencia o perspectiva que no es necesariamente basada en los hechos

P

plot / **argumento** *s.* la secuencia de eventos en una historia

poetic / **poético** *adj.* bonito, expresivo, sensible o imaginativo; como un poema

precise / **preciso** *adj.* exacto, certero; cuidadoso con detalles

problem / **problema** *s.* una dificultad; una cuestión para examinar y discutir

procedure / **procedimiento** *s.* la manera en la que se hace una tarea o un trabajo

progression / **progresión** *s.* una serie natural de eventos; un movimiento hacia adelante

purpose / **propósito** *s.* la razón por la cual algo existe o se hace

Q

quotation / **cita** *s.* un grupo de palabras copiadas exactamente de un discurso o texto

quote / **citar** *v.* escribir o decir un grupo de palabras copiadas exactamente de un texto o de las palabras habladas de alguien.

R

reader-friendly / **fácil de leer** *adj.* no complicado, fácil de entender y leer

reasonable / **razonable** *adj.* justo y sensato; el resultado de buen sentido, razón, y lógica; moderado, no extremo, ni muy bueno ni muy malo; no caro

relevant / **relevante** *adj.* conectado estrechamente, importante o significante al asunto en cuestión

research / **investigar** *v.* estudiar cuidadosamente la información sobre un tema; **investigación** *s.* el estudio cuidadoso de la información sobre un tema

resolution / **resolución** *s.* lo que ocurre para resolver el conflicto en el argumento de una historia

resource / **recurso** *s.* (en la investigación) un libro o documento que se puede usar como prueba en la investigación o para defender un argumento y ilustrar un punto; un lugar, una persona o una cosa que proporciona información u otras cosas; el lugar donde empieza algo, el origen

rhetorical devices / **técnicas retóricas** *s.* estrategias y técnicas (por ejemplo la metáfora e hipérbole) utilizadas por los escritores para crear un efecto o lograr un propósito

rhyme / **rima** *s.* la repetición de los mismos sonidos al final de las palabras, especialmente en la poesía

rhythm / **ritmo** *s.* el patrón de sílabas tónicas y átonas en el lenguaje oral y escrito, especialmente en la poesía

S

sense / **sentido** *s.* una de las cinco habilidades de visión, tacto, gusto, audición y olfato

sensory / **sensorial** *adj.* perteneciente o relativo a los cinco sentidos

setting / **escenario** *s.* el lugar y el momento de la acción en un cuento u otra obra escrita

solution / **solución** *s.* la respuesta a un problema

sonnet / **soneto** *s.* un poema de catorce versos, muchas veces con un patrón determinado de rimas

statement / **declaración** *s.* algo escrito o dicho que presenta información en una manera clara y definitiva

strategies / **estrategias** *s.* en un texto, tácticas o métodos literarios (como el flashback o el presagio) empleados por el autor para lograr un objetivo o efecto específico

structural / **estructural** *adj.* relativo a la forma que toma un objeto o la manera en la que parece un objeto

style / **estilo** *s.* una manera de hacer algo; una manera de escribir

support / **apoyar** *v.* defender las ideas con evidencia

suspense / **suspenso** *s.* una sensación de ansiedad e incertidumbre sobre lo que va a pasar en una historia u otra obra escrita

T

task / **tarea** *s.* un trabajo que se tiene que hacer

technique / **técnica** *s.* una manera de hacer una actividad o llevar a cabo una tarea, muchas veces con destrezas específicas

theme / **tema** *s.* una idea, asunto o propósito principal en una obra literaria

thesis / **tesis** *s.* una idea o teoría que se expone y que se discute de una manera lógica

transition / **transición** *s.* el cambio entre partes, lugares y conceptos

V

valid / **válido** *adj.* razonable y lógico y por lo tanto vale la pena tomarlo en serio; aceptable como verdadero y correcto

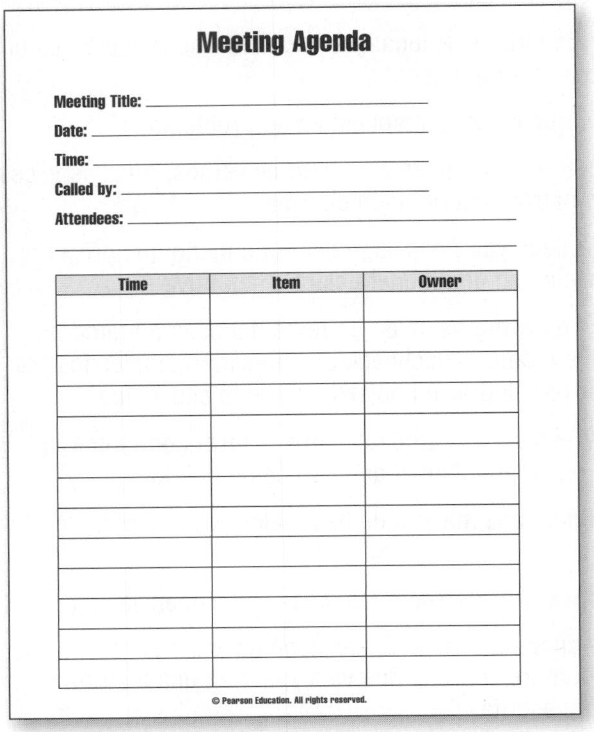

Meeting Agenda

Meeting Title: ______

Date: ______

Time: ______

Called by: ______

Attendees: ______

Time	Item	Owner

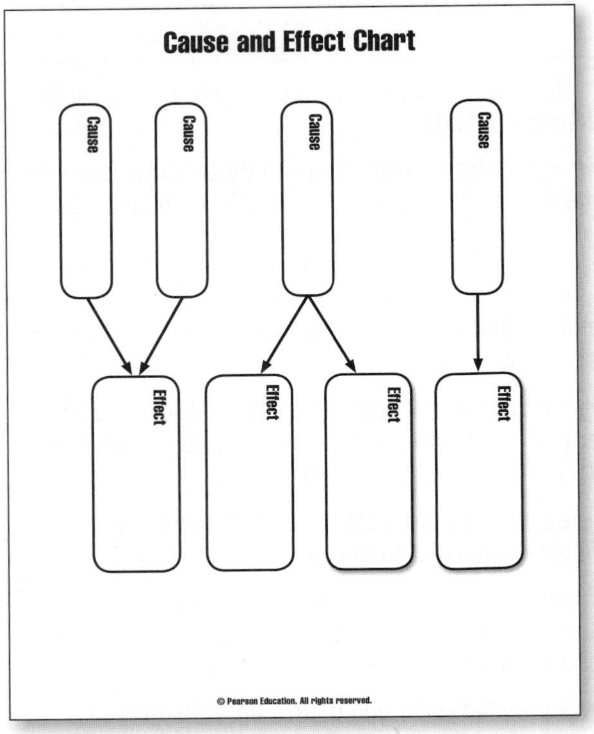

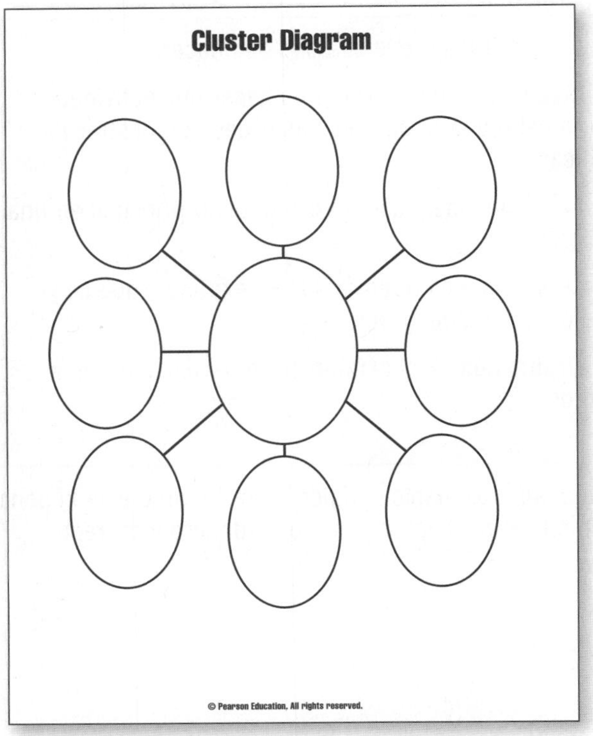

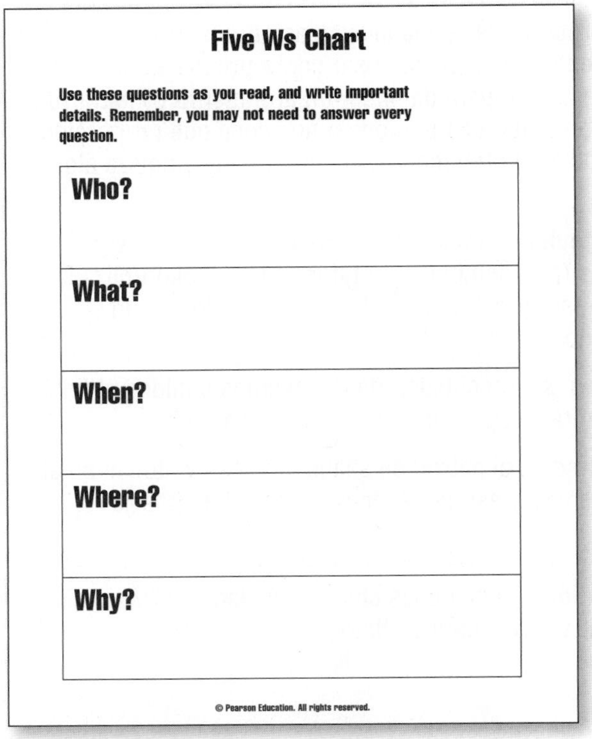

Five Ws Chart

Use these questions as you read, and write important details. Remember, you may not need to answer every question.

Who?
What?
When?
Where?
Why?

Resource Go online for printable versions of these graphic organizers.

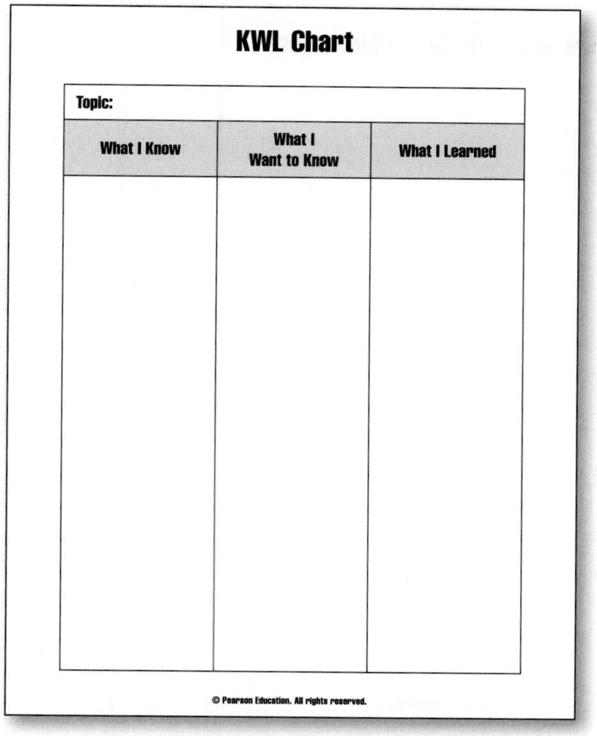

KWL Chart

Topic:		
What I Know	What I Want to Know	What I Learned

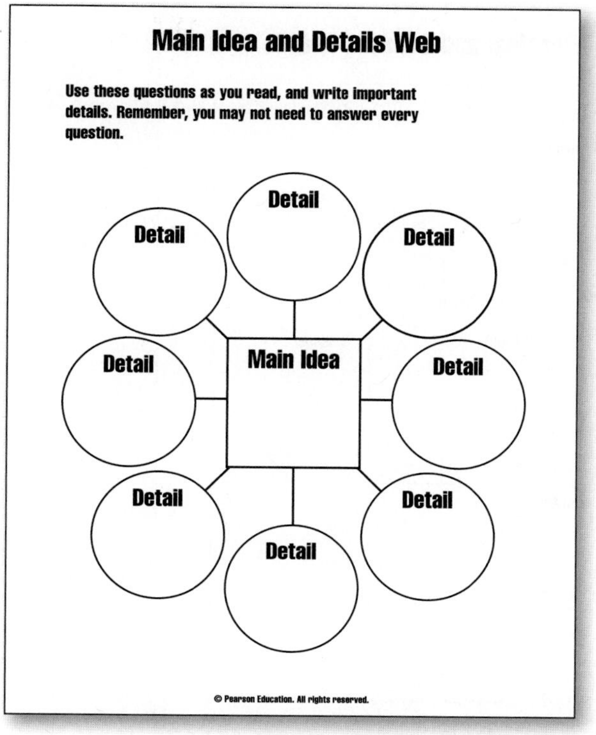

Main Idea and Details Web

Use these questions as you read, and write important details. Remember, you may not need to answer every question.

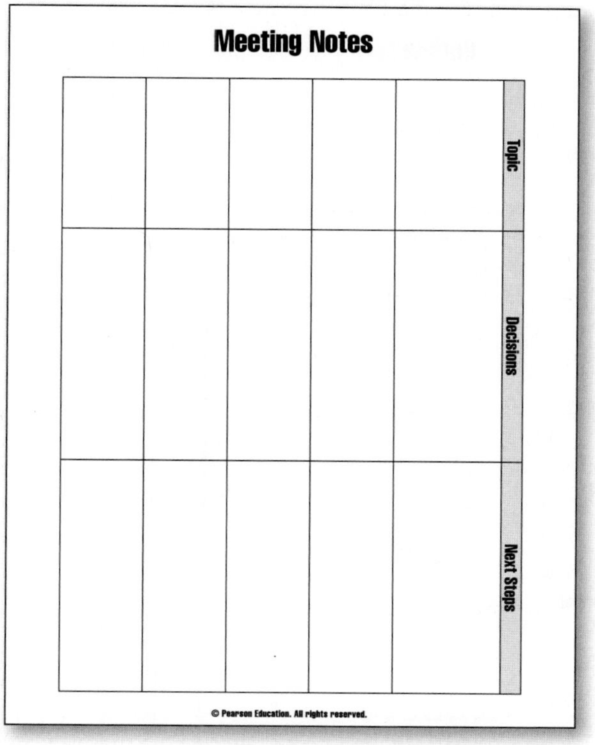

Meeting Notes

					Topic
					Decisions
					Next Steps

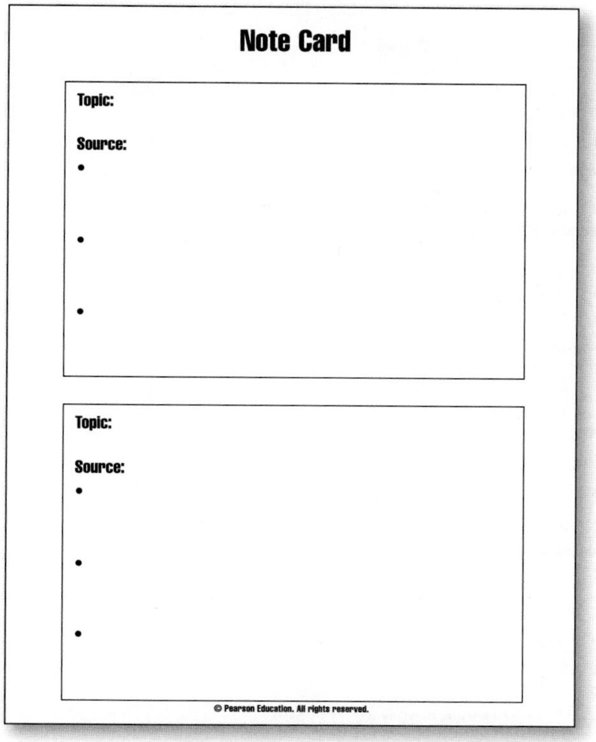

Note Card

Topic:

Source:

-
-
-

Topic:

Source:

-
-
-

Problem and Solution Chart

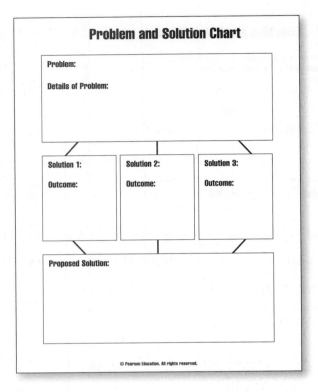

Problem:

Details of Problem:

Solution 1:

Outcome:

Solution 2:

Outcome:

Solution 3:

Outcome:

Proposed Solution:

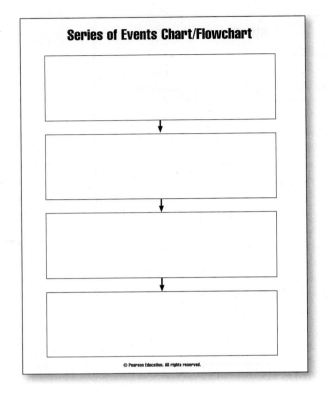

Series of Events Chart/Flowchart

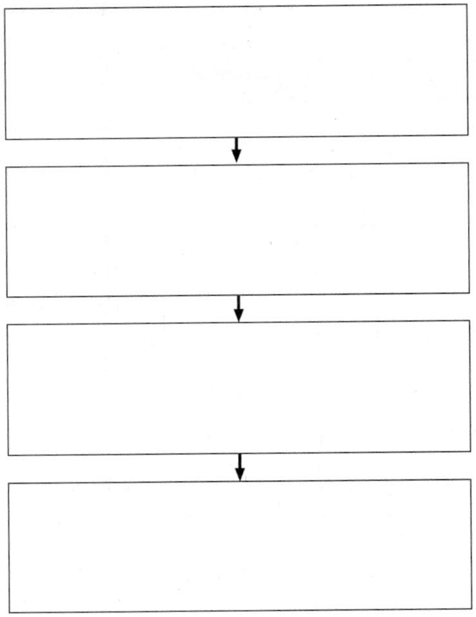

Source Card

Source Number: ______________
Source Name: ______________
Kind of Source: ______________
Author(s): ______________
Editor (when applicable): ______________
Publisher: ______________
Publication Date: ______________
Publication Location: ______________
Other Information ______________

Source Number: ______________
Source Name: ______________
Kind of Source: ______________
Author(s): ______________
Editor (when applicable): ______________
Publisher: ______________
Publication Date: ______________
Publication Location: ______________
Other Information ______________

Outline

Topic I. ______________

Subtopic A. ______________

Supporting details
1. ______________
2. ______________
3. ______________
4. ______________

Subtopic B. ______________

Supporting details
1. ______________
2. ______________
3. ______________
4. ______________

Topic II. ______________

Subtopic A. ______________

Supporting details
1. ______________
2. ______________
3. ______________
4. ______________

Subtopic B. ______________

Supporting details
1. ______________
2. ______________
3. ______________
4. ______________

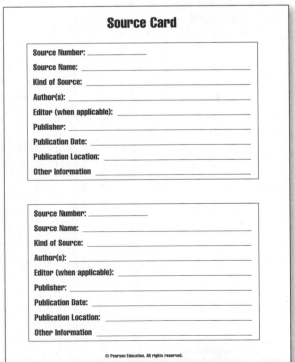

Steps in a Process Chart

Steps	Details
Step 1:	
Step 2:	
Step 3:	
Step 4:	
Step 5:	

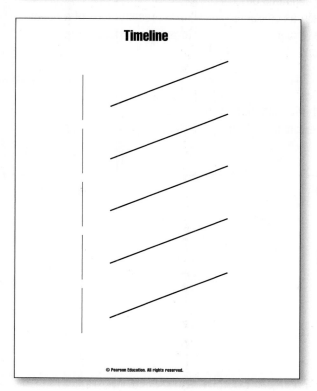

Storyboard

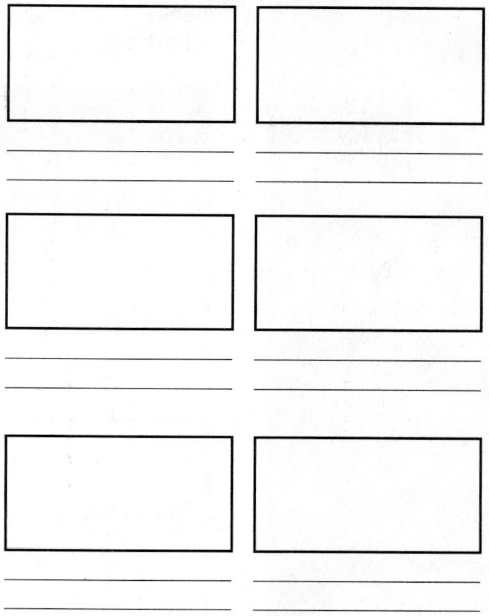

Timeline

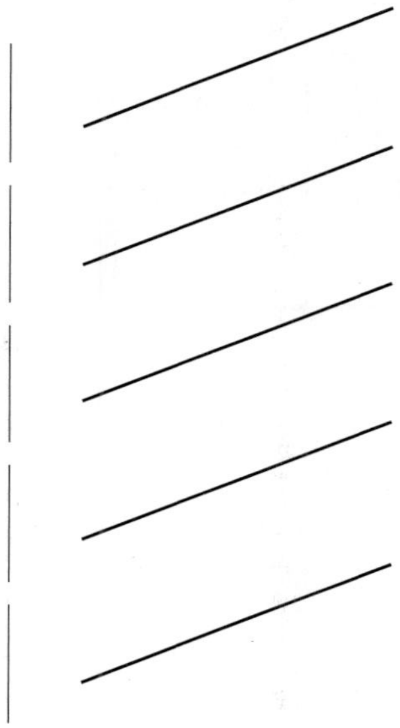

Venn Diagram

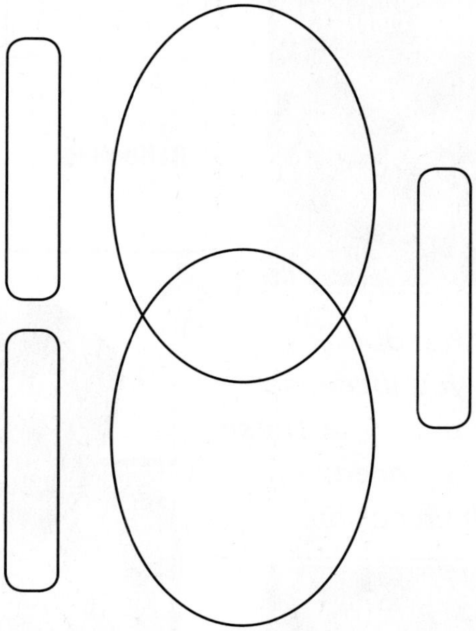

Listening and Speaking Handbook

Communication travels between people in many forms. You receive information by listening to others, and you convey information through speaking. The more developed these skills are, the more you will be able to communicate your ideas, as well as to comprehend the ideas of others.

If you improve your listening skills, it will become easier to focus your attention on classroom discussions and to identify important information more accurately. If you develop good speaking skills, you will be better prepared to contribute effectively in group discussions, to give formal presentations with more confidence, and to communicate your feelings and ideas to others more easily.

This handbook will help you increase your ability in these two key areas of communication.

Listening

Different situations call for different types of listening. Learn more about the four main types of listening—critical, empathic, appreciative, and reflective—in the chart below.

Types of Listening

Type	How to Listen	Situations
Critical	Listen for facts and supporting details to understand and evaluate the speaker's message.	Informative or persuasive speeches, class discussions, announcements
Empathic	Imagine yourself in the other person's position, and try to understand what he or she is thinking.	Conversations with friends or family
Appreciative	Identify and analyze aesthetic or artistic elements, such as character development, rhyme, imagery, and descriptive language.	Oral presentations of a poem, dramatic performances
Reflective	Ask questions to get information, and use the speaker's responses to form new questions.	Class or group discussions

Using Different Types of Questions

A speaker's ideas may not always be clear to you. You may need to ask questions to clarify your understanding. If you understand the different types of questions, you will be able to get the information you need.

- An **open-ended question** does not lead to a single, specific response. Use this question to open up a discussion: "What did you think of the piano recital?"
- A **closed question** leads to a specific response and must be answered with a yes or no: "Did you play a piece by Chopin at your recital?"
- A **factual question** is aimed at getting a particular piece of information and must be answered with facts: "How many years have you been playing the piano?"

Participating in a Group Discussion

In a group discussion, you openly discuss ideas and topics in an informal setting. The group discussions in which you participate will involve, for the most part, your classmates and focus on the subjects you are studying. To get the most out of a group discussion, you need to participate in it.

Use group discussions to express and to listen to ideas in an informal setting.

Communicate Effectively Think about the points you want to make, the order in which you want to make them, the words you will use to express them, and the examples that will support these points before you speak.

Ask Questions Asking questions can help you improve your comprehension of another speaker's ideas. It may also call attention to possible errors in another speaker's points.

Make Relevant Contributions Stay focused on the topic being discussed. Relate comments to your own experience and knowledge, and clearly connect them to your topic. It is important to listen to the points others make so you can build off their ideas. Work to share the connections you see. For example, say whether you agree or disagree, or tell the goup how your ideas connect.

Speaking

Giving a presentation or speech before an audience is generally recognized as public speaking. Effective speakers are well prepared and deliver speeches smoothly and with confidence.

Recognizing Different Kinds of Speeches

There are four main kinds of speeches: informative speeches, persuasive speeches, entertaining speeches, and extemporaneous speeches.

Consider the purpose and audience of your speech before deciding what kind of speech you will give.

- Give an **informative speech** to explain an idea, a process, an object, or an event.
- Give a **persuasive speech** to get your listeners to agree with your position or to take some action. Use formal English when speaking.
- Give an **entertaining speech** to offer your listeners something to enjoy or to amuse them. Use both informal and formal language.
- Give an **extemporaneous speech** when an impromptu occasion arises. It is an informal speech because you do not have a prepared manuscript.

Preparing and Presenting a Speech

If you are asked to deliver a speech, begin choosing a topic that you like or know well. Then, prepare your speech for your audience.

To prepare your speech, research your topic. Make an outline, and use numbered note cards.

Gather Information Use the library and other resources to gather reliable information and to find examples to support your ideas.

Organizing Information Organize your information by writing an outline of main ideas and major details. Then, when you deliver your speech, write the main ideas, major details, quotations, and facts on note cards.

When presenting your speech, use rhetorical forms of language and verbal and nonverbal strategies.

Use Rhetorical Language Repeat key words and phrases to identify your key points. Use active verbs and colorful adjectives to keep your speech interesting. Use parallel phrases to insert a sense of rhythm.

Use Verbal and Nonverbal Strategies Vary the pitch and tone of your voice, and the rate at which you speak. Speak loudly and emphasize key words or phrases. Avoid consistently reading your speech from you notes. Work to maintain eye contact with the audience. As you speak, connect with the audience by using gestures and facial expressions to emphasize key points.

Evaluating a Speech

Evaluating a speech gives you the chance to judge another speaker's skills. It also gives you the opportunity to review and improve your own methods for preparing and presenting a speech.

When you evaluate a speech, you help the speaker and yourself to learn from experience. Listed below are some questions you might ask yourself while evaluating another person's speech or one of your own speeches.

- Did the speaker introduce the topic clearly, develop it well, and conclude it effectively?
- Did the speaker support each main idea with appropriate details?
- Did the speaker approach the platform confidently and establish eye contact with the audience?
- Did the speaker's facial expressions, gestures, and movements appropriately reinforce the words spoken?
- Did the speaker vary the pitch of his or her voice and the rate of his or her speaking?
- Did the speaker enunciate all words clearly?

Listening Critically to a Speech

Hearing happens naturally as sounds reach your ears. Listening, or critical listening, requires that you understand and interpret these sounds.

Critical listening requires preparation, active involvement, and self-evaluation from the listener.

Learning the Listening Process Listening is interactive; the more you involve yourself in the listening process, the more you will understand.

Focus Your Attention Focus your attention on the speaker and block out all distractions—people, noises, and objects. Find out more about the subject that will be discussed beforehand.

Interpret the Information To interpret a speaker's message successfully, you need to identify and understand important information. You might consider listening for repeated words or phrases, pausing momentarily to memorize and/or write key statements, watching non-verbal signals, and combining this new information with what you already know.

Respond to the Speaker's Message Respond to the information you have heard by identifying the larger message of the speech, its most useful points, and your position on the topic.

Note: Page numbers in **boldface** refer to pages where terms are defined; *italicized* page numbers refer to writing applications.

Grateful acknowledgment is made to the following for copyrighted material:

Cengage Learning, Inc.
"An Overview of Blues Ain't No Mockin Bird" by Theresa M. Girard. From *Gale Literary Resource Center.* Copyright © 2009 Gale, a part of Cengage Learning, Inc. Reproduced by permission www.cengage.com/permissions.

The Christian Science Monitor
"Big Decisions in Little Hands" by Marilyn Gardner from *Christian Science Monitor 11/23/2005.* Copyright © 2005 The Christian Science Monitor. Used with permission of The Christian Science Monitor (www.CSMonitor.com).

Doubleday, An imprint of Random House, Inc.
"Homelanding" by Margaret Atwood from *Good Bones and Simple Murders.* Copyright © 1983, 1992, 1994 O. W. Toad Ltd.

Alfred A. Knopf, Inc., A Division of Random House, Inc.
"Dream Deferred" from *The Collected Poems of Langston Hughes* by Langston Hughes. Copyright © 1994 by The Estate of Langston Hughes. Used by permission of Alfred A. Knopf, a division of Random House, Inc.

Phoebe Larmore
"Homelanding" by Margaret Atwood from *Good Bones and Simple Murders.* Copyright © 1992, 1994 O. W. Toad Ltd. Used by permission of the author.

McClelland and Stewart, Inc.
"Homelanding" by Margaret Atwood from *Good Bones And Simple Murders.* Copyright © 1983, 1992, 1994 O. W. Toad Ltd. Used with permission of the publishers.

National Council of Teachers of English (NCTE)
"Mistakes are a fact of Life: A National Comparative Study" by Andrea A. Lunsford and Karen J. Lunsford translated from *bcs.bedfordstmartins.com/lunsford/PDF/Lunsford_article_Mistakes.pdf.* Copyright © NCTE. Used by permission of National Council of Teachers of English (NCTE).

Harold Ober Associates Incorporated
"Dream Deferred" from *The Collected Poems of Langston Hughes* by Langston Hughes. Copyright © 1994 by The Estate of Langston Hughes. Used by permission of Harold Ober Associates Inc.

Random House, Inc.
"Special Glasses" by Billy Collins from *The Trouble With Poetry and Other Poems.* Copyright © 2005 by Billy Collins. All rights reserved. Used by permission of Random House, Inc.

Note: Every effort has been made to locate the copyright owner of material reproduced in this component. Omissions brought to our attention will be corrected in subsequent editions.

Image Credits

Illustrations:
Tom Garrett

All interior photos provided by Jupiter Images. Except

90: © GoodShoot/age fotostock; 144: © Darren Greenwood/age fotostock; 222: © Monty Rakusen/age fotostock; 228: © NASA.